Democracies in Flux

Democracies in Flux

The Evolution of Social Capital in Contemporary Society

EDITED BY ROBERT D. PUTNAM

OXFORD
UNIVERSITY PRESS

2002

OXFORD
UNIVERSITY PRESS

Oxford   New York
Auckland   Bangkok   Buenos Aires   Cape Town   Chennai
Dar es Salaam   Delhi   Hong Kong   Istanbul   Karachi   Kolkata
Kuala Lumpur   Madrid   Melbourne   Mexico City   Mumbai
Nairobi   São Paulo   Shanghai   Singapore   Taipei   Tokyo   Toronto
and an associated company in Berlin

Library of Congress Cataloging-in-Publication Data
Democracies in flux: the evolution of social capital in contemporary society/
Eva Cox . . . [et al.]; edited by Robert D. Putnam.
p. cm.   Includes bibliographical references and index.
ISBN 0-19-515089-9
1. Social capital (Sociology).
2. Civil society.
3. Democracy.
I. Cox, Eva, 1938–
II. Putnam, Robert D.
HM708.D46 2002   302—dc21   2001047552

9 8 7 6 5 4 3 2 1

Printed in the United States of America
on acid-free paper

CONTENTS

Democracies in Flux

INTRODUCTION

**ROBERT D. PUTNAM
AND KRISTIN A. GOSS**

From Aristotle to Tocqueville, political and social theorists have stressed the importance of political culture and civil society. In recent years interest in these themes has revived, in part because the difficult births of market-oriented democracies in formerly Communist lands have underscored the cultural and sociological preconditions for such institutions. Ironically—just at the moment of liberal democracy's greatest triumph— there is also unhappiness about the performance of major social institutions, including the institutions of representative government, among the established democracies of Western Europe, North America, and East Asia.[1] At least in the United States, there is reason to suspect that some fundamental social and cultural preconditions for effective democracy may have been eroded in recent decades, the result of a gradual but widespread process of civic disengagement.[2]

This volume aims to contribute fundamental theoretical and empirical knowledge to our understanding of social change in eight advanced democracies: Australia, France, Germany, Great Britain, Japan, Spain, Sweden, and the United States. How has the character of civil society changed over the past fifty years, and why? This book is about social capital—that is, social networks and the norms of reciprocity associated with them—and how the profile of social capital is evolving in contemporary postindustrial societies. Because the concept of social capital may seem novel and perhaps academic, we begin with a few words about the term itself.

Nearly a century ago, L. Judson Hanifan, a young Progressive educator and social reformer trained at several of the best universities in America, returned to his native West Virginia, an impoverished state in Appalachia, to work in its rural school system. A Presbyterian, Rotarian, and Republican, Hanifan was no radical, but gradually he concluded that the grave social, economic, and political problems of the communities in which he worked could be solved only by strengthening the networks of solidarity among their citizens. He observed that older customs of rural neighborliness and civic engagement, such as debating societies, barn raisings, and apple cuttings, had fallen into disuse. "Gradually these customs became almost wholly abandoned, the people becoming less neighborly. Community social life gave way to family isolation and community stagnation."[3]

Writing in 1916 to urge the importance of renewed community involvement to sustain democracy and development, Hanifan coined the term "social capital" to explain why.

> In the use of the phrase social capital I make no reference to the usual acceptation of the term capital, except in a figurative sense. I do not refer to real estate, or to personal property or to cold cash, but rather to that in life which tends to make these tangible substances count for most in the daily lives of people: namely good will, fellowship, sympathy, and social intercourse among the individuals and families who make up a social unit. . . . The individual is helpless socially, if left to himself. . . . If he comes into contact with his neighbor, and they with other neighbors, there will be an accumulation of social capital, which may immediately satisfy his social needs and which may bear a social potentiality sufficient to the substantial improvement of living conditions in the whole community.

Hanifan went on to outline both the private and public benefits of social capital.   •

> The community as a whole will benefit by the coöperation of all its parts, while the individual will find in his associations the advantages of the help, the sympathy, and the fellowship of his neighbors. . . . When the people of a given community have become acquainted with one another and have formed a habit of coming

together occasionally for entertainment, social intercourse, and
personal enjoyment, then by skillful leadership this social capital
may easily be directed towards the general improvement of the
community well-being.[4]

Hanifan's account of social capital anticipated virtually all of the crucial
elements of later interpretations of this concept, but his conceptual
invention apparently attracted no notice from other social commentators and disappeared without a trace. During the rest of the twentieth
century the concept was independently reinvented at least six more
times. In the 1950s Canadian sociologist John Seeley and his colleagues
employed the term to point out that for an upwardly mobile suburban-
ite, "memberships in clubs and associations . . . are like negotiable securi-
ties (no less real for being psychological) which he may cash, transfer, or
use as collateral." Urbanist Jane Jacobs used the term in the 1960s to
emphasize the collective value of informal neighborhood ties in the
modern metropolis. In the 1970s economist Glenn C. Loury employed it
to highlight the inaccessibility of wider social ties to African Americans
as one of the most insidious legacies of slavery and segregation. French
social theorist Pierre Bourdieu defined it in the 1980s as "the aggregate of
the actual or potential resources which are linked to possession of a
durable network of more or less institutionalized relationships of
mutual acquaintance and recognition—or in other words, to membership in a group." German economist Ekkehart Schlicht used it in 1984 to
underline the economic value of organizations and moral order. Sociologist James S. Coleman put the term firmly and finally on the intellectual agenda in the late 1980s, using it (as Hanifan had originally done) to
highlight the social context of education.[5]

In recent years scholars in many fields have begun to explore the multiple sources and manifold consequences of varying stocks of social capital, and this work has grown exponentially. One search of the international social science literature found 20 articles on social capital prior to
1981, 109 between 1991 and 1995, and 1,003 between 1996 and March
1999.[6] One of the most striking features of the development of work on
social capital is the range of disciplines in which the concept has been
found useful—not merely in sociology and political science, where it
originated, but also in economics, public health, urban planning, crimi-
nology, architecture, and social psychology, among others.

While the pace and scope of this explosion of research make it impossible to summarize comprehensively the social, economic, medical, psychological, and political outcomes that have been linked to social capital,

the very range of the research is impressive. Studies from Tanzania to Sri Lanka to Italy have found that economic development under some circumstances can be boosted by adequate stocks of social capital. Studies in the United States and the United Kingdom have found that social networks, both formal and informal, reduce crime. Studies from Finland to Japan have reported strikingly consistent evidence of the powerful effects of social connectedness on physical health. Comparisons of regional governments in Italy and of state governments in the United States suggest that the quality of public administration varies with local endowments of social capital. Social capital has been studied in Andean Ecuador, medieval England, and cyberspace. Especially relevant to our project is the fact that recent work on social capital has echoed the thesis of classic political theorists from Alexis de Tocqueville to John Stuart Mill that democracy itself depends on active engagement by citizens in community affairs.[7]

Michael Woolcock and Deepa Narayan usefully synthesize much of this expanding literature:

> The basic idea of social capital is that a person's family, friends, and associates constitute an important asset, one that can be called on in a crisis, enjoyed for its own sake, and leveraged for material gain. What is true for individuals, moreover, also holds for groups. Those communities endowed with a diverse stock of social networks and civic associations are in a stronger position to confront poverty and vulnerability, resolve disputes, and take advantage of new opportunities.[8]

In short, there is mounting evidence that the characteristics of civil society affect the health of our democracies, our communities, and ourselves. There is also every reason to believe that the relevant characteristics of civil society—the contours of social capital—vary systematically across time and space. These two broad presumptions provide the starting point for this volume, though neither is systematically tested here. We begin with the assumption that social capital matters, and we ask how its characteristics have changed in the last fifty years or so in the economically advanced democracies.

The idea at the core of the theory of social capital is extremely simple: Social networks matter. Networks have value, first of all, for the people who are in them. In the language of microeconomics, networks have private or "internal" returns. The most familiar examples of this generalization are drawn from the sociology of labor markets, for a very common finding is that many—perhaps most—of us find our jobs because of whom we know as much as what we know. Some economic sociologists have even calculated the "cash value" of a person's Rolodex or address book, in the sense that one's income is determined by the range of his or her social connections, perhaps even more than by educational credentials. In that sense, social capital may rival human capital as a factor in individual productivity. Similarly, the very large literature on the effects of social support on physical and mental health refers largely to the private or internal benefits of social connections.

Another large (and growing) branch of literature on social capital refers, by contrast, to its "external" or "public" effects. One such effect is the common finding that crime rates in a neighborhood are lowered by social connectedness, so that even residents who do not themselves participate in neighborhood activities benefit from the deterrent effects of informal social capital. In that sense, social capital can be a public good. Hanifan (who wrote before the term "public good" had been coined by economists) described exactly this feature of social capital, for he argued that the legislators of West Virginia should in fact subsidize community centers because the benefits of this social interaction would not be limited to the people who made the direct investment of showing up at evening meetings.[9]

Dense networks of social interaction appear to foster sturdy norms of generalized reciprocity—"I'll do this for you now without expecting anything immediately in return, because down the road you (or someone else) will reciprocate my goodwill." Social interaction, in other words, helps to resolve dilemmas of collective action, encouraging people to act in a trustworthy way when they might not otherwise do so.[10] When economic and political dealing is embedded in dense networks of social interaction, incentives for opportunism and malfeasance are reduced. A society characterized by generalized reciprocity is more efficient than a distrustful society, for the same reason that money is more efficient than barter. Trustworthiness lubricates social life. If we don't have to balance every exchange instantly, we can get a lot more accomplished.

Social capital can thus be simultaneously a private good and a public good. In many instances of social capital, some of the benefit goes to bystanders, while some of the benefits serve the immediate interest of the person making the investment. For example, local civic clubs mobilize local energies to build a playground or a hospital at the same time that they provide members with friendships and business connections that pay off personally.

We describe social networks and the associated norms of reciprocity as social *capital*, because like physical and human capital (tools and training), social networks create value, both individual and collective, and because we can "invest" in networking. Social networks are, however, not merely investment goods, for they often provide direct consumption value. In fact, the very large international literature on the correlates of happiness ("subjective well-being" is the accepted jargon) suggests that social capital may actually be more important to human well-being than material goods. Dozens of studies have shown that human happiness is much more closely predicted by access to social capital than by access to financial capital. In fact, the single most common finding from a half century's research on the correlates of life satisfaction in countries around the globe is that happiness is best predicted by the breadth and depth of one's social connections.[11]

In the 1950s and 1960s a great debate raged in the discipline of economics—often termed "the debate of the two Cambridges," because it pitted English and American economists against one another—about whether physical capital was sufficiently homogeneous to be added up in a single ledger. A dentist's drill, a carpenter's drill, and an oil rigger's drill are all examples of physical capital, but they are hardly interchangeable. The same is true of social capital—it comes in many forms that are useful in many different contexts, but the forms are heterogeneous in the sense that they are good only for certain purposes and not others.

Your extended family represents a form of social capital, as do your Sunday school class, the people you meet regularly on your commuter train, your college classmates, the neighborhood association to which you belong, the civic organizations of which you are a member, the Internet chat group in which you participate, and the network of professional acquaintances recorded in your address book. It is even less clear in the case of social capital than it was in the debate of the two Cambridges about physical capital that we can simply "add up" all these different forms to produce a single, sensible summary of the social capital in a given community, much less an entire nation. Hence, the chapters in this volume describe the changing contours of social capital in various advanced democracies without attempting a simple summary of whether social capital in general is high or low.

If there is one enduring lesson from the early social capital debates, it is that we cannot assume that social capital is everywhere and always a good thing. Although the phrase "social capital" has a felicitous ring to it, we must take care to consider its potential vices, or even just the possibility that virtuous forms can have unintended consequences that are not socially desirable. That social capital can have negative externalities does not distinguish it in principle from other forms of capital. A nuclear power plant represents a massive investment in physical capital, even though radioactive leakage might mean that its net value for society is negative. The human capital of biochemists can be used to create lifesaving pharmaceuticals, but also to create biochemical weapons.

In short, we must understand the purposes and effects of social capital. Networks and norms might, for example, benefit those who belong—to the detriment of those who do not. Social capital might be most prevalent among groups of people who are already advantaged, thereby widening political and economic inequalities between those groups and others who are poor in social capital. Thus, in talking about different manifestations of social capital and changes in social capital over time, it is worth asking hard questions: Who benefits, and who does not? What kind of society is this form of social capital encouraging? Is more necessarily better?

Moreover, some forms of social capital are good for democracy and social health; others are (or threaten to be) destructive. Many cities in all the countries represented in this volume have organized neighborhood-based citizens' groups that meet regularly to accomplish a wide variety of purposes. One careful study of such groups in some American cities found that they increased government responsiveness to the organized neighborhoods and enhanced citizens' respect for government.[12] On the other hand, many American localities have had a different sort of citizens' group: the Ku Klux Klan and its less violent cousins, such as neighborhood groups that resist racial integration. With its century-old tradition of bigotry and racially motivated violence, the Klan represented a form of social capital that subverted the rules and traditions of liberal democracy. With its internal norms of trust and reciprocity, reinforced by a shared "self-defensive" purpose, the Klan—and its counterparts in other countries—remind us that social capital is not automatically conducive to democratic governance.

Since the forms of social capital vary greatly, social capital theorists have placed a high priority on developing a theoretically coherent and empirically reliable classification of different types and dimensions of social capital. Though we are still far from such a canonical account, at least four important distinctions have emerged from the scholarly debates. These distinctions are not mutually exclusive. Rather, they represent different yet complementary lenses through which social capital might be understood and evaluated.

Formal versus informal social capital. Some forms of social capital, such as parents' organizations or labor unions, are formally organized, with recognized officers, membership requirements, dues, regular meetings, and so on. On the other hand, some, like pickup games of basketball or people who gather at the same pub, are highly informal. And yet both of those constitute networks in which reciprocity can develop, and from which there can be both private and public gains. Early research on social capital concentrated on formal associations for reasons of methodological convenience, so it is worth emphasizing here that *associations constitute merely one form of social capital.*

Informal associating (say, family dinners) may be more instrumental than formal associations in achieving some valued purposes. Many scholars are actively developing new ways of identifying and measuring informal social capital, and the case studies in this book often touch on informal social connectedness. However, research on long-term trends in social capital inevitably depends on what evidence survives from the past, and thus the country case studies have been forced to emphasize formal (record-keeping) types of social capital.

Thick versus thin social capital. Some forms of social capital are closely interwoven and multistranded, such as a group of steelworkers who work together every day at the factory, go out for drinks on Saturday, and go to mass every Sunday. There are also very thin, almost invisible filaments of social capital, such as the nodding acquaintance you have with the person you occasionally see waiting in line at the supermarket, or even a chance encounter with another person in an elevator. Even these very casual forms of social connection have been shown experimentally to induce a certain form of reciprocity; merely nodding to a stranger increases the likelihood that he or she will come to your aid if you suddenly are stricken.[13] On the other hand, that tenuous, single-stranded bond is very different from your ties to members of your immediate family, another example of a thick social network.

The sociologist Mark Granovetter first articulated a closely related distinction between "strong ties" and "weak ties." Strong ties are defined in terms of the frequency of contact and closedness. If all of my friends are friends of each other and I spend a lot of time with them, we have a strong tie. I have a weak tie with someone with whom I have only a passing acquaintance and have few friends in common. Granovetter pointed out that weak ties are more important than strong ties when it comes to searching for a job. You're more likely to get a job through someone you don't know well than through someone you do know well, because a close friend of yours is likely to know the same people you know, whereas a casual acquaintance is likely to lead you to unknown opportunities. Weak ties may also be better for knitting a society together and for building broad norms of generalized reciprocity. Strong ties are probably better for other purposes, such as social mobilization and social insurance, although it is fair to add that social science has only begun to parse the effects, positive and negative, of various kinds of social capital.

Inward-looking versus outward-looking social capital. Some forms of social capital are, by choice or necessity, inward-looking and tend to promote the material, social, or political interests of their own members, while others are outward-looking and concern themselves with public goods. Groups in the first category are commonly organized along class, gender, or ethnic lines and exist to preserve or strengthen the bonds of birth and circumstance. Examples include London's gentlemen's clubs, chambers of commerce, contemporary labor organizations, and informal credit unions created by new immigrants. In the second category we find charitable groups such as the Red Cross, the U.S. civil rights movement, and the environmental movements that emerged in all advanced democracies in the 1970s and 1980s. It is tempting to judge the outward-looking or altruistic organizations as socially or morally superior to the inward-looking groups, on the grounds that the outward-looking groups provide clear public as well as personal benefits. We see the appeal of such an argument, but we believe it should be viewed with skepticism. Precisely because social capital is stubbornly resistant to quantification, we cannot say that an outward-looking youth service corps that clears an urban playground has somehow increased our stock of social capital more than, say, an inward-looking credit union that has allowed a new immigrant community to flourish.

Bridging versus bonding social capital.   Closely related to, but conceptually distinct from, the inward-outward dichotomy is the "bridging-bonding" axis. Bonding social capital brings together people who are like one another in important respects (ethnicity, age, gender, social class, and so on), whereas bridging social capital refers to social networks that bring together people who are unlike one another. This is an important distinction, because the external effects of bridging networks are likely to be positive, while bonding networks (limited within particular social niches) are at greater risk of producing negative externalities. This is not to say that bonding groups are necessarily bad; indeed, evidence suggests that most of us get our social support from bonding rather than bridging social ties.[14]

It is true, however, that without the natural restraints imposed by members' crosscutting allegiances and diverse perspectives, tightly knit and homogeneous groups can rather easily combine for sinister ends. In other words, bonding without bridging equals Bosnia. Ashutosh Varsh-ney has recently shown that violence between Hindus and Muslims in India is markedly reduced in communities where civic associations bridge this volatile religious cleavage.[15]

As a practical matter, most groups blend bridging and bonding, but the blends differ: They may include people of different socioeconomic classes but the same ethnicity or religion (many fraternal organizations fit here), or they may include people of different races but mostly or exclusively the same gender (for example, quilting circles and sports leagues).

Because social capital is multidimensional, and some of those dimensions themselves are subject to different understandings, we must take care not to frame questions about change solely in terms of more social capital or less social capital. Rather, we must describe the changes in qualitative terms. For example, within a given country one could imagine that the stock of social capital has become more formal but less bridging, more bridging but less intensive, or more intensive but less public-regarding. Or there could be truth in all three develop-ments. That is, a nation could simultaneously see growth in ethnically based social clubs, rainbow coalitions, and government-hating citizens' militias.

Theories of change in civil society have been at the core of sociology since its inception as a distinct discipline in the nineteenth century. Probably the single most dominant view has been that as society has become more modern, industrial, and urban, community bonds have atrophied. Industrialization changes the relations of production and provides incentives for people to leave the country for the city. Those developments, in turn, displace older forms of solidarity and social organization without replacing them (so the theory goes) with new forms of social capital befitting the new environment.

The thesis that modernization undermines community was in many respects at the core of the work of the classic founders of sociology—Durkheim, Tönnies, Weber, Simmel, and others. As we have already noted, L. J. Hanifan had the distinct impression that social capital had eroded in West Virginia in the last decades of the nineteenth century. This thesis was hardly unique, for as sociologist Barry Wellman observes:

> It is likely that pundits have worried about the impact of social change on communities ever since human beings ventured beyond their caves.... In the [past] two centuries many leading social com-

mentators have been gainfully employed suggesting various ways in which large-scale social changes associated with the Industrial Revolution may have affected the structure and operation of communities. . . . This ambivalence about the consequences of large-scale changes continued well into the twentieth century. Analysts have kept asking if things have, in fact, fallen apart. [16]

And as sociologist Pamela Paxton recently noted:

In fact, it could be argued that the birth of sociology occurred in concerns about potential declines in community due to industrialization and the advent of modernity.[17]

It became fashionable among academics in the last quarter of the twentieth century to debunk this so-called modernization theory. We too will find reason to question it, for it fails to account for important continuities, as well as important changes, in patterns of social capital in each of our countries. However, we should not gainsay that it is a powerfully parsimonious attempt at synthesis of the extraordinarily complex changes that swept across much of the world during the nineteenth and twentieth centuries. The question to which modernization theory was an answer—how are social relations affected by industrialization and urbanization?—was an intelligent, even inescapable one.

It was the great observer of American society Alexis de Tocqueville who first took up our particular challenge: to examine changing social mores and bonds with the premise that such changes had implications for the performance of democracy. Writing in the 1830s, Tocqueville observed how, following the 1789 revolution in his native France, an aristocratic, communally oriented society tended to give way to a democratic, individualist society. Individualist democracy, Tocqueville suggested, could take two different forms. The first was a form of atomistic despotism, in which politically equal citizens, newly freed from aristocracy's ties to patrons above and servants below, tend to their own self-interest and thereby leave the door open for a few rulers to grab and centralize their power. The second possible democratic form is liberal, decentralized, and participatory. Public-spirited mores and institutions of civil society, such as those Tocqueville saw in the United States, serve as a check on the centrifugal forces of democratic equality.[18] These insights notwithstanding, Tocqueville offered no deep theory of how changes in civil society either caused or made possible the transition from the aristocratic state to the democratic state.

Later in the nineteenth century European sociologists reformulated Tocqueville's polarity. Sir Henry Main distinguished between traditional society, based on status, and modern society, based on contract. For Ferdinand Tönnies, the fundamental sociopolitical divide was between *Gemeinschaft* (community) and *Gesellschaft* (society). Emile Durkheim differentiated between mechanical solidarity, which characterizes societies of social similars organized in tightly knit and insular collectives, and organic solidarity, which characterizes societies in which diverse individuals play different roles, each indispensable to the larger whole. Georg Simmel compared social relations in the traditional town and in the modern metropolis.

Each of these social theorists captured a different facet of the same fundamental social transformation: modernization. Each, of course, oversimplified. For example, these theorists made few attempts to distinguish between different forms of traditional societies and different forms of modern societies. Likewise, they did a poor job of distinguishing among different dimensions of change: Was the breakdown of traditional forms of community felt primarily in the world of work, family relations, civil society, government institutions, or some combination thereof? Yet for all their vagueness, these theorists did share the general view that the decay of community bonds is inevitable in modernizing societies and that institutions must be created to fill the void.

Many people—political leaders, social philosophers, and ordinary citizens—believe that the turn from the twentieth century to the twenty-first century is witnessing a fundamental social transformation perhaps unmatched since industrialization. This transformation has many dimensions, with some attracting greater comment and concern than others. In many advanced democracies, for example, social scientists and others have documented changes in the performance of democratic institutions, especially the weakening of political parties, the rise of media- and poll-centered campaigns, and the sharp decline in public confidence in government. There have also been changes in the structure and performance of economies, particularly with respect to the welfare state and income stratification. Although the second half of the 1990s was a time of economic growth for most Western democracies, that growth has been accompanied by an erosion of many nations' income security and social programs, and in a number of countries by a simultaneous and probably historically unprecedented growth in the gap between the well-to-do and everyone else.

Changes have occurred in other sectors of society as well. At least since the 1970s, the Western democracies have seen an overhaul in family structure—many fewer "traditional" two-parent families with children—prompted by divorce, delayed marriages, and more births out of wedlock.[19] At the other end of the scale, globalization is rapidly integrating the world's economy, bringing new prosperity to many parts of the world, but also undermining national autonomy. Even popular culture has undergone major shifts. Fueled by television, the end of the Cold War, and the opening of global markets, Western commercialism has spread eastward, from Los Angeles and New York to London, Prague, Moscow, and Shanghai. This has prompted the beginnings of the homogenization of popular culture.

And yet vast population movements have had an equal and opposite effect. The migrations of Asians and Latin Americans into the United States and Canada, of North Africans into France, of Turks and Bosnians into Germany, of Albanians and Iraqis into Italy, and of Koreans and Filipinos into Japan have diversified the demography and cultures of these democracies and are likely to do so still more in the future. In some respects the growing ethnic heterogeneity of the established democracies (as well as the nativist backlash that has often accompanied this change) is the most striking commonality among the societies represented in this volume.

All of these changes—in governmental, economic, social, and cultural norms—have had a ripple effect on civil society. In some cases, these transformations have spurred the growth and spirit of grassroots institutions, while in other cases, civil society has suffered. Some of these transformations may be conducive to social trust and harmony, while others may be corrosive of them. Some of these cultural shifts (for example, the integration of immigrants) might be intelligently managed to protect or even create social capital, while others (for example, family breakdown) will prove more difficult to translate into social-capital-building opportunities. Put another way, some twenty-first-century transformations are amenable to social-capital-oriented policy interventions, and some are not especially so. Likewise, some of these transformations are hurtling forward in an irreversible trajectory (for example, the development of computer technology), while other transformations may prove to be cyclical (say, the yawning income gap in many Western democracies).

With these caveats in mind, this project aims both to describe social capital and its evolution in eight democracies and to speculate about how this evolution has, or has not, been influenced by the larger sociopolitical context.

What accounts for change in social capital and civic engagement?

Conventional accounts, of which modernization theory is the most relevant, have described a trajectory that begins with the industrial revolution and the technological innovations accompanying it. The mass movement of people from cohesive rural areas to big, anonymous, atomistic cities translates into an overall decline in community and social capital.

This account clearly captures important common features of social change in Western nations between 1750 and 1950. And it may offer some inspiration for our efforts to understand the changes in contemporary postindustrial societies. On the other hand, close research has shown that a simpleminded interpretation of this theory drastically underestimated the ability of humans over the longer run to adapt existing forms of social capital and to create new forms to fit new circumstances.

Our self-assigned task here, however, is not to articulate another linear or one-dimensional theory of change in social capital that would be more carefully tailored to present conditions. Nor do we aspire to identify a common driving force behind changing stocks of social capital. Indeed, our studies raise serious questions about whether either aim would bear fruit. The nations in this study have been buffeted by many of the same social and economic forces but have seen dramatically different changes in social capital. Some nations have seen growth in voluntary associationalism, for example, while others have seen declines. This paradox reminds us of the advantages of comparative analysis. Cross-national case studies help to rule out, or at least raise questions about, certain conventional "universal" theories of causality while opening our minds to the possibility that multiple factors may be at work in different places to produce similar outcomes. In this volume, we take an empirically grounded first step toward identifying and analyzing the range of possible ways in which social capital has changed in the postwar era and the different factors responsible for instigating or perpetuating those changes. Because each author is attentive to the peculiarities of his or her national case, each highlights somewhat different causal processes, but common interpretive threads run through the various chapters. We consider, and find support for, a number of driving forces.

Technological innovation is certainly one of them. The second half of the twentieth century saw the rapid spread of inventions and innovations scarcely imagined when the century began. There are new technologies for entertainment (notably television), for communication (cheap and nearly universal long-distance phone service, fax machines, electronic mail), and for information (the Internet). These new technologies have had myriad effects on social capital. On one hand, they have no doubt enhanced our ability to maintain our social networks even across vast spaces. On the other hand, they have also facilitated a withdrawal of some people from civic and social life. It is hardly surprising that technology's effects on social capital building are mixed.

Another force influencing a nation's stock of social capital is the social or political entrepreneur. Leadership matters, because leaders build institutions through which social capital can germinate and grow. Unions organize because some enterprising worker—or enterprising federation—decides to organize them. Citizens' groups form because someone learns, often from personal experience, that public policy needs to change. Reading groups form because a couple of friends decide it would be fun to widen their social circle. Granted, entrepreneurs do not succeed unless the product they are selling—associationalism—is both in demand and undersupplied. The more interesting question isn't whether leaders affect the stock of social capital, but rather what affects the stock of leaders.

Hovering above individual leaders, and also influencing social capital, is the state. By that we mean both the institutions of government and the particular polices that those institutions promulgate. Some states have provided tax subsidies to voluntary organizations, making it easier for them to form and attract members, while other states have actively discouraged such associations. Some states are relatively open, fragmented, and decentralized, providing a political structure conducive to citizen-group participation in public affairs. Many states, by providing mass public education, have encouraged the formation not only of human capital but also of social capital, since education is a powerful predictor of civic engagement. And some states directly involve associations, such as unions and business organizations, in the making and implementing of public policy, thereby enhancing their sense of purpose and solidarity.

The myriad ways in which the state encourages or discourages the formation of social capital have been underresearched. Does trustworthy government—that is, a state whose officials are honest and effective in responding to citizens' needs—increase social trust? Do certain types of economic policies—say, those aimed at mitigating income inequality—facilitate the building of social capital across class lines? Does having a state church affect the type or amount of social capital in the polity? Such questions represent some of the many largely unexplored frontiers in social capital research, and while not resolved in this volume, each is illuminated by cases represented here.

Another underexplored question is to what extent war contributes to social capital. At first blush, the possibility that an event defined by violence, destruction, and death could seed peaceful cooperation for public ends seems illogical. But upon closer inspection, the connection is less surprising. Durkheim, Simmel, and other founders of the social sciences understood that shared crises create shared interests and shared identities. War creates social problems and individual needs that government has neither the infrastructure nor the extra resources to address. During the U.S. Civil War, for example, voluntary associations and church networks shuttled thousands of orphaned children to foster homes in the frontier West. After the Civil War, battleground nurses formed the American Red Cross, whose volunteers today continue to provide relief services during wartime and peacetime. As the case studies of Germany and (to a lesser extent) Japan in this volume illustrate, wars also may mark a transition from one form of government that is inhospitable to social capital to another that allows social capital to flourish.

Finally, of course, sociodemographic changes can influence a nation's types and stock of social capital. Building and maintaining social capital requires time, energy, and in some cases civic skills. Where individuals choose or are forced to deploy their resources in other places—in demanding jobs, for example—social capital is likely to suffer. The same is true when growing populations do not have the opportunity to learn civic dispositions, or when rapid mobility or long-distance commuting undermines social connectedness.

The authors in this study are social theorists in their own right. Several of them couple their accounts of the dynamics of social capital in their specific country with a wider account of how social capital should be conceived. Thus, for example, Offe and Fuchs begin their essay with a broader typology of the dimensions of social capital, while Pérez-Díaz emphasizes a distinction between "civil" and "uncivil" social capital. At this stage of the debate about social capital, it seems more productive to encourage those voices, no matter how dissonant, rather than to force a false theoretical unity. What unites us, above all, is a shared concern to understand patterns of social change and their implications for our democracies.

This volume will shed light on these various causal factors. But more important, it will provide for the first time a panoramic view of social capital in advanced postindustrial nations. As part of a global economy, the nations examined in this volume are influenced by many of the same economic and social forces. At the same time, they differ across the range of historical experience, economic organization, and democratic structures. Moreover, even when similar forces have impinged on all our countries—the advent of commercial television, the divorce revolution, urban sprawl, the movement of women into the paid labor force, the growth of the Internet, and many more—the timing of those changes has varied among our countries, in some cases by decades. It is not surprising, then, that the features of social capital in these countries have converged in some ways but diverged in others.

In this book we seek to bring to bear on these questions detailed evidence, both qualitative and quantitative, from eight different countries, covering roughly the period from the end of World War II to the end of the twentieth century. Our countries represent a broad sampling of advanced, postindustrial democracies from Western Europe, North America, and East Asia. Because of the unique importance that Tocqueville's America has played in theories of what we now call social capital, we include two essays on the United States, one more directly comparable to the other national case studies in its focus on the last several decades of the twentieth century and the second taking a longer historical view.

We should warn the reader now that we render no simple verdict. Indeed, we do not entirely agree among ourselves on what concepts are best suited for framing questions of change. A collective volume necessarily lacks the simple clarity that a single-author study can often produce. On the other hand, in an area such as ours, in which serious research programs are just getting under way, the diversity of perspectives and insights that a collection of creative scholars can provide is an even more valuable asset. We hope that the reader will benefit from this diversity in framing his or her own approach to this complicated but portentous subject.

1

GREAT BRITAIN: The Role of Government and the Distribution of Social Capital

PETER A. HALL

One of the most striking findings to come from social science in recent years reports an apparent erosion within the United States, normally the most civic of nations, in the propensity of individuals to engage in community affairs, to trust one another, and to associate together on a regular basis.[1] As the introduction to this volume indicates, this shift in interpersonal relations may have broad consequences. The purpose of this chapter is to examine the trajectory of such patterns of sociability, and thus of social capital, in Great Britain over the past fifty years. Following the definition of social capital popularized by Robert Putnam, my focus is on networks of sociability, both formal and informal, that bring individuals into regular contact with one another, and on norms of social trust, understood as the generalized willingness of individuals to trust their fellow citizens.[2] Although measurement problems necessitate an emphasis on membership in voluntary associations, I will also consider trends in other forms of sociability, including participation in charitable endeavors and informal relations with neighbors or friends.

The British case is an unusually interesting one. Overall levels of social capital there seem to have remained relatively robust for the past fifty years, but disparities among social groups in the distribution of social capital have widened over the period, drawing attention to the distributive dimensions of a phenomenon often seen largely as a collective good. Although social capital is often treated as a feature of civil society with an impact on governance but largely social roots, developments in Britain suggest that the causal arrows also run in the other direction: Governments can affect the level of social capital in a nation.

Britain provides a natural case for assessing whether the decline in social capital is primarily an American phenomenon or a broader trend affecting the developed democracies. The nation has long had some of the densest networks of civic association in the world. As one historian observes: "No nation can lay claim to a richer philanthropic past than Britain."[3] Civic organizations flowered during a nineteenth century that Trevelyan described as "the age of Trade Unions, Cooperative and Benefit Societies, Leagues, Boards, Commissions, Committees for every conceivable purpose of philanthropy and culture," adding that in England "not even the dumb animals were left unorganized."[4] Of the countries they examined during the 1950s, Almond and Verba found that, along with the United States, Britain still had the most civic of cultures, characterized by high levels of social organization, trust, and political participation, and even those critical of social organization regard Britain as a polar case.[5] Moreover, the many cultural and political similarities between Britain and the United States render it propitious terrain for testing some of the explanations that have been advanced for changes in the level of social capital.

My analysis will proceed in three steps. In the next section, I will assess overall trends in the level of social capital in Britain during recent decades, encompassing as much of the period since 1950 as possible. Then I will make an effort to explain these trends and draw some general conclusions about the causal factors that lie behind changes in social capital. Finally, I will explore how various dimensions of democratic politics are related to levels of social capital in Britain and discuss some general implications of this case for the understanding of social capital.

TRENDS IN SOCIAL CAPITAL

As conceptualized here, social capital turns primarily on the degree to which people associate regularly with one another in settings of relative equality, thus building up relations of trust and mutual reciprocity. Therefore, it can be created through formal or informal patterns of sociability, and it should be reflected both in the levels of general trust in others that people express and in their commitment to voluntary work in the community.

Membership in Voluntary Associations

At the core of this definition of social capital is membership in voluntary associations that may be dedicated to a variety of purposes, ranging from the recreational or social to the religious or political, but which share two key features: They involve their members in at least some face-to-face interaction with others (a factor of importance, since it is from such interaction that the capacity for generalized reciprocity is said to follow), and they engage their members in common endeavor (thereby nurturing the capacity for collective action, of long-standing importance to democracies).[6] Therefore, changes in membership of voluntary associations should provide one of the best indicators of trends in social capital. Figure 1-1 reports total membership levels for all the relevant organizations for which I was able to secure long runs of data, divided into various types, and the indices in Figure 1-2 display the rate of membership growth per organization aggregated by type of organization.[7]

Several patterns are apparent. First, membership has risen in some types of organizations and fallen in others. Traditional women's organizations, which tend to be oriented toward homemakers, have experienced the most striking declines in recent years, while environmental organizations, whose membership has quadrupled since 1971, have made the greatest gains.[8] Among youth groups, sports clubs, and service and recreational associations, some organizations have lost members, while others have gained. Second, despite fluctuation and the decline of some organizations, overall levels of membership in secondary associations have not eroded to any substantial degree over the long term. Figure 1-2 suggests that average membership has grown among all the types of organizations other than traditional women's associations at a rate that generally exceeds population growth. Third, although the long-run pattern shows modest expansion, there was some decline in membership during the 1980s, especially among youth organizations and a few service organizations, such as the Red Cross and St. John's Ambulance Society. After rising for most of the postwar period from 9.5 million members in 1951 to peak at 12.9 million in 1980, membership in trade unions also declined to 9.6 million in 1991.

In sum, average membership levels among most kinds of organizations seem to have risen at least enough to keep pace with population growth and rising levels of educational achievement through the postwar period. Moreover, data tracking membership in organizations that have been in existence for some time may understate the overall levels of organizational affiliation in British society. A survey of the directory compiled by the National Council for Voluntary Organisations shows

Figure 1-1: Trends in Total Membership of Various Kinds of Organizations, 1951–1991 (in thousands)

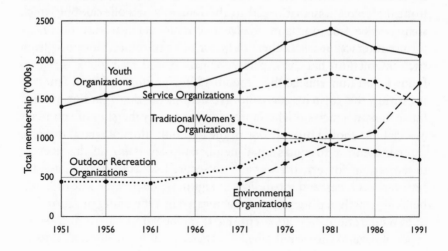

Figure 1-2: Index of Growth in Membership (1971=100)

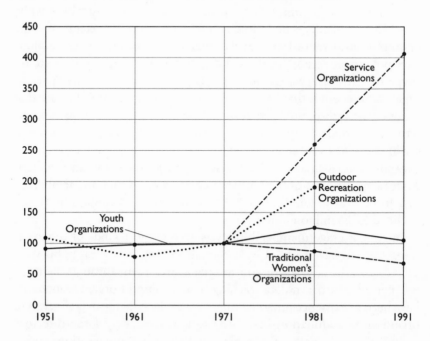

Source: *Social Trends* (London: HMSO, various years).

that large numbers of new voluntary associations have been created in Britain during the past three decades.[9] The Wolfenden Committee, appointed to look into the voluntary sector in 1976, found that over half of the voluntary associations in the five regions it examined had been created since 1960, and a more recent study of 1,173 national voluntary organizations in 1992 observed that while a quarter of them had been established before 1944, about another quarter were founded in the 1970s and a further quarter in the 1980s.[10] This is confirmed by Knapp and Saxon-Harrold, who observe a 27 percent increase in the number of voluntary organizations during the 1980s, reflecting the creation of three thousand to four thousand organizations a year.[11] In some cases, these are organizations formed around newly popular causes, such as environmentalism; in others, they reflect an increase in types of cooperative endeavors that have been rendered more important by social change, such as preschool playgroups, which now mobilize over 1.4 million volunteers in Britain.[12]

The available survey data present a very similar picture. The first row in Table 1-1 displays the average number of associational memberships reported by representative samples of the British electorate at four points during the postwar period.[13] The results are strikingly consistent with the aggregate data. They reveal that the average number of associational memberships among the adult population grew by 44 percent between 1959 and 1990, rising most rapidly during the 1960s but subsiding only slightly thereafter.[14] As the data for associational memberships among those at each of three levels of educational attainment suggest, the size of this increase is largely an artifact of rising educational levels within the populace as a whole. However, it is significant that associational membership does not decline among those at any given level of educational attainment.

The first of the broad conclusions we can draw from this is that overall levels of associational membership in Britain seem to have been at least as high in the 1980s and 1990s as they were in 1959, and perhaps somewhat higher. Even when the respondents' levels of education are held constant, the basic inclination of the vast majority of the British populace to join associations remained roughly the same in 1990 as it was in the 1950s.[15]

These results are consistent with the evidence from a wide range of national and local studies conducted over recent decades in Britain. In what remains the definitive study of political participation in Britain, Parry and colleagues found that two-thirds of the population belonged to at least one formal association and 36 percent belonged to two or more in 1984–85, while others estimate that 3 million Britons serve on

Table 1-1: Trends in Associational Membership

	1959	1973	1981	1990
All people	.73	1.15	.87	1.12
GENDER				
Men	1.05	1.46	.93	1.13
Women	.43	.90	.81	1.11
EDUCATION				
Primary	.60	.97	.64	.67
Secondary	.88	1.48	.76	1.04
Postsecondary	1.58	2.05	1.74	2.18
SOCIAL CLASS				
Upper middle	1.13	2.24	1.57	2.15
Nonmanual/clerical	.82	1.36	.89	1.34
Skilled manual	.70	1.02	.63	.79
Low-skilled manual	.53	1.02	.57	.65
AGE				
30 or under	.63	1.14	.71	.90
Over 30	.75	1.16	.98	1.19

Note: The cells report the average number of associational memberships per person in each group.
Source: 1959, the Civic Culture Survey; 1973, the Political Action Survey; 1981 and 1990, the World Values Surveys.

associations' committees each year.[16] Detailed case studies by Bishop and Hoggett found 300 groups with an average membership of 90 for a population of 85,000 in a suburb of Bristol and 3,000 men playing organized soccer every Saturday morning in a locality of Leicester with a population of 68,000. Knight's survey of voluntary social service organizations in fourteen localities found 3,691 such organizations serving 946,000 people, in ratios that varied from 1 per 165 local residents in a Scottish town to 1 to 361 residents in an inner-city neighborhood.[17]

Charitable Endeavor

Support for charitable endeavor is another important dimension of social capital. Volunteer work tends to bring individuals into direct contact with their neighbors and represents an important form of civic engagement. Accordingly, we may find some indicators here for the state of social capital in Britain.

The number of charities formally registered in Britain has risen

steadily to 166,503 in 1991, as has the amount of money donated to charitable organizations, which was roughly £5 billion or £10 per person in
1993.[18] Even more important, large proportions of the British populace
engage in voluntary work each year, usually oriented toward the provision of social services for the sick and elderly or the education and recreation of the young. One study found that 17 percent of people had
engaged in some form of voluntary work in 1976 and that 9 percent did
so on a weekly basis.[19] Although one must be cautious about comparability over time, some surveys found even higher numbers in the 1980s
and 1990s. In 1981, 23 percent of respondents to the General Household
Survey reported doing some voluntary work in that year, and Goddard
found that a quarter of the populace had done some voluntary work in
1992, with 15 percent normally participating twice a week or more, to
produce about 20 million hours of voluntary work each week in the
United Kingdom.[20] Other studies report that as many as a third of all citizens are now doing some voluntary work each year.[21] Although much of
this work involves collecting money for charities, about a third of all volunteers have also served on a committee, and most of the work involves
face-to-face contact with others in their neighborhood.[22]

These figures will not surprise anyone familiar with small and
medium-sized British cities, where three or four charity shops, staffed by
volunteers and selling goods for Oxfam, Barnardo's, or another charity,
are usually visible on the main streets. An in-depth study of three towns
for the Wolfenden Committee found substantial numbers of voluntary
organizations in each (82 organizations and 2,000 active volunteers in
a population of 50,000; 112 organizations and 2,500 active volunteers
in a population of 60,000; 239 organizations and 4,000 active volunteers
in a population of 265,000).[23] In general, most recent studies of the voluntary sector in Britain conclude that it is extensive and vibrant.

Informal Sociability
Participation in formal associations and voluntary work, of course, do
not constitute the only source of social capital. The networks of face-to-
face contact on which social capital depends can also be based on regular
interaction with others in less formal settings, such as those that involve
socializing with friends, conversation with neighbors, and informally
organized but regular activities undertaken with others. Many studies
neglect these kinds of informal sociability because they are much harder
to measure, but there is some basis for assessing trends in them in
Britain.

Time budget studies provide the most important source of data on

Table 1-2: Changes in the Use of Time (Average Minutes per Day)

General Use of Time Pursuits Associated with Social Capital

	Leisure at home	Leisure beyond home	Radio	TV	Sport	Civic duties	Social clubs	Pubs	Visit friends	All
Men in full-time employment										
1961	209	69	23	121	4 (9)	6 (15)	4 (10)	4 (16)	19 (43)	37
1975	207	102	5	126	7 (19)	4 (12)	8 (17)	14 (39)	21 (57)	54
1984	209	98	3	129	10 (31)	3 (13)	5 (16)	13 (41)	8 (60)	39
Women in full-time employment										
1961	173	61	16	93	2 (6)	2 (9)	1 (4)	0 (3)	24 (55)	29
1975	183	82	3	103	1 (6)	3 (11)	6 (13)	3 (17)	27 (69)	40
1984	188	90	2	102	2 (17)	7 (21)	2 (6)	10 (32)	21 (75)	42
Women in part-time employment										
1961	207	72	21	98	1 (11)	8 (13)	1 (2)	1 (4)	30 (35)	41
1975	221	99	4	112	2 (6)	5 (18)	3 (9)	3 (14)	33 (69)	46
1984	222	89	2	121	5 (17)	5 (21)	2 (9)	4 (20)	26 (75)	42
Women not in paid employment										
1961	257	70	25	125	1 (4)	5 (13)	1 (5)	0 (2)	34 (64)	41
1975	268	116	6	132	1 (5)	5 (16)	4 (10)	3 (14)	42 (81)	55
1984	286	95	3	147	3 (16)	6 (17)	3 (11)	4 (21)	29 (79)	45

Note: The figures in parentheses represent the percentage of the group participating in this activity. The samples for 1975 were taken in 1974–75 and for 1984 in 1983–84.
Source: Adapted from Jonathan Gershuny and Sally Jones, "The Changing Work/Leisure Balance in Britain, 1961–1984," in John Horne et al., eds., Sport, Leisure and Social Relations (London: Routledge and Kegan Paul, 1985), 9–50.

informal sociability. Table 1-2 reports the average number of minutes per day that individuals drawn from a representative sample of the British populace and divided according to their employment status spent on a variety of leisure activities in 1961, 1974–75, and 1983–84. Over this period as a whole, the amount of leisure time available to most people increased substantially as a result of reductions in working time and the diffusion of labor-saving devices.[24] However, it is notable that most groups chose to use this leisure time outside the home rather than inside, thereby expanding their scope for sociability. Although many people spent more time watching television, this usually replaced time that had been spent listening to the radio.

The six right-hand columns in Table 1-2 display the time spent on the type of activities outside the home that might be said to contribute to the formation of social capital. The total amount of time spent on such activities increased substantially through the 1960s and early 1970s and then declined slightly in the subsequent ten years, but it remained at least as high in 1984 as it had been in 1961. In general, the proportion of people participating in each of these activities (indicated in parentheses) also increased, sometimes substantially. These data tend to contradict suggestions that the British have become increasingly "privatized" or focused on "home life" over the postwar years at the expense of contact with people outside the home.[25] Instead, even a conservative interpretation would suggest that there has been some expansion in informal sociability over the past forty years.

In Britain, the public house has long been one of the most important institutions associated with informal sociability. Most neighborhoods contain several such establishments, and for many decades a visit to the pub was not only a regular feature of life for large segments of the population, but one that provided an opportunity to converse with friends and neighbors. In 1953, a national survey found that a third of all men went to the pub more than once a week and another 16 percent went once each week, although the equivalent figures for women were only 4 and 11 percent.[26] In 1957, 47 percent of all respondents to a national survey reported visiting a pub in the past week.[27] What has been the fate of this vehicle for informal sociability?

Unfortunately, the data available on trends in the use people make of pubs are very limited. The number of public houses in Britain fell substantially from 1900, when there were 102,189 (or 31.69 per 10,000 people), to 66,057 (or 13.45 per 10,000 people) in 1978, despite a small revival during the 1970s. However, as Table 1-2 indicates, both the number of people visiting pubs and the amount of time they spend in them seem to have risen between the 1950s and the 1980s. Roughly speaking, these figures suggest that just under half of all men spent an average of an hour and a half each week in a pub during the 1980s. Moreover, women are now much more likely to visit a pub than they were in the 1950s. In 1986, 47 percent of women reported that they had visited a pub in the last month, compared with 65 percent of men.[28] At a minimum, the pub seems to remain an important vehicle for informal sociability, at least among some segments of the British populace.[29]

Generation Effects

Although overall levels of social capital do not seem to have declined substantially in Britain since the war, it may be that they have fallen among the younger generations. If so, we can expect overall levels of social capital to decline over time, as older generations are replaced by newer ones. The possibility must be taken especially seriously because Putnam finds precisely such a generational effect in the United States, where he contrasts the activism of a "long civic generation" born between 1910 and 1940 with the lower levels of civic engagement he finds among the generations born after 1940.[30]

Disentangling generational effects from life cycle effects and period effects is notoriously difficult.[31] We can begin by examining Figure 1-3, which reports average levels of associational membership, church membership, and social trust among different age cohorts in Britain aggregated from their responses at five different points in time (1959, 1973, 1977, 1981, and 1990). Figure 1-3 shows a general rise since the turn of the century in the inclination of successive age cohorts to participate in voluntary associations, which peaks with the cohort born between 1940 and 1944 and falls thereafter. At first glance, the chart seems to indicate that the postwar generations are less engaged in civic endeavor than the

Figure 1-3: Levels of Associational Membership, Social Trust, and Church Membership by Date of Birth

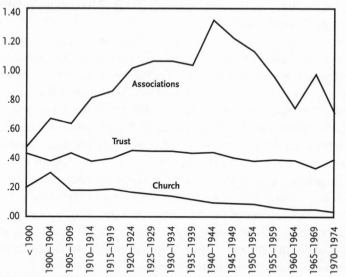

Note: The lines in the figure represent the average number of associations to which the respondents belong, the percentage reporting that they attend church regularly, and the percentage expressing social trust as defined in note 35. As appropriate, the left-hand scale should be read as a percentage or as the average number of memberships on a scale from 0.0 to 1.40.
Source: Civic Culture Survey 1959, Political Action Survey 1973, Eurobarometer study 1977, World Values Surveys 1981 and 1990.

Table 1-3: The Average Number of Associational Memberships of Different Generations at Various Ages

Age	Interwar Generation	1940s Generation	1950s Generation
20–25	.64		.87
25–30	.62	1.05	1.00
30–35	.94	1.17	1.00
35–40	1.07	1.22	1.33
40–45	1.27	1.22	
45–50	1.28	1.47	

Note: The interwar generation was born between 1919 and 1939, the 1940s generation between 1940 and 1949, and the 1950s generation between 1950 and 1959.
Source: Survey data from the 1959 Civic Culture Survey, the 1973 Political Action Survey, the 1977 Eurobarometer study, and the 1981 and 1990 World Values Surveys.

interwar generation and have become progressively less engaged with each successive generation.[32]

However, closer inspection suggests that the impression conveyed by Figure 1-3 may simply be the artifact of data limitations and a strong life cycle effect. As many studies have confirmed, civic involvement increases substantially with age, rising from relatively low levels in a person's teens and twenties to peak in one's forties and fifties.[33] Since the last point from which the data for Figure 1-3 could be drawn was 1990, the organizational involvement of those born after 1950 is sampled only during their teens, twenties, and thirties, before they have reached what would normally be their peak levels of organizational involvement.

Therefore, in order to separate life cycle effects from generational effects, I have drawn three generational groups from the sample—those born during the interwar years, those born during the 1940s, and those born during the 1950s—and examine the organizational involvement of each at different ages. The results, reported in Table 1-3, show that at any given age, those in the 1940s and 1950s generations tend to belong to at least as many associations as those in the interwar generation did at that age. By and large, this is also the case when the level of education of the population is held constant.[34] These results lead me to conclude, at least tentatively, that we do not see the same generational effects in Britain that Putnam finds in the United States; at least, the 1940s and 1950s generations display as much civic engagement as their interwar counterparts.

Social Trust

A slightly different picture emerges when we consider levels of social trust, understood as the general inclination of people to trust their fellow citizens.[35] Here there are two key developments. First, overall levels of social trust declined between 1959, when 56 percent of respondents said they generally trusted others, and 1990, when only 44 percent said they did. There is almost certainly a period effect here of some magnitude. Second, the erosion in social trust has been more substantial among some groups than others. Table 1-4 indicates that the decline in social trust has been greater among the working class than the middle

Table 1-4: Trends in Social Trust

Percentage Who Display Social Trust

	1959	1981	1990
All people	56	43	44
Gender			
Men	56	45	46
Women	56	42	42
Education			
Primary	50	37	42
Secondary	64	42	41
Postsecondary	79	60	62
Social class			
Upper middle	71	58	57
Nonmanual/clerical	54	48	45
Skilled manual	55	40	39
Low-skilled manual	51	33	38
Age			
30 or under	56	41	37
Over 30	56	45	46

Note: The cells report the percentage among each group responding "In general, you can trust other people" rather than "You can never be too careful," excluding responses of "Don't know," "It depends," and "Other."
Source: 1959, Civic Culture Survey; 1981 and 1990, World Values Surveys.

class. But most striking are the differentials among age cohorts when 1959 is compared with 1990. In 1959, those under the age of 40 were substantially more trusting (61 percent expressed social trust) than those over 40 (52 percent). By 1990, we find just the reverse: Although 47 percent of those over the age of 40 expressed trust in others, only 40 percent of those under the age of 40 did so, and this proportion declines steadily with each younger age cohort to reach only 32 percent of those between 18 and 29 years of age in 1990.

This decline in the proportion of the population expressing social trust is not purely generational. It shows up in all age groups, including those born during the interwar years, 61 percent of whom expressed trust in 1959 compared to 46 percent today. However, the experience of growing up in a period marked by low levels of social trust could leave its mark on the younger generations.[36] The erosion of social trust is something of an anomaly, given that other indicators of social capital do not show a similar decline, and I will return to the issue. For the moment, however, I turn to the problem of explaining why levels of social capital on all other indicators have remained reasonably high in Britain.

EXPLAINING LEVELS OF SOCIAL CAPITAL

General Causal Theories

On most of the measures examined here, social capital has not declined in Britain to the degree that Putnam finds it has in the United States. This divergence between the British and American cases has important implications for our understanding of the causal factors that might affect levels of social capital. In the first instance, it provides support for a number of the arguments advanced by Putnam.[37] Several trends common to the industrialized democracies that might otherwise be thought to erode social capital appear less important in light of the British case. These include the expansion of the welfare state, suburbanization, the growing participation of women in the labor force, and changes in family structure marked by higher rates of divorce and more single-person households. Postwar Britain has experienced each of these developments without a corresponding erosion in levels of social capital.[38]

The British case also raises questions about the causal impact of television on social capital.[39] Despite the fact that British citizens watch over two and a half hours of television per day on average, they still manage to maintain levels of sociability and community involvement commensurate with those of the late 1950s, and the generations that grew up with television do not display significantly lower levels of community involvement than their predecessors. This suggests that television viewing need not be entirely corrosive of social capital. To some extent, it seems simply to have replaced an analogous activity popular in the interwar years, listening to the radio (see Table 1-2).

Nevertheless, it is hard to imagine that levels of social interaction outside the household would not be higher if television did not exist, and there is at least tenuous support for this in the finding that the working classes, who are much less active in community associations, watch approximately a third more television than the middle classes.[40] In addition, the major effects of television may already have occurred by the late 1950s, which is the base point for most of the data reported here. There were 4.5 million television sets in Britain by 1955 and 10 million (or 211 for every 1,000 inhabitants) by the end of the decade. As early as 1953, 29 percent of the people in Derby, a fairly typical British town, owned a television, and detailed studies of working-class life in the 1950s provide some evidence that television viewing had already cut into the time that people would otherwise spend socializing with others.[41] Thus, the available British data cannot be said to contradict the contention that the spread of television tends to depress levels of social interaction in the community. Instead, it simply suggests that television viewing need not erode that involvement altogether.

Explaining the Resilience of Community Involvement

The outcomes in the British case present us with a difficult explanatory problem. Although levels of community involvement measured by associational membership, charitable endeavor, and informal sociability appear to have declined in the United States, they have remained resilient in Britain. How might this be explained? What can we learn more generally from the British case about the causal factors that lie behind social capital?

As noted above, a number of potential explanatory factors can be rejected relatively easily. Television did not come more slowly to Britain than to the United States; the first transmissions were undertaken in 1939, and by the mid-1950s, it was widely watched by the populace. Changes in female labor force participation rates, working time, and family structure are roughly similar across the two nations and largely uncorrelated at the individual level with community involvement.[42] What has generated such stability, and perhaps even some growth, in community involvement in Britain over the postwar years?

Close inspection of the case suggest that three factors have been of prime importance. These are (1) a radical transformation in the educational system, marked by a massive expansion of both secondary and postsecondary education; (2) a change in the overall class structure of British society, driven by economic and political developments, which has altered the distribution of occupations and life situations across the populace; and (3) characteristically British forms of government action that have done much to encourage and sustain voluntary community involvement. Although I cannot establish their relative importance with precision without a comparative study that is beyond the scope of this one, there are good reasons to believe that all three factors have been crucial to the maintenance of social capital in Britain.

The Educational Revolution

It is well established that each additional year of education increases the propensity of an individual to become involved in community affairs, whether by joining an association or by providing voluntary work for the community.[43] Moreover, the effect of each additional year of education on the propensity for community involvement increases as one moves upward to higher educational levels. In both 1959 and 1990, securing a postsecondary education meant that an individual was almost twice as likely to become involved in the community than an individual who had only a secondary education. As the population becomes more highly educated, it becomes more engaged in community affairs.

In this context, the radical transformation of the British educational system that took place between the 1950s and the 1990s is of great significance. In large measure, that transformation has sustained the level of associational involvement in Britain in the face of countervailing pressures. These educational reforms are well described elsewhere. In essence, by the 1980s, they transformed the British system of education from one that was deeply segregated by class and gender, focused on primary and secondary schooling, and provided very little postsecondary education during the 1950s into one that provided most individuals with secondary education and supplied many more from a much wider range of family backgrounds with postsecondary education.[44] Although most of the industrialized nations took similar steps, the scale of change was substantially greater in Britain during this period than in many other nations. Over three decades, Britain moved away from an educational system that was highly stratified by class background and provided far fewer years of schooling on average than did the United States and toward one that now converges on American levels of performance.[45]

This process of educational reform gave rise to three developments of considerable significance for levels of social capital. First, it greatly expanded the number of people who secure a secondary or postsecondary education. Second, it vastly increased the educational levels that women attain. Third, it substantially altered the class composition of those with postsecondary education. Table 1-5 provides an overall picture of these effects, reflected in the differences between representative samples of the electorate drawn in 1959 and 1990.[46] In those thirty years, the proportion of British citizens with a secondary education more than doubled, and the proportion with some postsecondary education increased from 3 to 14 percent. By 1990, the number of women with postsecondary education was virtually equal to that of men, compared with a ratio of 1 to 4 in 1959. Although class differences remain substantial, the number of those born into the working class who secure secondary or postsecondary education has increased noticeably.[47]

There are two paths whereby these changes in the educational system affect levels of social capital in Britain. The first is an aggregate effect based on increases in the number of people with higher levels of education. This increases community involvement because those who have secured higher levels of education seem to have a greater propensity for civic engagement. Since the 1950s, this effect has raised the level of community involvement by about 25 percent over the level that could have been expected without educational reform.[48]

Table 1-5: Changes in Levels of Education Among Various Groups, 1959–1990

Highest Level of Educational Achievement	All		Men		Women		Middle Class		Working Class	
	1959	1990	1959	1990	1959	1990	1959	1990	1959	1990
Primary	63	24	58	25	68	22	39	13	74	32
Secondary	34	62	38	61	31	64	53	60	26	64
Postsecondary	3	14	4	14	1	14	8	27	0	4
N	934	1470	448	683	446	87	286	645	648	825

Note: Cells indicate the percentage of the group with each level of educational achievement.
Sources: 1959 Civic Culture Survey and 1990 World Values Survey.

In addition, however, by diversifying the pool of those receiving higher education, educational reform has also increased the average impact of each additional year of higher education on the recipients. In the 1950s, when higher education was largely restricted to male children from the upper middle class, it tended to increase their community involvement by about 76 percent—a far from negligible figure.[49] But what higher education could add to the propensity of this already privileged group to participate in the community was limited by the fact that many other elements of their socialization already inclined them in this direction. When the system of higher education was expanded to take in a broader range of people from more diverse class backgrounds, many of whom did not have the benefit of these other socializing factors, the average effect of exposure to postsecondary education on the propensity for community involvement increased dramatically. In the 1990s, exposure to higher education increased community involvement by 110 percent. In short, not only do greater numbers of British citizens benefit from postsecondary education today, but the average effect of higher education on community involvement is substantially greater than it was during the 1950s.

The importance of this educational revolution is especially apparent in the case of women. One of the most striking features of the British data is that while community involvement by men increased slightly between 1959 and 1990 (by about 7 percent), the community involvement of women more than doubled (increasing by 127 percent) to converge with the rates of men. Social capital has been sustained in Britain largely by virtue of the increasing participation of women in the community. This effect might result from any of three long-term developments: the increased exposure of women to higher education; the growing participation of women in the labor force; or more general changes in the attitudes and social situation of women, partly under the influence of the feminist movement. We cannot altogether discount the importance of the last two of these. However, the data suggest that greater access to higher education is by far the most important factor.[50] By 1990, 14 percent of women had some postsecondary education, compared with barely 1 percent in 1959. Moreover, although women with a primary or secondary education were not significantly more involved in the community in the 1990s than they had been in the 1950s, women with a postsecondary education were two and a half times more involved than they had been in the 1950s. Expanding the access of women to higher education seems to have had a major impact on levels of social capital in Britain.

The Impact of Changes in Class Structure

Social class must be an important dimension of any analysis of social change in postwar Britain. On one hand, class divisions have long played a crucial role in the social consciousness and collective life of Britain.[51] On the other, there have been dramatic changes in the British class structure over the past fifty years, at least some of which are likely to have broad implications for social capital.[52] Issues of social class are especially relevant to this analysis because there are deep differences in how people in different class situations are connected to the community. Although some of these can be explained by levels of education, they have more extensive social roots.[53] We find such differences in both formal and informal patterns of sociability.

On average, people in the middle class have twice as many organizational affiliations as those in the working class (see Table 1-1), and they are likely to be active in twice as many organizations. Goldthorpe found that 52 percent of those at the top of the class structure had held office in an association versus 19 percent of those in the bottom two class categories.[54] Professionals are also three times as likely as manual workers to participate in volunteer endeavors.[55] Moreover, while social clubs and trade unions dominate the associations to which members of the working class belong, those in the middle class develop affiliations with a much wider range of organizations. The latter are likely to join new associations at frequent intervals, accumulating memberships over their lifetimes, while those in the working class join fewer associations but stay in them for long periods of time.[56]

The patterns of informal sociability of the working class are likely to revolve around close contacts with kin and with a small set of friends closely connected with each other. On the whole, these are likely to be friends of long standing, often old school friends. By contrast, the social networks of the middle class tend to be more extensive and diverse. They are likely to see twice as many colleagues from work outside the workplace on a regular basis; they draw their friends from a more diverse range of sources, and those friends are often not closely connected to each other. Perhaps surprisingly, those in the middle class are also likely to know twice as many of their neighbors fairly well than do those in the working class, and a much smaller number suffers from a complete absence of social support. Finally, people in the middle class seem less likely to limit their interaction with friends to a particular sphere of activity, preferring to engage them in multiple kinds of endeavors.[57]

In sum, although there are significant variations inside each class and recent research seems to contradict the older assertion that members of the working class suffer from a serious lack of social connections, the patterns of sociability that the two principal social classes display are quite different.[58] Many of these differences are relevant for social capital.

In Britain, at least, the level of social capital seems to be most strongly sustained by the middle class. It is members of that class who are likely to develop diverse networks of friends and to mobilize them for new endeavors, and it is the middle class who participates most actively in the widest range of formal associations, joining new ones to advance more recently developed objectives. These modalities conform more closely than do working-class patterns of sociability to classic conceptions of how social capital works. Moreover, these differences appear to be widening over time. Table 1-1 suggests that while the average number of organizational affiliations among the working class has remained roughly constant over the past thirty years, those of the middle class have increased by about 60 percent.

These observations are especially consequential because the size of the middle class itself has increased dramatically in Britain since 1950. Although we are accustomed to thinking of the class structure as something that is relatively fixed, notwithstanding some individual mobility up or down within it, recent studies indicate that the class structure of Britain has changed profoundly since the Second World War. This transformation has been driven by the decline of an older manufacturing base, the expansion of employment in a burgeoning public sector, and the rise of the service sector. As a result, many blue-collar or manual-labor jobs have disappeared, and there has been rapid growth in professional and white-collar positions that provide their incumbents with material perquisites and a workplace context associated with the middle class. Goldthorpe describes the essential change as the growth of an increasingly substantial "service class." Although there is some contention about precisely how the boundaries between classes should be drawn, there is general consensus on the orders of magnitude involved. Samples drawn from the British Election Studies, for instance, suggest that those in the working class fell from 51 percent of the adult population in 1964 to 36 percent in 1987, while those in professional or managerial occupations associated with the "salariat" rose from 19 percent to 29 percent and the proportion in other nonmanual occupations rose from 14 percent to 20 percent.[59] In short, as the number of white-collar positions expanded in the decades after the war, substantial numbers of people born into working-class families moved into middle-class occupations.

If the upwardly mobile still maintained working-class patterns of sociability, this shift in class structure would have had little effect on levels of social capital in Britain, at least until several generations had passed. If those moving up in the class structure ended up being more socially isolated by virtue of this movement, the consequences for levels of social capital would have been genuinely deleterious. But there is strong evidence that the upwardly mobile adopt the sociability patterns of the class into which they move. New entrants into the middle classes have had roughly the same number of organizational affiliations and friends as did people born into that class.[60] Indeed, as might be expected, they are slightly less likely to draw on kin and more likely to draw on membership in voluntary associations for sociability than those who are middle class from birth. As Goldthorpe suggests, the very magnitude of the shift in postwar British class structure probably contributed to these results. If only a few individuals had been upwardly mobile, they might have found themselves isolated in social terms. Since hundreds of thousands of people experienced this kind of upward mobility in recent decades, however, the sense of social isolation that any one of them might have experienced was reduced.

In sum, the massive shift in socioeconomic structure that Britain experienced in the postwar years may have helped to sustain levels of social capital by increasing the number of middle-class positions in the class structure and putting larger numbers of people into those positions, ones that tend to be associated with more extensive communal involvement.

The Effects of Government Policy

Although its impact is more difficult to quantify, a third factor also seems to have made an important contribution to the maintenance of high levels of social capital in Britain. I refer here to the presence of particular kinds of government policy. Since the beginning of the twentieth century, British governments have made substantial efforts to cultivate the voluntary sector, notably by using it to deliver social services to a degree that seems striking in cross-national terms.[61] Successive governments have devoted substantial resources to this objective.

It is common to assume that the development of publicly provided social benefits under the aegis of a welfare state displaces voluntary endeavor on behalf of the poor or disabled. Indeed, many early British reformers asked the government to provide social benefits precisely in order to free the working classes from dependence on the paternalistic charities operated by the upper classes.[62] However, the reformers lost this fight: From their inception, many of the social programs of the British government have been designed to preserve a substantial role for voluntary endeavor. To an extraordinary extent, these programs have used local volunteers, working in tandem with professionals, to deliver social services. In keeping with this emphasis, over the years a number of other policies have also nurtured the voluntary sector.

Although the major social reforms of the 1905–14 Liberal government were believed by many at the time to herald the end of mutual aid societies and the frenetic philanthropic activity that had characterized the nineteenth century, Lloyd George's budget of 1914 made provision for grants to voluntary organizations active in maternity, child care, home help, and work with the blind.[63] As one analyst observes, "Relationships between the state and the voluntary sector in the interwar years were already marked by increasing interdependence."[64] In 1929, the public authorities provided 13 percent of the income of charitable associations in Liverpool, and in 1932 the London County Council took steps to develop closer working relationships with voluntary organizations. By 1934, fully 37 percent of the income of registered British charities came from the state, normally in the form of payment for services they provided to the community, and Macadam could hail an emerging "new philanthropy" characterized by active cooperation between voluntary associations and public authorities.[65]

While radical, the social reforms of the postwar Labour government reinforced these patterns. The Disabled Persons (Employment) Act 1944, the National Health Service Act 1946, the National Assistance Act 1948, and the Children Act 1948 all made provision for volunteers to deliver social services. A Ministry of Health circular at the time observed, "It will clearly be to the advantage of local authorities to make use of voluntary organisations which are providing satisfactory services, and to coordinate their work with the authorities' own services."[66] Prime Minister Clement Attlee declared: "We shall always have alongside the great range of public services, the voluntary services which humanize our national life and bring it down from the general to the particular." After two famous reports setting the standards for British social policy, William Beveridge produced a third celebrating the role of voluntary endeavor and urging support for it.[67]

This stance was endorsed by subsequent Conservative governments. In 1956, the Younghusband Committee found that voluntary activity was an "integral part of the health and welfare services," with over three-quarters of all local councils making use of voluntary organizations to deliver services to the blind, the elderly, and unmarried mothers.[68] A comprehensive history of British philanthropy from 1660 to 1960 noted that the intervention of the state in the twentieth century had "extended rather than reversed the tradition of voluntary effort."[69] Moreover, the

1960s and 1970s saw even more rapid growth in public programs utilizing voluntary endeavor, notably in the spheres of poverty, urban renewal, and child care, where they were closely allied to a host of new voluntary associations, such as Shelter and the Child Poverty Action Group.[70] The Local Government Act of 1972 authorized local authorities to spend up to 2 pence on the rates of local taxation to fund voluntary organizations, and the same year saw the establishment of the Volunteer Centre and the Voluntary Services Unit in the Home Office to coordinate and enhance the role of volunteers in the provision of social services.[71]

Although operating from multifarious objectives, the Conservative governments of 1979–97 reinforced this trend by encouraging local government to contract out a wide range of services to nonprofit organizations in order to reduce the size of the state sector. Shortly after taking office, Prime Minister Margaret Thatcher declared, "I believe that the voluntary movement is at the heart of all of our social welfare provision," and between 1976 and 1987, the income of the voluntary sector from fees and grants almost doubled.[72]

By 1994–95, 12.5 percent of the income of voluntary associations in Britain (£687 million) came from local authorities, while central government provided another £450 million (not including funding for housing), much of which went to organizations delivering social services in the spheres of community care, family welfare, education, and recreation.[73] Although many of the organizations receiving these funds employed professional staff as well as volunteers, government funding apparently did not erode their voluntary character. Leat, Tester, and Unell found that local voluntary associations receiving large amounts of public money utilized more volunteers than those receiving fewer funds. Moreover, Hatch's inquiry into the origins of voluntary organizations in three towns found that public officials provided the impetus for creating more of them than did any other source.[74]

In short, British governments have worked to ensure that voluntary activity flourishes, using volunteers alongside professionals for the delivery of social services. This commitment has been accompanied by large public expenditures, including grants and fees for services, to associations that mobilize voluntary action on the local level. All indications are that these policies have made a major contribution to sustaining the kind of associations that augment the level of social capital in Britain.

Explaining Changes in Social Trust

The one indicator for social capital to have fallen over the postwar years is that measuring the generalized trust people express in others. We can expect a variable based on people's attitudes to fluctuate more than ones that reflect behavior, but there is also a secular trend here analogous to one that Wuthnow finds in the United States (see his chapter in this volume). Social trust seems to have declined among all groups between 1959 and 1980 and to have reached especially low levels among the young. How is this to be explained?

We can begin by considering two factors that might seem to be prime culprits: (1) urbanization, since residents of large urban areas are exposed to more crime and may be less familiar with their neighbors, and (2) a "Thatcher effect," since the Conservative governments of the 1980s deliberately advanced a new "individualism" to replace the "collectivist" spirit said to have been dominant in British society up to the 1980s.[75]

When closely examined, however, neither of these factors proves to be an adequate explanation. In the data sets used for this study, residence in larger urban areas *is* associated with lower levels of social trust for most people except those in the upper middle class, as one might expect. However, the proportion of the British population living in urban areas peaked in 1951 and has actually declined slightly since then.[76] Britain has not become a more urban society during the postwar period. It seems unlikely, then, that urbanization lies behind lower levels of social trust.

As Table 1-4 indicates, the data do not lend much support either to the hypothesis of a Thatcher effect, since levels of social trust remained broadly stable from 1981 to 1990. The one group that displays a potential Thatcher effect is composed of individuals age 30 or younger, whose levels of social trust fell substantially during the 1980s. Suggestions that the extended period of Conservative rule may have been especially alienating for the young, leading to lower levels of social trust, receives at least some support from the fact that, compared to any other group, substantially greater proportions of them voted for the Labour Party in the 1997 election.[77] But a Thatcher effect could ultimately explain only a limited amount of the decline: Even among the young, levels of social trust dropped more substantially between 1959 and 1981 than they did between 1981 and 1990, when Thatcher was in office.

What else might have mattered? Fully resolving this question would demand research that is well beyond the scope of this paper.[78] However, there is support for three broad kinds of propositions in the data assembled for this study, and they might be used to guide further inquiry.

First, shifts in a person's *material position* may lower his levels of social trust by reinforcing a sense of disadvantage vis-à-vis others and removing him from networks that provide social integration. Prime

candidates for these kinds of material changes include divorce, movement to a larger city, or unemployment; and these experiences are associated with lower levels of social trust at the individual level in all the
surveys examined here.[79] Wuthnow finds similar evidence that such factors affect social trust.[80]

Accordingly, changes in the performance of the economy may be
responsible for some of the change in aggregate levels of social trust over
the postwar period. There is a striking contrast between 1959, when 56
percent of the populace expressed trust in others and the younger age
cohorts were substantially more trusting than their elders, and the 1980s,
when only 44 percent of the populace expressed such trust and the
young were the least trusting of all. Economic conditions and perceptions of those conditions were very different across the two periods. In
1959, rationing had just ended, the economy was booming, and levels of
unemployment were negligible. Harold Macmillan had just won reelection on the campaign slogan "You have never had it so good." Perhaps
most telling, in 1959, only 5 percent of the populace believed that their
personal material situation was likely to worsen over the next year, and
the young were even more optimistic than the old. Those age 18–24 were
preoccupied with material prosperity and identified disproportionately
with the middle class. More than two-thirds believed they would be better off in two to three years' time, compared with only a third of their
elders.[81]

In 1981 and 1990, by contrast, rates of unemployment were close to 10
percent and almost twice as high among those under the age of 25. In
both years, large portions of the populace believed that the economy or
their personal material situation was likely to worsen over the next year,
and feelings of economic confidence were especially low among the
young.[82] Satisfaction with one's financial situation correlates strongly
with levels of social trust at the individual level. There is at least some
evidence, then, that rising levels of unemployment and shifting perceptions of the economy may have contributed to the decline in social trust.

A second set of factors linked to the character of *social integration*
may also have affected levels of social trust in Britain. I use the term
"social integration" to refer to the ways in which people relate to others
and, notably, to how they understand their own role in society.[83] This
understanding is closely related to the expectations individuals have of
others, and there is substantial evidence that it shifted in Britain during
the postwar years. Therefore, changes in the character of social integration may have lowered levels of social trust.[84]

The shifts in social integration to which I refer are those commonly associated in Britain with movement from a collectivist society to a more individualistic one. Their roots lie in the changes in social structure I have already described and associated shifts in social values. In the 1950s, British society was still highly stratified along class lines. Social class and class-based movements provided the principal reference points for social relations. Many members of the working class were deferential toward authority figures and those in superior class positions. Others belonged to solidaristic working-class communities that looked to collective vehicles, and class-based organizations in particular, such as the trade union movement and Labour Party, for improvement in their social situation.[85]

During the 1960s and 1970s, however, social attitudes shifted dramatically. A "romantic revolt" against traditional sources of authority, linked to the rise of postmaterialist values, reduced the deference of the general population.[86] Voting along class lines became less common.[87] And even those who supported organizations that were traditionally class-based seemed to do so for instrumental purposes rather than out of feelings of class solidarity.[88] On a wide range of dimensions, social relations became less oriented to class divisions and more oriented to individual achievement.

In many respects, this movement was liberating. Class origins no longer had such a profound effect on social destinations. Society as a whole became less stratified. However, the transformation of a traditional social order also has some less desirable effects. It renders the social position of many people less secure and their relations with others less certain. In this case, it went hand in hand with the decline of working-class organizations and the erosion of solidarism among working-class communities. The growing emphasis on individual achievement may have sharpened people's sense that opportunism is a pervasive feature of society and an important component of social advancement. Taken together, these trends could lead to some decline in overall levels of social trust.

Without better time series data, it is difficult to test this proposition. However, there is some evidence that the values of the British populace may have shifted away from ones stressing communal solidarity and toward ones that put more emphasis on personal opportunism. Let us distinguish between value systems according to a dimension that can be labeled "other-regarding" versus "self-regarding." I use these terms to refer to the degree to which, when faced with a trade-off between self-interest and the collective interest, an individual believes it morally justifiable to give priority to self-interest. On one side of the spectrum are those who believe that behavior that is personally advantageous but harmful to the collectivity is wrong. On the other side are those inclined to endorse such behavior. The latter may also be more likely to endorse moral relativism rather than moral absolutism.

I focus on this dimension of the value system because it relates logically to a person's level of social trust. Those who believe that a range of behaviors damaging to others is justifiable are presumably more likely both to engage in such behavior and to expect it from others. Accordingly, they should trust others less. And this is precisely what we find in individual-level data: Those whose value systems are self-regarding tend to have significantly lower levels of social trust.[89]

Has this type of shift in values been occurring in Britain on a large

Table 1-6: The Incidence of Moral Relativism and Self-Regarding Attitudes Among Age Cohorts

Percentage in Each Group Saying the Behavior Is Never Justified	Age 30 or Less	Over Age 30
Claiming government benefits to which one is not entitled	55	78
Avoiding the fare on public transport	40	68
Cheating on taxes	40	60
Buying stolen goods	49	80
Keeping money one finds	30	59
Not reporting damage to a parked car	35	62
Lying	26	49
Littering	41	69
Percentage endorsing moral relativism	78	58

Note: Cells report the percentage who respond "Never" when asked if the indicated behavior is justified. Moral relativism is measured by agreement with the statement "There can never be absolutely clear guidelines about what is good and evil. What is good and evil depends entirely upon the circumstances of the time" as opposed to the statement "There are absolutely clear guidelines about what is good and evil. These always apply to everyone whatever the circumstances."
Source: Data combine responses to the World Values Surveys in 1981 and 1990.

scale? Although we do not have data with which to track such values throughout the postwar period, we can exploit differences across age cohorts to assess whether a shift has taken place. In general, a person's basic values tend to be formed when he is young and to persist as he grows older. Therefore, it is notable that those under the age of 30 in Britain in 1981 or 1990—namely, those who grew up in a society more oriented toward individualism—are not only less trusting of others than their elders, but more inclined to embrace self-regarding values than those who reached maturity in an earlier, more collectivist era. Table 1-6 presents some interesting evidence.

Of course, some of the variation in values indicated in Table 1-6 may be attributable to a life cycle effect: We can expect the young to be less respectful of social norms. But several considerations suggest that these figures do not simply reflect the effects of youth but pick up longer-term shifts in values likely to persist. [90] First, the young do not simply endorse a range of antisocial acts. They also express more support for moral relativism. Since moral relativism is not a position normally associated with the young, whose idealism has been linked at many historical moments with moral attitudes that are more absolutist than those of their elders, the higher levels of moral relativism that the young now express may reflect a broader social movement in this direction. Second, the willingness of people *of all ages* to describe a range of antisocial acts as justifiable increased between 1981 and 1990. Although that shift was small, because a decade is a brief period of time from the perspective of long-term value change, this figure could indicate a secular trend of greater magnitude. Third, on the one indicator available for comparison with earlier decades, which asks whether it is justifiable to keep money that one has found, there has been a substantial shift across the entire populace consistent with a shift toward more individualistic values.[91]

In short, there are some indications that developments shifting the character of social integration in Britain may have led to changes in social values that militate against social trust. The political scientist Ronald Inglehart has drawn our attention to the importance of shifts in values, especially among the young.[92] However, he looks for the rise of postmaterialist values that evoke a certain social optimism. It may be that those who grew up in Britain during the 1970s and 1980s display another set of values that are far less attractive from the perspective of social integration.[93] This is a subject that merits further investigation.

Finally, the decline of social trust in Britain might be attributable to changes in the *character of the associations* to which people belong. The most anomalous aspect of the findings of this study, of course, is the observation that levels of social trust seem to have declined while membership in secondary associations remains high. This finding calls into question the close association that Putnam and others posit between the presence of secondary associations and high levels of social trust. However, it may be that the character of associational life has changed in such a way as to render membership in secondary associations no longer so conducive to trust. Two types of change are relevant here. The associations to which people belong may involve them in fewer face-to-face interactions of the sort that build social capital.[94] Alternatively, associations dedicated to the public interest may have declined in favor of ones serving mainly the needs of their members, and the latter may not forge the feelings of communal solidarity that feed into social trust.[95]

Some evidence points to the potential importance of these propositions. Although divorce, unemployment, and relocation to a larger city tend to depress levels of social trust, levels of trust drop less substantially among those who belong to two or more associations than among those who belong to only one or none. The direction of causation here is uncertain: Those who are more trusting may simply join more associations. But it is likely that those who belong to more than one association experience more face-to-face interaction by virtue of their memberships, and this may help sustain their social trust. If so, the decline in social trust in Britain may be linked to a movement away from associations that provide regular contact with others and toward ones that do not, even though overall levels of associational membership remain high.

At least some organizations dedicated to the public interest have experienced noticeable declines in membership in Britain. By the end of the 1980s, for instance, barely 5 percent of the electorate belonged to a political party, compared with about 10 percent at the beginning of the 1960s.[96] Only 22 percent of the populace declared themselves members of a church in 1980, compared with 28 percent in 1980, and church attendance has fallen even more substantially.[97] Although trade union membership remained robust through the 1970s, it declined by about 25 percent during the 1980s, and there are some indications that the attachment of members to their unions is increasingly instrumental.[98] The character of civic engagement in Britain may have shifted away from organizations dedicated to the public interest, in whatever way that is construed, and toward those oriented primarily toward the instrumental purposes of the individual. However, there are some countertrends, most obvious in the striking growth of the environmental movement, much of it dedicated to a broad public interest.

Whether shifts in the character of British associations are responsible for an erosion in levels of social trust is not an issue that can be resolved here. However, I raise it to suggest that beneath the apparent stability of associational membership in Britain, changes may be taking place that will ultimately affect the quality of civic engagement there.

SOCIAL CAPITAL AND POLITICS IN BRITAIN

Britain is also a good case in which to test some of the propositions about politics that are associated with theories of social capital. Because levels of social capital have been resilient there, most theories predict that levels of political engagement in Britain should have remained high as well.[99]

Political Participation in the Aggregate
In general, the data bear out this prediction with regard both to *political participation*, whether electoral or nonelectoral, and to *political attentiveness*, measured in terms of the interest people show in politics and

Figure 1-4: Interest in Politics and Political Activism in Britain, 1950–1997

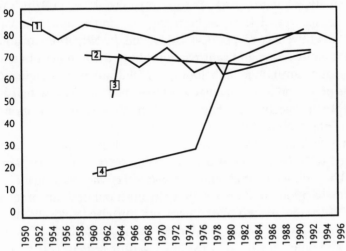

1 Electoral turnout
2 Talk about politics
3 Interested in politics
4 Active in politics

the frequency with which they discuss it. Figure 1-4 indicates that electoral turnout has remained broadly stable since the mid-1950s—almost three-quarters of the British electorate still vote—and the number of British citizens who engage in some form of political participation beyond voting has risen dramatically. Most of this increase reflects the growing number of people who sign petitions, but between 1974 and 1990, the proportion of citizens who joined a lawful demonstration, a boycott, or an unofficial strike also doubled, reaching almost 15 percent of the populace.[100] Using slightly narrower measures, Parry and Moyser found that 24 percent of adults were active in politics beyond voting in 1984–85.[101]

Similarly, political attentiveness has not declined much in postwar Britain. The percentage of adults who never discuss politics with others was no higher in 1990 than in 1959 (30 percent), and the proportion who frequently discuss politics with friends remained broadly stable between 1970 and 1990 at 15 to 19 percent.[102] The portion of the populace expressing some interest in politics rose steadily during the 1960s, declined slightly during the 1970s, and rose again during the 1980s to reach 69 percent in 1990, compared with 53 percent in 1963.[103] These figures reflect levels of political interest and activism consistent with a healthy democracy.

A substantial body of evidence also suggests that these levels of political participation and attentiveness follow from the high levels of associational activity, voluntary work, and informal sociability in British society. At the individual level, in both the 1981 and 1990 World Values Surveys, attentiveness to political issues and participation in politics showed a statistically significant relationship to the number of associations to which an individual belongs.[104] Mabileau and colleagues confirm this point and a strong correlation between political participation and informal sociability, while Gerard finds a similar relationship between volunteering and political activism.[105]

When we turn to two other dimensions of political behavior normally associated with the vitality of democracy, however, the picture is more mixed. These dimensions are those of *political efficacy,* by which I mean citizens' perceptions about their ability to affect political outcomes, and *political trust,* understood as the levels of confidence citizens have in their political leaders or institutions. By the 1990s, feelings of political efficacy and political trust reached low levels in Britain. Less than half the electorate expressed confidence in Parliament or the civil service, and barely half expressed confidence in the legal system.[106] Levels of cynicism about politicians have been high in recent decades. In 1974 and

Table 1-7: Changes in Feelings of Political Trust and Efficacy Among the British Electorate

Percentage Agreeing with Each Statement	1959	1974	1986
People like me have no say in what the government does.	58	61	71
Politics and government are so complicated that one cannot understand what is going on.	58	74	69
If Parliament passed an unjust law, I could do nothing about it.	34		46*

* Measured in 1990.

Source: Richard Topf, "Political Change and Political Culture in Britain, 1959–87," in John R. Gibbons, ed., *Contemporary Political Culture* (London: Sage, 1989), 56, and World Values Survey 1990.

1986, about two-thirds of the electorate agreed that politicians are interested only in their votes rather than their opinions, tend to lose touch with the people quickly once elected, and cannot be trusted to place the needs of the country above the interests of their own party.[107]

There is controversy about what these figures mean. Some argue that feelings of political trust and efficacy fell sharply in Britain between the 1950s and the 1970s, while others maintain that they were always low and have remained stable.[108] Unfortunately, few indicators comparable over time are available, and we must be cautious about extrapolating from those that are.[109] Table 1-7 collects the available measures. It shows that the proportion of the electorate expressing feelings of distrust or inefficacy increased from 1959 to the 1980s by a consistent 10 percent on each indicator.

What might explain this decline in political trust? Since levels of sociability have remained relatively stable, the decline is puzzling from the perspective of theories of social capital. However, the British data are revealing. First, they indicate that membership in associations alone does not seem to maintain levels of political trust. At the aggregate level, political trust has declined while associational membership has remained stable. In the survey data, although membership in formal associations shows a statistically strong relationship to political activism and political attentiveness among individuals, it is not strongly correlated with their levels of political trust.[110]

However, *political* trust is closely associated with *social* trust. At the aggregate level, the two have fallen in tandem since 1959, and there is a strong correlation between the two at the individual level. It should not surprise us that an unwillingness to trust others would be associated with an unwillingness to trust public officials. The lines of causation remain elusive. Declining social trust may erode political trust or vice versa, or a common set of factors may depress both.[111]

These findings suggest that there may be only a loose coupling between membership in secondary associations and feelings of social trust, despite the close connections often posited by theories of social capital. At a minimum, they confirm that an active associational life does not inoculate a society against political distrust. Political trust may fluctuate in response to many factors, including the performance of the government, even when patterns of sociability remain stable.[112]

This loose coupling contains some good news for democratic politics. It implies that moderate increases in social and political trust need not portend a collective retreat from political engagement.[113] Levels of political participation remain high in Britain, despite low levels of trust in politicians and political institutions. And political trust is not strongly correlated with political participation at the individual level. In fact, some of the new forms of political participation that have become popular in recent years seem to thrive on distrust. Analysis of the 1981 and 1990 World Values Surveys shows that those who were active in the new social movements devoted to environmentalism, nuclear energy, or feminism had less political trust than those who not active in them. New social movements can channel discontent with existing leaders and institutions into effective political participation.

In sum, the British polity may be less trusting in the 1990s than in the 1950s, but that has not impoverished its political life. On the contrary, perhaps by virtue of being able to draw on rich associational networks, many people have turned their discontent into constructive, if wary, political engagement. Swampy, the countercultural hero of environmentalists during the 1990s, had a very different public image than did Harold Macmillan, but he offered a model of political engagement for the young that was equally influential.

Distributive Issues

The portrait of the British polity that emerges from this study is not, however, entirely rosy. Although aggregate levels of social capital and political engagement remain high in Britain, they are distributed very unevenly across the population. For the most part, political activism and the associations that sustain it have remained middle-class phenomena and the preserve of those in middle age. The aggregate figures for social capital summon up an image of a polity uniformly crisscrossed by organizational networks and participatory citizens. But the more accurate image is of a nation divided between a well-connected group of citizens with prosperous lives and high levels of civic engagement and other groups whose networks, associational life, and involvement in politics are very limited.

This division has been present to some degree for decades. What is most worrisome, however, is that discrepancies in levels of social capital and civic engagement between the connected and the disconnected have not diminished over time, as social convergence theories might predict. Instead, they have grown since the 1950s. The two groups who face marginalization from civil society are the working class and the young. In 1959, the average person in the working class belonged to almost two-thirds as many associations as someone from the middle class. By 1990, he belonged to less than half as many. In 1959, the average Briton under the age of 30 belonged to 84 percent as many associations as an older person. By 1990, he belonged to only 75 percent as many. As Table 1-4 indicates, significant differences in levels of social trust parallel these divides.

Differences in access to social capital are reflected in lower levels of political engagement among the working class and the young. By 1990, members of the middle class were twice as likely as members of the working class to participate in politics beyond voting, and their political attentiveness was substantially higher. The figures for the young are even more striking. In 1959, only 27 percent of those under the age of 30 said they never talked about politics (close to the average for all respondents). By 1990, 42 percent said they never talked about politics (ten points above the national average). Between 1974 and 1993, regular newspaper readership by people between the ages of 15 and 34 fell by 25 percent, while dropping only 5 percent for the population as a whole.[114]

There is cause for concern for both groups, if perhaps less for the young. They may become more politically engaged as they age, and some young people may be tied into patterns of sociability so informal that studies do not detect them. The principal danger is that their current levels of distrust and disengagement will prove to be a generational phenomenon that persists over time.

However, the trajectory facing the working class looks considerably worse. The available evidence on patterns of sociability suggests that the informal friendship networks on which many in the working class rely are not structured in such a way as to be an effective substitute for associational membership, at least from the perspective of social capital. Members of the working class tend to have fewer friends, each associated with a specific endeavor, rather than wide networks of contacts available for many purposes.

In addition, the distinctive friendship patterns and the associational ties of the working class are especially vulnerable to secular trends. Their friends and organizational memberships tend to be drawn heavily from the local community. Thus, movement to another locality of the sort that economic restructuring demands can erode their social capital dramatically. All the surveys utilized here indicate that while movement to a large urban area does not reduce levels of social trust among the middle class, it does so among the working class. Similarly, the working class draws its organizational affiliations disproportionately from trade unions and workingmen's clubs, and so recent declines in trade union membership have taken an especially heavy toll on the associational life of the working class. As the solidaristic communities associated with traditional industries decline, workingmen's clubs are disappearing, along with other social networks once important to those communities.

Caution must be exercised in extrapolating from these observations, since it is easy to overgeneralize from the few portraits of working class life available. Many individuals may have more substantial resources than this overview suggests. However, the fact that associational membership remained flat among the working class during a period in which it grew dramatically among the middle class implies that the levels of social capital available to ordinary working people in Britain may be unusually fragile in the face of contemporary social trends.[115]

CONCLUSION

Britain is an interesting case for analysts of social capital. It provides an example of an economically advanced democracy in which levels of social capital, at least on most indicators, have not declined significantly in recent decades. This poses an explanatory problem to which I have responded by emphasizing the importance of an educational revolution, transformation in social structure, and forms of government action especially characteristic of Britain. However, observations of general importance for our understanding of social capital can also be drawn from this case.

In the first instance, the British experience tends to confirm a number of propositions already advanced in the literature on social capital. It suggests that the preservation of social capital in the form of an active associational life is associated with the maintenance of high levels of political engagement. It casts doubt on explanations for the decline of social capital that are based on the growth of the welfare state, rising rates of female labor force participation, increasing divorce rates, or other secular trends as prominent in Britain as elsewhere.

At the same time, this case raises questions about prominent contentions in the current literature. Although the evidence is far from conclusive, it suggests that extensive television viewing need not always be deeply corrosive of social capital. It suggests that patterns of sociability and attitudes of social trust—two phenomena normally seen as intertwined dimensions of social capital—may be coupled only loosely together. Indeed, in Britain, there seem to be two distinct constellations of variables: Social trust tends to co-vary with political trust, while patterns of sociability co-vary with political participation. There is an indication here that social and political trust may respond to a range of factors other than organizational connectedness, and they may decline to a moderate extent without eroding organizational networks or political engagement.

Finally, this case generates propositions that can be used to take inquiries about social capital in new directions. To date, the literature has emphasized how levels of social capital affect the performance of governments.[116] However, the British experience points to causal lines that run in the other direction. It seems that governments can have a substantial impact on levels of social capital. The policies of successive governments in the spheres of education and social service delivery seem to have been central to sustaining levels of social capital in Britain. We should look more closely at the way in which policies of various types build or erode social networks of various types, and at the impact of government more generally on the generation or degeneration of social capital.

The British experience also highlights the distributive dimension of social capital. The very term "social capital" draws our attention to those respects in which social networks provide a collective resource of benefit to all in society. Such benefits clearly exist. But social capital is not only a public good. It can also be a "club good," that is, one of most benefit to participants in the networks that constitute it. As such, its distribution across the populace becomes a salient issue.

Although all may have benefited from Britain's capacity to maintain high levels of social capital since the war, some seem to have gained more substantially than others. Even in the 1950s, there were differences between the social capital available to the working and middle classes, and those disparities appear to have widened, rather than narrowed, since then. Since social capital is an important resource, this is yet another respect in which secular trends have increased disparities in the resources available to those at different positions in the British class structure. Moreover, because of class-based differences in the character of social capital, these disparities may grow in the coming years. The British case reminds us that we should be attentive not only to changes in the aggregate level of social capital, but to the way in which it is distributed across the populace. In this, as in other processes of social organization, some may be organized "in" and others "out" by the same set of developments.

The finding that levels of social trust have declined in Britain while membership in secondary associations remains robust raises some intriguing questions. It draws attention to the possibility that the character of British organizations may have changed. Membership may no longer entail as much face-to-face interaction as it once did, and organizations oriented to the public interest may have been replaced by ones oriented primarily to the provision of services for their members. Trends such as these could have important implications for the quality of democracy in Britain. However, we do not yet have an adequate theoretical or empirical base for assessing them.

In particular, we need a more developed sense of precisely how different kinds of social organizations contribute to the functioning of the political system. Current conceptions of social capital, like their republican forebears, evoke the ideal of a dense, participatory democracy in which close personal ties provide individuals with capacities for collective action. But there may be ways of operating an effective democracy in an age of new media that do not require as much face-to-face interaction among the citizenry as this traditional conception contends. Organizations that promote environmental concerns or care for the elderly that do not bring their members into much direct contact with one another may still be effective intermediaries capable of ensuring that the government remains responsive to the citizenry. Democracies replete with opinion polls may not need political parties that have a large membership base. But networks of personal interaction could still be important to individuals for a variety of purposes, including collective action at the local level, where the national media and public authorities might not otherwise be involved.

In sum, while this study has been able to answer some questions about the trajectory of social capital in Britain, it raises others that demand attention. On the surface, Britain seems to have retained substantial reservoirs of social capital, but the past fifty years have also seen subtle changes in the texture of collective life whose full implications we are only beginning to appreciate.

2

THE UNITED STATES: Bridging the Privileged and the Marginalized?

ROBERT WUTHNOW

According to popular accounts, social capital in the United States has been declining steadily since the 1950s. Having won World War II, then containing Russian aggression, and building new homes in the suburbs that were favorable to child rearing, churchgoing, and community involvement, Americans gradually settled into a complacency that would threaten to undermine the very foundations of their historic democratic freedoms. By the late 1960s, civic-mindedness was already being transformed into self-interestedness: Apart from the few who temporarily became social activists, protesting racism and the war in Vietnam, a generation came of age with little else to think about besides television, themselves, and their personal ambitions. In this view, the decline of social capital was largely a middle-class phenomenon; it characterized all but the older generation, that stalwart cohort who had learned through the trials of World War II to put country first, and it was rooted in suburban sprawl, the demise of the traditional male-breadwinner family, and too much television. But it was mostly a moral problem, a failure on the part of vast numbers of middle-class Americans to turn off their television sets, take their children firmly by the hand, and sign up for memberships at the YMCA, Jaycees, League of Women Voters, PTA, community soccer league, local Methodist church, or whatever other organizations that would have drawn them out of their living rooms and into more vibrant interaction with their friends and neighbors.[1]

My argument is that these popular views are only partly correct. While many important forms of social capital have declined, newer ways of connecting with friends and neighbors—including volunteering and joining small groups—have emerged. Moreover, the decline that has afflicted such traditional manifestations of civic involvement as membership in voluntary associations, voting, and taking part in electoral politics has been concentrated most heavily among the socially and economically marginalized, not among the more privileged segments of the middle class. These differential rates of decline, together with the fact that nearly all forms of social capital (old and new) remain heavily slanted toward the privileged rather than the marginalized, raise, in my view, an important normative question: Can social capital in the United States be developed in ways that do a better job of bridging the privileged and the marginalized than appears to be the case at present?

THE DEBATE ABOUT SOCIAL CAPITAL

Since Tocqueville's famous analysis of American democracy in the 1830s, the United States has generally been thought to depend for the very foundation of its social well-being on voluntary associations, mediating groups, and what has recently come to be known as social capital.[2] In recent years, there has nevertheless been a growing number of reasons to believe that social capital is declining and, with this decline, that American democracy itself may be in jeopardy.

One reason to suspect such a decline is that a wide variety of social observers, both in public life themselves and in universities, have pointed to the possibility of declining civic participation in recent years. For example, one commentator summarizes the recent debate by observing that during the 1960s, "the culture of the streets, the sidewalks and the porches was chased indoors by the arrival of television and air conditioning. Technology and the market economy multiplied choices and helped loosen neighborhood ties. And the cultural revolution . . . , hostile to all rules and authority, produced the hyperindividualism and the narrow generational worship of 'rights' and 'choice.'"[3]

A similar argument was made recently by Cardinal Roger Mahony of Los Angeles, who writes of "family breakdown, child abuse, random violence, rising rates of illegitimacy, increased misery and despair among the poor, and, not least, an abortion rate of 1.5 million a year, coupled with growing efforts to legalize, through euthanasia, the direct killing of the elderly and others deemed inconvenient" as clear evidence that civil society in the United States is nearing collapse.[4]

A reviewer of a scholarly book on the subject concludes, "Rarely has the need for confidence in democracy and our fellow citizens been so imperative, and rarely has the evidence for such confidence been so weak."[5] In virtually the same language, another writer asserts, "The issue that underlies our politics and our society in the 1990's is the moral, social and cultural erosion of the past quarter century in American life. It is the gradual disappearance of safe streets, stable families, secure employment, and the enduring relationships with relatives, neighbors, merchants and co-workers that make an ordered life possible. It is the unraveling of the strands of community—of what many are now calling civil society. This unraveling is not a figment of middle-aged Baby Boom nostalgia. It is real."[6]

In addition to such statements by public leaders, opinion polls demonstrate that a large proportion of the American public is also convinced that civic-mindedness is waning and that civil society is now perceived to be in danger of being engulfed by selfishness and greed. For example, a national survey of baby boomers (age 18 to 44) conducted in 1987 revealed that only 21 percent considered their generation better in terms of "being a concerned citizen, involved in helping others in the community," whereas 53 percent thought their parents' generation was better in this way; in contrast, 53 percent said their own generation was more "cynical about politics" (compared to 29 percent who thought their parents' generation was more cynical), and, not surprisingly, 77 percent said the nation was worse because of "less involvement in community activities.[7] Similarly, a 1992 survey of the U.S. labor force showed that "the breakdown of community" was thought to be a "serious" or "extremely serious" social problem by 76 percent of the respondents. Even more (81 percent) thought "selfishness" was a serious problem in America, and virtually everyone (91 percent) said this about "the breakdown of families."[8]

Yet another reason to take seriously the debate about declining social capital in the United States is that evidence has already been marshaled to suggest that such a decline is occurring. Reviewing a wide variety of evidence, Robert Putnam concludes that membership in many conventional secondary associations, such as fraternal organizations and nationality groups, has declined by 25 to 50 percent over the last two or three decades, that socializing with friends and neighbors and spending time in organizations are down by at least as much, and that significant declines have also occurred in levels of public trust, in voting, in participation in political activities, and in church attendance.[9]

Although there are reasons to suspect that social capital is declining in the United States, there are nevertheless reasons to remain cautious about such assertions. For one, the decline of civil society is not simply an empirical question, but one that has political and ideological overtones. As the foregoing quotes illustrate, public officials, religious leaders, and journalists are not above voicing concerns about the direction of America as a basis from which to launch appeals about how to make the society better. Public perceptions of decline may be deeply influenced by such rhetoric and, as in debates about the decline of family or the decline of religion, we must exercise caution in assuming that there was actually a golden age when things were better.[10]

Another reason to be cautious is that the empirical evidence itself is far from uniform in the picture of American society that it presents. As subsequent sections of this chapter will show, specific instances of change are sometimes difficult to assess because of difficulty in comparing surveys with different designs and question wordings; surveys seldom permit analysis of trends over more than about a twenty-year period. Because some studies of social capital have demonstrated stability over long periods of time, we must avoid drawing hasty inferences from evidence covering only a few decades.[11]

Beyond these considerations, theoretical concerns also suggest the need for as careful and objective an approach to the question of social capital as possible. With the United States at or near the upper end of advanced industrial democracies on some measures of social capital, care needs to be exercised in determining whether some decline (however undesirable such a decline might be in principle) could be sustained without serious negative effects. For instance, drawing on a 1981 multination survey conducted for the Leisure Development Center, the political scientist Sidney Verba and his colleagues report that the United States ranked number one among the twelve advanced industrial nations studied in the percentage of population who were members of voluntary associations, who did work for voluntary associations, who were members of religious organizations, and who did work for these organizations. In comparison with Great Britain and West Germany, for example, the United States was substantially higher on voluntary membership (76 percent versus 52 and 50 percent) and on doing work for voluntary associations (34 percent versus 21 and 21 percent).[12] Calculations from the 1990–91 World Values Surveys of association memberships and trust also show that the United States ranks near the upper end of both these measures.[13] The reason these comparisons are interesting is that no absolute threshold has been established in the literature on social capital and democracy to permit assertions about when enough is enough or below which democracy may be in jeopardy. Put simply, the United States may have been overinvested in social capital and is now adjusting to levels more comparable to those in other industrial democracies.[14]

Before turning to empirical data, we must also look critically at what we mean by the concept of social capital. In the broadest sense, an inventory of social capital is impossible to conduct because virtually any kind of social network relationship and set of social norms counts as social capital.[15] As with any broad concept, however, the idea of social capital has emerged within a specific intellectual tradition, and its meaning is restricted by the concerns embedded within that tradition. In the United States, social capital has been regarded as a particular kind of relationship within communities that could be used by the people in those communities to strengthen their communities, to mobilize resources needed to solve social problems, and to make their voices heard in larger political arenas. Jane Jacobs' discussion of the uses of parks and sidewalks and neighborhood gatherings in cities and Glen Loury's treatment of extended families and churches in African-American communities were formative examples.[16] James Coleman's theoretical treatment of social capital focused especially on the rational choices about social exchange from which cooperative relationships and trust might emerge.[17]

Four general categories of social capital emerge from this literature: associations, trust, civic participation, and volunteering. Unlike social relationships that are limited to the nuclear family, for example, or that occur strictly in corporate board rooms or in government offices, these kinds of social capital serve as "mediating structures," in the terms of Peter Berger and Richard Neuhaus, linking individuals together in voluntary bonds of attachment that depend neither on kinship nor on economic incentives, and forging relationships that can then be used to improve their communities, solve some of their own social problems, and mobilize themselves as collective actors in the democratic process.[18] Each of the four, in turn, has multiple attributes that are worth considering as relevant aspects of the total stock of social capital in a society.[19]

Associations

Associations, such as parent-teacher associations, fraternal orders, veterans' associations, and gun clubs, are relevant partly for the sheer symbolic value of their existence. For instance, reports of political rallies in the nation's capital often emphasize the *number* of organizations represented, even if some have virtually no members and others have thousands of members, simply because large numbers of organizations give the appearance of widespread support for a particular cause. Similarly, democratic processes in communities are sometimes shaped by demands that all interested parties (associations) have "a place at the table," even though some organizations are more powerful than others.[20] Some associations may, for these reasons, be little more than paper entities, and yet they are significant for symbolic purposes as well as for the fact that some collective energies have been expended to create them. More important, *memberships* in associations are relevant because large numbers also have symbolic appeal and may mean more person-hours available to carry out programs, better-filled coffers, a permanent staff, and so on. In addition, *active memberships* are important because actual participation generally brings people into contact with one another, creates trust, and permits specific goals to be pursued. Other important factors include the degree to which associations are concerned with the general good rather than pursuing only the interests of their members, the degree to which social skills and democratic procedures may be modeled and learned within the association, the extent to which associations are embedded in territorial units (such as neighborhoods) that permit extra-associational ties to be established and that correspond with relevant political jurisdictions, and the extent to which memberships interlock with other associations and provide bridges for interaction among diverse segments of the population.

Trust

Trust is thought to be an essential element of healthy democracies, because democracy depends on people being willing to put their own destiny in the hands of "the people." Distinctions between trust in institutions and trust in individuals are helpful.[21] The former, which is sometimes described more aptly as confidence in institutions, points to the fact that much of contemporary life depends less on informal, interpersonal transactions than on the norms and social structures in which these specific transactions are embedded. To the extent that purchasing food is accomplished easily because of federal food and drug regulations, this activity may become more difficult if confidence in the federal government or in the courts erodes. Trust in individuals is, in turn, distinguishable in terms of the specificity or generality of the individuals in question. Within a family, neighborhood, or small community of acquaintances, one may say that most people can be trusted because deep knowledge of those particular individuals has been established over a period of time (one knows which neighbors can be trusted and under what conditions).[22] In more general terms, where detailed knowledge is lacking, trust is likely to be a function more of some primordial or philosophical view of human nature.[23] Trust of this kind may be higher or lower because of ideas about sin that one learned in Sunday school or about human progress that one learned in school; it may also vary depending on whether or not a person experienced loving relationships within the family as a child or not. And yet moderate, conditional levels of trust are more consistent with most theories of democracy than are overly optimistic, blind, universal ideals of trust, which may encourage faith in totalitarian leaders and not ensure the operation of effective checks and balances.

Civic Participation

Civic participation is most fruitful when directed toward activities that contribute directly to the political process (thus distinguishing them from participation in associations that may improve the community but do so through nonpolitical means). In the United States, civic participation is generally taken to include a variety of activities, ranging from voting to more active and informed types of political participation such as donating money to political organizations or campaigns, contacting public officials, doing party or campaign work, or participating in political rallies, marches, or protests.[24] Variations also occur in the level of political organization at which these activities are directed (e.g., federal, state, local), in the extent to which they focus on electoral politics or on other aspects of governmental functioning (such as work in government bureaus or use of the legal system), and in the extent to which they are explicit (such as putting candidate rating sheets in churches) or implicit (such as including a comment about a political issue in a prayer delivered at a church).

Volunteering

Volunteering, finally, overlaps with associations (to the extent that much of it may be done for associations) and with civic participation (in that one may volunteer for a political rally), but volunteering has been conceptually and empirically distinguished in the United States as behavior that is unpaid, generally not done for strictly political purposes (partly because some nonprofits are forbidden to engage in such activities), and often directed toward helping the needy.[25] Volunteering has been thought to promote democracy for some of the same reasons as simply participating in associations (for example, hearing about issues or learning leadership skills). But volunteering is also regarded as an activity that helps solve social problems through nongovernmental means, thus promoting self-sufficiency among communities and deterring dependence on government that could encourage the rise of totalitarian regimes or of bureaucracies that were no longer responsive to the public's needs. Volunteering varies in terms of whether it is actually concerned with serious social problems or simply focused on the interests of one's own family and friends. Volunteering varies, too, in terms of the total number of people in a society who are involved in it, the number of hours these people devote to it, and whether their volunteering is performed through associations or individually. In addition, charitable giving is generally considered relevant to volunteering because such funds are used by organizations to address social problems, hire professionals, and pay staff that may be needed in order to mobilize volunteers.

Now that we have introduced the four major kinds of social capital, we will examine whether in fact it is declining.

IS SOCIAL CAPITAL DECLINING?

Associations

The number of associations in the United States has risen steadily in recent years, and this trend probably reflects longer-term increases as well. As compiled in the *Encyclopedia of Associations*, the number of national nonprofit associations of all kinds rose from 14,726 in 1980 to 22,510 in 1994, the latest year for which data are available. Of these, the most numerous were classified as trade, business, and commercial nonprofit associations (rising from 3,118 to 3,768 in these years). Associations concerned with public affairs grew especially rapidly (from 1,068 to 2,169), as did health and medical associations (from 1,413 to 2,331). In comparison, labor unions and Greek letter societies showed relatively little growth.[26]

Despite growth in the raw number of associations, membership in formerly strong kinds of associations appears to have fallen in recent decades. As a percentage of the nonagricultural workforce, membership in labor unions declined from a high of 33 percent in 1953 to 29 percent in 1975, and then to a low of 16 percent in 1992, after which the trend stabilized.[27] Membership in parent-teacher associations declined from 33 per 100 schoolchildren in 1960 to 15 per 100 schoolchildren in 1976, reached a low of 13 in 1982, and rose only to 16 by 1992.[28] Despite a growing national population, membership in many other associations has fallen as well. For example, Putnam reports declines in membership of such national organizations as Elks, Boy Scouts, Shriners, Federated Women's Clubs, Lions, Jaycees, and the League of Women Voters.[29] Moreover, among those organizations for which data were available, membership had generally risen during the 1960s, whereas virtually all of these organizations registered declines during the 1980s.[30]

Of course, membership figures for specific organizations capture only a small fraction of total involvement in associations in the United States. It is for this reason that data from national surveys, in which questions about membership in broad categories of organizations are asked, is useful. These surveys provide comparable data only for the past two decades but offer a fairly systematic means of assessing trends over this period.[31]

The most detailed data on organizational memberships comes from a question in the General Social Surveys, conducted by the National Opinion Research Center at the University of Chicago, that is asked by showing respondents a hand card on which fifteen kinds of organizations (such as church-affiliated groups, sports groups, etc.) are listed. A yes is recorded by the interviewer for each type of organization of which the respondent claims to be a member. These questions were asked in fifteen of the years between 1974 and 1994.[32] Responses to the items in 1974 and in 1994 are compared in Table 2-1.

Church-affiliated groups elicit the highest proportion of yes responses. In 1974, 42 percent of the public claimed to be members of these groups, and this figure declined to 33 percent by 1994. Sports groups followed by professional and academic societies, labor unions, and school service clubs are next in order of membership. Although it would be tedious to consider the figures for all the intervening years in detail, several conclusions can be drawn.

First, comparisons of 1974 and 1994 figures show that membership in five of the fifteen kinds of organizations declined (church groups, labor unions, school service clubs, fraternal groups, and hobby or garden clubs), and in one of these (church groups) the decline was five or more percentage points.

Second, over the same period, the figures for membership in five kinds of organizations (sports groups, professional and academic groups, service clubs, literary or artistic groups, and school fraternities or sororities) increased, although only one (professional and academic groups) increased by more than five percentage points.

Third, there is some indication that a low point may have been reached around 1991, with some rebound in organizational member-

Table 2-1: Association Memberships

Question: Now we would like to know something about the groups or organizations to which individuals belong. Here is a list of various organizations. Could you tell me whether or not you are a member of each type?

	1974	1994	Change
Church-affiliated groups	42	33	-9
Sports groups	18	22	4
Professional/academic	13	19	6
Labor unions	16	12	-4
Service clubs	9	10	1
School service groups	18	16	2
Fraternal groups	14	10	-4
Youth groups	10	10	0
Hobby or garden clubs	10	8	-2
Literary, art, discussion	9	10	1
Veterans' groups	9	8	-1
School fraternities/sororities	5	6	1
Political clubs	5	5	0
Farm organizations	4	4	0
Nationality groups	4	4	0
Other	11	10	1
Any groups	75	71	-4
Number	(1,484)	(502)	

Source: General Social Surveys.

ships in more recent years. For instance, twelve of the fifteen kinds of organizations showed slightly larger figures for 1994 than for 1991.

Fourth, if a kind of stock market game is played with these figures, counting gainers and losers from one year to the next, the overall picture is as follows: 74 of the 210 organizations showed declines, 67 showed increases, and 69 displayed no change. As the large number of decreases and increases suggests, there was also considerable fluctuation in the data, rather than strictly linear decreases. For instance, membership in church groups (the item that showed the largest decline) dropped two points, then one point, then three points, then six points, after which it rose eight points, then dropped four points, increased six points, dropped ten points, dropped five points, then rose eight points, and after that stayed virtually constant.

Fifth, the percentage of people who are involved in associations of any kind has decreased and has done so in significant measure. In 1974, 75 percent of the sample claimed membership in at least one kind of association, whereas this figure had slipped to 68 percent by 1991 (and then increased modestly to 71 percent in 1994).

Further analysis of these data indicates that membership in fourteen of the fifteen kinds of organizations declined between 1974 and 1991 when level of education is taken into account.[33] When education is not taken into account, this number falls to ten. However, sampling tolerances must also be considered; despite the fact that two national samples are combined, yielding nearly 2,500 cases, only five of the fifteen relationships are statistically significant, and one of these indicates an increase rather than a decline.[34] Specifically, church-affiliated groups, labor unions, school service groups, and fraternal groups appear to have declined, while it is unclear that any of the other kinds of associations have declined.

More will be said in later sections about the sources of decline and about other kinds of associations, but the single conclusion that emerges from these descriptive data is that some decline in association membership between the early 1970s and the 1990s is indisputable, and yet it appears not to have taken place across the board, including all specific varieties of associations, but is most clearly evident in the fact that a growing proportion of the American population is not involved in *any* associations.

Trust

More than forty national surveys since 1948 have asked questions about trust. The most frequently used question asks respondents, "Generally speaking, would you say that most people can be trusted, or that you can't be too careful in dealing with people?" The two major surveys— National Election Surveys (NES) and General Social Surveys (GSS)— clearly suggest a decline in trust (see Table 2-2). The National Election Surveys show that trust was lower during the 1970s than in the 1960s, and that it was lower in 1992 than in the 1970s. These patterns are consistent with popular impressions of changes in the political climate more broadly. The sharp decline in trust between 1968 and 1972 corresponds to the growing unrest surrounding the United States' involvement in the Vietnam War. The modest rise between 1974 and 1976 corresponds with a common interpretation of Jimmy Carter's successful bid for the presidency as a signal that the country was putting Vietnam and Watergate in the past.[35] The NES figure for 1992 (45 percent) is only slightly lower than the average for the three 1970s polls (49 percent) but suggests further erosion of trust. The GSS figures cover a shorter period but suggest similar patterns. Perhaps because of Watergate, a decline appeared between 1973 and 1975, which was then reversed in 1976. After some fluctuations during the 1980s, the two most recent figures are lower than any in previous years.[36]

Results from surveys in the 1950s, it might be noted, are not comparable to ones since the 1960s because of different question wordings; nevertheless, these earlier surveys also suggest that trust may have been higher than in more recent years. When asked simply, "Do you think most people can be trusted?" 65 percent in a 1948 survey said yes (30 percent said no, and 5 percent said don't know); that figure rose to 68 percent in 1952, was 65 percent in 1954, rose to 75 percent in 1957, and was 77 percent in 1964. In comparison, when the same question was asked in 1983, only 56 percent said yes.[37]

One of the most serious limitations in the data on generalized trust, however, is that little qualitative research has been done to aid in interpreting what people may mean when they answer questions about trust in surveys. The most commonly used survey question requires respondents to choose between saying that most people can be trusted and saying that one can't be too careful in dealing with people. Yet a national survey conducted in 1997 in which respondents were given the opportunity to respond separately to these statements found the following: 62 percent agreed that "most people can be trusted," and 71 percent agreed that "you can't be too careful in your dealings with people." In other words, most respondents seem not to regard these as contradictory or as mutually exclusive statements.[38] A result such as this does not, of course, diminish the importance of the fact that fewer choose the trusting response now than did so in the past; yet it does suggest that surveys are probably not measuring the full complexity of how people think about trust.

Questions seeking to gauge confidence in institutions and in the leaders running these institutions have been asked more than five thousand times in public opinion polls in the United States over the past forty years. Most of these questions pertain to specific issues and do not provide evidence of social trends. Over the same twenty-year period as the evidence on associations and trust in people, however, comparable questions have been asked about confidence in the people running several kinds of institutions. Confidence in people running "the executive branch of the federal government" offers evidence on trust in the public sector, confidence in people running "major companies" gives a measure of trust in the private for-profit sector, and confidence in people with leadership positions in "organized religion" is the best available measure over the same period of confidence in the private nonprofit or voluntary sector (of which organized religion composes the largest share).[39]

Table 2-2: Trust in People

Percentage who say most people can be trusted

	NES	GSS
1964	54	
1966	54	
1968	56	
1972	47	46
1973		46
1974	48	
1975		39
1976	53	44
1978		39
1983		37
1984		48
1986		37
1987		44
1988		39
1989		41
1990		38
1991		38
1992	45	
1993		36
1994		34

Source: National Election Surveys, General Social Surveys. Question asked in both: "Generally speaking, would you say that most people can be trusted, or that you can't be too careful in dealing with people?"

While most of the data suggest caution in drawing conclusions about a linear erosion of confidence in major American institutions, the exception appears to be in the political arena, where mistrust of the federal government has not yet returned to its pre-Watergate levels. Indeed, other survey questions point directly to this long-term impact: In May 1973, as the Watergate story was beginning to emerge, 58 percent of the public said it had reduced their confidence in the federal government at least somewhat; this figure rose to 67 percent by August 1973, and nearly a decade later (in 1982), 66 percent still said that Watergate had reduced their confidence in the federal government this much.[40]

That mistrust of the political arena has eroded over the long term is also evident from results in National Election Surveys. On the standard Trust in Government index included in these surveys, the proportion who scored high has declined sharply since the 1960s.[41] Much of this decline took place during the Vietnam War, when high scorers fell from

65 percent of the public in 1964 to only 41 percent in 1972; Watergate precipitated a further decline (to 26 percent in 1974), and the lowest figure was reached in 1980 (19 percent). During the 1980s, trust in government rose temporarily to pre-Watergate levels (37 percent in 1984 and 30 percent in 1988), but then fell to 21 percent in 1992.[42] Mistrust of government, therefore, appears largely to be influenced by specific events, rather than simply reflecting an overall downward trend.

Civic Participation

Given the dramatic decline in public trust of government over the past three decades, we might expect civic participation also to have decreased, especially to the extent that such activity was directly involved with political campaigns, working for political parties, writing to officials, and the like. Most of the evidence does point to a decline in this kind of social capital; however, there are also some exceptions.

Civic participation directly concerned with electoral campaigns has been measured over a four-decade period by the National Election Surveys. Standard questions ask respondents whether, during the campaign, they "talk to any people and try to show them why they should vote for or against one of the parties or candidates," "go to any political meetings, rallies, dinners, or things like that in support of a particular candidate," "work for one of the parties or candidates," or "wear a campaign button or put a campaign sticker on [their] car."[43] Participation rates differ considerably between major (presidential) elections and minor elections, so trends are best considered separately for each kind of election.

As shown in Table 2-3, civic participation during major elections did not decline between 1952 and 1992; indeed, talking to or trying to influence others was ten percentage points higher in 1992 than in 1952, and working for political parties or candidates showed steady increases, while attending meetings or rallies remained constant. Only the use of campaign buttons and bumper stickers, which peaked during the Nixon-Kennedy race in 1960, experienced a long-term decline. In contrast, civic participation during minor or midterm elections gives clearer evidence of decline. Whereas three of the four measures showed increasing involvement between 1958 and 1970, all four of them registered declines between 1970 and 1990.

Another view of change in political participation, shown in Table 2-4, is that activities such as signing a petition, attending town meetings, attending political rallies, and serving on committees or as officers of local organizations have all declined since 1974. Less common activities, such as running for office, writing an article to the newspaper, making a

Table 2-3: Political Participation

	Talked to/ Influenced Others	Attended Political Meetings	Worked for Party or Candidate	Button/ Bumper Sticker
Major Election Years				
1952	28	7	3	-
1956	28	7	3	16
1960	34	8	6	21
1964	31	9	5	16
1968	33	9	6	15
1972	32	9	5	14
1976	37	6	5	8
1980	36	8	7	7
1984	32	8	9	9
1988	29	7	9	9
1992	38	8	11	11
Minor Election Years				
1958	17	-	-	-
1962	18	8	4	10
1966	22	-	-	-
1970	27	9	7	9
1974	16	6	5	6
1978	22	10	6	9
1982	22	9	6	8
1986	21	7	3	7
1990	17	6	3	7

Source: National Election Surveys.

political speech, and participating in a group concerned with governmental reform, also appear to have declined, although the percentages involved in these activities are quite small. Taking into account all dozen activities asked about, the proportion of the public who has participated in no such activities rose from 48 percent in 1973 to 62 percent in 1994. More detailed analysis of these activities suggests that a sharp decline may have occurred in the aftermath of Watergate, that patterns were relatively constant from about 1978 to 1990, and that most activities fell again during the early 1990s.[44]

Still another indication of change in civic participation is provided by Verba and colleagues, who report national comparisons in 1987 with earlier figures for 1967. Other than voting, their measures include a dozen kinds of civic participation, ranging from persuading others how to vote

Table 2-4: Political Participation, 1974 and 1994

Percentage who have done each in the past year

	1974	1994
Signed a petition	36	26
Attended a public meeting on town or school affairs	21	12
Written your congressman or senator	16	12
Attended a political rally or speech	11	6
Served on a committee for some local organization	10	6
Served as an officer of some club or organization	10	6
None	50	56

Source: Roper Surveys.

and attending a political meeting or rally to contacting local or national officials and working with others on local community problems. Of the twelve such measures included in their study, ten showed higher percentages of involvement in 1987 than in 1967, one showed no change, and only one declined.[45]

As might be expected, figures on voting itself generally show significant declines in voter turnout. For instance, turnout during presidential elections included 58 percent of the voting-age population in 1952 and again in 1960 and 1964, but declined to 45 percent in 1988, rose only to 51 percent in 1992, and fell to 49 percent in 1996. During congressional-year elections, a similar decline occurred, from 45 percent in 1962 (and in 1966) to 33 percent in 1986 and 1990. The most significant decreases in both types of election occurred between 1968 (or 1970) and 1972 (or 1974), corresponding to the heightened dissatisfaction with the Vietnam War in these years and, perhaps coincidentally, with the inclusion of 18-to-21-year-olds among voters. After these declines in the early 1970s, voter turnout has remained at about the same levels for the past two decades. In short, civic participation, by most indications, has declined, confirming what many social observers have suggested: that Americans are increasingly disenchanted with politics, even though they may continue to be involved in their communities in other ways.

Volunteering

Volunteering for soup kitchens, at churches, and for special causes, such as helping the handicapped or building low-income housing, has become one of the most important ways in which Americans participate in their communities. This kind of social capital has actually increased over the past two decades.

The best data on trends in volunteering come from a Gallup question that asks, "Do you, yourself, happen to be involved in any charity or social service activities, such as helping the poor, the sick, or the elderly?" The percentages who said they had served in these ways rose dramatically from 26 percent in the late 1970s to 46 percent in the early 1990s.[46]

Summarizing briefly, there has been some decline in social capital in the United States over the past two or three decades; however, evidence does not indicate that social capital has declined drastically or to radically low levels, nor does it show that social capital of all kinds has declined. Membership in associations is the specific kind of social capital that has declined most noticeably, especially between 1974 and 1991. Although some kinds of association show no decline, it is evident that a smaller proportion of the American public belongs to at least one organization (at least the kinds asked about in General Social Surveys) than was true two decades ago. This decline, moreover, is particularly interesting because association memberships are often regarded as a primary form of social capital that helps to predict other activities, such as voting and political participation. Trust has also declined, but the data suggest caution in estimating the seriousness and universality of this decline. Trust of government appears to have dropped, whereas trust of corporations and of religious organizations has not, and rising mistrust of government appears, on the surface at least, to be linked to specific events. Civic participation has dropped, but it also appears to be more of a mixed story than has been portrayed in the popular literature: Most figures on voting show declines, but some do not, and this ambiguity is even more the case for activities such as talking with others about politics, signing petitions, and attending rallies. Finally, there is little evidence to suggest that volunteering has been declining over any significant period of time; in fact, what evidence is available suggests that volunteering has probably increased.

In assessing the various explanations for the decline of social capital, we must pay attention to the decline of association membership, especially the fact that fewer Americans than in the past are involved in any kind of organization. After determining which explanations for this decline are most significant, we can consider whether these factors affect other measures of social capital.

EXPLAINING THE TRENDS

From one perspective, social capital is like economic capital in that it does not merely exist; indeed, it can easily be squandered by people who are either too lazy or too preoccupied with interests of their own to contribute to its creation.[47] Social capital is thus said to "erode" or decline, or to be dissolved or to dissipate, often through the inaction or inattention of people who lead dissolute lives or who willingly (or out of necessity) break social ties and violate social norms.

This view of social capital can be found in Tocqueville, who favored voluntary associations in the United States because they provided a barrier against individualism, against the overweening pursuit of self-interest, and against the crowd behavior that might be produced by public opinion itself. It was not dissimilar to the view of Protestant moralists during the same period, who argued that churches and other civic associations were needed to provide proper moral instruction to the growing multitudes.[48] In social theory, Durkheim's interest in secondary associations as a way of promoting social solidarity in opposition to the rising cult of the individual falls within the same perspective, as did the work of Robert Nisbet, William Kornhauser, and others in the 1950s and early 1960s who wrote about the dangers of mass society in which people took their cues from the mass media and from national leaders but who did not expend sufficient energy themselves to form alliances and shape their own opinions.[49] More recently, Robert Bellah and his associates have written about the dangers of living in a society where a language of self-interest is the only common form of public discourse because people have not committed themselves to the moral memories of their communities.[50]

In these various versions, totalitarian leaders and the manipulators of mass media pose threats to democracy, but the primary responsibility for maintaining social capital rests in the hands of citizens themselves. If an analogy with the factors of economic production (labor, management, capital) can be drawn, responsibility for decline in social capital is thus primarily to be sought in the laboring population. Such trends as the growing inclusion of women in the labor force or the lengthening of time spent on the job are thus of interest because they signal a diversion of labor away from time spent participating in voluntary associations or engaging in civic activities. Similarly, dissolution of marriages or people breaking residential ties with their families and neighborhoods is relevant because these activities point to a "loner mentality" that reduces commitment to associations. By the same token, people sitting at home engrossed in soap operas also signals a dissolute (lax, immoral) laboring population, rather than a commitment to working for the benefit of the community. These, then, are the kinds of explanations to which attention must be directed.

Associations

As shown earlier, the clearest evidence of decline in association memberships is in the percentage of the American public who belong to at least one association of any kind, and the sharpest difference occurred between 1974 and 1991, when this proportion dropped from 75 percent to 68 percent. In addition, it is worth noting that the proportion who were involved in only one association remained virtually constant. Thus, the shift was largely away from holding multiple memberships toward holding no memberships at all.[51]

The effects of standard measures of malaise (or dissolution) on social capital have been examined by Robert Putnam, who found that the erosion of membership in associations cannot be explained by the fact that more people are working longer hours at their jobs; nor is it accounted for by the inclusion of women in the paid labor force, by dissolution of marriages, by residential mobility, or by suburbanization. Aging or cohort effects may be a factor, although these require further interpretation. In addition, Putnam found that economic conditions seem not to be a factor, and education, as already noted, appears to have a positive effect on group memberships.[52]

As an independent assessment of these factors, Table 2-5 shows the percentages of people with each of the relevant social characteristics who were members of at least one kind of association in 1974, the same figures for 1991, and the percentage point decline between the two years. The results generally support Putnam's conclusions. The decline in association membership was about the same in all the various categories but suggests several interesting patterns among certain subgroups of the population. One of these patterns is among people who were separated or divorced: They were already less likely than married, widowed, or never-married people to belong to groups in 1974, and they remained at this level in 1991. The fact that their numbers increased in the population (from 8 percent to 14 percent in the surveys) means that some of the overall decline in group memberships can be associated with marital dissolution. Another pattern worth noting is that never-married people registered a decline that was slightly above average; their proportions in the surveys also increased (from 12 percent in 1974 to 21 percent in 1991).

In view of assertions about the possible effect of larger numbers of women being included in the labor force (37 percent of women in the 1991 study worked full time, compared to 27 percent in the 1974 survey), it is interesting to note that association memberships declined *less* among women in the labor force than among women who kept house. Because the proportion who kept house declined from slightly more than half of all women in 1974 to fewer than a third in 1991, it is reasonable to assume that the characteristics of these women may also have changed (i.e., it was more the norm to keep house in the earlier period than in the latter). What the comparisons among women suggest most clearly is that association memberships may be a function of two factors: having contacts with other people outside the home (in this case through the workplace), and having enough time to capitalize on these contacts (thus women who work part time are more likely to be in associations than women who work full time).

Otherwise, the data in Table 2-5 give little support to standard arguments about social dissolution. Comparisons of those working fifty or more hours a week with those working forty to forty-nine hours show that the decline among the former was less than it was among the latter

Table 2-5: Association Memberships by Social Characteristics

Percentage who belonged to at least one organization

	1974	1991	Change
Married	77	69	−8
Widowed	74	76	2
Divorced/separated	63	65	2
Never married	70	60	−10
Work full time (women only)	73	69	−4
Work part time (women only)	77	75	−2
Keeping house (women only)	68	57	−11
Work 50+ hours per week	80	71	−9
Work 40–49 hours per week	79	67	−12
Work less than 40 hours per week	76	73	−3
Age 25–34	76	63	−13
Age 35–44	79	67	−12
Age 45–54	75	74	−1
Age 55–64	78	71	−7
Age 65+	76	70	−6
Regional mobility	75	68	−7
Regional stability	75	68	−7
Urban	74	66	−8
Suburban	75	68	−7
Other	76	70	−6
Town/rural	71	67	−4

Source: General Social Surveys; association membership includes all items in Table 2-1.

(although both groups declined more than those who worked fewer than forty hours a week).[53] Age groups also provide only a partial interpretation of the decline. In these data, the 35-to-44-year-old category became a larger segment of the population (rising from 18 percent of the total in 1974 to 24 percent in 1991). Yet the percentage point decline for this category was no greater than that of younger people, and the decline among people in their late fifties and sixties was greater than among people in their late forties and early fifties. Nor is there any obvious cohort effect (from comparing each group in 1974 with the next older group in 1991).[54] Finally, neither changing residences from one region to another nor living in suburbs appears to be associated with significant differences in the likelihood or decline of group memberships.[55] Not surprisingly, a multivariate analysis that includes all these variables fails to explain (or even reduce) the trend between 1974 and 1991.

An alternative explanatory perspective comes from taking more seriously the idea that social capital is *capital,* and like other forms of capital, it may be distributed unequally; indeed, it may have a tendency to become more unequally distributed over time, unless other checks are in place, and its role may be one of exclusion rather than inclusion. This perspective, of course, is more consistent with Marx than with Tocqueville or Durkheim, but it is also compatible with recent discussions of cultural capital that emphasize how the arts, literature, and schooling serve to draw symbolic boundaries between those who have socially acceptable skills and those who do not.[56] By analogy, social capital may be said to function in an exclusionary way when it consists of limited networks that provide valuable information to some people but not to others (old-boy networks, for example) or when associations set up expectations about membership that cannot easily be met by everyone.[57]

In this view, a possible reason for the decline in social capital is that existing social arrangements have become systematically more exclusionary, causing some segments of the population to feel unwelcome and to cease participating, or failing to provide the resources that people need to engage in civic activities. In contrast to the erosion perspective, the exclusion approach focuses less on the moral commitment of the laboring population and more on whether or not this population has the resources necessary for participating in organizations, as well as on the possibility that organizations are less than democratic in their actual functioning. It raises the possibility that if people are no longer joining Kiwanis as often as they did in the past, it may be indicative of some problem with Kiwanis rather than with the population.

On the surface, there may be little to recommend this theory, especially in light of the fact that most voluntary associations are truly voluntary, that most are avowed proponents of democracy, and that cultural trends over the past half century have been toward greater inclusion along lines of gender, race, ethnicity, and lifestyle and toward greater tolerance of diversity. Nevertheless, associations operate according to implicit norms as much as according to formal statements of purpose, and these expectations may inadvertently favor some and exclude others. For example, considerable cultural capital is needed to participate in most organizations, and this capital depends greatly on what people bring with them, rather than simply being learned once they arrive. Leadership skills, the ability to speak comfortably in medium-sized groups, familiarity with organizational rules, and the capacity to make small talk about the right subjects are all examples of such capital. The rise in levels of education that has taken place over the past half century is but one important development that may have established implicit norms in organizations that inadvertently exclude potential members who do not have the kinds of cultural capital that is associated with higher education.[58]

As we see in Table 2-6, this alternative perspective is supported by the data. Five variables are examined to provide comparisons between those who have had fewer socioeconomic privileges and those who have had greater privileges: whether the income of the family in which one was raised was below average, average, or above average; father's level of education; respondent's level of education; respondent's race; and the number of children one had been responsible for raising. The patterns for all five variables are clear, consistent, and striking. In each case, those with fewer socioeconomic privileges were more similar in social capital to those with greater socioeconomic privileges in 1974 than they were in 1991. The decline in association membership was always more pronounced among those with fewer socioeconomic privileges to begin with than it was with people who already had greater privileges.

For example, among those raised in lower-income families, 72 percent were members of associations in 1974 (only 8 percent fewer than among people raised in above-average-income families); but by 1991, those from low-income backgrounds had declined in association memberships by seven percentage points, whereas those from high-income backgrounds had declined by only three points. Thus the eight-point spread that had been present between the two groups in 1974 became a twelve-point spread by 1991. Virtually the same pattern is evident for father's education. In 1974, association membership was about equally likely among people whose fathers had less than a high school education and among

Table 2-6: Marginalization and Social Capital

Percentage who belonged to at least one organization

	1974	1991	Change
Family income at age 16			
Below average	72	65	−7
Average	74	66	−8
Above average	80	77	−3
Father's education			
Less than high school	74	65	−9
High school graduate	78	69	−9
College graduate	76	83	7
Respondent's education			
Less than high school	65	53	−12
High school graduate	77	66	−11
College graduate	91	88	−3
Race			
Black or other	73	56	−17
White	75	70	−5
Number of children			
Three or more	77	67	−10
One or two	74	69	−5
None	71	67	−4
Marginalization Index			
High	67	49	−18
Medium high	75	67	−8
Medium low	75	68	−7
Low	78	77	−1

Source: General Social Surveys; association membership includes all items in Table 2-1.

people whose fathers had graduated from college; by 1991, association memberships were much less likely (eighteen percentage points) among people from low-education backgrounds than among people from high-education backgrounds. Similarly, African-Americans and white European-Americans were about equally involved in associations in 1974, but by 1991 there was a large disparity between the two. Having lower education oneself and having raised a larger number of children showed similar patterns.

The Marginalization Index shown in Table 2-6 was constructed by combining the previous five variables (shown in the table).[59] Like its component variables, it demonstrates that disparities in association membership were greater between the more marginalized and the less marginalized in 1991 than they had been in 1974. The decline in association memberships among the most marginalized was eighteen percentage points, those of the medium groups were eight and seven points, and that of the least marginalized group was only one point.

One way of thinking about these patterns is to say that virtually all of the decline in association memberships between 1974 and 1991 took place in the more marginalized segments of the population rather than among people who had the most privileges already. Put differently, had things gone as well for everyone as they did for people from affluent backgrounds, for people whose fathers had good educations, and for people who had college degrees, there would have been hardly any decline in this kind of social capital at all. Indeed, further analysis of the data shows that the increased role of marginalization in 1991 explains away the relationship between year and membership.[60]

Why have marginalized groups seen such a decline? One possible interpretation is that it was their lack of social capital in the first place that *caused* some Americans to become marginalized. But this interpretation makes little sense intuitively and none when we consider the data. Intuitively, it is difficult to imagine why not being a member of a sports club or the PTA would have led a sizable segment of the American population to slide downhill in socioeconomic status over a seventeen-year period. But that is also not what the data show. Education and number of children are the only variables over which respondents themselves had any control. It was their race, their father's education, and the income of their family of origin that were the best predictors of how much their segment of the population would decline in association memberships.

The interpretation that makes best sense of the data is that life became harder for marginalized Americans between 1974 and 1991 and thus made it more difficult for them to participate in community organizations. Some evidence to this effect can be seen in Table 2-7. Comparing 1991 to 1974 shows that more of the marginalized had become widowed or divorced, were elderly, were in the bottom third of the overall distribution of incomes in the United States, and were isolated from their friends, families, and neighbors. They had also become more pessimistic about life. Under such conditions, it is probably not surprising that their association membership also declined. Some were unable to pay the dues required to belong to associations; others were elderly people who were unable or afraid to travel to attend meetings; others had lost the more personalized social capital (friends and family) who had

Table 2-7: Profile of the Socially Marginalized

	1974	1991	Change
Percentage of the marginalized in each year who were:			
Widowed	13	19	6
Divorced or separated	11	18	7
Age 65 or older	24	33	9
In bottom third on income	48	69	21
Never socializing with friends*	22	28	6
Never socializing with neighbors	29	45	16
In low contact with relatives**	19	36	17
Pessimistic about life***	54	68	14

*Never spend a social evening with friends outside their neighborhood
**Spend a social evening with relatives less than once a month
***Agree that the lot of the average man is getting worse

Source: General Social Surveys.

drawn them into associations or who had helped with raising children and meeting other needs so that belonging to an association was possible; and others probably found themselves uncomfortable in organizations that were now populated more by people with better educations and higher incomes.[61]

Labor Unions and Religion

In addition to these general patterns, it is also instructive to consider labor unions and church-affiliated groups separately. The decline in labor union membership between 1974 and 1991 occurred only among men. Conditions in the wider economy are partly responsible for this decline; for example, fewer men are employed in the manufacturing sector than previously, and more jobs have shifted to the service sector. Women's membership in unions, in contrast, has partly been stabilized by employment in segments of the public sector that have shown growing rates of unionization.[62] Among men, the effects of marginalization that have just been examined are also evident with respect to union membership.

Among men who scored high on the Marginalization Index, 34 percent were union members in 1974, compared to only 15 percent of those who scored low on the index; in 1991, the respective figures were 21 percent and 11 percent. Clearly, union membership was one kind of social capital that was more prevalent among the less privileged, and it has remained so;

nevertheless, like other kinds of association, it has also declined more among the less privileged than among the more privileged.[63]

Trends in religious participation are more difficult to explain, at least partly because participation in religious organizations in the United States is enormously complex and varied. In the GSS data, membership in church-affiliated groups declined by eight percentage points (from 42 percent to 34 percent) between 1974 and 1991. None of the dissolution variables considered earlier provided an explanation as to why this drop occurred; nor did any of the marginalization variables.[64] In addition, no obvious patterns emerged when separate analyses were conducted among people who were in different traditions or who attended services more or less frequently.[65] The only variable that provided insight, in fact, was whether or not respondents had been reared in fundamentalist denominations.[66] Among these respondents, the decline in church-affiliated membership fell to six percentage points, whereas among those who were reared in liberal denominations, the decline increased to thirteen points. A logistic regression analysis of the data also demonstrated that an interaction term involving fundamentalist background and year was able to reduce the effect of year to an insignificant relationship.[67] Substantively, this finding is consistent with other research suggesting that baby boomers raised in liberal denominations were more likely to become apostates as adults than baby boomers who were raised in theologically conservative settings.[68] This conclusion also seems compatible with the fact that liberal denominations have declined in membership over the past thirty years more than conservative denominations have.

Caution is suggested in putting much stock in this particular finding, however. The reason is that the church-affiliated group question in the GSS is ambiguous. To some respondents, it may mean nothing more than being a member of a congregation or denomination, while to others it means involvement in anything from a church choir to a Boy Scout troop that uses the church basement as a place to meet. Indeed, the ambiguity of this question was demonstrated by a GSS question in the mid-1980s that asked which of these various meanings the item had, on which respondents were about evenly split between church membership in general and involvement in a particular group.[69] The reason this ambiguity is important is that church membership is known to have declined, partly because of independent and evangelical churches that emphasize attendance more than membership and partly because mainline Protestant and Catholic churches have begun undercounting members as a way of minimizing apportionment dues charged by denominational offices.

Thus, in spite of the commonly held view that religious involvement is declining, most students of the subject have been reluctant to offer blanket generalizations about decline. In fact, church attendance rates in the United States have remained virtually constant over more than half a century, except for a small upward shift during the 1950s that is commonly attributed to the postwar rise in birthrates and a temporary boom in church construction; certainly for the 1970s and 1980s, when other forms of social capital appear to have declined, church attendance was steady.[70] In addition, church membership, even after the small declines that have been registered since the 1960s, is still higher than at any time during the nineteenth century or the first half of the twentieth century. Cohort analyses and studies of the shifting composition of denominations also hint at little overall decline in religion as a form of social capital.[71]

What has declined in American religion is loyalty to specific denominations, congregations, or faith traditions. Americans are more likely to switch faiths than they were in the 1950s or 1960s, for example, and they overwhelmingly say that people should make up their own minds about religion and can be good Christians or Jews without belonging to congregations.[72] There have been long-term declines in the percentages who raise their children to have loyalty to the church and who have grown up in households in which strict observance of daily religious rituals was customary. Fewer Americans now than during the 1960s believe that religion can answer their problems or believe that the Bible should be taken literally. Qualitative oral history evidence suggests that many Americans are less territorial in their sense of the sacred, preferring to shop around and to be eclectic, rather than identifying the sacred with their particular congregation or community. To the extent that religious capital has declined, therefore, it is probably in a more subtle, qualitative shift in the meaning of religious belief and attachment, which of course is difficult to demonstrate with statistical data.[73]

Trust
Trust, as discussed, registered decline in the standard "trust in people" question and in questions about confidence in the federal government, which we attribute at least in part to the Watergate scandal in 1973, but not a decline in questions about confidence in major companies or organized religion. The decline of trust in people is most in need of explanation, since it should not necessarily reflect views of government, and since it is assumed in most writing on social capital to be a form of capital itself and to be heightened by involvement in associations. From

extensive analysis of the available data, two tentative conclusions are in order.

First, trust in other people is much more a function of socioeconomic privilege than it is of involvement in associations; indeed, its apparent relationship with the latter appears to be a spurious function of its relationship with the former. Specifically, in the 1991 GSS data trust in people was positively correlated with the number of associations to which respondents belonged, controlling for age and sex, but when the Marginality Index was introduced into the equation, this relationship became statistically insignificant.[74]

Second, the rather sizable differences between the more privileged and the marginalized on trust appear to have remained relatively constant in recent decades. In the National Election Surveys (which include the trust question over a longer period than the GSS), an overall decline of eleven percentage points was registered between the highest year (1968) and the lowest (1992). On the two measures of social status available in these data (race and education), the differences between groups within the same year, however, were greater than the difference between the two years. Specifically, in 1968, 60 percent of white respondents expressed faith in people, compared with only 25 percent of black respondents (in 1992, the figures were 49 percent and 18 percent). Similarly, in 1968 only 35 percent of grade-school-educated respondents expressed faith in people, compared with 55 percent of high-school-educated respondents and 76 percent of college-educated respondents (in 1992, the figures were 25, 36, and 57). These findings suggest that any discussion focusing only on decline in trust is missing the more essential fact that trust has been, and remains, quite differentially distributed across status groups.[75]

These conclusions are worth emphasizing because they contradict the conventional view that social capital is a resource that the marginalized may be able to use even if they do not have other resources. If the hope is that association memberships are enough to build trust despite an absence of other socioeconomic resources, however, that hope appears to be ill founded. It is not the case that trust was more equally distributed a few decades ago than it is now. Trust has simply remained at low levels among less privileged groups such as blacks and those with lower levels of education. The larger impact of declining trust in government on trust in people is also important to acknowledge. This impact suggests that trust in people is a function not only of firsthand social relationships, or even of social status, but of national leadership.

If an analogy can be drawn from discussions of economic capital, it might be said that trust appears to be a function of management (and of capital) more so than of labor. That is, management at the national level can build (or erode) trust, not only in government itself, but in people. The reason for this is that national leaders serve a symbolic role, heightening the public's willingness to believe that human nature is good when their leaders are trustworthy, and undermining that confidence when leaders behave less admirably. The implication for leaders should be clear: If the public is less willing to trust human nature, it is not because the public is spending less time in voluntary associations; it is because leaders themselves are not living up to the public's expectations.

Civic Participation

Civic participation, as we saw, appears to have declined in some studies but not in others. Both kinds of studies nevertheless point to the importance of privilege and marginalization in understanding levels of civic participation. In the National Election Surveys, political participation among whites increased slightly between 1968 and 1992 (from 37 percent to 41 percent), whereas it declined significantly among African-Americans (from 40 percent to only 29 percent). The same pattern was evident when respondents' level of education was taken into account: Among those with college educations, there was no change (51 percent in both years), whereas among those with high school educations there was a six-point decline (from 36 to 30 percent), as there was among those with less than a high school diploma (from 23 to 17 percent). Voter turnout shows an even sharper divergence: a decline of thirty-three percentage points between 1964 and 1992 among persons without high school diplomas, and a decline of twenty-six points among high school graduates, compared with a decline of only eight points among college graduates.[76] These patterns are similar to the ones seen earlier concerning the declining associational involvement of Americans in marginalized segments of the population. Other evidence also suggests that some of the decline in electoral turnout may be a function of so-called neighborhood effects that dampen civic participation because of high concentrations of joblessness, crime, and other social problems in particular communities.[77]

Volunteering

The decline in volunteer work, finally, is difficult to explain because the evidence of decline is limited to a couple of surveys conducted in the early 1990s, whereas surveys conducted over a longer period, as we saw, suggest strong growth in volunteering. It is possible, though, to examine the relationships among volunteering, association memberships, and

social status, and thus to speculate about the extent to which volunteering is rooted in the same factors as other forms of social capital. Data
from four national surveys conducted by Independent Sector between
1987 and 1993 show that volunteering is clearly more likely among the
privileged and less likely among marginalized groups. Those with lower
levels of education, those with lower family incomes, and blacks and
Hispanics were less likely to volunteer than people with higher levels of
education and income and whites, and these differences were evident
both in volunteering within the past year and in volunteering within the
past month. Moreover, when these differences were taken into account,
some of the decline evident in overall figures between 1989 and 1993 was
explained.[78] Not surprisingly, people who belonged to associations were
more likely to volunteer than those who did not belong to any associations, and this was the case both for religious organizations and other
kinds of organizations. More interestingly, in the two surveys that asked
about nonreligious organizations (1991 and 1993) members showed
steady rates of volunteering, whereas nonmembers' volunteering
declined.[79] Further analysis of the data also shows that marginalized
groups are much less likely to be involved in organizations than privileged groups, and that marginalization explains some of the apparent
effect of organization membership on volunteering.[80]

NEW FORMS OF SOCIAL CAPITAL?

Critics of the argument that social capital in the United States can chiefly
be understood in terms of its decline have suggested that there may be
new varieties of association and of civic participation that are missed in
trend assessments simply because they were not present when earlier
studies were designed. Thus, for example, these earlier studies did not
include questions about support groups or the use of electronic technologies for communication—forms of social capital that were nonexistent or not as prominent then as they are now. There is some reason to
take this suggestion about new forms of social capital seriously, especially because many of the survey questions from which trends can be
inferred were drawn from research conducted in the 1950s and 1960s.
More important, the history of voluntary associations in the United
States has always been characterized by the appearance of new kinds of
organizations, some of which flourished for relatively brief periods (but
with significant effects), and by the decline of other forms.[81] In the
1830s, for example, benevolent associations emerged, spreading rapidly

in urban settings, only to be replaced by charity organizations, as they were called, and by the settlement house and farm colony movements a half century later.[82] Similarly, American religious history has been characterized as a struggle between "winners" and "losers," such as the so-called popular denominations (Methodists and Baptists) in the 1840s in opposition to the declining eastern seaboard denominations (Episcopalians and Presbyterians), or between "churches" and "upstart sects" at the end of the nineteenth century, or in terms of schisms and mergers in the twentieth century.[83] Mutual-aid societies and volunteer fire companies have been replaced by life insurance companies and professional firefighters in many communities, and ethnic associations (such as Landsmanschaftn) have ceased to play as significant a function among second- and third-generation Americans as among immigrants and first-generation Americans (but in their place, Korean churches and Hispanic Pentecostal assemblies are flourishing).[84] Certainly, the labor union movement, which now appears to be in decline, was a rising form of social capital in the United States in the 1930s that would likely have been missed by survey questions designed in the 1880s.

The General Social Surveys list of voluntary associations is intended to be comprehensive, especially insofar as it includes an "other" category. However, it is well established in survey research that "other" categories are not likely to prompt as thoughtful responses as the presence of specific items. One indication of what may be missing in the GSS list comes from comparing it with a comparable survey conducted in 1990 among registered voters. It showed that 27 percent of respondents belonged to "business or civic groups," 15 percent belonged to "community centers," 18 percent belonged to "neighborhood improvement associations," and 15 percent belonged to "issue or action oriented groups."[85] None of these memberships would have likely have been captured by the GSS categories.

An indication of the possible effects of omitted groups on estimates of trends is provided by the World Values Surveys, which were conducted in 1981 and 1990.[86] The categories included in the two years are not strictly comparable, but they do cover a greater variety of memberships than the GSS—for example, human rights organizations and environmentalist groups in addition to unions, professional associations, church-affiliated groups, and so on. The result of this broader inclusion of groups is that more of the American public appears to be involved in at least some group than in the GSS (82 percent in 1990 rather than 68 percent). Moreover, the proportion involved actually rises (from 73 percent to 82 percent) over the period.[87]

Another indirect indication of the likelihood that newer groups are being missed in surveys using questions designed a quarter century ago comes from a 1992 survey in which women were asked to choose the type of organization they would be most likely to join. Although a majority chose conventional ones (religious groups, 22 percent; community groups, 20 percent; and parents' groups, 16 percent), a third selected other kinds of groups, such as self-help groups (14 percent), a group for social change (10 percent), or a women's group (9 percent).[88]

A related issue has to do with the value and validity of membership data from national organizations. For example, membership in parent-teacher associations appears to have dropped dramatically (from more than 30 members per 100 schoolchildren in 1960 to about 15 in 1992) when figures are taken from the PTA national headquarters.[89] Such a dramatic decline, however, may in part be offset by the fact that other kinds of parents' organizations are not represented in these figures. In a national survey conducted in 1993 for the PTA, for example, 35 percent of parents with school-age children claimed to be members of the PTA, but another 22 percent were members of PTOs, 12 percent belonged to booster clubs, and 15 percent were members of other parents' groups.[90] Similarly, membership figures from specific civic and service organizations, such as Lions and Jaycees, suggest decline in social capital.[91] Yet in surveys that mention such organizations as these specifically but that allow respondents to include membership in similar organizations, declining involvement is not evident; for instance, a national poll in 1960 that asked about "service clubs like Lions, Exchange, Rotary, Kiwanis" found that 4 percent of Americans were members, whereas a 1986 survey that asked about "civic clubs like Kiwanis or Rotary" showed that 11 percent of the public were members.[92] Such data do not indicate conclusively that alternative organizations have grown, but the possibility at least needs to be entertained.

Of course, not everything that attaches the label of "association" (or community or neighborhood) to itself should be regarded as a viable form of social capital, especially when novelty renders its significance as a means of generating social interaction unproven. For example, neighborhood watch associations have apparently grown dramatically over the past quarter century, at least judging by the fact that 42 percent of the public said in a 1984 survey that neighborhood watch programs had been established in their communities.[93] Yet, as Robert Putnam has observed, these may represent little more than "a kind of sociological Astroturf, suitable only where you can't grow the real thing."[94]

Another kind of voluntary association that has risen in recent decades is the special-interest group, especially ones oriented toward championing the rights of particular segments of the population in the political arena, such as black caucuses, gay activists, women's rights groups, and political action committees.[95] Between 1960 and 1985, approximately 1,500 such associations were founded; indeed, in the latter year, four out of five of all such associations had come into being since 1960.[96] Moreover, the growth of such organizations appears to have prompted similar groups to appear in other sectors of the society that had previously been organized around different axes. For example, in religion, approximately 800 nationally incorporated special-purpose groups had come into existence by 1985, a figure that rivaled the total number of denominations, and collectively such groups had elicited at least some involvement by a third of the population.[97]

Some of the larger of these special-interest groups have attracted sizable memberships; for example, the American Association of Retired Persons is estimated to include approximately 20 percent of the adult public among its members. Yet it is correct to point out that many such organizations do little to promote social capital because membership may consist of little more than sending in a check once a year and receiving a seldom-read publication in return.[98]

Also, one special interest—the so-called religious right—that has attracted much media attention over the past fifteen years needs to be viewed carefully. Specific organizations, such as the Christian Coalition (headed by television preacher Pat Robertson), have grown (between 1992 and 1994 Christian Coalition membership climbed from half a million to nearly 1.5 million).[99] However, surveys conducted since the mid-1970s suggest little or no growth in the overall proportion of Americans who identify themselves as "born again" Christians, as religious "conservatives," or as people who believe in a literal interpretation of the Bible; indeed, over a longer period, biblical literalism has declined significantly.[100] Nevertheless, studies provide strong evidence that conservative or evangelical Christians, who had been below average in voter turnout and political participation prior to 1973, became more civically active in these ways after 1973, especially during the presidential campaigns of Jimmy Carter and Ronald Reagan.[101]

Among the various developments in recent decades, small support groups are perhaps a more significant kind of capital building mechanism. These include many religious groups, such as home Bible study groups, prayer fellowships, and house churches; therapy groups; a wide array of self-help groups and twelve-step groups (such as Alcoholics Anonymous); and other groups such as book discussion groups and hobby groups that may serve a supportive function. Although some of these groups are likely to have been captured by the General Social Survey questions about membership in voluntary associations, many go under different labels, do not consider themselves to be "organizations," or in surveys fail to evoke responses unless mentioned specifically. Anecdotal evidence from national leaders who supply study materials for such groups, as well as increases in the number of bookstores devoted to such materials, have given the impression that such groups have grown substantially, and historical research shows that many of them originated only in the late 1960s and early 1970s.[102]

There is also statistical evidence that membership in some kinds of support groups has grown dramatically. Twelve-step groups, including any group that uses or follows an adaptation of the famous twelve steps to recovery on which Alcoholics Anonymous was based (such as Al-Anon, ACOA [Adult Children of Alcoholics], Alateen, or Gamblers Anonymous) are required to register and provide periodic information on attendance at meetings to the General Services Board of Alcoholics Anonymous. Membership in Alcoholics Anonymous itself (which was founded in 1935 and became a national phenomenon only in the 1950s) grew from approximately 445,000 in 1979 to approximately 980,000 in 1989, and then reached 1,127,471 in 1992.[103] Most twelve-step groups average approximately twenty to twenty-five members who attend weekly, and the variety of such groups has become more specialized in recent years. Al-Anon (founded in 1951) grew from 1,500 groups in 1981 to 1,900 (with approximately 500,000 members) in 1990; in the same year, there were 1,300 ACOA groups, none of which existed prior to 1982.[104]

An estimate of the larger self-help movement, which includes groups for the bereaved, for people with disabilities and health needs, for parents, and for victims of crime and domestic violence, comes from figures compiled by the fifty state-level self-help clearinghouses, whose task is to provide annually updated lists of local self-help groups and to obtain information from these groups about memberships, goals, and activities. In 1976, membership in all such groups nationally was estimated at 5 million to 8 million people; in 1988, the comparable figure was 12 million to 15 million members.[105] Another way of estimating the growth of self-help groups is by comparing the results of a 1984 Harris poll with more recent results. In the 1984 study, only 3 percent of the adult public said yes when asked, "Are you now participating in a mutual support self-help group for the purpose of aiding you in coping with a specific problem or problems of everyday life?" In comparison, a 1992 Gallup survey found that 10 percent of the public was participating in a "small group that meets regularly and that provides caring and support for its members" and described their group as a "self-help group."[106] Although these questions are not strictly comparable, they are consistent with the estimates drawn from other sources.

In addition, cross-sectional data suggests that a large proportion of the people who are involved in small, supportive groups belong to a group that is best described as a Bible study or prayer group. Such groups meet in homes or at churches, often informally, and they may or may not be a formal part of the church's activities. Directly comparable surveys asking about Bible study groups have not been asked in different years, but one comparison appears to be relatively accurate: It shows that in 1982 only 19 percent of the public was involved in Bible study groups, whereas by 1994 this figure had risen to 33 percent.[107]

Volunteer work is another arena in which changing forms of social capital are evident. The number of Red Cross volunteers, for example, suggests that civic involvement is declining.[108] Some of this decline, however, is probably a result of volunteers focusing on other activities (especially in view of the fact that overall volunteering appears to have risen except in the past few years). For instance, the number of Salvation Army volunteers increased from 1.1 million in 1987 to 1.25 million in 1991 and to 1.7 million in 1995.[109] More dramatically, Habitat for Humanity came into existence in 1976, and during its first decade volunteers constructed approximately 1,000 houses annually; in 1991, 10,000 houses were built; and in 1994, 30,000 houses were built.[110] New ways of enlisting volunteers through existing institutions have also appeared. Among high school students, for example, 27 percent were in schools that encouraged community service in 1985, whereas this figure rose to 55 percent by 1992.[111]

Another change that must be considered is the shifting character of interpersonal relationships. If "community" is defined territorially as the neighborhood, then there is clear evidence that social contacts within such communities have declined in recent decades. For example, General Social Survey results show that 72 percent of Americans spent a social evening visiting their neighbors at least once a year in 1974, but that this figure declined to 62 percent by 1991; frequent contact (defined by visiting once a month or more) also declined (from 61 percent to 50 percent).[112] Yet the next question in the GSS asks about spending a social evening with friends who live outside the neighborhood; here, 81 percent and 82 percent in the two time periods, respectively, have done so at least once a year, and the proportion who do so once a month or more has actually risen slightly (from 63 percent to 67 percent).[113] Comparing the two kinds of activity also suggests that neighborly and extra-neighborly contact was about even in 1974, whereas by 1991 the balance had shifted outside the neighborhood.[114]

The likelihood of this shift continuing is also evident in national polls. For example, a 1991 Barna poll that asked, "If you wanted to make new friends, where would you be most likely to find the people who would become your new friends?" found that only 12 percent of Americans said in their neighborhood, compared with 45 percent who said at work, 49 percent who said at church, 18 percent at school, 20 percent at social or exercise clubs, and 18 percent at community organizations.[115]

We must also consider other means of maintaining social relationships besides in-person contact. Telephone contact has made it possible for people to give counsel and seek advice, discuss politics, and share information over greater distances that when social capital was of necessity concentrated in local communities.[116] Most of the impact of telephone use occurred well before the period under consideration, and yet even in the past few decades evidence shows that social capital in the sense of people interacting with one another by telephone has increased. For example, between 1977 and 1987 the proportion of the public who made at least one long-distance call (to someone more than 100 miles away) in the past month rose from 57 percent to 68 percent.[117] How important telephone contact is as a form of social capital is evident from a national survey in which 56 percent of the public had called a relative or friend on the phone just to talk the day before.[118] In this study, 24 percent of Americans also said they had car phones or cellular phones.

The same survey showed how prevalent the mass media is as a means of staying in touch with social issues and other national events. Two Americans in three read a daily newspaper regularly, and 52 percent had read one the day before; 64 percent had watched news on television the day before, and of these, 82 percent had watched for at least 30 minutes and 40 percent had watched only the news.[119] Other evidence suggests that extended hours of television viewing dampen civic engagement, unlike frequent newspaper reading, and that newspaper reading has declined.[120] Nevertheless, it is clear from this study that television is also a significant means by which Americans keep abreast of news. And to the extent that the problem with television is conceived to be growing numbers of people sitting passively for long hours doing nothing but watching television, it is worth observing that it is not entirely clear that larger and larger proportions of the U.S. population are devoting major portions of their day to viewing television. For example, a national survey conducted in 1964 found that 19 percent watched television four or more hours a day; between 1982 and 1993, national surveys found comparable figures of 20 to 23 percent.[121] Also worth noting is the commonly mentioned fact that far more people have televisions on for long stretches during the day (and night) than actually watch them; for instance, a 1993 survey showed that 23 percent personally watched four or more hours a day, whereas 59 percent had a television on this long or longer.

The same study also provided evidence of the extent to which computing technology is giving some Americans new ways of maintaining social relationships. Of all adults in the labor force, 62 percent use a computer at least occasionally at work, and of those in school, 75 percent use a computer sometimes. Nationally, 36 percent of Americans own a personal computer, and, in all, 30 percent of the adult public have a PC and personally use it at least every few weeks.[122] Having a PC and using it to be in contact with others, of course, are different things; nevertheless, the study also suggests that networking has become a fact of life for perhaps at least 10 percent of Americans. For instance, approximately 15 percent of all Americans have PCs with modems; about 10 percent use a computer at work or at school to connect with computer bulletin boards, information services, or the Internet; and 9 percent of the population uses some type of online service.[123]

THE CONSEQUENCES OF CHANGE

While the complexity of trends among the various kinds of social capital examined make broad conclusions difficult, the evidence does suggest some worrisome trends for the future of American society. The decline observed in association memberships between 1974 and 1991 is likely to have negative consequences for a number of other desirable social characteristics, particularly insofar as this decline appears to be most serious among people who are already socially marginalized. Insofar as volunteering is encouraged by membership in associations, a decline in memberships may be especially unfortunate. Most volunteering is targeted toward serious social problems, and much of it (by the privileged and by the marginalized alike) is directed toward needs in low-income areas or among people with other disadvantages.[124]

Any consideration of the consequences of declining association memberships must also take account of the contextual effects of this kind of social capital. To take a widely cited example, teenagers whose neighbors go to church have been found to do better in school than teenagers whose neighbors do not attend church, taking into account most characteristics of teenagers' own families.[125] Another study that demonstrates contextual effects of a different kind is a longitudinal study of students in twenty high schools that found that individual risk-taking behavior (binge drinking, smoking, illicit drug use, and sexual activity) was reduced when social capital in the form of high levels of involvement in extracurricular activities among seniors was present.[126] Still another example is that high school students whose friends are church members are more likely to engage in community service activities, taking into account whether or not they themselves or their mothers or fathers are church members.[127]

These contextual effects, of course, are likely to diminish as a result of any decline in the likelihood of one's neighbors, classmates, or friends belonging to churches or participating in other extracurricular activities. Yet contextual effects demonstrate that social capital on the part of some accrues to the benefit of others. Put negatively, it is possible for people to be "free riders," receiving informal benefits without actually participating in organizations themselves. Viewed differently, however, contextual effects also suggest that not everyone need be involved in organizations for a relatively healthy society to exist. Some people may have no inclination to spend their time going to church, and yet enough people doing so may be sufficient to spread the benefits of this kind of social capital to others.

The question that must be asked is when enough is enough, and for that matter, can there be too much investment in social capital? This possibility is raised by the fact that most adults (even in the United States, where joining is allegedly the norm and is relatively high compared to other countries) seem not to belong to very many organizations. Indeed, fewer than one man in five belongs to more than three organizations, as does fewer than one woman in seven (according to the GSS data). In addition, more organizational memberships are associated with diminishing marginal gains as far as other kinds of civic goods are concerned. For example, voting is significantly higher for both men and women among those who belong to one organization than among those who belong to no organizations. But additional memberships contribute little for women and do so for men only a small amount after two organizations.[128]

Besides the consequences of decline, we must also consider the possible effects of those kinds of social capital that have grown in recent years. Of the newer kinds, cyberinteraction (through the use of computer net-

works, e-mail, and online services) has been one of the more controversial. Proponents argue that it promotes greater interaction by reducing
the cost and inconvenience of having to meet people in person or being
available for personal telephone calls. Critics raise a number of concerns:
Community is no longer territorially based, so cyberinteraction upsets
and challenges the idea of territorial government; there is more room for
selectivity, so instead of having to listen to and confront people with different views, people can simply interact with those who think the same
way; people may be more involved in virtual reality and less involved in
actual reality in their communities; overall use remains quite small, even
if there are benefits; and as far as Internet and e-mail correspondence
between citizens and elected officials is concerned, politicians are probably too busy to respond, so citizens can receive information but not
interact as much as they would like; in addition, computer bulletin
boards may provide forums for extremists.[129] Clearly, cyberinteraction
is at a fairly early stage in its development, and so further attention will
need to be directed to these concerns in the future.

The evidence from small support groups is relatively more straightforward. Although observers have worried about the homogeneity, casu-
alness, and self-interestedness of these groups, research shows that
members of small groups participate actively and over periods of at least
several years, that they develop close affective bonds with other group
members, that they discuss a wide range of issues (including civic and
political issues), and that group members are more likely than average to
be involved in other kinds of volunteer and community service activities, even taking account differences such as church attendance, age, education, and gender.[130] It is nevertheless worth considering the possibility
that some kinds of small groups may be less conducive to this kind of
community activity than others.

Table 2-8 uses national data from the 1992 Small Groups Survey to
assess the possibility that a changing composition of such groups may
have positive or negative consequences for other kinds of civic engagement. Because groups can be described with a number of overlapping
labels, respondents in the survey were asked to indicate whether or not a
list of labels applied to their own group (if they were in more than one
group, they were asked to focus on the group that was currently most
important to them). Among these labels were "Sunday school class,"
"Bible study group," "self-help group," "anonymous group," and "special-
interest group." By comparing those who said each label did or did not
apply (see the vertical comparisons in the table), it is possible to see
whether or not different kinds of groups have different consequences for

civic engagement. Among the items included in the survey, the three that focused most directly on civic engagement had to do with volunteer work in the community, becoming more interested in social or political issues, and participating in a political rally or campaign.[131] At the bottom of the table is a typology that divides group members (mutually exclusively) into those belonging to a Sunday school class, Bible study group, self-help group, or special-interest group, based on how they answered the previous questions.[132]

The top panels of the table suggest that Sunday school classes are very slightly more likely to elevate each of the three kinds of civic engagement, compared to people in groups that do not use this label; that members of Bible study groups, in contrast, are slightly less likely than

Table 2-8: Civic Engagement by Small Group Type

	Volunteer Work (%)	Interested in Social Issues (%)	Taken Part in Politics (%)	Number
Is group a . . .				
Sunday school class				
Yes	46	45	13	(274)
No	44	42	12	(709)
Bible study group				
Yes	42	42	11	(445)
No	46	44	14	(542)
Self-help group				
Yes	49	51	12	(268)
No	42	40	12	(704)
Anonymous group				
Yes	35	44	11	(83)
No	45	43	12	(888)
Special interest				
Yes	52	48	15	(458)
No	37	38	10	(522)
Typology				
Sunday School	46	45	13	(261)
Bible study	35	37	7	(200)
Self-help	40	48	15	(152)
Special interest	50	42	14	(352)

Source: Wuthnow, Small Groups Survey, 1992; question (asked only of group members): "As a result of being in this group, have you . . . become involved in volunteer work in your community, become more interested in social or political issues, participated in a political rally or worked for a political campaign?"

members of other kinds of groups to engage in civic activities; that self-help group members are relatively more likely than other group members to do volunteer work and take an interest in social issues (but are no different on political participation); that members of anonymous groups are less likely than others to do volunteer work (but are no different on the other two measures); and that special-interest group members are comparatively more likely to be civically involved on all three measures.

In the lower panel, where group members are forced into one or the other type of group, Bible study group members are clearly less likely than Sunday school class members to be involved on each of the three civic items; self-help group members are more civically involved than Bible study group members but less likely to volunteer than Sunday school class members (though equally likely to engage in the other two activities); and special-interest group members are most likely to volunteer, but slightly below the others on having become more interested in social issues. The two methods of making comparisons among kinds of groups are thus fairly consistent with each other: Among religious groups, Sunday school classes seem to be somewhat preferable to Bible study groups in generating civic involvement; among nonreligious groups, both self-help and special-interest groups seem to increase civic involvement, with neither one being the clear preference; anonymous group members are relatively infrequent in these data but appear to be somewhat less civically inclined, at least in terms of doing volunteer work in the community.[133]

We can speculate from these data that if current trends in the composition of small groups were to continue, there would be adverse effects on civic involvement. Specifically, a shift from Sunday school classes to Bible study groups—which some observers believe is occurring—could have such effects. Of course, it should be noted that many members of Bible study groups perceive their civic involvement to be increasing, and thus participation in Bible study groups is probably a positive factor compared with no group membership at all. Nevertheless, Sunday school classes appear to be more conducive to civil engagement than Bible studies. And this conclusion is consistent with ethnographic observations in the two kinds of groups and with interviews with clergy. Bible study groups are generally smaller, more homogeneous, informal, and driven by members' personal concerns, whereas Sunday school classes are more likely to be larger, more heterogeneous, formal, and didactic or clergy-led. As far as self-help groups and special interests are concerned, however, it does not appear that their growth would significantly dampen civic engagement. Indeed, both kinds of groups include many people who believe their civic involvement has increased as a result of their groups. Anonymous groups could detract from community involvement, but their numbers are relatively small compared to the larger small-group phenomenon. Finally, the data suggest that small groups may be much more effective in generating one-on-one efforts to do volunteer work and to help the needy than in mobilizing people to participate directly in political activities. Of course, these conclusions must be considered tentative, given the sparseness of the data.

In keeping with the earlier discussion of the effects of marginalization on social capital, a more serious question to ask is whether or not newer forms of social interaction, such as support groups and electronic forms of communication, also contribute to the unequal distribution of social capital. With respect to e-mail and computer networking, it seems relatively clear that these media are highly stratified by type of occupation and by education and income, and they appear likely to remain so as long as frequent technological innovations require significant expenditures of time and money.

Support groups are a more interesting phenomenon in this regard. On one hand, virtually no monetary costs are required; their ideology is often that of helping people with special needs; and in reality, membership in support groups is spread evenly enough that no major segment of the population is currently without a significant number of members. On the other hand, people join small groups because they are already connected with networks of people who invite them and make them feel at home; these groups are oriented more toward psychological and emotional needs than toward physical and economic needs; and it requires a certain degree of cultural capital, such as knowing how to speak in a group of twenty to thirty people, for members to feel comfortable in these groups.

There is, in fact, evidence that support groups are part of the wider retreat of social capital from marginalized categories of people, rather than an antidote to this trend. This evidence comes from comparing dropout rates among people who have ever been in small groups and taking into account whether those people were from lower, middle, or higher socioeconomic strata. Specifically, among people with less than a high school degree, 50 percent of those who have been in a small group at some time in their adult life are no longer in a small group, whereas this figure drops to 46 percent among those with high school degrees, to 36 percent among those with some college education, to 28 percent among college graduates, and to 25 percent among those with graduate degrees.[134]

Nor is this pattern limited to support groups. A similar pattern appears in another national survey in which respondents were asked whether or not they "belonged to a youth group or something similar" when they were young; included in the survey was another set of questions about current membership in voluntary associations as an adult (nine broad types were listed). Among those who had been involved in a youth group, only 20 percent of those with less than a high school education were currently involved in any voluntary association, compared with 33 percent of those with a high school diploma, 48 percent of those with some college, and 73 percent among college graduates; 51 percent of all whites fit this pattern, compared with only 32 percent of blacks.[135]

One clue as to why people with lower levels of education may be more likely to drop out of voluntary organizations is evident in the small-groups survey. Although most current members of small groups express satisfaction with their groups, those with less education are more likely to feel uncomfortable than those with more education. Specifically, 21 percent of those without a high school diploma say they feel like they "don't quite fit in," compared to only 9 percent of those with college degrees. Another clue comes from a national study of participation in nonpolitical organizations, which found that low-income members were considerably less likely to learn civic skills as a result of being involved in these organizations than were upper-income members.[136]

CONCLUSIONS

To the extent that social capital has declined in the United States over the past two decades, a significant share of this decline has occurred among marginalized groups whose living situations have become more difficult during this period. Part of this decline may be attributable to the fact that people need to feel entitled in order to take part in the political process, and they need to feel that their participation will make some difference. Part of the decline is also due to the fact that people need other resources in order to create social capital, not least of which are adequate incomes, sufficient safety to venture out of their homes, and such amenities as child care and transportation.

As the United States has undergone a significant expansion in the education levels of its citizens, new forms of social capital have emerged that make it easier for people to participate who may have moved from one community to another, or who have demanding jobs. Social skills help to make people comfortable in these groups and organizations, and the networks that emerge may be helpful for exchanging professional favors or elevating one's prestige in the community. But these associations have not been fully successful in bridging socioeconomic levels or in drawing in marginalized people.[137]

How much social capital exists in a society, these considerations suggest, is only one of the important questions needing to be addressed. With association levels and volunteering at comparatively high levels by cross-cultural standards, the United States may well have enough social capital left to function as a democracy with little loss of effectiveness. What kind of social capital a society is able to create is probably the more important question. At present, significant attention in the United States needs to be devoted to creating social capital that does a better job of bridging between the privileged and the marginalized.

3

UNITED STATES: From Membership to Advocacy

THEDA SKOCPOL

Americans take great pride in their democratic accomplishments—
and also worry about them more than any other people on earth.
Changes since the 1960s preoccupy the worriers right now, and much
discussion focuses on whether Americans are dropping out of voluntary
associations or creating very different kinds of groups. This focus in
hardly surprising, because the United States has long been known as a
"nation of joiners," as Arthur Schlesinger put it in a famous 1944 article.[1] If participation in voluntary groups is no longer so prevalent, then
late-twentieth-century America could be experiencing a worrisome sea
change.

Schlesinger was writing in a well-worn vein. Visiting the fledgling
U.S. republic way back in the 1830s, the French aristocrat Alexis de
Tocqueville declared in words that have been quoted again and again
that "Americans of all ages, all stations in life, and all types of dispositions are forever forming associations. . . . [I]f they want to proclaim a
truth or propagate some feeling by the encouragement of great example, they form an association. . . . [A]t the head of any new undertak-
ing, where in France you would find the government or in England
some territorial magnate, in the United States you are sure to find an
association."[2] In effect, Tocqueville described a nation of organizers as
well as joiners. His *Democracy in America* portrayed voluntary groups

both as schools for active citizenship and as sources of leverage in relation to government.

Tocqueville put his finger on something enduringly central to America's democratic vitality. To be sure, the nineteenth-century United States was the world's first mass electoral democracy. By the 1830s, most white men, regardless of class, had gained the right to vote. And nineteenth-century American voters turned out at very high rates. Between 75 percent and 90 percent of those eligible to vote actually participated in incessant rounds of local, state, and national elections for most of the 1800s.[3] Early mass suffrage, rather than anything about voluntary associations, might therefore seem to cement America's place in the annals of democracy. During the twentieth century, however, Americans have come to vote much less than the citizens of many other nations, and U.S. political parties have done less and less to mobilize citizens into the political process.[4] Nevertheless, until recently, membership in voluntary associations continued to offer millions of Americans pathways into community and public affairs.

In *The Civic Culture,* Gabriel Almond and Sidney Verba argued that the United States around 1960 was still an unusually participatory democracy, a nation where ordinary citizens were highly engaged in public affairs at both the local and national levels.[5] Using survey data on the attitudes and self-reported behaviors of citizens of Germany, Britain, Italy, Mexico, and the United States, Almond and Verba's analysis revealed that Americans were intensely involved in voluntary groups. American men around 1960 were more likely than European men to hold multiple memberships and participate actively as group officers or committee members, and American women were far more involved as members and activists than any other set of female citizens. American participation in voluntary associations carried a special civic punch, concluded Almond and Verba.

Why was this true? Almond and Verba speculated that U.S. voluntary groups might be organized in distinctive ways.[6] But they could not pursue this line of reasoning with data from attitude surveys. Using historical, organizational, and institutional evidence, this chapter probes matters *The Civic Culture* left unresolved: What was special about U.S. voluntary associations? How could they foster a special degree and kind of popular democratic engagement? To investigate these issues is not mere antiquarianism. Recent changes in U.S. civic life come into sharp relief only in juxtaposition to prior patterns.

WHY AMERICAN ASSOCIATIONS WERE SPECIAL

The argument I will develop here is sufficiently new that it helps to state it boldly at the outset. From the era of Tocqueville's *Democracy in America* through the time of *The Civic Culture,* influential voluntary groups in America took a characteristic form. Rarely were groups strictly local; yet broader groups were not just centered in national headquarters, either. Instead, *translocal but locally rooted membership associations* were at the core of classic civic America. Moral reform movements; farmers' and workers' associations; fraternal brotherhoods devoted to ritual, mutual aid, and service; independent women's associations; veterans' groups; and many ethnic and African-American associations—all were organized in this way. Historically, what made U.S. associationalism distinctive was the linking of thousands of local, face-to-face groups into powerful, translocally organized networks—many of which closely paralleled the local-state-national constitutional structure of the U.S. federal government, including its representative aspects.

Most classic U.S. voluntary groups recruited members across class lines. Of course there have been labor unions that recruited only among wage earners, as well as professional and business groups and other sorts of elite associations. But for decade after decade in U.S. civic life until recently, major voluntary associations involved considerable popular participation and mobilized people of different occupational and class backgrounds into the same or parallel groups. Local clubs or lodges offered countless leadership opportunities to average members, and even persons of nonelite background could move up ladders of organizational leadership into state and national positions. Because of their structure and cross-class patterns of recruitment, American associations served as schools for democratic citizenship, providing an unusually large number of citizens with chances for active participation and democratic leverage.

DATA ABOUT THE BIG PICTURE

In preparing to write this chapter, my goal has been to understand and characterize empirically the changing universe of voluntary groups across epochs of U.S. history, examining group changes in relationship to large-scale transformations in the economy, culture, and government and politics. Easier said than done. Formidable research obstacles stand in the way of anyone who aims to probe the changing array of U.S. voluntary associations. There is no one place to go to look up the facts, no straightforward data set to analyze. And previous research is dismayingly disconnected. Some scholars have explored the associational life of particular communities, while others have traced individual organizations. From such partial studies it is very difficult to gain any sense of overall trends or causal processes. Consequently, this chapter draws from studies that map aggregate associational dynamics across long periods of time. Each individual study has its limitations, but the studies can be calibrated against each other and supplemented with other information.

The social historian Richard Brown tallies the spread of locally present churches and other voluntary associations in late colonial and early national America from 1760 to 1830.[7] His data are about Massachusetts (including Maine, which was part of Massachusetts until 1820). Despite this geographical restriction, Brown's work surveys many types of associations in places of all sizes. Most other scholarship on early American associations focuses primarily on the seaboard cities of Boston, New York, Philadelphia, and Charleston, biasing findings toward the most elite-dominated groups.

Moving forward in history, in their study "Association-Building in America, 1840–1940," Gerald Gamm and Robert D. Putnam count numbers of churches and voluntary groups present in twenty-six cities of different sizes.[8] The places in Gamm and Putnam's project are spread across the United States and classified by their populations in 1890 into three size categories: five big cities (St. Louis, Boston, San Francisco, Milwaukee, and Denver), ten medium-sized cities, and eleven small cities. Data comes from official city directories published yearly to help people navigate their way within and among localities. Comparing some of these directories against other sources of information convinces me that they often leave out (or delay listing) labor unions or groups restricted to women or racial or ethnic minorities. Not surprisingly, groups of most interest to employed, mainstream men are the ones that appear soonest and most consistently in the directories. Still, we can learn about urban trends from this study.[9]

This chapter also draws heavily upon the civic engagement project I am working on with a team of students. The core of this research has been an effort to discover all of the largest voluntary membership associations in U.S. history from 1790 to the present. Using a wide variety of directories, books by historians, and primary documentary sources, my associates and I found the names of many large voluntary associations apart from political parties and churches. Then we asked whether each group ever (even briefly) enrolled 1 percent or more of American adults as members, according to whatever definition of membership that group used. If groups formally restrict membership to men or women, then 1 percent of the adult male or adult female population is the benchmark. But no other relaxations of the demanding size criterion have been made. Groups restricted to particular occupational, racial, or ethnic groups are included in our master list only if they enroll 1 percent of the entire U.S. adult population.

The list we have developed so far appears in Table 3-1, with groups listed chronologically in order of their founding (*not* according to the dates at which they crossed the 1 percent membership threshold).[10] For each group on our master list, we are developing a complete quantitative and qualitative profile, gathering information on origins and development, membership, activities and resources, and relationships to government, political parties, and religious institutions. In this chapter, I present preliminary findings from this research.

How can we synthesize insights from diverse data sets? I have taken steps to calibrate the relationship between Gamm and Putnam's data set and the set of very large associations documented in my own civic research. In one sense the Gamm and Putnam study is incommensurate with mine. About a third of all the groups Gamm and Putnam found in their twenty-six cities between 1840 and 1940 are religious congregations, a type of group not directly included in my project. But roughly another third of Gamm and Putnam's groups are fraternal and veterans groups (and their female partners). Such groups also make up about two-fifths of the large membership associations included in Table 3-1. Translocal associations devoted to brotherhood rituals, mutual aid, and community influence were historically at the core of U.S. civil society. So it is not surprising that they are a large presence in both these studies.

Another way to situate the Gamm and Putnam data on locally present groups is to see *what kinds* of groups appear in the city directories they used. Elsewhere my colleagues and I report the results of an analysis of the thousands of locally present voluntary groups that appeared in directories around 1910 for the twenty-six cities examined by Gamm and Putnam.[11] That date was chosen because Gamm and Putnam report that locally present voluntary groups were most numerous in relation to city populations about that time. We found that, on average, more than three-quarters of all locally present associations were church congregations, union locals, chapters connected to very large voluntary federations, or chapters of somewhat smaller national or regional voluntary federations. Only a small proportion of voluntary groups in early-twen-

Table 3-1. Large Membership Associations in U.S. History

Common name	Founding date	Ending date	National, state, and local units?
Ancient and Accepted Free Masons	1733		
Independent Order of Odd Fellows	1819		x
American Temperance Society	1826	1865	x
General Union for Promoting Observance of the Christian Sabbath	1828	1832	
American Anti-Slavery Society	1833	1870	x
Improved Order of Red Man	1834		x
Washingtonian Temperance Societies	1840	c. 1848	
Order of the Sons of Temperance	1842	c. 1970	x
Independent Order of Good Templars	1851		x
Young Men's Christian Association (YMCA)	1851		x
Junior Order of United American Mechanics	1853		x
National Teachers Association/ National Education Association (NEA)	1857		x
Knights of Pythias	1864		x
Grand Army of the Republic	1866	1956	x
Benevolent and Protective Order of Elks	1867		
Patrons of Husbandry (National Grange)	1867		x
Ancient Order of United Workmen	1868		x
Order of the Eastern Star	1868		x
Knights of Labor	1869	1917	
National Rifle Association (NRA)	1871		x
Ancient Arabic Order of the Nobles of the Mystic Shrine	1872		
Woman's Christian Temperance Union	1874		x
Royal Arcanum	1877		x
Farmers' Alliance	1877	1900	x
Maccabees	1878		x
Christian Endeavor	1881		x
American Red Cross	1881		
Knights of Columbus	1882		x
Modern Woodmen of America	1883		x
Colored Farmers' National Alliance and Cooperative Union	1886	1892	x
American Federation of Labor/ AFL-CIO from 1955	1886		
American Protective Association	1887	c. 1911	x
Loyal Order of Moose	1888		
Woman's Missionary Union	1888		x
Woodmen of the World	1890		x
National American Woman Suffrage Association	1890	1920	x
General Federation of Women's Clubs	1890		x
American Bowling Congress	1895		x

Table 3-1 (continued)

National Congress of Mothers/			
National Congress of Parents and Teachers (PTA)	1897		x
Fraternal Order of Eagles	1898		x
German American National Alliance	1901	1918	x
Aid Association for Lutherans	1902		
American Automobile Association (AAA)	1902		x
Boy Scouts of America	1910		
Veterans of Foreign Wars of the			
United States (VFW)	1913		x
Ku Klux Klan (second) (KKK)	1915	1944	x
Women's International Bowling Congress	1916		x
American Legion	1919		x
American Farm Bureau Federation	1919		x
Old Age Revolving Pensions			
(Townsend movement)	1934	1953	
Congress of Industrial Organizations (CIO)	1938	1955	
National Foundation for Infantile			
Paralysis/March of Dimes	1938		
Woman's Division of Christian Service/			
United Methodist Women	1939		
American Association of Retired			
Persons (AARP)	1958		
Greenpeace USA	1971		
National Right to Life Committee (NRLC)	1973		x
Mothers Against Drunk Driving (MADD)	1980		x
Christian Coalition	1989		x

Source: Civic Engagement Project, Harvard University.

tieth-century U.S. cities were purely local groups, specific to a given city or county. Roughly half, in fact, were church congregations or parts of the very largest membership associations listed in Table 3-1—and such congregations and chapters of very large federations were the most stable groups, the voluntary associations most likely to persist over time.

The fact that most of the locally present groups tallied by Gamm and Putnam were parts of translocal associations makes sense in light of the central conclusion of this chapter: American civic history is a primarily story of federated association building, with local groups taking shape within broader movements and translocal organizational frameworks.

VOLUNTARY ASSOCIATIONS IN EARLY AMERICA

Much of what made the United States civically distinctive was emerging by the time Alexis de Tocqueville visited in the 1830s. The roots of American civic vitality lie at the intersection of contentious representative politics in a new republic, competitive religious evangelism in a country without any officially established religion, and the remarkable intensification of commerce and communication in an expanding nation, even as life for the vast majority still proceeded on farms or in very small towns.

The Story of Massachusetts and Maine

Richard Brown documents changing patterns of voluntary activity before and after the American Revolution—with the revolution understood as a process of political contention and institution building that stretched from the 1760s through the 1790s.[12] As the thirteen American colonies rebelled against Britain and pulled themselves together into an independent, federal republic, they fashioned propitious institutional circumstances for a flourishing civil society, at once locally rooted and translocally interconnected.

In early America (as in many other developing countries, no doubt) a minimum threshold of small-town development was necessary before groups that people could choose to join were able to coexist with families and initially monopolistic churches and town meetings. Before truly voluntary groups could proliferate, Richard Brown argues, there had to be concentrations of two hundred to four hundred families, with at least 20 percent of the men in a total population of one thousand to two thousand persons engaged in nonagricultural occupations.[13] But there was nothing automatic about this socioeconomic threshold, which was surpassed by dozens of places in Massachusetts/Maine well before the Revolution. Despite that, relatively few voluntary groups were created during colonial times. As Brown's statistics show, prior to 1760 there were only a few dozen voluntary groups apart from churches in all of Massachusetts/Maine, and more than a third of them were located in Boston, the colony's capital and its single substantial city.

The associational story changed dramatically once the American colonies aroused themselves to separate from Britain. Between "1760 and 1820 . . . over 1,900 voluntary associations were created" throughout Massachusetts/Maine, and during "the 1820s at least seventy were founded each year."[14] This increase far outstripped population growth, and mostly occurred after 1790, as a wide variety of associations spread across Massachusetts and Maine. Charitable and missionary groups were part of the waves of foundings, along with political groups, lyceums, moral reform efforts, professional and trade associations, Masonic lodges, and new kinds of churches (chiefly Methodist and Baptist).

At first only a few of these groups, such as the Masons and most churches, were formally linked in translocal organizations. But many more spread through movements in which people in one locality modeled their efforts on similar undertakings elsewhere. Although women rarely organized separate translocal associations in this early period, recognizably similar female benevolent groups appeared in many towns, and the American Female Moral Reform Society, founded in New York City, eventually encompassed 445 auxiliaries across greater New England.[15] Meanwhile, male promoters disseminated explicit models and instructions for founding and operating community associations. A prime example was Josiah Holbrook, who traveled, spoke, and published to promote lyceums, that is, voluntary community institutions intended to promote adult education, sponsor traveling lecturers, and support the emerging "common" public schools and their teachers. In 1826, Holbrook published guidelines for the establishment of lyceums, along with a detailed plan for local, county, state, and national lyceums, with all levels above the local to be based on representatives sent from below.[16]

More striking than the sheer rate of increase of voluntary groups in Massachusetts/Maine was the geographical pattern of foundings.[17] All kinds of voluntary groups in Boston increased more than 650 percent between 1760 and 1830, yet the rate of increase was 920 percent for the rest of Massachusetts/Maine. The picture is even more clear-cut when churches (as well as what Brown calls "profit-seeking" groups) are left aside. Nonchurch associational foundings in Boston went from 14 prior to 1760 to 121 between 1760 and 1830 (roughly a 760 percent increase). However, such foundings in the rest of Massachusetts/Maine went from 24 prior to 1760 to 1,281 more between 1760 and 1830—an explosive increase of more than 5,000 percent!

During and (especially) soon after the American Revolution, what Brown calls an "urban" pattern of society—involving choice of association and extralocal connections and awareness—encompassed people in and around even the tiniest places across Massachusetts and Maine. "In colonial America," Brown notes, "urban society was a highly restricted phenomenon, limited to port towns that were also administrative centers," places such as Boston, New York, Philadelphia, and (to a degree) Charleston. Urbanity penetrated parts of the hinterland only via elites "who were in touch with the [colonial] capital as an occupational necessity."[18] But by the 1830s, "urban society had developed a broad social and geographic base in the countryside," as an amazing range of communities became home to a variety of voluntary associations and public institutions.[19]

Localism and insularity were being challenged, if not actually destroyed. People remained bound to the old organizations of family, church, and town, but now they possessed additional ties. . . . Sometimes the contact was direct, if they traveled to a meeting or convention or if outsiders came to them as part of a political campaign, lyceum, temperance or missionary association. More often, the contact was psychological, coming from memberships in countywide or statewide organization and the publications such activities produced.[20]

Going National

Although this transformation may have happened soonest and most intensively in the northeastern United States, similar changes soon spread across the expanding new nation and involved people from many backgrounds.[21] By the time the Civil War broke out in 1861, the United States, despite its enormous contentiousness and regional and ethnic diversity, had developed a recognizably national civil society.

From the 1830s through the 1850s, lyceums spread from New England into the upper South and (especially) into the Midwest east of the Mississippi River.[22] Vast moral crusades and temperance movements inspired the creation of thousands of interlinked local and state societies.[23] To name only those temperance efforts that gained the most prominence prior to the Civil War, by 1834 the American Temperance Society claimed some 5,000 societies and 1 million members in the East and Midwest. The Washingtonian crusade, which reached out for working-class members and reformed "drunkards," claimed some 6,000 members and 10,000 societies in the early 1840s. The Washingtonians were soon succeeded by the more institutionalized Order of the Sons of Temperance, which by 1860 was a truly continent-spanning federation boasting some 2,398 local divisions and 94,213 members spread across more than three dozen state divisions in the North, South, and across the Mississippi River into Iowa and California.[24] By the 1850s, the Independent Order of Good Templars (IOGT) began its climb to national prominence. Open to women as well as men for both leadership and membership, by 1860 the IOGT claimed more than 50,000 members grouped into about 1,200 lodges spread across twenty states (including Alabama and Mississippi in the deep South).[25]

Fraternal orders also spanned the nation prior to the Civil War, despite the outburst of a temporary but fierce furor against Masons and other "secret societies" that peaked in the 1830s.[26] From colonial times, Masonic lodges sank roots everywhere in America; local lodges were founded immediately upon the arrival of military garrisons in each new territory, and new sovereign grand lodges were chartered just as each state joined the Union.[27] The Masons were a relatively elite fraternal association, yet they were soon followed by other fraternal organizations involving many more working-class and white-collar Americans of various ethnic and racial backgrounds—sometimes joined together in the same groups, at other times enrolled in fraternal associations with parallel structures and purposes.[28]

Destined to become the model for many subsequent brotherhood associations in the United States, the Independent Order of Odd Fellows (IOOF) was launched from Baltimore, Maryland, in 1819. Originally a British fraternal and mutual aid association, the Odd Fellows took an organizational step that the (basic) Masons never did. As American Odd Fellows broke away from the British Manchester Unity Odd Fellows, they created the U.S. IOOF as a fully three-tiered federal structure capped by a national-level sovereign grand lodge, formed from representatives sent from state-level grand lodges with jurisdiction over local lodges.[29] Perfectly suited to U.S. conditions, this federated structure encouraged rapid growth. In 1830, American Odd Fellows met in 58 lodges spread across Maryland, Massachusetts, New York, Pennsylvania, and the District of Columbia. Over the next three decades, this fraternal organization, originally limited to the eastern seaboard, spread across the continent. By 1860, there were more than 170,000 U.S. Odd Fellows meeting in more than 3,000 local lodges in thirty-five states in all regions of the nation.[30] As the author of the 1852 edition of *The Odd-Fellow Text-Book* proudly declared: "From town to town, from city to city, from state to state, has this Order spread, and thousands upon thousands of the best men of our nation have been gathered to its folds."[31] The Odd Fellows admitted only whites, yet, like the Masons, they built some bridges across religious denominations and across early Euro-American ethnic groups. Centered among native-born Protestants, the Masons accepted some Jews, and both Masons and Odd Fellows allowed German-speaking and other immigrant local lodges to organize within their predominantly English-speaking orders.[32]

If not on such a spectacular scale as the Masons and the Odd Fellows, other U.S. fraternal organizations also made rapid headway prior to the Civil War. Claiming descent from societies of patriots at the time of the American Revolution, the racially and ethnically exclusionist Improved Order of Red Men (IORM) was founded in Baltimore in 1834. Red Men were white Christians who dressed up like Indians and dated their order from 1492, when Columbus arrived in America. By 1860 almost 10,000 of them were meeting in ninety-four "tribes" spread across the "reservations" of Maryland, Pennsylvania, Virginia, Ohio, New Jersey, Missouri, Kentucky, Delaware, and the District of Columbia.[33]

Not to be outdone, in 1836 Irish-Americans founded the American branch of the Ancient Order of Hibernians, which was organized in eight states of the East, South, and Midwest by 1861.[34] During the 1840s, German-Americans in New York City launched the Order of the Sons of Hermann and the Order of Harugari, two (eventually transstate) beneficial and cultural federations dedicated to defending German culture and German-Americans from nativist attacks during widespread Know-Nothing agitations.[35] What is more, German-Americans established their own Independent Order of Red Men in 1850, a fraternal group that met in federated "stamms" rather than "tribes."[36]

In addition to Germans and Irish, African-Americans were the other large U.S. minority. With the exception of some temperance orders, white-dominated U.S. voluntary associations shunned blacks as members. But African-Americans built vast orders of their own exactly paralleling the groups from which they were excluded. Prince Hall Masonry originated in 1775, when British Masons chartered a Negro Masonic lodge in Cambridge, Massachusetts.[37] Even before the Civil War, free blacks spread this fraternal empire across eighteen states, including "most of the Atlantic coastal states as far south as Virginia, and many midwestern states . . . [and] Maryland, Virginia, and Louisiana, the centers of the free Negro population" of the South.[38] In 1843, African-Americans in New York City under the leadership of seaman Peter Ogden launched the Grand United Order of Odd Fellows (again with the aid of a lodge charter from England). By the early 1860s, about 1,500 African-American Odd Fellows were meeting in about fifty lodges scattered across more than half a dozen Eastern states.[39]

A final indication of early American associational vitality is also worth mentioning. Using a 1975 encyclopedia of national U.S. voluntary associations, sociologist Charles Green identified fourteen functional types of U.S. voluntary associations and inquired as to when each type first emerged. He found that groups representing twelve out of the fourteen types had already been created by Americans prior to 1850 (and groups of the remaining two types appeared before 1870).[40] Examining possible causes for such early associational variety, Green concluded that "the growth rate in the number of types" of national voluntary associations paralleled the growth in the total population living in places with 2,500 or more inhabitants, and also paralleled the expansion of the proportion of all Americans living in such places. Like Richard Brown, in short, but with a different kind of data, Green shows that early American associational differentiation was linked to elementary urbanization. Complex associational development preceded by many decades the emergence of huge metropolises and "large-scale commercial and industrial development."[41]

The Roots of a Dynamic Civil Society

What happened in early America? Why was civil society so sharply and precociously transformed, as communities of all sizes established voluntary groups with remarkable simultaneity—and many groups became linked in translocal organizations?

As Richard Brown argues, many aspects of the American breakaway from British imperial control fueled the growth of a democratic civil society. The Revolutionary War and subsequent struggles over a new U.S. Constitution disrupted taken-for-granted loyalties, brought geographically dispersed sets of Americans into contact with one another, and undermined prior city monopolies (during colonial times, for example, all Massachusetts print shops were based in Boston, but during the Revolution printers multiplied and dispersed to other parts of the region).[42] Once victory and nationhood came, the ongoing political routines of the representative polity pulled Americans into broader, competitive involvements. Elections were held for statewide and national offices, and fledgling political parties competed for support, linking some citizens in each place to fellow Federalists or Jeffersonians elsewhere. In the wake of the American Revolution, ideals of active citizenship spread—encouraging popular mobilization, fueling a need for information, and spurring citizens to organize within and across localities.

Early America was also swept by the religious enthusiasms of the Second Great Awakening. Religious proselytizing started during late colonial times and accelerated during the early national period. Here it is important to underline that the United States—in contrast to most other countries of that time—had no governmentally established church monopoly. Under the Constitution and the Bill of Rights, competing denominations were free to preach and proselytize. This open, competitive situation for religion encouraged evangelical movements on a regional-to-national scale.[43] Traveling evangelical organizers, especially Methodists and Baptists, spread out across the land.

Early Methodist circuit-riding clergy, above all, pioneered new methods of associational organization.[44] Moving from place to place, they inspired local leaders to found and sustain new congregations, and then tied those bodies together into federations espousing shared worldviews and moral purposes. As the Methodists spread their word and founded tens of thousands of local congregations in even the tiniest places, other religious denominations had to reach out and organize, too, lest they shrink and die.[45] Through competitive emulation, a new model of association building spread across early America—one that assorted lay associations soon adopted.

Ready social communication allowed early Americans to create sustainable, interconnected groups. Widespread literacy and newspaper reading facilitated communication, argues Richard Brown, echoing Tocqueville's observation that "[n]ewspapers make associations, and associations make newspapers. . . . [O]f all countries on earth, it is in America that one finds both the most associations and the most newspapers."[46] But Tocqueville did not appreciate all of the conditions that facilitated communication and hence association building. An active and centralized arm of the early U.S. national state—the postal service—played the key role in this development.

Prior to the American Revolution, the colonies had a rudimentary postal system comparable to that in many European countries, with larger cities loosely tied together, especially along the Atlantic coast. This changed soon after the founding of the republic, when Congress passed the Post Office Act of 1792, which "admitted newspapers into the mail on unusually favorable terms . . . prohibited public officers from using their control over the means of communication as a surveillance technique," and "established a set of procedures that facilitated the extraordinarily rapid expansion of the postal network from the Atlantic seaboard into the transappalachian West."[47] By 1828, as historian Richard John points out, "the American postal system had almost twice as many offices as the postal system in Great Britain and over five times as many offices as the postal system in France. This translated into 74 post offices for every 100,000 inhabitants in comparison with 17 for Great Britain and 4 for France."[48] In the 1830s and 1840s, the system accounted for more than three-quarters of U.S. federal employees, and most of the 8,764 postal employees in 1831 and the 14,290 in 1841 were "part-time postmasters in villages and towns scattered throughout the countryside."[49]

The postal network was shaped by U.S. government institutions. Congressional representation based in states and local districts gave members of the Senate and the House of Representatives a strong interest in subsidizing communication and transportation links into even the remotest areas of the growing nation—yet in a carefully calibrated way. Legislators wanted mail and news to be carried into even the smallest communities, and they also wanted to be able to travel to and from the national capital. Hence, they subsidized stagecoach travel and set cheap postal rates. Postal rules also allowed for the free exchange of newspapers among editors, so that small newspapers could pick up copy from bigger ones. But at the same time, rate structures were fine-tuned to prevent eastern seaboard papers from outmarketing provincial news sheets.

To take advantage of postal subsidies, voluntary groups disseminated their messages in newspaper (and later magazine) format, greatly facilitating organization. One of the first great moral reform movements in America—briefly embodied between 1828 and 1832 in the General Union for Promoting the Observance of the Christian Sabbath—was devoted to trying to stop the opening of post offices and transportation of the mails on Sundays. Ironically, this movement depended on the very federal postal system it sought to challenge. It relied on the mail to spread tens of thousands of pamphlets and petitions to its potential followers. The same was true of other great voluntary crusades in the pre–Civil War era, including the temperance movements and the popular drive against slavery that helped to spark the Civil War.[50]

The Federal State as Civil Model

There was a final, equally crucial, way in which U.S. governing institutions influenced association building. The United States was put together by the Founding Fathers as a federal state, and the country had written constitutions that explicitly parceled out nested jurisdictions to administrative, representative, and judicial bodies at three (sometimes four) levels of sovereignty: the national government, state governments, and local governments (sometimes counties, too). From early national times, American civil associations began to imitate this local-state-national structure. Table 3-1 shows that more than two-thirds of all very large U.S. membership associations developed national-state-local federated structures that paralleled U.S. governing arrangements. Large and small translocal associations also produced detailed constitutions, regularly debated and modified. American voluntary associations had printed by-laws for each local unit, formal constitutions for each state association or grand lodge, and elaborately detailed constitutions for the national or supreme level of their group. Although it is not possible to provide a detailed analysis of such constitutions in this chapter, several points are worth making based on my reading of dozens of them. Associational constitutions often boasted of imitating the U.S. government's representative features and functional divisions. Thus local associational units were empowered to elect officers and representatives to state bodies, while local and/or state units sent representatives to national bodies—just as U.S. senators were originally appointed by state governments. Associations had elaborate rules for electing leaders and adjudicating disputes.

Associational constitutions also included explicit rules about the establishment of state and local units and the flow of members into them. Unlike fraternal groups in other nations, for example, U.S. fraternal associations required a potential member to apply to the lodge nearest his residence, or have its written permission to apply elsewhere. Traveling "brothers" had to have formal documentation from their local and state units to be admitted as visitors away from home. Just as Americans had to establish their voting rights in their local communities and states, so too did they have to establish their memberships in translocal associations through their home communities. American associations may have encouraged outward ties, but they did not allow rootless cosmopolitanism.

The national and state jurisdictions of fraternal associations maintained elaborate zoning rules. New local lodges were required to have the endorsement of previously chartered units in their vicinity, as well as the approval of the relevant state jurisdiction. The point of these rules was to embed members in local groups and—perhaps even more significantly—to manage the creation of local groups so as to avoid unnecessary fragmentation or duplication. State-level authorities encouraged would-be organizers of local units to meet and work together, rather than competing. They also ruled against applications for new local lodges if they thought there was not a sufficient pool of potential members in the area to sustain additional units.

These rules meant that during the earliest stages of the development of an associational network, local units were likely to be spread out, recruiting members across town lines. To attend early group meetings, Americans traveled amazing distances under poor transportation conditions. If and when an association matured and became very popular, then local units might be able to multiply—to the point where each town or village or urban neighborhood could hold conveniently located meetings. But new units could be added only with permission from higher authorities, and only when majorities in neighbor units approved. When associations went into decline, the process of contraction was similarly managed, allowing members of clubs or lodges that closed to join groups in neighboring areas or become at-large members of state associations. Classic American associations thus tended to be relatively cross-local in membership toward the beginning and the end of their life cycle, and most locally rooted at their height.

From the start, voluntary association building in America was as much a matter of regional social movements and translocal organizing efforts as it was a series of local undertakings. Local people took heart from regionally and nationally spread exemplars, and they valued formal connections to higher-level representative governing structures. Local group founders were at times recruited and inspired by traveling "agents" sent out from state and national headquarters. Even more frequently, perhaps, they came from the ranks of in-migrants, people newly arrived in particular towns or regions who aspired to found new lodges or clubs similar to those in which they had previously participated in their communities of origin. Either way, though, local founders had to proceed within explicitly institutionalized, "constitutional" rules of the game—rules that discouraged fragmentation even as they protected state and local sovereignty within the unified whole.

CIVIC AMERICA IN THE INDUSTRIAL ERA

If substantial waves of voluntary group formation occurred before 1861, scholars agree that even greater bursts gathered force after the Civil War—expanding some older associations and creating many new groups destined to persist through much or all of the twentieth century. What kinds of associations proliferated as the United States modernized, and what actors and processes shaped group emergence and expansion? Established wisdom in the social sciences might lead us to expect fundamentally new growth processes as America made the transition from a society of farms and small towns into a metropolitan, industrialized powerhouse. But in fact associational patterns first established prior to the Civil War were renewed during the century after that conflict.

The Limited Impact of Economic Modernization

Standard explanations for associational modernization focus on emerging actors responding to new stresses and opportunities offered by corporate industrialization and the growth of big cities. Scholars of a Marxian persuasion see industrialization and large-scale urbanization as motors of class differentiation and conflict. Workers are likely to form unions; capitalists may band together in business associations. Such organizations are likely to originate in big cities and then spread outward along lines of commerce and manufacturing activity. Associational innovation and expansion should follow lines of economic growth.

Other modernization theories posit different causal mechanisms. Durkheimians see voluntary associations as mechanisms of social integration, substituting in industrial societies for ties of family and neighborliness in preindustrial villages. One version of such reasoning appears in the historian Robert Wiebe's influential synthesis, *The Search for Order, 1877–1920*.[51] The key actors in Wiebe's drama are rising "new middle class" professionals and businesspeople situated in expanding metropolitan centers. In "response" to the unsettling transformations of immigration and rapid population growth and urban concentration, these modernizing elites fashioned new professional and trade associations and social service groups. In Wiebe's portrayal, the United States around 1900 was transformed from an agrarian society of "island communities" into an industrial nation knit together by corporations, bureaucracies, and relatively centralized associations led by managers and professionals.

Some data support Marxian and/or Durkheimian expectations about U.S. associational modernization. Translocal associations were mostly launched from the more industrialized states of the Northeast and Midwest, and such groups often spread into each state via the largest city or a highly commercialized region. Professionals, businessmen, and mobile workers such as railroad men were often the carriers of new associational ideas.

Occupationally based associations proliferated as well. Figure 3-1, borrowed from Gamm and Putnam, shows trends in the incidence of various kinds of associations per thousand population across twenty-six U.S. cities from 1840 to 1940. Clearly, labor unions increased sharply after 1880, and business groups proliferated, too, though more gradually. Gamm and Putnam's counts are confirmed by listings of statewide groups in issues of the *Maine Register*.[52] These yearly directories document a sharp increase of business and professional groups across the twentieth century, and especially from 1920 on. The numbers of such associations rose very steeply as ever narrower occupational and market segments organized themselves.

Elite "service groups"—chiefly Rotary Clubs, Exchange Clubs, and Lions Clubs—also spread across cities from the early through the mid-twentieth century.[53] Such clubs accepted only a few leading people from each business or profession within the community (although "professions" could be defined very narrowly to expand membership). Some argue that elite service clubs replaced cross-class fraternal associations, because business and professional people grew tired of evening-long rituals, preferred shorter lunchtime meetings, and wanted to network

Figure 3-1 Densities of U.S. Voluntary Associations Listed in City Directories, 1840–1940

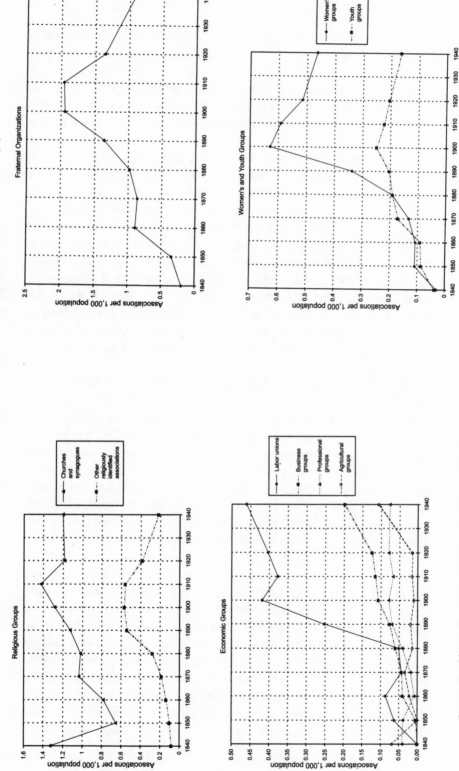

Source: Gerald Gamm and Robert D. Putnam, "The Growth of Voluntary Associations in America, 1840–1940," *Journal of Interdisciplinary History* 29 (4) (Spring 1999): 511–57.

among themselves rather than reaffirm "brotherhood" with blue-collar wage earners and white-collar employees.[54] But this cannot be the whole story, because as America industrialized, certain fraternal groups (such as the Masons) renewed themselves, while others (such as the Knights of Columbus, the Moose, the Elks, and the Eagles) grew to new prominence, with simplified rituals and new emphasis on community outreach.[55]

Occupationally linked associations and elite service clubs were not the only kinds of groups that flourished between the Civil War and the mid-twentieth century. As Figure 3-1 displays, Gamm and Putnam document sharp increases in city directory listings of religious congregations, religiously connected associations, fraternal and sororal groups, and independent women's groups from the mid-1800s until around 1900 or 1910. Extraordinarily steep increases are reported for fraternal and women's groups in the late 1800s. Although Gamm and Putnam document dropoffs in the incidence of such listings after the turn of the century, the numbers of religious and fraternal groups per thousand population remained much higher than the incidence of occupationally linked groups through the end of the Gamm and Putnam data series in 1940.

Clearly, Marxian and Durkheimian arguments do not fully account for patterns of U.S. associational growth during the industrial era. Labor unions, business and professional groups, and other associations explicitly linked to corporate-industrial growth grew but did not become hegemonic, because long-standing kinds of membership associations also survived or renewed themselves. The universe of large U.S. associations was different by the mid-twentieth century than it had been a century before, but it remained kindred to the previous universe. Economic modernization added new kinds of associations to the mix, yet the substratum of cross-class membership federations persisted.

There is a ready rejoinder to this argument: Modernizing America may have maintained a peculiar profile of associations—heavy with religious and moral associations, fraternal organizations, and veterans' groups and auxiliaries. But maybe such groups grew in response to modernizing forces. However, statistical hypothesis testing by Gerald Gamm and Robert Putnam raises doubt about this rejoinder. Making maximal use of the variation across places and decades in their data about group listings in city directories, Gamm and Putnam test the notions that foreign immigration, inflows of domestic migrants, industrialization, and/or urban expansion explain why some of their cities experienced greater increases in numbers of associations than others.

They went into their research expecting that bigger, more industrial, northeastern cities might experience sharper increases of associational incidence, and that cities experiencing rapid inflows of migrants might also show disproportionately more associational growth. But Gamm and Putnam found very much the opposite.

Through 1910, associations proliferated beyond population growth across all twenty-six U.S. cities studied by Gamm and Putnam. Yet within this overall expansionary pattern, cities in the South and West added more associations per capita than those in the East, slower-growing cities developed more associations per capita than faster-growing cities, and small cities gained more associations per capita than medium-size cities, which in turn gained more than the largest cities. "The civic core was in the periphery," Gamm and Putnam conclude, speculating that denizens of small- and medium-size cities may have created and maintained more associations because, in contrast to big-city dwellers around 1900, residents of small cities did not have access to "industrialized" modes of entertainment such as movies or amusement parks.[56]

With better data and analytical techniques, Gamm and Putnam recapitulate findings in Murray Hausknecht's 1962 book *The Joiners*. Yet Hausknecht's hypotheses about why associations were so prevalent in smaller American communities went beyond considerations of entertainment, raising the crucial issue of citizen leverage in democracy. "[V]oluntary associations may induce in the individual living in a small town a greater sense of 'potency,'" reasoned Hausknecht, "a sense that . . . 'his vote counts.' Some associations may be important for the community as a whole, and in a small town it is easier to get a feeling that this is so."[57] Hausknecht's point takes on added significance when we recall that the vast majority of U.S. voluntary groups around 1900 were not merely local. They linked local people into state, regional, and national activities, as well as allowing them to meet close to home. Members of translocal associations could learn about and contribute to civic undertakings on a much broader scale than local units alone could have managed.

The entertainment value of groups in towns and small cities was more than local, too. Officers and members prized opportunities to travel to district, state, or national conventions. Important social and economic advantages likewise accrued to associations that managed to spread across many places. Insurance societies could spread economic risk by including people from various places. Perhaps most important, Americans, especially young men, changed residences frequently and

Figure 3-2: Foundings and Cumulative Incidence of U.S. Membership Associations

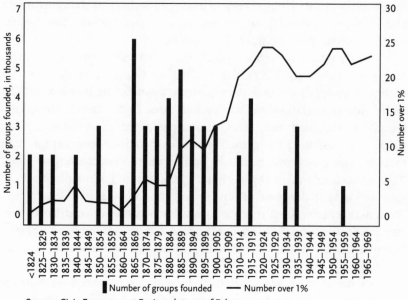

Number of groups founded   —— Number over 1%

Source: Civic Engagement Project data as of February 11, 2000.

traveled constantly, so they were glad to find familiar groups in new places. People transferred memberships from place to place, founded new units if none already existed, and visited clubs or lodges when they arrived for business or pleasure. City and associational directories recorded the day(s) of the week or month when groups met, precisely so that visitors from out of town could make their way to meetings.

Bearing in mind that locally present associations were typically parts of translocal networks, we can better pinpoint the timing and causes of associational change. The Skocpol group data arrayed in Figure 3-2 highlight the periods when the (eventually) largest translocal membership associations were launched in unusual numbers. This figure also graphs the cumulation of large U.S. associations whose memberships had surpassed 1 percent of the adult population by the given date. As Figure 3-2 shows, disproportionate numbers of associations that would eventually have very large memberships were founded in the decades right after the Civil War. Gamm and Putnam' study registers, in large part, the local proliferation of units connected to the new nation-spanning associations that came into being between 1860 and 1890. By the second decade of the twentieth century, more than twenty large membership associations coexisted, and the vast majority were rooted in thousands of local groups spread across villages, towns, and cities of all sizes.

War and Political Contention as Motors

Social scientists typically presume that the "real" or "basic" causes of long-term social change are economic. But wars and political contention also shape societies and cultures. For modern American civil society, wars and periods of intense group contention brought more group foundings, growing memberships, and vital new undertakings.

America's most ambitious and ultimately most successful associational launchings came at the end of the Civil War and during the next quarter century, and this same period brought amazing growth to membership federations already in place before 1861. This seems counterintuitive. By far the largest and most destructive U.S. war, the Civil War tore apart preexisting federations such as the Odd Fellows, the Sons of Temperance, and the Independent Order of Good Templars. It diverted adult energies and took millions of lives, leaving much of the South economically prostrate.

But the Civil War also spurred translocal associationalism. During the conflict, fraternal organizations such as the Masons and Odd Fellows attracted many new members among young men headed into or already in military service—perhaps because these brotherhoods had well-established methods for aiding members away from home.[58] Immediately after the war's end, moreover, divided U.S. membership federations quickly reunited. Voluntary federations were, after all, better positioned to reknit North-South ties than the regionally polarized political parties. During the war, the Odd Fellows left chairs for southern grand lodge representatives sitting symbolically empty at each of their national conventions, called the names of the absent state delegations, and mailed reports to those delegations. The southern grand lodge representatives returned to their waiting seats within months of the war's end.[59] It would take years longer to put the U.S. national government and political party system back together.

Throughout the later nineteenth century, most new American voluntary associations were launched from the Northeast and Midwest (and late in the century, some spread from the West).[60] The defeated and economically distressed South was not a leader in postwar association launching, and memberships and numbers of local units lagged there as well. But the fact remains that, in the wake of the Civil War, American association builders were determined to link North and South just as much as East and West. They thought in terms of national unity and regeneration, and worked hard to make this vision real. Most large-membership voluntary associations launched in the post–Civil War era took the form of local-state-national federations, and most spread their institutional networks across virtually all of the U.S. states within two to three decades after their founding.

For many association builders, the Civil War had an energizing and visionary effect, connecting them to one another and to a larger sense of purpose and possibility. During the conflict, men came together in great armies and women volunteered for war support or relief work. Connections were forged within states and across states, reinforcing the model of nested federalism as the best organizational way to get things done. As the war ended, the strengthened sense of national purpose and connections could be shifted, especially by the victorious northerners, toward bold efforts at nation building and sectional reconnection.

Destined to burgeon quickly into America's third largest fraternal group, the Knights of Pythias was launched in 1864, during the war, by a federal clerk who devised a ritual about mutually sacrificial brotherhood inspired by the classical tale of the friendship of Damon and Pythias.[61] Similarly, the Patrons of Husbandry (or Grange) was the inspiration of a U.S. Department of Agriculture official who, on a postwar inspection tour of the ravaged South, imagined the benefits of a nationwide fraternity for farm families. (Interestingly, Grange founder Oliver Kelley was able to open doors in the South by using his ties to fellow Masons.)[62] The creators of the American Red Cross were women and men who had run the Union war relief efforts of the U.S. Sanitary Commission and wanted to continue their efforts in new ways after the war.[63] Former participants in the Sanitary Commission also helped to launch the leading national women's association of the post–Civil War period, the Woman's Christian Temperance Union (WCTU).

WCTU organizers were determined to create a nationwide association powerful enough to influence public opinion and government actions at all levels.[64] Like other temperance groups right after the Civil War, the WCTU organizers were appalled by the drinking habits of ex-soldiers returning home and worried that federal taxes on liquor, which helped finance the war, had become entrenched. The only way to develop sufficient power to fight these evils, temperance people thought, was to create (or strengthen) federated voluntary organizations that paralleled the government itself and reached into every congressional district.[65] During the 1880s, therefore, chief WCTU organizer

Frances Willard traveled through every U.S. state and visited hundreds of cities and towns. She visited the Far West and repeatedly toured the South, leaving in her wake new local and state unions throughout the nation.[66]

Further waves of association launching came in the later 1880s and 1890s. One late-century dynamic was the proliferation of fraternal groups aiming to provide insurance to members. Many never grew very large. Some were deliberately limited to potential memberships thought to be relatively healthy; others represented breakaways from previously established insurance orders (westerners frequently broke away from aging eastern orders); still others (such as the Order of the Iron Hall, 1881–91) represented little more than thinly disguised Ponzi schemes. Such "insurance fraternals" sometimes proved actuarially unsound and hence short-lived.[67]

Another, more civically relevant dynamic grew out of fierce ethnic contention. The late 1880s and 1890s were a time of nativist agitation, as native-born American whites organized against recent immigrants and Catholics.[68] In response, many ethnic-American federations were established. They served to unite local groups for self-defense and assertion of American credentials, and stimulated the further spread of local and state ethnic associations. In general, trends of associational creation reveal that periods of nativist agitation in U.S. history—the 1840s and 1850s, the 1890s, and the 1920s—were also periods when large numbers of ethnic-American groups were launched or expanded.[69]

Tellingly, however, ethnic-American groups tended to structure themselves and operate very much like the Protestant- and native-born-dominated associations with which they were contending. Every group claimed to represent good Americans and godly people. Group badges and banners almost invariably featured U.S. flags (sometimes one U.S. flag crossed with the flag of the nation from which immigrants hailed), and group mottos championed similar patriotic and ethical values. Almost every association sought to spread local and state units within regional or national federations. U.S. membership associations, in short, may have championed diverse racial, ethnic, and religious group identities. But they did so in ways that fostered similar experiences and expressed shared American citizenship.

World War I was yet another period of concentrated associational launchings; twentieth-century giants such as the American Legion and the American Farm Bureau Federation emerged right at the end of that conflict, and so did many smaller associations. Perhaps more important, the First World War also proved an auspicious watershed for many previously established groups. But this was not true for all such organizations; identified with the foreign enemy, once vibrant and growing German-American associations largely collapsed during World War I.[70] After America entered the war in 1917, the approximately one-tenth of the U.S. population who was of German descent switched to non-ethnic-identified groups or relabeled existing groups in ostentatiously "American" ways.

As some groups suffered, many other voluntary associations burgeoned through close partnership with federal wartime mobilizations. In this way, the Red Cross and the Young Men's Christian Association experienced explosions of membership, volunteering, and local chapter building. The Knights of Columbus cemented its Americanist credentials by providing social services for military personnel.[71] During and soon after World War I, this Catholic fraternal federation used its new government partnership and legitimacy with the public to attract millions of members, gaining ground on Protestant rivals. Ever since, the Knights of Columbus has remained a leading American association.

The Twentieth Century

By the 1920s, the United States had become an industrial nation, and the data in Figure 3-2 document that about two dozen large-scale membership associations coexisted from then on. Of course, the mix of large associations changed over the decades. Some older groups (such as the Sons of Temperance, the IOGT, and the Grand Army of the Republic) declined or went out of existence. Others were never more than temporary blips on the radar screen, perhaps because they died after reform crusades (abortive, as in the case of the Knights of Labor, or successful, as in the case of the National American Woman Suffrage Association). Still other groups became briefly huge during periods of heightened ethnic or racial tension.[72] Meanwhile, though, other groups emerged or flourished, often benefiting from junctures of welfare-state building as well as wartime mobilization.

Today's conservatives claim that the growth of modern social provision has crowded out voluntary efforts.[73] But many of America's membership associations pressed for public social programs in the first place, and then prospered by helping government deliver benefits or services to millions of people. The Grand Army of the Republic grew along with generous state and national provision for Union military veterans and survivors.[74] The Grange and American Farm Bureau Federation were just as closely involved with public programs to aid farmers.[75] Independent women's associations—including the WCTU, the General Federation of Women's Clubs, and the National Congress of Mothers (later the PTA)—were closely involved with local, state, and national efforts to help mothers, children, and families.[76] The Fraternal Order of Eagles and the Townsend movement pressed for federal benefits for the elderly, and more recent associations of retirees have grown along with the resulting public programs.[77] Labor unions needed the U.S. government's help to establish themselves fully, and in turn became supporters of New Deal economic and social programs. And the American Legion championed the nation's most generous social program for young families, the G.I. Bill of 1944.[78] From the Civil War through the post–World War II era, voluntary membership associations have complemented the U.S. version of the modern welfare state.

Labor unions (including industrial as well as craft workers) finally gained a substantial foothold in U.S. civil society during the 1930s and 1940s. Yet this same period was stressful for other large groups. To cope with fiscal shortfalls as memberships aged, fraternal associations that had narrowly specialized in insurance frequently merged, died, or were absorbed by profit-making companies. Socially oriented fraternal organizations also declined. Americans could not afford dues during the Great Depression, and then they concentrated on mobilizing for a war abroad. Some associations experienced an irrevocable decline in this era. The Odd Fellows, for example, one of the nation's oldest fraternal groups, revived only slightly after 1945, and then continued to fade.

Yet a number of preexisting membership groups, including fraternal organizations, revived after World War II. Despite shrinkage since the 1960s, the Masons remain, to this day, on the list of groups enrolling more than 1 percent of American adults, and the Eastern Star remains a very large group predominantly enrolling women. More telling, when data are examined beyond the end of Gamm and Putnam's series in 1940, many U.S. associations launched from the 1850s through 1920 turn out to have prospered across much of the first two-thirds of the twentieth century. These include fraternal groups such as the Elks, the Moose, the Eagles, and the Knights of Columbus (as well as the Masons and the Eastern Star); veterans' associations such as the Veterans of Foreign Wars and the American Legion; a variety of church-connected associations; male and female bowling federations; the American Federation of Labor (which united with the Congress of Industrial Organizations in 1955 to become the AFL-CIO); and community-oriented groups such as the Red Cross, the Boy Scouts, the YMCA, and the National Congress of Parents and Teachers (PTA). As late as the 1960s and 1970s, many of these associations were still growing, as were hundreds of smaller federated membership groups with the same ways of doing things. World War II, like previous major wars, reenergized many American membership groups.

Taken together, a modernized set of federated membership associations formed the integument of post–World War II civil society for ordinary Americans. Most membership federations had local groups that met weekly, biweekly, or monthly, and new officers were periodically elected at every level of group governance. Except for the unions and farm groups, membership associations included men or women from a considerable range of occupational and social backgrounds. All popularly rooted groups structured two-way interactions between leaders and led, and between local and supralocal activists. The continuing vital involvement of millions of men and women with a remarkable range of membership associations surely influenced the answers U.S. citizens gave to Almond and Verba's survey, allowing Americans to emerge as the most participatory group of citizens discussed in *The Civic Culture*.

CIVIC AMERICA TRANSFORMED

History may explain why Almond and Verba found Americans to be strong civic participants around 1960, but in another sense the civic world these authors celebrated may now be "history." The American associational universe that so entranced observers from Tocqueville to Almond and Verba has been revolutionized during the last third of the twentieth century. A version of the professionally focused "modernization" that Robert Wiebe mistakenly argued triumphed early in this century has finally taken hold at the end.

About three-quarters of the large membership voluntary federations listed in Table 3-1 still exist, yet most of the surviving older associations soldier on with shrunken networks and dwindling, aging memberships. The PTA and the General Federation of Women's Clubs, the Masons and the Elks, and the great veterans' federations and their women's auxiliaries are no longer "where the action is" in U.S. society or politics. The once-hefty labor unions have declined, from enrolling more than a third of the labor force in the 1950s to less than a sixth now.[79] Meanwhile, new waves of national associational launchings have dwarfed in sheer volume even the waves that occurred after the Civil War. In 1959, *The Encyclopedia of Associations* listed almost 6,000 national associations in the United States; the number grew to more than 10,000 by 1970, to nearly 15,000 by 1980, and to almost 23,000 in 1990 before stabilizing at about that level thereafter.[80] In these recent launchings, a different type of group predominates: the professionally led advocacy group.

True, a few new membership federations rooted in local- and state-level face-to-face meetings have been created in recent times, particularly right-wing associations such as the National Right to Life Committee and the Christian Coalition. Also, some very old membership federations have recently grown enormously, notably the National Rifle Association, on the conservative side of the partisan spectrum, and the National Education Association, on the liberal end of the spectrum. But very few large-membership groups have been launched or revivified since the 1950s—especially *not* multipurpose groups that span class and partisan divides and combine local and translocal activities. Recently growing groups have narrower missions, and either no members at all or else thin memberships based on computer-directed mailings to individual constituents who send checks in the mail. The biggest of all is the American Association of Retired Persons, which was founded in 1958 and grew rapidly in the 1970s and 1980s.[81] Most new professionally led advocacy groups are much smaller—often amounting to little more than headquarters operations in Washington, D.C., or New York City.

The recent American "advocacy explosion," as political scientist Jeffrey Berry aptly calls it, includes several components.[82] The civil rights struggles of the mid-1950s and 1960s enfranchised southern blacks and spawned new organizations devoting to advancing opportunities for African-Americans. In the aftermath of this democratic watershed, additional "rights revolutions" gave new, organized voice to feminists, homosexuals, and a plethora of racial and ethnic minorities. Rights movements started as grassroots efforts from below, but many subsequently evolved into professionally led advocacy or social service organizations. Sociologist Debra Minkoff documents that groups acting on behalf of women and racial or ethnic minorities burgeoned sixfold between 1955 and 1985, from less than 100 to nearly 700. During the 1970s and 1980s, moreover, the mix of groups shifted sharply from cultural, protest, and service associations toward policy advocacy groups and service providers also engaged in advocacy.[83] In contrast to earlier ethnic associations and female partner groups, contemporary rights-advocacy groups aim to highlight what makes their constituencies special and different from other Americans.

Another watershed has been the proliferation of public interest advocacy groups, which seek to shape public opinion and influence legislation on behalf of causes ranging from environmental protection (for example, the Sierra Club and the Environmental Defense Fund) to the well-being of poor children (the Children's Defense Fund), getting big money out of politics (Common Cause), and cutting public entitlements (the Concord Coalition). Public interest groups markedly proliferated in the 1970s, and at first the expansion was decidedly liberal.[84] But more recently conservative advocacy groups have gained ground.[85] Some public interest causes, such as the environmental movement taken as a whole, include local activities and face-to-face membership groups as well as lobbying arms in Washington, D.C. But most do not (and even the environmental movement has become more professionally directed over time).[86] Equally important, cause groups usually rely on check writers skewed toward the upper end of the U.S. income distribution.[87]

The final wave of the recent U.S. associational explosion was, in a sense, a response to the previous two. Trade and professional interests could not sit idly by while supporters of various rights movements and public interest efforts were organized. During the 1970s and 1980s, thousands of business and professional advocacy groups organized anew, or opened offices in Washington. The members of these associations are often other organizations, not individual citizens. Following legal changes in the mid-1970s, business and professional advocates reinforced their lobbying efforts by forming political action committees to channel contributions to electoral candidates.[88]

Why Has It Happened?

Why are so many staff-led associations flourishing in late-twentieth-century U.S. civic life? A few hypotheses can be suggested. Some scholars point to changes in communications media, arguing that the rise of television and computer-directed mailings makes it possible for professionals in centralized offices to recruit mailing-list members, or conduct associational affairs without members or elected leaders. Certainly such changes—which have swept through both electoral politics and associational life—have made it possible for professionally run, thin-membership advocacy groups to operate. But the development of new federated membership groups such as the Christian Coalition and the recent resurgence of the AFL-CIO union movement show that new technologies do not rigidly determine group operations. If the leadership will is there, new technologies can energize multiply tiered membership groups.

Another factor, surely, has been the willingness of wealthy patrons and tax-exempt U.S. foundations to channel grants to advocacy groups, freeing them from the dependence on membership dues as a principal funding source that characterized many influential U.S. voluntary associations prior to the 1960s.[89] When association builders could not be leaders without recruiting self-renewing mass memberships, they had incentives to travel around the country, hold face-to-face meetings, and recruit and encourage intermediate leaders who could carry on the work of member recruitment and retention. Nowadays, it makes more sense for leaders in New York City or Washington, D.C., to prepare mass mailings or write grant applications to foundations.

Transformations in gender identities and class relationships surely matter as well. Most large U.S. voluntary associations (founded or growing) from the 1800s through the 1950s were cross-class, single-gender affairs. In most of these associations, business and professional people joined together with white-collar folks and perhaps with more privileged farmers and craft or industrial workers. Yet it was usually men *or* women, not both together, who formed and led these cross-class and transregional associations, especially in the eras between the Civil War and the 1950s. Segregated male and female roles offered broad, encompassing identities through which hundreds of thousands or millions of Americans could band together across regional and class lines. Male military veterans and better-educated women outside the paid labor force were key leaders of voluntary federations. Both kinds of people were resourceful, socially respected, and spread out geographically.

But these conditions have disappeared during the last third of the twentieth century. Cohorts of males coming of age in the last third of the century are much less likely to have served in the military.[90] What is more, America's bitter experiences during the war in Vietnam broke the continuity of young male identification with martial brotherliness. A sharp divide was created between World War II veterans and their sons, whereas previous generations of American sons seem to have idealized their fathers' experiences from the Civil War through World War I. This break in "manly traditions" occurred just as the feminist revolution and the accelerating entry of wives and mothers into the paid labor force forced the renegotiation of gender identities and the redivision of labor between husbands and wives.

Meanwhile, things have changed for educated American women. College-educated U.S. men have always tended to crowd into metropolitan centers, but in past eras better-educated women went everywhere to teach school, then got married and had to stop teaching. Thus well-educated married homemakers were to be found in every community across all states, and they became mainstays of voluntary life everywhere. But now better-educated women pursue nationally oriented careers, have less time for associations without occupational links, and crowd into the same cosmopolitan centers as do educated career men.

By the 1970s the United States had developed a very large professional-managerial upper middle class, full of men and women who see themselves as specialized experts rather than as "trustees of community."[91] Elites like this are more oriented to giving money to staff-led national advocacy organizations than they are to climbing the local-state-national leadership ladders of traditional membership voluntary associations. Metropolis-centered "modernization" has finally arrived, and the new civic world is dominated by professionals and managers as well as business elites.

American government and politics have changed, too. The U.S. federal government has *not* become steadily bigger as a taxer and social spender. But federal regulatory activity has vastly expanded since the 1960s, and activities in Washington have become much more professionalized. Congressional staffs grew and committees became more numerous and decentralized, offering many more sites of possible influence over legislation or administrative implementation. Seizing such opportunities, staff-level advocacy and lobbying groups took much of the action away from more cumbersome popularly based voluntary federations. All the more so, given that congressional representatives were increasingly seeking reelection with the aid of pollsters and media consultants and advertisements on television, eschewing the reliance they had formerly placed on voluntary federations as lifelines to voters in their districts. Ordinary citizens are less and less likely to be mobilized into parties or civic groups; instead, the wealthier among them are repeatedly asked to write checks.[92]

All in all, the very model of what counts as effective organization in U.S. politics and civic life has changed very sharply. No longer do most leaders and citizens think of building, or working through, nationwide federations that link face-to-face groups into state and national networks. If a new cause arises, entrepreneurs think of opening a national office, raising funds through direct mail, and hiring pollsters and media consultants. Polls are used to measure disaggregated public opinion, even as advocacy groups emit press releases about hot-button issues, hire lobbyists to deal with government—and engage in incessant fundraising to pay for all of the above. Organizational leaders have little time to discuss things with groups of members. Members are a nonlucrative distraction.

So What?

Some would argue that the transformations I have just described are for the best. Why mourn the decline of huge membership federations that were often racially exclusive or gender-segregated? Broad-gauged membership groups tried to do so many different kinds of things at once—from community service to recreation and national policy advocacy—that they may not have done any one thing optimally. Arguably, too, their policy efforts did not add up to "the public interest." As time went on, groups such as the American Legion, the unions, and the American Farm Bureau Federation seemed to become aligned with partial and self-interested causes.

New forms of group activity have their advantages, the argument continues. Americans today, especially young people, have little time to attend ritualistic meetings. They are better-educated and want flexible individual options. Maybe an associational world of small, intimate support groups, combined with lots of national offices to which checks can be sent in support of selected causes, is preferable for Americans today.

Valid as some of these points may be, they overlook valuable aspects of the old civic America that are not being reproduced or reinvented. America's new civic world of professionally led advocacy groups is very oligarchical. Arguably, the wealthiest and best-educated Americans are much more privileged in this new civic world than their (less numerous) counterparts were in the traditional world of cross-class membership federations. Of course, better-educated and wealthier men, and women married to them, have always been on top. But in the past they had to interact with citizens of middling means and prospects. Average Americans also had chances to participate and work their way up in associations that built bridges across classes and places, between local and translocal affairs. Now the bridges are eroding. Ordinary citizens have fewer venues for membership in associations with real clout. Meanwhile, the most powerful Americans are interacting—and arguing—almost exclusively with one another.

Perhaps the United States had a unique pattern of state and society from the nineteenth through the mid-twentieth century. Not only was America the world's first manhood democracy and the first nation in the world to establish mass public education, but it also had a uniquely balanced civic life, in which markets expanded but could not subsume civil society, and governments at multiple levels deliberately and indirectly encouraged federated voluntary associations. In classic civic America, millions of ordinary men and women could interact with one another, participate in groups side by side with the more privileged, and exercise influence in both community and national affairs. The poorest were left out, but many others were included. National elites had to pay attention to the values and interests of millions of ordinary Americans.

Now that old civic America is coming to an end. And for all that the post-1960s United States is more racially inclusive and gender-integrated, it remains to be seen whether the emerging civic world of professionally dominated associations without members can sustain or renew the vitality of American democracy.

4

FRANCE: Old and New Civic and Social Ties in France

JEAN-PIERRE WORMS

As in most other developed countries, questions are repeatedly being asked in France about threats to its social cohesion and challenges to its democratic ideals. French people commonly denounce the pressures of globalization and individualism for eroding civic and social ties. Many within France feel that the country is particularly vulnerable because such erosion primarily attacks the two structural elements pivotal for its republican model and for its internal and external security: the state and salaried employment.

The French nation-state is more than a thousand years old, the oldest in Europe. For ten centuries, in every circumstance of a turbulent history, subjection of all citizens to identical administrative constraints of the state machinery was relied upon to unify the nation: same taxation, same judiciary, same public services and utilities, same rights and duties for every citizen everywhere. The degree to which centralized political power and homogeneous administrative rules served as instruments of national unity has not been equaled anywhere, and Tocqueville aptly noted that replacing a monarchy by a republic only accentuated this distinctive feature of France. Thus today, the fact that France has based the foundations of its national identity, the structure of its civil society and the conditions of its sovereignty on the dignity and power of the state is undisputed by critics and supporters of the French republican model alike.

Less often mentioned is the specific manner in which the French built their highly developed welfare state and its systems of solidarity. There are two ways in which money can be collected for public social security (health insurance, unemployment benefits, family allowances, retirement pensions, and other types of protection against social risks): through taxation, that is, participation of the national budget, or through compulsory standardized subscriptions of interested parties to ad hoc mutual funds. Paradoxically, considering the traditional preeminence of the state regarding public responsibilities, France relied not on financing through the national budget and management by the public service but almost exclusively on standardized compulsory contributions to specialized funds by different sectors of employment, and on management by representatives of the interested parties. In the case of salaried employment the funds are cofinanced by employers and employees and comanaged by their elected representatives. Such heavy reliance on employment alone for financing the French welfare state probably explains why the rise of unemployment is felt to be particularly threatening to French social cohesion, all the more so considering the size of the French social budget: France's public social expenditure represents 29 percent of GDP compared with 23 percent in Germany and Italy, 20 percent in England, and 12 percent in the United States and Japan.[1]

The form of the debate is also typically French, involving a heated intellectual confrontation of radical theoretical conceptualizations. A social capital approach might help bring less ideological considerations to the debate.

SOCIAL CAPITAL IN FRANCE

The Scope of the Conceptual Framework

In general terms, social capital refers to the networks, norms, and values that individuals or groups mobilize in formal or informal relationships in order to cooperate to achieve a common purpose.

In a narrow sense, social capital refers only to social resources created and embodied in groups joined voluntarily by individuals and involving regular face-to-face meetings—for example, a formal, voluntary, nonprofit association, or an informal group of friends, neighbors, or churchgoers. In a wider sense, however, such social resources can also be created and embodied through relationships occurring within groups to which one belongs not only or mainly of one's own free will but through chance, constraint, or process of social ascription, for instance, a family, a company, an ethnic community, a neighborhood, a city, or a nation. Opening still wider the scope of the conceptual framework, social capital can be seen to be created in completely different types of groups where face-to-face relationships are rare, irregular, or even accidental and where they can vary greatly in intensity: subscribers to a charity, commuters on public transport, participants in public demonstrations.

I shall deliberately adopt the wider, more inclusive definition while being extremely careful not to blur specific characteristics of each set of relationships, as all these groups have extremely porous frontiers and numerous overlapping areas. Disentangling networks of relationships is obviously necessary, however practically difficult and theoretically risky it may be; but analyzing their interrelations is no less essential. An even more important reason why I chose the inclusive conceptual framework is that norms and values elaborated in one area are often put to use in another. Thus, for example, the French demographer Emmanuel Todd convincingly connected long-term regional differences in political orientations to historically rooted differences in family structures and norms, and the sociologist Renaud Sainsaulieu ascribed differences among socioprofessional categories regarding norms of authority and cooperation in general to the different working conditions in which each group learned, through repeated personal experience, the relative relevance of these norms for guiding daily behavior at work. I do realize, however, that what is gained in extending the scope of analysis will be lost in precision of focus and security of demonstration, a classic but inescapable social science dilemma.

Group and Societal Cohesiveness
The social cohesion of a society can be measured at various levels: within each of its groups and communities, on the one hand, and between these different groups and communities, on the other. The internal cohesion of each particular group does not automatically induce strong cohesion in the global society. In each case, therefore, it is important to identify precisely the community where social capital is formed and used; to consider whether it is employed primarily in internal relations, external relations, or both; and to determine whether it is self-centered or other-oriented social capital. Indeed, one of the main questions I shall try to answer is whether the general assumption that French social capital is on the wane refers to diminishing social capital within the primary groups of French society or to the groups' lack of connection with each other and with public institutions.

Received and Created Social Capital

The social capital of any group is always a two-sided affair: social capital offered to individuals by the group (preexisting communication networks, well-established cooperative norms and values) and social capital created by individuals and beneficial to the group (networks they create or activate through participation, norms, and values they perpetuate and change by joining them, referring to them, and utilizing them). Social capital is a volatile product of social exchange in a dynamic supply-and-demand relationship. If preexisting social capital offered to individuals is perceived by them to be irrelevant for the ends they are pursuing, if the advantages it may procure are not the ones they are looking for, such social capital may wane for lack of use. When analyzing diminishing social capital in different areas of French society, I shall be careful to question the relevance of preexisting sites of social capital for the intended beneficiaries and pay particular attention to new forms of social capital they may be creating to replace those abandoned. It may be that the decline in civil society so often lamented is in fact balanced by new forms of social capital.

Social Capital and the Political System

It has often been convincingly argued, notably by Robert Putnam, that a great deal of social capital in a society will enhance political democracy and economic performance by increasing the capacity of individuals to cooperate in a common endeavor, diminishing the costs of transactions between them (in terms of time, effort, rigidity of procedures, and money), and encouraging them to work together for the commonweal.

The relationship between social capital, the political system, and general institutional performance is indeed crucial, but it is a complex one. Just as the state is the product of society, the reverse is also true. On the one hand, a society progressively creates its state, that is, the institutions and rules required for peaceful cohabitation of its groups and for the production, defense, and distribution of common assets. Yet, on the other hand, public rules and institutions of the state enunciate common norms that "glue" the components of society together and create a feeling of belonging and a desire to participate in a common citizenry. At the same time, however, the state divides citizens into categories with specific rights and duties, specific group interests to defend and promote, and specific social identities. These groups will act together, form networks of cooperation, and create norms and values best suited to deal with the manner in which their problems are handled by the state. In this sense, social group dynamics are the product of the state, just as much as the nation as a whole is. The workings of a political system in a society will influence the nature of its social capital as much as the nature of its social capital will influence the performance of its political system.

Analyzing this dialectical relationship is particularly relevant in France, where the state has played a crucial role in shaping civil society. I shall specifically explore the following question: Is the apparent waning of French social capital a sign of the actual erosion of civic and social ties, or is it a sign of slackening links between state and society and, consequently, a more autonomous (or perhaps more mature) civil society and citizenry?

These are only some of the numerous issues suggested by a social capital approach to analyzing the past and present state of French civic and social ties. For clarity of presentation, I shall move from the narrower sense of the concept to the wider one. I shall start with associations and proceed to more informal ties associated with proximity; I shall then deal with the two fundamental institutions where social ties and social norms are formed and developed, the family and work; and I shall conclude with social and civic ties in the public arena, namely, moral and civic values, public institutions, and political participation.

ASSOCIATIVE SOCIAL CAPITAL

A Growing Associative Sector

The relative weakness of France's network of associations, compared to other European countries and the United States, is often noted and attributed to the dual influence of Catholic culture and a centralized state. Figures confirm that France lags behind the United States and Scandinavian countries considerably, but also behind Germany, Belgium, the United Kingdom, and Ireland in membership, number of volunteers, and donors (with fewer donors giving smaller amounts). The average contribution of a Frenchman is nine times less than that of an American.

The influence of church and state cannot be denied; they have competed for control of civil society for centuries, leaving little room for citizen initiative. Throughout the nation's history the state has staged a constant battle against any form of intermediary structure likely to fragment society and stand between central authority and private citizens. Independent voluntary associations have always been prime targets, but each period has added new ones. In the Middle Ages, feudal lords and free cities were targeted; during the monarchy (the ancien régime) it was regional parliaments and Protestant and Jewish minorities; during the revolution it was the church, Catholic congregations, and trade corporations; during the nineteenth century, it was political clubs, learned societies, Masonic lodges, and workers' mutual aid associations. The 1901 Law on Associations repealed a law that had required people to obtain dispensation from the Ministry of the Interior before creating an association, but at the same time it obliged associations to register at a prefecture to acquire legal status and capacity, such as the ability to rent premises, employ staff, sign commercial contracts, and so forth.

In spite of these impediments, and contrary to what most people believe, a dynamic but limited associative sector always existed in France, simultaneously countervailing and extending the power of the state and the church for charitable, health, or educational purposes. Learned societies and benevolent and leisure associations were created by the provincial urban bourgeoisie throughout the nineteenth century. Their main function was to structure the bourgeois elite in the provinces and accord it visibility and civic legitimacy. At the same time, many cooperative and mutual aid societies were created by the working class, influenced by the ideas of French utopian socialists. These constitute two important historical sources of the contemporary French associative movement.

Since the freedom of association was legally recognized in 1901, the associative sector has grown considerably. From 1901 to 1960 the growth was relatively moderate; 12,633 new associations were registered in 1960, the first year national statistics were gathered. It is estimated that during this first period, annual registration of new associations in prefectures rose at an average rate of 1.8 percent per year. This growth stemmed largely from two sources.

The first source was "social christianism," which particularly affected health and social charities and services. For centuries the Catholic Church had a quasi monopoly over institutions caring for the poor and those suffering from all types of social, physical, or mental handicap. As these functions of solidarity became recognized as part of the public responsibility of a welfare state, new social rights, public benefits, and services were created, and associations were entrusted with their management. Many of them inherited the professional know-how of previous Catholic institutions. The second source was the secular left, which influenced the creation of many new associations under the auspices of the Popular Front, particularly in youth movements, holiday camps, and

Table 4-1: Annual Registration of New Associations

YEAR	NUMBER	YEAR	NUMBER	YEAR	NUMBER
1908	About 5,000*	1978	35,025	1990	60,190
1938	about 10,000*	1979	31,222	1991	58,840
1960	12,633	1980	30,543	1992	70,403
1965	17,540	1981	33,977	1993	62,736
1970	18,722	1982	40,228	1994	65,056
1971	23,361	1983	46,857	1995	65,588
1972	26,257	1984	48,040	1996	67,528
1973	22,403	1985	47,803	1997	62,646
1974	22,153	1986	50,607	1998	62,708
1975	23,753	1987	54,130	1999	58,293
1976	25,622	1988	50,650		
1977	33,188	1989	60,630		

* Rough estimate since national computation started in 1960

Source: Ministère de l'Intérieur.

so forth (éducation populaire) and in popular tourist associations (tourisme social), which developed considerably after the passage of a 1937 law delineating the right to an annual paid vacation.

The number of new associations created each year rose dramatically from the 1960s on, with a 4 percent increase annually between 1960 and 1970, a 5 percent yearly rise between 1970 and 1980, and an annual increase of 5.5 percent between 1980 and 1990; it has since stabilized at around 5 percent, with some 60,000 new associations created each year, as one can see in Table 4-1.

In the last twenty years more than a million new associations have been officially registered. There is no way of knowing how many ceased to exist in the same period, as many do not bother to declare the end of their activity, since this negligence is of no consequence to them. The official estimate of 700,000 active associations remains plausible but unproven. To this figure we should add numerous de facto associations that do not require official registration for their activities, do not need to open a bank account or employ salaried staff, and so forth.

Other figures indicative of the vitality of the associative sector refer to the number of people it employs (the equivalent of 800,000 full-time jobs, 4.2 percent of total employment) or to the weight of its total expenditure in the national GDP (3.3 percent). More significant still is its contribution to job creation: One out of every seven net new jobs created in the French economy during the 1980s was created in the associative sector.[2]

Associations and the Welfare State

In my view, the growth of the welfare state stands out as the single most obvious explanation of the exceptional growth of the associative sector since 1960. This runs contrary to the often-advanced theory that associations develop to fill the gaps left vacant by the welfare state and, conversely, are crowded out by the development of the welfare state. In many cases, this theory fits reality: Numerous associations were formed in response to an emerging social need and helped to give it form, consistency, and visibility until it was picked up by the political system, transformed into a political demand, and dealt with by the creation of a new social service. This is particularly obvious with services dealing with various forms of social, physical, or mental handicap. However, the reverse is also true, as we see in the statistics of registration of new associations. Every peak in the curve corresponds to a political decision extending the welfare state by the creation of new social or civil rights or new social services. This interdependency of state and associative development deserves closer scrutiny.

Part of the growth of the associative sector is the result of sheer administrative expansion in the guise of associative legal status. Use of

Figure 4-1: Annual Registration of New Associations and Laws Extending the Welfare State

1. Law granting hunting and fishing associations the privilege of delivering permits
2. Law on adult professional education opening new opportunities for associations
3. New subsidies for services for the elderly rendered by associations
4. New legal possibilities for the development of local independent noncommercial radio stations run by associations
5. Transfer of optional school sports activities to associations
6. Legal recognition and financial help to intermediary associations for the unemployed
7. Inner-city programs heavily leaning on local associations

Source: Edith Archambault, *Le secteur sans but lucratif* (Paris: Economica, 1996).

associative status by public services in order to escape constraints of administrative regulations and political accountability is not specifically French—the British coined the word *quango* for these quasi–nongovernmental organizations—but it certainly blurs the vision of the real growth of genuine associations. Membership figures present a truer picture of reality, as they are much less subject to pollution by the "quango factor." The available data all point at least to stability and more probably to a slight increase in gross associative membership in recent years, belying the crowding-out theory. As a rough estimate, SOFRES, a prominent polling institute, suggests a significant rise in membership between 1978 and 1994, from 39 percent to 46 percent of the adult population. Two of the most reliable public research institutions, INSEE (National Institute of Statistics) and CREDOC (a specialized research extension of the Commissariat au Plan), conducted separate and much more precise analyses of associational participation. The INSEE study concludes that there has been relative stability in overall membership between 1983 and 1996 (around 43 percent of the total population over 14 years of age); CREDOC notes a slight rise (from 44.4 percent of the total population over 18 years of age in 1978–80 to 45.6 percent in 1990–92). [3]

Close analysis of Figure 4-1 points to three different ways in which growth of the public domain will induce growth of associations. First, when the state recognizes and organizes new group interests and social rights, it encourages members of such groups to form associations in order to better promote their interests and defend their rights. This is a classic lobbying function, probably more developed in other European countries and in the United States than in France, but it undoubtedly played a role in the creation of new associations in the wake of all the new legislation cited in Figure 4-1.

Second, when new legislation delimits and regulates a new area of civic involvement open to citizen initiatives (e.g., the laws mentioned in points 1 and 4 of Figure 4-1), it incites citizens to seize the opportunity for new collective action. This was obviously so with a 1982 law that opened the FM radio spectrum to independent private radio stations *(radios libres)*. Commercial radio networks quickly occupied all the space they could on the national level; independent noncommercial radio stations run by associations mushroomed at the local level, creating links to information, dialogue, and active participation in community affairs for all sorts of groups. This was also the case with a 1965 law on fishing and hunting that authorized the organization of such activities by local associations within the general framework of state regulations. These associations are still numerous and strong in rural France and closely correspond to the sort of associations Robert Putnam identifies as the typical embodiments of social capital (the bowling league model). They are, however, much weaker in large cities, and their aggregate weight has therefore diminished as the country has become more urbanized.

Third, when the state transfers partial responsibility for joint management of new public services to associations, alongside state administration, it requires active associative participation by the interested population. This is the case with most new social legislation dealing with problems of economic, social, or civic alienation and, specifically, of legislation earmarked in points 2, 3, 5, 6, and 7 of Figure 4-1, which gave rise, in all cases, to numerous new associations. This is also the case for the long-established social services for the young, the aged, and the physically, socially or mentally handicapped. [4]

The recent legislation on *revenu minimum d'insertion* (RMI) illustrates the dialectical relationship between the state and associations. It combines a guaranteed minimum income (a system of complementing an individual's existing sources of income with a contribution from the national budget up to a guaranteed minimum level) with a contractual arrangement between representatives of local government, civil society, and the individual regarding his or her efforts toward personal social and economic reinsertion (that is, achievement of an income permitting self-sufficiency: adequate housing, education, health care, and so on). Responsibility for the social work involved lies with local associations; financial responsibility for covering the costs such work involves lies with local governments. The concept was first elaborated and publicized by a prominent charitable association. Its chairman was nominated to the Economic and Social Council; there he wrote and steered in the council's assembly a report on poverty that inspired new legislation, which in turn relied on associations for the insertion dimension of its implementation.

This type of codevelopment of welfare state and associations has been reinforced by the present crisis situation in which growing state demands on associations reflect increasing difficulties in adjusting public policies to the ever more diverse, complex, and changing social needs of a society undergoing rapid and traumatic transformations in all areas of its development, as the rest of this chapter will show abundantly.

Such joint responsibility for public policies takes the form of explicit contractual arrangements linking associations and state bureaucracies and, with decentralization, associations and local governments. Both these trends, contractualization and decentralization, have obvious positive consequences on social capital formation by associations; they also have their drawbacks. Rigid contractual terms, instead of combining two different types of public legitimacy on an equal footing, often curb an association's freedom of movement, reducing it to a kind of public service agency. It loses a great deal of its internal democratic quality and its capacity to mobilize civic energies of free citizens on a voluntary basis, its principal contribution to social capital. The amount of public financing (more than 50 percent of total resources) was already characteristic of the French associative movement. Contractualization can increase dependence and loss of civic representativity, and so can decentralization when local governments copy (and often caricature) the type of relationship the state has traditionally established in France with civil society.

However, changes in the number and types of associations cannot be explained only by the nature of their relation to the welfare state. Other factors are at play, and these can be revealed by examining qualitative changes in the social issues stimulating collective action on the part of citizens and in the nature of citizens' involvement with these issues.

Old and New Issues for the Associative Movement

In order to analyze qualitative changes in the associative movement, we will need to differentiate the various types of associations and see how each one has evolved over time. Different typologies have been used by different authors, but none is entirely satisfactory. I shall often refer to three large categories of associations for the purposes of argument. Although no real-life association will ever fit perfectly into one of these categories, they represent useful distinctions for further discussion.

Associations that offer services and organize collective activities of a public service nature for large segments of the population. These are, in a sense, the associative arms of the welfare state. The two dominant sectors of the French associative movement, the social service and health associations and the sociocultural associations, belong here; together they represent between 70 and 90 percent of the French associative movement. The social service and health associations—which run most social and sociomedical services in France, with the notable exception of hospitals and clinics—are where France's Catholic heritage is most noticeable. The sociocultural associations run numerous services for specific publics or the general public, including youth clubs, cultural centers, *éducation populaire*, leisure activities, and especially *tourisme social;* this is where the secular heritage is most noticeable.

Associations that represent, promote, and/or defend the sectoral interests of members. This broad category includes a great variety of interest groups, such as parents, homeowners, tenants, landowners, professionals, employers and trade associations, labor unions, veterans, and members of hunting and fishing associations. Together they represent 10 to 20 percent of the associative movement.

Associations formed to defend a policy orientation or a cause. This category covers an equally diversified group of associations, including associations concerned with the environment, women's rights, other civil and social rights, job preservation and creation, local economic and social development, as well as national and international humanitarian movements, religious associations, political discussion clubs, and learned societies. These "voice" associations have great visibility but represent only a small fraction of the associative galaxy.

The changes over time that we shall observe reflect variations in:

- The respective weight of each of these three groups within the total associative movement
- The inner composition of each of them
- The nature of civic involvement of their members, users, and supporters

Analyses over time of numbers of yearly registrations of each type of association offer our first evidence of what has occurred. Two studies are of particular relevance. The first one, by Michel Forsé, divided associations into twenty types and compared the "birthrate" (number of yearly registrations) of each type in 1960, 1977, and 1982.[5] From this data I have selected several types of associations that clearly stand out from the rest by virtue of their high birthrate in a given year or the increase in their birthrate during a specified period (see Table 4-2).

In 1960 the four dominant areas in which new associations were created clearly belong to the first group listed above, public-service-type associations operating in conjunction with the welfare state. (Note that the high number of private schools created by associations in the postwar years paralleled the development of public education and did not alter the domination of the public sector in this area.) The year 1960 is in the middle of twenty-eight years of remarkable economic expansion. From the end of the Second World War to the 1973 oil shock, the yearly rate of growth of France's GDP oscillated between 3 percent and 6 percent, averaging 4.5 percent; unemployment was virtually unknown. This explains why this period is often referred to as "the thirty glorious years."

Table 4-2: High or Increased Birthrates of Associations in 1960, 1977, and 1982

1. EXCEPTIONALLY HIGH BIRTHRATE IN 1960		2. EXCEPTIONALLY HIGH BIRTHRATE IN 1977		3. EXCEPTIONALLY HIGH INCREASE IN BIRTHRATE, 1960–1977	
Type	Number of new associations	Type	Number of new associations	Type	Increase
1. Leisure	2,300	1. Sports	6,637	1. Elderly persons	From 169 to 2,451 (x 14.5)
2. Sports	2,008	2. Leisure	5,535	2. Parents	From 309 to 1,330 (x 4.3)
3. Social	1,203	3. Social	2,578	3. Political clubs	From 230 to 982 (x 4.3)
4. Schools	1,024	4. Elderly	2,451	4. Religious	From 142 to 595 (x 4.2)
		5. Arts	2,439	5. Arts	From 600 to 2,439 (x 4.1)
		6. Social clubs	2,025		

4. EXCEPTIONALLY HIGH BIRTHRATE IN 1982		5. EXCEPTIONALLY HIGH INCREASE IN BIRTHRATE, 1977–1982	
1. Sports	7,237	1. Independent radio stations	From 19 to 1,285 (x 67.6)
2. Leisure	4,863	2. Employment and economic development	From 568 to 1,692 (x 3)
3. Arts	4,116	3. Association-run schools	From 103 to 213 (x 2.1)
4. Social	3,558	4. Occupational training and research	From 1,464 to 2,599 (x 1.8)
5. Occupational training and research	2,599	5. Arts	From 2,439 to 4,116 (x 1.7)

In 1960, associational social capital was essentially part of the general process of collective social integration of society through its organization and management by the state, which was so characteristic of the French republican model. Nearly the whole of the associative sector depended on state finances and regulations for its development.

In 1977, quasi-public-service associations in sports, leisure, and social services still dominate the associational scene. The years of exceptional growth have also been years of welfare state development. However, new types of associations that belong to the two other categories enumerated above came to the forefront—those that defend sectoral interests or defend a cause. In fact, all five types of association with the most rapid growth in birthrates between 1960 and 1977 belong to these last two groups, such as associations for the elderly or for parents (associations defending sectoral interests) and political, religious, or arts associations (associations defending a cause). The "thirty glorious years" saw the growth of materialist values of self-interest as well as postmaterialist ones of universal bearing and of their implementation in associations.

In France, as elsewhere, years of growth promising relative affluence produced the rapid development of individualistic values. Apparently this move took two directions: selfish orientations mobilized civic energies for getting the best possible slice of the cake, and altruistic orientations combined a search for autonomous personal development and universal good (perhaps resulting from the influence of the May 1968 "cultural revolution"). There appeared to be a move in this period from received state-produced social capital to created society-produced social capital, and, within the latter, to self-centered as well as other-oriented social capital.

In 1982, France was in the throes of social and economic difficulties that began with the oil shock of 1973 and were to last for twenty-five years: The growth of GDP remained on average below 1 percent annually, and unemployment reached 13 percent. The trend has again reversed since 1998, but it is obviously too early to evaluate how this will affect social capital formation. In 1982, the country was about to engage in policies of strict financial discipline under the guidance of a left-wing government. Traditional sports, leisure, and social-service associations were still in the forefront of associational creativity. Postmaterialist values were still present and apparently growing in spite of social difficulties; arts activities were more than ever the source of new associations, moving from fifth to third place. But new preoccupations appeared, closely related to the circumstances of the time, resulting in creation of associations dealing with employability (occupational training and research) or with fighting social exclusion (knitting social ties). Section 5 of Table 4-2 confirms this, with two easily explained exceptions (independent radio stations were created in great numbers in the wake of new legislation permitting them, and private schools, which had previously dropped drastically from 1,204 new ones in 1960 to 103 in 1977, picked up again slightly in the midst of heated political debate over a project to unify public and private educational institutions); the two new types of associations showing the highest rate of development both dealt directly with citizens' efforts to create new jobs in the market economy—a sure sign of a dynamic civil society actively involved in tackling problems of general interest and not only relying on government to do so. A crisis situation can also increase the dynamism of a society, even in France.

Decreasing birthrates of certain types of associations promoting group self-interest tell the same story. Whereas one could expect difficult times to result in higher mobilization of selfish collective interests, the trend points in the opposite direction. The two types of associations with the greatest increase in birthrate between 1960 and 1977, both embodying self-centered social capital, receded in the next period.

Between 1977 and 1982, new associations for the elderly fell from 2,451 yearly to 1,126, and parents' associations dropped from 1,330 to 1,104. Yet in 1982, not only were there more old people, but they were in better health and relatively more prosperous than before; also, education was perceived more than ever as the passport to employment. Relative desertion of associations in these two areas seems to indicate neither a fall in their potential "market" nor a lack of civic interest (or even self-interest) on the part of their potential members, but rather a retreat from a type of civic investment embodied in traditional forms of collective action linking self-interest and state protection, as well as a move from self-centered to other-oriented social capital.

The second study dealing with birthrates of associations was done by Jean-François Canto on behalf of the Conseil National de la Vie Associative (CNVA), an official representative consultative organ.[6] Though Canto used a different classification of associations (eight large groups comprising fifty-seven types) and worked on the percentage of total new yearly registration and not on absolute figures, the conclusions drawn from his study are strikingly similar to those drawn from Forsé's. Canto measured registrations in three periods: between 1975 and 1986, between 1987 and 1990, and between 1994 and 1995. With the same purpose of analyzing the more dynamic types of associations, I have isolated in Table 4-3 the twelve types (out of fifty-seven) with the highest increase in birthrate between the first two periods and then analyzed how they fared between the second and third periods.

None of those twelve types are from the sociomedical category of quasi-public-service associations, which dominate the scene, and only two are from the sociocultural category. And none belong to the interest-group category. Nearly all of the fastest-growing associations of the recent crisis period belong to the third category (defending a cause or asserting views and cultural identity in the public arena), representing the emerging forms of social capital.

Most of the trends of the period 1975–90 continued up until 1995: nine out of the twelve types undergoing the fastest increase in birthrate between the first two periods were still increasing between the second and third periods (types 2, 3, 5, 6, 7, 8, 9, 10, and 12). Among those nine, seven participate in the promotion of personal development, whether through the expression of ideas and identity (types 6, 9, and 10) or through leisure, cultural, or educational activities (types 3, 5, 8, and 12); two indicate a growing involvement in actions of solidarity, in France with the unemployed (type 2) or with developing countries (type 7).

The three types of associations that did not continue to grow reflect

Table 4-3: Percentage of Total Registrations of 12 (out of 57) Types of Associations with Significant Changes in Birthrates at Three Periods in the Last Twenty Years

TYPE OF ASSOCIATIONS	% OF TOTAL NEW REGISTRATIONS		
	1975–1986	1987–1990	1994–1995
1. School and university sports associations	1.35	4.27	0.99
2. Employment-related associations	0.54	1.24	2.45
3. Research and training associations	1.00	1.87	2.15
4. Theater and dance associations	2.39	4.36	2.58
5. Publishing, library, philosophical, and literary associations	2.22	3.90	5.20
6. Alumni associations	1.35	2.35	3.41
7. Third World and international solidarity associations	1.69	2.71	4.60
8. Tourism associations	0.84	1.33	1.52
9. Political clubs	1.68	2.64	3.21
10 Religious associations	1.09	1.60	1.79
11. Economic development associations	4.39	6.03	5.00
12. Visual and graphic arts associations (painting, cinema, TV, photography)	2.16	2.62	3.34

specific circumstances: Optional school and university sports were no longer run by those institutions in 1994; economic development associations had already reached a remarkably high level, and so a great deal of the new associations in this area have switched toward helping the unemployed (type 2); and development of cultural activities is still rising, but interest has partly switched from theater and dance to music, especially among the young (music-related associations grew from 3.57 percent of the newcomers in the 1987–90 period to 4.30 percent in the 1994–95 period).

Identifying some of the big "losers" is no less significant. Apart from school and university sports, the five main types of associations with a marked reduction in growth (as measured by percentage of total number of associations created) were elderly persons' associations (from 2.05 percent to 1.16 percent), hunting and fishing associations (from 2.03 percent to 0.96 percent), and associations defending narrow corporate interests, such as craft and retailers' associations (from 2.05 percent to 0.96 percent), homeowners' associations (from 1.51 percent to 1.39 percent), and landowners' associations (from 0.25 percent to 0.13 percent).

The trends Forsé observed in the period 1960–82 have been confirmed and focused in the 1975–95 period analyzed by Canto. The dynamism of associative creation seems to have moved from the traditional sectors of quasi public service and defense of sectoral corporate interests to new activities more in tune with the needs and desires of citizens today: personal development in cultural and leisure activities, promotion of civil and social rights, and active solidarity with the disadvantaged. Little doubt is left as to the new dynamics of French social capital formation, indicative of a very active potential in civil society. However, fragmented as it is, and with its orientation toward values of personal autonomy and chosen solidarities so foreign to French cultural and institutional traditions, its capacity to link up with public institutions of representation and government and irrigate French political democracy will not come naturally and may be a very serious political challenge in the future.

Who Joins Associations, Why, and How?

Leaving associations as such in order to turn our attention to the individuals who join them should throw additional light on the nature of social capital in France. The two surveys by INSEE and CREDOC confirm trends regarding the type of associations rising or declining in the last twenty years, and they offer interesting indications as to the nature of their membership.

Table 4-4: Associations with Significant Rise or Decline in Membership Since 1978

TYPE OF ASSOCIATION	INSEE		MEMBERSHIP % CREDOC		
	1983	1996	1978–1980	1984–1986	1990–1992
Sports					
(% of total respondents)	15	18	15.3	18.9	19.4
Cultural*					
(% of total respondents)	5	7	12.2	11.6	16.6
Humanitarian					
(% of total respondents)	2	4			
For the elderly					
(% or respondents over 60)	21	16			
Parents					
(% of respondents with					
at least one child					
of school age)	12	8	10	8.2	8.1
Unions					
(% of respondents with					
present or past					
working experience)	14	8	9.7	6.8	6.8
Veterans					
(% of total respondents)	5	3			

* CREDOC counts cultural and leisure associations in the same category

Source: INSEE Première no. 542 ; CREDOC, *Consommation et modes de vie*, no. 78.

They confirm the rising attraction of leisure, sports, and cultural activities as well as new humanitarian associations such as those offering help to AIDS victims, immigrants, and Third World countries, and those opening avenues for self-development and new forms of solidarity. They also confirm the diminishing attraction of interest groups, notably parents' associations, unions, and associations for the elderly, as well as of certain types of "voice" associations, whether traditional (political parties) or heirs of the 1968 social movement (women's rights groups, consumers' associations). Table 4-4 gives the INSEE figures with CREDOC figures when the items are similar.

The INSEE survey also offers interesting new qualitative elements of information. The first one relates to the degree of participation in the management of associations. Contrary to the general perception, the level of participation measured in terms of active versus passive membership has risen between 1983 and 1996 in all eleven types of associations in the survey except two: associations for the elderly and sports clubs.

In the case of associations for the elderly, which many healthy and active people over 60 are deserting, not only does their membership decline, but it gets older, is in worse health, and is less active. In the case of sports clubs, the continuous rise in number and membership reflects the rapid growth of demand for sports activities and not a rising interest in the associations as such. In fact, many of the clubs have gained exclusive control of access to their sport (a monopoly over the facilities or over the right to practice), transforming their members into nothing more than users of a public facility; whatever social capital they induce is often nearer to the one created among commuters in public transport than among enthusiasts of a common endeavor.

If on the whole, however, active participation within associations is rising (in 1996, 46 percent of members of at least one association describe themselves as "active participants"; 41 percent did so in 1983), who are these active participants?

Membership has traditionally been biased in favor of the educated bourgeoisie. That income still plays an important role is evident in the 1996 INSEE study, which showed that 58 percent of the wealthiest quarter of the population are members of at least one association, compared with 33 percent of the least wealthy quarter. This is due not only to financial constraints but also to sociocultural ones, particularly level of education. However, it is interesting to note that the influence of education on association membership is weaker today than in the past. One might have thought that the rise in associative activities was the result of a general rise in the level of education; apparently this is not so, as the differ-

Table 4-5: Variations in Associative Membership According to Education, 1983 and 1996

		LEVEL OF EDUCATION (FROM NO QUALIFICATION TO UNIVERSITY)						
		1	2	3	4	5	6	7
MEMBER OF AT LEAST	1983	30	38	44	50	53	60	67
ONE ASSOCIATION (%)	1996	32	39	43	47	52	52	60

Source: INSEE Première, no. 542.

Table 4-6: Membership in Parents' Association According to Education

	LEVEL OF EDUCATION			
	1	2	3	4
Members of a parents' association (% of respondents with at least one child under 16)	9	17	24	32

Source: CREDOC, Consommation et modes de vie, no. 78.

ences in association membership according to level of education are smaller than they were. Dividing the population into seven groups, from the lowest to the highest level of education, the INSEE study obtained the results shown in Table 4.5.

Association membership and access to its social capital is less a privilege of the educated than it was. However, it remains an element of social prestige that reinforces the social status of already privileged categories, thereby reproducing the initial social utility of associations for reflecting the pretense to superior civic virtue of an enlightened elite.

The decreasing difference over time in membership between the least and best educated reflected in Table 4-5 appears to be much more the result of a fall in membership of the best educated (−8 percent and −7 percent for the highest two levels) than of a rise in membership of the least educated (+2 percent and +1 percent for the lowest two levels). In other words, the best educated are deserting associations faster than the least educated are joining them. However, as the total number of the best educated has increased with the general rise in education, and as they are still more apt to join associations than the average citizen, the same INSEE study registered a relative stability in average association membership (around 43 percent), and other studies could point to an overall rise in association membership.

The influence of education differs from one type of association to the next. It remains strongest for parents' associations—twice more than in the average case. This is one of the most striking results of the CREDOC study. For the purpose of this study, respondents were divided into four levels of education, from the lowest to the highest: Table 4-6 shows the huge differences among them regarding membership of parents' associations.

Access to compulsory free universal public education has always been presented as the great leveler of French society—the golden gate to equality of citizenship. The French republican model has positioned the state school as an institution towering above civil society and, on principle, ignoring all of its cultural and social specificities. Teachers pride themselves in not allowing external influences (including parents' demands) to influence the life of the institution and what they teach. However, numerous studies have shown how formal anonymous egalitarianism perpetuates social inequalities instead of abolishing them. Raymond Boudon first demonstrated that this is as much the product of parents choosing different educational itineraries for their children within the educational institution as the result of discrimination by the institution. The quality of relationships between parents and schools is therefore crucial.

Table 4-6 shows the dramatic lack of involvement of uneducated parents with schools—precisely those parents whose children are in greatest need of educational benefits and who expect most from the schools (expectations of schools grew more among the least educated between 1981 and 1990 than among any other group, according to the European Value Surveys). Uneducated parents are apparently so intimidated by the educational institution that only a small minority of them can envisage the possibility of dialogue and join the instrument of such dialogue—a parents' association. That this is not the result of them working more hours is proved by the fact that unemployed parents participate even less in parents' associations. This lack of involvement is exacerbated by the leadership of parents' associations, where parents who are themselves teachers often hold leadership positions, arguing they are in a better position to achieve the association's aims because of their inside knowledge. One could not find a better example of the way social capital is produced and shaped by the state through its relationship with civil society. If the French school system is to reestablish its role of social integration, it will have to change its institutional behavior, reaching out more to parents of all backgrounds.

On the whole, however, the influence of education on associative social capital has diminished, and, indeed, other sociodemographic variables show the same trend toward greater homogeneity of associative

Table 4-7: Rate of Joining in 1983 and 1996 by Age and Gender

PERCENTAGE OF RESPONDENTS WHO ARE MEMBERS OF AT LEAST ONE ASSOCIATION	AGE					GENDER	
	15–24	25–39	40–49	50–64	over 64	Male	Female
In 1983	32	47	50	41	45	52	34
In 1996	45	43	46	46	45	50	39

Source: INSEE Première, no. 542.

membership. Whereas joining associations used to be more developed in medium-sized provincial cities and in rural areas, the rate of joining is now more or less the same in Paris and large and smaller cities as in rural areas, although the balance between various types of associations differs greatly according to place of residence.

Regarding gender and age differences in membership, which have also tended to diminish, as Table 4-7 illustrates, closer analysis is required.

The slight decline in men's rate of joining is apparently linked to the decline of types of associations (e.g., political parties, unions, and veterans' groups) in which men had a much higher rate of membership than women. This decline is partly compensated for by men's higher level of membership in the ever-growing sports associations. The rise in women's membership is significant in all types of associations but more so in the growing sectors of humanitarian, social solidarity, and cultural associations.

More significant still is the changing pattern of participation of various age groups in associative activities. In 1982, the 25–50 age group had the highest rate of membership, with middle-aged, educated, bourgeois males dominating the scene. Those over 65 tended to participate in associations for the elderly and veterans' clubs. Fifteen years later, things had changed considerably. Those over 65 were more active and in better health; they deserted elderly persons' associations, which were stigmatized as ghettos for old people, and joined associations manifesting their active belonging to the wider society. With earlier retirement from work (by law and necessity), the rise in participation of the 50–64 age group partakes of the same trend toward an actively involved and socially meaningful retirement. The formation of bridging or other-oriented social capital lies heavily on the shoulders of the over-50s today.

While the 25–50 age group shows signs of declining interest, there has been an unexpected explosion in membership of the under-25 age group (with growth of 13 percent), mostly in sports and cultural activities. Boxing, martial arts, and music associations, in particular, are the types of groups joined by many of the deprived youth of French cities and the strongest vectors for the formation of their social capital (though it is often a fragmented, self-centered social capital). Another part of the explanation for such a spectacular rise in young people's membership in associations is that in many cases, volunteering has become a substitute for work in providing unemployed youth with social identity and status. A great number of adult associations make use of such a free, available labor force. Thus young people also participate in the formation of other-oriented social capital by necessity: associative social capital by proxy of work-associated social capital.

The general feeling among many old established associations is that the young are turning away from associations. Their leaders are quick to complain and to blame young people's individualistic, hedonistic values and lack of concern for general welfare. The reality is infinitely more complex, as we begin to see. The basic fact is that forms of associative sociability are rapidly changing. The young do not invest in the same associations as their elders, nor in the same way or for the same reasons; their elders ignore or misunderstand this. A number of case studies combining survey material and participant observation illustrate the point.[7] The young are shown to be no less concerned with ethical questions and motivations than were preceding generations, but many factors—the widening generation gap, difficulties of social and professional integration, a general feeling of not being heard or understood—prompt them to search for other forms of socialization and social involvement removed from the adult world, including existing associations.

The under-25 generation is not congenitally unfit for associative activity; their sociability within groups in their immediate vicinity is high. Young people do nearly everything collectively in closed communities with considerable inner social capital. Groups also serve as vehicles for contact with the outside world to negotiate with social or other public services or to oppose them—a form of critical investment in global social capital.

There are many areas where young people invest in altruistic collective action when they feel specifically concerned (e.g., AIDS, drugs, violence, racism), but they also do so for wider humanitarian causes (e.g., human rights, the environment, civic and social rights, the Third World).

These groups rarely adopt the institutionalized form of registered association except when dealing with local authorities who demand it.

Informal rules of sociability replace formal constraints. They are present in areas where established associations are not, and engage in types of collective investment also unknown to the more traditional associations. To some extent they are exploring new territories for future social capital.

When involved in collective action today, young citizens want to simultaneously satisfy a strong need for sociability, make a meaningful and effective contribution to social solidarity, and engage in personal development. This complex set of motivations can be satisfied only if they retain constant personal control of the nature and form of their public engagement. They will resist the coercion of any form of enrollment. Such extreme personalization of collective involvement disturbs traditional concepts of associations as well as of trade unions and of all other institutionalized forms of social capital. And such attitudes of the young are spreading to other age groups. In what is often mistaken for a decrease in quantity of social capital, a qualitative change seems to be under way in the trend toward individualization—a type of privatization of social capital formation.

Sports activities illustrate this point. More people today practice a sport outside associations; these informal sports activities develop even faster than sports associations, yet are still practiced collectively—one rarely goes cycling, motorcycling, walking, or skiing alone. There are innumerable soccer or basketball teams with no club affiliation, creating regular conflicts with municipalities and sports associations. This does not imply resistance to collective forms of social activities; it illustrates the difference between the desire of the young and of many adults to be and act together (as well as their capacity to do so) and the institutional structures they are offered. Such offered social capital seems irrelevant to them.

Another illustration of this discrepancy is the way some people move constantly from one association to another—what administrators of associations call "zapping" (also a term that describes using a remote to switch TV channels rapidly). Traditionally, associations are founded and organized around global projects to be realized over an indefinite period, irrespective of specific action. However, citizens, and the young particularly, now join associations because they are interested in specific action aimed at immediate, concrete results, and they will prolong membership only if they are satisfied with results and interested in the following step; otherwise they will join another association. Association leaders consider this conduct to be incoherent, but in fact it expresses a desire for personal coherence, for step-by-step control of one's social investments.

Preservation of personal integrity and opportunities for personal development have become the main motivation for asserting one's presence in any form of collectivity. This can produce a kind of juxtaposition of fragmented self-centered elements of social capital not easily interconnected. The difficulty is increased by the extreme volatility of associative loyalties and interassociative mobility. But this is the basic material offered by the emerging youth culture from which to build a civic society. The material is there; it is the engineering know-how that seems to be lacking.

CHANGING PATTERNS IN OTHER FORMS OF SOCIAL CAPITAL

Forms of social capital are closely related to particular historical circumstances and to the respective positions of different generations in them. Unlike England, where the war effort drew together government and civil society and produced an enormous stock of social capital, France came out of the war with a thoroughly depleted stock of social capital. The Nazi occupation and Vichy collaborationist government destroyed a great deal of French civil society. The vast majority of French citizens neither engaged in active resistance nor collaborated but retreated into individual survival strategies, keeping cautiously clear of any civic commitment.

After the war, heirs to the resistance movement, real or putative, took control of government and civil society positions of responsibility and started rebuilding the cities, the economy, and social capital, amidst great instability of political institutions in the throes of decolonization. For fifteen to twenty years this task absorbed the energy of a relatively small generation of inspired bureaucrats and technocrats. They had come to monopolize most positions of power in the state and civil society by the time the vast baby boom generation came of age to claim access to social recognition and positions. The arduous task of reconstruction and decolonization was completed, and growth was there to stay; why shouldn't "everything be possible," as the May '68 slogan proclaimed? The clash of two generations—a small, hardworking, modernizing generation, probably better epitomized by Georges Pompidou than by any other public figure, and a vast, privileged new generation, taking all the benefits of their predecessors' efforts for granted but feeling excluded from the right to enjoy them fully—is probably one of the main sources of the 1968 cultural revolution and of the emergence of postmaterialist values and social movements (women's liberation, ecology, moral and sexual autonomy) that rapidly came to dominate the culture. The generation that reached adolescence and adulthood after 1975 and especially in the 1980s clearly moved away from the optimistic idealism and moral audacity of the '68 generation. The experience of social harshness, disillusionment with Mitterrand's promise of a "changed life," and disgust with rampant political corruption has produced a pragmatic skepticism that is the hallmark of the young of today and pervades the general mood of the country.

Changes in social, moral, and civic norms and values are apparent in many other areas than formal associations, areas where new forms of social capital are also being produced. They are also revealed in numerous opinion surveys and particularly in various CREDOC studies[8] and in the European Value Surveys carried out in 1981 and 1990.[9] Before discussing how the new cultural dimensions of French social capital affect the working of our political democracy, a quick overview of three crucial areas where social capital is supposed to be diminishing is in order: poor suburban communities (especially those with large immigrant communities), the workplace, and the family.

Social Capital in Deprived Suburbia

The rapid growth and industrialization of the economy in the postwar years resulted in accelerated urbanization and huge demand for immigrant workers. In 1946 France was still a largely rural country, both demographically and culturally; the urban population was just over 50 percent of total population in 1946, while it is more than 75 percent today. And France moved from 40 million to 60 million inhabitants in the last fifty years, with a quarter of the additional population coming from immigration. The combination of these demographic upheavals produced a group of suburbs that house a disproportionate majority of these immigrants. Ethnic, social, and spatial segregation coincide, concentrating the most acute problems of exclusion, polarizing the most xenophobic and racist fears and fantasies. An exhaustive appraisal of neighborhood community relations is obviously out of the question in this chapter, but closer analysis of such suburbs is of particular interest for our purpose. Public opinion generally holds that total anomie is their inescapable lot. However, in-depth case studies point to quite a different diagnosis: Social exclusion does not automatically breed anomie but rather leads to a disconnected, incomplete form of social integration.

Close observation of tenement housing reveals a labyrinth of discreet but active sociability networks. Whereas established associations seem unable to take root in such environments, many small formal or informal associations do. Locked in a form of social exile, inhabitants fall back on the immediate vicinity to create primary sociability networks indispensable for personal and social identity. Small-scale social integration does take place in most high-rise buildings. Networks of sociability between neighbors help solve daily practical problems or defend against outside threats: mobilization of tenants against expulsion for unpaid rent, mothers associating to protect children from racketeers and dope pushers on the way to school, men exchanging odd jobs at home, young people organizing motorbike excursions and music and sports groups. Indeed, there is far more activity than one might imagine. At the same time they form a closed set of networks unconnected to larger society, breeding fragmented social capital.

Crossing social and functional frontiers, meeting people from other milieus and types of activity, is vital for communication between elective networks of the private sphere and more institutionalized ones in the public sphere. This is particularly difficult in the public settlements on city outskirts where the bulk of poverty is concentrated. Public and private neighborhood services are rare in these areas, and sports and other facilities as well as local employment are almost nonexistent; therefore neighbors do not meet each other when going to work, school, public services, shops, cinemas, and stadiums. With all these facilities outside and in different places, the local community can never be a local society, nor can it be a political community. People in them have no say in their government; they are governed by others elsewhere. These are hardly favorable conditions for integration into the wider society. All social rehabilitation experiments with deprived people and areas prove that success always depends on the capacity of the proponents of such policies to identify and join forces with informal local sociability networks. Unfortunately, large businesses and social or administrative organizations often seem incapable of the type of relationship required for bridging the widening gap between growing pockets of social exclusion and mainstream society, between community self-centered fragmented social capital and institutional other-oriented social capital.

The problems of social integration of the immigrant population of these suburban settlements are no different from those of their neighbors of French origin, only more extreme. The unemployment rate of the immigrant population is twice that of the indigenous population. It is not lack of cultural integration that blocks social integration but the reverse. Muslim Algerians illustrate this point. They are the victims of more prejudice and more brutal rejection than any other immigrant community. Thus the reality of their problems and attitudes on questions of cultural and social integration is of great relevance. A recent in-

depth study of young second-generation Algerians by the National Institute of Demographic Studies (INED) provides precise information on
three of the most significant indicators of cultural integration: religion,
school achievement, and choice of spouse or companion. [10]

Religion

On the whole, second-generation Algerians show a lower level of religiosity than the average French citizen, suggesting a belief that assimila-
tion in a secular country demands that all personal religious references
be abandoned. There is, however, a small minority of practicing Muslims whose stated motivations for strong religious involvement include
difficulty with French society and difficulty with parents.

At first sight, assertion of a strongly Islamic identity signals revolt
against society's withholding of socioeconomic integration and retreat
in the protective shell of fundamentalism: a minute but conspicuous
group actively and publicly opposes basic French values. But for the
most part, however, such identity assertion is less a rejection of integration than provocation to obtain it—a form of blackmail. The attitude of
girls wearing a head scarf to school was particularly revealing. The
republican concept of equal access by all citizens to the public system of
education precludes pupils showing any external sign of a distinctive
identity, notably religious identity. Insisting on wearing such a clear
assertion of Islamic faith was received as a provocation to the basic principles of the school system. Yet there was no demand for Koranic
schools; these girls merely wanted to enter the regular secular school of
other French children, yet without relinquishing their identity.

Nor is asserting Islamic identity always a sign of submission to parents; it is often the exact opposite, an effort to restore the injured dignity
of a family subjected to unemployment and social exclusion.

The motivation of the vast majority of young second-generation
Algerians who clearly refuse all religious affiliation is also ambivalent.
While 60 percent of young women and 70 percent of young men say
either that they never practice their religion or do not have a religion at
all, just as many declare that they respect Ramadan and food strictures.
Some of this is undoubtedly an assertion of respect for their culture of
origin and for their parents' way of life, unrelated to any religious fervor.

These attitudes demonstrate a strong desire to integrate the republican model of secular citizenship while simultaneously maintaining a
link with the original culture, an integral part of their identity. This
explicit demand for mixed identity is so clearly articulated that it might
well remain an intrinsic feature of French citizenship. Should this be the

case, it will call for readjustment of the French ideal republican model to make it more complex and flexible, better adapted to an emerging multicultural national identity. As one person said in a recent interview, "We have long known how to mix french fries with couscous."

School, School Friends, and Companions

The data on school achievement and companionship confirm the success and rapidity of integration of second-generation Algerians; their school results are identical to those of the average French pupil of similar socioeconomic background, suggesting integration in scholarly achievement as well as in personal friendships. The most revealing feature lies in the data of their love life and, later, choice of spouse or companion. Among those with both parents born in Algeria (this group has kept the strongest ties with the mother country), 50 percent of married men and 24 percent of married women have chosen a spouse of French origin. For the unmarried of the same group with a regular girlfriend or boyfriend, the same mix is observed for men, but for women, 32 percent choose someone of French origin; either the younger unmarried girls are more disposed to choose or accept a companion outside their community than was the older married generation, or parental influence makes them revert to traditional conduct when marrying. Less stable love relationships are even more open to intercultural exchange—another survey found that three-quarters of young people of Algerian origin had had a love affair outside their community.

Responsibility for difficulties encountered in turning so dynamic an integration process into complete success is clearly not theirs but that of the host country, which must address two specific areas: unemployment and racism. How could integration not be hampered when one-third of young immigrants are unemployed, when the majority live in deprived urban districts, when upward social mobility is so difficult and when so many still confront insidious or even blatant racism?

Racism

Indeed, immigrants are also the prime target of racism and xenophobia. They are often subjected to spot checks by police based solely on their physical appearance. The search for illegal immigrants makes potential suspects of all. Rampant racism in civil society is no less present and is undoubtedly the main obstacle to complete integration. It remains high, as shown by the last annual report on racism of the national committee for human rights.[11] Twice as many French people find immigrants a burden rather than an asset; 60 percent state they "no longer feel at home," and an equal number say that "there are too many Arabs and Muslims in France." The same proportion admits having occasionally uttered racist remarks. Eighty percent blame immigrants for the racism they encounter, and 50 percent even understand voting for the right-wing political figure Jean-Marie Le Pen for that reason. Forty percent admit personal dislike for North Africans.

It seems paradoxical that immigrants of Algerian origin are the prime target of so much racism, even physical violence, given the exceptional dynamism of their cultural integration. However, it may be precisely because this particular community is integrating so rapidly that it seems so threatening to the more insecure elements of French society.

This grim picture is tempered by other considerations:

- Violent racist acts, especially against North Africans, which had risen during the eighties, began to drop in the early nineties, and fell much more rapidly in the last two years of the decade.
- The opinion that there are too many immigrants in France (especially Arabs and Muslims) also fell in the nineties.
- The possibility of native-born French children marrying immigrants is accepted by more people.
- More significant than any other data is the finding that the greater the proportion of foreigners in a city, the less xenophobia and racism there is. Close relations with immigrants are the best antidotes to racism as Table 4-8 illustrates.

This finding contradicts many preconceived ideas. It is true that the National Front has garnered large numbers of votes in the poorest districts, which house the highest proportion of immigrants as well as the most vulnerable segment of the French working class. Yet a detailed analysis has found that the National Front gains most of its votes in homogeneous suburbs or blocks of flats, where most people are of French ancestry, than where cohabitation prevails.

The same general conclusion about the relationship between the number of foreigners in a city and the amount of anti-immigrant hostility found there emerges when analyzing problems of immigrant integration from the immigrant and host population point of view. This indicates that a new concept of the French republican model could be slowly emerging. According equal dignity to the diverse cultural communities composing the nation appears to be the only way to re-create a set of common universal values on which social cohesion and democracy could flourish. This involves a new way of combining community-

Table 4-8: Racism According to Percentage of Foreigners in City

TYPICAL OPINIONS ON RACIST ISSUES	% OF FOREIGNERS IN CITY			
	< 1%	1–4%	5–10%	> 10 %
In France today, there are too many:				
Arabs	74	84	64	47
Muslims	70	62	59	46
One no longer feels at home in France	60	60	53	44
I admit being racist	50	40	39	36
Believe immigrants to be an asset:				
For the economy	13	27	34	40
For intellectual and cultural life	36	44	44	58
Declare feeling sympathy for:				
Young French citizens of North African origin	54	51	53	58
North Africans	47	46	48	59
Declare themselves ready to:				
Boycott racist shops	31	35	40	43
Take part in antiracist demonstrations	19	24	31	30
Financially help antiracist organizations	17	22	20	24
Join antiracist organizations	19	22	23	24
Judge the quality of a democracy by its capacity to integrate immigrants	61	61	59	73

Source: Commission Nationale Consultative des Droits de l'Homme, 1997.

centered social capital with national social capital. Bridging social capital requires strong foundations for the individual pillars of the bridge as well as a robust span across them.

Work-Associated Social Capital

A great deal of social capital in modern societies is obviously formed through work relations. [12] Personal and group identities, norms of sociability, networks of friendships, and collective solidarities created at work are important components of social capital, just as industrial relations are essential cogs in the institutional framework of a democracy. No review of the state of social capital in France could be complete without an assessment of work-associated social capital.

The Downfall of Unskilled Workers and the Disruptive Effects of Unemployment

Postwar reconstruction accelerated industrialization, and sustained growth produced a significant increase in the number of jobs available.

The rapidly expanding work market easily absorbed the rural exodus and the baby boom's children and even required an external labor force. The rural and immigrant workers who filled the need were unskilled and thus perfect fodder for a Taylorized organization of mass production in which each unskilled worker is required to perform repeatedly a limited number of automatic gestures, analyzed, prescribed and rationally organized on an assembly line by management experts. France plunged into this form of scientific organization of labor; not only did it compensate for the lack of skills in the new labor force and the demands of a rapidly expanding market for mass-produced, standardized products, but it also required the type of command appreciated by our engineers, weaned on the peculiar French notion of the elite as having a monopoly over rationality. This produced a labor force heavily loaded with blue-collar workers (around 35 percent), and among them, a large proportion of unskilled workers (around two-thirds).

The crisis shattered this type of job development. The number of unskilled jobs fell sharply, as intelligence and creativity were increasingly required of workers. Above all, industrial jobs shrank drastically and service jobs increased correspondingly: In 1974 industry employed approximately 40 percent of the labor force and the service sector 50 percent. Today it is 25 percent and 70 percent respectively. It is easy to imagine the violent impact of sudden, massive layoffs on a large pool of unskilled industrial workers. The highest rate of unemployment and of precarious employment and the worst stigma of social exclusion are to be found among them.

The marginalization process of unskilled workers excluded from the labor force by technological change was accelerated by two newcomers on the work market: more and better-equipped young people and a rapidly growing number of women. Young people with diplomas bumped unskilled and older workers downward in the labor force or even out of it altogether. And the massive arrival of young educated women on an already saturated labor market exacerbated global competition for all jobs (very unequally, to be sure, given the gendered specialization of numerous jobs) and helped push the less skilled deeper into unemployment. This phenomenon has much wider cultural implications. Its sheer size is striking: Of the four million new arrivals in the workforce in the last twenty years, nine out of ten are women. In 1973, one woman out of two between the ages of 25 and 50 was working. Now, four out of five are present on the labor market—even nine out of ten single women, thereby attaining a rate of activity almost equal to that of men. This is a clean break from the bourgeois model of the housewife previously dominant in the 20th century. It is clearly the result of both a qualitative evolution of job supply (due to changes in the work process) and a quantitative evolution of job demand (women wanting the security of a supplementary income for the family budget in these difficult times). Nevertheless, they are relatively minor considerations compared with the major social and cultural factor of women's presence, by right, on the labor market in a society where work and the income it procured were essential elements of role differentiation in the family and in the wider society.

The structure of earned income has also been profoundly modified by the decrease of Taylorian organization of work, the increased importance of the service sector, the increased demand for intelligence and creativity among workers, and the arrival of better-educated people on the work market.

While the average income of the liberal professions increased (by 40 percent in the last ten years), as did that of managerial staff (though far less so), average income was more or less stable for skilled and office workers but reduced for unskilled workers. This widening disparity in earned income has had obvious repercussions on social identity. The deteriorating condition of unskilled workers inevitably affects the quality of social ties in France, a country where 50 percent of the labor force has less than basic vocational training. Not only does unemployment take its highest toll on them, but when they do work, they earn less than they did before. This creates the feeling of being handicapped and condemned to a form of social exile. Isolated, they transmit this feeling to their children, who also are deprived of social upward mobility.

Age also accounts for high discrimination in the labor market at both ends of the spectrum. In spite of a general rise in their standard of education, young people still face difficulties when looking for work, as their training often does not correspond to needs in the labor market. The lack of on-the-job training in many French companies is also responsible. In 1998, a quarter of young people on the labor market were looking for work, and three-quarters of those working held precarious jobs; indeed, they held 42 percent of precarious jobs against only 4 percent of stable ones, a proportion higher than in any other European country Thus the young carry most of the burden of workforce "flexibility."

At the other end of the spectrum, ill equipped for adapting to change but having attained relatively high wages, older workers are often the first to be dismissed and have great difficulty in finding new jobs once they are let go. Stable employment is largely the privilege of the 30–45 age group.

Consequently, unemployment (real or anticipated) spreads across wide sections of society, resulting in generalized fear of downward social mobility. In answer to a survey asking to which social group one belongs today and to which one will belong tomorrow, 23 percent of those in upper brackets thought that they might regress, while 57 percent of people from middle brackets and 72 percent of those in lower brackets believed they might slip down the ladder.

Fear of unemployment and a pessimistic image of the work market inspire behavior that makes the system even more rigid (for example, people refuse to change jobs because they fear losing employment), to the detriment of general economic performance and job creation. The lack of optimism regarding one's personal future also breeds an attitude of withdrawal into oneself and the decision to opt out of any sort of work-associated social capital. For a minority it may lead to militant rejection of present society and joining radical political groups at both ends of the political spectrum representing, in both cases, self-centered and highly disconnected social capital.

New Demands for Personal Development at Work

Attitudes about work and the types of benefits and gratifications expected from work are also crucial for the work-associated norms and values constitutive of social capital. The obvious question is whether these attitudes and expectations are congruent with the changing circumstances of the different components of the work force. This will prove not to be the case for a large group of workers, gravely impeding their capacity to create and use work-associated social capital.

The more work is considered scarce and the more people fear losing it, the greater its value. The French are almost unanimous in declaring work to be among the most important elements of their lives. This has been verified by the European Value Surveys of 1981 and 1990 and by many other surveys. Contrary to frequent assertions, work does not seem destined to lose its preeminence in society anytime soon, at least in people's minds.

But people's attitudes toward work and what is expected from it have changed considerably. Whereas work used to be the prime vehicle for collective social status, on which work-associated social capital could prosper, its value today is primarily linked to the opportunity it offers for autonomous personal development. This is apparent in the European Value Surveys as well as in other amazingly convergent surveys. Items indicating a positive opinion of opportunities for personal development at work all registered a gain of between 7 and 15 percentage points in the last ten to fifteen years, particularly among the young.

The value placed on personal autonomy can be traced to the cultural revolution of the sixties but also to the ideology of triumphant liberalism of the eighties. It is more indicative of a desire to make a place for oneself than of an interest in questioning the existing social order. Acceptance of the system is coupled with a demand for greater participation. People's claim to greater recognition of personal ability goes hand in glove with their recognition of the owner's right to run the company. The generalization of liberal economic values has integrated personalization of work values, glorification of personal success, and business enterprise and rehabilitation of money.

Such an emphasis on individual responsibility in the workplace and on fashioning identity through work obviously greatly increases the onus of the unemployed, especially considering how far the new image of what makes work worthwhile has spread in all sectors, including among the unemployed. If the unemployed (as well as other highly vulnerable social groups, such as unskilled workers) attach relatively less importance to these various factors of personal development and more to material advantages, their basic cultural references regarding work are the same, and they develop in the same direction as those of other social groups. One can imagine the pain caused by such discrepancy between individual expectations and the work market's capacities to satisfy them.

Unions and Industrial Conflicts

Let us consider the result of such tension on work-associated social capital, especially in two areas where it is created and used: unions and industrial conflicts. The considerable fall in union affiliation in France— already the weakest in Europe—must be addressed first. Membership is no more than a third of what it was twenty years ago—5 percent in the private sector, 12 percent in the public sector. When entering the workforce, young people and women pointedly avoid union membership, which fluctuates around 1 percent for these two groups of newcomers. Almost none of the unemployed are unionized; they feel as abandoned by the unions as by other representative bodies. Opinion polls well reflect this. Trust in unions is shattered in all socioprofessional groups, and more so among the most vulnerable, unskilled workers.

The severity of the crisis in unionization is partly explained by unions' structural features. Numerous national professional statutes following vertical divisions of industrial sectors and subsectors have produced union structures unequipped to deal with horizontal mobility and unable to protect workers' interests as they move from one employer to the next. Nor are they capable of taking heed of workers' new aspirations for personal development and recognition of individual performance. What is more, matters relating to practical needs, organization of work, training, and other services unions can offer their members have been neglected, whereas they are obvious factors in union resilience in neighboring countries. Thus, unions no longer reflect the changing aspirations of the working class. They are trapped in a vicious circle: the less they are representative, the less they have clout with management and government; the less they are able to promote the cause of members, the less trust people have in them.

There are two exceptions to the general slump in affiliation. The CFDT (a secular offshoot of the Christian labor movement) has deliberately chosen to adapt its organization and policy orientation to the changing circumstances of the time, paying greater attention to individual demands and supporting policies of reform and modernization (even when proposed by a conservative government) when they coincide with proposals of their own platform. Not surprisingly, CFDT is the only union with rising membership and has moved ahead of all other unions for the first time in the history of the labor movement, despite much criticism of its shift to the center. This constitutes a true revolution on the French social scene.

In contrast, new leftist unions of dissidents, mainly from the Fédération de l'Education Nationale (FEN) and the CFDT, violently oppose any change in existing social and labor legislation and favor systematic radicalization of conflicts—a time-worn minority strategy. Support for the leftist unions used to come from the young, educated, and relatively privileged; it now comes from the older, unskilled, and unemployed, whereas the educated young are far more likely to support reformist unions. Discontent of the underclass has become the ferment of extreme radicalism of leftist unions and parties, and of the National Front on the right.

Recent industrial conflicts reflect unions' loss of power. Conflicts are now much more likely to take the form of wildcat strikes and explosions of discontent rather than of organized industrial action. The street, more often than the workplace, is the stage for conflicts today. This is illustrated by a big drop in working hours lost to labor conflict. Whereas economic growth fed countless industrial conflicts, during the last twenty years the number of such clashes has dropped. Even the December 1995 social upheaval only drew a limited number of strikers (public transport and some postal workers); all efforts to extend the strike failed. The congestion in Paris streets was spectacular because everybody was going to work—by car, on motorbikes, bicycles, roller skates, walking, and hitchhiking—in an atmosphere of unusual conviviality. Public sympathy was due more to anger against the arrogant incompetence of all mediating or governing bodies, including unions, than to approval of the specific motives of strikers. Today, striking is frequently an expression of civic rather than industrial discontent. Lack of work-associated social capital produces sporadic eruptions of civic energy in the public arena, revealing the need (that is not yet an explicit demand) for a structured link between organized work sociability and receptive business and public institutions.

Family Ties and Social Capital

Roles within the family, between spouses and between generations, reflect patterns of authority and cooperation that obviously influence roles and relationships in the wider society no less than they are influenced by them. [13] Without even trying to unwind the multiple causal relationships between social capital formation within the family and that outside the family, it is nevertheless important to analyze whether the trends that can be observed in family relations are in any way comparable to the ones detectable elsewhere.

Couples

Families are going through changes of similar magnitude to those observed in associations, local communities, and the workforce. Married and unmarried couples among the young are equally common; divorce and separation are on the rise; couples have fewer children, often outside marriage, and the number of single parents is increasing; there are more numerous and public homosexual couples; sexual freedom is rising, as is its acceptability. Age-old precepts that defined the family are publicly disdained or scorned. Acceptance of these deviations is even wider than their practice.

The great variety of marriage models has turned diversity into a norm; there is a large consensus for personal choice of a family model, though this does not mean license. Quite the contrary: moral pressure often increases when individual responsibility replaces institutional guidelines. This is confirmed by changing attitudes of young people between 1981 and 1990. More choose to live outside marriage but show greater respect for its moral premises.

Two distinctly opposed models emerge on the wider European scene where this trend is even more prevalent: the Mediterranean Catholic model (particularly in Spain), where there is great conformity to the institutional prescriptions of marriage coupled with great freedom in conduct and opinion, and the Scandinavian Protestant model, which combines great institutional liberty with very exacting private morality. Both models, of course, exist in all countries, but the mixes are different. A general shift toward a more tolerant version of the Scandinavian model, creating greater homogeneity, is discernible within each country as well as between them. It is notably so in France.

Contrary to what might be imagined, the family remains the brightest star of French values, as it does for the rest of Europe and the United States of America. The European Value Surveys showed this. But the last decades have seen considerable role changes. Women have acquired professional status comparable to that of men and thus have gained a great deal of autonomy, but not necessarily equality. Theirs is the burden of household chores and responsibility for children's education. Most women today stop working after giving birth to a third child—not after the first or second, as before. Reconciling family and professional activities remains the exclusive "privilege" of women. There are others: 90 percent of single-parent families are headed by a woman (in the case of divorce, this is as often determined by courts as by the divorcing couple's decision). The responsibility of caring for seriously handicapped elders practically always falls to women (in 85 percent of cases).

Attitudes seem to evolve faster than conduct and may anticipate further changes. An opinion survey conducted in 1978 and again in 1994 showed important changes in attitudes: In 1978, 31 percent favored equal professional involvement of couples, 37 percent preferred a lower level for women, and 30 percent considered that housework and children required the full-time presence of a woman. Preference for full professional equality had risen to 54 percent in 1994; only 19 percent were in favor of full-time homemaking.

Neither the intensity of relationships nor the strength of the social tie appear to be diminished by these changes, however unstable the situation of the couple might be in these times of transition. There is, however, an important qualitative change—a move from a tie imposed by convention to one resulting from periodical reassertion of personal choice. This tie is not necessarily weaker because it is less permanent or institutionalized.

Children and Adolescents

Observation of parent-child relationships suggests that the rejection of the traditional authoritarian model of education prevails in France as elsewhere. Each member of the nuclear family benefits from greater autonomy and an enlarged personal domain. This is even noticeable at mealtime: The family does not always eat together, nor do they always eat the same food. Here, however, attitudes seem to be lagging behind behavior. The European Value Surveys show that normative judgments remain very traditional. The French consider it important for children to be taught the virtue of "obedience," "concentration on work"—certainly not "independence." France is among the last in Europe to adopt liberal values on the education of children.

Adolescents' relations with their family vary considerably with social status. This is probably the set of relationships where the greatest class differentiation is to be found in social capital formed in the family.

A minority of privileged "traditional" youth reproduce parental models. They come from families holding positions transmissible from parents to children through professional or social status: inherited networks constituting what Pierre Bourdieu calls social capital, instruments of privileged access to positions of economic, social, and political power.

A large group of middle-class or lower-middle-class young men and women are faced with great difficulty in entering a work market that is clearly biased against them. Thus they prolong their university studies and continue to live with their parents. After the postwar reformist student generation, after the libertarian generation of the affluent years, this generation of students falls back on their family and the university for a status unavailable elsewhere.

A third group, still a minority but rapidly growing, is made up of delinquent poor youth going through the mill of social exclusion, crippled and stigmatized. Their personal experience is one of broken families, violent surroundings, low-quality housing, and lack of successful integration in the school system. Low self-esteem is the result of passive acceptance of their own image reflected in such degraded circumstances; on the other hand, the violence they perpetrate on their immediate surroundings often is an expression of refusal to identify with them, a strategy of self-assertion through differentiation. Much energy goes into the creation and survival of the peer group, with tremendous solidarity among members; they invest vast amounts of social capital exclusively inside their peer group and exclude all external social structure, including their own families.

Grandparents

Grandparents are essential to the preservation of family social capital, particularly in situations in which cherished family values and ties are subjected to the disintegration of stable institutionalized roles and to the brutality of economic and social aggressions. While the traditional peasant model of three generations cohabiting has almost vanished, relations with their parents remain important for young couples, especially once they have children. Grandparents give financial help and look after children but also impart family history, an important function in a situation where uncertainly about the future breeds a renewed quest for roots. Statistics show this clearly: one out of two couples with children see their parents at least once a week (two out of three when the members of the couple are under 25). When physically separated from children and grandchildren, old people escape loneliness because of constancy in these relationships—even when a spouse dies. The number of people over 60 living alone has doubled in the last twenty years. Yet the vast majority declare they do not feel lonely. Socializing with friends and neighbors has increased so much that old-age sociability has become a characteristic of society today. Family social capital reinforces participation of those over 60 in other forms of social capital and vice versa.

A break does occur when the very old become physically dependent. Too heavy a burden for their families, most move to an institution or stay in their home with necessary professional help. Family and friendly ties continue, though often more tenuously. Statistically, this break most often takes place after the age of 80. Whereas 75 percent of the total population declare they never feel lonely, only 45 percent say so after 85. The very old also present an extremely high rate of suicide. They drop out of family social capital and of society simultaneously.

The general picture that emerges from this cursory description of relationships between members of the French family today is very different from that of twenty or thirty years ago. Each family member has gained greater autonomy. Some live together longer, others less. Although the family appears to be dispersed, it has rarely been so close and enjoyed such strong attachments. It is an irreplaceable haven for emotional ties and personal identity and has again become one for help in the face of adversity.

But it is not the same family. It is as much a chosen relationship as an inherited one. The ties that compose its social capital are elective, even more important than any imposed by blood or tradition. This is re-created and re-invested social capital rather than social capital received and hoarded. Trends of social capital formation within the family are strikingly similar to those in neighborhood communities, the workplace, and associations. In family ties as elsewhere, a distinction appears clearly between the less privileged, for whom the family is above all else a protective haven—self-centered, segmented social capital—and the more privileged, for whom it is also, and sometimes primarily, a stepping-stone for personal advancement in the wider society—bridging, other-oriented social capital.

SOCIAL CAPITAL IN THE PUBLIC DOMAIN

How can such private social capital irrigate networks of public social capital? This depends greatly on the form and dynamics of the public domain. I shall first examine public order—no public domain can exist without it. I shall then deal with the values (religious, moral, civic) that motivate individuals to enter the public domain. I shall conclude with an analysis of political attitudes and conduct: institutional perception, electoral behavior and other forms of direct action.

Public Order in Question

The greatest threat to the social tie does not come from organized crime, which is stabilized and contained at a level without danger to civil peace (about 65 offenses per 1,000 inhabitants per year). It comes, rather, from minor delinquency and incivility, which create a sense of insecurity and diminish trust in others—an essential ingredient of social capital.

If violence polarizes fear, feelings of insecurity emanate from the attacks on personal property that constitute the vast majority of misdemeanors. Such misdemeanors have considerably increased in the last fifteen years, whereas physical threats and violent acts remain a minute fraction of offenses.

Since trust represents the core value of social capital, it is clear that feelings of insecurity can have a devastating effect on social capital formation. Feelings of insecurity do not necessary mean real insecurity. Statistics show that feelings of insecurity depend less on reality of experience or of the risk of being the victim of a misdemeanor than on the degree of social isolation of the putative victim. The more one owns, the more there is risk of one's property being attacked, yet feelings of insecurity diminish with wealth; the more one is absent from one's home, the more one's property is at risk, yet those who stay at home are more frightened of being robbed.

Feelings of insecurity also depend greatly on social proximity to perpetrators of petty misdemeanors and civil disorder. Such disorder has exploded during the years of crisis among the unemployed young from derelict suburbs, including destruction of letter boxes, graffiti, littering, loud noise, aggressive, and deliberate rudeness, all acts targeted at symbols of social order and social ties. Within deprived social groups, the young show a higher rate of civil misdemeanor and adults a higher degree of feelings of insecurity. The civil disorder they create works against their own people, destroying what remains of seriously damaged social capital.

When socioeconomic circumstances do not allow easy conversion of private, narrow, self-centered networks of sociability into wider, other-oriented social capital and when the intermediary supporting structures of social capital (associations, organized local communities, the work market, families) cannot fulfill a bridging function toward the public arena, those who feel excluded from access to social and civic participation will often turn their energy precisely against those failing channels of integration.

The public is apparently aware of the vicious circle of social capital destruction, as evidenced by their expectations regarding the relevant public institutions. There can be no clearer indication of the importance attached to problems of insecurity than the choice of public policies considered most appropriate to solve them:

- Law and order (with an additional demand for greater visibility and proximity)
- Education and economic development (jointly, as great expectations reside in the school system to solve employment problems, although it is also criticized for failure to do so)
- Social solidarity (the public appears to see no contradiction between the widely held idea that the unemployed should be responsible for finding work and the value attached to greater solidarity with victims of exclusion and support for a more redistributive tax system)

The general public understands problems of insecurity to be problems of social cohesion and demands institutions capable of consolidating the integrating functions of social capital. It also puts great trust in such institutions; the European Value Surveys suggest that institutions inspiring a great deal of trust include the police, the social security system, schools, big business, and the rule of law.

Toward a Secular Religion?

Religion has traditionally been the central glue of all societies. Is this still the case? Religion refers both to churches and, more generally, to religious belief. In France, as in the rest of Europe, churches have been shaken to their foundations and beliefs are changing.

France, along with Italy, Spain, Portugal, Ireland, and Belgium, is part of that Mediterranean and western fringe of Europe where Catholicism is nearly exclusive. Protestants are 2 percent of declared believers, Muslims recently moved just above them at 2 percent, Jews are 1 percent, and Buddhists and other denominations are 0.5 percent.

Among European Catholic countries, France is by far the least religious, and it is among the least religious altogether in the whole of Europe, Protestant countries included, with the largest minority of self-declared atheists and a majority declaring they never or almost never attend a religious service. Nor are the French prepared to have the church venture beyond its religious territory. France is the most secular country on the Continent, and religion itself is undergoing a process of secularization, akin to the Scandinavian model where religious values pervade all aspects of civil society but religious institutional practice is very low.

Popular estrangement from the church is increasing. As in the rest of Europe, there is an accelerated shift toward de-Christianization, measured in terms of trust in the church, belief in God or religious practice. The young are less religious than their elders, and both groups are less religious than their corresponding cohorts ten years earlier.

While France and the rest of Europe are becoming less religious, they are not abandoning spirituality or moral values. The quest for substitute spiritual values is manifest in the rise of belief in life after death and in the massive increase in belief in such phenomena as astrology, telepathy, soothsaying, spiritism, clairvoyance, and magic. However, three minority religions, Islam, Judaism, and Buddhism, are on the increase among native-born French citizens, perhaps because these religions are less hierarchical than Christian religions, especially Catholicism. Should this be so, it would show that estrangement from religion is targeted at institutions, not at spiritual values.

French religious beliefs and practices suggest complementary insights. Only a minority believe God is a "person"; the majority prefer to think of God as a "kind of spirit or vital force," and a large minority declare that they are "not sure what to think," revealing the rise of what has been termed "probabilism."

While 57 percent declare that they believe in God, only one out of four believes the existence of God gives meaning to life, death or suffering. For the majority of Christians it is here and now, on earth, that a search must be made for such meaning.

Changes in religious practice clearly indicate that relativist skepticism and worldliness now dominate the Christian scene. Church attendance is on the wane except for marriages, funerals and, less often, christenings—ceremonies where public demonstration of a social and symbolic tie linking a community is clearly more important than relation to God. This is further proof of the secularization of religion. Even these "social" religious ceremonies are diminishing, especially christenings: while 92 percent of children born in 1958 were christened, only 64 percent of those born in 1987 were christened.

Finally, Catholicism and other faiths are undergoing an amazing process of fragmentation: there are several Catholicisms, Buddhisms, Judaisms and Islamisms. Many accept this fragmentation in the name of the equal value of each denomination and understand that one can select elements from this huge supermarket of beliefs to compose a unique personal religious identity, a manifestation of one's personal freedom and responsibility.

Basic cultural traits already observed in other areas reappear in religious beliefs and practices. Within such practices, we see strong attachments to sociability and community identity, and rejection of institutions and doctrines that would impose meaning from above. The majority of believers will accept ties to God only if they have freely chosen the ties. With religious institutions rapidly waning, what remains of religion is primarily its role in social capital formation—not institutionalized predetermined social capital, but individually created social capital. Privatization of religious social capital is in keeping with secularization of religion.

Public Moral and Civic Values

Less religious but not less spiritual, France has not seen a decline in moral and civic values, though significant changes have also occurred in these realms. The first dominant tendency observed in religious life is true also of civil life: Any moral rule imposed from above is rejected, regardless of its origin. Personal responsibility has replaced all outside prescription. According to the European Value Surveys, a majority prefer pragmatic personal morality to any predetermined line of conduct. Two out of three reject the idea that there can be "a clear guiding line to know what is good and what is bad," and nearly all agree that "the meaning of life is to get the most out of it."

This individualized and pragmatic notion of moral values is reflected most in personal habits. Personal lifestyle choice is generally accepted, reflecting the triumph of moral values propounded by the generation of the sixties; general acceptance of a great diversity in lifestyles is probably where May '68 has made its deepest mark. However, generalization has blunted its original libertarian, subversive impact. The crisis generation of today has learned caution and moderation in judgment and behavior.

The combination of all these elements results in striking homogeneity of moral values among the great majority of those between 18 and 45, who exhibit calm, serene, moral liberalism and unaggressive modernism. This group is large and homogeneous enough to shape France's contemporary moral culture.

Another striking feature of this move toward greater homogeneity of attitudes among different generations can be observed in the civic orientation in favor of radical as opposed to gradual reforms. Choice in favor of radical reforms increased as the crisis years unfolded after the 1973 oil shock, but it appeared less and less determined by age and more and more by handicap on the labor market as manifested by lack of qualifications. Whereas in 1978 radicalism was vindicated more often by the young, especially the well-educated young, by 1991, it was vindicated by the less qualified, the well-educated young and old having become proponents of moderate gradual changes. The radicals of today are no longer the privileged youth but members of the underclass, young and old, a fact already noticed when analyzing work-associated capital.[14]

The moral values of personal responsibility are in tune with those of economic liberalism, free enterprise, and personal achievement. Nevertheless, tension has appeared within this modernist set of values: materialist orientations giving priority to values of economic achievement were opposed to postmaterialist orientations giving priority to values of cultural achievement, civic liberty, political participation, social solidarity, human rights, and respect for nature. These two rival moral orientations developed simultaneously during the crisis years, propelled by the same social group of young, educated, upper-middle-class citizens, with postmaterialist values slowly gaining ground.

These normative orientations present a complex picture of civic values: The primacy of the private domain is undoubtedly the dominant feature of the general picture. Whereas trust in family and friends is at an apex and still rising, trust in anonymous others is weak and diminishing.[15]

The majority of citizens now demand that clear and strict moral and civic values be firmly reasserted as permanent references for the public domain, trusting neither the inherent virtue of fellow citizens nor that of any institution to provide moral guidelines for society, even questioning the capacity and legitimacy of the latter to do so.

Three levels of public morality stand out from the European Value Surveys and other surveys:

- The first level comprises those in our immediate vicinity and is marked by rich interpersonal relations, a great deal of trust, exchanges, reciprocity, and cooperation—in short, a lot of social capital but of the self-centered kind, limited in time and location, and excessively fragmented.
- The second level comprises neighborhoods farther away where daily social activities take place—a disjointed and deregulated environment encouraging a general free-for-all of "me first and now" individuals fending for themselves and for instant satisfaction of their demands at the collectivity's expense. Public morality is low at this level, with considerable petty corruption and distortion of civic and moral codes, such as use of influence to gain illegitimate favor, jumping lines, cheating when and if possible, parking where forbidden, and working on the side, all justified because of the difficulties of life. This is where constant erosion of all types of social capital occurs.
- The third level is where the creation of values and universal principles of collective life are rooted, and where human rights and solidarity above all have attained unparalleled approval during the crisis. An ever-increasing majority absolutely condemns uncivic behavior affecting fundamental moral values and infringement of basic principles of social organization. Moral censure has regularly increased for cheating in elections, swindling the social security system, and evading taxes. Thus we see a clear sign of societal aspirations for high standards of civic morality that belie the petty civic amorality of everyday behavior in the public domain. These aspirations are a rich but dormant source of social capital, untapped for lack of suitable open public institutions.

Herein lies the central problem of a "missing link" between the third level of basic civic values, all the brighter on the horizon because untried, and the networks of mutual trust and high sociability at the first level, which cannot connect with each other or with institutional networks. Effective mediation between the lower and higher levels of French society is missing—this is a common failure of bridging social capital structures and of political institutions.

Political Institutions

Trust in political institutions is at historic lows. The parliament, administration, and political parties are among the least trusted institutions in the nation and continue to lose public trust and esteem.

France's political parties are losing members and public respect for many reasons, some of which are directly related to their role as a mediating link between citizens and the state that serves to convert local social capital into national civic capital. Their ideology, their form of organization, and the demands they make on their members are in total contradiction with the way citizens of today relate to politics and society. In theory, the French model of a mass political party (a party with a large number of organized activists) requires every concrete political demand and daily action to be referred to a global purpose and ideological framework defining the ideal society, the derived "correct" concepts, a hierarchical mode of organization, and precise rules of behavior of members. This model could not be in more direct contrast to the piecemeal, autonomous, issue-oriented approach favored by citizens today. Active, concerned citizens will be less tempted than ever to act through a political party unless fundamental changes occur in their organization and their relation to society.

Graduates of the Ecole Nationale d'Administration (ENA) and members of other elite corporate bodies of the civil service have achieved positions of power in all parties likely to govern, as well as in parliament, government, public administration, and big business. Arrogantly imbued with the certainly of their superior knowledge, they are accused of being deaf to the wishes and problems of citizens and incapable of solving them.

The public image of parliamentarians is even lower than that of political parties; they encounter the same criticisms as all political institutions (that they are distant, indifferent, impotent, arrogant), with two specific criticisms added: absenteeism and corruption at the local government level.

The judiciary inspired great expectations as it confronted political corruption and financial scandals, which were all the more disruptive because of the social difficulties the country was experiencing at the time. Proportionate disappointment ensued. Suspected of inefficiency, servility and bias, the judiciary is among the most discredited of all public institutions; it is also where reform is thought to be particularly urgent.

Practically all political institutions are subject to an extremely high degree of criticism and mistrust. Citizens feel that they are badly represented and badly governed. What appears to be disinterest in politics is actually rejection of dysfunctioning institutions and of the conduct of their self proclaimed servants.

A Highly Critical Electorate

The behavior of France's electorate confirms its political disenchantment. Abstention did not rise significantly over a long period since the beginning of the Fifth Republic (1958), although it has increased in recent elections. The number of protest votes is more significant by far, indicating a true crisis of electoral representation. In recent years extremist parties opposing basic values of pluralist democracy have received a significant fraction of the vote (up to 15 percent for the National Front). The number of votes for candidates with no hope of being elected, such as independent candidates or the candidates of very small parties, has also grown. Taken together, the votes for extremist candidates and unelectable candidates plus spoiled votes and deliberate abstentions add up to the number of votes necessary for a parliamentary majority. The consequence of this is that France, with a tradition of relatively high electoral participation, is now in a position of electing a parliamentary majority representing a minority of the electorate.

These negative voting patterns are not the sign of a lack of interest in politics; in fact, all opinion polls point the other way, indicating a very high level of information and interest. Continued dissatisfaction with elected representatives could provide a dangerous breeding ground for an extremist party. It is a clear signal from an active, critical and dissatisfied electorate, certainly not a sign of passivity.

Volatility is another clear sign of this discrepancy. A week before the parliamentary election of 1997, one-third of the electorate who said they planned to vote did not yet know for whom they were going to vote. The amount of increase in this electoral "nomadism" from one election to the next has surprised commentators, but this is no sign of incoherent conduct. Rather, it is the result of two phenomena: the fact that the existing political parties are less and less representative of important options facing the nation, and the fact that citizens are increasingly independent from political parties and want to elaborate their own political identity.

The referendum on the Maastricht treaty clearly illustrates the first point. Analyzing yes and no votes, a survey presented a contrasting picture of two coherent sets of political values and of two typified electorates. None of the distinctions reflected those between political parties.

The increased degree of autonomy of citizens and their versatile voting patterns combine three factors: a situation where the choices political parties offer are less and less relevant to the issues that concern the electorate, better-informed voters, and a desire for greater personal autonomy instigated by the same basic cultural values operating in all other areas. Structurally and functionally, political representation is ever more at odds with the nature of problems facing the nation and the choice they require as well as with the civic aspirations and potential of the electorate. A great deal of the social capital abroad in society remains untapped by political institutions of our democracy.

Active Citizenship on the Rise

Discontent with political institutions and critical and undisciplined electoral conduct do not indicate disinterest in politics. Rather, they reveal a craving for politics of another type, illustrated by rising involvement in forms of direct participation in politics.

The European Value Surveys note a significant rise in various forms of direct political action such as petitions, boycotts, and street demonstrations. The degree of French dissatisfaction with institutional politics is illustrated by the fact that France scores highest on all these counts.

Recent social conflicts and street demonstrations confirm these observations. Unions seem unable to control industrial or social conflicts, whether their outbreak, strategy, extension, or termination. Initiative always escapes them; "coordinations," or ad hoc coordinating institutions, emerge in their place. Unions and employers may even be targeted together in grievances. These "coordinations" are established by leaders who appear in the forefront of a conflict because of their active personal involvement and who generally fade into anonymity once the conflict has ended. Defense of narrow corporate interests is often the initial detonator of a conflict; but action succeeds only when it reaches beyond specific grievances and mobilizes public support on wider social issues colored with moral value (e.g., equal access to medical protection or to public services).

Other recent protests are even more illuminating. In 1997, people staged a protest against legislation by a previous minister of the interior that tightened conditions of entry and stay in France for immigrants, tightened police controls, increased general insecurity of immigrants, and threatened vital civil liberties; in 1996 they staged a protest against the National Front congress in Strasbourg. The large crowds at these events were not the customary ones seen in political demonstrations. While left-wing parties were hardly present, a great number of small local associations active on new social issues were there, along with many citizens who did not belong to any organization at all. A study of Parisian participation showed wide attendance by the educated upper middle class between 18 and 45 years of age, identified here as sharing postmaterialist values.

A link was established in Paris between these active civil and social rights associations and some traditional human rights associations such as the Human Rights League, but there were only very slight connections with unions or political parties, and none with the city government. Bridges have yet to be built between established institutions and networks of political and social representation and the emerging civic forces of active citizens motivated by exacting moral values. In Strasbourg, by contrast, in spite of unavoidable tensions, communication channels were established with city institutional networks. Perhaps the unusual profile of the mayor was a help: Strasbourg had the only female mayor of a large city, and she was a graduate of a Protestant theological seminary—not the typical French local *notable*. It is often on a political system's periphery that future central forms of political capital have to be experimented.

CONCLUSIONS

It is clear that France is suffering not from an all-around collapse of its social capital, nor from generalized political disaffiliation. Rather, it is going through a double crisis.

One aspect of this is a crisis of social redistribution of income and employment. A growing underclass is increasingly dissociated from a worried and shaken majority of participants in the process of modernization. In a society culturally more homogeneous than ever before, where modernist liberal values of personal autonomy and responsibility have gained unquestioned hegemony, sharing cognitive moral and civic references with the majority renders social and civic exclusion all the more painful for this growing minority.

The other aspect is a crisis of political representation, mediation, and regulation. Good government by an enlightened elite imposing on an immature citizenry a "general interest" embodied in the administrative rules and procedures of the state was historically the remarkably successful distinction of the French republican model. Now this has become its weakest feature. Not only are citizens less ready to accept this form of tutelage and more capable of doing without it, but the mediating institutions—unions, parties, local governments, and even large associations—have become so absorbed by their privileged access to the state, so analogous to the state in their type of organization, that they have become impervious to citizens' demands and greatly disqualified as proper vehicles for existing or potential social capital—the "missing link" syndrome.

These two crises are interconnected. France, however, has a number of assets—material, cultural, and political—that might be useful in an attempt to solve them.

On the material side are France's economic assets. Having come through the colossal and successful postwar effort of urbanization and industrialization, France has the capacity to enter the third industrial revolution with most of the painful work already done. Also on the material side is France's demographic dynamism. France has been, since the war and until recently, among the countries with the highest birthrate in Europe. Very little would be required for it to start again—future perspectives able to stimulate the desire of citizens to participate in the construction of their collective future with the benefit of the participation of a young immigrant population endowed with great cultural and demographic dynamism.

Among France's cultural assets is the fact that a modernist cultural revolution has been practically accomplished. A new set of values, presenting great homogeneity, is shared by most French citizens as well as by a majority in the European Union. This common set of values has three supporting pillars: personal autonomy and responsibility, economic initiative, social justice, solidarity, and cohesion.

Other cultural factors that might provide a resource for addressing these twin crises include the constructive dynamic tension that is at work between two versions of individualism at the core of cultural modernity. Particularist individualism is a move toward a selfish and frightened protection of private identities and interests against all possible encroachments, and it breeds not only the culture of the "me now" society but the National Front "national preference" policy and even the more respectable "nationalist" political forces. Slowly gaining ground against this is a universalist individualism, in which the assertion of personal choice in lifestyle and social and political orientations implies recognizing that right for others and a common involvement in active and personalized citizenship. It also implies elaboration of a common set of universal values for democratic institutional practice, social cohesion, and economic development. These humanitarian postmaterialist values would offer a good basis for such a democratic revival if disentangled from the 1960s utopia of a paradisiacal apolitical and metahistorical world community with no need for institutional regulation.

France's political assets include a population with significant civic potential. A relatively large group of citizens is prepared to invest in political renovation, evidenced by the creativity and dynamism present in associations and in civic events. They can be activated by the historical opportunity provided by the construction of a new Europe, a project that has sufficient dimensions to fire citizens' imagination and sense of purpose and to offer a perspective of exciting new social and democratic investments. Too, France's citizens appear to be far more open to change than has been previously surmised. The French incapacity to negotiate necessary changes democratically has been frequently noted and analyzed, and it has been asserted that social upheavals are the only way to make a path for change. However, this appears to be far more the result of institutional dysfunction than of cultural blockage—more the responsibility of the elite than of the ordinary citizen.

The priority seems to lie in institutional reform. It is urgent to forge links between the civic energy and social capital that are at the very foundations of French society and the rich stock of universal cultural values shared by most citizens. This involves developing links in the following areas:

- Between areas and processes of exclusion and those of inclusion (school and professional training, employment, housing, local government)
- Between minority cultures and communities (especially immigrant populations) and institutions of the host country
- Between new aspirations for personal development and all types of organizations and forms of collective action (business enterprise, unions, parties, associations)
- Between large and small associations, old and new ones, and between them and public institutions
- Most of all, between citizens and the state, between the untapped wealth of civic energy and capability and the dwindling legitimacy and efficiency of public institutions, between representative and participative democracy

Knitting new social ties in all these areas involves the building of bridges between old and new, between civil society and political institutions, between social capital in the making and long-established networks of social capital, and between the new culture of postmaterialist, universalist individualism and political democratic individualism. This social engineering project is the new frontier common to France and the rest of Europe.

To sum up, the French case suggests tentative answers to the three questions posed early in this chapter. The first question concerned the relation between the social capital of the primary group and that of global society. Contrary to the general assumption that they increase or decrease together, the French case shows a simultaneous process of growth of inner-oriented, self-centered primary group social capital and of reduction of other-oriented bridging and institutionally linked social capital. In other words, a low level of bridging social capital and of institutionally linked social capital does not automatically produce less primary group social capital, and indeed can result in the exact opposite.

The second question, related to the opposition between received and created social capital, requires a similar answer. Received social capital, embodied in many existing networks and norms of French society, seems increasingly irrelevant to citizens' emerging demands, attitudes, mores, and capabilities, and even more so to emerging social problems. While such social capital is waning for lack of use, many signs point to compensating dynamics that are creating new social capital in new areas and in new forms. One phenomenon obviously feeds on the other. But a new question arises: How does one convert newly created social capital into established offered social capital, since the latter is necessary, because of its greater visibility and permanence, for transmission of social capital from one generation to the next and for continuity of a society?

The third question relates to the respective roles of state and civil society in the production of social capital. Civil society is clearly undergoing a process of emancipation from the tutelage of the state in France. This is the source of a serious crisis in the public arena, as the instruments of social and political representation, including those of public regulation and government, forged in the traditional republican model, seem inadequate to channel the mounting forces of a more mature civil society into a new republican synthesis. This raises a new question for France: How can the country avoid opposing the relative inertia of public institutions to the dynamics of civil society and instead use the latter to revivify the former? How can the greater autonomy of civil society irrigate and enhance the democratic quality and economic performance of political institutions in a representative democracy? This is both a very old question and a very contemporary challenge everywhere, without a really satisfactory answer anywhere.

5

A DECLINE OF
SOCIAL CAPITAL? The German Case

**CLAUS OFFE
AND SUSANNE FUCHS**

There is no evident decline of social capital in Germany, or so we shall argue. But any such proposition is entirely contingent on the conceptualization employed, the measurement applied, and the available data.

SOCIAL CAPITAL: A CONCEPTUAL EXPLORATION

Social capital is conceptualized here as a collectively owned resource of local, regional, and national societies or segments thereof. This resource can vary as to the amount that is available; it can be smaller or greater, grow or decline. If a high amount of this collective capacity or resource is available and widely dispersed throughout a society, the returns are hypothesized to consist in the desirable effects of economic performance and "good government." This favorable effect is due to the fact that social capital, by definition, includes all those behavioral dispositions that help to reduce transaction costs (e.g., trust relations facilitate exchange) and to overcome the undersupply of public goods that results from the propensity to be a free rider (benefit from the collective efforts of others without contributing). Also, a dense network of associational activities is likely to unburden state and local governments. Variations of the level of political and economic performance across time and space can thus be explained, at least in part, in terms of the level and dispersion of social capital. The presence of social capital helps to make democracy work.[1]

However, it remains to be determined what the unit of ownership of collective capital is—a national society, a region, a city, a generation, a cohort, a socioeconomic category, or whatever. At any rate, it appears sociologically naive to assume that national societies are internally uniform and externally distinctive concerning their social capital levels. The same applies to regions and other subnational territorial units. Thus we need to determine what kind of unit or social category is the bearer of social capital.

The first problem we need to come to terms with is how to measure levels of social capital. We need operational indicators, or at least finer-grained conceptual components of social capital for the overall measurement that we can apply to the data available. We propose to use three such components: *associability, trust,* and *attention.* Taken together, they allow us to assess the complex set of attitudes, behavioral dispositions, and structural patterns that together make up what the theoretical variable social capital stands for.

Attention refers to a set of thoughts and opinions concerning social and political life. When we monitor what is going on or how others are doing, or are attentive to collective conditions, we display attention of this kind. The object of attention is anything belonging to public affairs in the widest possible sense. Attention, as we use the concept here, focuses upon the material well-being, moral conduct, personal development, esthetic qualities, and other features of the conditions of life of some collectivity—not necessarily of "everyone else," but still of a diffuse number of people who are considered fellow citizens and are perceived as belonging to a shared political community.

Attention in this sense, and taken by itself, is a property of individuals that does not necessarily involve any disposition toward actively caring for others or engaging in associative action within the political community. It just means being sensitive to the quality of public life, including symbolic practices affecting it, rather than turning a blind eye to whatever does not affect oneself. Attention is thus a rather weak disposition, as it does not automatically result in active involvement in associative life beyond the use of print and electronic media. But being attentive can also be a more or less bindingly prescribed moral and social norm (such as the norm that one does not start eating before everyone has been served). At any rate, attention appears to be a necessary cognitive precondition of any more activist form of civic responsibility. The opposite of attention is the cognitive condition of ignorance, indifference, and opportunistic belief formation.

Second is *trust*. Here we want to distinguish "thin" and "thick" varieties. Thin trust is just the absence of fear and suspicion concerning the likely behavior of (relevant) others. Categorical distrust and universalized resentment stand in the way of even thin trust. If a person anticipates hostile encounters, a breach of privacy, deception, unreliable or dishonest behavior, or similar kinds of risk (including that of ending up in the "sucker" position due to others' refusal to cooperate) as a likely experience to be expected from the interaction with strangers, not even the criteria of the thin version of trust are fulfilled. An obstacle to such interaction may also result from an agent's lack of trust in herself or himself, that is, the absence of confidence that one can cope with others and sustain interaction with them. The absence of the thin version of trust may also result from the strongly individualistic perception that trusting others may involve, as a rule, the missing of valued opportunities.

In contrast, the thick version of trust is present not only if a person holds the optimistic belief that most people are good-natured and benevolent most of the time and that, as a consequence, joining in a given activity is harmless in terms of both direct and opportunity costs, but also if there is reason to expect mutual intrinsic as well as instrumental benefits from cooperation with other people. The thin version of trust can be thought of as the necessary condition of one's willingness to join informal networks or formal associations and the thick version as the sufficient condition.[2] The latter is represented by the belief that joining with others is either intrinsically attractive (i.e., by yielding process benefits) or leads to desirable outcomes.

Finally, *associability* connotes one's actual engagement in informal networks or formal associations, such as sports clubs, environmental networks, religious associations, nongovernmental organizations (NGOs), or social movements. We wish, in order to be on the safe side, to define the types of associations that indicate the presence of social capital rather narrowly, thus excluding a number of phenomena (such as, on one hand, large-scale formal organizations and, on the other, primordial groups of families and relatives) that are conventionally subsumed under the general concept of collective actors. We return to these subdivisions of types of collective agents in a moment.

We expect to find positive (as well as possibly also negative) interrelations to prevail among our three components of social capital. Active membership can have a positive influence on attention, as the cause around which an association is organized will sharpen the awareness of its members concerning events and conditions relevant to this cause. Inversely, a strong subjective sense of relevance and corresponding level of attention concerning aspects of public life will facilitate the decision to join with like-minded others—at least unless attention gives rise to suspicion and distrust. Furthermore, people with a strong sense of trust (in either of its versions) will find the barrier to associative involvement easy to overcome, be it for the primary motive of the "pleasure of belonging" and interacting with others or for the relevance they attach to the goals and practices of particular associations, with the latter being a likely by-product of the taste-shaping and attention-directing impact of membership itself.[3] Finally, we assume that active membership has a positive influence on trust in either of its two versions, although the absence of even the thin version of trust will be a powerful obstacle to joining an association voluntarily. (Note that some forms of acting together, such as school classes, are typically not joined on the basis of a deliberate decision.) These assumed interrelations serve to highlight the fact that a society's associability—the number of associations that exist in it (or in a part thereof) at a given point in time, and the number of people that belong to them through voluntary membership—is an indicator of the presence of civic cooperative dispositions as well as a generator of such dispositions, as associations have the capacity to nurture and strengthen the very same dispositions to which they owe their existence.

However, not every type of (nominally voluntary) membership in any type of association constitutes a reasonably safe indicator of social capital. In order to avoid a systematic overestimate of social capital as indicated by membership, we wish to focus upon a type of membership and association that can safely be assumed to indicate (as well as generate) the collective quality that is summarily termed "social capital." In order to do so, we eliminate from the universe of associative forms of social life in which people can be or become members a number of types in order to arrive at a reasonably discriminating indicator. For the sake of convenience, we subdivide this universe of associative forms into primary, secondary, and tertiary ones, with secondary associative patterns being the only ones serving our purpose. We proceed then by providing reasons as to why the first and the third of these forms or patterns of association are not suitable as indicators (or accumulators) of social capital. The sociological typology of types and patterns of collective action is based upon the combination of two dimensions: Goals can be (relatively) fixed or variable, and membership status can be rigidly fixed or easily acquired and abandoned (see Figure 5-1).

Figure 5-1: A Typology of Forms of Collective Action

goals \ membership	fixed, hierarchically controlled	variable, contingent upon participants
fixed through inclusion/ exclusion	(mostly illegal) gangs, conspiracies	self-identified ethnic groups
variable, voluntary	firms, associations, political parties	civic associations, clubs

Primary associations include those involving family, kinship, ethnicity, and religion (see Figure 5-2, cell 2).[4] Most cases in this category of membership and belonging are, as far as their structure is concerned, nonvoluntary, or primordial. They are thought of and treated as constituted by blood, unquestionable tradition, or family descent and are inherently exclusive of strangers as well as automatically inclusive of non-strangers—thus being diametrically opposed to the egalitarian and open principles of civility, citizenship, and optional membership. This inclusiveness (precluding the exit option) and potentially even hostile exclusiveness (precluding the entry of strangers) also applies to marriage, which is, according to prevailing social and legal norms, a voluntary contractual constitution of a lasting exclusive relation between two persons. Sometimes this suggestion of irrevocable and exclusive belonging is employed metaphorically, as in the case of Mafia "families" (which in fact illustrate the hybrid of strategic goals and fixed membership; see Figure 5-1, cell 1).[5] The mutual obligations the members, or various categories of members, owe each other are typically different from those fulfilled in interaction with strangers. They are inspired by the particularistic sentiments of love, sympathy, and faithfulness to mandates of identity and tradition, rather than by a commitment to universal principles. Through whatever mechanism, crossing the border of membership (including that of an ethnically defined nationhood) in either direction is made impossible, dangerous, or deviant within such primordial associative patterns. This is one of their defining characteristics.

The other characteristic is the fact that primordial associative patterns are diffuse in their goals. There is no purpose (other than the maintenance of the associative pattern itself) that they have set for themselves and that they can pursue at the expense of other and potentially rival purposes. Families and other primordial groups are not founded for the purpose of achieving a particular objective. In contrast to enterprises and bureaucracies, they are functionally diffuse and can come to serve a broad and unspecified variety of purposes. This does not exclude the possibility that purposive associations emerge that are parasitic upon primordial ties, such as a family business, an ethnically circumscribed branch of trade or industry, or an association restricted to members of a particular religious community. Among the offshoots of primordial collectives, there may be also instances that would belong to our category of secondary associations (see below), such as ethnic folk dance clubs or charitable associations.

Tertiary associations include firms, interest associations, and political parties (see Figure 5-1, cell 3). In many respects, the common characteristics of these forms of cooperation are the reverse of the primary type. They have *fixed goals* and *variable membership*, and they must be able to vary their membership when necessary to meet their strategic goals.[6] They depend, for the sake of accomplishing their goals, upon replacing less productive workers with more productive ones, or upon winning new members. Again, citizenship is alien to the logic of this associative pattern, as membership is conditional upon their suitability, ability, or willingness to contribute to the good that the association is premised upon—be it profit, the promotion of some categorical interest, or political power. The medium of communication that ties members to the association is typically not spoken information, but rather written information and, most important, money—be it in the form of members of an interest association paying dues or in the form of a company paying wages in exchange for productive services performed. The predominance of the organization's purpose over its membership is typically provided for through a hierarchical structure of managers and officers whose mandate is to see to it, through the use of formal authority and control, that as much as possible of the members' activity does actually turn into contributions to goal attainment and as little as possible friction (potentially amounting to the phenomena of strikes or organized dissent) occurs in the process. Thus the members' activity is rather narrowly circumscribed by assigned function and hierarchical control.

However, these strategic forms of association can give rise to associative patterns that belong to our secondary type (see below).[7] For instance, workers of a company can form a club in order to pursue recreational activities. Even the company's management can initiate such associative activities as part of its labor relations or public relations strategy (as in the case of a company-sponsored soccer team), according to much the same logic that leads political parties to sponsor neighborhood festivities as part of their mobilization strategy. The history of left-ist political parties in particular is rich in examples of how capillary associative structures (appealing to members of occupational groups, that is, those interested in music, gardening, theater, sports, debating, neighborhood issues, women's and youth issues, etc., all belonging to cell 4 in Figure 5-1) have been formed, encouraged, and subsidized by strategic tertiary associations.

A problem of conceptual distinction is posed by the phenomenon of church organizations. On one hand, they are large-scale, hierarchical organizations that pursue, in addition to their theological mission, a variety of political and economic purposes. On the other hand, they encourage and give rise to a great variety of associative practices in which members (and possibly also nonmembers) can get involved. In the latter case, they represent a framework or stage of what we call "nested" associability, similar in its organizational structure to the company soccer club or the local chapter of a political party.

Secondary or civic associations are defined, as far as goals and objectives are concerned, by an intermediary position between the two types discussed so far (see Figure 5-1, cell 4). That is to say, their purposive orientation is not as diffuse as that of families and similar communities, but also not as specific as in tertiary formal organizations (compare Figure 5-2). They differ from the latter in that they never strive for profit through the marketing of their services, nor for the acquisition of formal positions of political power. Rather than having a goal that can be achieved through strategic action, civic associations have just a domain, such as sports, music, philanthropy, education, or political mobilization. They are expected by their members to be durable common concerns, not just single-purpose and short-term episodes of cooperation, such as communal weekend excursions. The specific goals, plans, and projects that are to be pursued in the association's activities are determined through the interaction of members, with the organizational hierarchy being either absent or comparatively flat and a fully professional staff of leaders and administrators being a rare exception. Every active member can relatively easily involve himself or herself in the goal-setting process. And the results of this process can oscillate widely between activities that are either entirely and exclusively for the internal consumption by members (such as in clubs) or, at the other extreme, designed to serve or influence a wider public (e.g., choral societies performing public concerts, social and political movements, parent-teacher associations).[8]

Concerning the composition and recruitment of members, civic associations are guided, according to our conceptualization, by the egalitarian principle of citizenship, a condition that is as distant from familial intimacy as it is from the functional anonymity of formal organizations. Civic associations are considerably more open, that is, easily accessible to outsiders who wish to join, than families and other identity-based communities, although we should expect to find a mixture of functional as well as identity-related admission criteria. For instance, an association devoting itself to the performance of chamber music will require its members to have some proficiency in playing a musical instrument, and youth groups, women's groups, and religious groups will normally restrict membership to those actually belonging to these social categories. Sometimes membership status is divided between active and supporting members, as in sports clubs. In spite of these restrictions, the civic nature of associations manifests itself in their being open to the admission of all qualified members, and admission is denied on the basis of abstract criteria, not *ad personam*.

Finally, concerning the *mode of interaction* between the association and its individual members, it is less formalized and less stringent than in either families (with their cement of strong passions, such as love, care, sympathy, or commitment to a religious belief or allegiance to strong traditions) or tertiary associations (kept together by purposive considerations of interest and relying mostly on written language—beginning with registration forms or written labor contracts—plus monetary interests). In contrast, both the level and kind of the involvement of members in clubs, movements, networks, church groups, local chapters of political parties, and the like is variable and unregulated. Such associations rely on voluntary engagement and also must be tolerant of temporary nonparticipation and noncontribution of members, and they make use of a variety of forms of involvement ranging from monetary contributions and involvement in planning debates to organizational help and active performance of the services on which the association specializes. In contrast to tertiary associations, civic associations rely strongly on horizontal oral communication, rather than written communication or hierarchically mediated oral communication.

Thus civic associations represent the unique combination of relatively diffuse and contingent operational programs that are to be continuously defined within the association's substantive domain and a similarly contingent membership that allows (with or without categorical restriction of access) strangers to cooperate for shared values and interests in a variety of ways. Absent from civic associations are the authoritatively defined objectives that are characteristic of tertiary formal organizations and the certainty of given members that is characteristic of

Figure 5-2: Different Types of Associations

	Primary	Secondary	Tertiary
Formalized	families, relatives	"face-to-face" associations	mailing list associations, associations of associations, firms
Not formalized	clans	new social movements, neighborhoods, informal networks	"nested associations"

families. It is this dual lack of certainty that members of civic associations must come to terms with. Indeed, instruction in the relevant skills for coping with these ambiguities and for resolving them in cooperative ways is the specific contribution of civic associations to the formation of social capital.

The activity of volunteering poses a special problem in mapping social capital. Volunteering is defined as the providing of services to recipients in need of these services that is motivated by this need and the side effects of its fulfillment alone, not primarily by material gain or instrumental considerations such as career advancement. Volunteer activities can occur both within the framework of civic associations or formal organizations and, in contrast, according to a entirely individualized pattern consisting in people helping other people outside of any associational framework. In the former case, the association itself can be the recipient of the services donated (as in the case of a person volunteering as the treasurer of a club); in the latter, the beneficiaries of these services are clients who do not belong to the association (as in the case of charitable services provided by civic associations). As all of these cases play a significant role as forms of civic engagement, and as they manifest the potential of activists for both attention and trust, we propose to include them in the broad category of social capital, although they do not necessarily, as just pointed out, involve associability.

A further case worth distinguishing within the category of civic associations is that of so-called self-help groups, which people join in order to obtain and provide help and mutual encouragement, often concerning health problems and issues of social well-being, on the basis of their own competence, experience, and (mostly) nonprofessional knowledge. Self-help groups (such as Alcoholics Anonymous) typically recruit members from those who are personally affected by the condition on which the help is meant to focus. As providing and receiving of help coincides within the membership, high levels of trust are presupposed by this type of associative activity, which leads us to include them in the broad category of generators of social capital.

Types of Civic Associations

We do not know at the present point whether a contribution to the (re)generation of social capital—and, as an indirect consequence, to economic performance and the quality of governance—is to be expected from all types of secondary civic associations alike. Neither can we deal here in any detail with the various typologies by which researchers have categorized these associations. No less than five potentially useful kinds of typologies come to mind.

- *Substantive domains.* Examples of such domains are religious, artistic, charitable, and many other concerns. We do not expect to find significant differences across these domains in terms of the "returns" on social capital (see the section "Social Capital and the Quality of Governance," below).
- *Degree of formalization of the membership role.* A typology using this criterion would range from clans, networks, and movements to highly formalized organizations with elaborate procedures of admission.[9] Again, there should not be a major difference across these types as far as the contribution to good governance and economic performance is concerned.
- *The distinction between inward-looking and outward-looking association.* The former generate collective goods of the kind of "club goods," serving exclusively their members. The latter, in contrast, also address themselves to agents outside the membership proper, be it the public in general that is to be served, educated, or influenced, or be it certain client groups or elite segments. The hypothesis is straightforward: The more outward-looking and public-regarding an association, the more it contributes to the hypothesized output of social capital (re)production.
- *The distinction between universalist associations and those that are not.* Truly universalist associations are those in which everyone is welcome; in contrast are associations that make admission contingent upon some acquired (e.g., occupational) or primordial (e.g., gender, age) property. The latter are expected to be less productive than the former.

- *The distinction between political associations and nonpolitical ones.*
  Political associations address either elites or nonelites, with a view to
  ultimately achieving some impact upon legislation and administration; nonpolitical associations have no such ambition. Again, the
  former are expected to score higher in terms of the overall impact
  on social capital, as they are supposedly more collectivity-regarding
  and less self-centered.

Mechanisms

The mechanism of social capital accumulation works in three directions.
First, in social settings where people are rich in the characteristics that
constitute associability, civic associations will be easily formed and are
likely to become a vigorous factor of public life. Second, where both
associations and the number of members are numerous, they will help
to spread these social and moral resources and encourage the dispositions that we have termed trust and attention. Third, both the presence
of these resources in itself and their spreading and reinforcement
through associational activities will yield a number of positive results
that must be seen to be a key factor in making democracy work, the
assumption here being that the skills and dispositions of initiative,
attention, trust, organizing capacities, and egalitarian attitudes as well as
toleration of strangers that are acquired and enforced within the life of
civic associations will spread beyond their respective social, substantive,
and temporal locus of origin and become a significant ingredient of a
democratic political culture, partly because the experience of the viability of civic association immunizes its members against a generalized
sense of powerlessness as well as against clientelistic expectations
addressed to a paternalistic and authoritarian state.

Effects and Functions

After having assessed, in conceptual terms, the nature of social capital,
we will now turn to its hypothetical consequences. We hypothesize that
if a given place's social capital stock is high, it will have a robust economy
and a good government. For this to be the case in a strong sense (i.e.,
social capital being both a necessary and sufficient condition of predicted desirable outcomes), two cases should not occur. First, good governance and good economic performance should not occur in the
absence of high levels of social capital; second, high levels of social capital should always be associated with favorable economic performance
and good governance. Assuming for the moment that there will be, as
expected, positive correlations between aggregate social capital levels

Figure 5-3: Social Capital—A Conceptual Framework

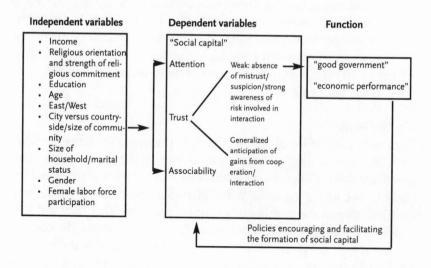

and indicators of both economic and political performance, it seems worth emphasizing that such empirical correlation also bears a bidirectional interpretation. That is to say, prosperity and good governance may contribute as much to social capital formation as the latter to the former. Good public policy (or, for that matter, good managerial strategy) can encourage, facilitate, and nurture the associative practices from which the accumulation of social capital results.

Finally, we need to understand the causal antecedents of social capital. It supposedly occurs in some strata—in some locations, regions, points in time, social and cultural milieux, religious groups, and so on—while it is absent in others. Thus we wish to check a variety of standard sociological variables concerning their impact upon the interrelated components of social capital, namely, attention, trust, and associability, as well as their combined impact upon the level of social capital and its change. The three sets of variables and their hypothetical interrelations are represented in Figure 5-3.

Not all of the questions and perspectives suggested by the conceptual map we have drawn so far can be pursued in the context of the present chapter. What we propose to focus upon are the independent variables, or causal antecedents, that determine the supply of social capital, as measured, for the practical reasons of the availability of data, predominantly in terms of attention, associability, and the willingness to volunteer (as well as the actual behavioral impact of that willingness).

DETERMINANTS OF SOCIAL CAPITAL: THE GERMAN CASE

A Decline of Associability?

We begin with a rough account of levels of associability—namely, membership in formal associations and volunteering—during the last four decades in Germany. We also try to shed some light on the situation in unified Germany after 1990 as well as on the effects of state socialist residues in the former East Germany. Here, two dimensions of the phenomenon of associability are of interest. First, how many people are actually involved at a given point in time? Second, how intense is such involvement? This latter dimension is complicated by a further distinction. On one hand, some people may participate more actively than others in a given type of association (say, a sports club). But on the other hand, associations may be subdivided according to the extent they typically presuppose active involvement, members' donation of time and other resources, and loyalty (with a religious sect probably being the extreme case of far-reaching demands an association makes upon its members).

It is the latter measure of intensity that interests us here. We assume that intensity of involvement is weakest, except for a proportionately small number of volunteer activists, in the case of dues-paying organizations such as political parties, trade unions, churches, and even automobile clubs.[10] Members in associations such as sports clubs and choral societies typically show more involvement, because these associations depend for the performance of their functions on members who do not just pay dues and receive services, but engage in active participation and donate their time, skills, and experience. Finally, the claims that associations (including informal networks) make upon the engagement of those involved in them are strongest and most demanding if (as in all cases of charitable activities) the beneficiaries of members' activities are not primarily other members (who benefit from each other's cooperation) but outside clients whom the association is designed to help, serve, assist, educate, or influence.

We now proceed to look at German trends in associability, keeping in mind the conceptual distinction just introduced. Membership in churches, political parties, and unions decreased, although not dramatically, in the course of the 1980s. In 1984, 50 percent of the citizenship of (West) Germany were registered members of the Protestant Church and 40 percent belonged to the Roman Catholic Church. In 1993, there was a drop to 45 percent for the Protestants, while the share of Catholics remained constant. At the same time, 13 percent of German citizens did not belong to any religious denomination.[11] These data, however, are strongly limited in their descriptive value, as they measure just the dues-paying (church tax) status of German citizens, not the degree of actual involvement of nominal members in religious life. Both churches, the Protestant more than the Roman Catholic, report an ongoing and steep decline in church attendance and other kinds of active religious life. Moreover, even nominal membership and dues paying has declined with unification, as only a minority (30 percent in 1993) of the population of the German Democratic Republic (GDR) belonged to a church.[12] In spite of having a strong measure of statist support, promotion, and pro-tection, Christianity's capacity for overall associational mobilization is clearly declining. That trend does not preclude, however, the capacity of both of these Christian denominations to stimulate a great variety of associative activities of a group-specific and/or issue-specific kind within their (largely nominal) membership.[13]

With regard to overall associational membership, it is safe to conclude that there is certainly not a decline, but at least a constant level of mem-bership in associations in (West) Germany over the last five decades. In 1953, 53 percent of those surveyed indicated membership in one or more voluntary associations.[14] In 1991, the figure was 58 percent,[15] and it was 55 percent in 1996 (West Germany only).[16]

These data on overall associational membership are generated by ask-ing respondents about their membership in what German law defines as a *Verein* (which refers to a range of phenomena somewhat more specific than the English term *association*). Technically, this term is restricted to *eingetragene* (registered) associations, involving some statutory pre-scribed internal structures as well as tax privileges and the license to insert the acronym *e.V.* (for *eingetragener Verein*) in its name. More col-loquially, however, *Verein* would also refer to associative activities that do not conform to these formal associational criteria. For instance, a group of people meeting regularly for bird-watching excursions may (or may not) be referred to by themselves, as well as others, as *Verein,* even if they are not technically an *e.V.* Thus, much seems to depend on the (largely unexplored) operative semantics that respondents apply in reporting their associative activities. As a consequence, when the ques-tion of membership in *Vereine* is posed (as has been routine in the sur-veys quoted above), chances are that, if anything, actual associative activities of a subformal nature are likely to remain partly underre-ported.[17]

While there is no indication that the level of associability and mem-bership has declined, changes have occurred in the distribution of such activities within the overall social structure, as well as in the type and thematic focus of associative activity. Over the last eighty or so years, the historical profile of associability in Germany seems to conform to the following pattern. In the Weimar Republic and up to the Nazi takeover of power, Germany was densely populated with associations of a markedly class-specific nature, with occupational interests, cultural pursuits, and religious affiliation being the focus of associations among both the middle class and the working class. Cultural associations (such as libraries, theater associations, and musical and choral societies) as well as interest-related associations (such as professional associations as well as adult education and training organizations) were often promoted by political parties, trade unions, cooperatives, and churches.

This rich variety of associative practices was rapidly destroyed by the Nazi regime through a policy of repression and prohibition, on one hand, and statist incorporation of societal associations with mandatory membership in state-controlled "chambers" and supervision of associative life, on the other. The erosion of the social, political, and religious basis of these associations had, however, begun well before the Nazi takeover of power in 1933—though least so within the Roman Catholic religious milieu. Roman Catholic political, cultural, and social associations even showed some capacity to immunize themselves from political repression and social erosion.[18] The Nazi regime itself (and in this respect similarly also the state socialist regime of the GDR, as both of them pursued strategies of authoritarian mobilization) relied on coerced associability, which, due to sanctions imposed for nonparticipation and positive ones for participation, led millions of people to join political, cultural, welfare, sports, paramilitary, and other mass organizations with a strong emphasis on collectivist (versus individual) concerns. This emphasis was epitomized by the slogan *"Gemeinwohl geht vor Eigennutz"* (collective welfare must take precedence over individual pursuits), adopted by both these regimes. As access to valued resources (such as subsidized vacation trips) was effectively monopolized by these state-controlled organizations, mandatory membership was strongly motivated by selfish and opportunistic reasons.

The associative structures of the interwar period, including most of the political, religious, and socioeconomic associations, were largely restored in West Germany by the 1950s. The military, economic, and moral breakdown of the Nazi regime, together with large-scale reshuffling and relocation of the postwar population and the predominance of individualist concerns with economic survival and success, meant that for some period after the war, there was a strong disinclination to join associations of any kind. The spirit of the time was proverbially captured in the defiant and highly popular phrase "*ohne mich*" (without me). Moreover, as postwar reconstruction, Western integration, and the "economic miracle" of the social market economy—the success story of the German version of welfare capitalism—evolved in the Adenauer years (1949–63), largely centripetal political forces caused the erosion of marked class divides, and socioeconomic groups lost their grip on the prevailing patterns of associability due to an apparent "end of ideology," which displaced the pattern of cleavages that followed class, political, and religious differences.[19] These developments manifested themselves, for instance, in the rapid decline of consumer cooperatives in the 1950s and their replacement by chain stores, to which people were related not as members but as customers.

A parallel change occurred in the specific purposes of associations. The 1950s saw a shift away from political concerns in the broadest sense toward a concern with leisure activities such as travel, sports, entertainment, and popular arts. The rise of ideologically amorphous leisure-related associative activities may be seen as corresponding to the substantial increase of free time that became available to average workers and citizens, beginning with the work-free Saturday being introduced in the manufacturing sector. The time spent on family-related activities has decreased with the trend toward smaller families, the increase in the amount of time children and adolescents spend outside the household, and the increase in the stock of labor-saving household appliances. To be sure, much of this increase in disposable time that occurred over the last generation is being absorbed by media consumption. But associative activities appear at least a plausible candidate for the use of some of this disposable time. It also seems to make some sense to assume that with the portion of time spent on the job decreasing, the impact that the work experience has upon extrawork (including associative) activities may also decrease, at least within broad ranges of levels of income and employment security. On the basis of this assumption, we would expect the political and ideological detachment of associations from parties, unions, and large interest associations that we actually find. On the other hand, media consumption is not the only alternative pattern of time use competing with associative activity. Take, for example, the case of physical exercise. If we suppose that the main motive for joining sports clubs is the pursuit of values such as fitness and health, we see that these clubs are faced with the competition of commercially supplied activities (e.g., fitness centers) serving the same purposes. An analogous point applies to commercial group travel. Furthermore, and as an alternative to media consumption, club membership, and the purchase of commercial services, there is also a host of leisure time activities offered by municipal adult education programs in which people can participate without joining an association.

Variations among different surveys apply also to data on volunteering, or associative activities designed to serve target groups outside of the association. Surveys from 1991–92 reported 12 million volunteers, which was 17 percent of the overall population above age 11,[20] while another survey indicated 16.4 million volunteers in West Germany, or 27 percent of the overall population above age 15 in 1994.[21] That means a 5 percent increase compared to 1985. Although these databases vary according to quality, method, and definition, they still provide a picture of the orders of magnitude involved. It seems safe to conclude that between a fifth and a sixth of the adult population participates (with varying levels of involvement) in some kind of volunteer activities. Five percent of the adult population are active in self-help groups, mostly of a health-related kind.[22] These proportions of voluntary service activisms are, if anything, not declining, and perhaps have even increased somewhat since the 1980s.

Given this sustained level of associative activity, at least in civil associations, and the increase in volunteering, we must turn to the question of what accounts for the robustness of civil engagement and its resistance to adverse factors, including the rise in individualism (the one most often cited). As the argument goes, strong individualists turn to the market (the supposedly quintessential arena of individual choice) and become intolerant of the binding commitments of associative action. This line of argument, however, is not as logical as it appears at first glance. In fact, individual choice may be practiced in the choice of associative networks joined as much as in the selection of commodities purchased. A strong emphasis on individual choice may thus affect the style of and motivation for joining and associative involvement, but not necessarily its level. While a collectivist style of associability is based upon a conventional sense of duty and commitment, individualists would engage in collective action according to individual tastes, emergent opportunities, and the contingent evidence of need.

Thus participation in helping and caring activities, especially among members of the younger generation, is said to be less motivated by ad hoc decisions based on specific cases of need. If this sense of concrete immediacy and urgency is generated, as well as the opportunity for intrinsic gratification derived from the helping activity provided, people's desire to participate in such activities may actually be greater and more widespread, though less readily visible, less formalized, and less durable than is the case with more conventional associative activities based upon an ethic of duty.[23] To be sure, the apparent increase of forms of associability and helping activities that conform to the less formal and more ad hoc pattern involves a measurement problem. The less formalized a type of associative action is, the fewer data are automatically generated by its existence and operation. Yet they are clearly within the range of phenomena in which social capital manifests itself, however small and transient they may be and how loosely they may be structured.

Although there are changes in the prevailing pattern and substantive focus of associational and volunteering activities in Germany, these can hardly be understood as an overall decline, either in associational activity in general or in the (small) subset of helping or other service-providing activities. In the following analysis we shall therefore be less concerned with quantitative changes concerning the level of associability and its determinants and more so with changes of the domains of associational activity as well as structural contexts and motivational underpinnings of such activity. These changes should become evident if we take a close look, to the extent the available data permit, at the divergences that occur in the cross-sectional dimension (seen by comparing different parts of the country and segments of the social structure, as well as in the longitudinal dimension across cohorts and generations).

Independent Variables and Hypotheses

In this section, we proceed as follows. First, we specify nine independent sociological variables, selected because they seem to be plausible determinants of levels of associative behavior. Second, within each of the variables, we formulate hypothetical positive as well as negative effects upon social capital and its components. Third, we present the available data that allow us to test the respective hypothesis that links each of the independent variables to social capital outcomes.

Household Income and Labor Market Status

We might assume that associability is a positive function of income. Such correlation could be explained by the greater salience of the interests of middle- and high-income earners that can be defended through associative action; they have simply more to lose than low-income earners, and can prevent such losses through associative action. Moreover, they are likely to be comparatively more familiar with associative practices, be it due to the correlation of higher income with higher age (and thus life experience) or to the fact that high income may itself be a consequence of organizational skills. On the other hand, a hypothetical correlation of income and associability might also be considered implausible, as high-income earners incur comparatively greater opportunity costs by spending their time on associative action, particularly as their high income allows them to buy in the market what others need to associate for. These speculations would suggest a negative correlation.

A positive correlation between high income and associability is confirmed by a number of studies. Scheuch analyzes data from 1991 and compares them with data generated in 1953 and 1979.[24] A correlation between associability and income is present throughout this time series, although the coefficients are declining over the period of observation. Relatively high income (i.e., DM 3,500–4,999 per month disposable household income in 1991, equivalent to roughly half these amounts in U.S. dollars) is a valid predictor for multiple membership in associations. Braun and Röhrig present basically the same findings for volunteering in helping and social service activities.[25] This correlation is particularly strong for women.[26]

A variable that is closely related to income is labor market status, as material well-being is a function not just of level of income but also of (anticipated) security of income and the availability of disposable time. The most favored case in the latter dimension is that of civil servants (Beamte) with practically tenured employment status. At the other end of the continuum we would locate the unemployed, with both level and security of income being low in their case, although they are high on disposable time. The data on the combined index of security, income level, and disposable time as a complex determinant of associability invite interesting speculations. Of all employed persons, 18.2 percent are involved in some kind of voluntary activity. Only 12.7 percent of the unemployed, however, are volunteering, which seems to indicate that having disposable time is just one among several factors favoring associative active. Among the employed, differences according to status show up: The most active group is those who are employed in the civil service (Beamte, 32 percent), followed by the self-employed (26 percent), white-collar workers (18 percent), and blue-collar workers (15 percent).[27]

Researchers have found a strong correlation between interest in politics and income level in both parts of Germany.[28] In West Germany, 63 percent of persons with a high income report a strong interest in politics, while only 38 percent of persons with a low household income report the same (for East Germany the figures are 65 percent and 49 percent).[29] We have not found any data suggesting turning points in the statistical association of income and associability; thus the negative hypothesis alluded to above can be dismissed as unsupported.

Religion

Religious orientation and strength of religious commitment are hypothesized to be positively correlated with social capital. Churches and other religious organizations act as catalysts of associational activity. For instance, by providing meeting rooms for environmental groups, they foster the development of cooperative skills and enhance the awareness of social problems. We shall examine two aspects of religion. First, we shall argue that Roman Catholicism should correlate more strongly with social capital than Protestantism, due to the stronger communitarian and less liberal-individualist aspects of Catholic doctrine. The positive correlation between Catholic church affiliation and level of associative participation could be explained by the fact that Catholic religious doctrine (arguably more so than most Protestant varieties of Christianity) inculcates an ethic of charity and advocates the taking of an active interest in the well-being of one's fellow community members. But it may also turn out that the two major denominations differ not in the level of associative participation, but only in terms of the preferred kind of association. Second, self-reported strong religious affiliation predicts higher levels of associability and of the two versions of trust across both of the major religious communities.

Religious commitment in general is a very strong predictor for membership in social service associations; this is in line with the Christian theological emphasis upon the duty to serve fellow human beings. In the associative sector, 31 percent of all volunteering members describe themselves as strongly committed to their church, while only 15 percent report a weak commitment and 11 percent no religious commitment at all. The relation is reversed, however, if interest in volunteering is scrutinized, with 37 percent of those who report an interest in volunteer activity (without being actually involved in one) reporting no church commitment and only 22 percent reporting a strong church commitment.[30] These data may suggest that religious commitment serves a strong catalytic function, as such commitment seems to activate associative dispositions, whereas these dispositions remain largely platonic on the part of those without religious commitment. Churches are uniquely capable of tapping the social capital of members, while people not belonging to a church face greater difficulties in investing their social capital. Such commitment, however, is highly unevenly distributed throughout the social structure. We cannot explore here, due to the lack of data, the intercorrelations that are known to exist between the variables of age, gender, and income, on one hand, and religious commitment and associative dispositions, on the other.

The positive impact of Roman Catholicism on associability has prevailed since the 1950s.[31] While 40.8 percent of the overall population in West Germany was Roman Catholic in 1991, 46.4 percent of all those who belong to more than one association were Catholics.

Education

Formal education in Germany has been provided through public schools for more than 150 years. The percentage of overall population obtaining a high level of formal education (*Abitur*, roughly equivalent to the U.S. high-school diploma) has increased continuously since the 1960s. Of those born between 1949 and 1951, 7.9 percent attended a university, while for those born between 1969 and 1971, the figure rose to 18.2 percent.[32] The expansion of formal education accelerated in the mid-1960s, when German political elites perceived a condition of *Bildungskatastrophe*, or higher-education emergency, causing a shortage of human capital. The participation rates in higher education increased in particular for girls, the rural population, and the working class.[33] The percentage of high-school graduates per cohort increased from 11.4 percent in 1970 to 30.9 percent in 1992.[34]

We also hypothesize that education, measured as years of formal schooling, has a positive influence upon social capital. We expect this because the school is the first nonfamilial context in an individual's life that trains, through both its explicit and hidden curricula, moral and cognitive capacities favoring cooperation. Length of education is also correlated to the socioeconomic status of the educated, with an independent effect of such status upon associability. Furthermore, schools and universities (as much as churches, work organizations, and perhaps also military organizations) must be understood as institutional environments that by virtue of their relative stability favor various forms of informal associability among peers and fellow members. One might object, however, that the overall effect of extended formal education can also strengthen individualistic and competitive dispositions, emphasizing status differentiation and thus perhaps undermining associability. Furthermore, it might be argued that the role of education in social capital formation is less than unique, given that a variety of readily accessible institutional contexts such as sports, music, and religion can also provide a locus for social capital formation that is equivalent (if not superior) to that provided by formal educational institutions, as at least some of those mentioned tend to deemphasize, unlike most schools, the role of competitive individualism expressed through the verbal code of communication.

The available data support, however, a positive correlation of educational attainment and associability even when the effects of these other contexts are controlled for. Stated in general terms, people with low levels of formal education are less likely to join associations than those with more years of schooling. Also, multiple membership is predominantly found among persons with a high level of formal education. This correlation, according to available data, has persisted since the 1950s.[35]

Volunteering also shows a positive correlation with level of education. This finding is valid for both East and West Germany: In 1994, 18 percent of the overall population in East Germany and 21 percent of the overall population in West Germany with a high level of formal education reported that they volunteered at least once a month, while only 5 percent (East) and 8 percent (West) with a low level of formal education reported such involvement.[36] Priller reports the same relation for participation in community affairs, citizens' groups, and political parties in East Germany.[37] The difference between persons with high levels of formal education and those with low levels is as much as 20 percentage points.

An exception to this rule is to be found in the associability of Catholic women. Catholic women with a low level of formal education are even slightly overrepresented in terms of involvement with associations (in 1991, 67.7 percent versus 66.5 percent in the overall population), while those with a high level of formal education are underrepresented.[38] We interpret these data to suggest that religious commitment, and particularly so in the case of Roman Catholicism, can work as a functional equivalent to formal education in promoting associability. But this appears to be the exception to the rule. Formal education is a very strong predictor for all kinds of voluntary participation, including unconventional forms of political and social participation. A high level of formal education fosters the self-reported willingness to participate in extrainstitutional forms (legal as well as illegal) of political protest.[39]

Unsurprisingly, attention (i.e., interest in politics, as a subset of interest in public affairs and community well-being more broadly defined) can be demonstrated to be a positive correlate of educational attainment. Very strong interest in politics was reported by 27 percent (East) and 35 percent (West) of the overall population in 1993. Of those strongly interested in politics, 57 percent (55 percent in the West) had a high level of formal education, while only 19 percent (25 percent in the West) had a low level of formal education.[40] The correlation between

Table 5-1: Gender, Age, Level of Formal Education, and Interest in Politics, 1970–1990

	INTEREST IN POLITICS														
	Strong					Medium					Weak				
	1970	1974	1980	1985	1990	1970	1974	1980	1985	1990	1970	1974	1980	1985	1990
Total	32.0	37.0	44.0	42.0	50.0	40.0	41.0	40.0	36.0	35.0	28.0	22.0	16.0	22.0	15.0
Male	46.0	50.0	56.0	55.0	62.0	37.0	37.0	37.0	30.0	27.0	16.0	13.0	9.0	14.0	10.0
Female	20.0	25.0	35.0	30.0	39.0	42.0	44.0	42.0	42.0	42.0	39.0	31.0	23.0	28.0	19.0
14–19	32.0	21.0	34.0	18.0	34.0	35.0	45.0	42.0	36.0	36.0	33.0	34.0	24.0	45.0	30.0
20–29	30.0	38.0	53.0	38.0	48.0	47.0	47.0	36.0	45.0	37.0	24.0	15.0	11.0	16.0	14.0
30–39	34.0	40.0	46.0	44.0	52.0	43.0	44.0	43.0	39.0	37.0	22.0	15.0	11.0	17.0	10.0
40–49	34.0	42.0	41.0	51.0	58.0	42.0	42.0	48.0	34.0	31.0	23.0	16.0	11.0	14.0	10.0
50–59	31.0	41.0	44.0	48.0	52.0	41.0	33.0	41.0	32.0	38.0	29.0	25.0	15.0	20.0	10.0
60–69	34.0	38.0	45.0	48.0	51.0	36.0	38.0	36.0	37.0	34.0	31.0	24.0	19.0	15.0	16.0
70+	29.0	30.0	40.0	39.0	47.0	25.0	31.0	31.0	28.0	32.0	45.0	39.0	29.0	33.0	20.0
Low level of formal education	16.0	21.0	29.0	18.0	26.0	36.0	38.0	39.0	39.0	40.0	47.0	42.0	32.0	43.0	34.0
Middle level of formal education	31.0	36.0	38.0	40.0	44.0	46.0	46.0	47.0	39.0	42.0	24.0	19.0	15.0	21.0	14.0
High level of formal education	59.0	55.0	60.0	55.0	66.0	34.0	38.0	33.0	32.0	27.0	10.0	7.0	7.0	11.0	6.0

Source: Klaus Berg and Marie-Luise Kiefer, *Massenkommunikation IV* (Baden-Baden, 1992), 340.

higher levels of formal education and attention is largely stable for the period 1970–90, as demonstrated in Table 5-1. The proportion of those expressing a strong interest in politics increases with the proportion of the highly educated in the overall population. The age effect, which here consists of a negative correlation between age and interest in politics, can partly be understood in terms of the higher average level of education of the younger cohorts.

Age

Age in this context is an approximate measure of an individual's position within the life cycle, consisting of stages that are conventionally distinguished as childhood, adolescence, adulthood, parenthood, retirement, and so on. As social capital is unlikely to be evenly distributed over the life cycle, age (and associated factors such as disposable income and disposable time) should turn out to be an important determinant of level and type of associative activity. Age, however, also measures (in combination with the point in time at which age is measured) the location of an individual life in historical time and the belonging of an individual to a particular age cohort or generation with its profile of collective experience and memory.[41] Given this duality of the underlying items measured by age, the well-known problem of interpretation emerges of assigning observed effects to either the generation effect or the life cycle effect. In other words, if we observe a certain distinctive behavioral pattern in, for example, people 60 years old, it remains to be determined whether this can be explained in terms of their age as such or in terms of the fact that this is their present age (that is, that they are 60 years old in 1997, as opposed to 60 in 1957). This distinction can also be referred to in terms of chronological versus chronometrical age.

In what sense does age determine associability, and how must such determination be interpreted? Scheuch's analysis of 1991 data suggests a direct link to the life cycle. Associability takes the form of an inverted U over the life course. Single association membership is the prevailing pattern among those 18 to 29 years of age. Multiple membership is the typical overall pattern among those age 30 to 59. In contrast, the population age 60 and older is underrepresented in associations relative to their share in the resident population.[42] Needless to say, this age-related overall pattern would likely be modified in numerous ways if we were able to cross-tabulate it with other variables, such as income, education, employment status, marital and family status, and size of community. This, however, cannot be explored here, as we lack the primary data required for such multivariate analysis.

Membership in sports clubs is most likely to occur during the school and university years, which may be read as a case of nested associability, that is, associative activity formed, encouraged, and subsidized by large-scale formal associations, such as companies, schools, or universities. In 1995, more than one of every two males in the age group 7 to 21 was a member of a sports club. Among females, no less than 45 percent of those age 7 to 14 years were members, with female membership rates sharply declining in late adolescence.[43]

Patterns of volunteering display a life cycle effect, too. Men are most active between the ages of 40 and 60 (26 percent), while women reach their peak of volunteer activity (19.5 percent) at a markedly later point, namely, between 60 and 70 years.[44] Adolescents and the elderly donate more of their time for volunteering than any other age category.[45] This must have to do with the greater amount of disposable time available to members of these age categories. Age also influences the type of voluntary work members prefer to perform. There is a trend toward an age-related dichotomy in voluntary work. Young women in the Catholic association of women are more interested in administrative responsibilities, while elderly women opt for charitable and helping kinds of activities.[46]

A number of surveys conducted in the late 1980s and early 1990s provide information on the associational practices of contemporary adolescents in Germany. In 1992 the Deutsche Jugendinstitut (DJI) conducted a survey of 4,005 adolescents and postadolescents between 16 and 29 years in East and West Germany. Of the sample, 54.7 percent (West) and 57.6 percent (East) did not belong to any associations. In its questionnaire, the DJI distinguished between the fully formalized intermediary system (e.g., unions, parties, professional organizations, church-related/religious organizations, sports clubs) and less formal networks, such as peace groups, feminist groups, environmental groups, other new social movements, women's groups, leftist militant groups (Autonome), rightist "skinheads," and groups engaged in self-help activities. About 21 percent, East and West alike, belonged to some of the fully formalized organizations; about 12 percent, East and West alike, belonged to some of the less formal networks. About 10 percent, East and West alike, belong to both types of associations.[47] Passive members and sympathizers were counted as nonmembers.[48] In the sample, 30.5 percent of male persons and 25.3 percent of female persons were a member of one fully formalized organization, and 14.6 percent of the males and 10.1 percent of the females were a member of two or more of the fully formalized organizations, sports clubs excluded.[49] Referring to the possible objection that membership in fully formalized organizations tends to be nonactive—

that is, dues-paying membership only—the DJI asked the question of how actively young trade union members participate in their union. It turned out that about 35 percent, East and West alike, described themselves as inactive members, while as many as 65 percent were engaged in regular or at least occasional participation.[50]

Activity in new social movements is to be found particularly among women between the ages of 16 and 29 in the East (58.3 percent versus 41.7 percent male) and the West (52.3 percent versus 47.7 percent male). Females are overrepresented in multiple activity in new social movements, too. High educational level is a strong predictor for (single and multiple) activity in new social movements for both sexes.[51] Regarding groups and networks who represent negative social capital—that is, who activate their members in aggressive and exclusionist ways against the rights of the wider community (or targeted segments thereof)—the sociodemographic characteristics are reversed: Activity in right-wing groups (e.g., skinheads) is a domain of young males with low educational status in East and West alike.[52] Militant leftist groups (e.g., *Autonome*) show a gender pattern similar to that of right-wing groups (although their gender gap is smaller), but the educational status is typically higher.[53] However, the percentage that is active in extremist political groups is very low in both East (2.8 percent rightist, 1.9 percent leftist) and West Germany (0.9 percent rightist, 1.5 percent leftist).[54] The sociodemographic characteristics of organized youth do not differ from the overall population: Males are slightly more active in fully formalized organizations, while females and persons with a high level of formal education are more active in less formalized networks.[55]

The IBM Youth Survey reports even higher numbers for associational activities of adolescents (14 to 24 years) than the DJI survey conducted in 1992, suggesting perhaps an overall increase (see Table 5-2).[56] Of the overall sample, 26.4 percent are active members, disregarding activities in private networks of families, friends, and neighbors. Women are more active in voluntary social services and environmental, feminist, and animal rights movements. Male adolescents, in contrast, are more active in trade unions and political parties. The data fit our hypotheses about the gendered distribution of sectors of associational activities (see the section on gender, below). In addition, educational level shows a strong impact upon the propensity to join associations. In general, East German adolescents do not differ in their associational behavior from their West German peers. As to overall levels of youth associability, there appears to be a rather significant decrease in membership over the period. While 55 percent of adolescents age 15 to 24 in 1984 were mem-

Table 5-2: Activities of Adolescents in Selected Groups, 1995

% (MULTIPLE ENTRIES POSSIBLE)	Absolute	SEX		AGE				LEVEL OF FORMAL EDUCATION		REGION		NATIONALITY	
		Male	Female	14–15	16–18	19–21	22–24	Low/middle	High	West	East	German	Other
N =	2,402	1,196	1,206	365	544	698	781	1,124	1,223	1,759	637	2,002	400
Private (family, friends, neighbors)	53.0	49.5	56.4	47.7	51.5	55.2	54.8	48.1	57.2	53.1	52.9	53.2	51.5
Voluntary social services	22.3	17.6	26.9	15.3	19.9	25.5	24.5	19.6	25.0	22.7	21.2	24.0	13.8
Environmental protection	20.9	19.6	22.1	25.5	19.5	21.8	19.0	19.0	22.8	21.2	20.1	21.0	20.3
Antifascist groups	10.3	11.0	9.6	8.2	13.4	8.9	10.6	9.6	11.1	10.1	11.1	8.5	19.3
Protection of animals	10.0	7.2	12.9	18.6	9.7	7.3	8.7	10.9	9.2	9.3	12.2	10.5	7.5
Church	9.7	7.7	11.6	12.9	10.8	9.3	7.6	9.0	10.1	10.6	7.1	9.2	12.0
Trade union	3.4	4.6	2.2	0.5	2.9	3.6	4.9	5.2	1.6	3.1	3.8	3.5	2.5
Peace movement	3.2	3.3	3.2	2.7	5.1	2.1	3.2	4.0	2.7	3.5	2.5	2.7	6.0
Citizens groups	3.2	3.5	3.0	1.9	3.1	3.7	3.6	3.4	3.1	3.5	2.5	3.2	3.3
Political parties	2.8	3.4	2.2	0.8	2.0	2.9	4.2	2.1	3.4	3.2	1.6	2.2	5.5
Groups assisting marginal social groups (e.g., homeless)	2.8	3.0	2.6	1.6	2.8	1.9	4.2	2.0	3.6	2.7	3.0	2.5	4.0
Women's movement	2.7	1.0	4.5	2.5	3.1	2.0	3.3	2.8	2.5	3.1	1.9	2.0	6.3
Cultural sector	12.2	12.0	12.3	6.0	10.3	14.0	14.6	8.3	15.5	12.0	12.6	10.6	20.0
Other	3.5	4.3	2.7	2.2	4.4	2.6	4.2	2.8	3.9	3.5	3.5	3.9	1.5
NA	20.6	23.8	17.4	28.8	19.7	17.5	20.1	25.0	16.5	20.3	21.4	20.4	21.5

Source: Courtesy of Karin Kürten, from ifep GmbH, *Tabellenband der IBM-Jugendstudie* (Köln, 1995), Tab. 21b.

bers of at least one association in West Germany, this figure went down to 43 percent in 1996.[57]

In order to pinpoint trends in youth associability over a still longer period, we turn to a comparison of three cohorts of 15-to-24-year-old persons, namely, the cohort born 1930–1939 and surveyed in 1954, the cohort born 1960–1969 and surveyed in 1984, and those born 1973–1982 and surveyed in 1996.[58]

Concerning the first two of these cohorts, the results from 1954 (36 percent) and 1984 (55 percent) showed an increase in the percentage of those with associational involvement.[59] This increase applied to male and female adolescents alike, with the gender difference also staying the same (15 percent in favor of men).[60] Also, the average number of memberships per person increased from 1.2 in 1954 to 1.6 in 1984.[61] At the biographical stage at which people reach early adulthood and approach labor market participation and/or family life, associational participation declined in both cohorts from age 20 on, though more slowly in the latter cohort, reflecting perhaps the dramatic increase in participation in tertiary education that occurred between these two cohorts, as well as a delay in the average age of marriage and parenthood.

This apparently robust trend is, however, not corroborated by the 1996 data on the youngest cohort. Members of this cohort, born between 1973 and 1982, show a remarkable decline in their pattern of associability. As stated, the portion of those indicating membership in any association decreased from 55 percent in 1984 to 46 percent in 1996 in West Germany. A strong loss of attraction to potential members seems to have occurred with types of associations that are devoted to political and broad social causes, such as the youth organizations of political parties and trade unions, but also the new social movements (civil rights, environmentalist, feminist, urban, Third World, etc.) of the 1970s and 1980s.

This curvilinear pattern can partly be explained, we submit, in terms of general political developments. In the 1950s, political mobilization, to the extent that it occurred at all and was not preempted by individual concerns with rebuilding economic success and private life, was largely annexed to and sponsored by political parties. This includes most notably the protest movements surrounding the issue of rearmament and international peace organized by leftist political parties, trade unions, and to some extent the Protestant Church. The appeals of these organizations were directed at their constituency in general and in no way specifically to the younger generation. In contrast, the second cohort grew up in the context of the aftermath of the various 1968 movements, which, in terms of the age composition of their constituency, constituted a distinctive youth movement that was both emancipated from the control and guidance of established political parties and sharply opposed to their leadership (as well as to their parent generation in general, with its perceived moral and historical failings). The youth movement of the 1960s was also comparatively unburdened by economic concerns and anxieties, as the youth involved had reached early adulthood under conditions of seemingly never-ending prosperity. The moral, political, and esthetic concerns of these movements were able to unfold considerable hegemonic potential, both for their peers and for the wider public, throughout the 1970s. This hegemony arguably did not end with the return of the conservative-led coalition in 1982, but crystallized into a political force of its own in the form of the Green party in 1980 and the political and cultural impact it gained from being the radical contrast to the newly installed conservative Kohl government. The historical peak in youth associability that our data show for 1984 can be attributed to the long-term effects of the 1967–68 mobilizations in the public space in general and in the educational system in particular.

However, the mid-1980s saw a rapid fading away of the oppositional impulses of both the new social movements and the new politics of the Green party. Beginning in roughly the mid-1980s, there emerged a number of political and social factors that must be held responsible for the decline in movement-style youth politics. These include:

- The withering away of the peace issue after the 1981–83 conflict over the deployment of nuclear missiles in Western Europe
- The settlement of the nuclear energy issue in the mid-1980s
- The dramatic rise of unemployment and welfare cutbacks
- The consolidation of the Christian-Conservative governing coalition
- The absorption of both feminist and environmental issues into the rhetoric and the platforms of both major parties
- The incorporation of countercultural lifestyles into the pattern of depoliticized consumerism
- The spread of neoliberal and postmodernist public philosophies

All of these factors contributed to the evaporation of the social and political legacies derived from the late 1960s and 1970s

This decline altered the entire landscape of issues, values, and collective actors, a change that was accelerated even further by the crumbling of the Berlin Wall in 1989 and the slow integration of East German society, in which there was, with the exception of various oppositional citizens' rights movements, no strong tradition of autonomous civic associability outside of the state-sponsored realm of large organizations.

This historical context leads us to the interpretation that the 1984 peak was in fact not representative of any secular trend, but simply a remarkably durable aberration that by the late 1980s had given way to decreased associability among the younger generation, which now neither is guided and mobilized by major political parties (as in the 1950s) nor can rely on patterns of mobilization of its own (as in the late 1960s to mid-1980s). Instead, the type of associative activity that seems to emerge in the 1990s (a period of increasing materialist concerns and values) can be characterized by a sense of deep distrust directed at the political class and a corresponding disinclination to get involved in the organizational forms and practices represented by it. We see among this group an absence of countercultural and otherwise oppositional ideas, motives, and movements, as well as a retreat into "soft" and informal associational practices. The associations to which they tend to belong lack the trappings of more formal ones: They do without statutes, officers, dues, admission procedures, and written communication. Examples of the kinds of associations they form include personalistic networks, friendships, quasi-families, user groups, cliques, and social gatherings—groups that are undemanding in terms of the commitments they expect their members to make.

The prevalence of this type of associational involvement differs between East and West Germany. Of a sample of persons age 15 to 24 interviewed as part of the first Youth Survey conducted after unification in 1991, 62 percent belonged to some network in West Germany, in contrast to just 42 percent of the adolescents in East Germany.[62]

The development of what we have termed attention—interest in politics and public affairs—is well documented over the last two decades. Table 5-2 shows the development of political interest in different cohorts (West Germany only). There is an overall increase of self-reported interest in politics in all cohorts except for the youngest one. Peaks of very strong political interest among the three youngest cohorts in the years 1970, 1980, and 1990 are possibly due to significant political events and conflicts having occurred at the time (such as unification in 1990), while political interest was found to be low among the cohorts surveyed in 1974 and 1985. All cohorts whose members had reached the age of 40 at the time of the respective surveys show a rather continuous increase of political interest from survey to survey.

While in West Germany the interest in politics of the middle and older generations was rather steadily increasing, the opposite applies to the younger cohorts in East Germany. Regarding the development of interest in politics by East German adolescents, Bischoff and Lang conclude that general interest in politics decreased considerably from 1981 to 1992.[63] This relative loss of interest in politics, however, can also be found among the younger generation in West Germany, with the only short-lived surge in interest in politics being recorded for every cohort (including the young) for those surveyed in 1990.[64]

Two negative predictors for adolescents' associative activity are suggested by the available data reviewed here: a low level of formal education and female gender. The effect of these two determinants is cumulative. Compared to their male peers, less-educated female adolescents tend to refrain more consistently from associational involvement. Another important finding is that today's adolescents are still more likely to engage in associational activities than were the members of the same age group in the 1950s, although the curvilinear trajectory implies that their associative activity declined compared to their peers in the 1980s. The secular increase can be partly explained by the massive overall increase in participation rates in postsecondary education and the positive impact that higher education is known to have upon associability. An additional element of explanation may have to do with the supply side of associational life, that is, the greater number (approximately 200,000 in 1973 and 659,400 in 1997), variety, and specificity of associations, each of which focuses on a relatively narrow set of concerns and interests without making any far-reaching presupposition about the values, identities, or backgrounds of potential members.[65] Similarly, perhaps a greater spatial density facilitates access (see the section "City Versus Countryside," below). The intuition guiding this speculation is that the more fine-grained and evenly populated the associational landscape becomes, the easier it becomes for potential members to find the right club and to overcome any reluctance to joining.

East Versus West

We have made the differences between East and West Germany as they affect the generation of social capital a major focus of our survey. The history of forty years of division of Germany into two states with mutually hostile and vastly different regimes, plus the recent experience of a sudden and unanticipated political unification, was bound, or so it appears, to yield differences in levels of social capital. We cannot, however, settle the important question of how robust these different mental and cultural legacies will be in the future, nor how rapidly these differences might evaporate.

We proceed as follows. First, we will review the patterns of associability that prevailed in the former GDR before 1989. It is by no means clear how the level of social capital that existed under the GDR regime can be accounted for. On one hand, one might argue that in a paternalistic, authoritarian, comprehensively state-controlled society with large-scale and mandatory state-sponsored membership associations, social capital had no real chance to emerge in the first place (nor was it widely perceived to be desirable) due to the absence of an autonomous sphere of civil society. Contrariwise, one might also expect that the widespread symptoms of shortages, malfunctioning, and repression may have helped to create attitudes and practices favoring mutual help, cooperative improvisation, trust, and solidarity—particularly in a society where major differences of socioeconomic status were unknown within a very large middle range of the working population.

Second, we will review the spread of associability and its patterns as they emerged in East Germany subsequent to the regime's breakdown and the economic and political unification crisis that followed it. One hypothesis concerning the impact of these events on levels of associability that fits common intuitions is a negative one: Inherited relations of trust and solidarity vanished with the old regime itself. The opposite expectation is also plausible, as the challenges and uncertainties of the new postunification situation seem to put a very high premium upon autonomous forms of cooperation and associative action within a nascent civil society.

Third, the impact of the wholesale transplantation of West German institutions upon associability in the former East German federal states, the new *Länder*, must be assessed. Here, the question is whether these institutions will foster similar levels of associability and trust as they exist in the old *Länder*, or whether distrust and a sense of powerlessness, alienation, and victimization will prevail that would make associative activity unlikely and breed hostility, nurtured by the very mixed results of the political and economic transformation

Priller analyzed citizens' associational activity in the political, social, and cultural sectors in the former GDR, using data from 1987.[66] He determined that membership in most associations was not optional and voluntary, but mandated by imperative political and economic considerations. For this reason, the organizational density of state- and party-sponsored sociopolitical and cultural membership associations in the GDR was very high. In general, membership depended upon citizens' preferences, background, or other individual variables to a small extent at best, while the type of activity pursued within the state-sponsored mass organization was in fact quite open to individual and collective choice. Often there were, however, such overwhelmingly powerful incentives attached to membership and sanctions attached to non-membership that individual choice, and the preferences guiding such choice, was at best of marginal importance. Only 5 percent (3 percent male, 7 percent female) of the GDR citizens were not members of any these official organizations.[67] Every third East German adult was a member of a political party, every fifth a member of the ruling party, Sozialistische Einheitspartei Deutschlands (SED). Membership in non-political (though equally state-sponsored) associations, such as sports clubs, offered the best opportunity to pursue leisure activities or to obtain goods and services in short supply. In addition, active membership in parties and organizations was deemed the only way GDR citizens could influence political and social change at the local and company levels.[68]

It would be wrong, however, to assume that membership and involvement in state-sponsored associations was either entirely coerced or opportunistic. In fact, organized volunteering was quite common in the GDR. In 1987, one out of every two citizens in the GDR reported having been involved in some kind of voluntarily assumed responsibility or activity—often of a work-related nature, such as serving on committees.[69] In contrast, the West German pattern of volunteering was largely confined to organizations and activity outside the job. In the GDR, however, job-related voluntary activity and, to a lesser extent, neighborhood and local community volunteering were expected and strongly encouraged, though usually not directly coerced. Only 12 percent of those surveyed volunteered because they felt obliged to perform such activity as a duty imposed upon them by their company or political officials. The vast majority gave other reasons for volunteering, such as "meeting other people" (27 percent) and "improving the quality of the neighborhood" (20 percent).[70] No doubt there was a considerable motivation for volunteering in the GDR, although these moral resources seem often to have been frustrated by the paternalism, inefficiency, and arrogance of the authorities.[71]

Many observers agree that liberal traditions and values of the middle class in the GDR survived the experience of forty years of state socialism to some extent and may be capable of being revitalized in the future.[72] The forms in which they survived were small and private personal networks based on trust, helping relations, family ties, and a more or less intensely felt opposition to the regime and its authorities.[73] Even when such opposition became an explicit theme of informal associability, as it did within groups and circles tied to the Protestant Church, the political critique of dissidents remained contained and strictly controlled by the vast state security system (Stasi) and its ubiquitous agents. Opposition groups were further weakened by the regime's practice of allowing or even pressing its key figures of dissident groups to exit to the West, sometimes banning them permanently from reentry. As a consequence, these groups and circles were effectively marginalized, rather than having had a chance (or even desiring to use the chance) to organize and mobilize a broad opposition movement.[74]

The sudden and unanticipated breakdown of the GDR in 1989 was bound to abolish, together with virtually every other institutional pattern, both its formal associations and its semioppositional private underground networks. In the mid-1990s, the level of participation of the citizens of the new *Länder* was considerably lower than was the case with citizens of the old *Länder* (the former West Germany). In 1993, 47 percent of the West German population (55 percent of males, 39 percent of females) were members of at least one association, while in East Germany only 26 percent (33 percent of males, 21 percent of females) were members.[75] In the countryside, where membership rates are traditionally high in West Germany (in 1993, 53 percent), only 21 percent of the population in East Germany were organized in 1993.[76] Sports was the major sector of associational activity in West Germany, with 28 percent of the West German population members of a sports club in 1993, while only 10 percent were members in East Germany.[77]

In 1990, 27 percent of the East German population reported some involvement in volunteering (29 percent among West Germans). That rate decreased continuously down to 17 percent in 1994, while the rate remained stable in West Germany.[78] The sociodemographic characteristics of volunteers in the East do not differ from those in the West: Women are less likely to volunteer than men, the age group of 41 to 50 years is the most active, and formal education is a strong predictor for volunteering.[79] In a time budget survey conducted in 1991–92, 9 percent of East Germans reported that they were active as volunteers, while 20 percent of the West Germans said they were active.[80]

Apart from the breakdown of most of the old associations and the underground oppositional networks, the East German participation gap must also be seen in the context of a period of sharply increasing unemployment.[81] Unemployment generally isolates people and undermines both trust in others and self-confidence. Second, as most associational activity and volunteering were tied to the enterprise and the workplace in the GDR, the disintegration of large parts of the industrial system, as well as the introduction of new managerial styles and constraints, was effective in destroying this multifunctional quality of the enterprise system of the old regime.

On the other hand, the condition of uncertainty and precariousness (including vast levels of open as well as hidden unemployment) that followed the breakdown of the old regime and unification would appear to provide strong incentives favoring self-help and other associational activities. In fact, the number of self-help groups in East Germany increased from 5,000 in 1992 to 7,500 in 1995. In spite of this increase, the density of such groups relative to the size of the population remains below that of the (largely middle-class-based) self-help groups found in West Germany (60,000 for 1995).[82]

As to attention, or concern for public affairs, in East Germany the share of persons indicating a strong political interest was higher in 1990 than the parallel figure for West Germany (57 percent versus 50 percent).[83] The exception to this was adolescents in East Germany, who were as interested as the West German adolescents. Attention, measured as interest in political affairs, was unsurprisingly very strong in both East and West Germany in 1990. A strong or very strong interest in politics was reported by 38 percent of West Germans and 41 percent of East Germans.[84] As early as 1991, however, this figure decreased dramatically, in East Germany to 26 percent and in West Germany to 33 percent.[85] One factor contributing to this decline in political interest was widely believed to be a sense of frustration, powerlessness, and alienation with the experience of the West German "takeover."

It is still too early to venture a prognosis concerning the future development of patterns of associability in East Germany. On one hand, associational activity, mainly in the form of self-help groups, increased, though this seems to be largely the result of incentives and support provided by federal and state agencies as well as large semipublic welfare agencies (Wohlfahrtsverbände). On the other hand, several factors, including extremely high levels of open and hidden unemployment, job insecurity, the very small portion of self-employed and entrepreneurial middle class, the fact that most large-scale membership associations (ranging from political parties to trade unions and professional or industrial associations) were widely perceived as quasi-colonial or at least largely unfamiliar transplants of West German origin, and finally the extremely weak attachment of people to religious life are likely to inhibit the rapid normalization of associational life in the former GDR.

City Versus Countryside

The impact of community size on associability produces two opposite expectations. First, people in small towns tend to know each other and are more directly and more uniformly affected by local issues. Hence trust and attention are in rich supply, and associational life flourishes as a consequence. Second and contrariwise, large cities enjoy the advantage that even very specialized concerns (say, the performance of sixteenth-century vocal music or the study of Swahili literature) will attract enthusiast audiences and potential activists with shared concerns. Despite the proverbial anonymity of urban settings, such highly specialized associations thrive on choice and the economies of scale, as well as on the comparatively low transaction costs of transportation and communication that only big cities supply. It is also conceivable that these two effects will cancel each other out, with the net result being that the number and type of associations will vary between small towns and large cities, rather than the level of associability. Again, the analysis of the data will have to demonstrate which of these hypothesized relations is actually supported by evidence.

In West Germany the relation between the size of a local community and its associability is very clear: The bigger a community is, the lower its membership rates are. So, for example, in 1993 membership rates were 53 percent in villages, 53 percent in small cities, 42 percent in middle-sized cities, and 39 percent in big cities.[86] In East Germany, however, this correlation does not hold true. In 1993 the membership rate was 21 percent for villages, 25 percent for small cities, 36 percent for middle-sized cities, and 28 percent for big cities.[87] Volunteering is most widespread in communities of between 2,000 and 10,000 inhabitants (20 percent of the resident population lives in such communities), while in big cities with more than 500,000 inhabitants only 14 percent are volunteers.[88]

In West Germany, the correlation of size of community and associability disappears, however, if membership in large-scale formal organizations (Verbände, e.g., automobile clubs or trade unions) is also taken into account, in addition to clubs (Vereine) and local associations relying more strongly on face-to-face interaction.[89] In fact, membership in tertiary organizations is more likely to occur in bigger cities, while membership in clubs and local associations is more widespread in smaller localities. Also, government-sponsored programs designed to promote associational and self-help activities are more likely to succeed in small rural communities. A policy evaluation study addressing one of these programs (which are increasingly popular among policy makers in the name of fiscal austerity) finds that it produced an increase of 52 percent in rural areas and only 35

Figure 5-4: Self-help Groups in Cities and in the Countryside, 1991

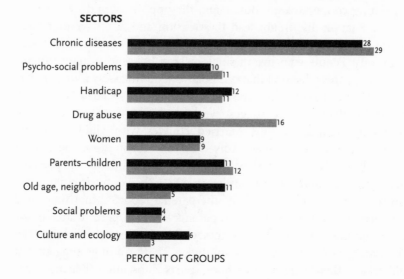

SECTORS

Chronic diseases	28 / 29
Psycho-social problems	10 / 11
Handicap	12 / 11
Drug abuse	9 / 16
Women	9 / 9
Parents–children	11 / 12
Old age, neighborhood	11 / 5
Social problems	4 / 4
Culture and ecology	6 / 3

PERCENT OF GROUPS

percent in larger cities.[90] The profile of issues on which self-help and volunteer social service groups focus tends to be surprisingly similar across all categories of size of community (cf. Figure 5-4).

Although there are still differences in associational patterns and thematic domains of associations depending on the size of the respective community, they do not seem to be very important and may be erased in the near future, as there are various policy initiatives to empower civic associability specifically in the countryside.[91]

Size of Household

If we build a scale that ranges from single-person households to couples without children to couples with children, we would expect that associability grows with household size. One conceivable reason for this is that family households with children generate both the opportunities and the need for associative action; another is that bigger, more complex households tend to broaden what we have called attention; a third is that intact families work as learning environments for social practices. Needless to say, these household types correlate to some extent with age and position in the life cycle.

In larger households a greater variety of aspects of social and political realities such as education, health, labor market, cultural activities, religious life, housing, and neighborhood issues are on the agenda. Moreover, the larger a family household is, the greater the benefits from interfamilial networks of help and cooperation can be expected to be, beginning with baby-sitting cooperatives.[92] But, again, the opposite could be true: An exhaustive family life might lead to seclusion and family-centeredness that leaves neither time nor need for associative involvements in the wider community. People who live in single-person households tend to have more time at their disposal that can be invested into associational activities, and the need to do so may result from feelings of social isolation.

Available data seem to suggest weak positive links between size of household and associability. Married couples with children in the household are more strongly involved in volunteering (20.7 percent of the overall sample) than married couples without children (18.2 percent) and singles (19.9 percent). In families in which the youngest child is less than six years old, 17.4 percent of the parents reported that they were volunteers. In cases in which both parents work, 16 percent are volunteers. In families in which the youngest child is between six and eighteen years old, 33 percent of parents volunteer. These findings suggest that children and their activities in school, sports clubs, and other organizations foster associational activities among their parents, even those who suffer severe time constraints.[93] The same relation proves to be valid for informal help networks that exist between neighbors and friends. In 1984, 48 percent of families with small children (age under 5 years) and 45 percent of single parents with small children reported that they provided help with child care for friends and neighbors, while only 20 percent of those couples whose children are between 13 and 17 years reported the same.[94]

There is also evidence for the reverse hypothesis. Bönner suggests that, on one hand, intense and complex family relations lead to a high degree of what we have called attention due to (1) intergenerational conflicts and debates over normative issues and (2) the extension of the range of concerns that, on the part of parents, typically includes issues (such as labor market prospects for new entrants) affecting the next generation only, while the younger generation is confronted with economic and health issues affecting their parents. On the other hand, however, such comparatively broader and more telescopic attention and awareness do not correspond with greater associational activity of parents living with children, be it due to the time constraints of family life or a lack of perceived need for social contacts outside the family.[95]

Gender

The most plausible and best-documented way in which gender is related to associability has to do with the domains men and women choose for their associative activities.[96] In consonance with traditional notions of gender identity, we would expect that women engage, as they do in their choice of occupations, in extrafamilial fields of collective and voluntary activity having to do with an extension of familial functions, such as education, (religious) charity, health, and indoor sports, while men prefer other fields of activity symbolically marked as male domains, such as politics and outdoor sports.

As to the level of associative activity, we might expect a greater home-centeredness among women, and thus lesser availability for participation. Moreover, being confined to the home (or middle-class suburb) diminishes the spatial opportunities of women for associative participation. Also, given the comparatively low labor market participation rate of women in Germany (see the section "Female Labor Market Participation," below), one might also expect women to have a greater amount of time at their disposal for joining and participating in voluntary associations. On the other hand, the social opportunities provided at and through the workplace must also be seen as a fertile soil for derivative associative activity of people working for the same company or in the same occupation

Gender differences may also be reflected in the form of association, ranging from a hypothetical male preference for a sharply demarcated membership role to a female pattern of loose, informal, nonthematic, and somewhat personalistic or "neighborly" mode of association.

Regarding associability in different substantive domains, women, when they join at all, are more likely than men to be members of church-related associations, parents' associations, and cultural associations.[97] Men prefer political parties and unions as types and domains of their associational activity. But sports clubs are the type of associations that attract the highest percentage of both men and women.[98]

The different types of engagement among the genders show a specific pattern, too. Caring activities in the neighborhood or neighborhood-related networks (e.g., church or parents' associations) are predominantly performed by women, whereas administrative and leadership responsibilities tend to be a male domain.[99]

Regarding the level of membership rates, women are still less likely to be members in an association than men.[100] The same is true for volunteering.[101] However, the difference between male and female membership rates decreased considerably over the last half century. Male rates exceeded female rates by 37 percent in 1953, by 27 percent in 1979, and by just 16 percent in 1993.[102] The is due to an increase in female participation, not a decline in male membership, especially in sports clubs.[103]

Gender has an impact not only on the type of association in terms of sector-specific associations (e.g., social versus political), on the type of engagement (e.g., caring versus administrative), and on the rate of membership of men and women, but also on the degree of formalization of the type of associations preferred by either gender. Women are more likely than men to be involved in informal, functionally diffuse helping networks. This might be explained as an extension of reproductive work, performed by women not only in the household itself but in the nearby environment, too (e.g., helping neighbors or caring for close relatives).[104]

Regarding political participation, so-called conventional forms (e.g., debating politics with friends, supporting parties or candidates) are still a male domain, while unconventional forms, such as participation in new social movements, attract a high share of (young) women.[105] In the conventional sphere, the male participation rate is twice as high as the female participation rate, while in the unconventional sphere, the differences between men and women decrease to 7–10 percent.[106]

An adjustment of gender-specific patterns of associability should have been the case in the former GDR, where female labor force participation was as high as 80–90 percent in the 1980s.[107] In the GDR in 1987, 93 percent of women (and 97 percent of men) have been members of an association or organization, though not always voluntarily. Nearly 100 percent of the employed persons have been union members (see "Female Labor Market Participation," below).[108] Apparently, workforce participation is a strong positive influence for associability that compensates for the negative influence of gender on associability.

Although women are still not participating as much as men do, the gender gap has decreased over the last forty years. This development seems to be due to a generational effect. Higher education and quota policies have had a positive impact on the participation rate of women (especially younger women); unconventional forms of participation, such as were opened up by new social movements in the 1970s and 1980s, created additional spaces preferred by women as a site of associative action.

Female Labor Market Participation

It has been argued that the impact of increasing levels of female labor market participation upon female as well as overall associability will be negative. This should be so mainly because of time constraints. Working full time imposes time budget restrictions upon women (even more so, given the gender distribution of household work, than it does in the case of men), which leaves women little or no free time for associative activities. This correlation, however, should be weakened by the spread of female part-time employment as well as general work time reductions. On the other hand, one might also expect that the job, while imposing time restrictions upon associability, also serves as a powerful activating communicative context and focal point from which associative activities emerge.

Female labor force participation has a strong positive influence upon formal as well as informal associability among women from all social strata.[109] This correlation may be explained by the diversity of people and interests that are to be encountered in the workplace, the access that coworkers provide to various forms and substantive fields of associational activity, and the durable social interaction that is necessitated by work organizations. In comparison to such organizations, neighborhoods typically provide less diversity and perhaps also less intensity and expected continuity of interaction, as such interaction, in contrast to interaction on the job, is always, at least within urban settings, under the proviso of unilateral discontinuation.

In East Germany, associative life (in both its more and less voluntary varieties) was closely tied to the enterprise rather than leisure-related and cultural foci of association. This pattern, together with a very high level of female labor force participation that implied a virtual absence of the male-breadwinner-cum-female-homemaker arrangement, provided for a largely gender-neutral access to associational life. After the East German state and its regime of labor and gender relations collapsed in 1990, the resulting loss of jobs affected men and women in massively unequal ways, with the female rate of unemployment increasing twice as fast during the first two years after unification as the male rate. On the basis of the well-documented causal effect of employment upon associability, a sharp decline of female associative involvement must be expected to result from this massive, persistent, and sharply gender-biased incidence of joblessness. This should be all the more the case since the population of the GDR had been used to an enterprise-centered pattern of associability.

SOCIAL CAPITAL AND THE QUALITY OF GOVERNANCE

So far we have discussed the standard sociological variables as they impact upon our central research interest: the incidence of associability, attention, and its assumed correlate of civic trust. We now proceed to shift the focus of the analysis and conclude with a discussion of the (assumedly favorable) implications of social capital. Such implications can, according to much of the current literature on this topic, be analytically thought of as affecting either the quality of governance or the level of economic performance. We look at these two dependent variables in turn.

The relation between social capital and good government moves in both directions. On one hand, we can focus upon the qualities of public policy that encourage, facilitate, and provide space for types of associations that generate social capital. On the other hand, we can focus upon ways in which strong associability can improve the quality (i.e., the efficiency, effectiveness, responsiveness, and fairness) of democracy and democratic governance.

Regarding the first of these two causal links, we can distinguish two ways in which (local, state, or federal) governments, legislatures, and political parties might contribute to strengthening associative activities. On one hand, they can provide favorable legal frameworks, tax incentives, and resources provided in kind (such as meeting halls or the services of consultants). On the other hand, policy makers can contribute to the emergence and robustness of associational life by refraining from preemptive and excessive state provision and bureaucratic administrations of those services and activities that civic associations are equally capable of performing (and often performing better). The principle according to which the state is called upon to exercise self-restraint and to give priority to smaller units (the family, local communities, self-governing welfare associations [Wohlfahrtsverbände], or occupational associations) is that of subsidiarity, with its highly influential roots in Roman Catholic social doctrine, but also in variants of libertarian-socialist and green-alternative traditions.

Under the impact of ubiquitous fiscal crises prevailing on all levels of government, there has been a strong advocacy (often under the slogan "from welfare state to welfare society") by both liberal and conservative politicians and policy makers of a withdrawal of governmental intervention and pleas for privatization or a new public-private mix. Such withdrawal, however, has typically resulted (by outcome or by intention) in the transfer of public function not to civic associations, but to the market. Emphasizing the adverse distributional impact and social injustices of this transfer, the social democratic political left has often vehemently resisted the anti-étatist moves launched by liberals and conservatives; instead, social democrats have typically called for the preservation of state responsibilities and the responsibilities of state-sponsored and state-financed agencies such as Wohlfahrtsverbände.

Within the framework of this rather sterile and ritualistic political conflict, both sides have missed new and promising approaches to the design of the interface between the state administration and the associational sector within civil society. Providing space for voluntary civic associations and putting to use their resources, material as well as moral, meets with the suspicion of conservatives, market liberals, and social democrats alike, if for different reasons. To the extent that all three groups are prepared to accept and support forms of collective action that are neither market-based nor part of the state apparatus nor purely private clubs, the firmly entrenched organizational pattern of the provision of social services within the German system of governance is that of *Wohlfahrtsverbände*. These associations are the key components of German welfare corporatism.[110] The most important of these corporatist associations are rooted in the milieux of Roman Catholic, Protestant, and social democratic working-class traditions. They are assigned the task and responsibility of providing a broad variety of social and health services and enjoy a virtual monopoly in these sectors. One-third of the financial resources needed for the performance of these functions is provided from federal and state budgets, one-third from the budgets of the social security agencies, and one-third from donations and members' dues. According to some observers, donations and dues accounts for only 10 percent of the budget of the *Wohlfahrtsverbände*.[111] A substantial part of the manpower employed in the provision of services consist of volunteers—about 1.5 million who donate their efforts without (full) monetary compensation. According to estimations of the *Wohlfahrtsverbände*, their number has stayed basically the same since the late 1970s.[112]

The performance of voluntary work *(Ehrenamt)* in the *Wohlfahrtsverbände* is voluntary in the sense that nobody can be forced to perform it. It is not voluntary, however, in the sense that the kind of tasks that are to be performed, as well as the division of labor according to which it is performed, is decided upon not by participants but by employed professionals and administrators *(Hauptamtliche)* who make up the staff of *Wohlfahrtsverbände*. Those administrators increased in number from 382,000 in 1970 to 937,000 in 1993, including the new *Länder*.[113] The *Wohlfahrtsverbände* can therefore be described as semipublic agencies (rather than voluntary associations). This hybrid structure puts the volunteers into the subordinate and dependent position of helpers (rather than members), a condition that is widely held responsible for the crisis of *Ehrenamt* and a significant decline in the manpower resources the *Wohlfahrtsverbände* are capable of mobilizing. Secularist and postideological trends and changes at the level of widely accepted social and moral norms have contributed to the decomposition of political and religious milieux; it has undermined the dispositions, most importantly the unquestioning acceptance of the duty of charity and solidarity, on the basis of which volunteering within hierarchical and often paternalist and authoritarian structures used to occur.

Voluntary services undergo complex structural changes.[114] First, there are no clear-cut dividing lines separating self-help activities (such as health groups or child care cooperatives) and the more traditional voluntary service sector (e.g., church-sponsored charity or social service activities organized by the German welfare associations [Wohlfahrtsverbände]). Second, the forces that motivated individual engagement underwent considerable change. Thus, both the associational forms in which services are provided and the motivational sources underpinning volunteering activities are at variance with the simplistic model of large and highly visible organizations activating and absorbing involvements, which in turn are motivated by a widely shared sense of duty and responsibility toward the community.[115]

The often diagnosed result of these cultural changes is an apparent mismatch between, on one hand, typical motivational dispositions to engage in voluntary social service and helping activities and, on the other, the structural opportunities within which these motives can be activated and accommodated.[116] What seems to follow from this diagnosis is a significant waste or underutilization of the moral resources of providing voluntary services.

A variety of surveys from the 1980s and 1990s deals with this mismatch and with the possibility of providing more appropriate structures.[117] All these surveys and projects converge on the finding that it is not egoistic individualism but a changing attitude toward volunteering that challenges existing structures and policies and leads potential volunteers to withhold their engagement, which they would be perfectly willing to supply if only more appropriate organizational opportunities were seen to be available.

On the basis of available surveys, the following portrait of the modern volunteer can be drawn. First, formal membership (including the duty to pay dues and donate time) is more readily accepted in associations that provide services and leisure activities to members only (such as sports clubs) rather than in associations providing help and services to outsiders. Second, if such engagement in the latter type of associations occurs, it is less motivated by a generalized and lasting sense of (social, political, or religious) duty than by a quid pro quo reasoning, with the quo being not material rewards but the gratifying opportunity for meaningful, creative, autonomous activities with strong socializing and expressive overtones. Third, the preparedness to supply such engagement is highly contingent and unevenly distributed across both the social structure and the life cycle. In particular, the longitudinal pattern of distribution seems to correspond to typical fluctuations of individuals' time budgets across the stages of adolescence, adulthood, parenthood, and retirement. Also, engagement in voluntary services follows the opportunities conditioned by, on one hand, the evidence of concrete need and, on the other, the contingencies of employment, marital status, family status, and geographic mobility. Because of these experiences and anticipations of fluctuation, it is widely considered unwise or unfeasible among potential volunteers to make lasting commitments and to join associational forms that presuppose the durability of commitment.

These observations seem to suggest that in order to deal with the mismatch between motivations and organizational opportunities, a much more flexible supply of the latter is called for than can be offered by the traditional practices of *Wohlfahrtsverbände*. More specifically, state authorities would have to avoid either of two fallacies in order to optimize the use that is being made of the motivational potential of volunteering. On one hand, it is the fallacy of authoritarian-bureaucratic and patronizing structures that reduce the role of volunteers to that of dutiful, subordinate helpers. On the other hand, the state must avoid the neoliberal fallacy of wholesale retreat. Given the highly contingent and fluctuating nature of the motivational potential for volunteering, attention must be focused upon opportunities for meaningful engagement, and the transaction costs of associational activities would have to be subsidized in ways that minimize the interference with the autonomy of volunteers. The familiar dilemma for state agencies is that between "doing too much" (that is, imposing programs that volunteers must simply implement) and "doing too little" (that is, failing to provide the framework, information, and auxiliary services on which a modern sector of self-help and voluntary services seems to depend).[118] Incidentally, models for many of these activating and enabling functions are to be discovered, apart from the religious and political organizations of Roman Catholicism, in the history of some leftist political parties, both communist (as in Italy's Partito Communista Italiano [PCI]) and social democratic (as in the Weimar Sozialdemokratische Partei Deutschlands [SPD]). As these models of nested, party-sponsored associability are unlikely to be revived under present conditions, the challenge is all the greater to invent and experiment with modern functional equivalents.

An example of a successful provision of auxiliary services is a "meeting point" project for self-help groups initiated by the Bundesminis-terium für Familie und Senioren. It was designed to provide consulting services, professional support, and mediation services addressed to vol-unteers and medical as well as social work professionals, support in pub-lic relations services, provision of rooms, information about monetary support, support in continuing education, and help in starting new self-help groups in thirty-seven communities in East and West Germany (1988–91 in the West, 1992–96 in the East). It was realized in collabora-tion with the county, city, and federal government and Deutscher Par-itätischer Wohlfahrtsverband, the most important nongovernmental actor that organizes volunteering in Germany. As a result of the pro-gram, the number of self-help groups increased considerably. In small towns and in the countryside, the increase was most substantial, amounting to 52 percent on average in the West and as much as 118 per-cent in the East.[119] Similar successes were achieved by programs initiated by the state Ministry of Social Affairs of Baden-Württemberg.[120]

As said earlier, the quality of governance is both a precondition for and dependent upon associational structures within civil society. Turn-ing now to the latter, or bottom-up, perspective, we wish to distinguish three ways in which the quality of democratic governance is contingent upon the density of associational life and the presence of social capital.

First, it seems relatively safe to assume (although conclusive evidence is hard to come by in the available survey data) that being a member of a political party, a formal association, a club, or a group of volunteers will have a formative impact upon members. Through interaction, discus-sion, and the information disseminated by the respective group, the capacity of the member/citizen to perform two functions will be enhanced: the capacity to cope with internal conflict and contribute to the maintenance of associational life, and the ability to pass reasonably informed judgment and to recognize and promote, vis-à-vis the outside world, his or her own interests and values as they relate to the substan-tive domain of a given association. Taken together, the Tocquevillean assumption is that membership in associations of (almost) whatever kind will, in addition to itself resulting from some measure of attention to public affairs, turn people into marginally better citizens by teaching them the routines of civilized conflict resolution as well as competent judgment about public affairs. To the extent that this assumption is not invalidated as excessively optimistic, these formative impacts of associa-tional membership, together with their conceivable spillover effects into other domains, would obviously count as a favorable contribution to the quality of democratic governance. According to Cusack, it is not the case, contrary to what is suggested by Putnam, that citizens engaged in associations are more satisfied with their (local) government.[121] But that does not preclude the speculation that they may have better reasons to be dissatisfied compared to their associationally less active fellow citizens. This would still speak for a favorable impact of associations upon governance (and, incidentally, against the measure of satisfaction as a reliable indicator of the quality of government).

Second, associations, by providing collective goods and services for their members and for external constituencies, increase the independence and self-sufficiency of all those who benefit from these goods and services. The more densely these goods and services are produced, and the more equitably they are distributed, the less there remains, due to this "unburdening" effect, to be done by governments, and the less likely it is that state-citizen relations will be deformed into inherently authoritarian relationships of dependency, paternalism, and clientelism. Therefore, strong and dense associations may help to immunize the citizenry from populist appeals and other dangers of the "politics of mass society."[122] Also, the less there remains to be done by government, the better governments can perform their core functions of protecting the life, property, and liberty of citizens. Again, the favorable effects of a dense associational life (and the consequent social capital) upon the quality of democratic governance are obvious.

Third, such favorable effects must still be weighed against two generalizable observations. For one thing, and as the data discussed in the section "Determinants of Social Capital: The German Case" demonstrate, people's access to and utilization of the associational production of collective goods are unequally distributed. Less privileged segments of the population (e.g., low-income groups, the less educated, women, the unemployed) are less likely to engage in civic associations and to benefit from their activities. For another, many associations appear to be exclusive (sometimes to the point of outright discrimination or cartelization) in their actual mode of operation, if not according to the letter of their statutes. Taken together, the associational landscape provides a highly uneven picture concerning both the social composition of the associations' members and the coverage of substantive domains and issues. Keeping in mind these features of associations, their favorable impact upon the quality of democratic governance must be held to be limited by these biases and inequities, at least if we take one of the qualities of such governance to be the assurance of equal citizenship. In conclusion, it seems safe to suggest that the quality of democratic governance is not determined, contrary to what enthusiasts of the idea of civil society sometimes seem to imply, by the level of civic associability and social capital alone. The legal and institutional structures of government and the underlying principle of universal citizenship, to the extent that they compensate for the gaps and inequities of the associational production of collective goods, play an independent and at least equally significant role.[123]

SOCIAL CAPITAL AND ECONOMIC PERFORMANCE

A positive correlation between social capital and economic performance (such as low unemployment and low rates of inflation) can be conceptualized in four ways. On the aggregate level, encompassing an entire territorial unit, a high level of social capital (i.e., a dense associational network in a given unit) can be thought of as either a precondition for or a result of good economic performance. Similarly, on the individual level, a person's intense associational involvement (including access to other persons providing interfaces between associations or networks) can be thought of as either a precondition for or a result of stable participation in economic life through employment, careers, and the level of disposable income resulting from such participation. The latter complex serves as an indicator of economic performance on an individual level.

Regarding the aggregate level and the interpretation of social capital as a cause of good economic performance, Putnam argues that, in the Italian case, "civic conditions seem gradually but inexorably to have brought socioeconomic conditions into alignment, so that by the 1970s socioeconomic modernity is very closely correlated with civic community."[124] Trust, a strong allegiance to the norm of reciprocity and the development of cooperative competencies, is seen as reducing transaction costs in market interaction through the readiness of people to share information, the informal enforcement of rules, and the "lubrication" of cooperation.[125]

Regarding the inverse correlation between social capital and economic performance—that is, the interpretation of social capital as a result of good economic performance on the aggregate level—the relation between the degree of civicness of a community and economic performance can be thought of in two ways. First, good economic performance enables persons to engage in life activities other than those aimed at economic gain, as secure employment and adequate earnings allow for the spending of time on social activities. Second, the experience of positive-sum games and economic slack that is typically associated with good economic performance diminishes the level of distributive conflict, socioeconomic marginality, and rivalry for economic opportunities. As a result of the harmony-enhancing impact of good economic performance, an increase in associability (and, in particular, associability centered on postmaterialist values) might be expected.

On the individual level, social capital may work as a precondition for economic success. Membership in associations and access to interassociational or internetwork links may facilitate the acquisition of jobs and other economic opportunities. Inversely, a dense net of social contacts may also result from stable membership in work organizations or secure market position. The workplace provides fertile soil for associability, as many associations and networks are formed by (long-term) fellow workers and colleagues employed by the same company, sometimes at the initiative of the company itself. As we have seen, this interpretation is strongly supported by the negative finding that the long-term unemployed, marginally employed, irregularly employed, discouraged workers, or people permanently outside the workforce (e.g., homemakers) are typically less often involved in associations than is the case with the active population (see "Female Labor Market Participation," above).

However, it also conceivable that conditions of bad economic performance (indicated by high levels of lasting unemployment with a broad incidence) create a situation of widespread precariousness that people affected by the labor market crisis compensate for by turning to various forms of associative cooperation as a source of nonmarket provision of goods, opportunities, and services, for instance, through barter networks and a rich variety of activities, partly illegal, within the *economia sommersa* (shadow economy). Similarly, economic precariousness of whole regions or segments of the population may contribute to associability, as unemployed people join together in order to represent their complaints and to strengthen their claims to employers and policy makers. In the new *Länder,* many self-help groups (*Arbeitsbeschaffungsmassnahmen,* or ABMs) have formed, mostly sponsored by the support made available through the German labor market agency, with the (often manifestly failing) intention of upgrading skills, developing work experience, and increasing employability, eventually resulting in the reemployment of members and clients. The formation of both barter networks and employability-enhancing self-help associations may be strengthened by the (involuntary) availability of lots of free time on the part of many of those affected by unemployment.[126] Some observers, however, have expressed the suspicion that instead of serving as a bridge to a new job, ABM schemes (particularly in the new *Länder,* where they are relied upon very widely due to special federal programs) tend to create meeting points for "failures," that is, forms of associability within which a culture of marginality, self-pitying, and despair is being nurtured. Should such suspicions turn out to be justified, this would invite the speculation that it is not associability as such but the degree of structural diversity within associations that makes for the desirable economic and political impact of social capital.

Inversely, acquisitive reasons for engaging in such cooperation may well vanish if the economy moves toward a restoration of full employment, income becomes less precarious, and the provision of goods and services can be ascertained through the market. Furthermore, we can also think of cases where high levels of associability are the result of—and, in turn, shape—strong preferences for noneconomic activities so that individuals' contribution to economic gain may diminish, as they feel they have better things to do than maximize their income by living up to strict standards of the work ethic.

Little evidence is to be found for the hypothesized positive correlations and either of the two applicable interpretations on the aggregate level in the case of Germany. Two surveys shed some indirect light on the relation between economic (and, in particular, labor market) performance and associational density.

The first of these surveys explores extraeconomic factors as they influence the unemployment rate in twenty-six districts of Germany.[127] These included thirteen districts with high unemployment rates and thirteen districts with low unemployment rates. No significant correlation was found to exist between employment levels and the importance that respondents assigned to local associational life in general. Regarding the importance assigned to good relations within the neighborhood, there is a noticeable difference between "strong" and "weak" districts, if in a perhaps slightly counterintuitive direction: In the strong districts, good neighborhood relations were considered less important than in the weak districts, as was the respondents' reported preparedness to help neighbors with problems such as renovation of apartments, construction work, and caring for children and sick persons.[128] This supports the interpretation that associational activity of the form of cooperation within the neighborhood is, apart from the greater availability of free time, driven by a substitution effect, as under conditions of precariousness people rely on help for the provision of services that they would probably buy in more prosperous circumstances.

Another survey supports this reasoning and extends it to kinds of associations that do not play a role in substituting for purchasable goods and services.[129] Unemployment levels and reported membership in clubs devoted to leisure time activities (such as bowling clubs) were compared within four government districts of Germany. It turned out that membership in such clubs was most frequent among residents (both male and female) of the region with the highest unemployment rate (Bremen, where it reached 11.5 percent in 1993), while in the district of Lower Bavaria (where unemployment was just 7.3 percent in 1993), reported membership in such clubs was negligible.[130] Could it be that high levels of associability correspond with poor economic performance—with the further possibility to be considered that strong regional preferences for associative activity conflict with and possibly even undermine the preference for maximum efficiency and economic gain?

At the individual level, the question is: Do individuals who rank high on a scale of associative involvement and participation in networks also rank high in terms of job security and economic success? If so, which way does the causal arrow point? Here, a stronger positive correlation is suggested by the few data that we were able to locate.

First, finding a (first) job is clearly facilitated by access to informal contacts, be they based upon family, school, neighborhood, or associations. Almost two-thirds of the respondents in a representative sample surveyed in 1980 found a new job, whether after being unemployed or after having decided to quit a previous job, through informal contacts of these various sorts, as opposed to the formal labor exchange of the labor market administration.[131] Another study focuses on the job search behavior of first entrants into the labor market and the success of their reliance on informal contacts. Again, the results suggest a very substantial role of this resource in successful job searches, as 44 percent of the respondents found their first job through connections, such as teachers at school, their own parents, the parents of friends, neighbors, and so on. These connections provide either information about opportunities or (in two out of three cases) substantial help in getting a particular job.[132] This survey of first entrants suggests that a person's access to networks is one important precondition for, rather than a result of, labor market success.

But the hypothesis that social capital—or, more generally, connectedness—is a result of labor market and other economic success also finds indirect confirmation. One survey looks at jobless persons in terms of the duration of their being registered as unemployed.[133] It turns out that long-term unemployment has a strong negative impact upon connectedness, measured in terms of the size of networks to which a person actually has access. Unemployment, as has been confirmed by many studies, increases social isolation.[134] Those who are unemployed for six years or more have access to networks that are on average just half the size of those networks that are available to persons who are unemployed for about eighteen months.[135] It thus appears that long-term unemployment creates a vicious circle, with the gradual loss not just of skills but also of other resources (i.e., informal contacts) that are of critical importance for regaining employment.

CONCLUSIONS

Throughout our exploration of social capital in Germany, we encountered the difficulty of determining whether the strength of social capital depends on individual properties of citizens (such as level of education), on collective properties of a local sort (such as shared cultural traditions and the presence of role models and opportunities), or on overall institutional properties of political and economic regimes (and the sense of efficacy they generate, as well as the opportunities they are seen to make available for promising and satisfactory kinds of involvement).

While our findings suggest that individual properties, such as level of education or employment status, make a significant impact on the level of social capital, the influence of collective properties is more difficult to assess. The fact that membership rates are particularly high in smaller communities may be read as evidence for the encouragement effect: The more people are seen to join, the easier others will find it to join as well, as the entry threshold is perceived to decline while at the same time the potential opportunity costs of not joining (e.g., the loss of access to information and useful social contacts) are perceived to rise.

As to the institutional properties of political and economic regimes, their impact upon levels of social capital appears complex and somewhat ambiguous. Clearly in cases of extreme social interventionism, where bureaucratic-paternalist provision of services suffocates and discourages civic activities, social capital declines. At the other extreme, a laissez-faire regime is likely to generate strong incentives for self-help, but it is also likely to result in the production of highly exclusive "club goods" for the benefit of members only, as opposed to collective goods that serve the entire community or at least have significant spillover effects. An optimal political regime, from the point of view of social capital formation, probably comes in between those extremes, as argued in the section "Social Capital and the Quality of Governance," above. This optimum would be defined by institutional arrangements within states or firms that provide opportunities (such as subsidized facilities), incentives (such as tax exemptions), and sufficiently open and pluralistic moral appeals (such as political advocacy for voluntarism) that encourage associative or volunteer activities without discouraging them through overly tight supervision and regulation. This optimum is what recent debates on "new subsidiarity" and a desirable road "from welfare state to welfare society" are aiming at.[136]

Regarding the patterns of distribution of associability and volunteering along a substantive dimension as well as social categories of actual participants, there is a clear shift from company-, party-, and church-sponsored (nested) associations to more autonomous and leisure-time-related associations, such as sports clubs. The latter, however, face significant competition from commercial suppliers of services. At the same time, even within clubs devoted to leisure-time activities, the relation of participants to the association tends to be transformed into that of clients (with comparatively weak commitments and with the exit option being relatively close at hand) as opposed to that of more robustly loyal members of encompassing religious, political, or even company-based groups.

Some groups who are underrepresented in terms of their associational involvement today, such as the less educated and low-income groups, used to be "captured" and mobilized into active participation by working-class organizations, such as trade unions and related associations. As these relatively homogeneous milieux are no longer clearly demarcated today and, consequently, large-scale sponsors of these milieux have virtually disappeared from the scene, a deprivation effect must be noted as a result. Thus the changing nature of associations and membership is likely to have an impact upon the structural distribution of associational participation. That is to say, those categories of the population who used to be relatively easily drawn into and mobilized by traditional milieu-based and party- or church-sponsored types of association seem now deprived of easy and conventional access to the benefits of associational life unless they acquire the middle-class skills of acting as prudent clients and consumers of what clubs have to offer. Apparently, being a part of these milieux used to work as a functional equivalent for high levels of these middle-class skills, which are partly acquired through education. Interestingly, class-specific and cultural selectivities of membership in associations is least significant where these associations focus upon nonverbal pursuits, such as is the case with sports, music, and religious worship, although there are some rather obvious internal differences as to which strata prefer which types of sports, musical, and religious styles and practices. Many of these practices, however, are also available as strictly individual pursuits without any associative implications, such as the practice of jogging, worshiping, or "bowling alone."

Differences in associative practices must also be accounted for in terms of gender. To be sure, the share of women among all members of associations has increased since the fifties as a consequence of increased rates of female participation in both higher education and the labor market, as well as a decrease in the size of households and families. Moreover, the rise of new social movements (including feminist movements) has improved the opportunity structure for female associability. Yet there is still a gender gap concerning both the level and the typical substantive domains of associability (see the section on gender), which may be accounted for by a decline of those movements and possibly also by a persistent female preference for small and informal networks of a more strongly personalistic type with associated expressive practices.[137]

But the preferred patterns of associability seem to undergo an overall structural change. There is some evidence for an "informalization" of associative practices, especially among the young. First, modes of participation, even in the more formal types of associations, appear to become less binding as the commitment of members declines in terms of durability and as participants relate to the association as clients, with an often transient and limited interest in the issues and themes on which the association focuses. Moreover, the attachment to the association tends to be more strongly mediated through personal ties to other members rather than through the cause the association stands for.[138]

Second, not only does the mode of attachment to formal organizations seem to lose its bindingness, but also a type of contact, communication, and cooperation is becoming common that strongly deviates from the pattern of a clearly bounded organization with members, entry procedures, and a formalized hierarchy. Such flat networks or webs of more or less lasting interaction are obviously limited as to the demands that can be made, as well as the cause-related loyalty expected, of those who at a given point in time feel attached to them, rather than being members in any tangible sense. On the other hand, this informality does not preclude a strong preparedness on the part of those attached to provide help and to share resources with other (recognized) members. The cohesion of such networks is more likely to be mediated by personalistic ties and shared histories of interaction than by some clearly defined thematic focus. Such webs of interaction and mutual loyalty are often highly homogeneous (and hence somewhat exclusive) in terms of age, gender, occupational affiliation, and level of education. Finally, to the extent these networks relate to public affairs at all, these affairs tend to be of a semiprivate and limited scope and do not typically involve matters of an encompassing social, political, and ideologically charged nature. This set of features of a somewhat intangible associability is illustrated by the findings of the most recent Youth Survey (1997), in which the young generation is portrayed as rather abstinent in terms of participation in conventional forms of political action although, at the same time, quite actively engaged in those informal social nets and webs.

We conclude with some suggestions for further research, applying both to the German case itself and comparative investigations such as the other chapters in this book. First, there is a remarkable lack of data on the less formal types of associative activity just discussed. These are methodically hard to elucidate due to their intangible nature and mode of operation. Second, it is not clear to what extent the involvement of persons in associations and networks is a matter of individual dispositions or, inversely, to what extent these dispositions are cultivated and activated as a result of the experience of associational activities and the observation of such activities on the part of others (as the intuition behind social capital theory seems to imply). This calls for more research. The spread and intensity of associative activities may furthermore be as much determined from above, that is, from the wider institutional context of civic life, as from below, that is, through the dispositions of individuals. Third, the question of cui bono must become one central focus of social capital research, as access to social capital and the beneficial outcomes of its operation is clearly very unevenly distributed within the social structure.

6

FROM CIVIL WAR TO CIVIL SOCIETY: Social Capital in Spain from the 1930s to the 1990s

VÍCTOR PÉREZ-DÍAZ

Following on from James Coleman, Robert Putnam has recently made "social capital" a fashionable term, and affirms that it is diminishing in the United States and possibly in other countries.[1] However, the term "social capital" needs some clarification, and the assumption of social capital's benign effects on liberal societies should be drastically qualified. The term denotes a combination of norms and networks of cooperation and sentiments of trust that may be of quite different character and serve quite different functions in the larger society. In this essay, I will propose a distinction between two very different kinds of social capital that may exist, "civil" and "uncivil" social capital, and I will explore the effects that these may have, with reference to developments in Spain over the last sixty years. But first a few words are in order on the context that frames these questions, in both its historical and theoretical dimensions.

Western liberal societies are in a post-totalitarian period and are learning to live with a market economy characterized by globalization, (partial) deregulation, privatization, and, so far, a large wave of prosperity. Welfare reform and the demise of the kind of capitalism that was regulated and strongly influenced by the state and corporatist institutions are part of this learning experience. People in many countries have associated the welfare state and the corporate arrangements of "managed capitalism" with the prosperity and stability of the post–World War II period; while they may learn to live without these, there is no way they can avoid a sentiment of malaise caused by their absence. Understandably, people affected by this malaise may tend to dramatize events and to think that the social fabric is being torn apart and social cohesion diminishing as they see the social compromises of the past revised. As they wonder why the political parties, unions and other professional associations, and churches that made those compromises lack now the will and the ability to uphold them, and as they point to people's detachment from these formal associations as one of the reasons for it, they may find in phrases such as "social capital is diminishing" a fitting statement of their anxieties.

However, an alternative view is to consider this malaise as merely another symptom of the birth pangs of a long transition toward a relatively homogeneous European and worldwide socioeconomic order and, therefore, to take a more positive attitude toward it. Instead of seeing the expansion of the market economy as an overwhelming process of commodification of the world (with the negative connotations of alienation and fetishism attached to it), we may consider it as possibly a step forward to an order of liberty and the type of social cohesion that goes with it, provided we learn how to adapt to it by looking to new forms of association or giving a new look to the old ones, and provided we take it as an opportunity to redefine solidarity.

Such a process of practical adaptation has to take place country by country and in particular traditions: in Western Europe, for instance, in the traditions of the liberal (Anglo-Saxon), social democratic (Scandinavian), and Christian democratic (Continental) welfare systems of the last hundred years. As Fritz Scharpf has suggested, there may be a diversity of solutions to the problem of adjusting European welfare systems to the international integration of product and capital markets (and in time, we may add, to that of labor markets), depending on the policy legacy and the local institutional (and cultural) constraints of the different countries.[2] At the same time, however, each country may learn from others' experiences, try what looks successful elsewhere, mix the components of various traditions, and end up with hybrid institutions and complex justifications for what it will do. Thus once solutions have been found in one country, they can be transmitted to others by means of cultural diffusion, translated into the local moral discourse, and adjusted to local circumstances, the result being that diversity may be compatible with a convergence of sorts.[3]

This process should go hand in hand with the development of a theory of social capital that makes a clear distinction between different types of social capital as they are related to different forms of solidarity, and that also explores the linkages of this theory with the classical problem of social integration in modern societies. This is what I attempt to do in this chapter by stressing the distinction between civil and uncivil kinds of social capital, and by doing so with reference to a theory of civil society.

I am interested in the process of transformation of each kind of social capital into its opposite as a given society goes through several historical stages; Spain, in particular, went from a civil war to a liberal democracy through an authoritarian experience. I have found Putnam's focus on norms and networks of cooperation and sentiments of trust to be useful in the Spanish case, but I am unsatisfied with a general tendency in the literature on social capital (and on civil society understood in a narrow sense) to reduce networks to a social fabric of formal associations, as well as to take verbal statements of trust or lack of trust (in people or in institutions) in answers to questionnaires as the main basis for assessments of the moral dimension of social capital. By contrast, a broad concept of networks would include what I call soft forms of sociability (such as families and family-centered networks, peer groups, and fiestas). By the same token, I am interested in actual behavior as an embodiment of tacit statements regarding attitudes, values, and norms; at the same time, I feel it indispensable to look into the discourses of justification (moral reasoning and explanations) attached to the various types of social capital. Finally, I think that some attention should be given to the role that the economy and politics play in these developments.[4]

CIVIL AND UNCIVIL KINDS OF SOCIAL CAPITAL

The networks, rules, and sentiments of which social capital is composed come to exist in diverse ways, and their effects vary depending on the type of social capital that we refer to. In general terms, it is impossible to imagine any stable social grouping without social capital of one sort or another, without bonds of trust and rules of cooperation. Micro societies (families) and macro societies (nations) alike cannot do without it, and of course, even groups such as the Mafia, patriarchal families subject to a despot, and totalitarian parties all have social capital of a certain kind. The point is, what kind or type of social capital is it?

For many, this has been, and is, linked to the general problem of the normative integration of society. Solutions to it have always remained sensitive to the changing character of social integration as it applies to "traditional" and "modern" societies, and to the transition from one to the other. In this chapter, I will tackle the issue of social integration from the viewpoint of a theory of civil society.

The ideal character of a civil society *sensu lato* is a hybrid, composed of (in Michael Oakeshott's terms) a "civil association," which is based on the participants' subscription to common rules while pursuing their own goals, and an "enterprise association," which is based on the participants' acceptance of common purposes (or, in other words, a "nomocratic order" and a "teleocratic order," respectively), though with a bias toward the civil association.[5] But the kinds of trust and solidarity appropriate to these two orders are different.

On one hand, there is the kind of trust typical of markets, voluntary associations, open public spheres, relationships with responsible public authorities subject to the rule of law, and plural societies. It is the trust appropriate to a community of free individuals who abide by the rules of individual conduct and of mutual respect and reciprocity that are required for the formation of spontaneous orders.[6] On the other, there is the kind of trust appropriate to a community of individuals united insofar as they are associates in a collective action with a common objective, and subordinate to a public authority insofar as it directs them in that action.

Likewise, Friedrich Hayek, arguing in a similar manner, insists that the sentiments and learned traditions of altruism typical of small groups or families are different from those typical of extended orders. Thus, the solidarity of the small group presupposes a relatively large measure of agreement among its members as to the objectives of the group and the methods for achieving them. This solidarity is of fundamental importance to a small group of people with similar habits, but unforeseen circumstances necessitate the very different form of social coordination of the extended orders based on rules, not on common ends (given that those ends will unite a complex society only in times of crisis).[7]

The kind of altruism applicable also varies according to the size and character of the group. In the small group, altruism corresponds to the shared purpose of attending to the visible needs of those whom one knows personally. But "the morals of the market lead us to benefit others not so much because we are oriented toward doing so intentionally, but because these morals induce us to act in such a way that this will be the effect which follows on from our actions," so that "the extended order makes our efforts altruistic in their effects" (and, therefore, offers the possibility for each one of us to add the intention to the effect).[8]

When it comes to connecting these two kinds of sentiments and morals, Hayek confines himself to offering some possibly prudent, but certainly very vague, advice: He warns us that if we apply the rules of microcosms to macrocosms, we will destroy the extended orders, but if we do the opposite, we will wipe out the microcosms. And he suggests that we learn the art of living in both worlds at the same time.

Rather than taking this recommendation at face value, I feel it invites us to move on to questions at the heart of the discussion of social capital: Is it necessary to combine the two sets of morals that are in operation here, and if so, how could it be done? On the one hand, we have the morals (and sentiments, and networks of social relationships) of the extended orders, which should prevail in a civil society due to its bias favorable to a civil association united by rules. This is where the morals of the economic markets (with their underlying morality of trust in the fulfillment of promises, and of a principle of reciprocity being applied to mutually beneficial exchanges) and the morals of the markets of intellectual and scientific debate belong. On the other hand, we have the various morals of the "associations as enterprise" or, in other words, of small groups or "tribal" groups (in a very large sense). Among the latter we find family morality, the morals typical of voluntary associations (for example, unions or firms), the moral feelings typical of local (provincial, regional) or religious or ethnic solidarity, and also a national morality of society "as a collectivity," be it national or plural.[9]

These "tribal" morals may be compatible or incompatible with a civil society. This means that while the morals of open or abstract societies imply the presence of a social capital of a civil kind, tribal morals (and the corresponding networks of cooperation and sentiments of trust) have, in this regard, much more ambiguous implications.

The point can be further elaborated by going back to the theories of Emile Durkheim on mechanical solidarity (which refers to a state of community bonding based on shared experiences and values) as typical of segmented (and "traditional") societies, and organic solidarity (which refers to a state of interdependency created by specialization of roles) as typical of modern societies, and to Parsons' comments on this.[10] Parsons believes that in Durkheim's thought (and within the tradition of that thought, in which he places himself), organic solidarity is not simply opposed to mechanical solidarity. Correcting or developing Durkheim, Parsons goes on to suggest that the organic solidarity typical of a highly differentiated society, in which exchanges usually take the form of exchanges in markets (or in extended orders), needs to be complemented by mechanical solidarity. For Parsons, the norms underlying these exchanges should be institutionalized (including mechanisms for sanctions and enforcement) and internalized. Enforcement involves some definition of the boundaries of society as a community (with its rules of membership), some common goals, and a government that attends to them and guarantees fulfillment of the norms by the use of force if necessary. In turn, the internalization of norms involves a socialization process and a common culture, that is to say, beliefs and sentiments shared by members of the society.

In my view, Parsons carries his reasoning too far, on the basis of two (related) assumptions. First, he believes that society as a community requires its members to share nothing less than a conception of the ideal society that they desire: a common definition of what a "good society" consists of.[11] Parsons' position seems excessive and inappropriate for a pluralistic society in which it is to be hoped (and desired) that people with very different visions of a "good society" would be able to compare and contrast their points of view and show reciprocal tolerance. Likewise, it seems to imply an overly robust state or government whose main role would be to steer society toward collective goals coherent with the supposedly shared (and why not unanimous?) vision of the ideal society. Second, Parsons understands that those feelings and beliefs, or supreme values, are related to the norms applicable to different sectors of society, its diverse communities (with less scope), and individuals (in their social roles, as Parsons points out) in such a way that the norms must be systematically subordinated to these supreme values. This vision implies an interpretation that is too rigid and not sufficiently plausible of what is to be hoped and, especially, what *ought* to be hoped from social integration in an open society.

Of course, if collectivities were to adhere to definitions of a "good life" that are incompatible with one another *together with* the urge to impose their views on others, it would be a recipe for civil war, as the Spanish case will show. Nevertheless, this does not preclude the existence of quite divergent, and even contrary, world visions, and different versions of what a "good society" means in a modern, complex society. The point is whether they can coexist with each other, and for this what is needed is not a set of common substantive values but just procedural rules.

Having said this, it must be recognized that Parsons is right both to insist on the need for accommodating the two kinds of solidarity and to express interest in the possible positive effects of mechanical solidarity on the integration of societies of extended orders. This leads him to underline the importance of rituals, which are dramatizations of people's commitments to values they all share when it comes to expressing and reinforcing (mechanical) solidarity in modern societies.

I must add that this reference to the importance of ritual gives us a clue to the interesting phenomenon of the difference in intensity of feelings of solidarity relative to the extended orders (and organic solidarity) and those relative to the collectivities (in Parsons' language) or small groups (bands or tribes *sensu lato*, in that of Hayek). Experience suggests that, normally, feelings are intense only if they refer to a particular object. Feelings of mechanical solidarity are those relevant to the family and to collectivities such as the tribe, the *ethnos*, the church, or even the nation, all of which can be perceived, in a manner tinged with affection, as the equivalents of huge families. This means that members can feel as if they have quasi-familial ties with them (like patriarchal or matriarchal extended families, or brotherhoods). The quasi-familial bond facilitates the transmission of feelings of (mechanical) solidarity from the family group in the strict sense toward much wider groups. Thus, in the classical accounts of Mediterranean societies, the seaman-merchant who arrives in a community as a stranger to trade is accepted on the basis of his adoption as guest, client, or member of the household of whoever is to be his protector, patron, and guarantor before the community, and it is through this almost familial hospitality that the stranger achieves some form of vicarious membership in the community.[12]

Hence, the most usual sentiment appears to be love (or hatred) of what is closest to us, and it gradually extends outward in a series of enlargements that preserve some part of their original familial nature. Hypothetically, this feeling could come to encompass the whole human race, like "one giant family" in the imagery of the great universal religions. Indeed, the media know that the best way to appeal for solidarity with the suffering of people in the Third World is, for example, by making the exotic appear domestic. This is accomplished by the immediacy of a scene in close-up on television, so that the protagonists of the news item can burst into the intimacy of the home, sit down at the table or in an armchair in the living room, and become, for one moment, parts (members) of the family community. The other side of the coin is that the kind of solidarity required, above all others, by the extended orders does perhaps exclude feelings that are too intense; it requires "weak ties," which allow and promote the fluid circulation of information in all possible directions, and which facilitate contacts between all sorts of people.[13]

This finally brings us to the complex and potentially contradictory role that the diverse forms of religious life can play with respect to the social integration of modern societies. While Parsons (and Durkheim) emphasizes the link between ritual (religious or otherwise) and the mechanical solidarity of society insofar as the latter is a particular, circumscribed community, Hayek is more interested in the link between the universal religions and society insofar as the latter is part of the extended orders. Both approaches tend to overlook the negative effects that religions can, and indeed frequently do, have: the reinforcement of tribalism against the extended orders, and the rupture of social solidarity when it falls victim to religious enthusiasm.

In other words, nations may behave in a civilized or an aggressive manner; religions may be tolerant or intolerant. Therefore we end up not only with a distinction between organic and mechanical solidarities, but also with a distinction within the latter, between the kind of mechanical solidarity that is compatible with a civil society and the kind that is not.

ACT I: SPAIN'S CIVIL WAR AND THE VICTORS' WORLD, OR SOCIAL CAPITAL OF AN UNCIVIL KIND (1930s–1950s)

In the following pages, I analyze the development and the transformations of social capital of various types in Spain over a time span of about sixty years. I wish to shed light on this process by showing its connections with other (political, economic, and socio-structural) dimensions of Spain's historical process. More particularly, I intend to explore the effects of political events and decisions, and long-term state actions, on the process of change and accumulation of social capital.

This entire period can be viewed as a drama in three acts, or three historical phases. My point of departure, or act I, is a moment of "zero solidarity," or, in other words, a moment of the apotheosis of uncivil social capital. This moment is the Spanish civil war of the 1930s, an event that can be interpreted as the antithesis of a civil society. However, I also consider the kind of social capital prevailing in the society that emerged from the war, the victors' world (which was a phase of political repression, economic autarchy, and social isolation, at least during the 1940s and early 1950s), to be similar in nature to that of the war itself. Act II is a period of fast economic growth, intense sociocultural transformations, and partial liberalization that stretches from the mid-fifties to the mid-seventies. In this act, the plot untangles with a change toward a more civil type of social capital, which coexists with the kind inherited from the war but builds the stock from which the democratic transition will draw in the final phase. Thus in act III, Spain follows the normal path of Western societies, combining a relatively advanced market economy with the institutions of liberal democracy.

There is perhaps a tendency to start most analyses of social change of Western societies in the 1950s, disregarding World War II as well as its aftereffects. These analyses therefore concentrate on two periods that are differentiated, *grosso modo,* by the political turbulence of the late 1960s (the reactions to the Vietnam War and the events of May 1968, among others) and the economic crisis of the early 1970s. They refer to societies that constitute relatively well integrated national communities operating in a market economy and under a liberal democratic polity. Finally, they overlook earlier phases of participation in foreign (or civil) wars, or under the rule of authoritarian regimes, from which some of these societies have emerged.

Personally, I doubt that we shall be able to understand capitalist democratic societies in the postwar period if we ignore their points of departure—that is, the Second World War, the civil wars, and either the authoritarian regimes or, alternatively, the interclass pacts of the time. In other words, we cannot understand these societies without considering the genesis of the particular type of social capital that developed during that period and became manifest in the following one.[14] In the case of Spain, I certainly cannot overlook that previous phase, in which the two distinct types of social capital that I referred to in the first part of the paper came to the fore.

The Civil War

As a fratricidal experience, the Spanish Civil War was the apotheosis of mistrust, the breakdown of a community, and, as a consequence, the destruction of social solidarity. At the same time, it was the apotheosis of tribal solidarities within each of the two sides. Of the two types of social capital, organic solidarity went out the window, while mechanical solidarity blossomed and flourished.

It must be remembered that the civil war is not only the point of departure for the accumulation of social capital as seen from the scientific observer's point of view when looking back from a later point in time. It has in fact been a crucial reference point in the collective imaginary of the people involved in the process of accumulation of social capital in every one of its phases. Their political narratives, their institutions, and their social practices have all been influenced by the memories of that war, as well as by the intermingling of those memories with diverse normative feelings and propositions. The war is not only the point of departure but also the crucial formative experience of several generations. It pertains to the way they created their social capital and inverted that capital in shaping their civic engagement, and their reasons for doing so. For instance, for the leaders of the transition from authoritarian rule to democracy in the mid-seventies (born, most of them, between 1930 and 1950), the civil war became, in an explicit and ostensible manner, the basic negative referent for their decisions. It was a counterexample to be overcome and avoided. That is why what they preached was primarily consensus, reconciliation, and a plan for "building together" the country and its institutions.

The civil war involved two adversaries motivated by intense reciprocal hatred, but each containing important social capital. By the time the war started (after a period of intensification of sociopolitical and cultural conflicts in the preceding years), neither of them was pervaded by social capital of the civil-society type—though we must be aware of nuances on each side.

On the side of those who called themselves the Nationalists, several kinds of solidarities, mostly of the mechanical type, were cemented during this period. Examples include the solidarity of the Church, the army, the Falangist Party/movement, and the corporate villages (and Catholic agrarian associations) of the masses of small farmers that supported the Francoist army in the northern half of the country. There was also the solidarity of a business milieu prone to come to an understanding with an interventionist and protective state and opposed to foreign competition and workers' claims. All this brought together the explicit or tacit support of a wide sociopolitical coalition for a statist-corporatist social design, which combined the features of several different historical formations. Such a design was based upon intense national solidarity and dependent on Catholic doctrines and strong links of authority and hierarchy, but it was also based on equality, fraternity, and comradeship (among equal neighbors, brothers in arms, party affiliates, or members of a mystical body). This was the design of a teleocratic order in which activities were supposed to be subordinate to the common good, under the leadership of the state and in alliance with the Church, at least in the field of culture (that is, as regards beliefs, feelings, and morals). In this order there was no room for liberal democracy and, at least in principle (if only partly in practice), the market economy was to be subordinated to the common good of the authoritarian state.

On the Republican side, several tribes (or confederations of tribes) can be distinguished against a more complex and colorful background. Tension among them was sufficiently high to bring them, at times, to civil war within a civil war (in Barcelona in May 1937 and in Madrid in March 1939). One of these tribes was the anarcho-syndicalists, whose type of solidarity implied an order without a state (or very little state) in which trade unions and industrial or rural groups imposed their authority on individuals (which drove the subtribe of individualistic anarchists to despair). Another tribe was the rather unstable coalition of Communists and their socialist allies (led by Francisco Largo Caballero and, subsequently, by Juan Negrín). Their idea of solidarity was built on the image of a social movement led by the hard-core party nucleus imbued with the power of the state, oriented toward a transformation of the social order, and leading to a new collectivist order.[15] Even though these two tribes within the Republican side fought each other, both wished to promote what they called a social revolution, that is, the transition to a collectivist social order under the leadership of a strategic minority—the CNT-FAI (Confederación Nacional de Trabajadores–Federación Anarquista Ibérica) in the case of the anarcho-syndicalists, or the Communist Party, or the revolutionary socialists.

In their design for a good or desirable society and in the significance given to the term *solidarity*, both sides involved in the civil war stood on common ground, although they stigmatized each other, so that the Nationalists or the right were labeled as "rebels" by their enemies and the Republicans or the left were labeled as "Reds" by theirs. However, their visions of a good society shared several common elements.

Both sides considered liberal democracy to be a political system in crisis. It was despised by the nucleus of their leaders, who saw it as a system of the past, ready to be replaced by another. They thought the same about capitalism or the market economy: It had to be suppressed (from the leftist point of view) or subordinated to the common good and subjected to state surveillance (from the rightist point of view). The *Rechtsstaat* was to be tolerated or maintained insofar as it was compatible with the grand projects for the transformation of Spain (salvation, regeneration, revolution) that the contenders entertained. Obviously, both parties made eloquent appeals to a moral duty of solidarity, altruism, and sacrifice for the community (which we might call postindividualistic).

During the war, an extraordinary amount of social capital circulated within both camps. The civic engagement of the contenders could not have been greater. Feelings of solidarity within each party were intense, although they could not entirely suppress factional tensions such as those described among the Republicans. Most of the diverse moral codes in use derived from morals of solidarity and civic engagement, and social cooperation networks were tightly knit. At its worst, it was social capital of an uncivil kind pushed to the limits.

The levels of affiliation experienced by social and political organizations evidence this plethora of social capital. On the brink of war, membership in the CNT and the UGT (Unión General de Trabajadores), the two major anarchist and socialist unions, is estimated to have been around 2 million, and total union membership may have been as much as 2.5 million if we add on the smaller trade unions (out of a labor force of about 8.5 million and a wage-earning population estimated at about 5.5–6 million people). Catholic agrarian associations numbered around half a million people.[16] The Catholic Church had become the center of a network of associations such as Acción Católica, the congregations for the worship of the Virgin Mary, Catholic circles, cooperatives, trade unions, and savings banks, which included a large part of the social body. The main political parties (conservative, socialist, and republican) were mass parties with numerous and enthusiastic followers and very active members. Added to these were the minority parties with growing influence, such as the Communists and Falangists, whose ranks grew extraordinarily just before the war.

The civil war was not, therefore, the clash of millions of isolated individual produced by a previously anomic state, but (to a certain extent, as I shall show later) that of two blocks with intense internal solidarity, even though of an uncivil kind. Their internal solidarity was channeled into murdering a large number of their opponents and subduing the remainder. Both sides engaged in killing each other for three years (from July 1936 to April 1939), leaving an estimated 500,000 dead out of a population of about 18 million. It is of interest to note that there were two distinct kinds of death: in the front lines and in the rear guard. Of the latter, at least 20,000 deaths took place in the Republican area, and we may presume an even higher number in the Nationalist area.[17]

Most of the deaths in the rear guard resulted from what were called at the time the "walks" *(paseos)*. As the front advanced, the day's victors would seek out partisans of the vanquished, at home with their families. Armed (Falangist, Communist, anarchist, etc.) militias or soldiers came to a house, knocked on the door, asked for the man in question, and drew him away, telling his wife and children they were just going for a walk. Often he was shot against a wall on the outskirts of town (for example, against the wall of a cemetery for convenience), or in a busy, public spot as a public example. The identification of those selected for these walks was based upon affiliation with an association from which sympathy to the right or the left could be inferred (such as trade unions and professional or religious associations), membership in a political party, engagement in political activity, or the previous holding of public office.

In other words, the expression of solidarity on each side went hand in hand with an experience of terror. And the terror was not limited to a minority within each side but became a far more widespread phenomenon aimed at a large part of the population. In fact, electoral results from the period of the Republic show a predominant vote for parties and factions that played a secondary role after the outbreak of war: Catholic conservatives on the right, Republicans and moderate socialists on the left. Their leaders acquiesced with the main protagonists of the war but remained witnesses. The paradigmatic and rather pathetic case of this behavior was the Republican leader Manuel Azaña. In the critical moment of the spring of 1936 he pretended to take charge of the situation by becoming head of state. In fact he was taking on symbolic pre-eminence while limiting his responsibility for what was to come and was already clearly on the way.

Therefore, even though the civil war may be interpreted as the clash between two camps, each with a dense network of cooperation, subjected to intense indoctrination and each sharing morals of (mechanical) solidarity *ad intra*, this interpretation must be understood in the context of a society in which the majority, whatever its political ideals or sympathies, held comparatively lukewarm political feelings and was probably drawn into (or allowed itself to be drawn into) war. Seen from the perspective of the hard core of each side, this was therefore a majority to be watched and intimidated—and intimidation was the role of the *paseo*.

Consequently, society perceived the experience of the civil war through three interpretative prisms. The first, held by the hard cores of the two sides, was relatively clear and simple, but the majority of the population oscillated between the other two.

The hard core on each side held a Manichean interpretation of the war. For those who called themselves Nationalists, it was a matter of "saving" Spain from the "evil forces" of separatism, class struggle, and atheism. For the left, it was a matter of preserving freedom, justice and the law against the "evil forces" of the rebel military, reactionary priests, and capitalist oligarchy. For the majority of the country, which felt little enthusiasm for either side, the war was a cruel blow that they tried to comprehend in one of two ways: as a Greek tragedy, in which the two Spains inevitably collided after a century of enmity, or as a drama that could have been avoided if the political actors, ultimately responsible for the intensification of conflict in the mid-1930s, had behaved otherwise. The first interpretation of the war was prevalent in the last phase of Francoism and best suited the interests of the political class and the society of the transition to democracy.[18]

After three years of civil war, the two hard cores could be observed dragging a society along behind them that they tried to shape into a dense network of social cooperation and to indoctrinate with exalted (mechanical) solidarity, but which was presumably suffering from increasing fatigue. This would explain the relative enthusiasm and feeling of "liberation" of the Republican towns when the Nationalist army arrived in Madrid and Barcelona at the end of the war.[19]

The Spain of the Victors, and of the Vanquished

On the Spanish stage of the 1940s, two parallel but contradictory plots were unfolding, both onstage and backstage. Onstage, the scene of the victors' triumph was acted out. Society was organized in a teleocratic manner, oriented toward the goals of national greatness and unity (solidarity), economic state corporatism, and defense of the Catholic faith. The public authority was located at the center of the social order and came to arrangements with an array of sociopolitical and sociocultural forces that had supported it during the war.

The state rearranged the legal system to accommodate the extraordinary decisions needed to subdue the vanquished: It was a "state of [political] measures" rather than a "state of norms."[20] A set of laws (of 1939, 1940, and 1941) provided a legal basis for banning political parties and free unions. There were no firm procedural guarantees, at least until 1941. The government supervised interprovincial traveling and kept the country close to a state of war until 1947. The war finished in April 1939, but 270,000 people were recorded as being held in prison in December of that year, as were 84,000 in 1940 and 35,000 in 1945. This had dropped to 16,000 in 1950.[21] Thus a period of fear lasted for about ten to fifteen years.[22] It left its mark on people's attitudes toward politics and dissent even longer. It also filled them with resentment and taught them the bitter lessons to be learned about the dangers of radical politics, which were transmitted from one generation of the defeated to the next.

At the same time, as complements and assistants to the state, both the Church and the Falangist Party made an effort to engulf society. There were priests, monks, nuns, and seminarists, on one hand, and social activists, on the other; young and not so young people who had the right combination of feelings for heroism and opportunism were encouraged to join the ranks. This was a great moment for Acción Católica and the Congregaciones Marianas (two lay Catholic associations) as well as for the Sección Femenina and for Educación y Descanso (two associations linked to the Falange).[23]

Meanwhile, backstage, a very different and more complex scene was acted out, with three subplots relevant to my argument. First, economic life actually functioned in a mixed regime. The state intervened and regulated abundantly: It controlled prices and salaries, it imposed rigid rules for workers' dismissal, and it required licenses for imports and exports as well as for new industrial investments. But a corporatist structure was also set up between the state and the market, with a network of sectoral arrangements between civil servants and private managers. A few big banking groups became key, dominant players in this framework. In a highly regulated capitalist system, capital circulated through privileged credit channels, and an important sector of agrarian products, cereals, was subject to a demand monopoly by the Servicio Nacional del Trigo. Within most economic sectors, patron-client relationships developed. All in all, these conditions led to a not-so-smooth operation of the economy in the semiautarchy of the 1940s. Second, the Church had great autonomy in managing its associations and designing its own messages, although in the 1940s the distance separating it from the Francoist state, and the tensions between the two, were barely observable.

Finally, Spain was at this time predominantly rural and agrarian, with over 50 percent of the working population in farming. A majority of this population (though certainly not all of it) lived within the semitraditional structure of the corporate village and the open-field system. Corporate villages remained similar to those of the last third of the previous century, once the corporate village of the ancien régime had adapted to the selling off of community and ecclesiastical lands, the end of seignorial rights and the tithe, and the building of railroads.[24] This social structure rested on a type of solidarity relevant to my argument since, first, it combined aspects of organic solidarity with others of mechanical solidarity proper to a segmented society. Life in the village was familistic and locally oriented, but people followed an ethic of honor and neighborliness. This clearly distinguished them from the people Edward Banfield observed in southern Italy at the same time.[25] Second, it did not become fully integrated into a society dominated by church and state. Third, despite its inclusion in the state-controlled economic system of production and distribution of its main product, cereals, it retained its traditional links to relatively open agrarian markets at a regional or national level.

ACT II: THE GREAT TRANSFORMATION
AND THE EMERGING FORMS OF CIVIL SOLIDARITY (1950s–1970s)

Franco's Spain encompasses not just one historical period but two. A time of apparent stagnation and scarcity (during the 1940s and the first half of the 1950s) was followed by a time of unrest and growth (from the mid-1950s on). This was the result of a variety of socioeconomic and cultural as well as political factors, since crucial decisions were made at the time to change the rules of the game in the economy and social life, and to allow the country to open up to outside influences.

During this period, Spain's politics, economy, and culture underwent profound change. There was a new grand strategy on the part of the Francoist regime, a different public sphere, and new political actors. The Spanish economy came to be based on the industrial and service sectors (4.7 million people were employed in agriculture in 1960, 3 million in 1975, and only 1.1 million in 1995), and it became more open to world markets.[26] Intense migratory processes followed, as most people moved to cities (40 percent of the population lived in cities in 1950, 55 percent in 1970, and 65 percent in 1991).[27] Life in both rural and urban areas was thoroughly transformed, with new social mores and new forms of religious life.

This set of changes was related to the accumulation of two forms of social capital: one associated with the functioning of extended orders, less heavily regulated markets, greater social mobility, and cultural exchanges (all of which implied an increase in society's ability to regulate itself, limits to the public authority, and a margin for civic dissidence), and the other connected to a network of associations and social movements committed to doing some civic work in the public space. This accumulation of social capital (of both kinds) made possible in the seventies the kind of democratic transition that was perceived as creating neither winners nor losers—it was like an inverted mirror image of the civil war.

The development of social capital was the result of several factors. Chief among these was a series of political moves that changed the institutional framework of the state-society relationship, the economy, and culture. The Francoist state of the fifties had to adapt to the international environment in order to survive. It broke its diplomatic isolation of the forties and, feeling itself more secure, reduced the intensity of its repressive domestic policies. As noted previously, there were 84,000 people in prison in 1940 and 35,000 in 1945; this figure had dropped to between 4,000 and 11,000 in the period 1955–1970.[28] The last execution for crimes alleged to have been committed during the civil war took place in 1963. The state tried to normalize (or institutionalize) its political regime and to fully become an *estado de derecho* or *Rechtsstaat*. This made its activities easier to predict and opened spaces for social activities of various kinds and for civic dissidence, particularly from the mid-fifties on. By this time, there had been an administrative reform that reduced the discretionary powers of the administration, a law on collective bargaining (Ley de Convenios Colectivos, in 1958) that allowed for direct wage negotiations between entrepreneurs and workers (within limits), and a reform of the criminal code that decriminalized strikes.[29]

These legislative acts were combined with a radical change in economic policy that set the country along a path of increasing liberalization and integration in the European economy (an agreement of association with the European Community was signed in 1970). This change in policy led to economic growth at an annual rate of 7 percent for the period between 1962 and 1974. Real wages, profits, and private consumption went up, as did the resources allocated to the welfare state; a network of public hospitals was built, and the number of university students increased fourfold.

This double strategy of political institutionalization and economic liberalization, with increases in private and public welfare, also brought changes in the way the Francoist state conceived the basis of its legitimacy. While previously the state's legitimacy had rested solely on Franco's victory in the war, and the state's claim to be placed (together with the church) at the moral center of a (hierarchical, authoritarian) teleocratic order, it now attempted to combine that kind of legitimacy with a new sort. It appealed to the interests and sentiments of the new middle classes and a working class that was assumed to be feeling satisfied with the results of the economy while appreciating the need for law and order. The state now claimed to be the guarantor of the correct functioning of the economic and legal systems. At the same time, the state initiated limited political liberalization. It allowed independent candidates to stand in the *elecciones sindicales* (elections for positions on the *jurados de empresa*, or works councils, in all enterprises with ten employees or more); another law (Ley Orgánica del Poder del Estado, in 1966) cleared the way for public elections of one-fifth of the Francoist Cortes or parliament; a law on religious liberty was passed in 1967; and, above all, a new law (Ley de Prensa) put an end to the censorship of the press.

The government took this path in the belief that it could cope with a margin of dissent, because it had to adjust to internal and international pressures, and also because this strategy was consistent with some of its own ideological premises. The ideology of an "organic democracy" (or corporate democracy, as opposed to a liberal-individualistic one) made it difficult for the state to argue against free elections for some sections of the seats in parliament or positions on students' councils (in the universities) and on the *jurados de empresa* (workers' councils). As a Catholic state, it had to tolerate the autonomy of the Church and Catholic associations, and it felt inclined to allow free discussion of civic affairs provided it took place in private spaces. In 1954, the Francoist minister of information, Gabriel Arias-Salgado, put it this way: "A distinction is needed between freedom of expression in the terrain of individual autonomy, and freedom to divulge this same opinion in the terrain of the common good where it must be submitted to the state's control."[30]

The state's decisions to opt for a (pro-Western) foreign policy and to choose Juan Carlos de Borbón for the succession as head of state were consistent with their general strategy. These moves outlined a long-term scenario that, though somewhat ambiguous, indicated a profound transformation of the state itself. The immediate aims of the Francoist state, however, were those of reinforcing its present power base and substantially increasing its legitimacy. It did not achieve these goals. In general terms, the country reacted in a Tocquevillian manner: The more the state reformed itself, the more society pressed for new reforms. For two decades, different groups took advantage of the new institutional framework to increase their social capital, engaging in civic endeavors and exerting pressure on that framework.

During these years we can observe an increase in two kinds of social capital, which seem to reinforce each other: that of the extended orders and that of "civil" associations. The result was a virtuous circle that, as social solidarity increased, placed the Francoist state on the defensive. Spain took the path that would lead to the democratic transition and a new constitution, both understood as a sort of apotheosis of national reconciliation.

There was an increase in a diffuse form of social capital, a reservoir of trust, associated with the functioning of the extended orders. Economic growth (per capita income doubled between 1960 and 1975) took place in the context of an economy with less state intervention.[31] Between 1964 and 1974 the volume of exports went up 2.6 times, and that of imports went up 3.2 times.[32] There was full employment of the labor force (mostly of the male population), and collective bargaining was continuous and reached massive proportions. The population went on the move, both abroad (with 1 million Spanish workers emigrating to Europe) and within the country (2 million changed their residence from one province to another). For all sorts of reasons, Spaniards began to go abroad much more often: 1 million in 1959, 4 million in 1966, and 7 million in 1973. Many families became owners of their own homes (50 percent of families owned their homes in 1960, as did 63 percent in 1970 and 73 percent in 1981). Many bought a car—there were 67,000 automobiles in 1960 and 492,000 in 1970. Interpersonal contacts and dealings increased. The number of letters and parcels posted rose from 1.1 million in 1950 to 2 million in 1960 and 4 million in 1970. The number of telephones increased from 0.6 million in 1950 to 1.7 million in 1960 and 4.6 million in 1970.[33]

There was also better access to education and the mass media. Between 1964 and 1974, the number of students in primary and secondary schools went up 1.4 times; in professional schools, 1.9 times; and at university, 4.3 times. The new press law allowed a new kind of press with wider circulation. *Cambio 16,* an independent periodical with a bent toward social and political reporting, saw sales rise from 20,000 copies in 1972 to 347,000 in 1977.[34] Reading of the foreign press increased, too. By 1965, according to a survey, one-third of people with a university background in Madrid followed the news through the foreign press.[35] Also, the sixties was the period when television sets started invading Spanish households.

This tremendous opening of society, resulting from the move to a more market-oriented and mobile society, saw a dramatic shift in the ways of people's involvement in society. Social interaction became more frequent and more free, and increasingly it was framed by the rules of individual conduct in an open society.

It seems likely that a large part of Spaniards' behavior following these changes was shaped by a moral understanding that was at least partly influenced by the legal system. They had acquired a modicum of trust in the regular functioning of the judiciary in most nonpolitical matters, including civil and commercial law, administrative law, and labor law (which had a definite bias in favor of workers' rights with regard to dismissal clauses, for instance). They were also influenced by an ethic of reciprocity with various roots and origins (in Christian morality, but also in the traditional ethics of the corporate village; see, for instance, various local studies of the time).[36] At the same time, these rules were consistent with the workings of vast networks of family and friends, which led to the use of many semipublic spaces as forums for debates on public matters (as suggested by the *New York Times* correspondent Herbert Matthews in the late 1950s).[37]

Traditionally, most young people (and not only teenagers) had always been remarkably gregarious, organizing themselves into *pandillas* or peer groups in order to go out to bars, dancing, and festivities together. However, their margin for maneuver and self-regulation expanded considerably in the aftermath of the changes of the period. As morals became more permissive, intergenerational and intrafamily relationships became somewhat more egalitarian. Parents lost a degree of control they had had in the past over young people's behavior, and the latter took advantage of this to enter a more open market of emotional and sexual relationships, particularly in the parts of the country most affected by tourism. The increasing moral freedom found little favor in the eyes of Francoist conservatives, who were joined by a mixed bunch of social and civic activists of a very different political persuasion in a critique of the hedonist, consumer society.

These years also witnessed an increase in social capital in the form of commitments to various associations: political parties, unions, or religious associations with a marked quasi-political or civic dimension attached to them. The end result of these associative commitments was quite important in preparing the ground for the next historical phase of the democratic transition. At the same time, this result was somehow unintended. In fact, the explicit intentions of many who joined the associations and took on civic commitments were confused. They wanted freedom from an authoritarian political regime, Francoism, but at the same time many of them were motivated by a collectivist philosophy, which was in many respects—for instance, in its Marxist versions—contradictory to an order of freedom. But the point is that whatever their confused aims, their practical activities ultimately favored a nomocratic order (in Oakeshott's sense), an order of freedom. That is why the social capital they accumulated through their civic and associative undertakings reinforced, in its effects though not always in their intentions, the kind of diffuse social capital that is linked to the workings of extended orders.

In general, the new social movements that emerged within the Church and society (and even from within the Francoist state, as in the case of dissident Falangists) in the 1950s, 1960s, and early 1970s were oriented toward a kind of civic commitment that combined political dissent and social critique. They were harshly critical of the model of society that capitalism and, in their view, an amoral or immoral consumerism were producing. Such was the case, for instance, for two dissident groups who came from the Francoist camp, namely, clerics and Falangists.

The victory of the Nationalist camp in the civil war reinforced the clerics' traditional disposition to rule over the faithful both symbolically and morally through the administration of the sacraments and through rhetorical persuasion. At this time, they enjoyed a quasi-monopoly in religious authority (and the protection of the state), and were successful in generalizing the imposition of the sacraments (baptism, communion, marriage, and extreme unction, or at least religious burial). However, rhetorical persuasion was quite another matter.

In the conditions of social change and more individual freedom of the mid-1950s and 1960s, the clerics' message had to be adapted to the needs of different groups in society. Their message was affected by internal tension, too, both ideological and generational. Older clerics portrayed a post–Council of Trent religiosity that was militant, imbued with the spirit of a crusade, rooted in memories of the civil war, and supportive of the Francoist state. Middle-aged and younger clerics looked more to the rest of the European Church, which was adapting to the modern world. Some clerics allied themselves with the Christian Democratic parties, and there arose a group of progressive clerics.

A mechanism was at work in this process that consisted of elective affinities and of trial and error. Younger clerics tended to become progressive (in opposition to the moderate middle-aged generation and to the older one still supportive of Francoism). They found that, being progressive, they were more successful in influencing the new generations of workers, students, employees, or farmers, that is, their actual or potential flock. The clerics encouraged their associations and joined their movements, taking on the role of advisor or spiritual leader wherever possible. These associations saw themselves as fighters against the system in pursuit of a fairer (that is, more egalitarian) social order, and they put forward various theoretical justifications of claims of liberty that were partially instrumental and partially substantial (as the expression of a natural right of self-determination). Yet much more important than the theoretical justification of these claims, which was provided to some extent by clerics and which was hybrid and rather confused, was the fact that both clerical and secular people involved in these movements made effective use of individual freedoms, became accustomed to them, developed dispositions toward exercising them, and linked these habits to resisting the political and ecclesiastical authorities and to competing regularly with other associations for the support of the masses (a competition that had to follow some game rules).

These observations on clerics can also be applied to the dissident Falangists. Though in the forties the Falangists may have appeared to be the key element in the new Francoist regime, even then they occupied only a subordinate position. They never controlled the ministries in charge of economic matters and soon lost control of those in charge of education and culture, being demoted to the administration of an infant welfare state. Besides, the need for accommodation with the victorious democracies in the Second World War led Franco to reduce the visibility of the Falangists' symbols.

The second half of the fifties saw a revival of the Falangist Party, one that looked back to its anticapitalist roots. Leading figures in this revival were, on one hand, Falangists who used their control of parts of the welfare state apparatus to compete with other political families in the Francoist regime and, on the other, young Falangists who initiated dissident social movements. The relationship between the two was rather ambiguous. Those within the state lent partial support to an emergent union movement in order to have it as an ally (or as an instrument) against the other political families (considered to be conservative by the young Falangists) that had implemented the new economic policy of the late 1950s. Hence the disposition within the Falange to tolerate some dissidence in the union domain and in spaces that emerged as a consequence of the extension of the welfare state: public hospitals and, above all, the higher education system, which experienced considerable expansion in the sixties and in which an important student movement developed that provided a training ground for an emergent opposition political class.

In the case of higher education (as in the case of hospital physicians, urban associations, and others), the course of events followed the pattern already analyzed. The core of the student movement was formed by enthusiasts, bearers of an anti-Francoist and anticapitalist ideology and of a heroic and righteous character appropriate to people aiming at a radical transformation of reality and the establishment of a fair, egalitarian and "solidaristic" society (with the kind of solidarity characteristic of segmented societies). However, tolerance and pluralism within the dissidents' group, and the need to arbitrate compromises with more moderate people outside the group, who formed the bulk of the masses they aimed at mobilizing, called for moderation of the anticapitalist strategy and encouraged the habits and dispositions that ultimately relegated their collectivistic ideology to the background.

Something similar took place in the union movement, in which there were significant elements of associative fabric, collective action, and civic commitment. Economic growth transformed a traditional economy into an industrial one (for example, there were 2.6 million industrial workers in 1960 and 3.4 million in 1975).[38] This development was paralleled by a process of urbanization. The concentration in and around the cities of immigrants and workers in industry and the construction and service sectors provided fertile ground for associations and collective action, which were encouraged also by less repressive behavior on the part of the state and the abovementioned changes in the legal framework. Legal changes permitted the election of union representatives in firms, collective bargaining, and economic strikes. Works councils (*jurados de empresa*) had been elected on several occasions since the early sixties. Many of their members belonged to illegal but (for some time) semitolerated unions, of which the main one was Comisiones obreras (workers' commissions), created by Catholic, Falangist, and communist activists. Collective agreements eventually covered between 4 million and 5 million workers yearly. The number of strikes between 1967 and 1973 oscillated between 350 and 1,000 per annum (with a peak of about 1,600 in 1970). These caused a loss of between 2.5 million and 11 million man-hours a year.[39]

The increasing richness of the associative fabric of Spanish society in such different arenas as industrial relations, religion, and political dissent went hand in hand with the described rise in its exposure to foreign cultural influences and therefore to a more open and tolerant morality. Thus, the simultaneous processes of sociocultural change and political and economic liberalization set the stage for the turn away from uncivil kinds of social capital to an accumulation of various forms of the civil type, contributing to the forthcoming transition to democracy.

ACT III: LIBERAL DEMOCRACY, SOFT FORMS OF SOCIABILITY, AND MANAGING STRUCTURAL STRAINS (MID-1970s–LATE 1990s)

The democratic period extends from the first free elections in 1977 (or from a few months after General Franco's death in November 1975) up to the present day. Democracy brought about an enormous change in the institutional framework of Spanish life and, consequently, a change in the conditions of social capital accumulation. (It is for this period, and in some cases for several years prior to this, that we are beginning to have available a reasonable amount of statistical evidence.)

The arrival of democracy was experienced as a chance for national reconciliation between the two sides of the civil war and, to some extent, for the re-creation of the Spanish community. People were conscious of the difficult compromises required to attain reconciliation. In spite of the socioeconomic and sociocultural changes in the last twenty years of Francoism, memories of the civil war still haunted society, and an effort was needed to avoid confrontations that could lead to a return to civil strife. Thus, once it was clear that democracy was "the only game in town" after an attempted coup d'état in February 1981 had been successfully put down, the transition years, *grosso modo* from 1977 to 1982, were marked by consensus, as reflected in several political and social pacts.

Consensus was expressed in an array of practices, symbols, and discourses during the transition period. The constitution was understood as the cornerstone of a reconciled society. The king became a symbol of reconciliation that allowed for a peaceful and agreed transition from the Francoist regime to the liberal one. The Church, which had apologized for its partial responsibility in the civil war, and in striking contrast with its initial depiction of the war as a crusade against atheism, played now an emphatic role as an intermediary between the different parties involved in the negotiations.

A new center-right party (led by Adolfo Suárez) took over the government after the first free elections and ruled for almost six years, thanks in part to the successful transition and its rhetoric of moderation and conciliation. In fact, the whole of the political class was speaking this language, and in election after election, Spaniards punished those who dared to use a discourse of confrontation. Something similar happened in the union movement: Future works councils elections resulted in the marginalization of more radical unions that emphasized the discourse of class struggle.

These pacts, including the constitution and the regional and social compromises, were the result of compromises between the descendants of those in the different camps in the conflicts of the thirties: the right and the left, the employers and the unions, the church and the secular intelligentsia, the center and the periphery, the military and the civil power. Formal associations (political parties, unions, professional associations, etc.) enjoyed wide support in their social bases and public opinion, and were decisive in bringing about these compromises.

The main content of the pacts was the reconstruction of national solidarity, not on the basis of a common project but on the realization that there needed to be compromise among people with different views and interests. They had to live together within the institutional framework of an order of freedom. The compromise between the right and the left resulted in a constitution that established liberal democracy (with the expectation of a peaceful alternation in government of the right and the left) and in the recognition of the rule of law (with division of powers and a constitutional court). The compromise between civil power and the military resulted in the submission of the latter to the former and to the constitutional order, while at the same time the civil power committed itself to the unity of the country. The religious compromise resulted in the formal recognition of religious freedom and pluralism and in the separation of church and state. The compromise between the center and the periphery was crafted as a complex design of a "state with autonomous communities," that is, a decentralized system with very wide devolution of powers to regional authorities. The socioeconomic compromise (in the constitution and in several social agreements) led to the recognition of the market economy as the basic framework for economic activity together with a formal recognition of the union movement.

Taking this history as my point of departure, I now follow the path taken by Spaniards in the last twenty years from the viewpoint of social capital. I will analyze the relationship between some of the outcomes of the civic compromises made by Spaniards and their social capital, that is, their associations or networks of cooperation, including families. I regard the outcomes of this compromise as positive, and I see them as indicators of significant social capital. They are not only the solutions to collective problems but also the demonstration of a capacity to learn to live with structural strains or unsolved collective problems without civil strife.

Associations and Soft Forms of Sociability

The political, social, and economic changes of the 1950s–1970s prepared the way for the process of social capital accumulation of the civil type that has occurred since then. There has been a steady increase of associational activity, limited but significant participation in unions' activities and political life, fairly strong families, remarkable social life of an informal kind, and some readiness to help in the handling of political and economic crises (high rates of unemployment, financial and political scandals) that might have endangered the foundations of an order of freedom. These experiences have brought society's sentiments somehow closer to those characteristic of either organic solidarities or civilized mechanical solidarities.

It has become a commonplace among scholars to say that Spain lacks a social fabric strong enough to promote economic growth, social cohesion, cultural creativity, and a liberal polity.[40] Evidence for this diagnosis usually rests on a mix of two kinds of data: registered affiliations to formal associations, interpreted as suggesting a weak associative network, and answers to opinion polls, interpreted as suggesting the pervasiveness of sentiments of social distrust. I return later to the matter of the moral sentiments of the population, focusing first on the available evidence on associative ties.

In general terms, it may be argued that Spaniards seem more prone to participate in informal networks than in formal organizations, thus preferring close and soft types of social connectedness rather than larger organizations where individual participation is usually more limited and standardized. Sociologists and political scientists who have focused on mass organizations, with strong traditions and leaders who co-opt each other on a regular basis (such as political parties, trade unions, and churches), have misunderstood the associative basis of Spanish society, picturing it as individualistic or anomic. It may be further argued that people's lack of enthusiasm for large associations with a robust leadership (as may be assumed to be the case in parties, unions, and churches) may go hand in hand with a greater inclination to join associations of another kind, for instance, societal associations, examples of which include sports, recreational, cultural, and educational associations of various sorts.

Recent studies on the Spanish nonprofit (third) sector suggest a rather robust sector in both absolute and comparative terms. The Johns Hopkins Comparative Nonprofit Sector Project has estimated that the nonprofit sector in Spain had revenues (without volunteer input) amounting in 1995 to U.S. $25.7 billion, compared with a gross domestic product (GDP) of U.S. $559 billion.[41] This compares well with France, with revenues of U.S. $57.3 billion and a GDP of U.S. $1.5 trillion, and with Germany, with revenues of U.S. $94.4 billion and a GDP of U.S. $2.4 trillion. In all three countries the nonprofit sector amounts to about 4 percent of GDP. Furthermore, the share of revenue from private giving was considerably higher in Spain (32.1 percent) than France (7.5 percent) and Germany (3.4 percent). By contrast, grants from the public sector accounted for 32.1 percent of revenues in Spain, 57.8 percent in France, and 64.3 percent in Germany; and the share of fees and charges was 49 percent in Spain, 34.6 percent in France, and 32.3 percent in Germany.[42]

The Spanish third sector employed 475,000 full-time-equivalent paid workers, or 4.5 percent of all nonagricultural workers in Spain, and 9.8 percent of the adult Spanish population contributed their time to nonprofit organizations (which translated into another 253,000 full-time-equivalent employees).[43] In terms of employment, Spain's figures (4.5 percent of the nonagricultural labor force) are fairly similar to those of Germany and France (4.9 percent) and Austria (4.5 percent), below those of the Netherlands (12.6 percent), the United States (7.8 percent), and the United Kingdom (6.2 percent), but above those of Japan (3.5 percent), Finland (3.0 percent), and other Latin American and Central/Eastern European countries.[44]

Even if we are dealing with a field of research in which reliable statistics and data are hard to come by, the estimates of the Johns Hopkins

Project suggest an already strong sector of nonstate and nonprofit associations, and corroborate the general impression of a growth trend in a variety of societal associations in Spain during the nineties.[45]

In fact, there has been a remarkable increase in the number of new associations in Spain during the last thirty years. The average of new associations was about 1,000 a year in the first half of the 1970s, before the democratic transition, and it was about 5,000 between the mid-seventies and the mid-eighties. Afterward, the yearly numbers grew, with the average oscillating between 11,000 and 13,000 a year in the nineties.[46]

Against this background, we may consider the Spaniards' low affiliation with parties and unions less as an indication of a low level of involvement in politics and social affairs and more as conduct influenced by the historical circumstances in which the transition to democracy and the full emergence of unions and economic associations have taken place. These include the limited role played by the political parties during the long period of Francoism and during the transition itself, as well as the relative weakness of a tradition of local unionism in contemporary Spain.[47]

In fact, party affiliation is fairly low. A 1980 survey showed that 6 percent of the adult population was affiliated to a party, but several surveys from 1985 to 1993 suggested that the rate had fallen to between 2 and 3.4 percent.[48] It seems, however, that the main parties have somewhat increased the number of their affiliates during the 1990s, probably as the result of an increase in the intensity of party competition around the twin issues of unemployment and political and financial scandals.[49] In any case, the Spaniards seem deeply attached to a political system in which the parties continue to play a crucial role and have a definite influence and a passably faithful electorate.

Unions also have few affiliates. They started in 1977 with a membership equal to 27.4 percent of the wage-earner population, which had decreased to 11 percent by 1990. However, the candidates of the two main unions (Comisiones Obreras and Unión General de Trabajadores) have obtained about three-quarters of the total vote in works councils elections since the early eighties, are the leaders in the rounds of central and sectoral collective bargaining every year, and occasionally call for a general strike (sometimes, as in 1988, with astonishing success). Thus workers refuse to join the unions but stand in a complex position toward them: They support them, but their support is limited and their attachment to them is largely instrumental.[50]

By contrast, Spanish social capital seems to have a stronger base in family networks and other networks of informal cooperation. This is a form of sociability that can be labeled soft and is characterized by its weak ties. This may include communities of residence of various sorts, which range from corporate or quasi-corporate villages (which conserve some of their traditional traits in many parts of the Spanish countryside) to semiurban and urban neighborhoods and associations of housing owners in urban condominiums. It also includes apparently transient ad hoc communities established around a local fiesta (which combine, once again, traditional and modern characteristics), networks of friends, conversational communities *(tertulias)*, bands of young people who wander in the streets or gather in pubs and other public palaces *(pandillas)*, and certainly families (and extended families) and family networks.

There are no statistics about peer groups or *pandillas*, but though the statistician may be blind to them, *pandillas* are quite easy for any casual observer to see (and hear). We do know, however, that they usually play a leading role in sports, sports associations, and festive activities, and furthermore, that both the playing of sports and the number of fiestas have increased enormously. The percentage of people practicing a sport was 12 percent in 1968 and 35 percent in 1990, and the number of sports associations increased 4.5 times in the same period.[51]

The importance of local festivities has increased extraordinarily in the 1980s and 1990s, including the number of participants and activities, the splendor of the proceedings, and of course the expenditure, with young people almost always at their center. I am referring not only to the big events such as the Valencian Fallas, the Sevillian Holy Week, the San Fermines in Pamplona, or the pilgrimage to El Rocío, but also fiestas in other big or middle-sized cities and in small villages. (The practice of running bulls à la Navarrese has become particularly widespread, to the despair of animal lovers.) We have also witnessed the spread of the *movida*, referring to the groups that walk endlessly from one bar to another and from one discotheque to another all evening and most of the night. This is apparent in all sorts of towns on weekends (loosely speaking, as the weekend often begins on Thursday evening). Spain has, in fact, the highest number of bars per capita, at least in Europe, with 9,000 per 100,000 people.[52]

As already indicated, the family and family networks are the key institutions in the system of social integration in Spain, and the main component of its social capital. Families lessen the effects of unemployment, manage and mediate the relationship between their members and the welfare state, and configure the locus where a compromise between generations and genders takes place. It has been argued and amply documented that families constitute one of the pillars of the welfare system in Spain.[53]

The Spanish family keeps its children at home until a relatively advanced age and also cares for its elderly members. It is very frequent for children to continue living in the family home until well into adulthood: In 1994, 95 percent of male and 88 percent of female children between 16 and 24 years lived with their parents (as well as 41 percent of male and 29 percent of female children between 25 and 34). This frequency has clearly increased in the last twenty years: Among people born before 1960, 11 percent to 15 percent of them had left the parental home by their 20th birthday; the corresponding percentage for those born after 1970 is 4.5 percent.[54] Marriage has been postponed from an average of 26.5 years of age for men in 1975 to 28.3 in 1993, with 23.9 and 26.2 years of age as the corresponding figures for women. Only 19 percent of those over 65 live alone (with 5 percent in old-people's homes); the rest live with their relatives.[55] Though family size has diminished in recent years, it is still larger than that of most European countries: In 1991, the average household size was 3.3 persons in Spain, 2.8 in Italy, 2.6 in France, 2.5 in Germany, and 2.2 in Denmark. Households organize themselves around the family more often in Spain than in other European countries: 81 percent in Spain, 70 percent in Italy and France, and 59 percent in Germany and Denmark.[56]

Spaniards remain in close touch with other members of the extended family: In 1993, 64 percent of the adult population declared that they had some contact with their relatives every day or at least once a week, but also with neighbors (74 percent) and with friends who were not colleagues at work (75 percent). As a result, we can conclude that this is a highly sociable or gregarious society, in which feelings of isolation or loneliness seem rare: In a survey in 1971, 79 percent of adults stated that they had not had such feelings recently, and the same percentage was repeated twenty years later in another survey.[57]

Associations of various kinds, families and social networks all together suggest a fairly dense social fabric. This seems corroborated by the fact that the Spanish rate of suicide (a classical indicator of social anomie) is one of the lowest in the world: 4 per 100,000 people in 1989–1993 (15 per 100,000 in Denmark, 11 in France, 10 in Sweden, and 9 in Germany). The murder rate is also fairly low: 1.2 murders per 100,000 inhabitants (Sweden 1.7, Italy 3.6, United States 13.3, and Brazil 29.4).[58]

The Ideational Content: Civilizing Normative Conflicts
Associations in Spain have altered their missions toward providing less demanding goals, more tolerant attitudes, and looser criteria for membership. Families have developed into less oppressive environments for women

and youngsters; the Catholic Church has reduced its efforts to control the beliefs, practices, and private lives of its followers; both left- and right-wing parties have moderated their ideologies and their expectations of the political commitment of their members; and the nation itself has become a loose or common point of reference that allows for plural national identities in several regions (such as the Basque country or Catalonia).[59]

Although it is evident that economic factors do play a role in the prolonged stay of children in their parents' home, it is also important that the structure, morals, and inner workings of the family conform to a relatively egalitarian and nonauthoritarian pattern. Decision making in the family between 1966 and 1980 shows a clear tendency toward decisions made jointly by the husband and the wife in the following areas: visits to relatives and friends (up from 35 percent to 80 percent), expensive purchases (up from 21 percent to 75 percent), calling the doctor in case of illness (up from 26 percent to 70 percent), activities to be undertaken on holidays (up from 26 percent to 80 percent), and expenditure on food (up from 6 percent to 38 percent, with the wife making this decision alone in 54 percent of cases in 1980).[60] The normative consensus between parents and children seems to have increased in matters of religion, politics, and morals, reducing the oppressive character of family life.[61] Spanish families are thus fairly egalitarian in many respects, even though the main burden of domestic work and care of sick members of the family falls primarily on wives and mothers.

The radical change in the relationship between church and state due to democratization has diminished the visibility and influence of the clergy in the public sphere. Secularization has also tended to reduce such influence in Spanish homes (particularly in matters of contraception, as the very low birthrate shows). Thus, the effects of religion on Spaniards' public and private morals has lessened considerably, but what is being preached to them has also changed, as the Church has distanced itself from politics and leans toward a more tolerant morality.[62]

Commitment to a political party has also become less demanding, from the extreme of risking one's life to merely casting a vote. Today's left- and right-wing party stances are the result of long journeys of moderation and convergence toward the center. The Communist Party evolved from Leninism to Eurocommunism in the 1960s; the Socialist Party went from Marxism to a kind of social democracy in the 1970s; and a handful of figures from the Francoist regime founded the party that has since developed into the center-right option. Centripetal competition may be expected to blur the ideational differences between the main center-right and center-left parties even more in the future.

Today, even national identities allow looser involvements. Spanish national symbols, such as flags or hymns (or the Francoist slogan of *"España, una, grande y libre,"* "Spain, one, great, and free"), were changed during the transition to democracy, and their presence in everyday life has quickly declined. The 1978 constitution was the starting point for the long-term construction of a decentralized, quasi-federal administration, as well as the reconstruction (or even *ex novo* construction, in some cases) of national traditions in the periphery of the country, which has gathered particular impetus in the Basque country and Catalonia. This process has allowed a considerable proportion of Spanish citizens to claim plural identities, in which they combine regional, national, and sometimes European sentiments.

Sentiments of Trust

There is a widespread literature (in Spain and elsewhere) on stated verbal opinions of trust in a variety of social and political institutions, and in people, both leaders and fellow countrymen. On the basis of these indications (of vertical and of horizontal trust) general attitudes of trust or lack of trust are inferred, and then countries are compared and the evolution of those attitudes is traced along a period of time. But even though I may recognize the potential worth of these data, I will use these opinion data *cum grano salis* here, since in my opinion their significance depends on our ability to sort out two different elements underlying those verbal statements.

On one hand, these statements can be the reiteration of the clichés, commonplaces, or stereotypes current in the circles or communities the respondents belong to. They may want to show that they belong rightly to the group of reference, and repeat the appropriate statements (morally or politically correct). If this is the case, the opinion polls would reflect the dominant moral or political discourse of the age. And we may speculate that in a country such as Spain, in which we find among the cultural elites a curious combination of the residues of the culture of traditional Catholicism and of the immoderate left, both making the point of the injustice of modern society, the dominant discourse is pervaded by feelings of distrust of the morality of the world such as it is. Expressions of trust or lack of trust may be, then, mere opinions. On the other hand, these opinions may express (more or less) deep attitudes, but in this case we may assume that they will be consistent with the revealed preferences embodied in actual behavior—with values held and rules respected. Of course, one way to sort out these two elements is to combine opinion polls, observation of actual behavior,

and the analysis of people's discourses of justification as they try to rec-
oncile their verbal statements and their actual conduct. But short of this,
I can only point at the problem and at the need to do research on it, and,
in the meantime, to use the data selectively and put them into context.

In fact, the experiences of civil social linkages already referred to in
the previous section are likely to bear an influence on Spaniards' sentiments of confidence, belonging, and obligation, which seem to be widespread according to recent public opinion polls. A survey carried out in
April 1996 shows that 88 percent of the adult population think that
"there are basic rules to follow," and 91 percent think that "in the long
term it is better to be honest"; 87 percent believe that "one can always
find friends if one tries," and 70 percent disagree with the idea that "to
get on well with other people it is necessary to pretend"; 63 percent state
that they are not "pessimistic regarding the future," and another 63 percent think that "anybody can improve their standard of living if they
really propose to do so."[63]

These feelings of trust and references to elementary rules of civil life
are very likely to be reinforced by a feeling of belonging to a national
community and to a religious community. In both cases, however, these
sentiments are not extreme and do not imply any intense militancy.
These feelings of attachment may contribute to stability in a seemingly
integrated and peaceful society, in spite of the memory of a recent civil
war and Spain's reputed historical inclination to violence (in fact, in the
nineteenth century, civil wars were almost endemic in several areas of
the country, and military *pronunciamientos* were frequent).[64]

In surveys, Spaniards express a relatively high degree of pride in being
Spanish: 83 percent and 85 percent in 1981 and 1990, respectively. This is
somewhat higher than other European peoples' pride in their nationality, with the European average standing at 76 percent and 77 percent.
However, Spaniards' national identity coexists with strong local and
regional identities, especially in the case of the Basques and Catalans, a
majority of whom usually declare their identity to be plural or shared.[65]
Furthermore, a Spanish identity is compatible with a strong Europeanist
feeling, on one hand, while on the other it is notoriously lacking in any
strong linkage to discourses of national exaltation, which were comprehensively delegitimized by their association with the Francoist state, or
to any other form of aggressive or offensive nationalism. Even nationalism of a defensive nature is lacking, evidenced by the general reluctance
to undertake compulsory military service, leading toward the abolition
of this institution.

As regards the significance of religion, an immense majority of

Spaniards have continued to declare themselves Catholic over the last twenty years, which may tell us something about the permanence of religious feelings of a general character. However, the intensity of their religious observance, their involvement in worship, and the organizational apparatus of the church have dropped dramatically. In 1970, 64 percent of adult Spaniards declared themselves practicing Catholics, 32 percent nonpracticing Catholics, and 3 percent religiously indifferent or atheist; only 1 percent declared themselves to be followers of other religions. Curiously enough, the size of the last group did not vary in the following two decades—it was still about 1 percent in 1993. But in that year, practicing Catholics only amounted to 31 percent, nonpracticing Catholics to 54 percent, and the religiously indifferent or atheist to 14 percent. The most important change had already taken place by the second half of the seventies, by the time of the transition to democracy, because the percentages for 1993 are quite similar to those for 1978.[66]

Socioeconomic, cultural, and political changes in the sixties and seventies brought about a redefinition of Catholics' attitudes toward their church, causing not only a decrease in observance but also a substantial reduction in the number of people choosing a religious vocation. Figures for the total number of those in the priesthood in 1992 (111,000) are similar to those for 1962 (126,000); however, the figures for newly ordained priests dropped from 825 in 1962 to 220 in 1992, and the number of seminarists decreased from 7,972 in 1962 to 1,947 in 1992.[67] Once again, the main drop took place in the seventies.

A Behavioral Test of Social Cohesion: Managing Three Structural Strains

Adding these pieces of evidence together, scarce and fragmented as they may be, we get an overall impression that Spaniards feel they belong to a wider and often plural community with a bright future. They adhere to organizational objectives that have become less demanding with time, and they prefer informal social linkages and commitments rather than formal organizations, while establishing instrumental relationships when they do belong to the latter.

As a result, we are dealing with a peculiar type of social capital, embedded in social associations that differ from most of the ones usually considered to be bearers of social capital (such as environmental organizations, soccer clubs, churches, unions, parent-teacher associations, or fraternal groups). Furthermore, these associations also differ from the ones Durkheim envisaged as the pillars of modern organic societies: corporations.[68]

In contrast to Durkheim's supposition that organic solidarity would need strong formal organizations of an "old corporatist" or a "neocorporatist" kind to hold society together, the accumulation of this type of social capital in Spain in the second half of the century, without any such organizational pillars, has led to relative success in dealing with several demanding structural strains at the end of the century. Unemployment, the functioning of democracy, and the handling of political scandals are three critical problems Spanish society has faced in the last three decades.[69] I consider that finding a solution to these strains, or learning to live with them, is a symptom of the underlying presence of a relatively large amount of social capital of a civil kind, as expressed in the above-mentioned soft forms of sociability and the formal associations themselves.

Unemployment

As a result of profound economic crises and erratic economic policies of adjustment to an open and more competitive market environment, the rates of unemployment in Spain between 1980 and the late 1990s have rocketed above those of any other Western European country, challenging the country's social stability. In contrast with the growth years of the sixties, the transition to democracy occurred during the economic crisis that began in 1973. Yet even though recession continued well into the mid-eighties and was even deeper between 1991 and 1994, Spanish GDP in 1994 was 60 percent higher in real terms than it was in 1975, with only a slightly lower level of employment: 13.1 million employed in 1975 and 12.6 million in 1994.[70] Economic policy during these twenty years can be characterized as one of gradual adjustment to the new conditions created by Spain's integration into a more competitive global economy. A policy tradition centered upon curbing inflation has eventually evolved, first in a halfhearted way in the 1970s, and more energetically since the early 1980s (inflation, taken as the annual increase in the consumer price index, was 24 percent in 1977 and stands below 3 percent today). Spending policies have been more erratic, with continuous increases in public spending until the early nineties (up to 49.7 percent of GDP in 1993) and some restraint since then (46.9 percent of GDP in 1995).[71]

Economic policy in general, on the part of both the center-right and center-left governments, has followed the pervasive philosophy of the main international organizations in this field, though with considerable effort placed on not antagonizing the unions. Massive inflows of foreign investment helped in persuading the policy makers they were on the right path (though, in fact, a large chunk of this investment was used to finance the public debt derived from deficits incurred as part of the government's strategy to appease the unions). This economic policy tradition has included the privatization of many of the state-owned firms in the last five to six years (by both left-wing and right-wing governments) and the liberalization of the economy (of the capital and most of the product markets, and, more timidly, of the labor and the real estate markets).

This economic policy has been endorsed by the voters again and again, but it has given rise to the unexpected and undesired consequence of a spectacular increase in unemployment. Almost nonexistent under Francoism, and below 4 percent of the labor force at the arrival of democracy, it went up to 21 percent in 1985, back down to 16 percent in 1991, and up again to 23 percent in 1994.[72] Unemployment is much higher among young people and women (45 percent and 31 percent respectively in 1994). Though these data are the subject of controversy in Spain, they have been obtained with methods that are similar to those used in most Western countries.[73] These rates might be reduced by as many as 3 or 4 percentage points if we took into account the underground economy.[74]

The big question remains: How is it possible for a society to live for ten to fifteen years with such a high unemployment rate and no serious disruption of the social fabric? The answer to this question may shed some light on the problems of the *quantum* and the *quale* of the available social capital. In my view, the answer entails three components: One is related to the welfare state, another to the role played by the unions, and the third (and fundamental one) to the institution of the family.[75]

First, a significant extension of the welfare state has provided compensation or prevention mechanisms: unemployment subsidies (which have covered around half the registered unemployed), schooling (which has delayed youngsters' entry into the labor market; the number of university students, for instance, has trebled since 1975), and financial help to other members of the family of the unemployed (retirement or disability pensions, with an increase in the number of beneficiaries and in the per capita amount received).

Second, unions (which mainly represent the interests of the workers with stable contracts) have successfully resisted measures that would have made the labor market more flexible and would have allowed business adjustments to demand and costs via wages. Moreover, the unions have managed to delegitimize alternative discourses that could have articulated and justified a strategy suitable for young people that would have aimed at this kind of adjustment; they have been able to prevent the consolidation of such a discourse precisely by appealing to the value of solidarity. This strategy of distraction and confusion of young people is still meeting with considerable success.

Third, the relative success of the above mechanisms (the welfare state and union strategies) has depended on their compatibility with families' strategies. A tacit compromise based on intergenerational and intergender solidarity has developed within families. According to this, women have accepted a slow and gradual entry into the labor market in worse conditions than male workers. The female employment rate remained at a level of 41–45 percent of women between 16 and 65 years in 1990–94 (it was around 75 percent for male workers), and the percentage of women in fixed-term employment contracts was 38 percent (31 percent for male workers). Young people have accepted they will undergo the combined experience of unemployment (around 45 percent of the labor force under 25)[76] and fixed-term contracts (more than 90 percent of the contracts signed since 1984). In exchange, women and youngsters have shared an assortment of family incomes (wages, pensions, unemployment benefits), the family flat or house, and a sense of togetherness with the male (usually employed) heads of household and the rest of the family. The family has gathered resources together from (almost) all its members and redistributed them, apparently according to individual needs. Thus it appears to have helped to reduce the level of conflict between generations and genders; at the very least, it has postponed these conflicts.

The Functioning of Democracy

Although a majority of Spaniards claim to have scant interest in politics and a certain resistance toward the political class, in fact the high electoral turnout, the relative stability of the party system after two turnover elections, and permanent public support for democracy and the party system are evidence of a strong political system.

Electoral participation has remained fairly high, especially if we take into account the high frequency of elections and the voluntary character of the ballot. Abstention in general elections averaged 26 percent of the electorate, with higher rates in the second half of the eighties than in the hard-fought polls of the nineties. Abstention rates in regional elections have varied considerably: In Catalonia, for instance, the lowest rate was 36 percent and the highest 46 percent (with polls in 1980, 1984, 1988, 1992, and 1995). Abstention rates in the five local elections to date went from a low of 30 percent to a high of 40 percent, and in the three elections to the European Parliament from 32 percent to 45 percent (lower levels than those of France and the Netherlands, and similar to those of Germany).[77]

Spaniards' party preferences have remained fairly stable, with one notable exception being the decline of the Unión de Centro Democrático (UCD), the leading center party in the late 1970s and early 1980s. The Spanish party system has been an imperfect biparty system, with one dominant party on the center-left (the Partido Socialista Obrero Español or PSOE, the Spanish Socialist Workers Party) and another on the center-right, flanked by a leftist party (the Communist Party, now leading the coalition Izquierda Unida, the United Left), and several nationalist parties (above all the coalition Convergència i Unió or CiU, Convergence and Union, in Catalonia, and the Partido Nacionalista Vasco or PNV, the Basque Nationalist Party, in the Basque country). In general terms, the vote for the whole of the left and for nationalist parties has remained stable. The acute crisis and eventual disappearance of UCD at the beginning of the eighties may have reflected the disenchantment of its constituency with intense factionalism within the party leadership. Its successor in the electoral space of the center-right, Alianza Popular (People's Alliance), later to become the Partido Popular or PP (People's Party), went from 26 percent of the vote in 1982 to 39 percent in 1996.

Public support for democracy and the party system has remained firm. Levels of support for democracy as a legitimate political regime, preferable to any other alternative, have usually remained high (around 80 percent of the responses in surveys of the adult population). Most Spaniards declare themselves satisfied with the present functioning of democracy, with numbers that range from 40–45 percent in the early eighties to 50–70 percent in the early nineties. Despite low levels of affiliation, the public regards the parties as indispensable for democracy. Formulated in different ways in surveys ("Without parties there is no democracy," "Thanks to the parties people can participate in political life," or "Parties are necessary to defend the interests of the different groups [in society]"), this judgment has remained stable at a level of 60–70 percent of the responses between 1980 and 1992.[78]

The percentage of adults who declared themselves well informed on political matters varied between 24 and 31 percent between 1980 and 1989. This may mean that Spaniards' confidence in their civic competence has increased; those who stated they understood political matters (or rather disagreed with the statement "Politics is so complicated that people like me cannot understand it") went up from 22 percent to 36 percent in the same period, while in 1996, 37 percent of the adult population declared that they understood "the most important political issues of the country rather well."[79] However, there has not been a parallel increase in a feeling of political influence: In 1996, only 24 percent thought that the average citizen had much influence on political life.[80]

The sensation of lack of influence is coherent with an ambivalent feeling toward parties and the political class. On one hand, the politicians are voted in and considered to be indispensable (see above). On the other, people think that politicians are unresponsive to citizens—that "politicians are not concerned about what people [like the interviewee] think" (65 percent agreed with this sentence in 1989), and that public representatives "do not make any effort to fulfill the promises they make during campaigns" (60 percent agreed with that in 1996).[81]

Given this feeling that politicians don't listen to them, people logically declared a rather low interest in politics. The number of people who "talk frequently" about politics seems to have dropped from 15 percent to 9 percent between 1981 and 1990.[82] Those who stated they had "a lot" or "quite a lot" of interest in politics stayed at a level of 22–24 percent between 1988 and 1996. Apparently politics aroused positive feelings among 25–29 percent of the adult population, negative feelings among 4 percent, and indifference among 55–64 percent.[83] If we focus on the young, their declared interest was lower in the eighties, after democracy had been consolidated (11 and 18 percent in surveys in 1982 and 1989), than in the sixties, before the arrival of democracy (21 and 19 percent in surveys in 1960 and 1965), with a high point during the critical transition years (1975–77) when young people who said they were interested in politics reached levels of 30 to 45 percent.[84]

Political Scandals

In the nineties, political and financial scandals occupied the center of the public space. These included scandals connected with state terrorism, illegal financing of the political parties, and insider trading and other forms of corruption. First, it seemed that prominent members of the state apparatus were part of a plot that led to the assassination of twenty-eight alleged terrorists between 1983 and 1987—they had planned or given the green light for this, made public funds available, and then covered it up. Second, proof was supplied that the different parties had systematically engaged in the illegal funding of their activities, probably since the beginning of the transition, and that they had deliberately broken the laws (which they themselves had made) forbidding these practices. Third, it became equally obvious that insider trading, tax evasion and false accounting, and massive bribery in the adjudication of public works had been common practice during the long tenure in office of the

Socialist Party (since 1982).[85] After four years of unremitting scandal •
(and partly as a result of it) there was a change of government, and a
number of judicial proceedings were initiated.

Even though the nature of the scandals varied, they were all to do with
the definition and implementation of the game rules that affected the
accountability of the elites: of politicians to the electorate, of entrepreneurs to their shareholders, and of both before the law. In this regard,
these scandals provide us with three important insights.

First, they shed light on the tacit rules of the patron-client networks
that operated within an ill-defined establishment. These comprised
financial circles and the entire political spectrum, particularly the center-left (which was in power between 1982 and 1996), large segments of
the state civil and police apparatus, and a number of medium-size and
small entrepreneurs, but it could be traced right down to the innumerable practices of corruption and cheating of the welfare system by individual people. This could be interpreted as a pathological development
of a traditional pattern, under the stimulus of the new financial and
political conditions of the '80s (the buoyance of the financial markets
and the sense of impunity of the party in power). With the exception of
state terrorism, the process is similar to others observed in France, Italy,
Germany, or Japan (and with different political parties).

Second, these practices were checked neither by the parties nor by
other associations (unions and churches, for instance), but by the combined actions of some judges (in the spirit of the Italian *mani pulite*) and
journalists.

Third, judges and journalists were able to mobilize public opinion.
The reason for this can be traced to two factors. First, we have already
noted the public's ambivalence toward the political class; this made it
sensitive to the issue of political accountability. Second, the public was
also increasingly sensitive to the more general problem of law and order.
Already in the eighties, between 1982 and 1987, there was an increase in
the number of those who agreed with the statements "We should obey
the law even if this runs counter to our own interest" (from 61 percent to
65 percent), "Personal circumstances are not an excuse to break the law"
(from 53 percent to 58 percent), "We should tell the truth before a judge
irrespective of the consequences" (from 65 percent to 70 percent), and
"Most criminals get away unpunished" (from 53 percent to 66 percent).[86] This evolution of public sentiment took place against a background of a perceived increase in insecurity: Between 1978 and 1996 the
number of people who had been the victim of a crime at some point in
their lives rose from 11 percent to 46 percent.[87]

Living with widespread unemployment, building a new democratic regime, and purging the state of corrupt and criminal practices are three difficult tests that Spanish society has recently faced up to with a modicum of endurance and a certain amount of success. Although I am deliberately overlooking the normative conflicts that underlie these tests, I take it that the ability to manage these structural strains is an indication of the level and civic quality of the social capital present at diverse levels of this society.

CONCLUSIONS:
THE IRONIES OF CIVIL AND UNCIVIL TRANSFORMATIONS

Spain illustrates the complexity of the topic of social capital. We are dealing not only with social capital in general, but with a number of drastically different kinds. We have the civil kind of social capital attuned to the solidarity of extended orders (which Durkheim called organic solidarity), but we may also find social capital of a civil kind connected with the rules, networks, and sentiments of "enterprise associations" (in Oakeshott's terms, corresponding with a "civil variety" of Durkheim's "mechanical solidarity") provided that their ideational contents as well as their internal rules make them compatible with a civil society. Thus, organizations of all sorts (churches, unions, political parties, societal associations, social movements, and others, including economic firms) may be of a civil or an uncivil kind; they may even have various "degrees of civility."[88] They may transform themselves from a civil to an uncivil form, and vice versa. For instance, churches, parties, and unions acting in the Spanish Civil War were of a rather uncivil kind; yet most of them had begun to behave in a civil manner and demonstrate a basic civil character by the time of the democratic transition.

In other words, associations, and the whole of a country, may move from a situation in which there is a plethora of an uncivil kind of social capital to another in which social capital of a civil kind prevails. We can call this a "civilizing process," using Norbert Elias' term.[89] The opposite may equally well happen (as indeed it did in Spain between about 1900 and 1930, and especially after the 1910s). But the Spanish case suggests that the ways from uncivil to civil may be baroque and unintended. The second phase of Francoism may be read as an illustration of this. In a sense both Francoist elites and anti-Francoist dissidents were, to a point, brother-enemies, following a long-standing Spanish tradition. By this I mean that their cognitive, moral, and emotional orientations in regard to the need for a strong, authoritative assertion of their views of what a "good society" should be were not that dissimilar. In a sense, they were all clerics or the faithful in need of clerics, who were used to authoritative preaching and enjoyed it in all its various guises, right-wing or left-wing, truly religious or half secular and half millenarian, and they tended or tried to behave in the manner of strong and disciplined organizations.

However, the cunning of reason, through the workings of markets, consumerism, economic growth, outside influence, generational change, and other mechanisms, converted them into tame, domesticated, "civilized" specimens, ready to live and let live. This was accomplished not because of any self-reflective and explicit change in the ideational contents of the formal associations they had joined in the fifties, sixties, and seventies that then led Spaniards along the road of moderation, because the ideologies of those associations were far from being moderate. Rather, their "civilization" was due to the sheer fact of coming together, electing their leaders, bargaining with each other as well as with their adversaries, trying to enlarge their social bases by persuasion, and marking time waiting for the big bang (Franco's death) to happen. In the meantime, they were getting used to the background of those aforementioned factors: the markets, economic growth, outside influence, and generational change. In other words, it was, above all, the "tacit wisdom" (by analogy with Michael Polanyi's "tacit knowledge")[90] embodied in the practice and (in time) in habits of tolerance, and in an attitude of live and let live, that made those changes possible and led to the transformation of uncivil social capital into a civil kind.[91]

When liberal democracy came at last, we find that a stock of social capital of the civil kind had already been accumulated. This was a reservoir of goodwill on which the political and social leaders of the late 1970s would draw in order to make the democratic transition and consolidation successful.

At the same time, the Spanish case has also shown that, for the twenty years or so following the transition, even social capital of a civil kind may adopt various forms and allow for various patterns of sociability and association. Thus what we find now is not so much an explosion of new associations or the growth of those already existing, but rather the development of a pattern of soft forms of sociability around the family, family-centered networks, and peer groups, as well as occasional associations. The last are formed when people come together in order to transform an event into a ceremonial display and an exaltation of a *communitas* that is lacking, or almost lacking, in any instrumental orientation, as is demonstrated by the remarkable rise during this period in the frequency and importance of local fiestas that procure the direct (and often intense) participation of increasing numbers of people.[92]

There is also some irony in that these transformations from civil to uncivil forms of social capital (and vice versa) and these variations between organic and mechanical forms of solidarity suggest a revision of sorts of most of the conventional wisdom regarding the transition from traditional to modern societies. Soft patterns of sociability, family-centered networks, and the fiesta culture suggest the resilience of the cultural forms of the corporate villages of premodern times and, more generally, of the bilateral nature of northern Mediterranean kinship.[93] This allowed for significant autonomy on the part of the family unit as well as for an important stock of social capital (of a civil kind of sorts) leading to a significant degree of social stability at the local level, which lasted for about two millennia in many parts of the region. Moreover, at least in the case of corporate villages such as those of Castile, their solidarity was not reduced to its mechanical form, since they could accommodate economic, social, and symbolic markets of some importance and maintain complex and elaborate ties with the outside world. For all its limits, this form of rural life was, in many respects, more civil than the forms of life existing in the modern urban world of ideological politics, authoritarian parties and unions, and fanatic and well-organized churches.[94]

Of course, any situation at any time shows both light and darkness and has both its potentials and its limits, corresponding to a mix of social capitals of various kinds, civil and uncivil. At this point in the late 1990s, the accumulated stock of social capital, all components considered, has provided for significant social cohesion. A social fabric of networks and associations, together with sentiments of social trust, has gone hand in hand with a mellowing of the normative conflicts of the past. This has allowed the country to meet the challenge posed by some significant structural strains. Spain has lived with a huge unemployment problem apparently compatible with a modicum of social cohesion and a hopeful mood (though in the late 1990s unemployment seems in the process of being significantly reduced thanks to a wave of economic prosperity). Spain's democratic institutions are well and alive, at least in comparative terms, and the country is seemingly getting through a crisis in the application of the rule of law to its political class (not to speak of the ordeal imposed on so many by terrorism), for which there is a 50-50 chance of either ending well or following the path of dubious compromises, incremental progress, and periodic reversal to illegal/semilegal party funding and other abuses that other Western polities (such as

France, Germany, Italy, and Belgium, for instance, among others) seem used to.

Of course, in the end, the mix of civil and uncivil potential is always there in today's Spain, as in any other historical location. Civil societies are fragile institutional and cultural constructs, and the more we engage ourselves along the path of translating those constructs into reality, of "building" them, the more we realize that their foundations rest on shifting grounds. They are the shifting grounds of the coming generations to be socialized anew, and of the deep layers of authoritarianism, *ressentiment,* or fear of liberty that may be part of the character of the old (and new) generations and which may be at least partly favored by established practices and institutions that bear witness to a long-standing tradition of mechanical solidarity of an uncivil kind.

7

SWEDEN: Social Capital in the Social Democratic State

BO ROTHSTEIN

In no other Western country has Social Democracy had such a political influence as in Sweden. Having been in government for sixty of the last sixty-nine years, the party is not only the most successful among social democratic parties but one of the most successful democratic political parties ever. As a consequence of this unique power of its political left, Sweden stands out as extreme on many standard measures used in comparative politics.[1] To take a few examples, Sweden is at the top of the Organization for Economic Cooperation and Development (OECD) countries in public spending and taxes, in degree of unionization, and in voting turnout. Apart from such purely quantitative measures, it has been argued that the political and economic system in Sweden has been characterized also by important qualitative differences from comparable countries. From the 1950s until the early 1990s, Swedish society in general and its system of industrial relations in particular was branded by many observers with a special name: the "Swedish model."[2] One of the more important features of this model was an unusually close collaboration between the state and major interest organizations in the preparation as well as in the implementation of public policies.

In what now can be labeled the "standard theory" of social capital, the major idea is that social networks, informal as well as formal, create norms of trust and reciprocity that in turn make it less difficult to solve problems of collective action such as the provision of various forms of public goods. If the stock of social capital in a society or in a group is low, a situation metaphorically known as a *social trap* may occur. The logic of a social trap is as follows.[3]

1. Everyone stands to gain if almost everyone chooses to cooperate.
2. But if one person doesn't trust that almost everyone else is going to cooperate, it becomes meaningless for that person to cooperate, because the good that is to be brought about demands near-universal cooperation.
3. The implication is that it is rational not to cooperate if one doesn't trust that almost everyone else is going to cooperate.
4. Thus, effective cooperation for common purposes will occur only if one trusts that almost everyone else will choose to cooperate.
5. Without this trust, the social trap will prevail, implying that the agents will be in a worse situation even though they all realize that they would gain if they cooperated.

Agents who face a social trap are said to be in a *social dilemma*. Situations such as these are very common and range from protecting the environment in one's city by deciding to sort one's garbage (or not) and paying taxes to provide for public goods (or cheating the tax system) to avoiding civil strife between different ethnic groups in a country (or encouraging such strife). It makes no sense for a person to be the only one who sorts garbage, pays taxes, or refrains from ethnic discrimination if that person is convinced that most other people will not do the same, because the good that is supposed to be produced will then not materialize.

One interesting part of a social trap situation is that standard theories about rationality are of no use. In such theories, agents make choices after ordering their preferences to maximize utility. But what is a rational choice in a social dilemma depends not at all on the agents' preferences.[4] Instead, it is the expectation of what others are going to do that becomes decisive for the choice to cooperate or not. Thus the critical variable for avoiding a social trap is the level of trust in the group or the society, which, according to the theory about social capital, depends on the type and amount of social interactions. It is from such interactions that agents may learn whom to trust and establish cooperation with (and whom not to trust and avoid cooperation with).

There are several reasons why Sweden provides a particularly fruitful case study for the social capital theory. One is the relationship between, on one hand, the high level of its public spending and ambitious welfare-state programs and, on the other, the health of its civil society. Have Sweden's numerous and encompassing welfare programs made not only voluntary organizations but also other forms of informal social relations between individuals unnecessary and thereby fostered social isolation and anomie? Is there a "carving out" effect in which more social programs mean less civil society and thereby less social capital?[5]

Second, how has the close collaboration between the government and the major national interest organizations affected associational vitality? During the 1970s, several political scientists argued that this neocorporatism (in contrast to pluralism) would take these organizations' activities out of the voluntary sector because such groups were getting most of their money and their tasks from the government, thus making them more like government agencies than parts of any civil society.[6] A standard assumption in the research on neocorporatism has been that the government's support for and collaboration with the interest organizations has made the organizations' elites become more professional and less responsible toward their members, and that this in turn has resulted in a drop in members' activity.[7] On the other hand, it has also been shown that support from the government can strengthen the ability of interest organizations to organize potential members.[8] Sweden thus may provide us with an answer to the question of whether neocorporatism creates or destroys social capital.

Third, what has been the long-term trend in social capital in this social democratic polity? Robert Putnam and others have reported a surprisingly sharp decline in almost all major forms of social capital in the United States during the last two decades.[9] The differences not only in size and demography but also in many political and economic aspects makes a comparison between Sweden and the United States—what in comparative methodology is called a "most different design" approach—meaningful. The differences between the ideology of the dominant political parties and many public policies are striking.[10] This means that if the changes in social capital in the United States and Sweden were the same, then we could assume that politics at the national level would be of minor importance in explaining this phenomenon and that instead we should examine hypotheses such as changes in global ideological orientation. However, if we were to find great differences in the forms and trends of social capital in these two countries, then it may very well be the case that politics explains social capital as much as social capital explains politics.

Fourth, one of the most important arguments in the discussion of social capital is the existence of a positive relationship between social capital and a well-functioning and stable democracy. If, as I will argue below, there has been a decline in some important aspects in the performance of Swedish democracy, then we should expect that social capital, however measured, has also declined.

FROM A MODEL DEMOCRACY TO A PROBLEM DEMOCRACY

As in the other Scandinavian countries, the Swedish Social Democrats came to power during the crisis of the 1930s. Their program for handling the severe social and economic crisis got wide acceptance, leading to an uninterrupted forty-four-year period in which they were the governing party (1932–76). During the World War II period and again in 1951–57 the party led coalition governments, but the post of prime minister remained in the hands of the Social Democrats. The hegemonic position of the Social Democratic Party in Sweden was perhaps strongest during the late 1960s. Not only did the party reach one of its all-time high electoral successes in 1968, scoring just above 50 percent, but it was during this period that the term "Swedish model" became internationally recognized. For many observers, Swedish social democracy seemed to have found working solutions to some of the most intransigent problems facing modern capitalism.[11] The combination of democratic stability, popular legitimacy, considerable economic growth, a collaborative system of industrial relations, and a universal and generous welfare state were the central parts of this model.

The concept of the Swedish model covers a broader terrain than just the political system in Sweden, but it is safe to say that the Swedish type of democracy represents the specific political configuration of this model during the postwar period. According to many outside observers, as well as in the Swedish self-image, this was a society marked by high levels of trust, both vertically (between citizens and the elite) and horizontally (between individuals). Concepts such as consensus, collaboration, and cooperation were important ideological markers of Swedish society during this period. Thus, the image of this "model democracy" of the 1960s and 1970s was that citizens were, on a large scale, cooperating with one another in different nationwide popular movements such as the temperance movement, the free churches, the farmers' organizations, and the unions. The parties in the labor market collaborated in organizing peaceful industrial relations, and the ruling Social Democratic Party tried to form public policies in consensus with the parties in opposition and with major interest groups.[12]

Today, the general picture of Swedish democracy is very different. Most of the elements of the Swedish model have been abandoned or are in a state of crisis.[13] Most notably, the trustful collaboration between the major interest organizations in the labor market and the state disappeared during the late 1980s.[14] The participation of interest organizations in the creation of public policy by governmental commissions has become much less significant, and working compromises are seldom reached even when they do participate.

What evidence is there for arguing that the quality of Swedish democracy has deteriorated? An attempt to audit the Swedish democracy was carried out by a group of political scientists (including this author) in 1995. Measuring thirteen indicators, the report concluded that, on balance, there has been a qualitative deterioration in the way the Swedish democracy has worked during the last two decades, especially with regard to democratic control over the political agenda and control over economic resources.[15] I will, however, confine myself here to three types of data that are closely related to the social capital concept and which indicate a change for the worse in the quality of Swedish democracy.

Confidence in Central Political Institutions

One of the basic principles of a working democratic system is to make government and governance legitimate.[16] As shown by Sören Holmberg, Sweden is one of the countries where trust in politicians has gone down most dramatically. In 1968, 38 percent of the respondents agreed with the statement "The parties are only interested in people's votes, not in their opinions." In 1998, this figure had risen to 75 percent. This result is supported by other similar survey questions.[17]

It could be argued that this merely reflects the public's increasingly skeptical attitude toward all kinds of authority in the zeitgeist of the late 1960s and beyond, especially the way in which the media cover politics. It could also be argued that the increased mistrust has resulted from a series of political scandals or from an increasing distance between the electorate and politicians. In the SOM Institute's yearly surveys, which have been conducted since 1986, respondents have been asked about their confidence in the Riksdag (the Swedish parliament) and the central government. In 1986, 47 percent stated that they had confidence in the Riksdag, but by 1999, this figure was down to 27 percent. Regarding confidence in the government, the figures were 44 percent in 1986 and 22 percent in 1999.[18]

The evidence for a fall in Swedes' confidence in their central political institutions stands in sharp contrast to findings from a major international research project on beliefs in government in the Western European countries. Their data, which cover the period from 1981 to 1990, "do not demonstrate that there has been a widespread decline of the public's confidence."[19] Sweden is also alone among the Nordic countries to show a decline in political trust, which indicates that we need to look for country-specific explanations for the Swedish case. In other words, there is something special about the decline of political trust in Sweden.[20]

Political Participation

A vital aspect of any working democracy is the willingness of its people to spend time and energy in established forms of political activity. One of the central findings in the social capital approach is that social capital enhances political participation. Whereas for older generations such participation may be a question of habit and social pressure, for young people participation can be considered a more deliberate act. Here we find two opposing trends. On one hand, several surveys show an increasing interest in politics. On the other hand, people are turning away from traditional channels for political participation, such as political parties and interest organizations, and are turning toward temporary and single-issue organizations mobilizing citizens for particular causes (such as preventing the building of plants that process nuclear waste or organizing shelters for battered women).[21] Consequently, membership in the youth organizations of the political parties has declined sharply, from more than 220,000 in 1972 to below 50,000 in 1999.[22] There has also been some decline in membership in the political parties. In 1984, 13 percent of those 25 to 44 years old were members of a political party, whereas ten years later, this dropped to 6 percent.[23] Political scientists analyzing this trend have argued that the parties have changed character, from popular movements and member parties to voter parties. The work of volunteers has, to a large extent, been taken over by professional staff. Professional campaign and media activities have become more important than internal ideological debate, popular mobilization, and study circles. The study concludes that during the last two decades, members in political parties have become fewer, older, and less active.[24] Politics in Sweden is thus becoming a "spectator sport," even though more people claim to be interested in politics than ever before.[25]

The argument presented so far is not that Sweden's democratic stability is in a state of deep crisis, but that it seems reasonable to argue that there are clear signs of a qualitative deterioration concerning confidence in central political institutions and political participation. If a high level of social capital indicates a well-functioning democratic process and trust in the political system, we should then expect that social capital has deteriorated in Sweden.

CIVIL SOCIETY AND POPULAR MOVEMENTS

While survey data can tell us a lot about the current situation and how trust correlates with other variables at the individual level, the specifics of social capital in a country or region have long historical roots. It is therefore necessary to present a historical analysis of the specific development of the relations between civil society and the state in Sweden. Civil society is a broad concept, including sometimes both markets and family relations. I will here use a more confined definition of the concept as voluntary associations and other formal or semiformal networks outside the state, family relations, and market-based economic transactions. As such, civil society is understood, in the social capital approach, as the breeding ground for social trust.

An important historical research project about the Swedish nineteenth century labeled the latter part of the century as the "age of the associations."[26] Among these associations, the so-called popular mass movements (in Swedish, *folkrörelser*), such as the labor movement, the farmers' movement, the temperance movement, and the free churches,[27] played a very special and important role in state–civil society relations beginning in the 1860s.[28] To understand this, it is important to recognize that in Scandinavia, a popular mass movement was (and still is), to some extent, different from what in many other countries is understood as a voluntary organization. First, although the popular movements had strong local branches to secure mass participation, the movement as such was a united national entity, thereby linking individuals and local branches to the nation as a whole. Second, historically, the popular mass movements saw themselves as protest movements against the bureaucratic, clerical, aristocratic, and capitalist elite who dominated Sweden at the turn of the century. The idea of a movement implied that society should be changed and that the vehicle was mass organization from below. Third, a popular mass movement consisted of not one but a whole network of organizations. For example, the labor movement included (and still includes) not only the unions and the Social Democratic Party but also the consumers' organization, the tenants' organizations, the workers' educational organization, the organization of pensioners, the Scout organization, the workers' funeral organization, and so on.[29] Fourth, as organizations of both protest and self-help, the popular mass movements stood in sharp contrast to the charity organizations dominated by the middle and upper classes. Fifth, in the official Swedish mythology, the popular mass movements were the major schools of democratic and organizational training for the people.[30]

What seems to be unique about Sweden, as well as about the other Scandinavian countries, is the development of a very close collaboration between the state and the popular mass movements without destroying the autonomy of the latter.[31] To illustrate the historical pattern, I will focus on one aspect of the relationship between the state and the labor movement in Sweden, namely, the establishment of the National Board for Social Affairs in 1912. According to the commission that prepared the bill founding the board, the task of this agency was not primarily poor relief, a function handled by local authorities, but instead was nothing less than the so-called labor question. The commission argued that the problem was concentrated in the cities, where the rapid process of industrialization had led to a potentially politically dangerous situation with masses of workers who had become alienated from traditional local communities and other social bonds. The economic distress of workers in times of unemployment, the lack of a system of social insurance, and the many industrial disputes had become the major political problem. In the words of the commission:

> The feeling of solidarity that has emerged among the working masses, in itself praiseworthy, is limited to themselves and they do not appear to wish to extend it to the whole society in which they share responsibility and play a part. This obviously poses a national danger, which must be removed in the common interest of everyone. Everywhere the government therefore faces the difficult task of mitigating conflicts of interest and repairing the cracks that are opening in the social structure.[32]

The National Board for Social Affairs was established to handle this problem by implementing reforms in worker safety, labor exchanges, and social housing and by overseeing the system of poor relief managed by the local authorities. Its mandate was to handle the labor question, and the preferred method was to incorporate representatives from this new and threatening social class into the state machinery. As a result of the commission's proposal, the chairmen of the national trade union conference (the Landsorganisationen, or LO) and the employers' federation (the Svenska arbetsgivarföreningen, or SAF) were given seats on the board of the agency; following the corporatist principle, other representatives from the LO and the SAF were given seats on various subcommittees. The commission's argument supporting this arrangement was that the representatives from the organizations

> would behave as guardians not only of special interests but also of the interests of everyone, of society as a whole . . . It should certainly be expected that a representative body structured according to these principles, official and thus functioning with a sense of responsibility, should provide valuable support for the new social welfare administration.[33]

This mode of organizing the relationship between the state and the organizations was not a centrally commanded elite project because it had already been established at the local level when public employment exchanges were set up starting in 1902. A common pattern arose in which half the representatives in these local boards were taken from the labor movement and half from local employers' organizations. The boards had not merely an advisory role but full responsibility for operating the labor exchanges under the city councils. While a public and corporatist employment exchange system rapidly became dominant in Sweden, this was an exception in Continental Europe. In Germany, for example, control over labor exchanges was used as a major weapon in industrial disputes, with employers wanting to blacklist striking workers and unions wanting to block employers' labor supply. The question about labor exchanges was raised publicly for the first time in Sweden in 1895, in the city council of Stockholm. What is important in this case is that the local commission of inquiry explicitly warned against a development such as had taken place in Germany, where the question of control over the labor exchange system had become a major source of conflict between labor and capital. In addition, the local unions in Stockholm argued that if the exchanges were to function properly, it would be imperative that these exchanges be trusted by the employers as well as by organized labor, and for this, a corporatist mode of representation was needed.[34]

In a 1916 report to the government regarding the operation of the exchanges, the National Board for Social Affairs declared that "no objection has appeared from any quarter against the organizational principles on which the publicly operated labor exchanges were based." On the contrary, the board argued that it was these very principles that had made it possible for the system to grow and that had been pivotal for strengthening the confidence their operations enjoyed among both

employer organizations and unions, "which in our country have fortu-
nately abstained from utilizing the employment service as a weapon in
the social struggle, which in Germany has partially distorted the whole
issue of labor exchanges." The board also observed:

> Despite the sharp social and political conflicts that have emerged
> in other areas of public life between members of the employer and
> worker camps, on the boards of the labor exchanges the same per-
> sons have, in the experience of the National Board for Social
> Affairs, continued to cooperate faithfully in the interest of objectiv-
> ity.[35]

This type of corporatist relations spread quickly to other areas of the
Swedish state and came to dominate Sweden's political culture as an
integrated part of the Swedish model. Not only were the unions organized into the state, but many other voluntary organizations were also
integrated. For example, the temperance movement was given the
responsibility of handling the government's propaganda against widespread misuse of alcohol; the farmers' movement, the responsibility of
handling subsidies to farming; small business organizations, the responsibility of implementing subsidies to support small business; and so on.
A qualitative breakthrough came during World War II, when nearly all
parts of the wartime administrations incorporated the major interest
organizations of each policy area.[36] The argument that was put forward
repeatedly was that this would create trust among the members and followers of the organizations for the process of implementing the policy in
question.[37]

This illustrates that the relationship between voluntary organizations
and the state in Sweden generally has been one of close cooperation,
more so than of direct competition or open conflict.[38] Most importantly, the corporatist channel of popular influence over the state was
accepted by both the popular movements and the governing elite *before*
the democratic breakthrough in 1917. Up until the 1980s, the Conservative, Liberal, and Social Democratic Parties had all considered this type
of "democratic corporatism" to be the most politically effective way to
handle social and economic problems, arguing that it generated trust
between the parties involved and made it possible to secure both functioning compromises in the process of policy formulation and a smooth
implementation of public policies.[39]

One can hardly overestimate the importance of the popular movements for the type of democracy that has characterized the Scandina-

vian countries since the beginning of the twentieth century.[40] First as schools of democratic mass mobilization, where "members learnt how to handle a chairman's gavel and to accommodate themselves to majority resolutions," and second as intermediary and modernistic organizations, they filled the gap between the nation-state and the citizens by creating collective identities in an era in which the fall of the old estate order had left a huge social and political vacuum.[41] If there could be an "owner" of social capital in Sweden, it has been the popular movements.

It should be added that the dominance of popular movements meant that neither "friendly societies" nor charitable organizations came to dominate the organizational scene during the critical decades when modern Sweden was formed. This is not to say that such organizations did not exist, only that they played a minor role. It should perhaps also be added that many of the leading persons in the charitable organizations quickly got important positions in the governmental agencies that were established to handle the "social question," especially the National Board for Social Affairs.[42] Another reason for the minor role played by charitable organizations was their "state-friendliness." Instead of jealously protecting the right of their own organizations to handle social problems, they took a positive stance when public authorities stepped in.

The close collaboration between the state and voluntary organizations has sometimes led observers to question whether a civil society even exists in Sweden.[43] As will be argued in the next two sections, this is based largely on a misunderstanding of the specific configuration of state-society relations in Sweden. This misunderstanding is based on an approach that usually emphasizes conflict and competition at the expense of collaboration between the state and voluntary organizations. In any case, it would be difficult to argue that a voluntary organization that collaborates closely with the state creates less trust among its members than would one that refrained from contact with the government. The important questions are the type and quality of member activity, that is, whether it is voluntary and whether citizens are active for the "right" reasons.

THE ORGANIZATIONAL LANDSCAPE: AN OVERVIEW

In a comparison to citizens of most other nations, Swedes are highly organized. Data from a large survey with almost six thousand respondents conducted in 1992 show that 92 percent of all Swedish adult citizens belong to at least one voluntary organization. The average number of memberships per person, depending upon the measure, is between 2.9 and 4. More than half of the population (52 percent) consider themselves active, and 29 percent serve as an elected representative in a voluntary organization. Only 8 percent of the adult population stand outside the world of organizations. Sweden's degree of unionization is the highest in the world among capitalist economies; roughly 85 percent of the workforce is unionized, which is equivalent to 62 percent of the adult population. The sports movement, in which almost all sports clubs are organized, is second to the unions in number of memberships, with 33 percent, followed by consumers' cooperatives (32 percent), tenants' organizations (27 percent), and cultural organizations (12 percent).[44]

There is of course a difference between being a member and being active in a voluntary organization. The sports movement is the most successful of all, with one out of five Swedes active in its voluntary associations. "Being active" is of course a broad term, but it includes having an official position with some degree of responsibility in the organization or taking part in the organization's activities on a regular basis. Other organizations with high levels of mobilization (defined as active members in relation to the whole population) are the union movement (10 percent), cultural organizations (6.9 percent), tenants' organizations (5.9 percent), and recreational organizations (5.4 percent). Below 1 percent are the environmental, women's, and temperance organizations, along with the free churches. The Church of Sweden, in which until recently all citizens born in Sweden became members unless their parents stated otherwise, scores 1.8 percent.

"Trust, by keeping our mind open to all evidence, secures communication and dialogue," writes Barbara Misztal.[45] If this is true, there may be one specifically Swedish way of organizing people that should be of special interest for establishing social capital. This is the so-called study circles, which have been especially popular in the mass movements. Study circles are small groups of adults who usually meet one evening a week during a semester to educate themselves on a given subject. According to a recent report, the average number of participants is 8.6 and the average number of hours spent in each study circle is 35.6.[46] Study circles are organized by associations for popular education (which are part of most popular movements) on subjects ranging from foreign languages to cooking, computer knowledge, the European Union question, and rock music. Of course, many individuals participate primarily out of interest in the subject, but as many as 40 percent report that they participate for social reasons.[47] A recent study shows that 75 percent of the adult population has attended a study circle at some point and that around 10 percent participate on a regular basis. The importance of this type of activity is shown by the fact that each year about 40 percent of the adult population attend a study circle of some sort.[48]

As could be expected, there is a positive relationship between participating in study circles and activity in voluntary organizations, voting, and having a more civic-minded attitude in general.[49] Unlike most other forms of adult education, the associations for popular education seem able to recruit people with minimal educational backgrounds to their study circles. In Sweden, this activity is seen as one of the cornerstones of a viable democracy, and consequently, about one-half of the costs are covered by governmental funds.[50] The associations for popular education also arrange open lectures, evening debates, and various cultural activities.

To summarize, I quote a recent evaluation based on extensive qualitative and quantitative research: "The circles have an important societal function besides the learning that is going on and also besides what the participants say about the value of their social functions. It is quite clear that the study circles maintain a civic network right across all social borders."[51] The government's economic support for the study circles and the educational associations may thus be seen as an example of creating social capital from above.

How do social class, gender, and age relate to organizational activity? One of the most cherished arguments about the popular movements is that they have endowed the lower social classes with organizational assets that would work in a compensatory manner in relation to the resources commanded by more affluent citizens.[52] A study with data from 1986 showed that the picture was more complex and, to some extent, contradicted the established myth. On the one hand, there were no differences in organizational activity between workers and the middle class (i.e., salaried employees and self-employed) for many large and politically strong organizations, such as the unions and the consumer cooperatives. On the other hand, there were significant differences in several other strong organizations, such as the cultural and sports organizations. People from the middle class were also members of more organizations (3.8 compared to 2.6). None of the twenty-five types of organizations that were analyzed had more members from the working class than from the middle class.[53]

Gender differences are generally small when it comes to memberships. Men are, on average, members of 3.0 organizations, and women of 2.8 organizations; men are slightly more active in organizations (56 percent compared to 46 percent). This difference seems largely caused by a generation effect because there are no differences among the younger

Table 7-1: Organizational Activity Among Different Social Groups, 1992

CATEGORY	PERCENT ACTIVE IN ORGANIZATIONS
All (age 16–84)	51
Workers	41
Salaried employees/self-employed	60
Low education	42
Moderate education	51
High education	64
Young (age 16–24)	58
Homemakers	45
Gainfully employed	55

Source: Lars Häll, *Föreningslivet i Sverige* (Stockholm: Statistics Sweden, 1994), Table 3:4.

men and women (age groups 16–44). There are, however, some noteworthy differences in the type of organization men and women prefer to join. As could be expected, men are more active in, for example, motor organizations and in voluntary defense organizations, and women are more involved in church and charitable organizations.[54] Table 7-1 shows the percentage of those among different categories reported in a survey conducted in 1992 to be active in at least some organizations.

As can be seen from Table 7-1, there are important differences both between the social classes and between people with different levels of education. People of higher education and those of higher social class tend to be more active in organizations. Moreover, and contrary to the conventional belief, young Swedes are more active in organizations than the average person. In fact, people 16 to 24 years old have the highest percentage of active members of all age groups in this study. Here we do find a gender gap in that 15 percent more young men than young women report being active, but among women, the young are the most active age group. It should also be noted that only 45 percent of Swedish homemakers are active, compared to 51 percent for the average person and 55 percent for those who are employed. It should perhaps be added that in Sweden, this group is very small; in this study, only 2 percent (124 people) stated that they belonged to the homemaker category.

CHANGES IN THE ORGANIZATIONAL LANDSCAPE

Much of the discussion about voluntary associations and social capital is not about absolute levels but about changes over time. Robert Putnam's

Table 7-2: Organization Membership in Katrineholm by Social Class and Sex, 1950 and 1988, as Percentage of Total Population

| Number of | WORKERS | | | | SALARIED EMPLOYEES | | | |
| | Men | | Women | | Men | | Women | |
organizations	1950	1988	1950	1988	1950	1988	1950	1988
0	-	-	-	-	-	-	2	2
1–2	62	36	100	43	29	15	63	30
3–4	33	43	-	44	43	31	34	51
5+	5	21	-	13	28	54	-	17
Total	100	100	100	100	100	100	100	100
(N)	337	258	39	191	68	79	41	18

Source: Marek Perlinski, "Livet utanför fabriksgrinden och kontorsdörren," in Rune Åberg, ed., *Industrisamhälle i omvandling* (Stockholm: Carlssons, 1990).

research showing a steep decline in organizational membership and activity in the United States has gotten wide attention in the academic and public discussions about social capital.[55] Despite the great political differences between them, Sweden is one of the European countries in which cultural and lifestyle trends from the United States are quickly adapted. Thus there would be good reason to believe that the decline in organizational life in the United States that has been reported by Putnam would also occur in Sweden. In fact, the data show the opposite: During the postwar period, voluntary organizations have been growing in size, level of activity, and financial resources.[56] Of course, this growth has not been evenly distributed. Women's organizations, the free churches, and the temperance movement have lost members, while sports, retired citizens', union, and environmental organizations have grown. The growth of the sports movement has been especially impressive, from about 200,000 members in the 1930s to almost 3 million in the 1990s. Table 7-2 shows data from two studies of a typical Swedish middle-sized town, Katrineholm, conducted in 1950 and 1988.

There are some clear changes from 1950 to 1988. First, more people are members of many (i.e., more than five) organizations. Second, although men are members of more organizations, the gender gap is closing. This Katrineholm study reports very little change in the membership of different types of organizations, except for the temperance movement, which has lost most of its members, but growth of other organizations more than compensated for this loss.[57] The overall picture remains that hardly any Swedes fall outside the organizational world and that no decline in membership has occurred since the early

Figure 7-1: Changes in Organizational Memberships, 1981 to 1996

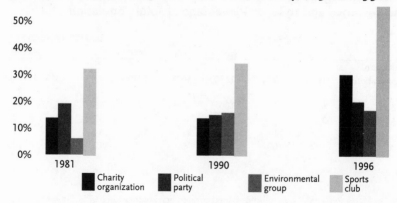

Source: Swedish section of the World Value Studies.

1950s. The Swedish sections of the World Value Studies from 1981, 1990, and 1996 shows a considerable increase in membership in charities, sports clubs, and environmental organizations and no decline in membership in political parties.

Some see weakness in Sweden's voluntary organizations not in terms of formal membership or level of resources but in terms of the activity of their members. As in the United States, many traditional popular mass movements have been accused of having mostly "paper" members.[58] Some organizations, such as the unions, have made membership, at least to some extent, an instrument of economic rationality rather than of civic engagement by using various selective incentives to increase mem-

Figure 7-2: Interest in Working in Voluntary Organizations

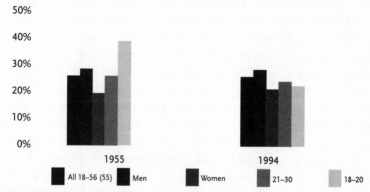

Source: Data from Forskningspruppen för samhälls-och informationsstudier (FSI), Stockholm (N 1955=2,050, N 1,994=650).

bership.[59] But as shown in Figure 7-2, from the 1950s to the 1990s there has been no general decline in the willingness to engage in voluntary organizations; if anything, more people are answering that they are interested in working in voluntary associations during the 1990s than four decades ago. The major changes are that women's interest in voluntary work has gone up, while the interest among the very young (18–20 years) has gone down.

In the Swedish sections of the World Value Studies, people were also asked if they had done any unpaid work in voluntary organizations. Sixteen different types of organizations were presented to the respondents in these surveys, conducted in 1981 and 1990. As can be seen in Figure 7–1, there is no general decline between 1981 and 1990 for the voluntary sector in this respect. On the contrary, human rights organizations, environmental groups, and especially sports organizations seemed to attract more people to voluntary work in 1990 than they did in 1981. It should perhaps be added that the period from 1988 to 1991 was a period of extreme economic boom in Sweden, which, among other things, caused a shortage in the labor supply in the labor market. This should, one could argue, decrease the willingness of people to do unpaid work, but the results from the World Value Studies show the opposite—no general decline could be detected.

This result is supported by Swedish Standard of Living surveys from 1968, 1981, and 1991 showing that the number of Swedes who live outside the world of voluntary associations did not increase between 1968 and 1991.[60] As for the study circles mentioned above, there has been considerable growth in these. The number of adults who participate each year increased from 15 percent in 1960 to around 40 percent in 1975, a level that was pretty stable until the mid-1990s.[61] However, two surveys with identical questions conducted in 1987 and 1992 show a considerable decline in membership and activity for most voluntary organizations between these years. The degree of mobilization (i.e., the percentage of the adult population who are active in the organizations), on average, went down by nearly 1 percent for each of the twenty-five organizations reported in these two surveys. Bearing in mind that the average degree of mobilization in 1987 was 3.7 percent for these organizations, this is a considerable decline for such a short period.[62]

These two studies also report a weakening of "affinity" (samhörighet) for the major types of organizations and popular movements. Table 7-3 shows the results of two survey studies in 1987 and 1992 asking people to what degree they felt affinity for different organizations and/or popular movements.

Table 7-3: Affinity with Different Organizations and Movements

Type of organization	1987	1992	Difference
Sports organizations	5.2	4.3	-0.9
Environmental organizations	5.6	3.8	-1.8
Organizations for international aid and solidarity	4.9	3.7	-1.2
The peace movement	5.8	3.1	-2.7
Organizations for popular education	3.6	2.7	-0.9
The Church of Sweden	3.3	2.6	-0.7
Consumer cooperative movement	3.3	2.3	-1.0
Women's movement	3.7	2.0	-1.7
Temperance movement	2.6	1.6	-1.0
Free churches	1.3	1.0	-0.3
Average	3.9		
(N = 2,701)		2.7	
(N = 5,902)		-1.2	

Respondents were asked: "In the Swedish society exist different types of organizations and movements. How strongly do you feel affinity with . . ." Responses were scored on a scale of 0 to 10, where 0 meant "feels no affinity with . . ." and 10 meant "feels very strong affinity with. . . ."

Source: Lars Häll, *Föreningslivet i Sverige* (Stockholm: Statistics Sweden, 1994), p. 26.

As can be seen, all of these organizations/movements lost support during this period, most clearly the peace, women's, and environmental organizations. The average percentage of people reporting affinity for any of these groups dropped from 3.9 to 2.7, which is a considerable change over a rather short period. How this can be explained, and what affinity really measures regarding social capital, are difficult questions. These results have been taken by several scholars as a clear sign of a major crisis for the voluntary organizations in Sweden.[63]

I believe that one can give a different interpretation of these figures about organizational affinity. What has changed may be not so much people's willingness to participate in voluntary organizations as their notion of collective identity in general, and the collective sense of belonging that traditionally has been the trademark of the popular movements. This argument is based on interpretations of several different empirical studies. First, the Katrineholm study reported an interesting shift among blue-collar workers. In the 1950s, workers saw themselves as members of the working class and of a labor movement committed to changing society. In the late 1980s, workers saw themselves as members of the middle class but not of a labor movement with a common goal. On the contrary, the study reported a sense of mass/elite cleavage within the labor movement. Second, a major survey report published in 1990 claimed that a new type of citizen, endowed with greater knowledge and resources, has emerged and that the educational level of these citizens makes it possible for them to question expert judgments.[64] The virtue held most highly by Swedish citizens was, according to this study, the ability to form one's own views independently of others.[65] Third, the yearly SOM surveys in which questions about membership and activity in unions, sports organizations, and "other organizations" are posed, show hardly any decline in membership or activity between 1987 and 1998.[66] This result is confirmed by yet another study about work in voluntary associations conducted in association with a recent government investigation into the state of Swedish democracy.[67]

Thus it seems that the notion of individual autonomy has gained popularity among Swedish citizens; available evidence suggests a trend in this direction. The proportion of citizens deeming themselves able to write a letter appealing an authority's decision increased from 45.1 percent to 68.5 percent between 1968 and 1987. Work by Thorlief Pettersson within the framework of a larger study of European values supplies evidence that the Swedish citizen of 1990 was substantially more individualistic than his counterpart of ten years earlier and resented impositions and restrictions on individual means of expression.[68]

One might expect this change in value patterns to be limited to the highly educated middle class, and it is true that individualistic attitudes are most marked in that social group. Interestingly, however, it was only among blue-collar workers that any palpable change took place between 1981 and 1990; both high- and low-level white-collar employees, in contrast, remained largely at their earlier high levels when it came to embracing individualistic values.[69] Accordingly, the proportion of workers with an individualistic viewpoint in general increased from 39 percent to 53 percent between 1981 and 1990, and those expressing an individualistic outlook toward their working life rose from 17 percent to 43 percent.[70]

One might assume that this new individualism would undermine forms of collective action (and also support for the universal welfare state); however, an individualistically minded citizen is not necessarily an egoistic citizen. Pettersson and Geyer argue that the new individualists do not hold the values assumed by neoliberals:

Compared with the less individualistically-inclined, moreover, they do *not* show any stronger interest in increasing today's wage differentials, they do *not* evidence any greater tendency to view the poor with a "they-just-have-themselves-to-blame" attitude, they do *not* show any stronger tendency to regard their fellow beings in

less of a spirit of trust and fellowship. . . . They are neither the irre-
pressible entrepreneurs imagined by the Neo-liberals, nor the selfish egoists supposed by the Social Democrats.[71]

Thus, it appears that collectivism/individualism and altruism/egoism
represent distinct and largely independent ranges of values among the
Swedish population. These largely younger and highly educated citizens
are, for example, no more critical of universal welfare programs than
were their more collectivistically minded brothers and sisters.[72] One reasonable interpretation of these findings is that a solidaristic rather than
an egoistic individualism has appeared. A concept such as "solidaristic
individualism" may seem to be a contradiction in terms, but the meaning is that solidarity does not necessarily imply collectivism. By "solidaristic individualism," I mean that individuals are willing to give support to other individuals but also to accept that they have other, different
values and want to engage themselves for different causes. This support,
however, is given under the condition that they can trust their fellow citizens to give the same support back for their own different lifestyles and
organizational efforts. There is some empirical evidence from other
sources showing that individual autonomy and social responsibility go
together. One such source is the analysis from the group behind the
European Value Study, which argues that while individualism is increasing, "individualism may involve identification with, and action on behalf
of others."[73]

One way to understand the diminishing affinity of Swedes for
most movements/organizations is thus not as a declining interest in
voluntary organizations but as an increasing demand for individual
autonomy and a willingness to construct lifestyles and worldviews
independently of large collectivities such as the old popular movements. My conclusion is thus that the decreasing level of affinity for
the major organizations/movements should not necessarily be taken
as a sign of decreasing willingness to engage in voluntary organizations, thereby diminishing the amount of social capital in Sweden. It
may instead reflect problems the old and established organizations
face in creating the type of collective loyalty that existed in the past. If
there is a crisis in the production of social capital, it must be manifested in changed patterns of activity, not just in changed attitudes of
this sort.

Evidence that a decreasing level of affinity does not necessarily translate into less social capital can also be drawn from a survey of those born
in the 1970s. This survey shows that although this generation has, to

some extent, turned away from traditional, hierarchical forms of organizational activity, they are more likely to engage in more temporary organizational forms (e.g., teams, action groups, local music clubs, etc.).[74] As shown in the Pettersson study, they are more individualistic but not less likely to engage in voluntary organizations; it is the form of organization that they demand (and produce) that has changed. Yet another reason for being skeptical of the conclusion that lower affinity means lower engagement in organizations, and thus a crisis for the organizations, is that even among blue-collar workers, affinity toward the union movement scores an average of only 3.5 on a scale of 0 to 10, and that among young women, affinity for the women's movement is as low as 1.7 on the same scale.[75] In sum, I think there is something strange with the way the affinity question has been interpreted and that it is not a very good indicator of activity in or support for the voluntary organizations. The available data seem to show that when old and established popular movements, such as the free churches and the temperance movement, have a declining stock of members, it reflects a changed composition of organizational life in Sweden more than a general decline in voluntarism.

How should this new organizational landscape be described? Based on their extensive study of voluntary organizations in Norway (which show the same general tendencies as in Sweden), Per Selle and Bjarne Øymyr have argued that the composition of the voluntary sector in the Nordic countries has changed dramatically since the 1940s. First, organizations have become less hierarchical; that is, the local units act more independently of the national organization, what organizational theorists call "loose coupling." Second, there has been a change from religious, temperance, and purely women's organizations to leisure and cultural organizations, while the economic organizations (unions and cooperatives) have largely stayed at their initially high level. Third, both the diversity and density of the organizational landscape have increased. There are many more organizations and many more different types of organizations in the 1990s than there were during the 1940s. Fourth, the 1990s are characterized by an increasing dynamism in the organizational world; that is, many organizations die, but even more new ones are created. Lastly, nowadays more people get organized in order to fulfill their own individual interests, while collective ideological movements, such as the temperance movement and the free church movement and probably also the labor movement, have become weaker. One way to describe this change is to say that the Scandinavian countries have gone from collective mass movements to "organized individualism."[76] There are good reasons to believe that this change in the organizational landscape has a connection to the type of individualism mentioned above. Choosing an organization may nowadays have more to do with the individual's deliberate creation of a specific lifestyle than with adherence to an established organized ideological collective.

Swedish Unions: A Special Case

Of all Swedish organizations, the union movement is the one with the most members, and next only to the sports movement, it engages the most people in activity. If there is a general crisis in the idea of popular movements in Sweden, we should be able to detect it here. As stated above, the degree of unionization in Sweden is unusually high, more than 85 percent. The variation in degree of unionization is, in fact, one of the most peculiar differences between Western capitalist countries. It is peculiar for two reasons. First, hardly any other important political variable show such a variation, with France at the bottom, with less than 10 percent in unions, and Sweden at the top. If it is rational, in any sense, to be a member of a union, then why are there more than eight times as many rational employees in Sweden than in France? Or, to follow the standard theory of collective action, if it is individually irrational to be a union member, then why should Swedes in particular be the most irrational people? Second, the level of unionization has changed dramatically during the whole postwar period. For example, the difference between the level of unionization in Sweden and that in the United States (the Swedish rate is more than five times the U.S. rate) was much smaller during the 1950s. The effects of the recent and much discussed globalization and internationalization of capitalism have come at the same time that the differences in degrees of unionization have continued to increase.[77]

The answer to this puzzle is, to a large extent, the existence of "selective incentives." It pays more in some countries for the individual to be a member of the union. As I have shown elsewhere, one such selective incentive seems to be of special importance in this case, namely, the degree of control unions have over unemployment funds. Figures from the late 1980s from eighteen OECD countries showed that the five countries with the highest degrees of unionization (Sweden, Denmark, Finland, Iceland, and Belgium) all had unemployment systems in which the unions had control over the administration of the unemployment insurance scheme, whereas in the rest, this was handled by governmental agencies. The results from multiple regression analysis showed that this explained 18 percent of the variation in the degree of unionization.[78]

The idea of giving the unions control over the unemployment insurance scheme is a very good illustration of the relationship in Sweden between voluntary organizations and the state. On one hand, the unions get a very powerful selective incentive to help them recruit members. On the other hand, the unions also handle the very difficult question of deciding who is really to be considered unemployed, that is, what type of work one has to accept or else risk losing the benefits. The government is thereby relieved of having to take responsibility for these very difficult decisions, and this is something that probably increases the legitimacy of the scheme—first, because it is the union officials and not the governmental bureaucrats who take these decisions, and second, because the union officials probably know more about each segment of the labor market and thus the opportunities their members have for finding suitable jobs.[79]

It should be added that this is not the only type of selective incentives the Swedish unions have been granted by the government. A vast number of industrial laws and regulations give the local unions a say over working conditions, the implementation of work safety regulations, and who has to go first when there is a shortage of jobs. In sum, this means that for many, if not most, employees, membership in the union is only formally a voluntary decision.[80]

On the other hand, this does not mean that instrumental motives are the only reason for becoming a union member. Surveys both from the late 1970s and from more recent years show that instrumental and solidaristic motives are equally strong when union members are asked why they decided to join.[81] Even so, an instrumental motive for joining a union may translate into activity in the next stage and thereby produce social capital. From the standpoint of producing social capital, there is nothing intrinsically bad in combining instrumental and noninstrumental reasons for organizational activity. After all, most people join choral societies in order to pursue a very instrumental and individual preference for singing, not to create interpersonal trust or to make democracy work.

What, then, has happened to union activity during the last two decades? Do the unions in Sweden consist of only passive paper members who see the union as something like a public insurance company controlled by professional bureaucrats, or do unions engage their members in activities that are likely to produce interpersonal trust? Before I try to answer this question, I would like to underline the diversity of the Swedish union movement. Although the blue-collar trade unions organized nationally in the LO are the largest unions, unions for salaried employees organized in the Tjänstemännens Centralorganisation

(TCO) and unions for professionals with academic educations organized in the Sveriges Akademikers Centralorganisation (SACO) have an almost equally high degree of unionization. Second, the Swedish union movement is both more centralized and more decentralized than is the case in most other OECD countries. The central organizations are very strong, but so are, in most cases, the local clubs in each workplace. By tradition, but also because of the laws regulating industrial relations, Swedish unions have a more direct presence in the workplace. The laws securing the rights of local union officials and the co-determination law have been especially important in this case.

A survey from 1993 shows that 36 percent of all employees had participated in at least one union meeting during the previous twelve months and that 19 percent had also spoken during a meeting. A similar study from 1988 shows a slight decrease in this type of union activity (45 percent and 20 percent). This report also shows that 14 percent of all LO members served as an elected representative, the figures for the two other national union organizations being slightly higher. Given the extremely high degree of unionization in Sweden, this means that a considerable part of the population as a whole (13 percent) is active or serves as an elected representative in the union movement.[82]

The Swedish Living Conditions report, which has survey data from 1995, shows similar results. Of the adult population, 36 percent had been in a union meeting during the previous twelve months, and 11 percent reported that they were active as union officials. However, the difference between 1976 and 1995 is significantly negative, −7.6 percent.[83] One explanation for this may be that during the mid-1970s, an unusually high number of new and important industrial relations laws that implied increased local activity had just been launched, such as the co-determination law and the work safety law. Another important factor that may explain the decrease in union activity is the rapid increase in unemployment in 1992.

In sum, it would not be correct to describe the Swedish union movement as a group of vibrant organizations in which a majority of their members are active, but it would be equally wrong to ignore the fact that 36 percent of the adult population go to a union meeting once a year and that 11 percent go to more than four meetings a year. The percentage reporting that they were active went down during the late 1970s, but it has been pretty stable (10–12 percent) since 1980.[84]

Informal Social Networks

One popular image of the Swedish society holds that Swedes, either because of their national character or because of the cradle-to-grave welfare state, had rather weak social ties.[85] I will leave the question of national character and concentrate on the latter problem, namely, what does a universal welfare state do to informal social networks? Interestingly enough, there are arguments from both the left and the right saying that there is an inverse relationship between these two. The argument from the political right is that when altruism and social problems are taken over by the government, people stop caring; compassion is shown only by paying taxes, and informal social networks are weakened. A recent major research project about the Swedish welfare state (financed by the employers' federation) concludes, among other things, that "the twentieth century has been a lost century for the civil society."[86]

The argument from the left is, in fact, very similar. According to Jürgen Habermas, the welfare state has "colonized" civil society and undermines what he calls "natural" forms of solidarity. Alan Wolfe argues that the Scandinavian type of welfare state "squeezes families, communities, and social networks."[87] Wolfe has further argued that a historical irony may exist here—when social obligations become public, intimate ties will weaken and "so will distant ones, thus undermining the very moral strengths the welfare state has shown."[88] What is somewhat peculiar with these arguments is that they are hardly ever substantiated by empirical evidence.

If it is true that the universal welfare state has been detrimental to informal social relations, then we should see a weakening of such relations since the 1950s in Sweden. However, the data show that there has been a strengthening of informal social ties during this period. The Katrineholm study with data from 1950 and 1988 concludes that "the people in Katrineholm have become more socially active. They are members of more organizations and socialize more frequently with their fellow workers, neighbors and friends."[89] The Swedish Living Conditions report, produced by Statistics Sweden and based on data from about 7,000 interviews from 1975 and 1995, gives the same type of result. Over this period, there is an increase of 12 points in the percentage of people who get together with friends each week (from 45.5 to 57.5). The positive changes are statistically significant for all age groups, except those from 55 to 64 years of age, where the increase is only 3 percentage points, but there is another significant 12 percent increase among those 65 to 74 years of age. The greatest increase has taken place among those 25 to 34 years of age (23.5 percent). Interestingly enough, the figure for women who are homemakers is lower (51 percent) than for women in general (56 percent), and this figure is also lower than for women who work full time (56 percent). It can be added that the number of people who report not having a close friend is down from 26 percent in 1979 to 19 percent in 1985; these changes are statistically significant for all age groups.[90]

This result is confirmed by data from another study, as shown in Figure 7-3 below. The number of people interviewed in this study is far smaller than in the Swedish Living Conditions study cited above, but the time span is greater, 1955 to 1995.

As can be seen, both men and women, young and not so young, seem to be more interested in socializing with friends in the 1990s than was the case in the mid-1950s. In the 1990s, hardly anyone reports being uninterested in socializing with friends.

One could argue, however, that the important part of the criticism of the welfare state mentioned above is not that people socialize too little but that in a time of distress they would not help the people with whom they socialize. People in a universal welfare state would, according to its critics, turn away from others in need and coldheartedly refer them to the welfare authorities.[91] Paying high taxes would morally relieve them from more traditional social obligations. There are, unfortunately, no data over time to test such a hypothesis; however, in a recent study, Karin Busch Zetterberg reports from a survey of 2,749 Swedish adult citizens (age 16–89) conducted in 1994 that more than one in every five adults (approximately 22 percent) regularly takes voluntary care of someone who is sick, handicapped, or elderly.[92] Of these 22 percent, about 5 percent took care of persons in their own household and about 18 percent cared for people who lived outside their household. The difference

Figure 7-3: Interest in Socializing with Friends

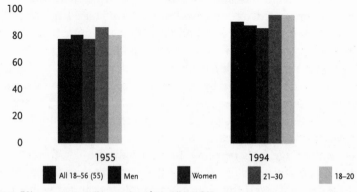

Source: FSI surveys. 1955 (N=1509) and 1995(N=1388).

between men and women was surprisingly small, as 23 percent of Swedish women and 20 percent of the men were voluntarily helping out. Age also had a small effect, varying from 20 to 25 percent between different cohorts. Social class, however, made a difference, with 31 percent caregivers in the upper class and 20 percent in the working class. The type of care given varies, of course, but sometimes included rather demanding tasks such as lifting and helping out with personal hygiene and medication.

"Still, when all is said and done, there is not and can never be any guarantee that stronger relations in civil society will create the practices that enable people to take personal responsibility for the fate of abstract others," writes Alan Wolfe.[93] I tend to agree, but I would add that Wolfe's fear that the strength of the Scandinavian welfare states would destroy such moral obligations seems unwarranted. Whether the amount of voluntary care in Sweden is high or low is, of course, difficult to say from this study, but it seems fair to conclude that the universal welfare state has not wiped out this sort of activity.

In most European countries, drinking establishments can serve as sites of community interaction. However, in Sweden there is no equivalent to the British pub, the German *kneipe*, or the French bistro. Historically, the severe restrictions on the selling of alcohol made such neighborhood places for socializing very rare. But there has been a rather remarkable change in this respect over the last thirty years. In 1967, the number of fully licensed restaurants was a mere 1,249 (which is about 1 per 6,400 individuals).[94] Thirty years later, this has increased seven times; that is, there are now close to 10,000 fully licensed restaurants in Sweden (which is about 1 per 900 individuals).[95] This increase has not taken place as a result of any legal change enacted by the Swedish parliament. Instead, according to experts in this area, it largely reflects a cultural change (Swedes becoming more Continental in their lifestyle), which has been reflected by a change in administrative practices.[96] There has, moreover, been no increase in alcohol consumption during this period, which means that the great increase in the number of fully licensed restaurants has not been caused by an increased demand for alcohol. Instead, it must reflect a change in social habits; that is, consumption of alcohol has gone from private to public. Survey data also show that going to restaurants has now become one of the favorite leisure time activities in Sweden. In fact, this is the leisure time activity with the highest increase between 1982 and 1995; in 1982, 25 percent of Swedes said that they had gone to a restaurant more than five times during the previous year, and in 1995, 41 percent said this (while only 9 percent reported going to a religious service

Figure 7-4: Social Isolation and Passivity

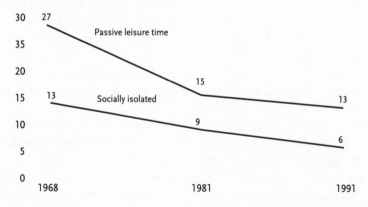

Source: Johan Fritzell and Olle Lundberg, *Vardagens villkor* (Stockholm: Brombergs, 1994), p. 226

more than five times a year). Although the young are the most frequent patrons in restaurants, the increase is significant in all age groups and highest among those 45 to 54 years of age, among whom it has more than doubled (from 16 to 34 percent).[97]

However, the effect of this type of activity on social capital remains unknown. There seems to be a strong connection over time between the decreasing activity in the temperance movement reported above and the increasing interest among Swedes in consuming alcohol in public places. I leave it to the reader to determine whether this type of change is good or bad for the creation of trust and social capital, but it is surely an indicator of an increased number of informal social contacts in Sweden. However, in the SOM survey data collected for this study, we found (to our dismay, we confess) no relationship at all between high levels of trust and high frequency of visits to restaurants (whether fully licensed or not).

Another kind of data that can serve as an indicator of informal social ties are generated by surveys on social isolation and on the activity level of people's lives. As can be seen in Figure 7-4, the number of people who can be characterized as living in social isolation or who are passive in their leisure time activity decreased considerably from 1968 to 1991.

Thus, much of the criticism of modern society and of the expansion of the welfare state for creating passive and socially isolated citizens seems inconsistent with these empirical findings.[98] But this rosy picture must be tempered by what seems to be a considerable increase in violent crime. According to the Swedish Living Conditions survey, the number of individuals who have been victims of or threatened with some form of physical violence increased by 35 percent between 1978 and 1995.[99] In sum, the hypothesis that high levels of social interaction creates high stocks of social capital, which in turn lowers the level of crime in society, is not corroborated by Swedish data.

SWEDISH CIVIL SOCIETY IN COMPARATIVE PERSPECTIVE

So far, we have tried to see what has happened over time with the voluntary sector and with more informal social relations in Sweden, and the conclusion is that although there has been a change in the composition and direction of this sector, we cannot detect a general decline in membership or activity during the postwar period. But time series data on this question must be supplemented with comparative data. How does the voluntary sector in Sweden fare compared to countries with different and/or less developed welfare states and more pluralistic political systems?

Thanks to two different comparative projects on the nonprofit sector and volunteering, we now have data with which to address this question. One of the most common ideas in the debate about civil society is that an encompassing welfare state would make people less willing to do unpaid work in voluntary organizations. If so, rates of voluntary work would be very low in countries with large welfare states, but such a hypothesis is not validated in a recent survey comparing eight European countries.[100] The two countries with the most extensive welfare policies, the Netherlands and Sweden, also have the highest scores in the volume of unpaid work in voluntary associations.[101] In response to the question "In the past year, have you carried out *any* unpaid work or activity for or with an organization that has nothing to do with your paid work and is not solely for your own benefit or the benefit of your family?" 36 percent of the Swedish population answered yes as compared to an average of 27 percent across other European countries.[102] This says something about frequency but nothing about the total volume of voluntary work. It may be that people do voluntary work every year but that the total amount is very small. According to this study, however, the Swedish population did not spend fewer hours a month in voluntary work than those of the other seven countries. In considering the type of organization in which the work was done, Swedes scored comparatively high on sports and recreation, trade unions and professional organizations, civil defense, international development, and human rights and peace, and, as could be expected, low on health, social services, child education, and community development. Surprising to this author was the finding that Swedes were slightly more active in religious organizations.[103]

Considering the general theory of the importance of social capital, the Swedish population also seems to volunteer for the right (i.e., noninstrumental) reasons. Of those Swedes who volunteered, 62 percent said they did so to "meet people and make friends," as compared to an average of 36 percent elsewhere in Europe, while only 6 percent said they did so because "it gives me social recognition and a position in the community," as compared to an average of 18 percent elsewhere.[104] At the same time, only 11 percent of the Swedish population agreed with the statement "If the government fulfilled all of its responsibilities, there should be no need for people to do unpaid work," as compared to an average of 37 percent in other European countries. And finally, in Sweden, 74 percent agreed that "engaging in unpaid work helps people take an active role in a democratic society," compared to the average of 62 percent. These results are confirmed by another recent comparative study that found that the per capita amount of voluntary work in Sweden is considerably higher than in France, Germany, or Italy.[105]

This research project also provides data about the way voluntary organizations are financed. Although the size of the nonprofit sector in 1990, measured in terms of expenditures as a percentage of GDP, was 4.1 percent in Sweden, the average of the eight countries in the study was 3.6 percent. By this economic measure, the nonprofit sector in Sweden is smaller than that of the United States or the United Kingdom, but it is larger than that of Germany, France, or Italy.[106] Even more surprisingly, although the average revenue from public payments was 42 percent for the countries compared, the Swedish nonprofit sector received only 29 percent of its funds from the government.[107] Accordingly, the Swedish nonprofits obtained 62 percent of their funds through earned income, the highest percentage among the eight countries (the average was 47 percent). The explanation for this is not that Swedes are more altruistic (they are not) or that Swedish nonprofit organizations are more successful in generating income on their own. Rather, as Lundström and Wijkström have pointed out, the nonprofit sectors in other countries are more dependent on public money to fund social services, health services, and elementary education, which, because of the universal welfare state, are relatively small concerns for Swedish nonprofits.

Considering informal social relations, the study by Busch Zetterberg mentioned above on the number of people who voluntarily help others in need makes a comparison with Great Britain possible. Figures from a comparable study in Great Britain based on a survey from 1990 show that this type of voluntary activity is higher in Sweden (22 percent) than in Britain (15 percent). If we compare the number of people who helped people outside their own household, the Swedish figure is 18 percent, while for Great Britain, it is 12 percent.[108]

Comparing surveys from different countries is always difficult because the wording of the question can be interpreted differently. In this case, there is also a four-year time span between the surveys. On the other hand, this is a question not about attitudes but about actual behavior, which means that the methodological problems should be fewer. Great Britain's welfare system is, moreover, far less universal than Sweden's, and Great Britain is also known for its many charitable organizations. We should thus expect higher figures from Britain, but the data show the opposite. Thus, it seems safe to conclude that these results from Sweden and Great Britain do not substantiate the claim that the more extensive and universal the welfare state, the less we will see of voluntary activity based on feelings of moral obligation. This is of course not to say that a more universal welfare state system *causes* more voluntarism, because we cannot control for other variables. How the causal mechanisms may work here is a more complicated affair.[109]

To summarize, in terms of membership, activity, and finances, the voluntary sector in Sweden is as large or larger than those in most other Western industrialized democracies, and Swedish political participation ranks among the highest. Moreover, the nonprofit sector in Sweden is less dependent on governmental funding and is better able to raise money on its own than are many comparable countries. What differentiates the voluntary sector in Sweden, as well as in the other Scandinavian countries, is its structure. While historical and political factors have made it weak in areas such as social service, health care, and elementary education, it is strong in the fields of sports, recreation, culture, adult education, and the labor market.[110]

THE TRUST SCENE

Being an active member of voluntary organizations and having lots of informal social contacts will, according to the general theory of social capital, serve to increase the level of trust in society. From the very first World Value Study in 1981, we know that Sweden and the other Scandinavian countries are high-trust societies. More people than elsewhere agree with the statement "Most people can be trusted" and disagree with the statement "You can't be too careful when dealing with other

Figure 7-5: Opinions about Trust in Other People, 1981 to 1997

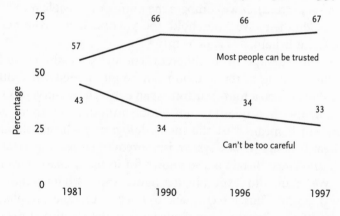

Sources: Data for 1981 and 1990 are taken from the Swedish sections of the World Value Studies (N = 876 and 994). In 1996, two different surveys were conducted in Sweden with this question, the third World Value Study (N = 957) and one made for this report by the SOM Institute
at Göteborg University (N = 1,707). The figures shown are the means from these two studies.
The data for 1997 are from a survey (N = 1,640) by the Forskningsgruppen för samhälls-och
informationsstudier.

people."[111] As shown in Figure 7-5, recent Swedish survey data do not
show a decline in the opinion about whether most people can be trusted.
On the contrary, generalized trust measured in this way has increased
between 1981 and 1997.[112]

In the four yearly SOM surveys conducted since 1996, we asked not
only the dichotomous trust question as stated above but also a question
for which respondents were asked to mark their opinion on a scale of 0 to
10 about whether or not other people could be trusted. The result has
been remarkably stable in these four surveys, indicating that the question
has a high degree of validity. The average for these years is that 12 percent
can be considered as "low trusters" (value 0–3), 29 percent as "middle
trusters" (value 4–6), and 55 percent as "high trusters" (value 7–10).[113]

We have also used the SOM survey from 1996 to analyze what other
variables may explain differences in levels of trust as measured on the
0–10 scale. To summarize the results of the statistical analysis from these
four data sets, the following variables had the highest (i.e., most positive) effect on individual trust: education, income, activity in organizations, satisfaction with democracy, accepting more refugees, and satisfaction with one's life. Controlling for all these variables, we also found

that confidence in the judicial system and the police had significant positive effects on individuals' trust.[114] In other words, people who indicate that they trust most other people are likely to have the following characteristics: They earn more money, have higher education, are more satisfied with their lives, are more tolerant toward immigrants, and have a more positive view of how the Swedish democracy works than the average person. Controlling for all these variables, they have also more confidence in how the police and the judicial system operate. This result is in accordance with similar survey-based analysis from the United States, so we can conclude that there are important cross-national similarities in the way trust can be explained at the individual level.[115]

Of particular importance is, of course, the relationship between trust and how people view the political system. As shown above, there is a significant correlation between the trust and degree of satisfaction with the Swedish democracy. In the group who expressed high trust (7–10 on the scale), 72 percent said they were "very satisfied with how Swedish democracy works," compared to 42 percent who said they were "very dissatisfied."[116]

The four SOM surveys also have questions about confidence in specific political institutions. People have been asked whether they had very high, high, middle, low, or very low confidence in a number of institutions (parliament, the public health care system, the public schools, the unions, major companies, the courts, the armed forces, the banks, the Church of Sweden, the government, the police, the Royal House, the media, and the European Commission). In order to capture the relation between individuals' social trust (i.e., their trust in other people) and their trust in institutions, we have analyzed how the variables are correlated. The result from the statistical analysis can be summarized in a number of points.

- Each one of the sixty correlations point in the same positive direction, so that the more a person trusts other people, the more he or she trusts institutions.
- All the correlations are weak, implying that there is a significant number of people for which this does not hold.
- The existence of these positive correlations does not say anything about how the causal mechanism operates or if there is a causal mechanism at work at all. It may be that trust in other people causes trust in institutions, but it can as well be that it is trust in institutions that causes trust in other people. Or these variables may not be related at all, that is, both can be caused by some other variable.[117]

One noteworthy result is that the strongest correlations we found are the ones between social trust and trust in the institutions of law and order, that is, the courts and the police. There seems to be no reason why there should be a causal mechanism between trusting other people and trusting these two particular institutions. One possibility is that the causal link runs the other way around; that is, if you trust the institutions that are supposed to keep law and order, you also trust other people. The argument runs as follows: In a civilized society, institutions of law and order (the police and the courts) have one particularly important task: to detect and punish people who are "traitors," that is, those who break contracts, steal, murder, and do other such noncooperative things and therefore should not be trusted. Thus, if you think that these institutions do what they are supposed to do in a fair and effective manner, then you also have reason to believe that the chance people have of getting away with such treacherous behavior is small.[118] If so, you will believe that people will have very good reason to refrain from acting in a treacherous manner, and you will therefore believe that most people can be trusted.[119]

Such an admittedly speculative interpretation of what causes people to trust others does in fact change what is usually thought about how the causal link operates, namely, that trust is caused by societal factors such as the vitality of voluntary organizations and other types of networks in civil society. If the above reasoning is correct, then trust in other people may have more to do with the way in which political institutions of this type are operating.[120] If people believe that the institutions responsible for handling treacherous behavior are fair and effective, and if they also believe that other people think the same of these institutions, then they will also trust other people. Social capital would then have its origin more in the political institutions than in societal factors.[121] This interpretation of what causes trust is supported by studies in which cross-national survey data on social trust have been correlated with data about the level of corruption and judicial efficiency in different countries. The results show that high levels of social trust are highly correlated to a low level of corruption and a high degree of judicial efficiency.[122]

Another result from the regression analysis of the SOM data is the significant effect of activity in organizations. Are people who are active in volunteer organizations and politics more trusting than those who are passive? Concerning the relationship between trust and membership in volunteer organizations, the general hypothesis also gets support from the Swedish part of the World Value Study. The more organizations people are members of, the more likely are they to trust others.[123]

To summarize so far, the overall picture of Sweden is that of a rather vital, growing, and changing civil society. In most respects, the amount of social capital seems to have increased since the 1950s. We can thus tentatively conclude that whatever the troubles in Swedish democracy, a decline in social capital, as it is usually conceptualized, is not likely to be the cause.

THE UNIVERSAL WELFARE STATE AND CIVIL SOCIETY

Why, then, hasn't the encompassing Swedish welfare state destroyed trust and social capital? One reason may be in the way the Swedish welfare state system has been institutionalized. Its main architects sought a social policy based on the idea of "people's insurance" that would supply all citizens (or in some cases all but the very rich) with basic resources without incurring the stigmatization associated with poor relief. They not only shunned the means-tested poor-relief system but also the class-segregated Bismarckian type of social insurance. The universal character of the welfare state may have two important implications for social trust. One is that people receiving support from the government cannot be portrayed as "other." Second, compared to means-tested programs, universal ones are far less likely to create suspicion that people are cheating the system.[124]

Language is, I believe, a problem here. The term "welfare state" is not an adequate description of social programs in Sweden. The word *welfare*—at least in the United States—implies targeted means-tested programs and connotes stigmatization of the persons receiving it.[125] For Sweden, "social insurance state" would be a more accurate term.

This is not to deny that there are parts of the Swedish welfare system that have been detrimental to social capital. As in other Western countries, a strong planning and managerial optimism, which could indeed take a rather paternalistic form, characterized welfare policy, especially in the late 1960s. High unemployment during the early 1990s increased the number of people who depend on means-tested social assistance. I argue, however, that the bulk of the programs, precisely because they are universal, are not likely to have a negative effect on civil society. In fact, if one looks very closely, leading theorists of civil society agree that general welfare programs cannot be seen as subversive of civil society. In their voluminous book on the political theory of civil society, for example, Jean L. Cohen and Andrew Arato write (in a well-hidden endnote):

> We fail to see how social security, health insurance, job training programs for the unemployed, unemployment insurance, and

family supports such as day care or parental leave create dependency rather than autonomy, even if the particular administration of such programs as AFDC (such as the man-in-house rule) do create dependency and are humiliating. But these are empirical questions. The theoretical issue behind such questions is the extent to which social services and social supports are symbolically constituted as welfare for "failures" or as supports for all members of the community.[126]

Although it is only given endnote status, Cohen and Arato accordingly perceive the fundamental distinction between general and means-tested social policies for civil society. There may be other negative (and positive) effects of a universal welfare state, but it does not keep people from participating in voluntary organizations or helping others in distress.

ORGANIZED SOCIAL CAPITAL AND THE DEMISE OF THE SWEDISH MODEL

So far, our study of Sweden has contradicted the conventional wisdom about social capital. The problems in the Swedish democracy with increasing mistrust of politicians and the central political institutions cannot be traced back to a decline in interpersonal trust, a decline in engagement in voluntary associations, or a fall in informal social networks. The question is, then, whether there is another way of understanding the importance of trust and social capital that would better fit the Swedish context. Instead of repeating the arguments above, I will develop a highly speculative argument that there is another type of social capital that has evaporated in Sweden.

My argument is that in a corporatist political culture where the collaboration between the major interest organizations (trade unions, employers' federations, farmers' organizations, etc.) and the state has been a dominant theme, citizen-to-citizen trust does not exhaust what should be understood as social capital. In order to make a corporatist political system work, we should look more to vertical forms of trust. This type of trust exists in three different forms: (1) trust between individuals in the organizations, (2) trust between the leaders of the organizations, and (3) trust between the leaders of these organizations and the state. Corporatism means power through organization, and I have therefore labeled these three types of vertical trust as *organized* social capital.[127] My argument is that it is the disappearance of such organized social capital that has rendered the Swedish model obsolete and has produced the problems mentioned above for Swedish democracy.

Sweden has not always been the land of compromises and negotiations. From the 1890s to the mid-1930s, the Swedish economy lost the most days of production because of industrial disputes of any Western industrial nation.[128] Especially during the 1920s, Sweden was marked by democratic instability and comparatively very high levels of industrial disputes. One way to understand this situation is, of course, from a classical Marxist perspective in which capitalist relations of production lead to an endemic class struggle between capital and labor. But from another perspective, the labor market can also be understood as a "tragedy of the commons" in which all parties know they would be better off if everyone would cooperate, but cooperation is not rational if you cannot trust others to cooperate. Short of replacing capitalism with socialism, two gains are possible from cooperating in industrial production: (1) both labor and capital will benefit if they work together to achieve increased productivity through technical rationalization, and (2) both parties will benefit if they keep production going and quality high, thereby gaining a solid reputation for reliability among customers and a potential competitive advantage over competitors. To realize these benefits and change capitalism from a zero-sum to a positive-sum game, cooperation between capital or management and labor must be established.[129] But without mutual trust, such efforts will fail, leading to a social trap in which both parties stand to lose.

Starting with a "historical compromise" during the late 1930s, the national federation of blue-collar trade unions (the LO) and the national employers' federations (SAF), solved the critical problem of collective action in the labor market by keeping wages (and consequently inflation) and industrial conflict under firm control through a system of centralized wage negotiations. Beginning in 1928, a particularly black year for the Swedish labor market because of the number of industrial disputes, the government invited the LO and the SAF to talk about what could be done to achieve a more peaceful labor market. After ten years of conferences and investigations, filled with problems and setbacks, these talks eventually led to what became known as the Basic Agreement in 1938. In the Swedish political culture, this agreement became famous and was given an almost mythical status, named after the small resort outside Stockholm where the final negotiations took place and the agreement was signed (the Saltsjöbaden accords).

As a cornerstone of the Swedish model, the Basic Agreement was foremost a symbolic regulation of procedures for negotiations and for the peaceful settlement of grievances. The most important result of the process and the agreement, however, was the new spirit of trust in which unions and employers recognized their common interest in peaceful labor market relations. As stated by the former chairman of the SAF, "the agreement was an effort to try to solve the conflicts on the labor market by wise self-restraint instead of violence."[130]

Many of the most important features of the Basic Agreement were in fact informal.[131] For example, the employers informally agreed to refrain from using strikebreakers and recognized the right of unions to organize and be recognized as an equal partner in the labor market. The LO tacitly agreed to control militant (read Communist) local unions and to implement central command over strikes and blockades. In return for the right to unrestricted unionization of the labor force, unions conceded employers the final say in the organization and direction of production; that is, they agreed not to interfere in the process of rationalization.[132] The symbolic character and informal content of the agreement made its implementation totally dependent on this organized social capital that became known as the "Saltsjöbaden spirit." As the former executive director of the SAF wrote in his memoirs: "The importance of the Saltsjöbaden negotiations cannot be overstated. Exaggerated notions of the opponent's ill will disappeared. . . . One also discovered that the parties had a number of common interests."[133]

The many problems involved in the process of creating and maintaining the Basic Agreement and the organized social capital it required should not be underestimated. Leaders on both sides had to convince their more militant members that the other party could be trusted to honor the agreement, and there is ample evidence that moving from class confrontation to class collaboration was not easy for either side.[134] It would not have been possible if there had not been a high degree of trust between members and leaders on each side.[135] As I have argued elsewhere, there are good reasons to believe that the many corporatist arrangements by the government described above, through which the parties in the labor market learned to cooperate despite intense industrial strife, created the type of trust that made the Basic Agreement possible.[136]

One important facilitating factor was the agreement between the parties to keep the state out of the labor market. One reason the employers' federation (the SAF) entered into the Basic Agreement of 1938 was that the LO leadership made it clear that they did not want the Social Democratic government involved in the process. Despite open conflict with the Social Democratic prime minister and the minister of social affairs, both of whom at that time were convinced that the labor market needed to be regulated through political means, at the critical moment the LO leaders opted for a solution in which the labor market organizations would handle problems on their own.[137] This assured the SAF that the LO would not use its political power (i.e., its very close connection with the government) in order to play a two-against-one game. The principle that problems in the labor market would be solved without political interference became a symbolic centerpiece of the Basic Agreement.

Because the agreement was in fact more symbolic than legally binding, it rested to a very high degree on personal trust between the leaders of the organizations. Many of the most important elements of the Saltsjöbaden accords were based on a mutual understanding that this new policy could be implemented only if both parties could be trusted to act in good faith. There are many examples in the memoir literature illustrating the importance of this type of trust. Consider how Bertil Kugelberg, the managing director of the SAF, in his memoirs describes his opponent, LO chairman Arne Geijer:

> Already after our first meeting with Arne I became firmly convinced that I had met a stable, discerning person whose word one could trust. Many years of company at the negotiation tables and on journeys never gave me any reason to doubt this first impression. He knew what he wanted, his statements were straight, and he stood by his word.[138]

Kugelberg and Geijer came to dominate the labor market scene from the late 1940s until 1966 and became personal friends. Kugelberg's memoirs, and others as well, are filled with evidence of this sort of personal trust and with descriptions of how visitors from employers and unions abroad found this situation peculiar. Beyond this trust at the elite level, there is ample evidence that both the union movement and the employers' federation invested a lot of effort in convincing their rank and file that this collaboration would be advantageous.[139]

THE BREAKDOWN OF ORGANIZED SOCIAL CAPITAL

The first signs of a breakdown in organized social capital came early in 1970. Under pressure from an increasingly radicalized society and a number of wildcat strikes, the LO leadership abandoned the principle of not involving the (Social Democratic) government in the regulation of industrial relations. Instead, they demanded (and got) about twenty new labor laws intended to strengthen their position vis-à-vis the employers. Tim Tilton, one of the leading scholars on Swedish Social Democratic ideology, underlines the break with former principles:

> The reforms did not simply represent the pragmatic middling-through or consensual politics, however; when the Labor Law Commission was unable to present an unanimous report in 1974, the Social Democratic government based its proposals upon the minority report of the LO and TCO representatives.[140]

Accordingly, the Saltsjöbaden accords were formally denounced in 1976. The most far-reaching proposal that came from the LO during this period of radicalization was the establishment of wage earners' funds. In their original form, they were intended to socialize all the major companies in Sweden by forcing them to divert part of their profits to funds that would be used by the unions to buy stock.[141] According to Tilton, the proposal "was not presented as just another incremental reform, however; it was heralded as the beginning of a new and more distinctively socialist epoch."[142] After seven years of unusually bitter political struggle, a much watered-down version of this proposal was established in 1983, only to be abolished by a Conservative-led government in 1992.

The altered strategy of the labor movement had two effects. First, the longer the debate over the wage earners' funds continued, the weaker popular support became for the proposal, not least among LO members. In 1976, about half of the LO membership supported the idea, while by 1983, this had sunk to about 17 percent.[143] Second, and most importantly, the new confrontational strategy of the LO produced a predictable change in strategy by the SAF. The SAF abandoned the central wage negotiations, began a vigorous and rather successful campaign supporting neoliberal economic principles, and withdrew from all corporatist boards and agencies. The situation between the parties today can best be described as endemic distrust, of which there are two clear signs.[144]

First, between the mid-1970s and the mid-1990s, there was no functioning system of wage negotiations. While the LO wanted to return to central negotiations, the SAF wanted to decentralize to the level of the individual company. The cause of this stalemate, according to the chairman of the SAF, was that "there is too little confidence in the Swedish labor market. And when there is no confidence, distrust will grow."[145]

His characterization of the situation was in accord with the LO's reason for resisting local wage setting—they feared arbitrary settlements because they distrusted the employers, believing they would take advantage of weak local unions.

The result of this failure to coordinate the wage formation process created a spiral of inflation and a series of devaluations of the currency that hurt the Swedish economy's international competitiveness. As a result, the Swedish economy fell from fourth in the OECD rankings of GNP per capita in 1970 to eighteenth in 1997.[146] This sharp deterioration of Sweden's economic performance may be the main explanation for why trust in the political institutions and leading politicians has fallen, since, as we have shown, social capital has remained stable.

Second, there has been a failure to reach any compromise on adapting labor laws to new demands for a more flexible organization of production. Despite prolonged efforts by the Social Democratic government to reach some form of agreement, the commission has failed to do so. Moreover, despite these efforts and the use of all available expertise on industrial relations, labor law, and labor economics (of which there is plenty in Sweden), the representatives on the commission failed to reach even a common understanding of the problem. As a result, the government enacted some heavily criticized changes that provoked open protests from the LO and were rejected as totally insufficient by the SAF.[147]

There are, of course, other explanations for the demise of the Swedish model. One is that the model broke down because of changes in the organizational landscape of the labor market. When organizations proliferated, that is, when it was no longer a game limited to the LO and SAF but also included a number of public-sector employers' organizations and a number of unions representing public-sector white-collar workers, coordination of wages and industrial disputes became much more difficult.[148] There is probably some truth in this explanation, but I have two caveats. First, the number of unions that had separate wage contracts was in fact higher in the 1930s. Second, other countries with many labor market organizations, such as Germany and Norway, have been able to coordinate wage formation.

Another explanation points at changes in production, technology, and international trade and finance: It is the "end of Fordist production," the demand for "flexible specialization," and/or the "internationalization of capital" that has undermined the model.[149] Changes in technology and in the economy are clearly important, but these explanations fail to reveal what it is about these particular changes that has produced confrontation instead of compromise in the labor market. Unions and employers in comparable countries such as Norway, Denmark, and the Netherlands have been able to control wages and inflation during the same period that the Swedish model failed in this crucial area.

I propose a different, admittedly speculative, explanation for the demise of the Swedish model. It did not expire because of changes in technology or in the international economy; it broke down because the organized social capital upon which it was built evaporated.

The connection between the demise of the Swedish model and the problems of Swedish democracy are not easily detected. My hypothesis is that there is an indirect causal link between the demise of the Swedish model and the problems of Swedish democracy. The argument is as follows: The Swedish model rested on a limited role for government. It left the parties in the labor market to sort out their problems by themselves. This limited role for the political sphere in the labor market was abandoned during the 1970s. The LO and the Social Democratic Party gave the electorate the impression that the political system would be able to increase social equality through the expansion of the welfare state, introduce economic democracy through the wage earners' funds, establish industrial democracy through the new system of labor laws, secure full employment through an active labor market policy and Keynesian economics, and so forth. The result in every one of these areas has been retreat or outright defeat. There were, as Jonas Pontusson has shown, definite limits to reformism.[150] The tentative conclusion is that the political system in Sweden is distrusted because the political hubris of the LO and the Social Democratic Party during the 1970s led them to abandon the Swedish model, which in turn created a sharp decline in the country's economic performance.

However, the purpose of my argument is not to blame the labor movement for the breakdown of organized social capital in Sweden. It may be that the unions, because of intense pressure from below and the unwillingness of employers to accept changes in the negotiation process, had no other option but to turn to their political allies. But it must also be said that this strategy of double envelopment, in which the LO and the Social Democratic Party pursued both economic democracy/socialism through the wage earners' funds and industrial democracy through new labor law legislation, was unprecedented outside of Sweden as well. It seems as if the dramatic change of strategy by the employers (and their political allies) came as a surprise for the labor movement. But if trust and other such social norms, as Jon Elster has argued,[151] must be understood as noninstrumental behavior, then the Marxism of the LO in the 1970s and the neoliberalism of the SAF of the 1980s are close cousins. Both ideologies rest on the same assumption, namely, that interest never lies. Thus, following the major lesson to be learned from game theory: If all actors act out of such an instrumental rationality, the social capital that is needed to solve problems modeled on the "tragedies of the commons" will not be produced.

8

AUSTRALIA: Making the Lucky Country

EVA COX

This chapter considers how social capital has contributed to giving our diverse populations the skills and incentives to work collectively, through developing a particular form of democracy in Australia. The data suggest this ability may come from a peculiar amalgam of civil society and the state, which has put the public sector and politics at the center of efforts to make a better nation.

The mix of structures, the institutional role of trade unions and religious organizations, and the links between formal and informal community groups provided the social fabric of the new nation when it was forged in 1901. The social fabric held through the twentieth century, with foreign wars, the Great Depression, waves of immigration, and bouts of racism.

Australia, like the United States, was a society of settlers. In Australia, however, the country was claimed as *terra nullius*, unowned territory, by the British Crown, formally denying land rights to the indigenous peoples. Federation by civil process in 1901 owed nothing to any war for independence, nor any civil war. The Federal House of Representatives, the chief arm of government, is elected from local single-member electorates, whereas the Federal Senate is elected from the states at large, following a republican model more like that of the United States.[1] Most of the states have two houses of parliament as well, which can suggest that the country's nineteen million people are overgoverned. Compulsory voting ensures voter involvement and feeds into the popular expectation that governments will act on the people's behalf. A recent poll showed 70 percent support for a benign view of government as being for the people.[2]

Australia, like Britain, had a nineteenth-century history of mutual aid, of collective effort to provide local services, and of an involved, established labor movement closely linked to the Australian Labor Party. There was, however, no hereditary aristocracy, as in Britain, nor big private fortunes, as in the United States, which ensured that the cost of settlement and major infrastructure has generally been publicly funded.

Australian politics and institutions rely more on government than those of Britain and the United States. It was the new federal government and courts that set up minimum wages and work conditions, in 1907.[3] Old-age pensions had been instituted in 1901, votes for women in 1902, and widows' pensions from 1926 on. Government was seen as the vehicle for reform, powered by political parties and by community and church groups.

Australia was hit hard by the 1930s Depression. The economy did not recover completely until the Second World War. Postwar fears of unemployment and consequent social division encouraged a substantial state welfare system, while reconstruction brought Australia her share of the developed countries' economic boom. Progress seemed inevitable, making Australia a desirable land for those who had settled there and for immigrants. She was the "lucky country." It was not until the 1970s that doubts about that luck arose.

Postwar Australia deemed herself underpopulated and set up a major immigration program that impacted greatly on population growth. The population increased by 11,501,442 between 1947 and 1999, and some 7,000,000 of these can be attributed to the net gain of immigrants and their children and grandchildren. The first waves of them came from war-torn Britain and other northern European countries. By 1997, 16 percent of Australians had been born in a non-English-speaking country, and the indigenous population was just 2 percent of the total population.[4] Most of the earlier European immigrants were needed in the burgeoning manufacturing industry and to build infrastructure. However, as the need for labor in these sectors fell off, the advisability of continuing immigration came to be questioned.

From the 1980s on, Australia has followed Britain and the United States in adopting the trend toward reduced public spending and market deregulation. In Australia, however, the policy was led by the Australian

Labor Party (ALP), in office from 1983 through 1996. As the ALP has always been allied to the union movement, to see it reducing government controls and government spending with neoclassical prescriptions created confusion about politics and the role of the state. This comes out in the opinion polls quoted later in this chapter. It is during this time, too, that data indicate a significant increase in distrust and disengagement from formal institutions such as the trade unions and political parties. Paradoxically, at the same time, pressure from community groups led to increased government action on human rights, sending fresh messages of social inclusion and civic responsibility.

There was an election and change of national government in 1996; the resulting coalition government was socially conservative and neoclassical in economic thinking, which renewed debate on the relative roles of the state, business, and volunteer sectors. New divisions perceived are between the haves and the have-nots and between the urban elites and ordinary country people (the rural "battlers").

The last three decades in Australia have integrated many newcomers, and there appears to have been slow movement toward a better relationship with its indigenous peoples. The wider acceptance of homosexuality and the advances made by feminism suggest that public policy and social culture have been keeping pace with each other. However, gaps are appearing. The "lucky country" tag has been part of the popular narrative of an egalitarian society, one that gave people a fair go. There is now a question about whether the loss of this type of optimism, and increasing levels of political distrust, are affecting the processes of democracy.

THE PUBLIC-PRIVATE COMPACT

Throughout the history of Australian civil society, there have been no sharp distinctions between state and community or between public and private. On an island continent of only nineteen million people, the size of the population, rather than the distances, has conditioned our perception of nationhood, our sense of community, and the interdependence of the institutions of government and community. Many state institutions have functioned in parallel with voluntary groups, either in collaboration or as alternatives. Formal political structures and the public service have always been permeable and closely related to community services and advocacy. The political culture sees government as representing, however poorly, the civic will in a range of republican assumptions that are peculiarly Australian.

One recent example is the establishment from 1973 through 1990 of public service units that represented special-interest groups such as women, indigenous peoples, and immigrants.[5] These units were originally designed to provide an internal advocacy process and were seen as an important formal means of representing minority views. They were within the system, linking community and government, and showed that people expected the government to represent the diversity within its boundaries, rather than present itself as a monolith of majority views.

Over the last twenty-five years, these specialist units have been largely responsible for public commitments to multiculturalism, for developing mechanisms against racism and sexism, and for working with the gay community on HIV/AIDS. Until recently, Australia could be seen as progressing toward a more civil society through a compact between community and state. However, these units have gradually been losing influence as state intervention in these areas has decreased, and in the last few years the special-interest units have become less visible. Some were abolished to respond to a perceived backlash from the "battlers." Voters' volatile behavior in recent state elections has been seen as a rejection of the special-interest groups and has made for a refocusing on the mainstream. There have been growing signs of racism, and this new intolerance indicates a new uncertainty in cohesion.[6]

A 1997 conference entitled "Measuring Progress" looked at the quality of life in Australia and at the reliability of current objective measures.[7] Better education, higher incomes, and more access to material goods are at odds with frequent reports that the inhabitants feel bad about their country and its future. In a June 1997 poll that was commissioned for the conference, people were asked, "Thinking now about the overall quality of life of people in Australia, taking into account social, economic and environmental conditions and trends, would you say that life in Australia is getting better, worse or staying about the same?" More than half thought the quality of life was getting worse, and only 13 percent thought it was getting better. While higher income earners and the young were more optimistic, they were still two to three times more likely to hold negative rather than positive views, as Table 8-1 shows. Other polls, some of which are treated further on in this chapter, show increasing unease about the future.

Data in this chapter suggest that there may have been an overall loss of social capital, indicated by recent resistance to change and rising general anxieties. Political cynicism is on the rise, and formal civic and political engagement is tapering off. However, at the same time, there has been growth in other forms of social activism, but not in those

Table 8-1: View of the Future, 1997

Group	Better (%)	Worse (%)	About the Same (%)
Total	13	52	33
18–24 yrs	15	44	39
50–64 yrs	10	57	31
Income < A$30K	9	59	31
Income > A$50K	19	42	37

Source: R. Eckersley, "Perspectives on Progress," in R. Eckersley, ed., *Measuring Progress: Is Life Getting Better?* (Collingwood, Victoria: CSIRO, 1998).

requiring ongoing commitments. The way people see their social relationships and involvements has changed. The assumption we start from is that a general climate of expectations and optimism and trust accumulation is influenced, in the Australian context, by the interrelation of community and state.

In Australia, government structures are significant to the formation of trust and to a healthy civic involvement. A comparison with the anglophone societies of Britain and the United States offers a chance to investigate whether fluctuations in social capital, and social capital formation in general, is linked to the differences between these three societies' state-community relations.

IS SOCIAL CAPITAL DECLINING IN AUSTRALIA?

Social capital, however defined, is generally agreed to be intrinsic to social functioning, in that it enables the members of a society to act collectively in solving their problems and working for their common good. Networks of social cooperation facilitate collective action. It is therefore useful to examine different social formations—to look at the shape, the sources, and the rates of growth in resilient social networks.

In investigating how civic involvement has changed in Australia over the past three decades, we look at the distribution of levels of engagement through volunteering and through membership in community groups. The data include levels of engagement in social and political activities where possible, including informal networks that depend on sociability among friends, neighbors, and whole communities. The data suggest that levels of sociability may be changing, with those groups who have more resources being more likely to have both the inclination and skills for finding opportunities for involvement in organizations. These groups are then more likely to develop and maintain levels of trust that accrue as social capital. Growing inequalities suggest that the more widely distributed social capital of the previous, more homogeneous society is being depleted at a time when it may be useful for dealing with economic change and growing diversity within the community. The gradual shrinking of government's role to that of a safety net has featured in many debates on the current social divides.

Participation and Engagement

Participation in, and engagement with, political and communal activities bring citizens into close contact with one another, and are clearly essential to the accumulation of social capital. These are among the most obvious indicators of social capital levels. Capacity building can be defined as learning that generates enough trust to make participants optimistic about their continuing involvement. The question is how various forms of engagement offer opportunities for learning democratic processes. The data in this part of the chapter cover volunteering, membership in organizations, and other forms of social participation.

Civic Engagement

The data collected suggest that most voluntary groups are experiencing a decline in membership, and that both men and women are spending less time in formal volunteering. Our data also suggest that people shop around for places to go, even to worship. Younger people in particular are involved in far fewer structured activities than previous generations. Short-term events and social movements may offer different experiences of collective action but fewer opportunities for ongoing learning of transferable social skills. As short-term involvement may not be recorded, nor necessarily listed by people when asked about their volunteering for community groups, data should be read with caution.

Levels of Volunteering

Formal volunteering still makes a significant contribution to civic life. The Australian Bureau of Statistics' Voluntary Work Survey 1995 was the first national survey of voluntary work ever undertaken. It shows that 17 percent of men and 21 percent of women, 19 percent of the population, offered their time in 1994.[8] However, state-based surveys by the bureau in Queensland and Victoria in 1982, and in South Australia in 1988, show that there have been changes.[9]

These figures show that the number of volunteers has fallen by almost a third over thirteen years, but not whether the fall was gradual or

Table 8-2: Levels of Formal Volunteering, 1982–1995, Victoria and Queensland

| | Men | | Women | |
	1982	1995	1982	1995
Victoria	27	18	30	22
Queensland	26	18	31	24

Source: Australian Bureau of Statistics, *Voluntary Work Australia*, Cat. No. 4441.0 (Canberra: 1995).

whether there was a sudden drop. A survey in the state of South Australia in 1988 showed participation of 28 percent, as against 20 percent in 1995.[10] These figures are for involvement in formal groups, and figures from a 1992 time-use study suggest that informal helping boosts the total to 23 percent.[11] Neither study looks at participation in newer but less formal events, nor in environmental activities.

A further survey in 2000 showed a rise in national volunteering rates since 1995, but the data are not comparable. The rise is not easily explained, as no group seems to have contributed particularly to it, but the trend has clearly reversed.

One reason often given for the decline in formal volunteering is the movement of women into the workforce. However, the data show that the number of men volunteering has declined along with their workforce participation.

Table 8-3 also shows that volunteering is highest among women who work part time. The higher rate of part-time work by mothers of preschool and younger school-age children may explain this, as they are more likely to be involved through their children. Men with dependent children, at 23 percent, and women with dependent children, at 30 percent, came out highest on participation.

Table 8-3: Levels of Formal Volunteering by Work Status by Gender, 1995

Employment Status	Men (%)	Women (%)	Total (%)
Working full time	18	17	18
Working part time	21	30	27
Not in the labor force	13	19	17
Total	17	22	19

Source: Australian Bureau of Statistics, *Voluntary Work Australia*, Cat. No. 4441.0 (Canberra: 1995).

Table 8-4: Volunteering by Occupation, 1995

Occupations	Male (%)	Female (%)	Total (%)
Manager/administration/professional	29	33	30
Paraprofessional	23	27	25
Clerical	20	23	22
Sales	17	17	17
Trades	13	16	13
Laborer/unskilled	12	18	13
Total	18	23	19
Not in labor force	13	19	17

Source: Australian Bureau of Statistics, *Voluntary Work Australia*, Cat. No. 4441.0 (Canberra: 1995).

Volunteering and Inequality

The higher the status of a person's occupation, the more likely he or she is to volunteer in formal organizations. Professional and white-collar workers volunteer more than those in trades or unskilled jobs, or those who are out of work. This could reflect demand, but it also suggests that the confidence to volunteer, and the related degrees of trust, is not equally distributed.

Volunteering also correlates with literacy rates. A 1995 survey showed that people with lower literacy were less likely to take part in formal volunteering. The participation rate in formal voluntary and community organizations for those in the lowest literacy group was 8.3 percent, rising to 14.7 percent at literacy level 2, and 18.5 percent at literacy levels 4 and 5.[12]

A survey of urban and rural communities in 1998 shows that volunteering in community organizations relates both to the density of population and to urban socioeconomic status.[13] In general, people living in the cities are volunteering less for community activities than are those in rural areas. Within the cities, people in areas of higher socioeconomic status have higher levels of involvement.

The same survey found that unemployed people and migrants, especially migrants from non-English-speaking countries, had much lower levels of formal volunteering. This was confirmed by another survey in Adelaide, and emerges also in the 1995 Australian Bureau of Statistics study.[14] Hughes suggests these results indicate that those who do not have a recognized place in society, who are personally vulnerable, or who lack the ability or opportunity to be involved in society may have lower levels of trust, which then affects their involvement in volunteering.[15]

When taken together, these figures show that volunteering correlates to social status, which raises issues about volunteering and the distribution of social capital. We suggest, in relation both to participatory options and to how social capital can bridge differences, that the more traditional forms of civic engagement may exclude the more marginal groups, who may then create alternative structures. Figures later on in this chapter on increasing inequality may explain some of the changing rates of participation over a range of civic activities.

Membership and Participation in Different Social Institutions

This section considers community groups and social movements, and their roles in engaging people in civic activities. Owing to the dearth of statistics, we have had to draw on surveys and reports that do not offer comparative data. There is enough material, however, to make well-based inferences about patterns and perceptions.

Community Groups and Social Movements

Membership numbers show that many traditional community groups, and even some social movements, are losing ground. Large-scale representative organizations such as the trade unions, traditional women's organizations such as the Country Women's Association, traditional youth movements such as the Scouts and Guides, and the traditional churches have shown declining membership over the last forty years.

Some have argued that traditional social movements have been losing out to recently emerged groups, such as women's movements and environmental groups. But these, too, have been losing both membership and some of their public support. As there are few records of membership trends in formal groups, some original data were collected directly from the organizations for this chapter. Service groups such as the Apex clubs and the Lions Clubs have seen substantial drops since their highs in the 1950s. The Country Women's Association membership dropped from 110,000 in 1955 to 48,000 in 1997. The Wilderness Society is down from 9,000 in the mid-eighties to 2,000 now. Generalist feminist groups have also lost active membership, but there are many smaller and more specialist groups that go unrecorded. Yet there are exceptions to the trend; in New South Wales for instance, there are 70,000 members of volunteer fire brigades, with recruitment considerably up since the big 1994 bush fires attracted extensive media coverage.

In terms of social capital, declining membership in social and community organizations must be taken in the context of the changes in Australian population and lifestyles over the period. The marked change in the ethnic makeup of the whole country, especially in the big cities, has influenced both the types of activities and their content, as have declining birthrates and greater mobility.

There has been a growth in events that involve large numbers of people, such as Clean Up Australia, fun runs, the Gay and Lesbian Mardi Gras, festivals, dragon boat races, and food fairs, which flourish outdoors in Australia's mild climate. The participation they offer is not necessarily based on relationships, but suggests a wider involvement in public social events, and may engender commitment and trust. These events call for intensive organizing and intimate collaboration, as in work on folding ribbons for sale to support HIV programs. They offer different types of interactions, with less emphasis on ongoing relationships, than do traditional organizations.

Activities such as Clean Up Australia, which offer participation without a membership structure, attract hundreds of thousands of participants who work alongside strangers for a day. Community greening projects are heavily reliant on an ongoing supply of volunteers. Landcare, which organizes repairs to the bush, has brought together members of environmental groups and farmers in country areas, though often for only limited periods. Activities for reconciliation between indigenous and nonindigenous Australians have involved many formal and informal activities, locally and nationally. These include public meetings, ongoing study groups, and an installation of 250,000 signed colored hands that is taken from town to town.

These new mass activities raise the question of how much civic gain their often transitory contacts provide. There are verbal reports that they may give people the confidence and motivation to transfer further efforts into community-based activities, but this has not been tested. How these activities reinforce communality and goodwill toward strangers is still in question, but their spread, together with big public events such as the Reconciliation marches, suggests that new forms of community politics may be emerging.

Many of these events have a media presence; they are publicized beforehand and written up afterward. They attract many people to a local event, thousands to a major one, so they may represent a wider mediated sense of belonging. They offer visibility and legitimacy for people who are media-savvy. A publicly promoted event is seen as legitimate; involvement is acknowledged and admired, and people feel they are doing good. Other activities may involve only those with common interests and resources. Some of these come from public funding through community arts programs, providing partnerships between community and the state, which funds festivals and other participatory pleasures where people share a space rather than work together. It is interesting to speculate what connecting threads these might create.

In a survey undertaken by my students in 1997, membership patterns in community organizations were shown to be mobile, with people both joining and leaving.[16] A survey of over two hundred people who were involved in their communities showed that they were each members of three organizations on average. However, 80 percent of them acknowledged that they had let two memberships lapse over the previous decade, suggesting that people move on as their interests change.

The data collected for the Australian Non-Profit Data Project indicate current activities in some nonprofit groups.[17] The data cover 1995–96 and identify thirty thousand nonprofit organizations that have both paid employees and volunteers. There are many more entirely voluntary nonprofit organizations, but the survey covered only "employing" non-profit organizations, as these are required to record their business, and there are no data for the rest. However, the results show that 373,000 hours were donated to groups in 1995, as well as over A$2 billion in cash—a significant output for a small country.

Religious Engagement

Australia has no established religion, but its religious makeup has been traditionally Anglo-Protestant and Irish Catholic. This predominance is shifting with migrations. Currently Buddhism is the fastest-growing denomination, followed by Islam; however the leading religions are still Christian. Churches and their many welfare affiliates work closely with government to deliver health care, education, and community services. They are all publicly funded, for these services at least. Table 8-5 shows falling church attendance overall, but this probably relates mainly to the major Christian denominations.

The National Church Life Survey of 1996 shows that most denominations have aging profiles and are losing members, but that the Pentecostals are drawing in younger members. The research also shows that

Table 8-5: Church Attendance

	1950s–60s	1970s	1984
Attend weekly	25%	20%	17%
Attend rarely/never	61%	67%	64%

Source: Mariah Evans, "World Wide Attitudes," Australian National University, Canberra, March 1995.

heavily involved churchgoers tend to be more sociable and to have more outside relationships as well as close friends within the congregation. These people are also the most likely to be tolerant of diversity within their faith group, and to be members of other organizations.[18]

The census data in Table 8-6 show a substantial increase in people declaring no religion. As many community organizations are church-based, this raises the question of the possible relationship between a more secular community and the loss of members by organizations that are both majoritarian and Christian. However, the changing ethnic basis of Australia, and the increased secular emphasis, raises questions about religion's contribution to social cohesion.

A recent study of social trust in different communities found that religious belief did not contribute to trust at the general or local levels.[19] In fact, declared atheists had higher levels of trust than those who described themselves as believing in God or a higher power. There were significant differences, however, between people of different denominations, reflecting different theological attitudes. Those religious people who see a sharp difference between "Christians" and "the world" are more likely to be distrustful of people they do not identify as "Christians."

Trade Union Membership

Trade union membership has also been dropping over the last decade. Official Australian Bureau of Statistics figures show that between 1984 and 2000 union membership has dropped from 46 percent to 25 percent of the workforce.[20] Unions maintain that the rate of decline has slowed, but this has yet to show up as a clear trend. There are changes in the roles of unions now, as new legislation reduces their official roles in both wage

Table 8-6: Identification with Major Christian Religions (or No Religion), 1947–1991

	1947	1971	1991
Anglican	38%	29%	23%
Baptist	1%	1%	2%
Catholic	19%	26%	26%
Pentecostal	0.5%	1%	1%
No religion	0.5%	6%	12%
Total population	8,400,000	13,500,000	17,500,000

Note: Amalgamations of various other Protestant groups make further comparisons difficult.
Source: Australian Bureau of Statistics, The Census of Population and Housing (1947, 1971, 1991).

setting and the resolution of disputes. However, much of the drop occurred in the period of Labor rule, when the unions were very much seen as a major influence on government. The changing gender base of the workforce and the growth of casualized work are often named as other factors in the decline, but the data parallel the loss of membership in other groups, which suggests at least partial causal overlaps.

Now that the centralized wage-fixing system is almost gone, enterprise agreements are being replaced by individual contracts, and unions have been redefined as just another player at the bargaining table. There is no evidence, however, that confidence in the unions has lessened as membership has declined. Starting from a low base, the attitude toward unions seems to have become marginally more positive.

Union membership is highest in the public sector and in a few skilled blue-collar areas. Changes in union and workplace structures mean that there is much less political and social action in the workplace than there was thirty years ago.

Political Involvement

Australia has compulsory voter registration and voting, so voter turnout is not a reliable indicator of political involvement. Compulsory voting is widely accepted; the 1996 Australian Election Survey showed that 86 percent of registered voters were likely to vote, even if voting were not compulsory. Only 3 percent replied that they would not vote.[21] This is confirmed by the fact that there are few spoiled votes in elections, with 95 percent valid voting even in often-complex preferential ballots.

There is a dearth of longitudinal data on political behavior and attitudes, except for the 1987–98 Australian National University election surveys. These span five elections and investigate views on the political process over a period of unprecedented change. The survey is mailed to several thousand electors randomly selected from the electoral rolls. The

Table 8-7: Trust in Trade Unions, 1983–1995

	1983	1995
A great deal	5	3
Quite a lot	20	22
Not very much	55	50
None at all	20	21

Source: Roy Morgan Research Centre, *World Values Study* (Melbourne: Roy Morgan Research Centre, 1983, 1995).

results show a low (and shrinking) level of active involvement in election campaigning and party membership in the four federal elections covered. From 1993 to the new data in 1998 there is a drop from over 3.4 percent participation to about 1.7 percent in 1996, with a small recovery to 2 percent in 1998. Yet the 1996 Australian Election Survey showed that 10 percent were at some time party members.[22]

Watching the Political News

Watching the political news is a primary indicator of attention. Most people get their news from TV, so a significant drop in political news watching suggests less engagement. Between 1987 and 1996, the Australian National University election studies showed a drop in those claiming a good deal of interest in watching the news, and a substantial rise in those uninterested in the elections. The figures below show the 1996 election as a low-level media event, even compared to other recent elections. In the 1998 election, interest was even lower. The attention to political issues is diminishing.

Attendance at political party meetings in the 1993 or 1996 federal election campaigns was miniscule, with just over 2 percent in 1998, according to the election surveys. The reduced involvement could in part be explained by the increase in professional campaigning and the use of direct mailings and media manipulation. There were few public meetings and little door-to-door canvassing, which has been replaced by targeted direct mailings.

Involvement Past and Present

Table 8-9, which is based on data from the Morgan World Values Survey in 1983, shows increasing involvement in politics, which would contradict the previous data, unless involvement had increased in the late eighties and then declined.

The table (Table 8-10) suggests that a substantial proportion of the population, particularly younger people, have not and do not intend to move into activism past the petition stage, and do not intend to be more radical than the older generations.

Other cross-tabulations on the 1995 data show interesting differences. Voters for the minor parties, the Greens and the Democrats, expect to be more active. Those who voted for the ALP were somewhat more active than were those who voted for the conservative coalition, but they were fairly evenly in agreement on petitions. These figures support the possibility that the professionalization of the large parties has reduced involvement.[23]

Table 8-8: Followed Election on Television, 1987–1996

	1987	1990	1993	1996
A good deal	51	42	41	31
Not much/none	16	21	20	31

Source: Australian National University, Social Science Data Archives, *Australian Election Survey* (Canberra: Australian National University, 1987, 1990, 1993, 1996).

Table 8-9: Participation in Political Activity, 1983–1995

Discuss Political Matters	1983 (%)	1995 (%)
Frequently	11	16
Occasionally	54	54
Never	35	31

Source: Roy Morgan Research Centre, *World Values Study* (Melbourne: Roy Morgan Research Centre, 1983, 1995).

Table 8-10: Involvement in Political Activity by Age, 1995

Have done	14–17 (%)	18–24 (%)	26–34 (%)	35–49 (%)	50+ (%)
Sign petition	57	74	80	84	78
Boycott	9	17	24	31	15
Demonstration	5	16	17	27	13
Unofficial strike	5	5	9	11	6
Wouldn't do					
Sign petition	2	4	4	3	9
Boycott	28	29	27	29	49
Demonstration	34	28	29	33	57
Unofficial strike	24	41	54	57	76

Source: Roy Morgan Research Centre, *World Values Study* (Melbourne: Roy Morgan Research Centre, 1983, 1995).

Practicing Democratic Processes?

A major factor in engagement is a sense of efficacy in society at large and in the political system. A survey in South Australia (Table 8-11) makes a significant connection between a sense of efficacy and voluntary involvement.[24] While the direction of the arrow of causality is not clear, we can reasonably assume that to some extent, trust in others and in the system is related to perceived efficacy. This is important in terms of the distrust of politicians set out in the next section.

Trust and Social Capital

The previous section showed some withdrawal from political engagement. This section looks at levels of trust in various sectors of society. The scope of this section is the expressions of generalized and particular trust, the fear of crime and of strangers, the expectations we have of the ideal society, and where the current system falls short. These are all indicators of how we feel about others, and they raise questions of how these feelings would impact the likelihood of engaging with others and getting involved in collective action for common purposes.

Generalized Trust

Table 8-12 is drawn from the Australian version of the International Values Study. There has been a significant fall in trust overall during the twelve years from 1983 to 1995. While a 7 percent drop is not grave, in the context of a loss of faith in many areas the figures indicate the possibility of wider problems.

Table 8-13 suggests that the areas that have lost trust are those most closely related to government, law, and finance institutions. Not all areas changed, as high trust was maintained for human service professionals—nurses, doctors, teachers, and even police, despite some public scandals.

Tables 8-14a and 8-14b both show declining levels of trust in government and in politicians.

The concern about politicians is confirmed in election polls. In the 1996 election survey, only 40 percent thought the federal government did the right thing most of the time, while 61 percent thought the ethical standards of politicians had declined in recent years. Results of the 1998 election study show similar results and confirm politicians' poor ratings.[25]

Trust in Democracy Itself

Most people still want democracy. In a survey on the preferred method of government, 84 percent gave democracy a positive response, and 82 percent thought it better than any other system of government; 49 percent thought it very good, and 35 percent fairly good. Alternative forms of government, however, had some level of approval; 41 percent had positive responses to experts, and—more worryingly—24 percent were positive about a strong leader, with no parliament or elections.[26]

Trust in Strangers and Other People

The measure of trust in strangers and other people involves the capacity of society to build bridges to those not perceived as "like us." The evi-

Table 8-11: Sense of Power in Volunteers/Nonvolunteers, 1998

I can influence decisions in my neighborhood

	Strongly agree (%)	Moderately agree (%)	Neutral (%)	Moderately disagree (%)	Strongly disagree (%)
Volunteers (N = 331)	7	25	42	13	14
Nonvolunteers (N = 2,093)	3	17	41	19	20

People can influence decisions that affect the neighborhood

Volunteers (N = 332)	26	40	26	4	3
Nonvolunteers (N = 2,094)	18	36	34	7	5

Source: F. Baum et al., "Volunteering and Social Capital: An Adelaide Study," *Volunteer Journal of Australia* 23, 3 (1998).

Table 8-12: Trust of Others, 1983–1995

	1983 (%)	1995 (%)
Most people can be trusted	46	39
Can't be too careful	52	59

Source: Roy Morgan Research Centre, *World Values Study* (Melbourne: Roy Morgan Research Centre, 1983, 1995).

Table 8-13: Belief in the Trustworthiness of Selected Professions, 1976–1996

Occupation	1976 (%)	1986 (%)	1996 (%)
Accountants	-	51	46
Bank managers	66	60	37
Lawyers	43	39	29
Business executives	22	23	17
Federal members of parliament	19	16	13
State members of parliament	21	17	12
Journalists	12	12	7
Schoolteachers	56	57	68
Police	52	56	55

Source: Roy Morgan Research Centre, Morgan Poll, no. 2893, 1996.

dence is mixed. There is a wide perception that racism is rising, and there are indications of increasing objections to immigration, particularly from Asia.

On the other hand, Table 8-15 shows little evidence of increased anxi-

Table 8-14a: Trust of Those in Government, 1983–1995

	1983 (%)	1995 (%)
A great deal	9	2
Quite a lot	47	24
Not very much	36	53
None at all	8	20
Don't know	0	2

Source: Roy Morgan Research Centre, *World Values Study* (Melbourne: Roy Morgan Research Centre, 1983, 1995).

Table 8-14b: Confidence in Political Parties and the Public Service

	Political Parties		Public Service	
	1983%	1995%	1983%	1995%
A great deal	-	1	7	4
Quite a lot	-	15	40	34
Not very much	-	64	45	50
None at all	-	18	7	10
Don't know	-	2	0	2

Source: Roy Morgan Research Centre, *World Values Study* (Melbourne: Roy Morgan Research Centre, 1983, 1995).

Table 8-15: Groups of People Not Liked as Neighbors, 1983–1997

	1983 (%)	1995 (%)	1997 (%)
Drug addicts	-	74	65
Homosexuals	34	24	17
People with AIDS	-	15	11
Immigrants	6	5	2
Different race	6	5	3

Source: Roy Morgan Research Centre, Morgan Poll, 1997.

ety about outgroups. In fact, some outgroups have increased in acceptability in recent years. These figures suggest that there is no particular built-in racism or even biases, and that such attitudes may be generalized expressions of anxiety, not related to action.

Fear of Crime

Lack of generalized trust may be a major cause of the recorded excessive fear of crime. There are widespread perceptions that crime is on the increase and the world is out of control, leading to increased calls for law and order. This is despite the fact that crimes such as personal assaults have actually decreased in Australia. Surveys suggest that people feel unsafe and so avoid public places and going out at night. This has been exploited in a series of state elections, where political parties have competed on law-and-order issues.

The article "Crime Perception and Reality" looked extensively at people's fears that they would become victims of crime, and correlated this with actual area crime rates.[27] Expectation of crime was well above any likelihood of it and did not even relate to any likelihood of being a victim. Those least at risk, older women, were often the most fearful. The authors conclude that the media, political exploitation of the issue, and social change are most likely responsible for the levels of concern expressed.

Fears for the safety of children may well be part of the same phenomenon. A 1992 survey of children in a fairly average suburb showed that 50 percent of parents of primary-school-age children and 12 percent of parents of younger secondary-school-age children did not think it safe to let them go to school without adult accompaniment.[28] Fear of attack and kidnap outweighed the danger of crossing busy roads, which suggests generalized rather than rational anxiety. Around half were concerned about kidnapping, which is very rare, albeit well publicized. A later article on the same data points out that assaults on young people in Victoria had declined by 35 percent in the decade prior to the survey.[29]

Similar attitudes toward avoidance of risky behavior also appear in the data from some of my own research and that conducted by my students.[30] The consistent pattern revealed by research into women's sense of safety is that women will avoid situations they see as putting them at risk. They will increasingly avoid going out at night, using public transport, and going into public spaces. This is despite the higher danger of assault by family members in their homes. In an aging population, the loss of access to public spaces that are easily shared across generations and genders may well decrease trust.

Other-Regarding and Social Expectations

The following indicators show people's expectations of society's basic responsibility to all its citizens. These are included because they may be related to loss of trust. The concept of fairness is related both to perceptions of self and to perceptions of the fate of others.

The idea that giving everyone a "fair go" should lead to a more egalitarian society has traditionally been part of a general optimism about the future in Australia. Polls indicate that the gap between the desire for a "fair go" and the perceived possibility of obtaining this is widening. A 1989 AGB McNair poll showed that 83 percent of respondents agreed that "Australia is becoming a less fair society, where the gap between rich

Table 8-16: Income and Wealth Should Be Redistributed Toward Ordinary Working People, 1987–1996

	1987 (%)	1990 (%)	1993 (%)	1996 (%)	1998 (%)
Agree	45	41	51	47	47
Disagree	34	35	26	25	25

Source: Australian National University, Social Science Data Archives, *Australian Election Survey* (Canberra: Australian National University, 1987, 1990, 1993, 1996, 1998).

and poor is getting wider."[31] One of the few time series, the Australian Election Surveys in 1987, 1990, 1993, 1996, and 1998 (Table 8-16), shows that the government is still seen as having the major responsibility in creating equality, with agreement percentages relatively constant. Disagreement, in fact, has decreased at a time when governments were stating their intention to reduce their redistribution efforts.[32]

Income distribution has changed over the past two decades. Market incomes have become more unequal. While welfare payments have increased, fewer individuals are eligible for them. Meanwhile, the proportion of income units that include earners has gone down. In 1979, 23 percent of households had no earners. This rose to 35 percent in 1995. In a later survey, the middle 40 percent of income earners lost out badly, while the top 10 percent increased their share of income.[33] The 1998 United Nations Human Development Report puts Australia just behind the United States as the second most unequal developed country based on incomes.[34] The contradiction between the egalitarian desire and the increasing inequalities are likely factors in the narratives of trust.

Other Factors Affecting Engagement

The decline in trust of politicians and other aspects of governance, and the fear of crime as indicated above, form part of an overarching set of narratives about life in Australia today. The next section looks at two aspects of daily life that may impinge on this set of stories: the media and how we use it, and the use we make of time—time for social activities as well as free time.

The Media

The media have changed in nature and range in complex ways over recent decades. In the early eighties, TV stations almost doubled coverage of news and current affairs, to a quarter of broadcast time. Newspapers went the opposite way and increased coverage of sports and entertain-

Table 8-17: Confidence in the Press and TV

	Press		Television	
	1983 (%)	1995 (%)	1983 (%)	1995 (%)
A great deal	3	2	-	4
Quite a lot	25	15	-	22
Not very much	59	61	-	59
None at all	12	22	-	15
Don't know	0	1	-	1

Source: Roy Morgan Research Centre, *World Values Study* (Melbourne: Roy Morgan Research Centre, 1983, 1995).

ment, their twenty pages rising to thirty-two. Some radio stations shifted from all music to all talk, and vice versa.[35] The 1992 Australian Bureau of Statistics time-use survey showed a drop in newspaper readership among the young; 40 percent of those over 65 years of age read newspapers, but only 8 percent of those between the ages of 15 and 24 do so.[36] Papers of record are still holding their own, but the tabloids are losing ground.

Industry groups perceive a loss of readership of about 30 percent since the eighties, based on the closure of other papers, so the overall picture is unclear.[37] But it is true that individuals who are more educated and in the upper socioeconomic groups still read newspapers, while others do not. The cancellation of one commercial current-affairs program and a shrinking audience for the genre suggest that TV reporting is also being thinned out. Again, this suggests growing inequality in access to responsibly presented news on political and social issues.

Believing the News

Table 8-17 shows that fewer people trust the media. This may tie in with the loss of audience for the TV programs and loss of readership for the tabloid press.

Polls show that confidence in the media, which was not high, has been dropping. Confidence in the print media is shown as 17 percent, in TV as 26 percent.[38] The Morgan Poll on occupations in 1996 showed that newspaper journalists and TV reporters were not rated high for ethics, at 7 percent, nor honesty, at 12 percent.[39]

CONCLUSIONS

Factors that May Affect the Distribution of Social Capital

Various factors are emerging as possible predictors of increase and decrease in social capital in Australia. This chapter has explored various types of participation, formal and informal, and has raised questions of how participatory processes affect the experiences of trust and mutuality. The data suggest that both opportunities and experiences may be skewed, as are other social benefits, meaning that certain groups within the society are more or less likely to have access to some forms of trust-building processes.

On the other hand, there appear to be more participatory events for fund-raising and public statements, such as cleanup days, the Gay and Lesbian Mardi Gras, the 40-Hour Famine Campaign, and homelessness sleep-outs.

These changes raise issues interesting to governments and other bodies who see that opportunities for people to grow trust and accumulate social capital require some careful planning. If societies become more unequal, and involvement and trust building become more the purview of the competent and confident, social cohesion is threatened, as then is democracy. The sections that follow explore some of these areas in more detail.

Inequality

It may be that increasing inequality and the perception of this are causal of the falling level of trust and lower formal involvement in the community, despite the overall rise in material well-being. The introduction of widespread market-based distribution of income and goods has increased inequalities in most developed countries, including Australia. Knack and Keefer also show that relatively flat income distributions correlate with high trust and civic norms.[40]

Inequality may also create a vicious circle, as perceived and actual economic difference relate to other social factors that include more isolation and less skill in sociability. Changes in community networks and in family relationships may reduce social contact with people outside the immediate social circle, because of financial or other stressors. This lesser social experience may in turn lead to loss of self-confidence and a decline in the ability to socialize. Voluntary involvement may offer opportunities to gain confidence, but it requires a certain level of trust to initiate this involvement. Opportunities to engage and to learn to trust may be lacking in the smaller and often more isolated household units of the present day.

Changes in Community Groups

The problems of involvement are exacerbated by changes in the structure of voluntary groups. The major, more visible groups often become employers and are substantially funded to offer professional services. This "third sector" has become a major player and, as identified by Lyons and colleagues, is a substantial economic factor in the overall system.[41] Many nongovernment groups are professionalizing because the calls on their services and the requirements of government funding demand it. These changes set up barriers both to using voluntary labor and to encouraging participation from those without professional skills. Many groups have become major providers of both government contracted and "user-pays" community services.

Groups that are involved in lobbying rather than in service to their members claim that the demands of the political processes require a level of professionalization. The advent of more professional lobbyists and of PR firms, hired by business and political groups to promote their views, makes it harder for groups to use "amateurs." Political parties and advocacy groups have also professionalized, which makes their senior ranks inaccessible to volunteers, and consequently of less interest to them.

The net effect of these changes may be that the experience of working together in formal groupings is less accessible to those with fewer skills and less confidence. While groups such as school parents' associations are still there, they again may often be the province of the more confident and the more competent. The less formal groupings that appear to be on the increase may not be easily accessible, precisely because of their informality. So as more people live alone or in smaller units and have fewer opportunities to become involved, they may suffer considerable inequities in the social experiences in which they could learn civic skills.

Sharing of Public Space

Involvement in sports and other leisure and cultural activities is often seen as contributing to a sense of social cohesion. The sharing of space, time, tastes, and activities offers a range of processes, from the companionable to the more involved. Many Australians are used to spending their time in public spaces in the company of strangers. However, economic issues may also create differences here: Museums and many galleries now charge, as do some parks, sporting arenas, and other once-free facilities. "User-pays" services and the loss of access to public areas raise interesting issues of how much of our social capital is built in the public sphere, where we can share our pleasures with strangers in safe spaces and see that others share our tastes and interests. While the experiences may be at a less intense level than working together, the loss of these spaces may make other forms of contact appear more difficult.

Making Social Capital Scripts

The problem with social capital is that it is not a definable entity, but a measure of processes between people. It is therefore identifiable only by indicators such as expressed attitudes, behavior, and the outcomes and outputs of group processes. The concept of overarching and middling narratives and personal scripts seems to offer the best metaphor for expressing the totality of social capital. Experiences are interpreted and create the possibility of learning, which in turn creates positive or negative expectations. The process may be best described through the concept of social capital narratives, both individual and group. These stories are mediated by cultural values and media images and are used to place the self and groups within the social system.

Items such as those collected here are not, in most cases, proof of social capital, but they add together into narratives that, if articulated, can indicate the possibilities of group behavior. If people's own scripts of daily life are based on assumptions of being cheated or imposed on, they will tend to distrust others, generally and within defined groups. There will always be those whose life experiences, dispositions, and beliefs will limit their spheres of trust, but if the proportions and the distribution of views of this kind become the habitus of larger groups, then the society and the community may be threatened with loss of social resilience.

Creating the Narratives

The role of the media in involving people in the issues and the processes of civil society has been discussed by Putnam and others.[42] In an island nation with few media sources other than our own, the national media play a significant role in the development of public narratives. Media are integral shapers, interpreters, and narrators of the views of the public; if it is not on the news, for many people it does not exist. The news is blurred with fiction and fantasy to create people's worldviews.

The notion of good citizenship is likely to be redefined by what is seen to be "sexy" in media terms. Certainly, the numbers of people who turn out for organizations and activities promoted through the media seem to be higher than for traditional organizations.

What Do the Data Suggest?

The Australian data show some contradictory indicators of whether social capital is declining, stable, or growing. The data collected in this chapter show rising distrust and disengagement from political and formal community processes. The last fifteen years show deteriorating levels of trust in anything to do with governance and the financial sectors and indicate diminishing participation in traditional service clubs. The same period has also been marked by official rhetoric about, and reductions in, the active role of the state.

There are indications through rising third-party voting that rural and outer urban voters are rejecting the two major parties, in particular rejecting many aspects of reduced government services and the deregulation of markets. Anecdotal accounts speak of rural and regional problems in areas where economic changes have hurt people. Other indicators, such as fear of crime and the desire to exclude risk or change, raise the question of what effects these trends will have on social cohesion. There are questions of whether the distribution of trust identified in the data is the cause or the effect of perceived loss of social cohesion. Households are more likely to be single-person and isolated, and thereby have fewer options for sociable interactions with those outside their circles of intimacy.

Social capital appears to be most functional in those population groups of wider economic options, who have the capacity to benefit from social change. There are also signs that people are still predisposed to expect improvement and goodwill from others. There has been growing involvement in community festivals, environment-repair events, and other intercommunal activities. This indicates strong residues of goodwill, and the possibility of inclusiveness such as has operated to make gradual improvements in the quality of life for most Australians since the end of the Second World War.

The last three decades in Australia have revealed a nation that has integrated many newcomers and is slowly moving toward a better relationship with its indigenous peoples. The last decade has seen wider acceptance of homosexuality and some moves toward reconciliation, which suggest that, until recently, public policy and social culture have been keeping pace with each other. However, the politicizing of inclusiveness and the reemphasis on the mainstream mean that wider political spaces are appearing between what are being referred to as urban elites versus the "battlers." The playing off of these differences by government, together with a dismissal of minority politics as "political correctness," sets up contradictions in the compact between community and state.

The data suggest that there are risks where a nation does not have the resilience to manage changes such as those driven by current technological and economic changes. The challenge for Australia is whether we can manage the increasing inequality in market processes, the expectations of fairness and redistribution by the state, and the shifting forms of community participation, yet remain democratic.

The role of the state is crucial, and local policy makers are now actively naming social capital production as part of their mission statements. Some are seeking policies to increase social capital. The implications are that social capital is a good, and there is considerable confusion about its nature and production. Government realizes that it is not the primary agent of social capital development, and it often sees its role as putting pressure on the declining traditional part of the community sector to make it happen.

There is a public policy failure here in not recognizing the importance of the state as arbiter and, through its partnership with the community, mediator and constraint on the market. Social capital may be the major enabler of democracy, but further work on indicators is needed to gauge the critical levels of distrust that can put democracy at risk.

These trends raise issues as to how far opportunities for participation and involvement may need to be generated formally, rather than being assumed to come about spontaneously. The Australian experience suggests a clear need for the state to provide the framework and the stimulus for access to these opportunities for those who are excluded and therefore unlikely to join in voluntarily. The building of social capital may depend on everyone having equitable and culturally appropriate opportunities for establishing the networks that will allow for linking and for cross-group cohesion.

9

BROADENING THE BASIS OF SOCIAL CAPITAL IN JAPAN

TAKASHI INOGUCHI

Japan is often cited as a country rich in social capital. For the last half century, its political system has allowed Japan to successfully adjust to and negotiate the epochal technological, demographic, economic, and social transformations that have taken place in a very short span. Similarly, over the same period, Japan's economic system has enabled it to emerge from the devastation and demoralization of war and defeat, when its per capita income fell to the lowest in Asia, to become the second largest economy in the world, with a per capita income among the highest worldwide. Can these democratic and economic outcomes over fifty years be attributed, even in part, to social capital, or to the propensity of individuals to engage in community affairs, to trust one another, and to associate on a regular basis?[1] In other words, can the high level of social trust and civic engagement account for the outstanding performance of Japan's democratic and economic systems?

In this chapter we shall examine the development of social capital as understood in terms of the networks of civic engagement in Japan over the past fifty years, keeping in mind the maturation as well as degeneration of its democratic institutions. This investigation will be informed by two questions: One, what are the forms, quality, quantity, and distribution of social capital? Two, what can account for the change in social capital?

Japan is an interesting case since it is one of the very few countries among non-Western nations that has been practicing democratic politics for as long as fifty years. The question I would like to address is whether social capital in fact plays a major role in facilitating the transition to democracy and consolidating its institutions. The examination proceeds in three steps. First I will assess overall trends in the formation of social capital in Japan over the past fifty years. I then will examine plausible explanations for these trends. Finally, I will try to speculate about the nature and direction of social capital in order to point out emerging features in Japanese political culture. The principal argument I shall make in this chapter has two aspects: (1) that Japan's social capital has increased under democracy for the last fifty years quite steadily, and (2) that Japan's social capital, accumulated over the last few centuries largely in particularistic face-to-face and group settings, has become more individualistic and broader than in the past, as such relations tend to be very complex and comprehensive in a highly industrialized democracy.

TRENDS AS SEEN IN THE ESTABLISHMENT CENSUS

The Establishment Census, conducted and published every three to five years since 1950 by the Statistics Bureau of the Management and Coordination Agency, contains macrostatistical figures on the number of nonprofit organizations and their members. The Establishment Census is focused on industrial and other business organizations. Therefore, only a somewhat elementary big-picture view of nonprofit organizations emerges from the census. The total number of nonprofit associations in 1996 was 6.7 million. Of these, fewer than 200,000 could be classified as either religious organizations, social insurance and welfare organizations, or associations not classified elsewhere.

Trends since 1951 suggest a number of features. The number of religious organizations was very high in 1951, 128,440, but declined to 90,000 by 1954 and has remained constant since. The number of organizations affiliated with the Shinto religion has declined steadily, from 55,939 in 1951 to 11,312 in 1996. The number of Buddhist organizations has remained virtually stagnant at 63,000 over the last forty-five years. Christian organizations have steadily increased in number, from 1,933 in 1951 to 6,280 in 1996. The overall number of believers is difficult to determine, since it is customary to follow the teachings of different religions for different occasions in Japan (wedding ceremonies tend to be held according to Shinto or Christian ritual, funerals and memorial services according to Buddhist ritual, and so forth). Followers of mainly Shinto and Buddhist beliefs form the vast majority, while Christians make up only 1 or 2 percent of the population (this has been a constant feature of Christianity in Japan since the mid-sixteenth century, when it was introduced to Japan from the West).

Statistics on social insurance and welfare organizations exist only for the period since 1969. The largest increase within this category was for nursery schools, 30,273 of which were registered in 1996. Also noteworthy is the spectacular increase in the number of organizations for the elderly and for people with mental or physical disabilities, registering 8,961 and 4,436 respectively in 1996 (increases of 40.1 percent and 33.5 percent from 1991 respectively).

The numbers for associations not classified elsewhere exhibit a number of features. Business associations registered a steady increase in number, from 5,448 in 1951 to 14,728 in 1996. Union associations registered a modest increase, from 2,218 in 1951 to 5,248 in 1996. Academic and cultural associations increased from 349 in 1951 to 942 in 1996. Political associations increased from 201 in 1951 to 840 in 1996. Overall, associations in this category showed a spectacular increase, from 2,002 in 1951 to 16,224 in 1996. They may be described roughly as "interest associations" involving organized interests of various kinds.

First, in comparison with figures for the United States, Japan's civic organizations are much more likely to involve business associations. The figures for the United States show many more civil and social associations. Recently, however, Japanese figures for civil and social service associations have been dramatically increasing, whereas the dominance of businesses associations has steadily dropped off. Second, the absolute number of business associations in Japan surpasses the number in America, despite the overall size of the American association sector. While U.S. antimonopoly laws discourage the formation of business associations, the Japanese symbiosis between business and bureaucracy has led to a proliferation of business associations.

There are three distinctive periods of Japanese political development: 1951–57, 1957–72, and 1972–96.[2] The first period was an era of "class struggle," showing the decline of business associations and a corresponding increase in union and other associations. This period saw the upsurge of the Japan Socialist Party and an increase in mass protest movements. The second period was characterized by an increase in the number of business associations and a decline in union associations; it was also marked by the dominance of the ruling Liberal Democratic

Party (LDP). In the third period, the LDP invigorated its support base by shifting from its traditional emphasis on the business and agricultural sectors to a focus on the large, somewhat amorphous middle-income strata.[3] During the third period, the number of business associations stagnated. In contrast, the number of associations not classified elsewhere rose. This category includes foundations, civic groups, and quasi-official bodies. The third period also saw the rise of nongovernmental organizations (NGOs). The governing LDP seems to be vigorously incorporating NGOs into its own fold.

Let us examine further the number and nature of the associations not classified elsewhere.[4] There are two broad categories within this classification: nonprofit organizations (NPOs) created through private-sector initiatives (NPO/PSIs) and NPOs created as affiliates of governmental organizations (NPO/SGOs). The former total 18,000 and the latter 7,000. Many NPO/PSIs were established in the period between 1945 and 1964, but since 1965 their number has leveled off. Newly established NPO/SGOs have been steadily increasing since 1945, most markedly in the third period. This is directly related to many local governments' policies of subcontracting their services for maintenance of public facilities and for the management of particular events to such organizations. These NPO/SGOs are established, in other words, to create and maintain social space for civic engagement on the grassroots level. This constitutes one arm of local governments' empowerment policies, which have been under way for the last two decades or so. There are about three thousand local (prefectural, municipal, town/township, and village) governments in Japan.

The NPO/PSIs, too, have been refurbishing themselves in the attempt to cope with what has been called the postindustrial malaise of the third period. In the late 1980s a major center-left/left-leaning weekly, the *Asahi Journal*, devoted a series of articles to a selection of about two hundred civic groups engaged in movements for the betterment of society. This series offers a useful summary of the number and characteristics of these civic groups.[5] These groups are involved with the environment and pollution (twenty-eight groups), nuclear power station safety (six groups), and peace and nuclear weapons (twelve groups). There were twenty-seven civic groups engaged in exchange and networking, and twenty groups organized on a strictly local basis. Two were involved with technology, fourteen with welfare and medical care issues, twenty-one in the areas of education and children, fourteen with women's issues, and eighteen in agriculture and food. There were seventeen civic groups involved with the Third World and international issues. The number of civic groups in the broad area of society was fourteen, and eight were of a broadly cultural nature. Most noteworthy with regard to these groups is the fact that they are all grassroots-based. A substantial number have transnational ties with groups of similar purpose abroad. We cannot go into the details of these civic groups here; suffice it to say that a reading of this series of articles confirms our belief that the often-heard characterization of Japan as consisting of governmental organizations (GOs) and nongovernmental individuals (NGIs) is not entirely correct and that nongovernmental organizations (NGOs) do exist in vibrant form.[6]

TRENDS AS SEEN FROM THE TIME-BUDGET SURVEY

The time-budget surveys conducted every five years since 1976 by the Statistics Bureau of the Management and Coordination Agency (and prior to 1976 by the Statistics Bureau of the Prime Minister's Office) provide a useful view of changes in people's engagement in civic activities. Notable trends are as follows. First, civic activities for neighborhoods and larger areas have been more or less constant, at 19.6 percent of dis-

Figure 9-1: Civic Activities

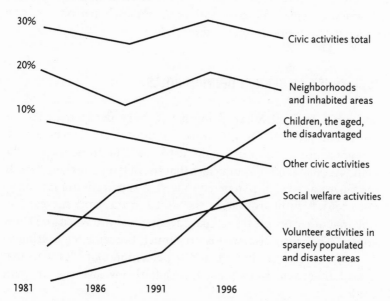

Source: Management and Coordination Agency, *Shakai Seikatsu Kihon Tokei (Basic Statistics of Social Life,* 1981–1996

posable time in 1981, 17.3 percent in 1988, 19.8 percent in 1991, and 18.8 percent in 1996. Second, social-welfare-related civic activities have been essentially the same over these years, at 3.0–3.1 percent. This is due largely to the contributions of women. Third, civic activities for children, the aged, and the disadvantaged have been rapidly rising, registering 1.7 percent in 1976 and 5.5 percent in 1996. The most active in this segment are women in their thirties and forties. Fourth, civic activities in sparsely populated areas and disaster areas registered a slow rise over this period, from 1.1 percent in 1976 to 2.1 percent in 1996.

The overall percentage of the population engaged in civic activities has been virtually constant over these years, at 26.0 percent of the total population in 1981, 25.2 percent in 1986, 27.7 percent in 1991, and 25.3 percent in 1996. Civic activities in the neighborhood and community do not seem to have been affected negatively by the onslaught of urbanization, industrialization, and market liberalization of the past fifty years, and the rise in civic activities among children, the aged, and the disadvantaged is dramatic. Increased participation among women, especially those in their early thirties, has contributed to the recent rise in civic activities. Among men, those in their early forties participate most in civic activities. In the large cities, fewer people engage in civic activities, but those who do tend to devote quite extensive amounts of time to this work, whereas a greater number of residents of rural communities and small towns participate in civic activities, but each person tends to devote a smaller amount of time to them.

POLITICAL TRUST AS SEEN IN OPINION POLLS

The National Character Survey, conducted every five years, asks the straightforward question "Do you think that most people can be trusted or that one cannot be too careful about them?" The trend seen in the surveys in 1978, 1983, and 1993 indicates that social trust has risen steadily from the fairly low level of 26 percent in 1978 to 31 percent in 1983 and 38 percent in 1993. A similar question was asked in the same survey: "Do you think that other people try to take advantage of you when you show a weakness?" The trend displayed is very much the same, registering 39 percent in 1978, 29 percent in 1983, and 25 percent in 1993.[7] It seems that social trust has been on a steady rise from a fairly low level over the past two decades.

More directly, regarding political trust, a question about democracy was asked in the same survey: "What do you think of democracy?" The percentage of people who chose "good" as an answer increased signifi-cantly between 1963 and 1993: 38 percent in 1968, 43 percent in 1973, and 59 percent in 1993. The following question, pertaining to politicians, demonstrates an unmistakable trend toward trust in democracy: "It has been said that in order to improve Japan, it is better to choose the good politicians that come forward and entrust them to resolve problems rather than for the people to debate the issues. Do you approve or disap-prove of this view?" In 1953, the approval rate was 43 percent; in 1958, it was 35 percent; in 1963, 29 percent; in 1968, 30 percent; in 1973, 23 percent; in 1978, 32 percent; in 1983, 33 percent; in 1988, 30 percent; and in 1993, 24 percent. This is a clear departure from what is called the "subject politi-cal culture," as discussed by Almond and Verba.[8]

Similarly, trust in political institutions is high. Surveys conducted by Joji Watanuki, Ikuo Kabashima, and other scholars report that people consistently confirm a strong confidence in elections, parliament, and political parties.[9] But all the figures show a decline since 1996. Trust in elections registered 67.3 percent in 1976, 77.9 percent in 1983, and 82.3 percent in 1993 and 1995. Trust in the Diet registered 58.3 percent in 1976, 65.5 percent in 1983, 65.9 percent in 1993, 71.0 percent in 1995, and 64.1 percent in 1996. Trust in political parties registered 56.5 percent in 1976, 70.1 percent in 1983, 68.2 percent in 1993, 71.3 percent in 1995, and 66.1 percent in 1996. The overall impressions we get from the above are that the political institutions of Japan's parliamentary democracy gained firm legitimacy and that public trust in democratic institutions was gen-erally high until 1996.

Figure 9-2a: Trust in Democracy

"What do you think of democracy? Which best approximates your view (good, depends on time and case, not good)? Please describe."

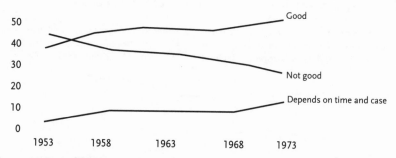

Source: Ministry of Education, Institute of Statistics and Mathematics, *Kokumin sei no Kenkyuu* (A Study of National Character), 1963–1993.

Figure 9-2b: Trust in Democracy

"What do you think of democracy? Which best approximates your view (good, depends on time and case, not good)? Please describe." (Ministry of Education, 1963–1993)

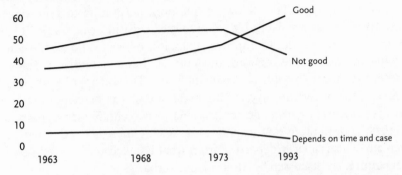

Source: Ministry of Education, Institute of Statistics and Mathematics, *Kokumin sei no Kenkyuu* (A Study of National Character), 1963–1993.

Figure 9-3a: Increasing Belief in Participatory Democracy

"It has been said that in order to improve Japan, it is better to choose the good politicians that come forward, and entrust them to resolve problems rather than for the people to debate the issues. Do you approve or disapprove of this view?"

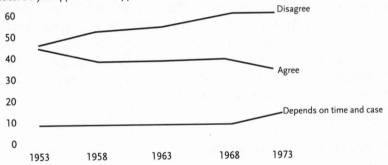

Source: Ministry of Education, Institute of Statistics and Mathematics, *Kokumin sei no Kenkyuu* (A Study of National Character), 1953–1973.

Figure 9-3b: Increasing Belief in Participatory Democracy

"It has been said that in order to improve Japan, it is better to choose the good politicians that come forward and entrust them to resolve problems rather than for the people to debate the issues. Do you approve or disapprove of this view?" (Ministry of Education, 1978–1993)

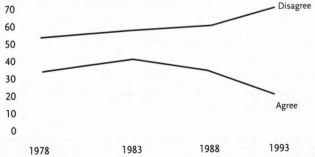

Source: Ministry of Education, Institute of Statistics and Mathematics, *Kokumin sei no Kenkyuu* (A Study of National Character), 1963–1993.

Table 9-1: Legitimacy of Institutions Related to Parliamentary Democracy

1. Elections make it possible for people's voices to be heard in politics.

	Agree	Disagree	Don't know/NA	Total (N)
1976	67.3	10.4	22.3	100% (1,796)
1983	77.9	6.7	15.4	100% (1,750)
1993	82.3	8.2	9.5	100% (2,320)
1995	82.3	9.5	8.2	100% (2,076)
1996	76.5	13.4	10.2	100% (2,299)

2. The Diet makes it possible for people's voices to be heard in politics.

	Agree	Disagree	Don't know/NA
1976	58.3	11.7	30.9
1983	65.5	11.9	22.6
1993	65.9	17.6	16.5
1995	71.0	16.5	12.6
1996	64.1	20.7	15.2

3. Political parties make it possible for people's voices to be heard in politics

	Agree	Disagree	Don't know/NA
1976	56.5	14.3	29.2
1983	70.1	9.4	20.5
1993	68.2	15.3	16.4
1995	71.3	16.0	12.7
1996	66.1	19.2	14.7

Source: Joji Watanuki, "Japan: From Emerging to Stable Party System?" Research Papers Series A-67, Institute of International Relations, Sophia University, Tokyo, 1997.

SOCIAL CAPITAL AND SOCIETAL/INSTITUTIONAL PERFORMANCE

This section presents trends in social capital by using two types of indexes. One is what I call the civic community index. The other is the societal/institutional performance index. The data used for this analysis are reported annually by the Social Policy Bureau (Kokumin Seikatsu Kyoku) of the Economic Planning Agency (1980–1995). Briefly, the framework by which the data are organized is as follows. Eight clusters focus on various aspects of people's lives: dwelling, spending, work, nurturing (children), health, recreation, learning, and association (social activity). Each cluster includes data that reflect the four criteria of concern: freedom, fairness, safety/security, and comfort. The data cover the period from 1980 to 1995. The unit of data is the prefecture. The results presented in Table 9-2 show how civic consciousness is facilitated by societal/institutional performance.[10]

Those with high spending and work scores tend to have low scores on

Table 9-2: Societal/Institutional Performance as a Source of Civic Community Consciousness

1. Civic Consciousness adj. $R^2 = 0.11$	Societal/Institutional Performance in Dwelling parameter estimate = 0.37 t-value = 2.6
2. Civic Consciousness adj. $R^2 = 0.46$	Societal/Institutional Performance in Spending parameter estimate = –0.72 t-value = 6.4
3. Civic Consciousness adj. $R^2 = 0.37$	Societal/Institutional Performance in Working parameter estimate = –0.82 t-value = –5.3
4. Civic Consciousness adj. $R^2 = –0.02$	Societal/Institutional Performance in Nurturing parameter estimate = –0.01 t-value = 0.1
5. Civic Consciousness adj. $R^2 = 0.00$	Societal/Institutional Performance in Healing parameter estimate = –0.17 t-value = –1.1
6. Civic Consciousness adj. $R^2 = 0.20$	Societal/Institutional Performance in Playing parameter estimate = 0.45 t-value = 3.5
7. Civic Consciousness adj. $R^2 = 0.07$	Societal/Institutional Performance in Learning parameter estimate = 0.32 t-value = 2.1

Source: Economic Planning Agency, Social Policy Bureau, *Shin Kokumin Seikatsu Shiryo* (New Indicators of Popular Lifestyles), 1980–1995.

civic consciousness, which is measured by the association categories. Those with high playing, dwelling, and learning scores tend to score high on civic consciousness. More specifically, those prefectures with better facilities and incentives for studying and recreational activities, as well as spacious housing, tend to score high on civic consciousness. To promote civic consciousness, a community needs to create places and occasions for civic engagement. This is where the NPO/SGIs briefly examined above come in. The nonprofit organizations that subcontract local government tasks for creating and maintaining facilities and carrying out special events seem to play a large role in promoting civic consciousness.

The lesson to be drawn from this analysis in terms of cultivating and maintaining civic consciousness is that we should pursue innovative and proactive policies toward the construction of physical and social space and psychological incentives for civic engagement. Those prefectures where people work long hours and spend a lot of money do not display high scores with regard to civic consciousness.

SOCIAL CAPITAL AND PARTICIPATION

So far I have examined either aggregate statistics or aggregated survey data. Here I will examine disaggregated data relating social capital to participation. Following Claus Offe's conceptualization, social capital can be conceived as composed of attention, trust, and associability.[11] What I try to do is to relate attention, trust, and affiliation to participation. The basic assertion of social capital theory is that good civic traditions, accumulated over the years, are conducive to high levels of participation and high levels of redistribution of resources to correct inequality. I shall focus here on the relationship between social capital and participation.

I measure attention by the frequency of TV news program viewing. Participation data are observed at three levels: national, prefectural, and district. Included are participation in civic activities, participation in local government-initiated group activities, interaction with elected politicians in terms of conveying grievances and prodding policy actions, attendance at political meetings, and involvement in political campaigning. A question was asked regarding each mode of participation. I then related the responses to trust at the three levels of politics. I present the results of cross-tabulation of the 1987 and 1991 data of surveys done by the Association for the Promotion of Clean Elections.[12]

For both data sets, the relationship between attention and participation is fairly clear. Those paying attention to news programs on TV tend to register a high degree of participation at all levels and in all areas. While there are somewhat weak associations between attention and participation in some areas and at some levels, the overall impression one gets from the cross-tabulated data is that attention strongly determines participation and vice versa. The oft-noted strong influence of the mass media, especially TV, seems to be real in this regard. The relationship between attention and affiliation with organizations (by which I mean reported mem-

Table 9-3: Speaking to a Person Who Seemed Lost on the Street

Voluntarily speak to a person who seemed lost on the street

U.S.	U.K.	Germany	Korea	France	Japan
60%	46%	43%	38%	34%	29%

Speak to a person who seemed lost on the street only when asked the way

U.S.	U.K.	Germany	Korea	France	Japan
38%	52%	55%	60%	63%	68%

Source: Shigeki Nishihira, *Yoron kara mita dojidaishi* [Contemporary history as seen from opinion polls] (Tokyo: Brain Shuppan, 1987).

bership in community associations, women's and youth associations, PTAs, agricultural cooperatives, trade unions, commerce and industry associations, religious associations, recreational associations, and other categories) is less strong than the relationship between attention and participation. This is so in part because these groups and the institutions they are affiliated with are not necessarily related to political causes. Many, in fact, have little to do with politics on a day-to-day basis.

The relationship between trust and participation shows an equally clear pattern. That is, the higher the level of trust, the higher the level of participation. Thus, when I compare the data from 1987 and 1991, it is clear that at the national level, trust was much lower in 1991 as compared to 1987, and in 1991 participation was much lower. In 1987, Japan was led by Yasuhiro Nakasone of the LDP, while in 1991 that party, though still governing, was in increasing disarray. Also clear is that at the lower levels of politics—that is, at the prefectural and district levels—the level of trust between 1987 and 1991 did not change much and the relationship between trust and participation was consistently high.

The relationship between trust and affiliation is less pronounced than the relationship between trust and participation because affiliation means potentiality, whereas participation is reality.

My attempt to relate attention, trust, affiliation, and participation in the framework of social capital through massive cross-tabulation of data leads me to suggest the following set of propositions.

First, the initial hypothesis of social capital theory, that the overall level of civic consciousness positively affects the participatory performance of democracy, seems to be supported. The higher the level of attention, trust, and/or affiliation, the higher the level of participation.

Second, the level of trust goes deeper as politics becomes more local and more established at the grassroots, and does not seem to be particularly susceptible to the vicissitudes of politics at the national level, perhaps with the noticeable exception of the LDP in 1987. Locally, trust is consistently high, and participation at the local level is much more closely correlated with it than is the case at the national level.

Third, the level of trust is high with regard to the Japanese system in general but not necessarily with regard to specific political actors and institutions. The level of affiliation at the local level is generally high, but this is not necessarily so at the national level. At the national level, the degree of attention and trust tends to be more strongly affected by the mass media, which accentuates certain events in national politics. This point has been made clear by Watanuki and Miyake, using the 1983, 1987, and 1991 data sets.[13]

SOCIOLOGICAL ATTRIBUTES AND PARTICIPATION

I will try to relate participation to some sociological attributes, including income, education, region, city size, family size, and TV watching. The data used are the same as those referred to in the preceding section. The initial hypothesis underlying this exercise is that these attributes more or less determine the level of participation, albeit with some notable exceptions.

Income and participation. Though never strong, there are positive correlations between higher income and political participation.

Education and participation. Of the four categories of educational achievement, the intermediate categories seem to have stronger positive correlations with political participation and affiliation. Those completing only compulsory education (through ninth grade) and those completing college education seem to participate and be affiliated less than those who have completed high school or technical school. Those with higher education seem to take into account other factors such as opportunity costs of participation.

Region and participation. The only area with consistently high rates of participation and affiliation is the Hokuriku region on the central part of Honshu Island, stretching from Fukui to Niigata. On this observation two hypotheses may be offered. One is an explanation based on political culture, akin to the one Putnam uses to account for the strong civil tradition in central Italy.[14] The Hokuriku region is noted for its large population of Jodo Shinshu Buddhists, known for their pragmatism, thrift, diligence, tenacity, and honesty. The other explanation involves the greater number of seniors' clubs and other types of community organizations in areas with a lower degree of urbanization; this may reflect conscious policy making.

City size and participation. There are discernible correlations between smaller city size and higher political participation and affiliation, as smaller size (above a certain limit) makes possible a more closely knit community and thus higher trust and attention among residents. At the same time, metropolitan areas exhibit a fairly high level of participation and affiliation, as they allow more room for functionally organized interaction and activities.

Family size and participation. Three-generation families exhibit the highest degree of participation and affiliation in general. They are most likely to be long-term residents of an area and hence more likely to be firmly embedded in local networks of activities and institutions.

TV watching and participation. There are clear positive correlations between TV watching and participation.

My examination of these cross-tabulated data leads me to suggest the following propositions. First, a country's overall level of wealth and knowledge is important to its accumulation of social capital. In the case of Japan, the country's literacy rate was among the highest in the world even between the seventeenth and nineteenth centuries and has risen continuously, now standing at around 98 percent (which is also the percentage of people subscribing to a newspaper). With regard to wealth, Japan achieved steady economic development over the last two centuries, especially during the last half century, and now ranks among the countries with the highest per capita income.

Second, nonetheless, an optimal size of city and family may be necessary to keep such accumulated social capital from being rapidly depleted. An overemphasis on freedom and mobility, efficiency, and scale of economy tends to result in disintegrating social cohesion and a jeopardized sense of community. Overemphasizing equality, security, and comfort tends to generate different kinds of negative social consequences, including excessive financial deficits and a diminished spirit of innovation, which may not help cities and families to maintain their self-rejuvenating capacity. The salience of the Hokuriku region's being ranked number one in terms of overall livability may have something to do with this proposition, as may its civic cultural traditions, which go back some five or six centuries.

PLAUSIBLE EXPLANATIONS FOR OBSERVED TRENDS

Social capital in Japan, as measured by the aggregate and survey data presented above, has been resilient over the past fifty years. Since confidence in the legitimacy of democratic institutions has been correspondingly high, the resilience of social capital may vindicate the theory of social capital as articulated by Putnam.[15]

More specifically, the number of nonprofit organizations has been rising steadily, especially civil and social associations at the grassroots level. In terms of time budgeting, people have consistently devoted the greatest amount of time to civic activities for neighborhoods and larger communities. In contrast, time devoted to civic activities for children, the aged, and the disadvantaged has been rapidly rising over the past decade.

Sociologically, Japanese participation in civic society can be sketched as follows: Women register a high level of civic activities in the latter half of their thirties, while men do in the first half of their forties. In urban settings, a small number of people devote a large amount of time to civic activities, while a proportionately larger number of citizens of rural communities devote small amounts of time to such activities.

The two questions regarding social trust and trust in democracy indicate that both have been steadily rising. Conversely, the number of people who see politicians as authority figures has been steadily declining over the years.

Trust in elections, parliament, and political parties has registered a steady increase over those same years, yet at a somewhat lower level than trust in democracy. Trust in politics and politicians is at an even lower level. The discrepancy between high support for the political system and the often glaring distrust in politics and politicians must be noted. Since this discrepancy has been the subject of quite a bit of attention and analysis, let me summarize the following three concepts first and then try to come up with some synthesis that can serve as a step toward making sense of social capital and democracy in Japan.[16] The three concepts are Watanuki's "cultural politics," Pharr's "videocracy," and my own "karaoke democracy."

Cultural Politics

On the basis of surveys conducted over half a century, Watanuki argues that certain patterns of incongruence between political party support and sociological attributes may be due to cultural factors.[17] Watanuki focuses on the underdevelopment of political parties and the party system. In contrast to the typical European country, in Japan lower income levels are not necessarily linked to left-wing party support; urban dwellers do abstain more from voting; the highly educated abstain more; the young do not necessarily support left-wing parties. In contrast to the United States, in Japan party identification does not play a strong role, postmaterialist voting patterns do not display significant generational effects, and personal support organizations (koenkai) of individual candidates in the district remain the locus of politics at the grassroots level. All these factors are related to the underdevelopment of political parties (by which I mean the relative inability of party headquarters to shape policy platforms and to discipline their own district-level candidates) and underdevelopment of the party system (by which I mean the weakness of policy competition between the governing party and the opposition parties). The underdevelopment of parties and the party system gives rise to the situation in which there is high confidence in the legitimacy and institutions of democracy and low trust in politicians and politics.

Party support patterns do not correlate neatly with patterns of economic well-being. In Europe, individuals in lower income strata tend to vote for left-wing parties, and those in upper income strata tend to support right-wing parties. In Japan, the long-term rule of the LDP found its base among farmers and small-business owners. The number of farmers and small-business owners shrank with the first phase of industrialization and market liberalization, but the LDP portrayed itself as a party representing and working for the socially weak in the population. This strategy worked brilliantly in the 1970s and 1980s, enabling the LDP to hold on to power even while most industrial democracies experienced a decline in one-party dominance.[18] Urban dwellers abstain from voting more often than rural dwellers in Japan, presumably because the latter feel a greater sense of community spirit and can connect voting more directly to benefits in public policy.[19] Voting participation by the highly educated is not steady or consistent. A more salient rise in right-wing voting is manifested among the young rather than among older voters, who experienced or remember the traumatic effects of war and are often wary of the LDP stance on security issues.

In the United States, party identification does play a strong role in determining party support patterns. But in Japan, individual candidates rather than party labels are a much more important factor in voting, except perhaps for the Japan Communist Party and the Komei Party (based on a Buddhist lay organization). Also, postmaterialist voting patterns—which reflect concerns such as freedom, equality, and the environment more than factors such as income and law-and-order issues— have been on a steady rise in Japan and have risen practically equally among voters in all age groups. Also, candidates' support organizations, which are independent of party organizations, play a major role in determining the outcome of elections in Japan.[20] This is vastly different from the United States, where adroit and aggressive TV advertising, which sells both party labels and individual candidates, does make a major difference.

Videocracy

Ellis Krauss and Susan Pharr have developed a thesis concerning the influence of the mass media on Japanese politics in the last twenty years, arguing that video legitimization does play a major role in Japanese politics and can account for the discrepancy between the generally high trust accorded to democracy and the perennially high distrust of politics and politicians.[21] The quasi-state television network Japan Broadcasting Corporation (NHK) carries news programs in which high-level politicians and bureaucrats are presented as shaping Japanese political development in an authoritative way. NHK has played a vital role in the nation-building process since the 1920s through the dissemination of a standard version of the Japanese language and by cultivating loyalty and solidarity. It is not significantly different from the role in nation building performed by state-owned radio in Indonesia, which fostered an "imagined community" (in Benedict Anderson's sense) in the latter half of the twentieth century.[22]

Recently, however, we have seen politics being presented in a new mode on television.[23] There is currently a proliferation of TV debate programs featuring prominent public figures who take advantage of the opportunity to engage in political rhetoric. Also, plenary and committee sessions of the Diet are now broadcast, exposing the weaknesses of politicians and bureaucrats in a sometimes devastating way—for example, when a cabinet minister, in a committee session, does not answer questions posed by the opposing party parliamentarian and instead calls upon a high-ranking bureaucrat who is also a member of the committee to answer, saying that the issue is too important or too delicate for he himself to respond to. It may be said that these developments have turned out to be too much for a political soil where video legitimization has long been practiced in more subtle forms.[24]

Karaoke Democracy

The term "karaoke democracy," coined by this author in 1994, is part of a theory that focuses on the dominance of the bureaucracy in Japanese politics.[25] Bureaucratic dominance in policy making and implementation in Japan is a tradition going back for at least four centuries, first in each of the approximately three hundred units of local government during the Tokugawa period (1603–1867), then in the central government unit of the modernizing state, launched in 1868.[26] When the Diet was established in the late nineteenth century, political parties were by definition the opposition, and the government was run by the central bureaucracy. Political parties and politicians were not held in high esteem, in large part because the government portrayed itself as representing the general, neutral, and enlightened interests of the entire nation, above partisan interests. Bureaucratic dominance has meant that parliamentarians rely heavily on bureaucrats for information and support regarding drafting of legislation, policy implementation, budgeting, and administrative guidance. Most politicians, except for the most influential 5 percent in the governing parties, do not have much role in the shaping of policy at a high level. Instead, they take care of their own constituencies, fine-tuning in response to the sentiments and grievances of their supporters (actual and potential) by bringing back "pork barrel" projects; attending meetings, funerals, and weddings; and finding jobs for the children of their constituents. Their "home style" requires them to spend an enormous amount of time in their constituency rather than in the Diet or in party headquarters in Tokyo.[27]

Even when appointed to the post of cabinet minister or prime minister, they are often forced by established custom to rely on briefings from bureaucrats in preparing their parliamentary speeches and interpellations. The main menu of government, in other words, is prepared by the bureaucrats. The politicians may then select from this menu the policies they want to support. In this sense it is like karaoke, which provides a catalog of songs from which to choose. Even if someone does not have a firm grasp of the song, he or she can read the lyrics appearing on the video screen and follow the melody that springs forth from the machine, simply following the lead of the karaoke machine. To carry the analogy over to the political realm, with this setup many people feel they can participate in politics, and nearly anyone can perform reasonably well. While this is an exaggeration, it does capture the sense of Japanese politics, in which the bureaucracy is dominant.

What makes karaoke democracy very distinctive is that over the past fifty years egalitarianism and antiauthoritarianism have been consistently strong, more than ten times stronger than in the United States or the United Kingdom, for instance.[28] The majority of people regard politicians with mild disdain and not with great respect for their authority. Politicians are seen to be not much different from anyone else; they are in a position of authority, but not because they are great or inspiring. They are there because the people want these individuals to work for them up there. The kind of deferential political culture observed in the United States and the United Kingdom does not seem to be strong in Japan. Perhaps the legacy of individualism, which flourished in Japan during the fifteenth and sixteenth centuries, is being slowly resuscitated, triggered by the relentless tide of globalization that permeates every corner of the world in the twenty-first century.

Comparing the above three theses leads me to note a similarity among them. All three point to the dissonance between high-level confidence in the legitimacy and framework of democracy and continuing distrust in politics and politicians. In addition to the above schemes explaining this dissonance, I will introduce Shigeki Nishihira's cross-national data and Toshio Yamagishi's thesis on results of cross-cultural comparisons relating to social capital. On this basis I will then develop a thesis of my own, that Japan's social capital accumulated over the last few centuries on the basis of face-to-face interactions in group settings, but now its basis is becoming both broader and more individualistic as Japan moves toward becoming a complex, highly individualized democracy.

Cross-National Surveys

Shigeki Nishihira presents comparative survey data findings in his attempt to elucidate the characteristics of Japanese political culture.[29] In surveys involving the United States, the United Kingdom, Germany, South Korea, and Japan, levels of satisfaction with family life, school life, working life, and friendship are consistently lowest or near lowest in Japan. Data of this kind suggest that Japanese individuals tend to shy away from social activity and be largely passive toward it.

In a specific setting, such as being confronted with a person who seems lost on the street, surveys show a pattern of Japanese having the most passive response (see Table 9-4). The degree of trust placed in social institutions shows a distinctive pattern (see Figure 9-4). Public trust in the judiciary, police, education, and the mass media is mildly higher than distrust, at 50–60 percent. Trust in the military and the executive and legislative branches of government is low, with only 20–39 percent expressing trust; trust is lowest in nongovernmental institutions such as labor unions, corporations, and religious organizations, at only 10–29 percent. In the United States, the highest trust is placed in military, religious, police, and educational institutions, at 60–79 percent. Next come political institutions (executive, judicial, and legislative), at 50–59 percent. Thus Japanese show very low trust in their political institutions in comparison to Americans. The European patterns fall in between those of Japanese and Americans.

Confidence in political institutions, as observed in a 2001 cross-national survey called the Asia-Europe Survey, gives a somewhat different picture (see Tables 9-5a, 9-5b). Japanese trust in most political institutions was lower in 2001, reflecting a trend that began in 1993, when the LDP ceased to be the governing party for a period of three years. Yet the two institutions that were relatively highly trusted in 1987, the police and the judiciary, remain highly trusted in 2001. The military had acquired a newly high level of trust by 2001. The civil service registered respectably high trust in 2001 despite a number of well-publicized corruption cases. It is very interesting to note that a high level of confidence in the military and the civil service is fairly common among the eight Asian countries under investigation. In this sense Japan is now no exception to this obser-

Figure 9-4: Trust in Social Institutions

%	U.S.	U.K.	Germany	France	Japan	Italy
80–90		Police Military				
70–80	Military Religion Police		Police			
60–70	Education	Judiciary Education	Judiciary	Police	Judiciary Police	Police Religion
50–60	Executive Judiciary Legislative		Military Legislative	Education Judiciary Military Religion Executive	Education Mass media	Military Education
40–50	Mass media Business firms	Religion Business firms Executive Legislative	Religion Education	Legislative Business firms		Judiciary
30–40	Labor unions		Labor unions Executive Business firms Mass media	Labor unions Mass media	Military Executive Legislative	Mass media Business firms Legislative
20–30		Mass media Labor unions			Labor unions Business firms	Executive Labor unions
10–20					Religion	
Average score of distrust	39.7%	40.4%	44.3%	52.2%	55.6%	56.5%

Source: Shigeki Nishihira, *Yoron kara mita dojidaishi* [Contemporary history as seen from opinion polls] (Tokyo: Brain Shuppan, 1987).

vation. Observed broadly among the nine European countries is the high level of confidence placed in the military and the police. The picture revealed in the 2001 data is more in harmony with the traditional modern Japanese image of the nonpartisan and the partisan in that nonpartisan institutions (courts, police, civil service, and military) are respected, while the partisan (parliament, parties, elected government, political leaders, big business, and mass media) are less highly trusted. When the Imperial Diet was convened in 1890, most parliamentarians belonged to the opposition parties. The government portrayed itself as the only public-spirited, nonpartisan, responsible body in society, whereas it portrayed the parliamentarians in political parties as driven by private interests such as profits and fame, intensely partisan and essentially irresponsible.

This pattern of a high level of confidence in the military, civil service, police, and courts and a low level of confidence in the parliament, parties, leaders, and government is quite common, whether in Asia or in Europe.[30] The general comparative picture of confidence in political institutions seems to be that the level of trust has declined somewhat across advanced industrial democracies.[31] Japan's pattern of confidence in political institutions is very similar to the European pattern, while among the eight Asian countries, Japan is more similar to South Korea and Taiwan, most dissimilar to Singapore and Malaysia, and has much in common with Thailand and the Philippines.

Cross-Cultural Experimental Data

Toshio Yamagishi provides a comprehensive account of cross-cultural comparisons of trust based on experimental data.[32] His experiments are akin to those of the prisoner's dilemma, in which selfish utilitarianism has its limits in maximizing the net benefits to each individual confronted with such a dilemma. In other words, he deals with experiments in which a scheme of cooperation or coordination is the only way to maximize the net benefits to each.

In his scheme, four persons receive 100 yen for participating in the experiment. Each of them is asked to make some donation to the other participants. The amount of the donation differs depending on the level of trust each places in the others. Among Japanese subjects, individuals with high trust make donations averaging 55 yen out of 100 yen received, while individuals with low trust make donations averaging 30 yen. Among the American subjects, high-trust individuals make donations averaging 35 cents out of 50 cents received, while low-trust individuals make donations averaging 20 cents. In both the Japanese and American cases, high-trust individuals make higher donations. In other words, his hypothesis is that high trust fosters social cooperation.

Yamagishi moves on to examine further the relationship between trust and punishment by establishing a framework for placing sanctions on noncooperative participants. He is interested in how subjects cooperate in setting up a scheme for punishing those subjects who fail to cooperate. The results are dramatically different from those obtained in experiments not involving sanctions. Low-trust individuals cooperate most when such a framework is instituted. In other words, the lower the trust one has in other persons, the more cooperative one is in setting up a scheme for placing sanctions on noncooperative participants.

In order to explain the eagerness of low-trust individuals to cooperate with other persons in experiments in placing sanctions, Yamagishi draws

Table 9-4a: Confidence in Institutions (Asia)

%	Japan	South Korea	Taiwan	Singapore	Malaysia	Indonesia	Thailand	Philippines
80–90				police courts government civil service military leaders			military	
70–80				parliament business parties media		civil service		media
60–70					government courts military leaders civil service	military media government parliament	business civil service media	
50–60		military	civil service		police parliament media business parties	police	courts	military civil service government courts
40–50	military courts police civil service	media	military leaders government business			leaders parties	police	parliament police
30–40			police courts civil service	police media courts		courts business	leaders parliament	leaders business parties
20–30	business media parliament	government	parties				government parties	
10–20	governement parties leaders	business	parliament					
0–10		leaders parties parliament						

Table 9-4b: Confidence in Institutions (Europe)

%	UK	Ireland	France	Germany	Sweden	Italy	Spain	Portugal	Greece
80–90									
70–80	military		business civil service					military	military
60–70	police	police military	police military	police		police business		media civil service business police	
50–60		civil service courts	media		police courts	military	police parliament		
40–50	courts business civil service	media	courts parliament government	courts military	business	media	military courts government media civil service	parliament government courts	police courts
30–40	parliament	business government parliament		parliament business leaders	military parliament civil service		parties leaders business	leaders	government business
20–30	media government	leaders parties	leaders	government civil service media	media government leaders	civil service courts government parliament		parties	media parliament civil service
10–20	leaders parties		parties	parties	parties	leaders parties			leaders parties
0–10									

Source: Nippon Research Center, *The Asia–Europe Survey*. Tokyo: Nippon Research Center for the project on democracy and political cultures in Asia and Europe, led by Takashi Inoguchi, funded by a grant from the Ministry of Education, Culture, Sports, Science, and Technology, for the period between 1999–2003 (project no. 11102000)

from experiments exploring internalized motivation.[33] In their experiments, kindergarten children were given felt pens to draw pictures. One-third of them were told that if they drew a good picture, they would be rewarded. Two-thirds of them were not given such instructions. However, half of the uninstructed group, or one-third of the entire group, was rewarded at the end of the session. The remaining children, who were told nothing about a reward, received no reward at the end. A few days later, the children were given felt pens again to see whether they would be eager to pictures this time around. The results were quite dramatic. Of the children who had previously been instructed on how to receive an award, 40 percent willingly drew pictures in the second round. Of the children who had not been given instructions, 80 percent willingly drew pictures the next time. In other words, children who were placed in a framework of participation conditioned on reward performed less willingly at the next opportunity than those who were not placed in such a reward structure. Without internalized motivation, trust is difficult to foster. Promising a reward does not necessarily ensure cooperation unless the meaning of cooperation is understood clearly. An open and voluntary framework, this evidence suggests, works better in fostering trust. In other words, when cooperation is facilitated by the carrot-and-stick method, not only is one's own internal incentive for cooperation enfeebled, but one also starts to think that other persons cooperate only because they are forced to do so. Trust declines when such a structure is used to promote cooperation. Since the removal of such a framework makes cooperation more difficult to obtain, further tightening of the structure is often required and enforced.

Michael Taylor goes further to assert that such a structure is like drugs.[34] Drugs facilitate cooperation, but they reduce the will for voluntary cooperation, and additional doses of the drugs are required to maintain the same level of cooperation. In other words, the use of the reward-and-punishment structure not only reduces the altruism that is necessary for voluntary cooperation but also destroys the commitments that are the fertile ground for fostering voluntary cooperation. Once family, kinship group, and community ties are destroyed by monitoring and regulation of individual behavior through the development of government and other public institutions, selfish interests tend to take over, replacing voluntary cooperation.

The Nishihira analysis of social trust and the Yamagishi theory of cooperation can be critiqued from three perspectives. One is the purely methodological perspective of unobtrusive measures; the second is a sociocultural view of differentiated expression of trust; and the third is a sociocultural perspective on the waning of normative control.

Unobtrusive Measures

It is important to recall that interviews and experiments are conducted in a set of artificial and abstract human settings. If Japanese social trust is created on the basis of face-to-face and group settings, as argued by sociologist Eshun Hamaguchi, artificial and abstract instruments such as interviews and experiments are likely to produce results that cannot be taken at face value.[35]

Interviews are conducted by asking questions, for instance, about social groups and institutions the respondents trust, but without any sort of concrete setting or clear orientation to an established set of social relations. In the absence of such specific, concrete links, the answers tend to be heavily slanted toward mistrust among Japanese respondents. Experimental data are no less obtrusive. The prisoner's dilemma games used for cross-cultural trust comparison have a set of features most inimical to Japanese. First, they involve an encounter with unknown persons. Second, subjects are not allowed to communicate with each other. Third, the rules are based on pure utility rather than on basic human trust. It seems that for this reason Japanese are noticeably more prone not to cooperate in the prisoner's dilemma game. It may be natural in that under conditions of anarchy, which the prisoner's dilemma game seems to symbolize, Japanese are prone to behave distrustingly, given that they are accustomed to rely heavily on contextualized rules of social interaction. The lack of specificity and concreteness, in addition to the unknown factor of the subjects and the rule that they cannot communicate with each other, means that such experiments cannot be used as an accurate measure of the trust people show in others. The call for unobtrusive measures is the lesson of this study.[36]

Differentiated Expression of Trust

In cross-national and cross-cultural comparisons, it is sometimes necessary to take into account sociocultural factors expressing sentiments such as trust. It would be useful to recall Albert Hirschmann's comparison of an American Jew and a German Jew.[37] They had known each other for many years but had been separated for a long time when they happened to meet again in New York City. The German Jew asked his American friend, "How have you been?" And the American Jew answered the question in a manner that symbolizes how people of different linguistic and cultural traditions use what seem to be the same words in different ways. The American Jew answered, "I am very happy. *Aber bin ich nicht so gluecklich* [But I am not so lucky]." It seems that in American society one has to sound positive, be it about one's life or one's trust in other persons, at least in the public domain, given the fact that God is supposed to have given America as the promised land of freedom and opportunity. One must be happy and positive. In an encounter with a stranger, the American must start positively, at least in terms of words and gestures. People should not offend others by giving an impression of mistrust. It could be dangerous. So they must sound friendly and as if they trust others.

In Japanese society, this demand to be positive does not seem to exist. Given the relatively homogeneous setting and the ease with which trust can be nurtured among Japanese in a specific and concrete bilateral and organizational setting, Japanese tend to start off with a rather cautious, awkward, or skeptical attitude toward remote social institutions and unknown persons (unless the strangers turn out to be associated with persons, groups, or institutions they know well).

As seen in Putnam's comparisons of Japanese and American responses, in Japan it is context-specific behavior and context-specific verbal response that are highly trusted.[38] It is in contextless situations that Japanese are less trusting. Therefore, the distinction between America and Japan is that Americans tend to display a relatively broader degree of trust in comparison to the Japanese.

The Waning of Normative Social Control

Social capital is not only a sociological concept but also a political science concept. The organizing principle and disciplining norms of a society are normally hard to change in the short span of half a century. If one is to be serious, one should broaden the span of observation to ten times that fifty-year span. Although we cannot use aggregate and survey data to investigate trends in social capital over the past five centuries, as we

Figure 9-5: Differentiated Expressions of Trust

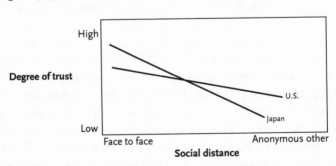

Source: Robert Putnam, "Democracy in America at Century's End," in Axel Hadenius, ed., *Democracy's Victory and Crisis* (Cambridge: Cambridge University Press, 1997), 27–70.

often can for the late twentieth century, it is important to grasp the nature and direction of change in political culture over a long span of time.

In approaching Japanese political culture, I want to emphasize the historical metamorphosis it has undergone over several centuries. Eiko Ikegami delineates with impressive skill the metamorphosis in early modern Japanese society from honorific individualism to honorific collectivism.[39] She analyzes the transformation of society's organizing and assessing principles in the sixteenth and seventeenth centuries. In medieval times, what mattered most was the individual capabilities of warriors. Thus a battle was prefaced by announcements by the leaders of their names, place of origin, and commitment to fighting for the honor of their name. Fighting was everything, and it was driven by the individual pursuit of honor.

When Japanese absolutism floundered midway through the sixteenth century, what emerged instead was the decentralized, quasi-feudal, highly bureaucratic Tokugawa regime. It demanded the collectivist pursuit of honor. The individualism of warriors was replaced by the collectivism of disarmed warrior-cum-bureaucrats honoring their collective organization, an organization derived from the structure and rules of the feudal lord's domains and family. Unlike in the case of European absolutism, despotic lords tended to be superseded by their bureaucrats, who ruled the territory honoring the spirit of a sort of extended family. They treasured loyalty, rectitude, honesty, diligence, commitment to the welfare of the populace, frugality, and physical and mental fitness to serve the collective cause. This spirit developed during the early modern period (from the seventeenth century to the mid-nineteenth century) and was inherited by the modern Japanese state, with the modern bureaucracy further extending and expanding this spirit into a version of nationalistic and collectivist spirit for the nineteenth and twentieth centuries. Thus honorific collectivism was further enhanced in modern Japan.

When the regime based on honorific collectivism was solidified in the seventeenth and eighteenth centuries, the challenge facing the Tokugawa shogun and the provincial lords was internal unity and stability. But with the arrival of Commodore Matthew Perry at Shimoda in 1853, the challenge facing Japan became how to cope with external threat, be it military, economic, or institutional. This was an entirely new challenge for the leaders of the Meiji state. They were assiduous in establishing a "wealthy nation and a strong military."[40] The key was the mobilization of nationalism under the emperor and the creation of a national bureaucracy meritocratically recruited nationwide. The Meiji bureaucracy was manned primarily by former samurai and their sons, who had lost their status and occupation after the Meiji state abolished class distinctions; they tended to be well educated, and their ideology of honorific collectivism suited the needs of the Meiji state. Thus the honorific collectivism of the early modern period was further developed in the modern period.

The modern Japanese state failed in its nationalistic outburst in 1941. But its leaders succeeded in getting the country to catch up with the West in terms of wealth and equality by 1995. Yet the problem of Heisei Japan (that is, Japan during the reign of Akihito, which began in 1989) is that Japanese have been gradually undermining the bastions of honorific collectivism. The guiding spirit of the nation seems to be changing slowly but steadily toward something that is increasingly neither honorific nor collectivist. Needless to say, the new guiding spirit is not likely to be entirely similar to the kind of individualism observed in the United States.

The success of the postwar Showa state in terms of catching up with the West, however, began to decrease the intensity of the nation's forward-directed drive. Having savored the fruits of achievement, people are far more cautious and averse to taking risks. On the issue of security, their basic starting point is to avoid involvement in conflicts. In direct investment, corporations may study an investment opportunity for ten years and still not take the risk. In domestic politics, they abhor the exercise of real leadership because it disturbs the comfortable web of vested interests. At both governmental and societal levels, this loosening of resolve is all the more apparent because it has coincided with the end of three global movements: the end of the Cold War, the end of geography, and the end of history.[41] The bipolar confrontation that formed the bulwark of the global security system has ended. The market, further empowered by borderlessness and globalization, now reigns supreme. And the social and transnational forces that were inadvertently suppressed by the Westphalian framework of nation-states have been unleashed.

These, in short, are three aspects of the metamorphosis Japanese political culture has undergone. A fourth is in the offing. In this process, individualism will be resuscitated to a significant extent and organizations will become more flexible and more functionally malleable, thanks to the individualist legacy of the fifteenth and sixteenth centuries as well as to the merciless forces of globalization that have been tangible at least since the Plaza Accord of the Group of Seven countries in 1985.

This brief summary of Japanese political culture in terms of content and direction can offer a broader, more long-ranging, deeper historical context in which to examine and assess social capital in Japan. Today, old, stylized images of Japanese society cannot remain tenable for long.

TOWARD THE NEW MILLENNIUM

There are three major pointers for understanding the nature of social capital in Japan in the new millennium. First is the dramatic rise in the number and activities of social and civic organizations over the past two decades. One good example is the huge number of volunteers that flowed into Kobe when a massive earthquake on January 17, 1995, left thousands dead and widespread devastation in the area. This phenomenon was impressive in its own right, but it is all the more remarkable because of the contrast with the generally inept and slow action taken by the central government.

For instance, AMDA, the Alliance of Medical Doctors in Asia, is a new kind of volunteer group. Headquartered in a small Catholic church in Okayama, west of Osaka and Kobe, it lists on its rolls 1,500 medical doctors and their staff throughout Asia, and it has participated in more than a hundred missions of humanitarian assistance and disaster relief throughout the world during the past fifteen years, including Kobe, Cambodia, Iraq, the Philippines, Ethiopia, Bangladesh, Nepal, Somalia, India, Indonesia, Mozambique, Rwanda, Chechnya, Sakhalin (Russia), the former Yugoslavia, Kenya, Zambia, Angola, and Mexico. Such organizations serve to erode the image that Japanese society consists only of governmental organizations and nongovernmental individuals .

The second pointer is the steady increase in the number of adherents to what are called postmaterialist values, such as participation and freedom, rather than order and economy. Inglehart argues that postmaterialism is closely related to generations and that the younger generations may be more easily influenced by postmaterialist values.[42] Trends in most industrial democracies during the last two decades seem to vindicate his argument. But, as demonstrated by Watanuki's important two-decade-long panel surveys, the number of Japanese adherents to postmaterialism has been rising steadily (3.6 percent in 1972, 7.6 percent in 1983, and 14.5 percent in 1993), with almost the same percentage increases across generations.[43] Thus the Japanese change in this regard has been very swift and substantial, with no need to wait for its effects on younger generations to become manifest.

The third pointer involves neighborhood-related civic activities such as autumn festivals, fire-prevention patrols in the wintertime, garbage-collection management, and Red Cross donations, all of which have been fairly resilient. Although neighborhood cooperation with police patrols has become more difficult in metropolitan suburban areas, this is due largely to the daytime absence of many residents. Although the frequency of and time spent on such civic activities have apparently decreased somewhat, civic consciousness is to a large extent alive and well. For example, garbage collection management is looked after remarkably well despite the huge space covered and the gigantic amount of waste produced daily.

These three very long-term pointers for understanding the nature of social capital in Japan in the coming millennium notwithstanding, we need to be more attentive to the historical and comparative complexities of social capital there. Of these, the following three issues should especially be noted: the historical comparison of primary determinants of the transformation of Japan and Germany, both formerly totalitarian/authoritarian societies; the seeming incongruence between the Fukuyama and Yamagishi conceptions of trust, and its conceptual resolution with Chinese-Japanese and Japanese-American comparisons; and the short-term difficulty of making the transition from honorific collectivism to cooperative individualism in Japan. In this chapter the primary comparison has been with the United States, as it is most familiar to the author as well as important to the other countries dealt with in this volume. Japan and Germany are distinguished from the rest in that they represent the triumph of democracy and civil society in the aftermath of totalitarian/authoritarian failures.

One obvious question is: How much of these trends toward civic engagement is due to socioeconomic modernization, politics, or other factors? My answer is that the socioeconomic modernization that fostered the rise of civil society, especially since the late nineteenth century, is apparently the primary contributing factor. Both Japan and Germany were latecomers to economic development in the nineteenth century, and they did well in catching up with the early starters; in the first two or three decades of the twentieth century, political and social liberalism made remarkable progress in both countries. Without the basis of economic development and social modernization, the rise of civil society over the last half century in both countries could not be properly accounted for. Yet a no less important factor in the equation in the mid-twentieth century was occupation by the Allied powers following the Second World War. During the occupations of the two vanquished nations, the leader of the Allies, the United States, exerted powerful political influence in the democratization and liberalization of political and economic institutions and of people's mind-sets. Change in the governing regime is not uncommon in defeated countries after major wars. The power basis of a regime is normally shattered by defeat, and the victor, victorious coalition, or international hegemonic culture prevails, permeating the values and norms of the domestic system of the vanquished. Furthermore, the much longer historical legacy before the late nineteenth century in both countries—that is, their long experience with decentralized political systems—seems to reinforce the rise of civil society following the waning of suppressive factors, such as the grip of the nation-state as the fashionable organizing principle (zeitgeist) and the predominance of a system of production geared to massive infusion of capital and efficient, concentrated use of labor. In other words, atavism plays a role in the rise of civil society in both countries.

Second, while the vigorous rise of civil society is quite visible, some constraints are also noticeable. They have much to do with the type of social capital that has been created. What is the type of social capital Japan has been good at producing? To characterize types of social capital, we may combine Francis Fukuyama's distinction between Chinese and Japanese types of trust and Toshio Yamagishi's distinctions between American and Japanese types of social capital.[44] Fukuyama compares what he calls high-trust and low-trust societies, focusing on the United States, Japan, and Germany on one hand and France, China, and Russia on the other. To make his distinction clearer, let me contrast Japan and China according to the terms he proposes. He argues that Japan transcends family and blood ties especially in business, as seen in the frequent practice of having an adopted son run and expand a firm, whereas Chinese do not quite transcend such ties, sticking more firmly to family and blood lines. According to him, Japanese trust is much wider than Chinese trust and enables the Japanese to mobilize resources on a wider scale and minimize risks inherent in business, thus contributing to prosperity beyond what is accounted for by such factors as technology, capital, and labor.

Yamagishi's comparison is made between Japanese and American trust. In what Fukuyama calls the high-trust society, Japanese and American trust can be distinguished as follows. American trust is broader and more open, whereas Japanese trust is narrower and more closed. American trust tends to be based on generalized reciprocity, whereas Japanese trust usually is restricted to known small groups, if not to narrow family and bloodline-defined groups. The key function of Japanese social capital among known small groups is to reassure, so that uncertainty and risks are minimized within the group and yet trust and risk-taking do not extend beyond the group. The key function of American social capital is to express trust so that cooperative and productive reciprocity can be generated. The former type of social capital can be called nonbridging, whereas the latter type can be called bridging. In the Japanese case, the task of risk assessment and risk avoidance in the uncertainty of social interaction is minimized within the group, whereas in the American case that task is inherent in social interaction of any kind. In terms of a sense of obligation, the stereotypical Japanese feels a very strong obligation only toward a narrow range of socially known others, whereas the stereotypical American feels a weaker obligation but toward a wider range of "socially anonymous" others. The former type of social capital can be called binding, whereas the latter type can be called extending.

Seen this way, the gap between Fukuyama's and Yamagishi's conceptions of social capital can be evaluated in a consistent fashion. The original puzzle posed by the Japanese data to Japan watchers and analysts seems to be resolved with conceptual clarity.

Third, the very challenges Japan now faces can also be explained in the same fashion. Japan may be in transition from relatively closed to relatively open social capital, from reassurance-oriented to trust-generating social capital, from binding to extending social capital. The transition is broadly in line with the transition from what Eiko Ikegami calls honorific collectivism in the Tokugawa-Showa periods (circa 1600–1989) to what Emile Durkheim might call cooperative individualism in the Heisei era (1989–) and beyond.[45] The transition is also in line with the transition from a mode of production based on massive mobilization of capital and labor in concentrated and concerted fashion to the mode of production based on creative innovation of technology and deft manipulation of capital.[46] The very success Japan achieved on the basis of relatively closed social capital, reassurance-oriented social capital, and binding social capital has started to function negatively in an age of globalization. Honorific collectivism and the state-led economic developmental model have become obstacles to further success. Therefore, the very success of the recent past may delay the transition from relatively closed to relatively open social capital in Japan. That may explain the difference between Japan and Germany despite their similar experiences in the twentieth century. In the Japanese case, societal collectivism and state-led development went to the extreme in the second and third quarters of the twentieth century, whereas in the German case, both ended by the mid-twentieth century. In Germany it lasted for a briefer period, and the state-led, collectivist German Democratic Republic was confined to a small territory, collapsing by 1989.

The degree of the tenacity of reassurance-oriented social capital in Japan can be glimpsed by looking at how the bad-loans issue has been handled and how voters responded in the upper-house elections on July 12, 1998, and July 29, 2001.[47] In 1998 the financial institutions with the greatest burden of bad loans are likely to be taken care of by the government (using tax funds), preventing them from going bankrupt. The government plan for recovery was clearly based on reassurance-oriented social capital. The logic is that the country must help the troubled financial institutions, since everyone makes mistakes, and also in order to keep depositors' funds intact. Japanese voters' performance at the polls in 1998 displayed their deep distrust of the reassurance-oriented policy package. The governing party, the LDP, lost its simple majority in the upper house by giving up a substantial number of seats to the opposition, especially the one-month-old Democratic Party, the Communist Party, and the Komei Party. The voters were angry at the dismal failure of the economic policy the government was conducting despite the deepening recession, steadily rising unemployment, and the steady slide of the Japanese yen vis-à-vis the U.S. dollar, and they were apprehensive about the future in an aging society when social policy programs are widely regarded as steadily eroding. In an interesting contrast to the 1998 Upper House election, the 2001 Upper House election produced a resounding victory for the Liberal Democratic Party during a period when the economy was continuously registering a lower level of performance. This occurred primarily because Prime Minister Junichiro Koizumi exercised strong leadership in persuading the electorate of the need to abandon the reassurance-oriented policy package and embrace instead the concept of structural reform, even though it carried the possibility of high risk in at least the short term. All the reassurance-oriented policy packages of the government during the late 1990s had not demonstrated any dramatic positive results. Preoccupied with bankruptcy and unemployment, these policies committed a large amount of government money to the rescue of noncompetitive sectors such as banks, public corporations, and construction firms but were unable to pull the economy upward. However, because these policies failed to get rid of a huge amount of bad loans and also did not increase the money supply, they wound up miring the government in deficit without producing any significant improvement. What Koizumi apparently wants is for the electorate to start to adopt a new mind-set, one focused less on reassurance and more on reshaping Japanese society.

It seems that the reassurance-oriented social capital of Japan cannot be made to disappear overnight, but the fact that its weaknesses have been revealed is a positive indicator of greater changes to come in the twenty-first century, allowing Japanese society to move on to the next aspect of Japanese political-cultural metamorphosis in a slow but steady process. Deciphering the multidimensional and multilayered nature of change in social capital in the new millennium will be one of the major research tasks for those interested in the resilience and longevity of democracy.[48]

CONCLUSION

ROBERT D. PUTNAM

In knitting together this quiltlike collection, I begin by summarizing the individual national analyses, highlighting both commonalities in the descriptions each author provides of his or her country and the differences in their theoretical perspectives. In the second half of this chapter I summarize some general themes—and questions—that emerge from our collaborative effort.

NATIONAL PATTERNS

Britain

Peter Hall discusses trends in a wide array of indicators of social capital in Britain. Membership in voluntary associations, he concludes, has been roughly stable since the 1950s, rising in the 1960s and subsiding only modestly since then. While some types of association have faded in importance in recent decades (traditional women's groups, unions, churches, and political parties), others (especially environmental organizations and charitable organizations) have expanded, so that the voluntary sector in Britain remains vibrant. Informal sociability also appears about as intense in the 1990s as in the 1950s, although perhaps slightly less than in the 1960s and 1970s. Rates of political interest and participation have remained relatively high. Moreover, Hall finds no intergenerational differences in British civic participation that might portend substantial changes (up or down) in the years ahead. On the other hand, he also reports a significant secular decline in social trust, particularly in younger age brackets, as well as some decline in political efficacy and political trust.

Hall contrasts the general stability in social participation in Britain with comparable declines in the United States, seeking to account for the transatlantic difference. He singles out three factors as especially important: (1) the massive expansion of the British educational system between the 1950s and 1990s that in itself boosted aggregate levels of civic involvement, especially among women, (2) changes in the British class structure that simultaneously enlarged the middle class and increased its long-standing predominance in British associational life, and (3) British government policy that cultivated the voluntary sector while expanding the welfare state. On the other hand, Hall finds some evidence that the decline in social trust may be indicative of a broader transformation of British social relations from collectivist to individualistic, and especially from class-based solidarity to achievement-based opportunism and from public-regarding groups to private-regarding groups.[1] In short, he raises the possibility that "beneath the apparent stability of associational membership" there may have been an erosion in the quality of collective life or civic engagement.

Yet more disturbing, Hall reports, is the evidence that Britain is becoming increasingly "a nation divided between a well-connected and highly active group of citizens with generally prosperous lives and another set of citizens whose associational life and involvement in politics are very limited." The latter, disconnected group is drawn disproportionately from the working class and the young, and while the age gap may prove transitory, Hall argues, the class gap is likely to grow. Thus, while Hall dismisses any simple thesis of uniform decline in British social capital in recent decades, he expresses concern about changes in the social distribution of social capital, as well as about the possibility that the rising forms of civic participation may be less suited to the pursuit of collective goods than the forms they are replacing.

Sweden

The backdrop to Bo Rothstein's analysis of trends in social capital in Sweden is the classic "Swedish model" of social democracy—referring to the ambitious welfare state and neocorporatist arrangements, based on the hegemony of the Social Democratic Party. During the 1960s this system produced an enviable combination of democratic stability, popular legitimacy, economic growth, and social welfare, but over the last quarter century Sweden has become exhibit number one in the European roster of "democratic discontent."[2] Rothstein summarizes evidence of Swedes' mounting discontent with their public institutions, along with a slackening of participation in politics, especially parties and traditional interest organizations, and a notable decline in economic performance during the 1990s. He argues that a key ingredient in the political dynamics that caused this deterioration was the collapse of what he terms "organized social capital," that is, trust within and among the major labor and business organizations. In turn, he traces this collapse to the "political hubris" of Swedish unions and the Social Democratic party during the 1970s, which led them to abandon the incrementalist, consensualist Swedish model.

But even if this specific form of organized social capital has indeed eroded, there does not seem to be evidence of damage to Swedish democracy; on most measures of civic engagement and social connectedness Rothstein finds impressive evidence of stability and even growth over the last half of the twentieth century. In global perspective Sweden ranks at or near the top of organizational involvement, political participation (at least as measured by voting), and social trust. Moreover, the available evidence suggests that both formal and informal social organization has, if anything, displayed increasing vitality in recent decades. Similarly, unlike the United States, Britain, and some other countries, social trust in Sweden appears to be stable or even increasing. Rothstein does find evidence of increasing individualism, as younger generations have turned away from traditional hierarchically organized forms of social activity, but rather than social isolation, they seem to have increased their involvement in shifting, temporary social activities— perhaps like what Robert Wuthnow in another context has referred to as "loose connections."[3] Rothstein argues that what has replaced collectivism among younger generations of Swedes is not egoistic individualism but solidaristic individualism.

Perhaps most intriguing for non-Swedes is Rothstein's account of the widespread incidence of study circles—small groups that meet weekly for educational discussions. This practice appears to be growing and involves an astonishing 40 percent of the adult population every year. (It is perhaps no accident that other studies have shown that Swedes and other Scandinavians spend much less time than citizens of other advanced nations watching television.)[4] As social capital theory would suggest, participation in such study circles appears linked to broader civic involvement. Equally intriguing is the fact that fully half of the cost of the study circles is covered by government funds.

Indeed, as Rothstein demonstrates, all aspects of the Swedish case study provide powerful evidence against the thesis that the welfare state necessarily undermines social capital. On the contrary, Sweden (along with its Scandinavian neighbors) leads the world not only in many measures of social capital, but also in public spending and taxation. Moreover, as Rothstein argues forcefully, the steady or even rising levels of social participation and volunteerism among Swedes over the last several decades is strong evidence against the claim that big government is necessarily the enemy of social capital. On the contrary, Rothstein argues that the universal (not targeted) social provision that has characterized the Swedish welfare state is entirely compatible with high levels of social capital.

Australia

Australia is, like the United States, a relatively new, settler, continental society, and in some respects the portrait that Eva Cox sketches of trends in Australian social capital is similar to my own portrait of trends in American social capital. Many long-term established voluntary groups have registered declining membership, and volunteering in formal organized settings appears also to have waned in recent years. Union membership and church attendance both fell significantly from the 1960s to the 1990s, and some recent data suggest a decline in political involvement, although other data imply that political protest activities have become more common. Both social and political trust seem to have declined in the last decade or two.[5] Australians, like Americans, seem to be spending more time watching television and less time socializing. Though sports participation is up—as it appears to be in many of our countries—Cox suggests this trend reflects individual fitness activities, rather than team sports. Even some newer feminist and environmentalist groups appear to have lost ground, though offsetting this trend, at least in part, has been a growth in episodic community events, such as festivals and "fun runs." On the other hand, Cox argues, these new ways of sharing public space may not serve the same social and educational functions that participation in more formal, more enduring organizations once did.

Like other authors, Cox emphasizes the social inequalities in the distribution of social capital in Australia, and she is particularly concerned that what I have termed bridging social capital may have been especially hard hit by the declines she describes. While she reports growing tolerance for homosexuals and nonwhite minorities, she concludes with concern that declines in distrust and disengagement may be linked to rising general anxiety about Australia's future.

Japan

Takashi Inoguchi finds stable or gently rising levels of civic engagement in Japan, especially as measured by such conventional Western indicators as nongovernmental organizations. Neighborhood groups—much the most common form of civic organization in Japan—appear roughly as important in the late 1990s as fifteen years earlier, and organizations serving children, the aged, and the disadvantaged have substantially increased. (One might speculate that the latter have risen in part to offset a weakening of more traditional Japanese social safety networks.) In the political sphere Inoguchi reports that over the last half of the twentieth century Japanese voters gradually shed their deferential "subject" orientation and became more enthusiastic democrats, while remaining quite critical of the foibles of their political leaders.

Inoguchi notes the striking fact that by conventional comparative measures of generalized social trust, Japan appears to be a low-trust society, not a high-trust society, as is often assumed by casual observers. Other researchers, led by Toshio Yamagishi, have shown that this is not merely a verbal matter, since in experimental settings (for example, facing prisoner's dilemmas with strangers) Japanese respondents are substantially less likely to cooperate and more likely to defect than are Americans in a similar setting. Inoguchi points out, too, that the Japanese are substantially less likely than Americans or even Europeans to volunteer assistance to a stranger in need on the street. Yet we know from other sources that in intimate circles social cohesion in Japan appears much higher than in comparable Western settings. Theoretically speaking, this important anomaly suggests (following Yamagishi) the possibility that the radius of social trust is narrower in Japan—that the Japanese do trust (and act in a trustworthy way) in a setting with other familiar actors, but that they are less trusting of (and less trustworthy toward) the generalized other. Whether or not that is the correct interpretation of the Japanese trust anomaly, Inoguchi reports a gradual rise in Japanese trust of the generalized other, suggesting that on this dimension, too, Japan may be gradually converging toward more Western forms of social capital.

In other domains, by contrast, Inoguchi's portrait of Japanese social capital remains quite distinct from the other country profiles in this volume. In all the other countries, for example, civic engagement and social connectedness are closely correlated with socioeconomic status, and in fact this inequality in the distribution of social capital may be increasing. In Japan, by contrast, Inoguchi reports that social participation is actually higher among less educated groups.

Partly because of the paucity of systematic data and partly for reasons of comparability to the other studies in this book, Inoguchi presents less evidence on trends in more traditional Japanese forms of social connectedness, such as *oyabun-kobun* (roughly speaking, patron-client) ties or informal ties with friends, neighbors, and co-workers. Thus, on the basis of the evidence here we cannot say for certain whether the aggregate level of social capital in Japan has increased over the last several decades or whether instead we are seeing a gradual shift from more traditional to more Western forms of civic engagement.

What is clear, however, is that the dynamics of social capital in Japan, as elsewhere in our survey, are determined more by the peculiarities of national history than by any single global modernization clock. This fact becomes clearest in Inoguchi's quick but thoughtfully provocative sketch of the successive stages through which Japanese political culture has moved over the last five centuries—from honorific individualism in medieval Japan to honorific collectivism under the Tokugawa and Meiji regimes. Inoguchi concludes that Japan may be in the early stages of a profound transformation in its social capital profile, with a dramatic increase in the vitality of civil society as well as of postmaterialist values of participation and freedom, a transformation from more closed forms of social capital toward more open forms that may be more effective in helping to manage the problems of a postmodern, internationally interdependent economy.

France

Jean-Pierre Worms describes a France facing two interlocking crises—a crisis of socioeconomic inequality in which an increasingly desperate minority of victims of social exclusion (disproportionately, though not entirely, Muslim immigrants concentrated in suburban slums) are "dissociated from a worried and shaken majority," and a crisis of political representation in which the populace is increasingly alienated from the political institutions of the classic French republican state. Within the various segments of civil society there is little evidence of a net decline in informal bonding social capital. While some of the principal social and political organizations—especially unions, political parties, and the Church—have experienced declining membership, gross membership in associations has been stable. Indeed, as in other modern welfare states public provision of social services has actually underpinned an apparent expansion of nonprofit social service organizations.[6] The last quarter of the twentieth century apparently witnessed a disproportionate growth in two somewhat different directions—initially rapid growth in organizations defending sectoral, self-oriented interests, and subsequently growth in organizations aimed at broader, more altruistic objectives, as well as personal development in the form of cultural and leisure activities. As in Britain after World War II, a primary impetus toward greater associational involvement appears to have been the postwar expansion of French education, for within the more educated categories one can see some slippage in rates of membership. Ironically, this tendency has reduced the traditionally strong link between social capital and more general social standing; as Worms summarizes the pattern, "the best educated are deserting associations faster than the least educated are joining them."

Like other countries surveyed in this volume, France appears to be characterized less by a global slump in civic associationism than by a generational shift away from some sorts of associative activity (especially in traditional formal organizations) and toward other sorts (especially informal, rapidly shifting affiliations), "a type of privatization of social capital formation." Similarly, within the increasingly marginalized French underclass, Worms notes the persistence of important forms of bonding social capital that do not, however, serve to integrate these groups into the wider society. The result, he concludes, is a general pattern of increase in self-directed, fragmented social capital and decrease in institutional, other-directed social capital. Thus, despite relatively stable levels of social capital in general, Worms diagnoses a worrisome lack of institutionalized mechanisms for linking private sociability with the wider public arena. This "missing link" between the rich sphere of private social capital and the increasingly discredited public institutions constitutes Worms' primary explanation for the disjunction between a relatively healthy civil society and the ailing institutions of the French state.

Germany

The impact of larger historical and political forces on patterns of sociability is particularly clear in the case of Germany, as described by Offe and Fuchs, in large part because of the extraordinary political disjunctures in Germany over the twentieth century. The backdrop to their detailed description of social capital in the contemporary Federal Republic is the powerful impact of the Nazi and Communist regimes on the structure of civil society, particularly their respective policies of coerced participation in state-organized associations. Broadly speaking, West Germany emerged from the "zero hour" in 1945 with its long-standing tradition of strong associationism in disarray. The struggles of the first half of the century had left a powerful sociopolitical culture of *ohne mich* (without me).

From that depressed level, it is hardly surprising that at least until the 1990s trends in sociopolitical participation in West Germany seem to have been upward, particularly among the younger generation and particularly in less formal types of sociability. The only important exceptions to this trend are two: (1) declining membership in the familiar triad of unions, parties, and churches, as in other advanced countries over the last several decades, and (2) an apparent disengagement of younger Germans from political and social organizations during the 1990s. It is still too soon to tell whether either or both of these exceptions may lead to a broader pattern of disengagement in the future, but at least during the second half of the twentieth century, trends in West Germany showed no net decline in social capital and more probably an increase. Like Rothstein in Sweden (and, in another context, Wuthnow in the United States), Offe and Fuchs do find evidence of a trend away from formal membership organizations and toward more transient and personalistic (but in some respects equally valuable) social ties.[7]

In the case of the former East Germany, the traumatic events of the decade after 1989 appear to have had a strongly negative effect on most measurable forms of social involvement, in part because of the sudden collapse of the older state-run organizations and their replacement by transplanted and perhaps quasi-colonial associational structures from the West, and in part because of the classic disengaging effects of severe unemployment.[8] Offe and Fuchs conclude that a rapid normalization of associational life in the former GDR is unlikely. Once again, the effects of large-scale events at the level of the state on the contours of civil society is especially plain.

Offe and Fuchs also provide a thorough accounting of the social distribution of social involvement, and in all essential respects the patterns they find are characteristic as well of social participation in the United States—more associational involvement (especially of a formal sort) among the more educated and more affluent, among those in the labor force, among the middle-aged, in smaller towns, and among men (especially in more-public forms of activity, though the gender gap is closing over time).[9] Offe and Fuchs, like other authors in this volume, conclude with some serious concern about the inegalitarian implications of this distribution of social capital.

Spain

Víctor Pérez-Díaz tells a fascinating story of the evolution of patterns of social capital in a Spain that has moved from civil war to authoritarianism to pluralist democracy. That history highlights the important distinction between what he terms civil and uncivil social capital (what I have termed bridging and bonding social capital). The two sides in the Spanish Civil War of the 1930s were bonded internally by strong ties, but during the previous decades, Pérez-Díaz reports, political actors on both sides had destroyed the country's nascent stock of civil social capital that bridged the ideological cleavages. Pérez-Díaz describes an almost classic case of strong internal ties of solidarity and fraternity and dehumanizing stigmatization of the enemy, as exemplified in the murderous *paseos*. The result was a civil war of great brutality and bitterness.

Under the Franco regime, however, social capital of a more civil sort was gradually accumulated, in part through conscious recognition by younger leaders on both sides of the negative reference point of the civil war, in part because of the emollient effects of economic modernization and internationalization, but also in part as the unintended consequence of the actions of a new generation on both sides of the older cleavage who created a new set of civic associations. Though "baroque and unintended," Pérez-Díaz concludes, "this accumulation of social capital (of both kinds) made possible in the seventies the kind of democratic transition that was perceived as creating neither winners nor losers—it was like an inverted mirror image of the civil war."

While formal associations of a more civil sort were decisive in the successful transition to democracy, Pérez-Díaz notes that in the subsequent quarter century the most vibrant part of Spain's stock of social capital has been instead the "softer" sorts of social capital embodied in family networks and other networks of informal cooperation. Like other authors in the volume, Pérez-Díaz notes a substantial decline in popular involvement in political parties, unions, and the church, but he argues that this decline is less important than the persistence and even growth of the softer forms of Mediterranean gregariousness. As evidence that Spain faces no social capital deficit, he adduces the success with which the young Spanish democracy has surmounted such serious crises as massive and sustained unemployment and a wide-ranging series of political scandals.

On one hand, Pérez-Díaz's chapter illustrates the important role that patterns of social capital (civil/bridging or uncivil/bonding) play as a backdrop to regime change—from fledgling, unstable liberal democracy to lethal civil war to authoritarian dictatorship and miraculously back to mature liberal democracy. On the other hand, his account of the Spanish case illustrates that socioeconomic change (in this case, classic modernization from poor and rural to relatively wealthy and modern), generational change, and political actions (sometimes intentional, more often not) all can have an important impact on the dynamics of social capital. From a broader comparative perspective—for example, from the perspective of those concerned with the aftermath of the equally murderous Balkan civil wars of our own time—Pérez-Díaz's account of this transition leaves the reader eager to learn more about the extraordinary Spanish success.

United States

Given the importance of the American case in current debates about trends in social capital, our volume includes two complementary essays. One, by Theda Skocpol, offers a wide-angle historical view; the other, by Robert Wuthnow, focuses specifically on trends over the last several decades of the twentieth century.[10]

Skocpol asks how America became by the middle of the twentieth century one of the most civically participatory countries in the world, in which locally rooted but translocal and cross-class membership associations played an unusually prominent role. The features of this distinctive civil society were, of course, already evident at the time of Tocqueville's famous visit in the 1830s—well before large-scale industrialization and urbanization, as she notes. Religious enthusiasms, political democracy, and the institutions of the federal state played important roles. The development of associational life was strongly boosted by the Civil War (at least in the North and among southern blacks). Indeed, the period bracketed by the Civil War and World War I appears to have been the most fecund in American history from the point of view of mass membership organizations. This was also the period of the American industrial revolution, but Skocpol argues that any simple modernization theory would miss the importance of wars and group contention in fostering associational growth.[11] Moreover, she argues that a central feature of American civic associations in this period was their fostering of shared citizenship even across persistent ethnic and class cleavages. Finally, she presents evidence that, historically speaking, American civic involvement was encouraged, not crowded out, by government activities.

This "classic civic" America, Skocpol concludes, remained vital until the middle 1960s, but over the last third of the twentieth century, mass-based, cross-class membership associations were steadily replaced by professionally led political advocacy groups with narrower missions and much more anemic membership involvement. She tentatively suggests several possible explanation for this watershed—changes in communications media, new sources of financial support for political advocacy, the abdication of educated men and women from their traditional roles as community leaders, the weakening of traditional institutions of civic mobilization. The newer structure of civic America is, she concluded, more oligarchical, dominated by professionals, and less likely to bridge different classes and places.

Wuthnow carefully reviews complementary evidence pointing in several different directions as regards these recent trends. He finds evidence of modest but significant decline in associational membership, especially if growth in educational levels is taken into account. This decline seems especially marked for unions and religious groups, two forms of social organization that, as we have already noted, have been fading in virtually all the countries represented in this volume. Social trust has unambiguously declined, but broader trust in institutions has been relatively stable, he reports, with the important exception of political institutions. Some evidence points as well to declining civic participation, though Wuthnow finds the evidence mixed. On the other hand, he also reports growth in volunteering over this period and in participation in some newer forms of social life, such as Bible study groups, special-interest groups, and (especially) self-help groups. He adds that a fuller accounting of trends in social connectedness would need to examine the effects of telecommunications and other non-place-based forms of community. In other recent work on related issues, Wuthnow has argued that the most important shift in American community life in recent years is not the disappearance of social connections, but a transformation from stable, long-term relationships toward more flexible, "loose connections."[12]

Wuthnow's most distinctive contribution is his argument that much of the recent decline in social capital in the United States is concentrated among marginalized groups, which in general had less social capital to begin with. His central thesis is that "existing social arrangements have become systematically more exclusionary, causing some segments of the population to feel unwelcome and to cease participating, or failing to provide the resources that people need to engage in civic activities." Decline in social trust, though common in all social categories, should be attributed, Wuthnow argues, to failings of national political leadership, not changes in grassroots social life. The central issue, he concludes, is one of the changing distribution of social capital and the relative decline of social capital that bridges the privileged and the socially marginalized.

COMMON THEMES

What do we know about trends in social capital in advanced democracies over the last several decades? A number of important common features are evident from very recent research on the advanced industrial democracies that make up the Organization for Economic Cooperation and Development (OECD).

Declining Electoral Turnout

As is well known, American electoral turnout began to decline in the 1960s, a trend that accelerated in the 1970s. Although that trend has been well established in the scholarly literature for several decades, for some years researchers disagreed about whether similar tendencies could be observed elsewhere in the OECD. Recently, however, a clear scholarly consensus has emerged: With a lag of roughly two decades after the American decline in turnout, electoral participation in virtually every other advanced industrial democracy has begun to retrace that decline.[13] As Martin Wattenberg summarizes the evidence: "In seventeen out of these nineteen [OECD] countries, recent turnout figures have been lower than those of the early 1950s. It is rare within comparative politics to find a trend that is so widely generalizable."[14] In broad terms, the decline has been from roughly 80 percent turnout in the 1950s to roughly 70 percent in the 1990s, but apart from the United States, these declines began in the 1980s and accelerated in the 1990s.

Levels of voter turnout remain relatively high in Europe, but as Peter Mair argues, "while an average turnout across Europe in the 1990s of more than 75 percent appears to belie any notion of substantial levels of mass disengagement, these new figures do tend to sustain the notion of a gradual erosion in popular commitment to conventional politics. In this sense, the increasing concern with declining participation which is being voiced by governments and political observers throughout western Europe seems not to be misplaced."[15] Similar declines in voting of approximately the same magnitude have also occurred in Australia, New Zealand, and Japan, though it is worth noting here that within Europe

Figure 10-1: Turnout decline in the OECD Nations (excluding Scandinavia)

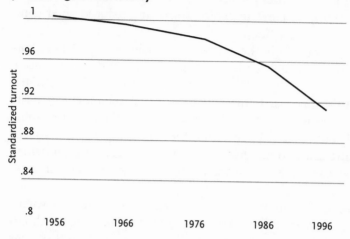

Note: Entries represent a three-year moving average of standardized turnout numbers, with the average turnout in the first two elections of the 1950s serving as a baseline for each country.

the decline in turnout is less marked in Scandinavia than elsewhere. The broad trend in electoral participation in the established democracies of the OECD is summarized in Figure 1.

This nearly universal decline in the single most important form of democratic political participation is all the more striking because it has occurred in the face of rapidly rising levels of education, and education is virtually everywhere a very strong predictor of political participation. As Wattenberg points out, "Based solely on demographic changes since the 1950s, electoral participation should be expected to show a generalized increase."[16] There is as yet no generally accepted explanation for this widespread slackening of electoral participation, although Mark Gray and Miki Caul have reported evidence linking these declines to a weakening of unions, mass political parties, and perhaps other mass organizations.[17]

Declining Public Engagement in Political Parties

Just as in the case of electoral participation, weakened partisan attachments appeared first in the United States in the 1960s and 1970s and then spread to other advanced industrial democracies in the 1980s, accelerating in the 1990s. Indeed, by the 1990s weakening partisan identification had become virtually universal throughout the OECD, including Australia, New Zealand, and Japan. Generally speaking, the decline appears to be concentrated in younger generations.[18] A concomitant trend is increasing volatility of partisan choice, suggesting reduced voter commitment to particular parties.[19]

This change came last in the newer democracies, such as Spain, Portugal, and Greece, probably because the initial effect of democratization is to increase activity by political parties. Similarly, as Dalton notes, "research on German partisanship stressed the development of party attachments in the immediate post-war decades; but then the dealigning process eroded these ties." By the 1990s the weakening of party attachment had progressed so far that a new term emerged in the German political vocabulary to refer to alienation from political parties: *Parteienverdrossenheit*.

Beyond this decline in partisan commitment among ordinary voters, recent research by several scholars has also made plain that the disengagement affects the party organizations themselves. These studies show evidence of dramatic declines in party membership in virtually all established democracies of the OECD, accelerating in the 1990s. Susan Scarrow reports that her review of a wide range of evidence from throughout the advanced industrial democracies of Europe, Asia, and North Amer-

Figure 10-2: Party membership in OECD nations declines, 1970s–1990s

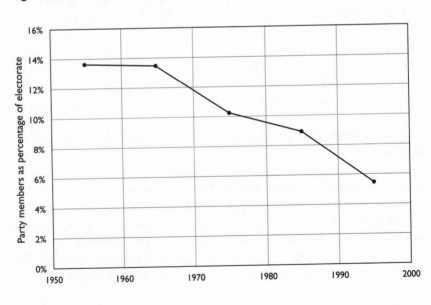

ica "yields a fairly general picture of party memberships in decline by the 1990s, whether membership is measured in absolute or standardized terms. . . . Parties' reports of generally falling enrolments are reinforced by responses from public opinion surveys about party membership."[20] Figure 2 summarizes this evidence.

Examining evidence specifically on Europe, Peter Mair concludes, "Not only have levels of party membership continued to decline as a proportion of the electorate, a trend which was already apparent at the end of the 1980s, but there is now also compelling evidence of a major decline in the absolute numbers of party members across all the long-established European democracies. . . . Across all of the long-established democracies, these party are simply hemorrhaging members."[21] Martin Wattenberg adds that "even in the United States, where the practice of formal dues-paying members never existed, grass-roots organizations were prominent on the political scene for over a century. Such organizations quickly began to wither during the early years of television."[22]

A similar pattern of nearly universally declining engagement in conventional politics appears in measures of participation in electoral campaign activities, such as attending a political meeting, working for a party or candidate, or simply talking to acquaintances about the election. Declines in conventional political participation are by now well established in the United States. However, as Dalton and his colleagues show, "declining campaign involvement is not a distinctly American phenomenon. . . . The trends for participation in party meetings or campaign rallies are down in virtually every nation. This is a clear indication of how elections have shifted from mass-based participation to vicarious viewing of the campaign on television."[23]

Dalton and Wattenberg summarize the general picture of citizen involvement in party politics throughout the OECD: "Today, mounting evidence points to a declining role for political parties in shaping the politics of advanced industrial democracies. Many established political parties have seen their membership rolls wane, and contemporary publics seem increasingly skeptical about partisan politics."[24]

Declining Union Membership

Another domain in which recent evidence makes clear a broad pattern of lowered social capital is organized labor. As early as 1990, Griffin, McCammon, and Botsko reported that "unions in more than three-fourths of the 18 largest, politically stable capitalist democracies experienced sustained declines or stagnation in the density of their organization from the late 1970s to the mid-1980s."[25] Just as in the case of party

Figure 10-3: Union Membership Rates Decline after 1980 (except in Scandinavia)

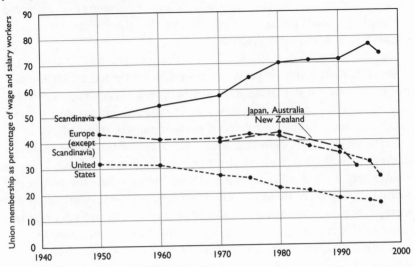

politics, these declining trends, which had begun in the United States in the 1960s, accelerated throughout the OECD after 1990. The only significant exceptions involve the four Scandinavian nations, where unemployment insurance, channeled through labor unions, has provided a powerful material incentive for continued membership. Trends in the established Asian industrial democracies mirror those in Europe. Figure 3 summarizes this evidence.

Declining Church Attendance, Especially in the 1990s

A fourth important domain of organized social life is religion. Here again the pattern of declining engagement mirrors those we have already seen in politics and the workplace. Church attendance in the United States rose to a peak in the 1950s and 1960s and then began a long, slow slump that by now has lasted nearly four decades. Similarly, between the 1970s and the late 1990s, church attendance declined in virtually every European country. Overall, the recent decline in European church attendance has been greater than that in the United States, though it perhaps began somewhat later. (Systematic survey evidence on church attendance in Western Europe is available only after 1970.) The evidence on declining religious engagement is summarized in Figure 4.

The evidence I have reviewed so far on mass participation in elections, political parties, unions, and churches represents the principal

Figure 10-4: Church Attendance Falls in Europe and America

social institutions for three primary spheres of community life—politics, work, and faith. For tens of millions of citizens in these established democracies, churches, unions, and political parties once represented a primary source of identity, social support, political leverage, community involvement, and friendship—in short, a primary reservoir of social capital. The universal decline of engagement in these institutions is a striking fact about the dynamics of social capital in advanced democracies.

In each case the trends outside the United States are parallel to trends in that country, though U.S. trends generally began two decades earlier. That twenty-year lag is possibly related to the fact that the major underlying causal factors that have been linked to the decline of social capital in the American case—commercial television, two-career families, and urban sprawl—also arrived later in the other countries of the OECD. In other words, the evidence just summarized is consistent with an interpretation that the general decline in social capital in the United States over the last third of the twentieth century is not unique; rather, its onset has simply been delayed in other advanced democracies.

On the other hand, case studies in this volume make clear that social capital dynamics do not follow a single global metronome. An experienced American politician once famously observed, "All politics is local," and similarly, students of comparative politics and society know that all good analyses are ultimately local in the sense that they must be grounded in the unique characteristics of specific societies. The chapters in this book abundantly confirm that truth.

Yet we also seek some common patterns in our understanding of the dynamics of social capital in contemporary democracies. The sphere of such comparative inquiry is a battleground on which genuine insights that speak both to local contexts and to broader theoretical concerns are hard won. In this concluding section, I seek to sketch some tentative generalizations suggested by our work—plausible hypotheses, but not yet confirmed truth.

At the most general level, our investigation has found no general and simultaneous decline in social capital throughout the industrial/postindustrial world over the last generation. No single global chronometer marks stages in the dynamics of social capital. In virtually all our countries 1945 was a moment of great significance—and thus a reasonable starting for our various investigations—but 1945 did not mean the same thing in Germany or Japan or Australia as in the United States or France or Spain. The 1930s witnessed disruption of social capital in many countries, but the meaning of the 1930s in Spain was quite different from that of the same period in Germany or Britain. Thus, when the curtain rises on our various histories, the national dramas are at quite different points.

National history clearly matters to dynamics. Thus, the starting point for our studies of European civil society is visibly different from that for the study of American society. Widening our geographic focus to encompass Australia and Japan only strengthens this point. The simple, pluralistic model of civil society as a multitude of overlapping interest groups has historically been more accurate of America than of Europe, where political society was traditionally organized into larger, more coherent, more encapsulated, largely class-based units of a corporatist sort and where the state has traditionally played a more visible role in social organization. Certain trends, such as expansion of the educated middle class, a rising culture of individualism, and the diffusion of mass electronic entertainment, may be common to all our countries. However, prior institutional and associational patterns in each inevitably condition possibilities for later change. Swedish civil society, with its legacies of national and class solidarities, is not likely to change in the same way as the more pluralistic American civil society or French civil society with its more *etatiste* tradition, and the three are not likely to end up in precisely the same place.[26]

Socioeconomic modernization plays some role in triggering changes in patterns of social capital, as Skocpol describes for America in the nineteenth century and Pérez-Díaz for Spain in the mid-twentieth century. Industrialization destroyed some forms of social capital (for example, villages) and created opportunities for new forms (for example, labor unions). An analogous process may well be under way now as the telecommunications and information revolutions sweep our countries, but we are still too close to the process to perceive it clearly.

However, at least as important as such economic factors are large-scale political factors, such as state structures and wars, both international and civil. The Nazi and Communist regimes in Germany coerced solidarity, and thereby discredited voluntary association and induced amoral familism. Democratization in Japan and Germany, in large part imposed from abroad, encouraged more engaged citizenry and the development of social capital. In Spain democratization and social capital (of the civic or bridging sort) appear to have co-evolved. Thus, broad-scale, exogenous regime changes have powerful effects on social capital. Our studies also reveal the impact of wars on contemporary patterns of social capital. Theda Skocpol and I have separately emphasized the sweeping effect of major wars on the evolution of civil society in America.[27] Wars (at least wars that are won) foster and reinforce national solidarity and often create generationally defined civic habits. Moreover, states at war often intervene in their domestic social arrangements in ways that have enduring consequences for social capital. In short, social capital is conditioned by political developments as much as the reverse.

Looking more directly at developments in our countries in recent decades, we can discern certain common patterns. As we have seen, waning participation in elections, political parties, unions, and churches seems to be virtually universal. These common patterns are especially important because of certain features of the declining institutions. These forms of social capital were especially important for empowering less educated, less affluent portions of the population. They also embodied broader social purposes—liberating the working class, saving souls, or achieving programmatic changes in society—not merely in their mission statements, but also in the lives of individual activists. These organizations preached solidarity with others. Thus, their decline may be linked with declining social trust that appears even in countries such as Britain, where associational membership as such does not appear to have declined.

Those common declines, however, seem to be offset at least in part by increases in the relative importance of informal, fluid, personal forms of social connection, what Rothstein calls "solidaristic individualism" and what Wuthnow has called "loose connections." Involvement in sports and other leisure groups seems generally to be growing. Also, new social movements in most of our countries won increased public engagement in the 1960s, 1970s, and 1980s, although evidence on their continuing growth or stagnation in the 1990s is mixed at best. Necessarily, the statistical evidence for this growth in informal social connectedness is less firm, since such forms of involvement leave fewer traces in formal records (or surveys). It is perhaps notable that in the one case for which we have the most abundant time series evidence on informal social capital—the United States—that evidence does *not* appear to support the hypothesized growth.[28] However, it is striking that most of our authors report impressionistic evidence in this direction. Assuming that subsequent research confirms this pattern, it provides the strongest evidence against the simple thesis that citizens everywhere are increasingly "bowling alone."

On the other hand, most authors in this volume fear that the new individualistic forms of civic engagement may be less conducive to the pursuit of collective goals. The older forms that are now fading combined individual fun with collective purpose, and they were multi-stranded, as in Catholic unions or party sports leagues. The newer forms of social participation are narrower, less bridging, and less focused on collective or public-regarding purpose. An important hypothesis that emerges from our initial survey is that the newer forms may be more liberating but less solidaristic—representing a kind of privatization of social capital.

Mounting discontent with political institutions is another common, though not universal, feature of our countries.[29] Most, though not all, contributors to this volume believe that the role of citizen is coming to be defined more as spectator than as participant. Parties and unions in most of our countries have tended to become hired professional agents for citizens and workers, not solidaristic social movements. The privatization of social capital occurring in most of our countries may distinctively undermine traditional forms of political participation, and many Europeans worry about the spread of American-style electoralism (and what Kirchheimer called catchall parties) to their continent. One way of describing this trend is a transformation from a social-capital-intensive politics to a media-intensive, professionalized politics. One consequence may be a reduction in opportunities for direct citizen deliberation and face-to-face encounters among people who do not agree.

Another issue raised, but not answered, in this volume involves generational differences in social capital and civic engagement. For many years a common narrative of postindustrial society has had as its hero the youngest generation—children of affluence who pursue postmaterialist values oriented toward participation, liberation, and idealism. "Man does not live by bread alone, especially if he has plenty of bread" is the way this broad thesis has been summarized by Ronald Inglehart. Inglehart has advanced this broad interpretation of modern society with vigor and persuasion, and much research has provided supporting evidence. In our work, by contrast, we find some evidence of a very different generation gap—evidence of a younger cohort singularly uninterested in politics, distrustful both of politicians and of the generalized other, cynical about public affairs, and less inclined to participate in enduring social organizations. Evidence of such a generational shift is strongest in the United States and Britain, but there are some hints of a similar trend in Germany, Sweden, Japan, and elsewhere.[30]

The trends in various countries are surely not identical, in part because of prior national differences: The U.S. generation that came of age in the 1960s and 1970s is distinctively less engaged than its predecessors, as I have argued at length elsewhere, whereas Offe and Fuchs show that the German generation that came of age in the same period was distinctively more engaged than its elders. Other evidence has confirmed the obvious fact that whereas the World War II generation in the United States was distinctively civic, their chronological counterparts in Germany, having experienced a very different pattern of socialization during the 1930s and 1940s, were distinctively uncivic.[31] Reflection on the U.S. case has suggested that commercial televised entertainment has played an important role in this trend, and the effects of the much more recent commercialization of television in Europe may turn out to be similar. However, the appearance of similar trends in Europe adds other potential explanations for generational change, as well, including the massive problems of youth unemployment and the consequent delay of delayed insertion into the workforce and adult life. As Pérez-Díaz points out, the family can provide an important cushion against the economic hardship associated with youthful unemployment, but the family is not a full substitute for a job.

Recent debates about trends in civil society have often featured the view that the growth of the welfare state has diminished social capital, as public policy has crowded out private action.[32] Contributors to this volume acknowledge instances in which this thesis has force; for example, in the United States there is some evidence that public provision has marginally reduced private philanthropy.[33] For the most part, however, the evidence in this volume appears, if anything, to support the opposite view: that the welfare state has helped sustain social capital rather than eroding it. For example, among the nations treated here, the United States (where much evidence favors the thesis of declining social capital) has nearly the smallest welfare state, whereas Sweden (where evidence most strongly disconfirms the thesis of declining social capital) has the largest welfare state. Other authors report evidence from Japan, France, and Britain, as well as the United States and Sweden, that social provision by government has had positive, not merely negative, effects on social capital.

The welfare state and other policies can encourage solidarity, both symbolically and practically. Public policies, such as British social provision or U.S. tax policy, can be designed specifically to encourage voluntary organizations. Skocpol argues that the U.S. state both created opportunity structures and directly encouraged social capital formation (e.g., the Farm Bureau, 4-H clubs for rural youth). The G.I. Bill, which provided free university education for American military veterans after World War II, provided a powerful boost to social capital in that generation, both by increasing rates of higher education and thus social participation among the sons of the lower middle and working classes and by reinforcing a norm of reciprocity. Recent research has shown that the beneficiaries of this government program, in effect, "returned the favor" by becoming more active in civic affairs in their later lives.[34] Crowding in (government reinforcement of social capital) can be as important as crowding out.

Most empirical research on social capital thus far has focused primarily on the quantity of social ties, but the social distribution of social capital is at least as problematic as trends in the overall quantity. At any given level of social participation (say, 30 percent of the population attending public meetings), the social distribution of that participation could be quite different. The 30 percent who attend meetings could be drawn more or less proportionately from different income, racial, and educational categories, in which case we would describe the distribution as egalitarian. Or the 30 percent who attend meetings could be drawn entirely from the more privileged social strata, rich, well-educated, and white, so that rates of participation would be quite different at different levels of the local social hierarchy. In some communities, the bank president, the bank teller, and the bank janitor all turn out for community activities, but in other communities only the president does.

Social capital is generally distributed unequally—more trusting, more joining, more voting, and so on among the better-off segments of society. Citizens who lack access to financial and human capital also lack access to social capital. (Japan may be an exception.) Social capital is accumulated most among those who need it least. Social capital may conceivably be even less equitably distributed than financial and human capital.

A recent unpublished survey of social capital in forty American communities found that the problem of inequality in access to social capital is greatly exacerbated in socially heterogeneous communities. In ethnically diverse places such as Los Angeles, college graduates are five times more likely to be politically involved than their fellow residents who did not get past high school. In smaller, ethnically less diverse communities such as in New Hampshire, the comparable class gaps in political participation are almost nonexistent. In terms of civic activity, there is not much difference between a high-tech executive in Los Angeles and a high-tech executive in New Hampshire, but there is a very substantial difference between a laborer in Los Angeles and a laborer in New Hampshire. Perhaps not coincidentally, the distribution of income is also much more egalitarian in New Hampshire than in Los Angeles. Since this research is still incomplete, the origins of these sharp differences in the social distribution of social capital are still somewhat obscure. However, it appears that ethnic heterogeneity and high rates of immigration are part of the story. If so, then the rapid increase in ethnic immigration in most OECD countries in recent decades may pose important challenges to both the quantity and the social distribution of social capital in all our countries.

Traditionally, many organizing efforts by unions, parties, and churches aimed to redress imbalances in the social distribution of social capital, but it is just those organizations that have most uniformly declined in recent decades. Several authors in this volume report disproportionate declines in forms of social capital that favored the less privileged and that bridged social and economic cleavages. Groups that organized the working classes—unions, parties, churches, and traditional women's organizations—have faded. The newer groups—sports groups, environmental groups, new social movements—appeal disproportionately to the younger, college-educated middle class. Skocpol argues that older associations, such as fraternal and veterans' groups, were more class-bridging than the functionally specific lobbying groups that replaced them. In short, there is reason to fear that inequalities in the distribution of social capital are being exacerbated both by trends within the associational field and by broader demographic trends.

Growing inequality in the distribution of social capital remains for now a hypothesis, not a confirmed generalization, but what might explain growing class gaps in social capital? First, as older solidarities fade, education and the civic skills and cultural capital that it fosters may have become relatively more important determinants of social participation. If, as a number of our authors believe, social capital that extends into the working class has been particularly disadvantaged by recent developments, that may be especially bad for equality. The apparent increase in class bias in social capital may be related to growth in income inequality noted in many advanced countries, as well as to growing ethnic fragmentation. Concern about inequalities, especially growing inequalities, in the social capital domain is perhaps the most important common thread throughout the national studies in this volume. Both for researchers and for activists, understanding the social distribution of social capital must be moved higher on our list of priorities. In that normative domain, as well as in the domain of social scientific research, the authors in this volume hope to contribute to setting the evolving social capital agenda.

NOTES

Introduction

1 See Susan J. Pharr and Robert D. Putnam, eds., *Disaffected Democracies: What's Troubling the Trilateral Countries?* (Princeton: Princeton University Press, 2000).

2 See Robert D. Putnam, *Bowling Alone: Collapse and Revival of American Community* (New York: Simon and Schuster, 2000).

3 L. J. Hanifan, *The Community Center* (Boston: Silver, Burdett, 1920), 9–10.

4 L. J. Hanifan, "The Rural School Community Center," *Annals of the American Academy of Political and Social Science* 67 (1916): 130–38, quotation at 130. For biographical information, see John W. Kirk, *Progressive West Virginians: 1923* (Wheeling, WV: Wheeling Intelligencer, 1923), 107. Ever the practical reformer, Hanifan was self-conscious about using the term *capital* to encourage hard-nosed businessmen and economists to recognize the productive importance of social assets. Having introduced the idea of social capital, he observed, "That there is a great lack of such social capital in some rural districts need not be retold in this chapter. The important question at this time is: How can these conditions be improved? The story which follows is an account of the way a West Virginia rural community in a single year actually developed social capital and then used this capital in the improvement of its recreational, intellectual, moral, and economic conditions." His essay, which included a list of practical exercises for community-based activists, was originally prepared in 1913 for West Virginia schoolteachers as "a handbook for community meetings at rural schoolhouses," and it was subsequently incorporated in Hanifan, *The Community Center*. We are grateful to Brad Clarke for first spotting this usage of the term "social capital" and to Anne Lee for tracking down Hanifan's biographical materials.

5 John R. Seeley, Alexander R. Sim, and Elizabeth W. Loosley, *Crestwood Heights: A Study of the Culture of Suburban Life* (New York: Basic Books, 1956), quotation at 296; Jane Jacobs, *The Death and Life of Great American Cities* (New York: Random House, 1961); Glenn Loury, "A Dynamic Theory of Racial Income Differences," in P. A. Wallace and A. LeMund, eds., *Women, Minorities, and Employment Discrimination* (Lexington, MA: Lexington Books, 1977), 153–88; Pierre Bourdieu, "Forms of Capital," in John

G. Richardson, ed., *Handbook of Theory and Research for the Sociology of Education* (New York: Greenwood Press, 1983), 241–58; Ekkehart Schlicht, "Cognitive Dissonance in Economics," in *Normengeleitetes Verhalten in den Sozialwissenschaften* (Berlin: Duncker and Humblot, 1984), 61–81; James S. Coleman, "Social Capital in the Creation of Human Capital," *American Journal of Sociology* 94 (1988): S95–S120; and James S. Coleman, *Foundations of Social Theory* (Cambridge: Harvard University Press, 1990). Except for a brief acknowledgment by Coleman of Loury's work, we can find no evidence that any of these theorists was aware of any of the preceding usages. For a comprehensive overview of the conceptual history of social capital, see Michael Woolcock, "Social Capital and Economic Development: Toward a Theoretical Synthesis and Policy Framework," *Theory and Society* 27 (1998): 151–208.

6 Ian Winter, "Major Themes and Debates in the Social Capital Literature: The Australian Connection," in Ian Winter, ed., *Social Capital and Public Policy in Australia* (Melbourne: Australian Institute of Family Studies, 2000), 17.

7 Anita Blanchard and Tom Horan, "Virtual Communities and Social Capital," *Social Science Computer Review* 17 (1998): 293–307; Anthony Bebbington and Thomas Perreault, "Social Capital, Development, and Access to Resources in Highland Ecuador," *Economic Geography* 75 (1999): 395–418; Marjorie K. McIntosh, "The Diversity of Social Capital in English Communities, 1300–1640 (with a Glance at Modern Nigeria)," *Journal of Interdisciplinary History* 29 (1999): 459–90; Deepa Narayan and Lant Pritchett, "Cents and Sociability: Household Income and Social Capital in Rural Tanzania," *Journal of Economic Development and Cultural Change* 47 (1999): 871–97; John Helliwell and Robert D. Putnam, "Economic Growth and Social Capital in Italy," *Eastern Economic Journal* 21 (1995): 295–307; Robert D. Putnam (with Robert Leonardi and Raffaella Nanetti), *Making Democracy Work: Civic Traditions in Modern Italy* (Princeton: Princeton University Press,199); Elinor Ostrom, *Governing the Commons: The Evolution of Institutions for Collective Action* (New York: Cambridge University Press, 1990); R. J. Sampson and W. B. Groves, "Community Structure and Crime: Testing Social-Disorganization Theory," *American Journal of Sociology* 94 (1989): 774–802; Robert J. Sampson, Stephen W. Raudenbush, and Felton Earls, "Crime: A Multilevel Study of Collective Efficacy," *Science* 277 (1997): 918–24; James S. House, Karl R. Landis, and Debra Umberson, "Social Relationships and Health," *Science* 241 (1988): 540–45; Lisa F. Berkman, "The Role of Social Relations in Health Promotion," *Psychosomatic Medicine* 57 (1995): 245–54; Teresa E. Seeman, "Social Ties and Health: The Benefits of Social Integration," *Annals of Epidemiology* 6 (1996): 442–51; and more generally, Partha Dasgupta and Ismail Serageldin, eds., *Social Capital: A Multifaceted Perspective* (Washington, DC: World Bank, 2000).

8 Michael Woolcock and Deepa Narayan, "Social Capital: Implications for Development Theory, Research, and Policy," *The World Bank Observer* 15 (2000): 225–49, quotation at p. 226.

9 Hanifan, *Community Center*.

10 The logic linking social capital and collective action is itself a topic of intense current scholarly activity. See, for example, Jacint Jordana, "Collective Action Theory and the Analysis of Social Capital," in Jan W. van Deth, Marco Maraffi, Kenneth Newton, and Paul F. Whiteley, eds., *Social Capital and European Democracy* (New York: Routledge, 1999); and Elinor Ostrom and T. K. Ahn, "A Social Science Perspective on Social Capital: Social Capital and Collective Action," report prepared for the Enquete Commission of the German Bundestag, 2001.

11 Michael Argyle, *The Psychology of Happiness* (London: Methuen, 1987); Ed Diener, "Subjective Well-Being," *Psychological Bulletin* 95 (1984): 542–75; Ed Diener, "Assessing Subjective Well-Being," *Social Indicators Research* 31 (1994): 103–57; David G. Myers and Ed Diener, "Who Is Happy?" *Psychological Science* 6 (1995): 10–19; Ruut Veenhoven, "Developments in Satisfaction-Research," *Social Indicators Research* 37 (1996): 1–46, and works cited there.

12 Jeffrey M. Berry, Kent E. Portney, and Ken Thomson, *The Rebirth of Urban Democracy* (Washington, DC: Brookings Institution Press, 1993).

13 Social psychologists have discovered that when a confederate "stranger" speaks briefly in the hallway to an unwitting subject, the subject is quicker to provide help when she subsequently "overhears" the confederate having an apparent seizure than if there had been no previous contact. See Bibb Latané and John M. Darley, *The Unresponsive Bystander: Why Doesn't He Help?* (Englewood Cliffs, NJ: Prentice-Hall, 1970), 107–9.

14 Nan Lin, Mary W. Woelfel, and Stephen C. Light, "The Buffering Effect of Social Support Subsequent to an Important Life Event," *Journal of Health and Social Behavior* 26 (1985): 247–63; Jeanne S. Hurlbert, Valerie A. Haines, and John J. Beggs, "Core Networks and Tie Activation: What Kinds of Routine Networks Allocate Resources in Nonroutine Situations," *American Sociological Review* 65 (2000): 598–618.

15 Ashutosh Varshney, *Ethnic Conflict and Civic Life: Hindus and Muslims in India* (New Haven: Yale University Press, 2001).

16 Barry Wellman, "The Community Question Re-Evaluated," in Michael Peter Smith, ed., *Power, Community, and the City* (New Brunswick, NJ: Transaction, 1988), 81–107, quotation at 82–83.

17 Pamela Paxton, "Is Social Capital Declining in the United States? A Multiple Indictor Assessment," *American Journal of Sociology* 105 (1999): 88–127, quotation at 88.

18 See Alexis de Tocqueville, *Democracy in America*, vol. 2, chapter IV.

19 Francis Fukuyama, *The Great Disruption: Human Nature and the Reconstitution of Social Order* (New York: Free Press, 1999).

1   Great Britain

This study benefited greatly from the skillful assistance that Maurits van der Veen provided with the data analysis. I am also grateful to Anne Wren, Virginie Guiraudon, Alvin Tillery, and Bonnie Meguid for help with the data collection, to Justin Davis Smith for sharing his library and wide knowledge with me, and to Tom Cusak, Dieter Fuchs, David Halpern, Joel Krieger, Ken Newton, Richard Rose, Rosemary C.R. Taylor, Perri 6, and the other contributors to this volume for helpful discussions about social capital. A somewhat different version of this chapter appeared in the *British Journal of Political Science* (July 1998).

1   Robert D. Putnam, "Bowling Alone: America's Declining Social Capital," *Journal of Democracy* 6 (1995): 65–78, and "Tuning In, Tuning Out: The Strange Disappearance of Social Capital in America," *PS: Political Science and Politics* 28 (1995): 664–83. For a view that significantly nuances this finding, however, see the chapter by Robert Wuthnow in this volume.

2   I focus in this chapter on social capital as defined by Putnam in "Bowling Alone," "Tuning In, Tuning Out," and *Making Democracy Work* (Princeton: Princeton University Press, 1993), and in James Coleman, *Foundations of Social Theory* (Cambridge: Harvard University Press, 1990), ch. 12. Note, however, that the term can be used to refer to other features of social organization not examined here. Cf. Peter A. Hall, "The Political Economy of Europe in an Era of Interdependence," in Herbert Kitschelt et al., eds., *Continuity and Change in Contemporary Capitalism* (New York: Cambridge University Press, 1999), and Pierre Bourdieu, "The Forms of Capital," in John G. Richardson, ed., *Handbook of Theory and Research for the Sociology of Education* (New York: Greenwood Press, 1983). Defined in these terms, social trust can be distinguished from generalized trust in institutions and from forms of trust that are transaction-specific and likely to be affected by the institutional arrangements governing those transactions. Cf. Piotr Sztompka, "Trust and Emerging Democracy," *International Sociology* 11, 1 (1996): 37–62; and Richard Rose, "Social Capital: Definition, Measures, Implications," paper presented to a workshop of the World Bank, 1996.

3   Frank Prochaska, *The Voluntary Impulse* (London: Faber, 1988), 86.

4   George Macaulay Trevelyan, *History of England* (London: Longman, Green, 1898), 616–17; cf. Derek Fraser, *The Evolution of the British Welfare State* (London: Macmillan, 1973), and David Owen, *English Philanthropy 1660–1960* (Oxford: Oxford University Press, 1964).

5   Gabriel A. Almond and Sidney Verba, *The Civic Culture: Political Attitudes and Democracy in Five Nations* (Princeton: Princeton University Press, 1963); Mancur Olson, *The Rise and Decline of Nations* (New Haven: Yale University Press, 1982).

6   Coleman, *Foundations of Social Theory;* Putnam, *Making Democracy Work.*

7   Figures 1-1 and 1-2 aggregate data for fifty-one separate organizations,

many of them organized in a confederal structure with local branches. Data primarily from *Social Trends* (London: HMSO), various issues.

8 Membership in the National Trust has been excluded from these figures since it is the least likely of the environmental associations to involve collective interaction among its members, but its membership, too, has increased by equivalent amounts.

9 National Council for Voluntary Organisations, *The Voluntary Agencies Directory* (London: National Council for Voluntary Organisations, 1996). Cf. National Council for Voluntary Organisations, *The NEST Directory of Environmental Networks* (London: National Council for Voluntary Organisations, 1993).

10 S. Hatch, *Outside the State* (London: Croom Helm, 1980); B. Knight, *Voluntary Work* (London: Home Office, 1993).

11 Martin Knapp and S. Saxon-Harrold, "The British Voluntary Sector," Discussion Paper 645, Personal Social Services Unit, University of Kent, Canterbury, 1989.

12 Jeremy Kendall and Martin Knapp, "A Loose and Baggy Monster: Boundaries, Definitions and Typologies," in Justin Davis Smith et al., eds., *An Introduction to the Voluntary Sector* (London: Routledge, 1995).

13 As in Putnam, "Tuning In, Tuning Out," the cells in Table 1-1 report responses to a question asking for the number of different types of associations to which the respondent belongs. For details about the samples and questions in the four surveys used in this research, see Almond and Verba, *The Civic Culture;* Alan Marsh, *Protest and Political Consciousness* (London: Sage, 1977); Samuel Barnes and Max Kaase, eds., *Political Action: Mass Participation in Five Western Democracies* (Beverly Hills: Sage, 1979); and Ronald Inglehart, *Culture Shift in Advanced Industrial Society* (Princeton: Princeton University Press, 1990).

14 In 1959, the percent of respondents belonging to one type of association was 31 and to two or more 17. The corresponding figures for 1973 are 29 and 25; for 1981, 31 and 21; and for 1990, 25 and 27. It is possible that the increase shown here for 1973 may be an artifact of the survey instrument, which presented respondents with an especially long list of potential kinds of associations.

15 When the 1959 results are recalculated using the distribution of educational attainment present in 1990, the average number of associational memberships for the sample as a whole is .94, still lower than the 1.12 reported in 1990. Because the list of types of associations presented to respondents varies somewhat from year to year, however, one must be cautious about attributing significance to small differences in the averages.

16 Geraint Parry et al., *Political Participation and Democracy in Britain* (Cambridge: Cambridge University Press 1992), 90; Perri 6 and J. Fieldgrass, *Snapshots of the Voluntary Sector* (London: National Council for Voluntary Organisations, 1992).

17 Jeff Bishop and Paul Hoggett, *Organizing Around Enthusiasms: Patterns of Mutual Aid in Leisure* (London: Comedia Publishing Group, 1986); Knight, *Voluntary Work*. It should be noted that this study excluded trade unions, sports clubs, and professional and church organizations. Cf. Katherine Gaskin and Justin David Smith, *A New Civic Europe? A Study of the Extent and Role of Volunteering* (London: Volunteer Centre, 1995); Justin Davis Smith, "What We Know About Volunteering: Information from the Surveys," in Rodney Hedley and Justin Davis Smith, eds., *Volunteering and Society* (London: National Council for Voluntary Organisations, 1992); Mark Abrams et al., *Values and Social Change in Britain* (London: Macmillan, 1985); Hatch, *Outside the State;* Julia Field and Barry Hedges, *A National Survey of Volunteering* (London: Social and Community Planning Research, 1987); Wolfenden Committee, *The Future of Voluntary Organisations* (London: Croom Helm, 1978).

18 Charities Aid Foundation, *Dimensions of the Voluntary Sector* (London: Charities Aid Foundation, 1994).

19 Wolfenden Committee, *The Future of Voluntary Organisations*, 35.

20 Eileen Goddard, *Voluntary Work* (London: HMSO, 1994).

21 Gaskin and Davis Smith, *A New Civic Europe*, 29.

22 Goddard, *Voluntary Work*.

23 Wolfenden Committee, *The Future of Voluntary Organisations*, ch. 3.

24 The length of the average working year in Britain fell from 2,900 hours in 1906 to 2,440 hours in 1946, 2,340 hours in 1982, and 1,800 hours in 1988. *Demos Quarterly* 5 (1995).

25 Cf. Ferdynand Zweig, *The Worker in an Affluent Society* (London: Heinemann, 1961); John Goldthorpe et al., *The Affluent Worker: Political Attitudes and Behaviour* (Cambridge: Cambridge University Press, 1969), 107; Howard Newby et al., "From Class Structure to Class Action: British Working Class Politics in the 1980s," in B. Roberts et al., eds., *New Approaches to Economic Life* (Manchester: Manchester University Press, 1985); R. E. Pahl and C. D. Wallace, "Household Work Strategies in Economic Recession," in N. Redclift and E. Mingione, eds., *Beyond Employment* (Oxford: Blackwell, 1985); and R. E. Pahl and C. D. Wallace, "Neither Angels in Marble nor Rebels in Red: Privatization and Working-Class Consciousness," in David Rose, ed., *Social Stratification and Economic Change* (London: Hutchinson, 1988), 127–49. It should be noted, however, that an increasing proportion of nonworking time has been devoted to child care among all segments of the population. See Jonathan Gershuny and Sally Jones, "The Changing Work/Leisure Balance in Britain, 1961–1984," in John Horne et al., eds., *Sport Leisure and Social Relations* (London: Routledge and Kegan Paul, 1985), 9–50.

26 T. Carter and J. S. Downham, *The Communication of Ideas: A Study of Contemporary Influences on Urban Life* (London: Chatto and Windus, 1954), 96.

27 George H. Gallup, ed., *The Gallup International Public Opinion Polls: Great Britain 1937–1975*, vol. 1 (New York: Random House, 1976), 415.

28 *Social Trends*, 1987.

29 It should be noted that pubs seem to play a more important role in informal sociability among the working class than among the middle class; in 1953, 34 percent of the working class visited the pub at least once a week, compared to 21 percent of the middle class (Carter and Downham, *The Communication of Ideas*). And one must bear in mind that the level of social interaction that takes place in pubs may have changed in ways not measured here. Cf. Mass-Observation, *The Pub and the People* (London: Hutchinson, 1987 [1943]), and Daniel E. Vasey, *The Pub and English Social Change* (New York: AMS Press, 1990).

30 Putnam, "Bowling Alone," "Tuning In, Tuning Out."

31 Life cycle effects reflect differences between the young and the old that disappear as people age. Generational effects are differences between age cohorts that do not change much over time. Period effects are those that affect all age cohorts but only for specific periods of time.

32 When the educational level of the populace is held constant, as in a similar diagram in Putnam, "Tuning In, Tuning Out," the participation rates of the interwar generation rise relative to those of the postwar generations, reinforcing this overall impression.

33 Putnam, "Tuning In, Tuning Out"; Parry et al., *Political Participation and Democracy in Britain*.

34 For data on this point, see Peter A. Hall, "Social Capital in Britain," *British Journal of Political Science* 29 (1998): 431.

35 The survey question used to assess social trust asks, in 1959, "Some people say that most people can be trusted. Others say you can't be too careful in your dealings with people. How do you feel about it?" and, in 1981 and 1990, "Generally speaking, would you say that most people can be trusted or that you can't be too careful in dealing with people?" Although this is a slim measure, it is widely used elsewhere to assess levels of social capital, and responses to it are closely correlated with the responses to related questions asking how much trust people have in the British, how much importance they attach to friends, and how lonely they feel as well as whether the respondent thinks people are inclined to help others, to be cooperative, to care about each other, and not to take advantage of each other—all measures for feelings of general social connectedness.

36 Cf. David O. Sears and Nicholas A. Valentino, "Politics Matters: Political Events as Catalysts for Preadult Socialization," *American Political Science Review* 91, 1 (1997): 45–65.

37 Cf. Putnam, "Tuning In, Tuning Out."

38 The share of social spending in gross domestic product rose from 14 percent in 1951 to 21 percent in 1980 (Peter Flora, ed., *Growth to Limits: The West European Welfare States Since World War II* [Berlin: de Gruyter,

1986]). The percentage of women in the labor force rose from 33 percent in 1951 and 35 percent in 1971 to 44 percent in 1994 (Department of Employment, *Labour Statistics* [London: HMSO, 1995]). The proportion of families headed by a single parent rose from 8 percent in 1971 to 23 percent in 1994, and the proportion of people living alone rose from 9 percent in 1973 to 15 percent in 1994 (Central Statistical Office, *Living in Britain* [London: HMSO, 1994]). The number of divorces granted rose from 30,500 in 1951 to 110,700 in 1971 and 165,018 in 1993 (Central Statistical Office, *Annual Abstract of Statistics* [London: HMSO, 1979, 1996]).

39 Putnam, "Tuning In, Tuning Out." Cf. Pippa Norris, "Does Television Erode Social Capital? A Reply to Putnam," *PS: Political Science and Politics* 29, 3 (1996): 474–80.

40 Nicholas Abercrombie and Alan Warde, *Contemporary British Society* (Oxford: Polity, 1994), 421.

41 Carter and Downham, *The Communication of Ideas*; Zweig, *The Worker in an Affluent Society*, 116–17, 208–9.

42 Cf. Gershuny and Jones, "The Changing Work/Leisure Balance"; Gaskin and Davis Smith, *A New Civic Europe?*

43 Parry et al., *Political Participation and Democracy in Britain*, ch. 4; Sidney Verba, Kay Schlotzman, and Henry Brady, *Voice and Equality: Civic Volunteerism in American Politics* (Cambridge: Harvard University Press, 1995); Putnam, "Tuning In, Tuning Out"; Davis Smith, "What We Know About Volunteering," 76.

44 See A. H. Halsey, *British Social Trends Since 1900* (London: Macmillan, 1988), chs. 6 and 7.

45 As one analyst famously observed, in the early 1960s, a working-class youth was more likely to spend time in a mental institution than to attend university in Britain (R. D. Laing, *The Politics of Experience* [London: Penguin, 1965]).

46 The figures derived from these samples mirror the aggregate figures quite closely. For instance, the number of full-time students in postsecondary degree programs in 1985 (600,000) was five times higher than it had been in 1955 (Michael Ball et al., *The Transformation of Britain* [London: Fontana, 1989], 293).

47 It should be noted that, while increasing the absolute numbers of those from the working class who secure secondary or postsecondary education, these changes have not eliminated class inequalities in access to higher education. Cf. A. H. Halsey et al., *Origins and Destinations* (Oxford: Clarendon Press, 1980).

48 This figure is calculated by comparing the actual average number of associational memberships for the sample drawn in 1959 with the level it displays when the distribution of educational attainment of the 1990 sample is substituted for the relevant marginals in the 1959 data. Except where

noted, in this section community involvement is measured by average number of associational memberships.

49 This is to say that in 1959, the average number of associational memberships reported by respondents with some postsecondary education was 76 percent higher than the number reported by those with a secondary education. The corresponding figure in 1990 was 110 percent. See Table 1-1.

50 Table 1-1 shows that most of the increase in women's associational memberships had occurred by 1973, that is, before rates of female labor force participation rose appreciably; and Table 1-2 indicates that the participation rates for and time spent on civic duties and other activities that contribute to social capital are roughly the same among women who are employed and not employed. Both of these observations suggest that although higher rates of female labor force participation have not diminished the level of social capital, neither have they substantially increased it.

51 Anthony Heath et al., *Understanding Political Change: The British Voter, 1964–1987* (Oxford: Pergamon, 1991); Geoffrey Marshall et al., *Social Class in Modern Britain* (London: Hutchinson, 1988); R. Pahl, *Divisions of Labour* (Oxford: Blackwell, 1984); Martin Bulmer, ed., *Working Class Images of Society* (London: Routledge and Kegan Paul, 1975); Samuel Beer, *Modern British Politics* (London: Faber, 1968).

52 John H. Goldthorpe, *Social Mobility and Class Structure in Modern Britain*, 1st ed. (Oxford: Clarendon Press, 1980); Samuel Beer, *Britain Against Itself* (New York: Norton, 1982); Joel Krieger, *British Politics in the Global Age* (Oxford: Polity, 1999).

53 When education is controlled, movement from the working class to the middle class increases the average number of associations to which a person belongs by about 50 percent, and movement from the lowest class level to the highest increases the number of such memberships by almost 150 percent.

54 John H. Goldthorpe, *Social Mobility and Class Structure in Modern Britain*, 2nd ed. (Oxford: Clarendon Press, 1987).

55 Davis Smith, "What We Know About Volunteering," 76; Peter Lynn and Justin Davis Smith, *The 1991 National Survey of Voluntary Activity in the UK* (London: The Volunteer Centre, 1992).

56 Goldthorpe, *Social Mobility and Class Structure*, 1st ed., ch. 7.

57 Ann Oakley and Lynda Rajan, "Social Class and Social Support: The Same or Different?" *Sociology* 25, 1 (1991): 31–59; Martin Bulmer, *Neighbours: The Work of Philip Abrams* (Cambridge: Cambridge University Press, 1986); Goldthorpe, *Social Mobility and Class Structure*, 2nd ed., ch. 7; Graham Allan, "Class Variation in Friendship Patterns," *British Journal of Sociology* 41 (1990): 389–92; M. Stacey et al., *Power, Persistence and Change* (London: Routledge and Kegan Paul, 1975); Goldthorpe et al., *The Affluent Worker in the Class Structure* (Cambridge: Cambridge University Press, 1969).

58 Ian Procter, "The Privatisation of Working Class Life: A Dissenting View,"

British Journal of Sociology 41, 2 (1990): 157–80; Pahl and Wallace, "Neither Angels in Marble nor Rebels in Red."

59 Geoffrey Evans, "The Decline of Class Divisions in Britain? Class and Ideological Preferences in the 1960s and 1980s," *British Journal of Sociology* 44, 3 (1993): 449–71; Heath et al., *Understanding Political Change.*

60 Goldthorpe, *Social Mobility and Class Structure,* 1st ed., 194, 204, and *passim.*

61 For an argument suggesting that government action may be important to social capital in other countries as well, see Sidney Tarrow, "Making Social Science Work Across Space and Time: A Critical Reflection on Robert Putnam's *Making Democracy Work,*" *American Political Science Review* 90, 2 (1996): 389–97.

62 R. H. S. Crossman, "The Role of the Volunteer in the Modern Social Services," in A. H. Halsey, ed., *Traditions in Social Policy* (Oxford: Blackwell, 1976); Maria Brenton, *The Voluntary Sector in British Social Services* (London: Longman, 1985), 20–21.

63 Brenton, *The Voluntary Sector,* 17.

64 Justin Davis Smith, "The Voluntary Tradition: Philanthropy and Self-Help in Britain, 1500–1945," in Davis Smith et al., eds., *An Introduction to the Voluntary Sector,* 25.

65 Elizabeth Macadam, *The New Philanthropy* (London: Allen and Unwin, 1934).

66 Brenton, *The Voluntary Sector,* 18.

67 Asa Briggs and A. Macartney, *Toynbee Hall: The First Hundred Years* (London: Routledge and Kegan Paul, 1984), 35–36; Davis-Smith, "The Voluntary Tradition," 28; William Beveridge, *Voluntary Action: A Report on Methods of Social Advance* (London: Allen and Unwin, 1948).

68 Brenton, *The Voluntary Sector,* 26.

69 Owen, *English Philanthropy,* 597.

70 Davis-Smith, "The Voluntary Tradition," 1; Brenton, *The Voluntary Sector.*

71 Brenton, *The Voluntary Sector,* 38–45; Nicholas Deakin, "The Perils of Partnership: The Voluntary Sector and the State, 1945–1992," in Davis Smith et al., eds., *An Introduction to the Voluntary Sector.*

72 Hedley and Davis Smith, eds., *Volunteering and Society;* Brian D. Jacobs, "Charities and Community Development in Britain," in Alan Ware, ed., *Charities and Government* (Manchester: Manchester University Press, 1989), 82–112; Knapp and Saxon-Harrold, "The British Voluntary Sector"; Ralph Kramer, "Change and Continuity in British Voluntary Organisations, 1976–1988," *Voluntas* 1, 2 (1992): 33–60.

73 R. Pinker, "Social Policy and Social Care: Division of Responsibility," in A. Yoder et al., eds., *Support Networks in a Caring Community* (Dordrecht: Martinus Nijhoff, 1985), 106; Kramer, "Change and Continuity," 38; Margaret Bolton et al., *Shifting the Balance: The Changing Face of Local Authority Funding* (London: National Council for Voluntary Organisations, 1994), 2.

74 D. Leat et al., *A Price Worth Paying? A Study of the Effects of Governmental Grant Aid to Voluntary Organisations* (London: Policy Studies Institute, 1986); Hatch, *Outside the State.*

75 Cf. Beer, *Britain Against Itself;* Peter Riddell, *The Thatcher Decade* (London: Martin Robertson, 1990).

76 Bruce Wood, "Urbanisation and Local Government," in A. H. Halsey, ed., *British Social Trends Since 1900* (London: Macmillan, 1988), 322–56.

77 Exit polls indicate that 57 percent of voters age 18 to 29 supported Labour, compared to 44 percent of the overall electorate (*The Sunday Times,* May 14, 1997, 16).

78 For recent suggestive analyses, see Claus Offe, "How Can We Trust Our Fellow Citizens?" in Mark Warren, ed., *Democracy and Trust* (New York: Cambridge University Press, 1999), 42–87; Eric Uslaner, "Democracy and Social Capital," in Warren, *Democracy and Trust,* 121–50; and Perri 6 et al., *Handle with Care: Public Trust in Personal Information Handling by Major Organizations* (London: Demos, 1998).

79 These relationships appear in statistically significant chi-square coefficients and in probit analyses that control for age, level of education, and social class.

80 See also Offe, "How Can We Trust Our Fellow Citizens?"

81 Mark Abrams and Richard Rose, *Must Labour Lose?* (Harmondsworth: Penguin, 1960); David Butler and Richard Rose, *The British General Election of 1959* (London: Macmillan, 1960).

82 *Gallup Political Index,* No. 249 (May 1981), Tables 2 and 7; David Sanders, "Why the Conservative Part Won—Again," in Anthony King et al., *Britain at the Polls 1992* (Chatham, NJ: Chatham House, 1993), 178.

83 Cf. W. Runciman, *Relative Deprivation and Social Justice* (Harmondsworth: Penguin, 1966).

84 Although he may not agree with my formulation, I am grateful to Richard Rose for insisting that I consider this dimension of the problem.

85 A huge literature develops such themes. For some important examples, see Eric Nordlinger, *The Working Class Tories* (London: MacGibbon and Kee, 1967); David Lockwood, *The Blackcoated Worker* (London: Allen and Unwin, 1958); Samuel H. Beer, *British Politics in the Collectivist Age* (London: Faber, 1969); and Runciman, *Relative Deprivation and Social Justice.*

86 See Beer, *Britain Against Itself.*

87 See Bo Saarlvik and Ivor Crewe, *Decade of Dealignment* (Cambridge: Cambridge University Press, 1983); James Alt, "Dealignment and the Dynamics of Partisanship in Britain," in Russell J. Dalton, Steven Flanagan, and Paul Beck, eds., *Electoral Change in Advanced Industrial Democracies* (Princeton: Princeton University Press, 1984); and Pippa Norris, *Electoral Change Since 1945* (Oxford: Blackwell, 1997).

88 Cf. John Goldthorpe et al., *The Affluent Worker in the Class Structure* (Cambridge: Cambridge University Press, 1969).

89 The indicators employed here (and reported in Table 1-6) were chosen from a longer list of possibilities according to the following criteria: All are acts that (1) an ordinary individual might himself have the opportunity to do, (2) could reasonably be expected to cause material but not bodily harm to others, at least indirectly, and (3) do not involve sexual behavior or the commission of a serious felony. As such, they bear on relatively normal behaviors in which the individual faces a conflict between self-interest and the interest of others, approximating what Harding and colleagues describe as moral judgments about self-interest. Note that this relationship between these indicators and social trust remains strong when a range of controls, including age, are applied. Cf. S. Harding et al., *Contrasting Values in Western Europe* (Basingstoke: Macmillan, 1986).

90 Cf. Sears and Valentino, "Politics Matters"; Stephen E. Bennett, "Why Young Americans Hate Politics and What We Should Do About It," *PS: Political Science and Politics* (1997): 47–53; Helen Wilkinson and Geoff Mulgan, *Freedom's Children: Work, Relationships and Politics for 18–34-Year-Olds in Britain Today* (London: Demos, 1995).

91 David Halpern, "Changes in Moral Concepts and Values: Can Values Explain Crime?" paper presented to the Causes of Crime Symposium, 1996.

92 Cf. Inglehart, *Culture Shift in Advanced Industrial Society,* and his many other works.

93 Of course, there is also some evidence that postmaterialist values have not been as prominent in Britain as in some other nations. Cf. Marsh, *Protest and Political Consciousness.*

94 Cf. Putnam, *Making Democracy Work.*

95 See the chapter by Claus Offe and Susanne Fuchs for this volume.

96 Ivor Crewe, Anthony Fox, and Neil Day, *The British Electorate, 1963–92* (Cambridge: Cambridge University Press, 1995), 122; David Butler and Gareth Butler, *British Political Facts, 1900–1994* (London: Macmillan, 1994), 518.

97 Peter Brierly, "Religion," in A. H. Halsey, ed., *British Social Trends Since 1900* (London: Macmillan, 1988), ch. 13.

98 Butler and Butler, *British Political Facts,* 370; Goldthorpe et al., *The Affluent Worker in the Class Structure,* chs. 5 and 6.

99 Putnam, "Bowling Alone," "Tuning In, Tuning Out."

100 Richard Topf, "Political Change and Political Culture in Britain, 1959–87," in John R. Gibbons, ed., *Contemporary Political Culture* (London: Sage, 1989), 88.

101 Geraint Parry and George Moyser, "A Map of Political Participation in Britain," *Government and Opposition* 25, 2 (1990): 147–69.

102 Max Kaase and Kenneth Newton, *Beliefs in Government* (Oxford: Oxford University Press, 1995), 47.

103 Crewe, Fox, and Day, *The British Electorate,* 153.

104 Controlling for social class, the relationship is statistically significant (p < .05) between associational membership and the importance attached to politics, interest in politics, frequency of discussion of politics, and political activism beyond voting.

105 Albert Mabileau et al., *Local Participation in Britain and France* (Cambridge: Cambridge University Press, 1989), 211; David Gerard, "Values and Voluntary Work," in Mark Abrams, et al., eds., *Values and Social Change in Britain* (London: Macmillan, 1985), 216; cf. Parry et al., *Political Participation and Democracy in Britain.*

106 The percentage of respondents in 1981 and 1990 expressing "a great deal" or "quite a lot" of confidence (as opposed to "not very much" or "none at all") was 41 for Parliament, 42 for the civil service, and 55 for the legal system. Cf. William L. Miller et al., *Political Culture in Contemporary Britain* (Oxford: Clarendon Press, 1996), 47–51.

107 The percentages agreeing with these statements are 70, 66, and 57, respectively, in 1986, and 67, 67, and 60 in 1974. Cf. Anthony Heath and Richard Topf, "Educational Expansion and Political Change in Britain, 1964–1983," *European Journal of Political Research* 14 (1987): 554; Topf, "Political Change and Political Culture in Britain, 1959–87," 56; Marsh, *Protest and Political Consciousness.*

108 Cf. Marsh, *Protest and Political Consciousness;* Dennis Kavanagh, "Political Culture in Great Britain: The Decline of the Civic Culture," in Gabriel Almond and Sidney Verba, eds., *The Civic Culture Revisited* (Boston: Little, Brown, 1980); Anthony Heath and Richard Topf, "Political Culture," in Roger Jowell et al., eds., *British Social Attitudes: The 1987 Report* (London: Gower, 1987), 51–70; Topf, "Political Change and Political Culture in Britain."

109 Critics of Almond and Verba's relatively positive portrait of the British in *The Civic Culture* point out that 83 percent of respondents to their survey agreed that "all candidates sound good in their speeches but you can never tell what they will do after they are elected"; Heath and Topf, "Political Culture," 54.

110 Political trust is measured here by the amount of trust the respondents expressed in Parliament, the civil service, and the legal system.

111 For some indication that shifts in political trust may depress social trust, see the essay by Robert Wuthnow in this volume.

112 Cf. Kenneth Newton, "Social Capital and Democracy," *American Behavioral Scientist* 40 (1997): 571–86.

113 Almond and Verba in *The Civic Culture* argued some years ago that a certain level of political skepticism was healthy for democracy, although high levels of social and political distrust might discourage political engagement or encourage engagement with antisystem parties and organizations. Cf. Seymour Martin Lipset, *Political Man: The Social Bases of Politics,* 2nd ed. (Garden City, NY: Doubleday, 1981).

114 Bob Tyrell, "Time in Our Lives: Facts and Analysis on the 90s," *Demos Quarterly* 5 (1995): 24.

115 Moreover, the expansion of the "salariat," which propelled many from working-class origins into the middle class, was fueled heavily by the expansion of the public sector, something that is now at an end. Cf. Goldthorpe, *Social Mobility and Class Structure*, 1st ed., 1980.

116 Cf. Putnam, *Making Democracy Work*; Tarrow, "Making Social Science Work."

2   United States

I wish to thank Doug Mills and John Evans for technical advice in analyzing the quantitative data; the staff at the Gallup Organization, Independent Sector, and the Princeton Social Science Reference Center for making data sets available; Natalie Searl for assistance in the research; and a number of friends and colleagues for comments and suggestions, especially Claude Fischer, Michael Moody, Edward Queen, Brad Wilcox, Brian Steensland, Angela Tsay, Sara Wuthnow, the members of the Religion and Culture Workshop at Princeton, the members of the Civil Society Reading Group at Princeton, Robert Putnam, and the other members of the Bertelsmann project.

1 The popular view of social capital's decline in the United States has been articulated most forcefully and with impressive empirical evidence in Robert D. Putnam, *Bowling Alone: The Collapse and Revival of American Community* (New York: Simon and Schuster, 2000). The present chapter is deeply indebted to Putnam's work and is intended as a partial corrective to his arguments, rather than as a refutation.

2 Alexis de Tocqueville, *Democracy in America*, 2 vols. (New York: Vintage, 1945 [1835]); on mediating groups, Peter L. Berger and Richard Neuhaus, *To Empower People* (Washington, DC: American Enterprise Institute, 1977); and on social capital, James S. Coleman, *Foundations of Social Theory* (Cambridge, MA: Harvard University Press, 1990), ch. 12. Several readers of an earlier draft of this chapter expressed reservations about the concept of social capital, particularly about how to identify the norms and networks that count as social capital and those that do not, as well as questions about its theoretical grounding in rational-choice perspectives on human behavior. These are reservations that I share. However, the present chapter can also be read largely without reference to these concerns by situating it in the context of recent concerns about civic involvement.

3 John Leo, "When Stability Was All the Rage," *U.S. News and World Report*, October 30, 1995, 27.

4 Roger Mahony, "Faithful for Life: A Moral Reflection," *Los Angeles Times*, September 28, 1995, B9.

5 David McCabe, "Review of *Democracy on Trial*," *Commonweal*, February 10, 1995, 18. Elshtain herself writes of American democracy as being "pre-

carious" and characterizes the present as a "culture of mistrust"; Jean Bethke Elshtain, *Democracy on Trial* (New York: Basic Books, 1995), ch. 1.

6 Alan Ehrenhalt, "No Conservatives Need Apply," *New York Times*, November 19, 1995, 15.

7 Rolling Stone Survey (September 1987), conducted by the Gallup Organization; results available on Public Opinion Online through Lexis-Nexis.

8 Robert Wuthnow, *God and Mammon in America* (New York: Free Press, 1994), 173.

9 Here and throughout this chapter, I draw extensively on Robert Putnam, "Bowling Alone: Democracy in America at the End of the Twentieth Century," Nobel Symposium on Democracy's Victory and Crisis, Uppsala, Sweden, August 1994 (March 1995 draft), a somewhat different version of which was published as "Bowling Alone: America's Declining Social Capital," *Journal of Democracy* 6 (1995), 65–78; and Robert Putnam, "Tuning In, Tuning Out: The Strange Disappearance of Social Capital in America," 1995 Ithiel de Sola Pool Lecture, American Political Science Association (September 1995); both papers were graciously supplied to me by Mr. Putnam.

10 This point has been made about families in Arlene Skolnick, *Embattled Paradise: The American Family in an Age of Uncertainty* (New York: Basic Books, 1991), and in Stephanie Coontz, *The Way We Never Were: American Families and the Nostalgia Trap* (New York: Basic Books, 1992); and about religion in Andrew M. Greeley, *Unsecular Man: The Persistence of Religion* (New York: Schocken, 1985).

11 Robert Putnam, *Making Democracy Work: Civic Traditions in Modern Italy* (Princeton: Princeton University Press, 1993), in my view at least points to the persistence of differences in levels of social capital among regions of Italy over approximately eight centuries.

12 Sidney Verba, Kay Lehman Scholzman, and Henry E. Brady, *Voice and Equality: Civic Voluntarism in American Politics* (Cambridge, MA: Harvard University Press, 1995), 80.

13 Putnam, "Bowling Alone," Figure 14; see also data from the World Values Surveys reported in other chapters in this volume.

14 Although the United States ranks high on various measures of civic involvement, an important conclusion to be drawn from the chapters in this volume is that the United States should not be thought of, as some interpretations of Tocqueville have tended to do, as being unique; despite different political traditions and structures, other advanced industrial societies, especially those in Western Europe, have also managed to sustain relatively high levels of voluntary associational activity (see especially the chapter by Bo Rothstein).

15 For example, an argument could be made that self-interested individualism is a norm that people in many communities share and that this norm helps the community solve its collective problems (by encouraging people

to take responsibility for themselves and to respect the privacy of their neighbors), yet social capital theorists seem reluctant to say that a norm of this kind is what they have in mind; similarly, loose networks that connect people over large distances and through infrequent contact seem not to receive as much credit among social capital theorists as tight networks that form enduring and diffuse bonds of attachment. For further discussion, see my book *Loose Connections: Civic Involvement in America's Fragmented Communities* (Cambridge, MA: Harvard University Press, 1998).

16 Jane Jacobs, *The Death and Life of Great American Cities* (New York: Random House, 1961); Glenn Loury, "A Dynamic Theory of Racial Income Differences," in Phyllis A. Wallace and Annette LaMond, eds., *Women, Minorities, and Employment Discrimination* (Lexington, MA: Lexington Books, 1977), ch. 8; and Glenn Loury, "Why Should We Care about Group Inequality?" *Social Philosophy and Policy* 5 (1987): 843–67.

17 Coleman, *Foundations of Social Theory*, 300–21.

18 Berger and Neuhaus, *To Empower People*; Elshtain, *Democracy on Trial*, 5, includes most of these ideas in her definition of civil society: "the many forms of community and association that dot the landscape of a democratic culture, from families to churches to neighborhood groups to trade unions to self-help movements to volunteer assistance to the needy." In the United States, social capital has generally been conceptualized to include participation in formal associations, rather than focusing as much on social networks, thus distinguishing its usage somewhat from that of Pierre Bourdieu, "The Forms of Capital," in John G. Richardson, ed., *Handbook of Theory and Research for the Sociology of Education* (New York: Greenwood, 1986), 241–58; but Bourdieu's emphasis on the stratification of capital is important in the present context.

19 I do not mean to suggest, however, that social capital, as operationally defined here, is sufficient for understanding civil society or democracy; for example, see Adam B. Seligman, *The Idea of Civil Society* (New York: Free Press, 1992); Jean L. Cohen and Andrew Arato, *Civil Society and Political Theory* (Cambridge, MA: MIT Press, 1992); and John A. Hall, "Genealogies of Civility," paper presented at the annual meeting of the American Sociological Association, New York, 1996.

20 Michael Moody, Department of Sociology, Princeton University, is examining the symbolic and practical aspects of representation "at the table" in his dissertation on California water management issues. The idea that organizational structures come into being for symbolic reasons is best developed in John W. Meyer and Brian Rowan, "Institutionalized Organizations: Formal Structure and Myth and Ceremony," *American Journal of Sociology* 83 (1977): 340–63; see also Paul J. DiMaggio and Walter W. Powell, "Introduction," in Walter W. Power and Paul J. DiMaggio, eds., *The New Institutionalism in Organizational Analysis* (Chicago: University of Chicago Press, 1991), 1–39.

21 Adam B. Seligman, *The Problem of Trust* (Princeton: Princeton University Press, 1997); I am grateful to Adam Seligman for making a draft of his manuscript available to me prior to publication and for several instructive conversations about trust. Francis Fukuyama, *Trust: The Social Virtues and the Creation of Prosperity* (New York: Free Press, 1995), is also helpful, but in my view fails to distinguish adequately among kinds of trust and between trust and other aspects of social capital.

22 This idea is similar to that of "strong evaluation," as developed in Charles Taylor, "What Is Human Agency?" in Charles Taylor, *Human Agency and Language* (Cambridge: Cambridge University Press, 1985).

23 For qualitative interview evidence on the complex ways in which Americans construct the meanings of trust, see Robert Wuthnow, "The Role of Trust in Civic Renewal," in Robert K. Fullinwider, ed., *Civil Society, Democracy, and Civic Renewal* (New York: Rowman & Littlefield, 1999), 209–30; on the social correlates of trust, see Eric M. Uslaner, "Faith, Hope, and Charity: Social Capital, Trust, and Collective Action," Department of Government and Politics, University of Maryland, 1996, and Andrew Kohut, *Trust and Citizen Engagement in Metropolitan Philadelphia: A Case Study* (Washington, DC: The Pew Research Center for the People and the Press, 1997).

24 See especially Sidney Verba and Norman Nie, *Participation in America: Political Democracy and Social Equality* (New York: Harper and Row, 1972); and Verba, Scholzman, and Brady, *Voice and Equality*, ch. 3.

25 Brian O'Connell, *America's Voluntary Spirit* (New York: Foundation Center, 1983); Jon Van Til, *Mapping the Third Sector: Voluntarism in a Changing Social Economy* (New York: Foundation Center, 1986); and Paul G. Schervish, Virginia A. Hodgkinson, and Margaret Gates, eds., *Care and Community in Modern Society* (San Francisco: Jossey-Bass, 1995).

26 U.S. Bureau of the Census, *Statistical Abstract of the United States: 1992*, 115th ed. (Washington, DC: U.S. Government Printing Office, 1995), 793. The number of associations was higher in 1994 than in 1980 in all sixteen categories listed; however, some decline in social capital may be indicated by the fact that the numbers in half the categories were slightly lower in 1994 than in 1990.

27 Barry T. Hirsch and John T. Addison, *The Economic Analysis of Unions* (Boston: Allen and Unwin, 1986), Table 3.1, 46–47, as reported in Putnam, "Bowling Alone," Figure 7.

28 Putnam, "Bowling Alone," Figure 8.

29 Ibid., Figure 9.

30 See the chapter in this volume by Theda Skocpol for further information on larger associations.

31 For an overview of these kinds of data, see Frank R. Baumgartner and Jack L. Walker, "Survey Research and Membership in Voluntary Associations," *American Journal of Political Science* 32 (1988): 908–28.

32 The General Social Survey was not conducted in 1995, and the 1996, 1998, and 2000 surveys did not include the questions about associational memberships. According to Tom Smith at NORC, interviewers are instructed to read the list of organizations to respondents; however, it is not known whether interviewers actually follow this instruction, nor is it known what the effect of increasingly lengthy interview schedules may be on the likelihood of interviewers following this instruction (these observations are based on discussions to which I have been party as a member of the General Social Survey Board of Overseers).

33 I compared memberships in 1974 and 1991 in order to capture the somewhat greater declines that are evident over that period than when the 1994 data are used. Following Putnam, I used logistic regression analysis to obtain a measure of the direction and significance of the time difference on membership in each kind of association. Models were examined for year as the sole independent variable and for the effects of year with levels of education controlled (year was recoded as a dummy variable with 1974 = 0 and 1991 = 1; education was a recode of the "degree" variable, with 1 = college graduate or higher, 2 = high school diploma, and 3 = less than high school diploma. Both sets of models are of interest for different reasons. The models with year alone are the best descriptive estimate of whether decline actually occurred in each kind of membership; the models with education controlled are, as Putnam has argued, of interest if one wishes to know whether social capital has declined for other reasons, taking into account the fact that rising levels of education have contributed some elevation in association memberships). The results, Exp (B), for year with education controlled and for year only, respectively, for each kind of group were as follows: church-affiliated groups, .658* and .694*; sports groups, .869 and 1.007; professional/academic, .955 and 1.308*; labor unions, .587* and .557*; service clubs, .837 and .998; school service groups, .642* and .776*; fraternal groups, .569* and .633*; youth groups, .740* and .816; hobby or garden clubs, .996 and 1.118; literary, art, discussion, .793 and .993; veterans' groups, .771 and .774; school frat/sororities, .761 and 1.019; political clubs, .686 and .836; farm organizations, .700 and .759; and nationality groups, 1.135 and 1.308 (note that coefficients less than one indicate decline; * means significant at or beyond the .05 level of probability using the Wald statistic).

34 Putnam, "Bowling Alone," Figure 10, and Putnam, "Tuning In," Figure 1, show association memberships with education controlled.

35 Statistical analysis of these changes are presented in Albert Bergesen and Mark Warr, "A Crisis in the Moral Order: The Effects of Watergate upon Confidence in Social Institutions," in Robert Wuthnow, ed., *The Religious Dimension: New Directions in Quantitative Research* (New York: Academic Press, 1979), 277–97.

36 I report results from the two survey organizations separately, even though

the question is the same, because of the discrepancies in results in the same year (especially in 1976 and in 1992); these discrepancies may be the result of different frames of reference established by previous questions in the surveys. See also Putnam, "Bowling Alone," Figure 12; and Eric Uslaner, *The Decline of Comity in Congress* (Ann Arbor: University of Michigan Press, 1993), 79.

37 These results are all available on Public Opinion Online from the Roper Center. All of the surveys were conducted by the National Opinion Research Center at the University of Chicago; the 1948 and 1952 surveys were election polls, the 1964 survey was Charles Glock's Anti-Semitism in America study, and the 1983 question was included in the General Social Survey. Further analysis of the NORC surveys is presented in Tom W. Smith, "Factors Relating to Misanthropy in Contemporary American Society," GSS Topical Report No. 29, National Opinion Research Center, Chicago, 1996.

38 These results are from my Civic Involvement Survey, a national study of 1,528 respondents conducted for me by the Gallup Organization in early 1997; for further detail see Wuthnow, *Loose Connections*.

39 For a discussion of religion in the nonprofit sector and of this sector's changing relationships to government and the for-profit sector, see Walter Powell, ed., *The Nonprofit Sector: A Research Handbook* (New Haven: Yale University Press, 1986), and Robert Wuthnow, ed., *Between States and Markets: The Voluntary Sector in Comparative Perspective* (Princeton: Princeton University Press, 1991).

40 From the *Gallup Opinion Index* (May 1973); *The Gallup Poll* (August 6, 1973); and *Newsweek* (June 14, 1982); all results are on Public Opinion Online.

41 This is a Guttman scale constructed by combining items about "how much of the time you think you can trust the government in Washington to do what is right," "government is pretty much run by a few big interests looking out for themselves," "people in the government waste a lot of money we pay in taxes," "quite a few of [the people running the government] don't seem to know what they are doing," and "quite a few of the people running the government are crooked."

42 See also Stephen C. Craig, *The Malevolent Leaders: Popular Discontent in America* (Boulder, CO: Westview Press, 1993).

43 Giving money to a political party or candidate is often included in National Election Survey indexes of political participation but is excluded here because the questions have been asked differently in each of the surveys.

44 Putnam, "Bowling Alone," Figure 2; and Steven J. Rosenstone and John Mark Hansen, *Mobilization, Participation, and Democracy in America* (New York: Macmillan, 1993). This conclusion is also based on my own analysis of these data. Robert Putnam supplied me with raw data that he

and Henry Brady have obtained from the Roper Center. A somewhat different picture of these data is presented in Karyln H. Bowman, "Democracy in America," *Public Opinion and Demographic Report*, March-April 1994, 83.

45 Verba, Scholzman, and Brady, *Voice and Equality*, 72. Being a member of a political club was the item that declined; their data also show a decline in voter turnout.

46 To my knowledge, this question was last asked in a Gallup survey in 1991; however, the same question was posed in a 1995 survey conducted by Princeton Survey Research Associates, and 54 percent responded affirmatively, up eight percentage points from a comparable PSRA survey in 1991.

47 Social capital is also like cultural capital in this view. On the production of cultural capital, see Richard A. Peterson, ed., *The Production of Culture* (Beverly Hills, CA.: Sage, 1976); and Robert Wuthnow, *Producing the Sacred* (Urbana: University of Illinois Press, 1994).

48 Paul E. Johnson, *A Shopkeeper's Millennium: Society and Revivals in Rochester, New York, 1815–1837* (New York: Hill and Wang, 1978).

49 Emile Durkheim, *Professional Ethics and Civic Morals* (London: Routledge, 1957); William Kornhauser, *The Politics of Mass Society* (New York: Free Press, 1959); Robert Nisbet, *The Quest for Community* (New York: Oxford University Press, 1953).

50 Robert N. Bellah, Richard Madsen, William M. Sullivan, Ann Swidler, and Steven M. Tipton, *Habits of the Heart: Individualism and Commitment in American Life* (Berkeley: University of California Press, 1985).

51 Whether some internal shift in the composition of memberships that may account for this trend is present warrants consideration. Exploration of this possibility using a variety of techniques, however, failed to provide any definitive conclusions. For example, a factor analysis of the fifteen kinds of association memberships in 1974 and in 1991 showed no distinct change in overall correlations among the items or in factor structure. An item-by-item analysis of the likelihood of holding multiple memberships if a person held membership in particular kinds of associations also failed to produce clues (most members of any single kind of association were also members of at least one other kind, and these proportions dropped uniformly between 1974 and 1991). The measure of association memberships used in the analysis summarized in the text is a dichotomous variable that distinguishes people who belonged to any of the kinds of association shown in Table 2-1 from people who did not belong to any of these associations.

52 Putnam, "Tuning In." The analysis done by Putnam focuses on mean number of associations, rather than the more delimited measure used here.

53 The proportion of people in the surveys who worked fifty or more hours a week increased from 17 percent to 24 percent, substantiating the claim in

other research that people are putting in more hours on the job. For more evidence, see Juliet B. Schor, *The Overworked American: The Unexpected Decline of Leisure* (New York: Basic Books, 1991), and Robert Wuthnow, *Poor Richard's Principle: Restoring the American Dream through the Moral Dimension of Work, Business, and Money* (Princeton: Princeton University Press, 1996).

54 The youngest age category (age 18 to 24) is always difficult to interpret because a substantial proportion are in college and are generally missed in surveys if they are living in dormitories or other group residences.

55 Regional mobility/stability was a dummy variable created by comparing the question about region in which the respondent lived at age sixteen with the question about current region (including all eight regions); place of residence was the NORC size variable, which compares people living in large or medium-sized cities with those living in suburbs of each kind of city, those living in independently incorporated areas, and those living in small towns and rural areas. Those living in suburbs increased in the samples from 23 percent in 1974 to 32 percent in 1991; there was no change in the likelihood of regional mobility (26 percent and 25 percent in the two periods had switched regions).

56 Especially Michele Lamont, *Money, Morals, and Manners: The Culture of the French and the American Upper-Middle Class* (Chicago: University of Chicago Press, 1992); also Pierre Bourdieu, *Distinction: A Social Critique of the Judgment of Taste* (Cambridge, MA: Harvard University Press, 1984); and Helmut K. Anheier, Jurgen Gerhards, and Frank Romo, "Forms of Capital and Social Structure in Cultural Fields: Examining Bourdieu's Social Topography," *American Journal of Sociology* 100 (1995): 859–903.

57 Pamela A. Popielarz and J. Miller McPherson, "On the Edge or In Between: Niche Position, Niche Overlap, and the Duration of Voluntary Association Memberships," *American Journal of Sociology* 101 (1995): 698–720.

58 Lamont, *Money, Morals, and Manners,* presents qualitative evidence that upper-middle-class men in the United States perceive volunteerism and voluntary association activity to be an indication of moral worth and a marker of social status; anecdotes about racial and religious exclusion in associations are, of course, abundant.

59 Respondents received scores of 3 for each of the lowest-privilege groups in terms of income, father's education, education, and number of children; scores of 2 for being in the middle group on each of these variables; scores of 1 for being in the high-privilege groups; and a score of 3 if they were nonwhite and 0 if they were white. Scores of 12 to 15 were considered high, those of 10 or 11 were coded as medium high, those of 7, 8, or 9 were classified as medium low, and those of 4 to 6 were categorized as low.

60 The variables used in a multivariate logistic analysis were a dummy variable for year (1991 = 1), for sex (male = 1), a three-category age variable (age 18 to 29, age 30 to 49, and age 50 and over), the Marginalization Index,

and an interaction term between this index and year. Interpretation of the coefficients is that association membership was lower in 1991 than in 1974, higher among men than among women, higher among older people, and lower among marginalized people. The effect of year is significant when sex and age are included and when marginalization is added; when the interaction term is added, the year effect becomes insignificant. The coefficient for the interaction term means that marginalization dampens association membership significantly more in 1991 than in 1974. The logistic coefficients were are follows: for Model A, year, .714***; male, 1.356***; age, 1.240***; for Model B, year, .677***; male, 1.309**; age, 1.356***; marginality, .737***; for Model C, year, .867; male, 1.307**; age, 1.356**; marginality, .805**; marginality * year, .834^; significance (Wald test): ^ < .09; * < .05; ** < .01; *** < .001; N = 2,483.

61 On other aspects of the worsening condition of the poor and of blacks, see Jennifer L. Hochschild, *Facing Up to the American Dream: Race, Class, and the Soul of the Nation* (Princeton: Princeton University Press, 1995), esp. ch. 10.

62 "Union Membership," *Forbes*, September 14, 1992, 302. Between 1955 and 1990, union membership in the private sector fell from 35 percent to 12 percent, whereas union membership in the public sector increased from 12 percent to 37 percent. On manufacturing and service, see Daniel Bell, *The Coming of Post-Industrial Society* (New York: Basic Books, 1976), 142; for more detailed analysis, see Hirsch and Addison, *The Economic Analysis of Unions*.

63 Because of smaller numbers of cases and less change, the gamma measure of association provides a simple test of the statistical strength of relationships reported in the text; the gamma for the year effect among those scoring high on the Marginalization Index is .304; those low on the index, .157.

64 The lack of an effect of the marginalization variables suggests that religious groups may be more egalitarian than nonreligious groups, a conclusion drawn by Verba, Scholzman, and Brady, *Voice and Equality*, 226.

65 The analysis of the variables summarized in the text (seventeen variables in all) was conducted by comparing the percentages in 1974 and in 1991 who were members of church-affiliated groups for each subcategory of each variable (e.g., Protestants and Catholics, or married people and divorced people) to see either if a particular subcategory declined more than others, or if it had been low at the start and then remained low but increased as a proportion of the total sample. No interesting differences were evident from this analysis, other than that the decline was somewhat larger among Protestants than among Catholics, which may be accounted for by the finding concerning fundamentalist background that is discussed in the text.

66 In the GSS, this is the FUND16 variable, which has been created by staff at NORC to separate denominations such as Southern Baptists and small

conservative sects from other denominations and, then at the liberal end, to distinguish Presbyterians and Episcopalians.

67 The logistic model with year, sex, and age showed a statistically significant coefficient for year, which became insignificant when a variable that multiplied FUND16 and YEAR was added to the model.

68 Dean Hoge, Donald Luidens, and Benton Johnson, *Vanishing Boundaries: The Religion of Mainline Protestant Baby Boomers* (Louisville: Westminster/John Knox, 1994); and Wade Clark Roof, *Generation of Seekers* (San Francisco: Harper San Francisco, 1993); also, from my own analysis of data on religious backgrounds.

69 When asked, "You said you were a member of a church affiliated group; is that group or organization the church (synagogue) itself, or some other group related to the church?" 52 percent said it was the church itself and 45 percent said it was a group related to the church. Verba, Scholzman, and Brady, *Voice and Equality*, 61, argue for considering church groups separately; see also David Horton Smith, "Voluntary Action and Voluntary Groups," *Annual Review of Sociology* 1 (1975): 249, and Aida K. Tomeh, "Formal Voluntary Organizations: Participation, Correlates, and Interrelationships," *Sociological Inquiry* 43 (1973): 96.

70 In the GSS, 36 percent attended religious services nearly every week or more often in both 1974 and 1991.

71 Michael Hout and Andrew M. Greeley, "The Center Doesn't Hold: Church Attendance in the United States, 1940–1984," *American Sociological Review* 52 (1987): 325–45.

72 Robert Wuthnow, *The Restructuring of American Religion* (Princeton: Princeton University Press, 1988).

73 I discuss trends in religion in greater detail in my book, *Christianity and Civil Society* (Philadelphia: Trinity Press International, 1997).

74 The trust in people question was not included in the 1974 General Social Survey; in the models based on the 1991 data, the effect of marginalization was about twice as strong, even when controlling for memberships, as the effect of memberships (without marginalization in the model).

75 The broader decline in trust of other people may also be a spillover effect from the public's growing distrust of government. Some evidence for this conclusion comes from logistic regression analysis of the 1968 and 1992 National Election Survey data: in the model with year, education, race, and age, year has a strong negative effect on trust (indicating that trust declined between 1968 and 1992); but in the model with these variables and including an interaction term involving year and trust in government, the effect of year becomes insignificant, while that of the interaction term is significant. In a more detailed analysis of the General Social Survey data, John Brehm and Wendy Rahn also suggest that interpersonal trust may be affected by institutional trust; see "Individual-Level Evidence for the Causes and Consequences of Social Capital," *American Journal of Political*

Science 41 (1997): 999–1024; see also Margaret Levi, "Social and Unsocial Capital: A Review Essay of Robert Putnam's *Making Democracy Work*," *Politics and Society* 24 (1996): 45–55.

76 For Americans age 25 to 44 with college educations, voter turnout among registered voters declined from 87 percent in 1964 to 79 percent in 1992, whereas it declined from 76 percent to 50 percent among those with high school educations, and from 60 percent to 27 percent among those without high school diplomas; see Bureau of the Census, "Voting and Registration in the Election of November . . . ," *Current Population Reports*, Series P-20, Nos. 143, 293, 322, 383, 440, 453, 466, and PPL-25. I am grateful to Robert Putnam for his summary of these reports.

77 Sidney Verba, Kay Lehman Schlozman, and Henry E. Brady, "The Big Tilt: Participatory Inequality in America," *American Prospect*, May-June 1997, 74–80; Peter F. Nardulli, Jon K. Dalager, and Donald E. Greco, "Voter Turnout in U.S. Presidential Elections: An Historical View and Some Speculation," *P.S.: Political Science and Politics* 29 (1996): 480–90; see also William Julius Wilson, *When Work Disappears: The World of the New Urban Poor* (New York: Knopf, 1996).

78 Virginia A. Hodgkinson and Murray Weitzman, *Giving and Volunteering, 1994* (Washington, DC: Independent Sector, 1994), Table 1.10, 41.

79 Ibid., Figures 1.20 and 1.21, 34.

80 Logistic regression analysis of the 1993 data (N = 1,509) shows that the Exp (B) coefficient for organization membership on volunteering is reduced from 4.77 to 3.89 when education level, race, and gender are controlled. Among persons with less than a high school diploma, only 16 percent belonged to a nonreligious organization, compared with 40 percent of high school graduates, 43 percent of those with some college, and 65 percent of college graduates; respective percentages for whites and blacks were 40 and 17.

81 See Theda Skocpol's chapter in this volume.

82 On benevolent societies, see Richard Lee Rogers, "A Testimony to the Whole World: Evangelicalism and Millennialism in the Northeastern United States, 1790–1850," Ph.D. dissertation, Department of Sociology, Princeton University, 1996; on settlement houses and land colonies, see Diane Winston, "Boozers, Brass Bands, and Hallelujah Lassies: A History of the Salvation Army," Ph.D. dissertation, Department of Religion, Princeton University, 1996; see also Robert Wiebe, *The Search for Order, 1877–1920* (New York: Hill and Wang, 1967), and Robert H. Bremner, *American Philanthropy*, 2nd ed. (Chicago: University of Chicago Press, 1960).

83 Roger Finke and Rodney Stark, *The Churching of America, 1776–1990: Winners and Losers in Our Religious Economy* (New Brunswick, NJ: Rutgers University Press, 1992); Robert C. Liebman, John Sutton, and Robert Wuthnow, "Exploring the Social Sources of Denominationalism: Schisms in American Protestant Denominations, 1890–1980," *American Sociological Review* 53 (1988): 343–52.

84 R. Stephen Warner, University of Illinois at Chicago, research in progress on new immigrant congregations.

85 *American at the Crossroads: A National Energy Strategy Poll* (Washington, DC: Alliance to Save Energy and Union of Concerned Scientists, 1990), a survey of 1,200 registered voters.

86 Ronald Inglehart, *Culture Shift in Advanced Industrial Society* (Princeton: Princeton University Press, 1990).

87 World Values Surveys, 1981, 1990; details are available on Public Opinion Online.

88 "Women's Voices," A National Study conducted for the MS Foundation for Women and the Center for Policy Alternatives by Greenberg-Lake Analysis Group (June 1992), from Public Opinion Online.

89 Putnam, "Bowling Alone," Figure 8.

90 Third PTA National Education Survey, June 1993; Public Opinion Online.

91 Putnam, "Bowling Alone," Figure 9.

92 Gallup Poll (March 7, 1960); Public Opinion Online (April 7, 1989), a national survey of 2,427 respondents conducted by the Interaction and Overseas Development Council.

93 Public Opinion Online (April 6, 1989).

94 Putnam, "Tuning In," Footnote 8.

95 Jack L. Walker, "The Origins and Maintenance of Interest Groups in America," *American Political Science Review* 77 (1983): 390–406; and Kay Lehman Schlozman and John T. Tierney, *Organized Interests and American Democracy* (New York: Harper and Row, 1986).

96 Wuthnow, *The Restructuring of American Religion*, 112.

97 Ibid., 140.

98 It can also be questioned whether or not people actually attend meetings or only hold memberships in the kinds of associations considered in Table 1; for a similar list, Verba, Scholzman, and Brady, *Voice and Equality*, 63, show that approximately 65 percent of members claim that they attend meetings; these figures range from 16 percent in veterans' organizations to 72 percent in literary or art groups.

99 Mary Beth Regan and Richard S. Dunham, "Gimme That Old-Time Marketing," *Business Week,* November 6, 1995, 76–78.

100 Paul DiMaggio, John Evans, and Bethany Bryson, "Have Americans' Social Attitudes Become More Polarized?" working paper, Department of Sociology, Princeton University, 1995; Robert Wuthnow, "The Restructuring of American Religion: Further Evidence," working paper, Department of Sociology, Princeton University, 1994; and on the decline of biblical literalism, Wuthnow, *Christianity and Civil Society*.

101 Robert Wuthnow, "The Political Rebirth of American Evangelicals," in Robert C. Liebman and Robert Wuthnow, eds., *The New Christian Right* (New York: Aldine, 1983), 167–85.

102 Kurt W. Back, *Beyond Words: The Story of Sensitivity Training and the Encounter Movement,* 2nd ed. (New Brunswick, NJ: Transaction Books, 1987).

103 Mary C. Dufour and Kathryn G. Ingle, "Twenty-five Years of Alcohol Epidemiology," *Alcohol Health and Research World* 19 (1995): 77–78; Bill Marvel, "Religion of Sobriety," *Dallas Morning News,* June 10, 1995, 1C.

104 Katy Butler, "Adult Children of Alcoholics," *San Francisco Chronicle,* February 20, 1990, D7; Sara Wuthnow, "Working the ACOA Program," in Robert Wuthnow, ed., *"I Come Away Stronger": How Small Groups Are Shaping American Religion* (Grand Rapids, MI: Eerdmans, 1994), 179–204.

105 "News Summary," *New York Times,* July 16, 1988, 1.

106 Robert Wuthnow, *Sharing the Journey* (New York: Free Press, 1994), ch. 3.

107 The 1982 data were collected in a survey of 1,483 respondents by the Gallup Organization asking, "Which, if any, of these are you involved in . . . Bible study groups?" The 1994 study was conducted among a sample of 3,800 respondents by Princeton Survey Research Associates for Times Mirror; it asked, "Please tell me which of the following activities, if any, you personally do. Do you . . . attend Bible studies or prayer group meetings?" Both questions are included in Public Opinion Online. The recent figure probably includes a somewhat broader response than the earlier survey; however, my research on small groups shows that upward of 90 percent of those who describe their groups as Bible studies also describe them as prayer groups.

108 Putnam, "Bowling Alone," Figure 9.

109 Public Relations Office, National Headquarters, Salvation Army.

110 Christopher Oleson, "Homesteading and Neighborhood Restoration Act," FDCH Congressional Hearings Summaries, May 25, 1995. As of 1995, Habitat for Humanity had local chapters in 1,148 cities and was said to be adding 8 to 15 new chapters each month.

111 F. M. Newmann and R. A. Rutter, "A Profile of High School Community Service Programs," *Educational Leadership,* December 1985, 65–71; Virginia A. Hodgkinson and Murray S. Weitzman, *Volunteering and Giving Among American Teenagers 12 to 17 Years of Age: Findings from a National Survey, 1992* (Washington, DC: Independent Sector, 1992), 71; see also National Center for Educational Statistics, "Community Service Performed by High School Seniors," *Education Policy Issues,* October 1995, NCES-94-743, which shows that 15 percent of high school seniors now report that they are required to perform community service. The Independent Sector report shows that the proportion of American teenagers doing any volunteer work during the year rose from 58 percent in 1989 to 61 percent in 1991.

112 For the full time series, see Putnam, "Bowling Alone," Figure 11.

113 The GSS data also show no change in the likelihood of spending social evenings with relatives: 89 percent did so at least once a year in both 1974 and 1991, and 73 and 72 percent did so respectively at least once a month.

114 See also Claude S. Fischer, *To Dwell Among Friends: Personal Networks in Town and City* (Chicago: University of Chicago Press, 1982).

115 Public Opinion Online, October 2, 1992.

116 Claude S. Fischer, *America Calling: A Social History of the Telephone to 1940* (Berkeley: University of California Press, 1992).

117 A Roper poll conducted in 1987; from Public Opinion Online.

118 Technology and Online Use Survey, Princeton Survey Research Associates, October 16, 1995; N = 3,603.

119 Ibid.

120 Putnam, "Tuning In."

121 The 1964 study was conducted by the National Opinion Research Center for Charles Glock's study Anti-Semitism in America, and the more recent surveys were conducted by the Gallup Organization; all are on Public Opinion Online. Several surveys conducted as part of the General Social Surveys during the 1970s show higher rates of television viewing, but this is probably because of differences in response categories. Nevertheless, the General Social Surveys also fail to indicate rising levels of television viewing, as evidenced by the fact that 34 percent watched four or more hours a day in 1974, compared with 32 percent in 1991.

122 Technology and Online Use Survey. The PC market has grown in recent years, of course; 35 percent of those who had a PC have had their PC less than two years.

123 Ibid. The study also showed that of all online users, 45 percent "communicate with other people through online forums, discussion lists, or chat groups," only 19 percent ever go online to play games, 44 percent do so to get information about hobbies, entertainment, and community activities, and 10 percent do so to engage in political discussions. In addition, of online users, 23 percent receive e-mail every day, 15 percent do so 3 to 5 days a week, 15 percent do so 1 or 2 days a week, and 12 percent do so every few weeks, 7 percent less often, and only 28 percent never do; 83 percent say they use e-mail to communicate with friends and relatives; of online e-mail users, 59 percent think they communicate more often with friends and relatives now than before they had e-mail; and of all online users, 23 percent say they've made an online friend or buddy that they've never met in person.

124 *A Measure of Commitment* (Washington, DC: Points of Light Foundation, 1995). Based on a national survey conducted in 1994, this brief report indicates that 85 percent of all volunteering is directed toward serious social problems, of which helping the elderly, children, and the disabled are the largest categories; 24 percent of respondents in the survey with high school educations or less were currently engaged in volunteer work directed toward serious social problems, compared with 57 percent of college graduates.

125 Cited in Putnam, "Bowling Alone."

126 Colleen M. McBride, Susan J. Curry, Allen Cheadle, Carolyn Anderman, Edward H. Wagner, and Bruce Psaty, "School-Level Application of a Social

Bonding Model to Adolescent Risk-Taking Behavior," *Journal of School Health* 65 (1995): 63–75.

127 My analysis of a 1991 national survey of teenagers; the survey is described in my book *Learning to Care: Elementary Kindness in an Age of Indifference* (New York: Oxford University Press, 1995).

128 In the 1991 General Social Survey, for example, the percentages of women with different numbers of memberships who had voted in the 1988 presidential election were, respectively, 49 percent among those with no memberships, 71 percent among those with one, 77 percent among those with two, 85 percent among those with three, and 80 percent among those with four or more; among men the comparable figures were 53, 65, 77, 80, and 86 percent.

129 For a review of these concerns, see James M. Pethokoukis, "Will Internet Change Politics?" *Investor's Business Daily,* November 15, 1995, A1.

130 Wuthnow, *Sharing the Journey,* ch. 11.

131 Self-report questions of this kind are not entirely satisfactory, but the relevant comparisons here are among people who were all in a small group of some kind and thus could respond similarly to the questions.

132 The typology places people in the Sunday school category if they said this label applied (on grounds that Sunday school classes are fairly distinct in tradition and style from all other groups); it then allocates residual group members, first into the Bible study category (on grounds that studying the Bible is generally a primary focus of any group that would elicit this label), and then into self-help groups, leaving the residual as special interest group members. This typology is discussed at length in my book *Sharing the Journey,* where further comparisons and validation are presented.

133 There are of course notable exceptions, especially among people for whom sponsorship of other members in an anonymous group constitutes volunteer work; for example, see one of the people featured in my book *Acts of Compassion.*

134 My analysis of the 1992 Small Groups Survey; the dropout rate among African Americans was 50 percent, compared to 37 percent among whites.

135 The 1993 Independent Sector Giving and Volunteering Survey; my analysis.

136 Verba, Scholzman, and Brady, *Voice and Equality,* 319.

137 This conclusion is similar to that of Verba, Scholzman, and Brady, *Voice and Equality,* 214, who write of "the distinct tilt of participatory input away from the disadvantaged."

3   United States

1 Arthur M. Schlesinger Sr., "Biography of a Nation of Joiners," *American Historical Review* 50 (1944): 1–25.

2 Alexis de Tocqueville, *Democracy in America,* ed. J. P. Mayer, trans. George Lawrence (Garden City, NY: Doubleday Anchor, 1969 [1835–40]), 513.

3 Paul Kleppner, *Who Voted? The Dynamics of Electoral Turnout, 1870–1980* (New York: Praeger, 1982).

4 John H. Aldrich, *Why Parties? The Origin and Transformation of Political Parties in America* (Chicago: University of Chicago Press, 1995), part 3.

5 Gabriel A. Almond and Sidney Verba, *The Civic Culture: Political Attitudes and Democracy in Five Nations* (Princeton: Princeton University Press, 1963), especially part II and chapter 11.

6 Ibid., 318–19.

7 Richard D. Brown, "The Emergence of Urban Society in Rural Massachusetts, 1760–1820," *Journal of American History* 61, 1 (1974): 29–51; Richard D. Brown, "The Emergence of Voluntary Associations in Massachusetts, 1760–1830," *Journal of Voluntary Action Research* 2, 2 (1973): 64–73.

8 Gerald Gamm and Robert D. Putnam, "Association-Building in America, 1840–1940," *Journal of Interdisciplinary History* 29, 4 (1999).

9 Gamm and Putnam claim that association building in modernizing America was mainly an urban phenomenon and did not occur to anything like a comparable degree in nonurban towns and village (with populations below 2,500). This claim is in tension with Richard Brown's empirical findings, and it fails to take into account that urban associations often recruited members from surrounding areas outside city limits. More important, Gamm and Putnam's claim is based on skewed and incomplete data. They count Masonic lodges and Episcopal churches per thousand population for their twenty-six cities versus the nation as a whole. But those groups were among the most elite and urban-centered of hundreds of cross-class associations. One would expect Masonic lodges and Episcopal churches to be unusually concentrated in cities. Had Gamm and Putnam looked at larger and more popular associations—such as Methodist churches and the Independent Order of Good Templars—the picture would have been very different, as I have discovered using Maine state directories that list associations in small cities versus towns and villages within counties.

10 Most of these associations became very large within one to a few decades of their founding, but some (such as the National Education Association and the National Rifle Association) did not cross the 1 percent mark until a century or more after their establishment.

11 See Theda Skocpol, Marshall Ganz, and Ziad Munson, "A Nation of Organizers: The Institutional Origins of Civic Voluntarism in the United States," *American Political Science Review* 94, 3 (2000): Tables 3 and 4.

12 Brown, "Emergence of Urban Society."

13 Ibid., 47.

14 Ibid., page 38.

15 Anne Firor Scott, *Natural Allies: Women's Associations in American History* (Urbana and Chicago: University of Illinois Press, 1991), chapter 1; and Carroll Smith-Rosenberg, *Disorderly Conduct: Visions of Gender in Victo-*

rian America (New York: Knopf, 1985), 120.

16 Holbrook's plan appears in *Annals of American Education* (Boston) 6 (1836): 474–76 and 7 (1837): 183–84. See also John A. Monroe, "The Lyceum in America Before the Civil War," *Delaware Notes: Bulletin of the University of Delaware* 37, 3 (1942): 65–75. During the 1830s Holbrook's organizational plan briefly took shape under the "national lyceum," but then the higher levels melted away, while local units continued to operate as sponsors of traveling lecturers into the post–Civil War period. See Carl Bode, *The American Lyceum: Town Meeting of the Mind* (Carbondale, IL: University of Illinois Press, 1968).

17 In this paragraph I am working with data presented in Brown, "Emergence of Urban Society," Table 1, 40–41.

18 Ibid., 31.

19 Ibid., 32.

20 Ibid., 43.

21 Ibid., 32.

22 Bode, *The American Lyceum*, section 2; David Mead, *Yankee Eloquence in the Middle West: The Ohio Lyceum, 1850–1870* (East Lansing: Michigan State College Press, 1951).

23 My characterization of the temperance movement and temperance societies draws from data collected for the Civic Engagement Project, and also from memos and unpublished papers by Bayliss Camp, graduate student in sociology, Harvard University.

24 Samuel W. Hodges, "Sons of Temperance—Historical Record of the Order," in *Centennial Temperance Volume: A Memorial of the International Temperance Conference Held in Philadelphia, June, 1876* (New York: National Temperance Society and Publications House, 1877), 572.

25 William W. Turnbull, *The Good Templars: A History of the Rise and Progress of the Independent Order of Good Templars* (n.p., 1901), 38.

26 Kathleen Smith Kutolowski, "Freemasonry and Community in the Early Republic: The Case for Antimasonic Anxieties," *American Quarterly* 34 (1982): 543–61; Lorman Ratner, *Antimasonry: The Crusade and the Party* (Englewood Cliffs, NJ: Prentice-Hall, 1969).

27 In this and all discussions of specific large groups, I draw upon Civic Engagement Project data. On the early Masons, see also Dorothy Ann Lipson, *Freemasonry in Federalist Connecticut, 1789–1835* (Princeton: Princeton University Press, 1977).

28 On the cross-class nature of American fraternalism, see the discussion and synthesis of data in Mary Ann Clawson, *Constructing Brotherhood: Class, Gender, and Fraternalism* (Princeton: Princeton University Press, 1989), chapter 3.

29 The process is recounted in Theodore A. Ross, *Odd Fellowship: Its History and Manual* (New York: M. W. Hazen, 1888), chapters 1–3.

30 Ibid., 36 and chapter 14.

31 Paschal Donaldson, *The Odd-Fellows' Text-Book*, 6th ed. (Philadelphia: Moss and Brother, 1852), 9. On page 14 Donaldson cites Alexis de Tocqueville in support of the value of a "moral" association such as the Odd Fellows—proving that Americans were entranced with the French man from a very early date.

32 Lynn Dumenil, *Freemasonry and American Culture, 1880–1930* (Princeton: Princeton University Press, 1984), 10–13; Clawson, *Constructing Brotherhood*, 129–33. Catholics were not barred from the Masons and Odd Fellows, but the Church strongly opposed their joining. Later in the nineteenth century, when southern and eastern European immigrants arrived, native-Protestant-centered fraternal associations became less welcoming to ethnic members and lodges.

33 Charles H. Lichtman, ed., *Official History of the Improved Order of Red Men*, rev. ed. (Boston, MA: Fraternity Publishing Co., 1901), 314–15.

34 John T. Ridge, *Erin's Sons in America: The Ancient Order of Hibernians* (New York: AOH Publications, 1986).

35 Albert C. Stevens, *The Cyclopaedia of Fraternities* (New York: Hamilton Printing and Publishing Company, 1899), 234–35, 282–84.

36 Ibid., 262.

37 William Alan Muraskin, *Middle-Class Blacks in a White Society: Prince Hall Freemasonry in America* (Berkeley: University of California Press, 1975).

38 Edward Nelson Palmer, "Negro Secret Societies," *Social Forces* 23, 2 (1944): 208. Palmer adds that the "three years following the end of the Civil War saw the inclusion of every southern state in the Negro Masonic ranks," after the slaves were freed.

39 Stevens, *Cyclopedia of Fraternities*, 236–37.

40 Charles S. Green III, "The Emergence and Growth of American National Voluntary Associations, 1790–1970," paper presented at the annual meeting of the Southern Sociological Society, Knoxville, March 1980.

41 Brown, "Emergence of Urban Society," 48, stresses this point.

42 Ibid., 43.

43 Roger Finke and Rodney Stark, *The Churching of America, 1776–1990* (New Brunswick, NJ: Rutgers University Press, 1992).

44 Donald G. Mathews, "The Second Great Awakening as an Organizing Process, 1780–1830: An Hypothesis," *American Quarterly* 21, 1 (1969): 23–43.

45 This is brilliantly argued and documented in Finke and Stark, *The Churching of America*.

46 Brown, "Emergence of Urban Society," 518.

47 Richard R. John, *Spreading the News: The American Postal System from Franklin to Morse* (Cambridge, MA: Harvard University Press, 1995), 31.

48 Ibid., 5.

49 Ibid., 3.

50 Ibid., chapters 6–7; Jed Dannenbaum, *Drink and Disorder: Temperance*

Reform from the Washingtonian Revival to the WCTU (Urbana: University of Illinois Press, 1984).

51 Robert H. Wiebe, *The Search for Order, 1877–1920* (New York: Hill and Wang, 1967).

52 The *Maine Register, State Year-Book and Legislative Manual* has been published annually in roughly the same format since 1870, by various Portland publishers. It includes data on statewide associations, and on local groups, too, between the 1870s and 1920s.

53 Jeffrey A. Charles, *Service Clubs in American Society: Rotary, Kiwanis, and Lions* (Urbana: University of Illinois Press, 1993).

54 Charles, *Service Clubs in American Society;* Clifford Putney, "Service Over Secrecy: How Lodge-Style Fraternalism Yielded Popularity to Men's Service Clubs," *Journal of Popular Culture* 27 (1993): 179–90.

55 Dumenil, *Freemasonry and American Culture,* discusses the movement of modern Masons from "ritual to service."

56 Gamm and Putnam, "Voluntary Associations in America."

57 Murray Hausknecht, *The Joiners* (New York: Bedminster Press, 1962), 18–19.

58 Masons met regularly while in the Civil War military units. In addition, R. W. Ralph J. Pollard, *Freemasonry in Maine, 1762–1945* (Portland, ME: Grand Lodge of Maine, 1945), 77–79, recounts a number of stories about Union military men from Maine who were aided by southern Masons while they were Confederate prisoners of war. "Numberless stories are told," he says, "of how the gentle touch of Masonry softened the rigors of war."

59 Ross, *Odd Fellowship,* 158–79.

60 This is based information about the founding locations for large membership groups on the Civic Engagement master list, and also on an analysis done by Cameron Sheldon for fraternal associations listed in Alvin J. Schmidt, *Fraternal Organizations,* Greenwood Encyclopedia of American Associations (Westport, CT: Greenwood Press, 1980). In this compilation, 330 out of 528 entries for U.S. fraternal organizations give founding locations.

61 Jno. van Valkenburg, *The Knights of Pythias Complete Manual and Text-Book,* rev. ed. (Canton, OH: Memento Publishing Co., 1886), xvi, 17, 381–84.

62 D. Sven Nordin, *Rich Harvest: A History of the Grange, 1867–1900* (Jackson: University of Mississippi Press, 1974), 4.

63 Charles Hurd, *The Compact History of the Red Cross* (New York: Hawthorne Books, 1959), chapters 3–4.

64 Ruth Bordin, *Woman and Temperance: The Quest for Power and Liberty, 1873–1900* (Philadelphia: Temple University Press, 1981).

65 For a clear-cut statement by a Right Worthy Grand Templar of the IOGT, see Turnbull, *The Good Templars,* 88.

66 Ruth Bordin, *Frances Willard: A Biography* (Chapel Hill: University of North Carolina Press, 1986), chapter 8.

67 Much of the fraternal upsurge Gamm and Putnam record from their city directories for 1890, 1900, and 1910 may be due to such short-lived insurance experiments. I suggest this based on preliminary analysis of data from Stevens, *The Cyclopaedia of Fraternities*, and Schmidt, *Fraternal Organizations*, as well as perusal of city directories. This raises questions about a method that treats the sheer proliferation of numbers of groups per capita as a gauge of civic vitality. Groups that persist and grow may well be more significant than lots of short-lived failures.

68 Seymour Martin Lipset and Earl Raab, *The Politics of Unreason: Right-Wing Extremism in America, 1790–1970* (New York: Harper and Row, 1970), 81–104.

69 This is based on the analysis of founding dates for various types of fraternals listed in Schmidt, *Fraternal Organizations*.

70 Stephen Thernstrom, ed., *Harvard Encyclopedia of American Ethnic Groups* (Cambridge, MA: Harvard University Press, 1980), 422–23 (in the essay "Germans").

71 Christopher J. Kaufman, *Faith and Fraternalism: The History of the Knights of Columbus, 1882–1982* (New York: Harper and Row, 1982), chapter 8.

72 These included the Improved Order of Red Men, the American Protective Association, the Junior Order of United American Mechanics, the German-American Alliance, and the second Ku Klux Klan.

73 For a bald version of this argument very much at odds with the evidence in this chapter, see Michael S. Joyce and William A. Schambra, "A New Civic Life," in Michael Novak, ed., *To Empower People: From State to Civil Society*, 2nd ed. (Washington, DC: AEI Press, 1996).

74 Stuart McConnell, *Glorious Contentment: The Grand Army of the Republic, 1865–1900* (Chapel Hill: University of North Carolina Press, 1992).

75 Nordin, *Rich Harvest*; John Mark Hansen, *Gaining Access: Congress and the Farm Lobby, 1919–1981* (Chicago: University of Chicago Press, 1991).

76 Theda Skocpol, *Protecting Soldiers and Mothers: The Political Origins of Social Policy in the United States* (Cambridge, MA: Belknap Press, 1992), part 3.

77 Henry J. Pratt, *The Gray Lobby* (Chicago: University of Chicago Press, 1976).

78 William Pencak, *For God and Country: The American Legion, 1919–1941* (Boston: Northeastern University Press, 1989); Richard Seelye Jones, *A History of the American Legion* (Indianapolis and New York: Bobbs-Merrill, 1946); Theda Skocpol, "The G.I. Bill and U.S. Social Policy, Past and Future," *Social Philosophy and Policy* 14, 2 (1997): 105–9.

79 Jeffrey M. Berry, *The Interest Group Society*, 3rd ed. (New York: Longman, 1997), Figure 2.4, page 27.

80 Frank R. Baumgartner and Beth L. Leech, *Basic Interests* (Princeton:

Princeton University Press, 1998), 103. I have updated these counts to 1999 to conclude that there was little net change in the 1990s.

81 Charles Morris, *The AARP* (New York: Times Books, 1996).

82 Berry, *The Interest Group Society,* chapter 2.

83 Debra C. Minkoff, *Organizing for Equality: The Evolution of Women's and Racial-Ethnic Organizations in America, 1955–1985* (New Brunswick, NJ: Rutgers University Press, 1995), chapter 3, especially Figures 3.1 and 3.2, page 62.

84 Jeffrey M. Berry, *Lobbying for the People: The Political Behavior of Public Interest Groups* (Princeton: Princeton University Press, 1977).

85 Berry, *The Interest Group Society,* 34–37.

86 Robert Cameron Mitchell, Angela G. Mertig, and Riley E. Dunlap, "Twenty Years of Environmental Mobilization: Trends Among National Environmental Organizations," in Riley E. Dunlap and Angela G. Mertig, eds., *American Environmentalism: The U.S. Environmental Movement, 1970–1990* (New York: Taylor and Francis, 1992), 11–88.

87 For example, according to Andrew S. McFarland, *Common Cause: Lobbying in the Public Interest* (Chatham, NJ: Chatham House Publishers, 1984), 8, from "the beginning, Common Cause's subscribers tended to be upper-middle-class whites; they were well educated, middle-aged, financially secure, and disproportionately from the Eastern Seaboard and Pacific Coast states."

88 Berry, *The Interest Group Society,* 19–29.

89 Ibid., 80–85; Jack L. Walker Jr., *Mobilizing Interest Groups in America: Patrons, Professions, and Social Movements* (Ann Arbor: University of Michigan Press, 1991); Michael T. Hayes, "The New Group Universe," in Allan J. Cigler and Burdett A. Loomis, eds., *Interest Group Politics,* 2nd ed. (Washington, DC: CQ Press, 1986), 133–45.

90 Data from Robert D. Putnam.

91 Steven Brint, *In an Age of Experts: The Changing Role of Experts in Professional Life* (Princeton: Princeton University Press, 1994).

92 Steven J. Rosenstone and John Mark Hansen, *Mobilization, Participation, and Democracy in America* (New York: Macmillan, 1993); Sidney Verba, Kay Lehman Schlozman, and Henry E. Brady, "The Big Tilt: Participatory Inequality in America," *The American Prospect* 32 (1997): 74–40.

4   France

Special thanks are due to Nicolas Mariotte, who gathered and analyzed masses of data for this chapter. Discussion with him was always most stimulating.

1 The data on the cost of social security refer to 1993 and are from ILO; the data on social protection expenditures and receipts refer to 1991 and are from Eurostat. Quoted in Lester M. Salamon and Helmut K. Anheier, *The Emerging Sector: An Overview* (Baltimore: Institute for Policy Studies,

Johns Hopkins University, 1994).

2 All figures quoted are from Edith Archambault, *Le Secteur Sans But Lucratif* (Paris: Economica, 1996). This book is the result of the French contribution to the Johns Hopkins comparative nonprofit sector project. Other figures quoted in the Johns Hopkins study are equally impressive. For example, the French associative sector has the highest percent of total employment of all countries studied with the sole exception of the United States. In another example, between 1981 and 1991, French associations' employment increased by 40 percent, while overall French employment rose much more slowly. In other words, associations were 3.76 times more successful in adding new jobs than the rest of the economy in the eighties, compared with 2.9 times in Germany and 1.87 times in the United States. For further information on the French associative movement, see Bénédicte Halba and Michel Le Net, *Bénévolat et Volontariat* (Paris: La documentation Française, 1997); CNVA, *Bilan de la Vie Associative en 1994–1995* (Paris: La documentation Française, 1996); Marie-Thérèse Chéroutre, *Exercice et Développement de la Vie Associative* (Paris: Conseil Economique et Social, 1993).

3 *INSEE Première* 542 (September 1997); *Consommation et Modes de Vie* (CREDOC) 78 (June-July 1993). The contrast between the rapid growth in the number of new associations every year and the relative stability in the proportion of French adults engaged in them is easily explained. The total adult population has grown considerably since 1960 as a result of the thirty-year postwar baby boom, roughly coinciding with years of exceptional economic growth requiring a vast influx of immigrants (the population of France was 40 million in 1945 and 60 million fifty years later). Therefore, the same proportion of adults who join associations actually represents a vast increase in number. Such an increase in gross membership was absorbed by new associations rather than by the growth of old ones. Two qualitative changes are also part of the explanation: development of multiassociational membership (i.e., belonging to more than one association) and interassociational mobility.

4 The proportion of services to the handicapped rendered through associations is impressive. For handicapped children, the figure is 88 percent; for handicapped adults it is 90 percent; for children or adolescents in trouble the figure is 33 percent; for the homeless it is 86.5 percent. The source for this data is a report by Marie-Thérèse Chéroutre to the thirteenth annual conference of the Association pour le Développement de la Documentation sur l'Economie Sociale (ADDES), Paris, November 1997.

5 The twenty categories used by Michel Forsé are sports, religious, private schools, political, socioeducational, heritage (*patrimoine*), vocational training and research, arts, alumni, parents, employment and economic development, knitting social ties (*renouer les liens sociaux*), leisure, social services, elderly, environment, owners and tenants, civil and social rights,

professional, association-run local independent noncommercial radio stations. Michel Forsé, "Les Créations d'associations: un indicateur de
changement social, observations et diagnostics économiques," *Revue de
l'OFCE* 6 (1984). Quoted in Halba and Le Net, *Bénévolat et volontariat.*

6 Jean-François Canto, "Les créations d'associations," in CNVA, *Bilan de la
vie associative en 1982–1992* (Paris: La documentation Française, 1993), and
CNVA, *Bilan de la vie associative en 1994–1995* (Paris: La documentation
Française, 1996).

7 The research department (Mission Recherche) at the Ministry of Social
Affairs sponsored many of them. The most relevant one on this point is
summarized in "Nouvelles Dynamiques Habitantes et Enjeux de Citoyen-
neté," Migrations Etudes working paper, Paris, June 1996.

8 See particularly "Les grands courants d'opinions et de perceptions en
France de la fin des années 70 au début des années 90," Rapport CREDOC
no. 116, March 1992; "L'évolution des différences d'opinion entre groupes
socio-démographiques," Cahier de Recherche CREDOC no. 41, February
1993; "Un tour d'horizon des aspirations et valeurs des Français telles
qu'elles résultent des enquêtes extérieures au CREDOC," Département
conditions de vie et aspirations, CREDOC, May 1996.

9 Results from this research project were analyzed in two remarkable publi-
cations by a group of social scientists (P. Bréchon, L. Chauvel, O. Galland,
Y. Lambert, Y. Lemel, E. Millan-Game, H. Riffault, L. Roussel, and J.-F.
Tchernia), in Hélène Riffault, dir., *Les valeurs des Français* (Paris: Presses
Universitaires de France, 1994), and "Les valeurs des Européens," *Revue
Futuribles* 200 (1995).

10 Michèle Tribalat, *Faire France* (Paris: La Découverte, 1995).

11 Commission Nationale Consultative des Droits de l'Homme, *1996. La lutte
contre le racisme et la xénophobie* (Paris: La documentation Française,
1997).

12 Figures for this section are taken from a variety of sources, among them:
for statistics, INSEE, OECD, and the Ministry of Labor and Employment;
for opinion surveys, CREDOC and the European Value Survey; for qualitative analysis, *L'Etat de la France 96–97* (Paris: La Découverte, 1997), and
various issues of *Alternatives Economiques.*

13 Figures for this section are taken from various sources, among them *Population et societé;* INSEE and CREDOC publications; the European Value
Survey; and the works of Agnès Pitrou, the most prominent family sociologist in France.

14 This is one of the most significant results of CREDOC studies. The following graph illustrates the whole story (CREDOC, *Cahier de Recherche* no.
41):

Percentage in Favor of Radical Reforms

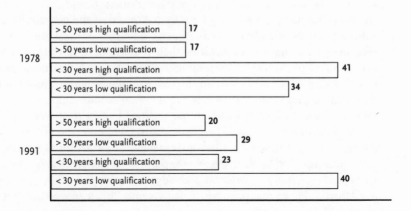

15 Friends, according to the European Value Surveys, were the third most valued element in life, after family and work, and the importance attached to
them grew between 1981 and 1990. Regarding the comparative level of trust
between the family and generalized others, the following tables clearly
indicate the very high level of trust of one's family and distrust of generalized others. Distrust is significantly reduced when the others are specified
as fellow countrymen.

General Trust

Most people can be trusted	21
One is never too careful when dealing with others	72
Don't know	7
Total	100

Source: *European Value Survey* (French results, 1990)

Trust in Family and in the French in General

	Family	The French
Total trust	57	6
Some trust	36	51
Neither one nor the other	2	20
Not much trust	3	17
No trust at all	1	4
Don't know	1	2
Total	100	100

Source: *European Value Surveys* (French results, 1990)

5 Germany

1 Robert D. Putnam, *Making Democracy Work* (Princeton, 1993).

2 On the other hand, people may be fully convinced of the desirability of voluntary forms of collective action but at the same time lack the "thin" version of trust that would motivate their participation. In this case the behavioral response will be not joining an association but contributing to its cause through donations or, in the case of political parties, voting for them. An intermediate category is the nominal membership, in which members limit their participation to paying dues but shy away from more active forms of involvement. This silent involvement may be motivated by services the association performs for its members or other forms of selective incentives. See Mancur Olson, *The Logic of Collective Action: Public Goods and the Theory of Groups* (Cambridge, MA, 1965).

3 See Albert O. Hirschmann, *Shifting Involvements: Private Interest and Public Action* (Oxford, 1982).

4 The inclusion of religious associations is potentially controversial. Reasons for doing so are twofold. First, in most societies most people acquire the religion they confess through primary socialization within their family of origin. Second, at least within Christianity, all human beings are conceived of as "God's children," thus constituting a "family of mankind."

5 Other cases in which family metaphors are invoked include feminist "sisterhood" and trade unions' "brotherhood," both of which imply the significance and inescapability of some belonging and some bonds of solidarity the violation of which amounts to betrayal.

6 Even if the goals are changed, they do so at the initiative of those formally entitled to change the goals (be it a board of directors or the delegates at a party convention), not the membership as a whole.

7 This coincidence of two associational patterns occurs typically in educational institutions. They represent, on one hand, purposive formal organizations guided by the implementation of a curricular regime. On the other hand, they give rise to informal associative practices of peer groups of students.

8 It is worth noting not only that civic associations can be "nested" within formal organizations pursuing strategic purposes but also that civic associations of amateurs can evolve into formal business or professional practices. The latter is the case when movement activists transform themselves into entrepreneurs or political party activists. See John Case and Rosemary Taylor, *Co-ops, Communities and Collectives: Experiments in Social Change in the 1960s and 1970s* (New York, 1979).

9 We propose to cast our net rather widely in the informal direction in order to avoid the optical illusion that whatever is not a formal, registered, and easily visible association therefore does not count as a manifestation of associability at all.

10 See Robert D. Putnam, "Tuning In, Tuning Out: The Strange Disappear-

ance of Social Capital in America," *Political Science and Politics*, December 1995, 666.

11 *Statistisches Bundesamt 1994. Datenreport* (Bonn), 553.

12 Ibid.

13 Membership in political parties has also decreased in West Germany, if only very slightly. In 1980, 4.3 percent of the adult population were members of a political party, while in 1996, 4.1 percent reported party membership. Trade unions have lost members, too. In 1980, 18.6 percent of all employees identified themselves as union members, while in 1996, the figure had fallen to 16 percent (Sigurd Agricola, *Vereinswesen in Deutschland. Eine Expertise des Bundesministeriums für Familie, Senioren, Frauen und Jugend* [Stuttgart, Berlin, and Köln, 1997], 33).

14 Erich Reigrotzki, *Soziale Verflechtungen in der Bundesrepublik. Elemente der sozialen Teilnahme in Kirche, Politik, Organisationen und Freizeit* (Tübingen, 1956), 164.

15 Erwin K. Scheuch, "Vereine als Teil der Privatgesellschaft," in Heinrich Best, ed., *Vereine in Deutschland. Vom Geheimbund zur freien gesellschaftlichen Organisation* (Bonn, 1993), 167.

16 Agricola, *Vereinswesen in Deutschland*, 32.

17 An even greater underreporting of less formal associational activity results from studies that focus exclusively on registered associations and the membership figures reported by them. At any rate, measuring the extent of less formal activity seems to call for more fine-grained and costly methods of data gathering.

18 See M. Rainer Lepsius, *Demokratie in Deutschland* (Göttingen, 1993), 25–94, and Ulrich Herbert, "Arbeiterschaft unter NS-Diktatur," in Lutz Niethammer et al., *Bürgerliche Gesellschaft in Deutschland* (Frankfurt am Main, 1990), 447–71.

19 See Helmut Schelsky, *Der Mensch in der wissenschaftlichen Zivilisation* (Köln, 1961), and Daniel Bell, *The End of Ideology: On the Exhaustion of Political Ideas in the Fifties* (Glencoe, IL, 1960).

20 Manfred Ehling, "Ehrenamtliches Engagement. Erfassung in der Zeitbudgeterhebung des Statistischen Bundesamtes und Möglichkeiten der Weiterentwicklung," paper presented at the INIFES Workshop: Messkonzepte der Kräfte zivilgesellschaftlichen Zusammenhalts, BMBF, Bonn, December 4–5, 1997.

21 *Süddeutsche Zeitung*, December 27, 1997.

22 Joachim Braun, "Selbsthilfepotentiale in den alten und neuen Bundesländern und ihre Aktivierung durch Selbsthilfekontaktstellen," in Joachim Braun and Ulrich Kettler, eds., *Selbsthilfe 2000: Perspektiven der Selbsthilfe und ihrer infrastrukturellen Förderung* (Köln, 1996), 54.

23 The motivational basis for helping appears, however, to differ between East and West Germany. In East Germany, the older pattern of a generalized duty and collectivist commitment to the community seems (still) to

be comparatively more strongly adhered to, while the more individualized pattern of helping on the basis of concrete evidence of need and according to personal circumstances is less prevalent (see Michael Vester et al., *Soziale Milieus im gesellschaftlichen Strukturwandel. Zwischen Integration und Ausgrenzung* [Köln, 1993] for data on West Germany, and Michael Vester, Michael Hofmann, and Irene Zierke, eds., *Soziale Milieus in Ostdeutschland. Gesellschaftliche Strukturen zwischen Zerfall und Neubildung* [Köln, 1995] for data on East Germany). In the East, participation in helping activities is likely to continue to be motivated by a sense of obligation to the community, at least for some time into the future (Stefan Hradil, "Eine Gesellschaft der Egoisten? Gesellschaftliche Zukunftsprobleme, moderne Lebensweisen und soziales Mitwirken," *Gegenwartskunde* 2 [1996]: 293).

24 Scheuch, "Vereine als Teil der Privatgesellschaft," 171.

25 Joachim Braun and Peter Röhrig, *Praxis der Selbsthilfeförderung* (Frankfurt am Main, 1987), 63f.

26 See Joachim Winkler, *Das Ehrenamt* (Schorndorf, 1988), 95.

27 Norbert Schwarz, "Ehrenamtliches Engagement in Deutschland. Ergebnisse der Zeitbudgeterhebung 1991/92," in *Wirtschaft und Statistik* 4 (1996): 264.

28 Klaus Berg and Marie-Luise Kiefer, *Massenkommunikation IV* (Baden-Baden, 1992), 168.

29 Ibid., 341f.

30 Braun and Röhrig, *Praxis der Selbsthilfeförderung,* 63; see also Deutsche Bischofskonferenz, *Frauen und Kirche. Eine Repräsentativbefragung von Katholikinnen* (Bonn, 1993), 164, 170, 174.

31 Scheuch, "Vereine als Teil der Privatgesellschaft," 169.

32 Heiner Meulemann, *Werte und Wertewandel* (Weinheim and München, 1996), 431.

33 Ibid., 145.

34 *Statistisches Bundesamt 1995. Datenreport* (Bonn), 54.

35 Scheuch, "Vereine als Teil der Privatgesellschaft," 170; Reigrotzki, *Soziale Verflechtungen in der Bundesrepublik,* 174.

36 Helmut K. Anheier and Eckhard Priller, *Der Nonprofit-Sektor in Deutschland. Eine sozialökonomische Strukturbeschreibung* (Berlin, 1995), Tab. 25; see also Schwarz, "Ehrenamtliches Engagement in Deutschland," 264, and Winkler, *Das Ehrenamt,* 100.

37 Eckhard Priller, "Veränderungen in der politischen und sozialen Beteiligung in Ostdeutschland," in Wolfgang Zapf and Roland Habich, eds., *Wohlfahrtsentwicklung im vereinten Deutschland* (Berlin, 1996), 298.

38 Katholische Frauengemeinschaft Deutschland, ed., *kfd Mitglieder-Umfrage 1991* Köln, 1992), 48.

39 IPOS (Institut für praxisorientierte Sozialforschung), *Einstellungen zu aktuellen Fragen der Innenpolitik 1995* (Mannheim, 1995), 60f.

40 *Statistisches Bundesamt 1995. Datenreport* (Bonn), 618.

41 The specific profile of a generation can be shaped by either or both of two conditions, opportunity structures and self-identification. The first has to do with the economic, military, educational, family-related, media-related, demographic, and similar contexts under which a cohort enters adolescence and adulthood. The second results from explicit cultural or political conceptualizations of the "collective self" of a generation and its conflict with or allegiance to previous generations (as in the "generation of '68"). Both contexts and symbolized identity by which members of a generation relate to these contexts should provide interpretive clues to statistical findings.

42 Scheuch, "Vereine als Teil der Privatgesellschaft," 170.

43 Deutscher Sportbund, *Bestandserhebung 1995* (Frankfurt am Main, 1995), 3.

44 Schwarz, "Ehrenamtliches Engagement in Deutschland," 262.

45 Ibid.

46 Katholische Frauengemeinschaft Deutschland, *kfd Mitglieder-Umfrage 1991*, 87; see also Bundesministerium für Familie, Senioren, Frauen und Jugend, *Bedeutung ehrenamtlicher Tätigkeit für unsere Gesellschaft. Antwort der Bundesregierung auf die Grosse Anfrage der Fraktionen der CDU/CSU und der F.D.P.* (Bonn, 1996), 111.

47 Helmut Schneider, "Politische Partizipation—zwischen Krise und Wandel," in Ursula Hoffmann-Lange, ed., *Jugend und Demokratie in Deutschland* (Opladen, 1995), 299f.; see also Wolfgang Kühnel, "Orientierungen im politischen Handlungsraum," in Deutsche Shell, *Jugend '92* (Hamburg, 1992), 2:69, and Deutsche Shell, *Jugend '97* (Hamburg, 1997), 4:79, 137f., 200.

48 Schneider, "Politische Partizipation," 298.

49 Ibid., 287.

50 Ibid., 289.

51 Ibid., 295f.

52 Ibid., 296f.; see also Wolfgang Melzer, *Jugend und Politik in Deutschland* (Opladen, 1992), 133.

53 Schneider, "Politische Partizipation," 297f.

54 Ibid., 296f. Despite the denial of the existence of neofascist orientation among GDR youth, both skinheads and anti-Semitic actions were common phenomena. In 1988, 2 percent of GDR adolescents reported themselves as members of skinhead groups; 4 percent reported that they sympathize with skinheads. See Wolfgang Brück, "Jugend als soziales Problem," in Walter Friedrich and Hartmut Griese, eds., *Jugend und Jugendforschung in der DDR. Gesellschaftspolitische Sozialisation und Mentalitätsentwicklung in den achtziger Jahre* (Opladen, 1991), 199.

55 Schneider, "Politische Partizipation," 299f.

56 ifep GmbH, *IBM Jugendstudie '95. Tabellenband* (Köln, 1996), Tab. 21b.

57 Deutsche Shell, *Jugend '97* (Hamburg, 1997), 357.

58 Ibid.; Jürgen Zinnecker, *Jugendkultur 1940–1985* (Opladen, 1987).

59 Zinnecker, *Jugendkultur 1940–1985*, 254.

60 Ibid., 255.

61 Ibid.

62 Melzer, *Jugend und Politik in Deutschland*, 48f.; see also Bundesministerium für Familie, Senioren, Frauen und Jugend, *Jugendliche und junge Erwachsene in Deutschland* (Bonn, 1995), 7:68–70.

63 Peter Bischoff and Cornelia Lang, "Ostdeutsche Jugendliche und ihr Verhältnis zur Politik in den ersten fünf Jahren nach der Wende," in Sozialwissenschaftliches Forschungszentrum, Deutsches Jugendinstitut, and Hans Böckler Stiftung, *Jugendliche in den neuen Bundesländern. Sozialreport 1995.* Sonderheft 2 (1995), 20–25.

64 Ibid., 20f.

65 The 1973 figure is from Thomas Ellwein, "Die grossen Interessenverbände und ihr Einfluss," *Aus Politik und Zeitgeschichte* B 48/73 (1973): 22, while the 1997 figure is from Agricola, *Vereinswesen in Deutschland*, 30.

66 Priller, "Veränderungen in der politischen und sozialen Beteiligung in Ostdeutschland."

67 Ibid., 287.

68 Ibid.; Horst Poldrack, *Soziales Engagement im Umbruch. Zur Situation in den neuen Bundesländern* (Köln, Leipzig, 1993), 33.

69 Priller, "Veränderungen in der politischen und sozialen Beteiligung in Ostdeutschland," 289.

70 Ibid., 289f.

71 Ibid., 290f.

72 Poldrack, *Soziales Engagement im Umbruch*, 31.

73 Ibid., 11; see also Martin Diewald, "'Kollektiv,' 'Vitamin B' oder 'Nische'? Persönliche Netzwerke in der DDR," in Johannes Huinink et al., *Kollektiv und Eigensinn. Lebensverläufe in der DDR und danach* (Berlin, 1995), 223–60.

74 Detlef Pollack, "Sozialethisch engagierte Gruppen in der DDR. Eine religionssoziologische Untersuchung," in Detlef Pollack, ed., *Die Legitimität der Freiheit. Politisch alternative Gruppen in der DDR unter dem Dach der Kirche* (Frankfurt am Main, Bern, New York, and Paris, 1990), 145.

75 *Statistisches Bundesamt 1995*, 560.

76 Ibid.

77 Ibid., 559.

78 Priller, "Veränderungen in der politischen und sozialen Beteiligung in Ostdeutschland," 299.

79 Anheier and Priller, *Der Nonprofit-Sektor in Deutschland*, Tab. 25.

80 Schwarz, "Ehrenamtliches Engagement in Deutschland," 262.

81 The number of employed persons declined from almost nine million to less than six million in the GDR/new *Länder* from 1989 to 1996.

82 Ingo Becker and Ulrich Kettler, "Zwischen Euphorie und Ernüchterung: Die Selbsthilfelandschaft in den neuen Bundesländern fünf Jahre nach der Wende," *Selbsthilfegruppe Nachrichten* 1996: 66.

83 Berg and Kiefer, *Massenkommunikation IV*, 346.

84 *Statistisches Bundesamt 1992*. Datenreport (Bonn), 635.

85 Ibid.

86 *Statistisches Bundesamt 1995*.

87 Ibid.

88 Schwarz, "Ehrenamtliches Engagement in Deutschland," 262.

89 Heinz Sahner, "Vereine und Verbände in der modernen Gesellschaft," in Heinrich Best, ed., *Vereine in Deutschland. Vom Geheimbund zur freien gesellschaftlichen Organisation* (Bonn, 1993), 72.

90 Joachim Braun and Michael Opielka, *Selbsthilfeförderung durch Kontaktstellen* (Stuttgart, Berlin, and Köln, 1992), 11f.

91 See ibid.; Joachim Braun and Ulrich Kettler, *Selbsthilfe 2000: Perspektiven der Selbsthilfe und ihrer infrastrukturellen Förderung* (Köln, 1996); Jörg Ueltzhöffer and Carsten Ascheberg, *Engagement in der Bürgergesellschaft. Die Geislingen-Studie* (Stuttgart, 1995); Jörg Ueltzhöffer and Carsten Ascheberg, *Bürgerschaftliches Engagement in Baden-Württemberg. Landesstudie 1997* (Stuttgart, 1997); Thomas Klie et al., *Bürgerschaftliches Engagement in Baden-Württemberg. 1. Wissenschaftlicher Jahresbericht 1996/1997* (Stuttgart, 1997).

92 This pattern of associability for the sake of cooperative self-provision of services has been much less prevalent in the GDR, as child care and other service facilities were generously provided by the state authorities and enterprises in order to make mothers available for full-time workforce participation.

93 Schwarz, "Ehrenamtliches Engagement in Deutschland," 263.

94 Martin Diewald, *Soziale Beziehungen. Verlust oder Liberalisierung?* (Berlin, 1991), 181f.

95 Karl H. Bönner, "Gleichaltrige: Die Bedeutung der Peer-group in verschiedenen Entwicklungsalterstufen," in Rainer Ningel and Wilma Funke, *Soziale Netze in der Praxis* (Göttingen, 1995), 68.

96 Christoph Sachsse, *Mütterlichkeit als Beruf* (Opladen, 1986); Gisela Jakob, *Zwischen Dienst und Selbstbezug* (Opladen, 1993).

97 Regarding church-related associations, see Caritas, *Dokumentation zur Auswertung des Tätigkeitsberichtes 1991* (Freiburg, 1991), and Caritas, *Auswertung der Tätigkeitsberichte 1994* (Freiburg, 1996).

98 Verena Mayr-Kleffel, *Frauen und ihre sozialen Netzwerke. Auf der Suche nach einer verlorenen Ressource* (Opladen, 1991), 114.

99 Ibid., 124; Ursula Rabe-Kleberg, "Wenn der Beruf zum Ehrenamt wird. Auf dem Weg zu neuartigen Arbeitsverhältnissen in sozialen Berufen," in Siegfried Müller and Thomas Rauschenbach, eds., *Das soziale Ehrenamt* (Weinheim and München, 1988), 96; Heide Funk, "Weibliches Ehrenamt

im Patriarchat," in Siegfried Müller and Thomas Rauschenbach, eds., *Das soziale Ehrenamt* (Weinheim and München, 1988), 120; Sigrid Reihs, *Im Schatten von Freiheit und Erfüllung. Ehrenamtliche Arbeit in Bayern* (Bochum, 1995), 135–37.

100 See Scheuch, "Vereine als Teil der Privatgesellschaft," 169; *Statistisches Bundesamt 1995*, 560; Mayr-Kleffel, *Frauen und ihre sozialen Netzwerke*, 114f.; Elisabeth Noelle-Neumann and Egdar Piel, *Eine Generation später. Bundesrepublik 1953–1979* (Allensbach, 1981), Tab. 41; Sahner, "Vereine und Verbände in der modernen Gesellschaft," 66f.; Anette Zimmer, Andrea Burgari, and Gertraud Krötz, "Vereinslandschaften im Vergleich—Kassel, München, Zürich," in Anette Zimmer, ed., *Vereine heute—zwischen Tradition und Innovation* (Basel, Boston, and Berlin, 1992), 180f.

101 Schwarz, "Ehrenamtliches Engagement in Deutschland," 262.

102 The 1953 data is from Reigrotzki, *Soziale Verflechtungen in der Bundesrepublik*, 169; the 1979 data is from Noelle-Neumann and Piel, *Eine Generation später*, Tab. 42; and the 1993 data is from *Statistisches Bundesamt 1995*, 560.

103 Scheuch, "Vereine als Teil der Privatgesellschaft," 169.

104 Mayr-Kleffel, *Frauen und ihre sozialen Netzwerke*, 124f; see also Diewald, "'Kollektiv,' 'Vitamin B' oder 'Nische'? Persönliche Netzwerke in der DDR," 253.

105 See Samuel H. Barnes et al., *Political Action: Mass Participation in Five Western European Democracies* (Beverly Hills, 1979); Ute Molitor, *Wählen Frauen anders?* (Baden-Baden, 1992); Beate Hoecker, *Politische Partizipation von Frauen* (Opladen, 1995).

106 Molitor, *Wählen Frauen anders*, 157f.

107 Christiane Ochs, "Frauendiskriminierung in Ost und West—oder: die relativenErfolge der Frauenförderung. Eine Bestandsaufnahme in den beiden ehemaligen deutschen Staaten," in Karin Hansen and Gertraude Krell, eds., *Frauenerwerbsarbeit* (München and Mering, 1993), 48.

108 Priller, "Veränderungen in der politischen und sozialen Beteiligung in Ostdeutschland," 286f.

109 See Molitor, *Wählen Frauen anders*; Regina Berger-Schmitt, "Arbeitsteilung und subjektives Wohlbefinden von Ehepartnern," in Wolfgang Glatzer and Regina Berger-Schmitt, eds., *Haushaltsproduktion und Netzwerkhilfe* (Frankfurt am Main, 1986); Mayr-Kleffel, *Frauen und ihre sozialen Netzwerke*, 121.

110 See Rolf G. Heinze and Thomas Olk, "Die Wohlfahrtsverbände im System sozialer Dienstleistungsproduktion," *Kölner Zeitschrift für Soziologie und Sozialpolitik* 33, 1 (1981), S94–114; Rolf G. Heinze and Thomas Olk, "Sozialpolitische Steuerung: Von der Subsidarität zum Korporatismus," in M. Glagow, ed., *Gesellschaftssteuerung zwischen Korporatismus und Subsidarität* (Bielefeld, 1984); Rudolph Bauer, *Wohlfahrtsverbände in der Bundesrepublik* (Weinheim, 1978).

111 Eberhard Goll, *Die freie Wohlfahrtspflege als eigener Wirtschaftsfaktor. Theorie und Empirie ihrer Verbände und Einrichtungen* (Baden-Baden, 1991).

112 Thomas Olk, Thomas Rauschenbach, and Christoph Sachsse, "Von der Wertgemeinschaft zum Dienstleistungsunternehmen. Oder: über die Schwierigkeit, Solidarität zu üben. Ein einführende Skizze," in Thomas Rauchenbach, Christoph Sachsse, and Thomas Olk, eds., *Von der Wergemeinschaft zum Dienstleistungsunternehmen* (Frankfurt am Main, 1995), 13.

113 Holger Backhaus-Maul, "Vom Sozialstaat zur Wohlfahrtsgesellschaft? Über organisiertes Engagement, Verbände und Sozialstaat," *epd-Dokumentation 52/96* (1996): 9.

114 Thomas Olk, "Zwischen Hausarbeit und Beruf. Ehrenamtliches Engagement in der aktuellen sozialpolitischen Diskussion," in Siegfried Müller and Thomas Rauschenbach, eds., *Das soziale Ehrenamt* (Weinheim and München, 1988), 25.

115 See Deutsche Shell, *Jugend '97;* Martina Gille et al., "Das Verhältnis Jugendlicher und junger Erwachsener zur Politik: Normalisierung oder Krisenentwicklung?" *Aus Politik und Zeitgeschichte,* B 19/96, 3 (1996): 12; Christa Perabo and Hessisches Ministerium für Umwelt, Energie, Jugend, Familie und Gesundheit, "Freiwilliges soziales Engagement in Hessen," positionspapier, Wiesbaden, 1996; Rainer Zoll et al., *Nicht so wie unsere Eltern!* (Opladen, 1989); Rainer Zoll, ed., *Ein neues kulturelles Modell* (Opladen, 1992); Thomas Ziehe, *Zeitvergleiche. Jugend in kulturellen Modernisierungen* (Weinheim and München, 1991); for the former GDR, see Lindner 1991.

116 Claus Offe and Rolf G. Heinze, "Am Arbeitsmarkt vorbei. Überlegungen zur Neubestimmung 'haushaltlicher' Wohlfahrtsproduktion in ihrem Verhältnis in ihrem Verhältnis zu Markt und Staat," *Leviathan* 14, 4 (1986), 483f.

117 See Aktion für Gemeinsinn, e.V., *Was bedeutet Gemeinsinn heute?* (Bonn, 1995); Joachim Braun, Ulrich Kettler, and Ingo Becker, *Selbsthilfe und Selbsthilfeunterstützung in der Bundesrepublik Deutschland* (Köln, 1996); Braun and Kettler, *Selbsthilfe 2000;* Braun and Opielka, *Selbsthilfeförderung durch Kontaktstellen;* Warnfried Dettling, *Politik und Lebenswelt* (Gütersloh, 1995); Rolf G. Heinze and Matthias Bucksteeg, "Freiwilliges soziales Engagement in NRW: Potentiale und Förderungsmöglichkeiten," in Ministerium für Arbeit, Gesundheit und Soziales des Landes Nordrhein-Westfalen, *Zukunft des Sozialstaates. Freiwilliges soziales Engagement und Selbsthilfe* (Düsseldorf, 1996); Hessisches Ministerium für Umwelt, Energie, Jugend, Familie und Gesundheit, *Expertengespräch: Freiwilliges soziales Engagement* (Wiesbaden, 1996); Karl Otto Hondrich and Claudia Koch-Arzberger, *Solidarität in der modernen Gesellschaft* (Frankfurt am Main, 1992); Ministerium für Arbeit, Gesundheit und Soziales des Landes Nordrhein-Westfalen, *Zukunft des Sozialstaates. Freiwilliges soziales Engage-*

ment und Selbsthilfe (Düsseldorf, 1996); Perabo and Hessisches Ministerium, "Freiwilliges soziales Engagement in Hessen"; Ueltzhöffer and Ascheberg, *Engagement in der Bürgergesellschaft;* Ueltzhöffer and Ascheberg, *Bürgerschaftliches Engagement in Baden-Württemberg.*

118 Eckart Pankoke, "Subsidäre Solidarität und freies Engagement. Zur 'anderen' Modernität der Wohlfahrtsverbände," in Thomas Rauschenbach, Christoph Sachsse, and Thomas Olk, eds., *Von der Wertgemeinschaft zum Dienstleistungsunternehmen. Jugend- und Wohlfahrtsverbände im Umbruch* (Frankfurt am Main, 1995), 75.

119 Braun and Opielka, *Selbsthilfeförderung durch Kontaktstellen,* 236; Braun, Kettler, and Becker, *Selbsthilfe und Selbsthilfeunterstützung in der Bundesrepublik Deutschland,* 77.

120 See Konrad Hummel, ed., *Bürgerengagement. Seniorengenossenschaften, Bürgerbüros und Gemeinschaftsinitiven* (Freiburg, 1995); Klie et al., *Bürgerschaftliches Engagement in Baden-Württemberg;* Ueltzhöffer and Ascheberg, *Engagement in der Bürgergesellschaft;* Ueltzhöffer and Ascheberg, *Bürgerschaftliches Engagement in Baden-Württemberg.*

121 Thomas R. Cusack, "Social Capital, Institutional Structures, and Democratic Performance: A Comparative Study of German Local Governments," paper presented at the Conference on Social Capital and European Democracy, Milan, October 3–6, 1996, 40; Putnam, *Making Democracy Work,* 76–82, 176, 182.

122 See William Kornhauser, *The Politics of Mass Society* (Glencoe, IL, 1959).

123 See Thomas R. Cusack and Bernhard Wessels, "Problemreich und konflikgeladen: Lokale Demokratie in Deutschland fünf Jahre nach der Vereinigung," *Institutionen und sozialer Wandel,* FS III (1996): 96–203.

124 Putnam, *Making Democracy Work,* 153.

125 Ibid., 171.

126 A further version in which economic precariousness and marginality leads to associability must be mentioned. To wit, some authors (e.g., Wilhelm Heitmeyer et al., *Die Bielefelder Rechtsextremismus-Studie* [Weinheim and München, 1992]) believe that the condition of economic decline and high levels of (youth) unemployment in the new *Länder* is an important factor in accounting for neofascist gangs and movements—a clear case of what we have called "negative" social capital.

127 Meinhard Miegel, *Wirtschafts- und arbeitskulturelle Unterschiede in Deutschland* (Gütersloh, 1991).

128 Ibid., 56.

129 Günter Tempel, "Regionale Kulturen in Deutschland—Ergebnisse einer Sekundärauswertung von Umfragedaten," Universität Bremen, ZWE Arbeit und Region, Arbeitspapier Nr. 11, 1993.

130 Ibid., 35.

131 Heinz-Herbert Noll, "Arbeitsplatzsuche und Stellenfindung," in Helmut Knepel and Reinhard Hujer, eds., *Mobilitätsprozesse auf dem Arbeitsmarkt*

(Frankfurt am Main, New York, 1985), 286.

132 Heinz-Herbert Noll, "Arbeitsmarktressourcen und berufliche Plazierung," *Mannheimer Berichte* 22 (1983): 638f.; see also Mark Granovetter, "The Strength of Weak Ties," *American Journal of Sociology* 78 (1973): 1360–80; Mark Granovetter, *Getting a Job: A Study on Contacts and Careers* (Cambridge, MA, 1974).

133 Klaus Gröhnke et al., "Soziale Netzwerke bei Langzeitarbeitslosen. Duisburger Beiträge zur soziologischen Forschung," Gerhard-Mercator Universität, Gesamthochschule Duisburg no. 2/1996, 1996.

134 A. Goldsmith, J. R. Veum, and W. Darity Jr., "The Psychological Impact of Unemployment and Joblessness," *Journal of Socio-Economics* 25 (1996): 333–58.

135 Ibid., 49.

136 See Dettling, *Politik und Lebenswelt*.

137 See Mayr-Kleffel, *Frauen und ihre sozialen Netzwerke*, 124f.; Molitor, *Wählen Frauen anders*, 175.

138 See Deutsche Shell, *Jugend '97*, 324f.

6 Spain

1 James Coleman, *Foundations of Social Theory* (Cambridge, MA: Harvard University Press, 1990). The contribution of Robert Putnam in "Bowling Alone: America's Declining Social Capital" (*Journal of Democracy* 6, 1 [1995]: 65–78, where he discusses the concept in regard to the United States—he had earlier applied the concept to Italy, for which see Robert Putnam, Robert Leonardi, and Raffaella Naneti, *Making Democracy Work: Civic Traditions in Modern Italy* [Princeton: Princeton University Press, 1993])—should be viewed in the context of a growing literature dealing with the reciprocal influences between economy and sociology. See, for example, the reasoning of Kenneth Arrow on the need for trust in order for contracts to be fulfilled, and the importance of what he calls a "business morality," in Richard Swedberg, *Economics and Sociology* (Princeton: Princeton University Press, 1990), 139.

2 Fritz Scharpf, "The Viability of Advanced Welfare States in the International Economy: Vulnerabilities and Options," Max-Planck-Institut für Gesellschaftsforschung Working Paper 99/9, September 1999.

3 An argument suggesting a limited convergence around the recognition of the four pillars of the welfare system (families, the state, for-profit groups, and nonprofit organizations) and around a blend of liberal and communitarian arguments can be found in Víctor Pérez-Díaz, Elisa Chuliá, and Berta Álvarez-Miranda, *Familia y sistema de bienestar: La experiencia española con el paro, las pensiones, la sanidad y la educación* (Madrid: Fundación Argentaria/Visor, 1998).

4 The assessment of the role of politics is a matter of balance and of empirical research. Thus Putnam suggests that social capital is related to a tradi-

tion of civic engagement (or participation in the affairs of the city), and he believes he has found such a tradition, based on social capital, in the civic humanism of the cities of northern Italy, in contrast with those of the south. Though this is not the place to discuss the Italian case, a word in defense of Putnam against some of his critics is in order here. It may well be that Putnam leaps to conclusions about the Middle Ages, contemporary times, and the connections between them, and that he does not pay sufficient attention to the influence of the state (and the political class) and the economy in the formation of social capital, as Sidney Tarrow suggests, following Cohn and others (Sidney Tarrow, "Making Social Science Work Across Space and Time: A Critical Reflection on Robert Putnam's "Making Democracy Work," *American Political Science Review* 90, 2 [1996]: 389–97). It is obvious, anyway, that any attempt to explain a phenomenon as complex as that of the Italian case requires careful consideration of those political and economic factors. However, such criticism may prove tangential to Putnam's central theoretical concern, which is the role of social capital, when it comes to explaining a tradition of civic engagement. We could even be led astray by this criticism were it to result in the reduction of social structure and culture (networks and norms as well as sentiments) to mere by-products of political and economic factors, thereby reducing to irrelevance a large part of the tradition of sociological debate on the problem of social integration.

5 Michael Oakeshott, *On Human Conduct* (Oxford: Clarendon Press, 1990). For the distinction between a broad understanding of civil society (the original Scottish view; see also Ernest Gellner, *Conditions of Liberty* [New York: Allen Lane, 1994]) and a more narrow or restricted use of the term (close or equivalent to the "third sector" of nonstate and nonprofit associations), see Víctor Pérez-Díaz, "The Possibility of Civil Society: Traditions, Character and Challenges," in John Hall, ed., *Civil Society: Theory, History, Comparison* (Cambridge: Polity Press, 1995), 56–79, and Pérez-Díaz, "The Public Sphere and a European Civil Society," in Jeffrey Alexander, ed., *Real Civil Societies: Dilemmas of Institutionalization* (London: Sage, 1998): 211–38

6 Friedrich von Hayek, *Law, Legislation and Liberty,* vol. 2 (London: Routledge and Kegan Paul, 1976).

7 Friedrich von Hayek, *The Fatal Conceit* (Chicago: University of Chicago Press, 1989), 19.

8 Ibid., 81.

9 Talcott Parsons, *Sociological Theory and Modern Society* (New York: Free Press,1967).

10 Emile Durkheim, *De la division du travail social* (Paris: Presses Universitaires de France, 1967 [1893]); Parsons, *Sociological Theory and Modern Society.*

11 Parsons, *Sociological Theory and Modern Society,* 8.

12 Julian Pitt-Rivers, *The Fate of Schechem, or the Politics of Sex: Essays in the Anthropology of the Mediterranean* (Cambridge: Cambridge University Press, 1977), 94ff.

13 Mark Granovetter, "The Strength of Weak Ties: A Network Theory Revisited," *Sociological Theory* 1 (1983): 201–33.

14 For example, the social capital of the American generation of World War II; see Michael Schudson, "What if Civic Life Didn't Die?" *The American Prospect*, March-April 1996, 17–20.

15 Here, for this purpose only, I disregard the political sectors led by Indalecio Prieto and Manuel Azaña, who were moderate socialists and left-wing Republicans. Although they played a relatively minor role once the war started, their testimony is of crucial importance for understanding the normative conflicts that led to the war.

16 Juan J. Linz, "La realidad asociativa de los españoles," in Fondo para la Investigación Económica y Social de la Confederación Española de Cajas de Ahorro, ed., *Sociología española de los años setenta* (Madrid: CECA, 1971).

17 Gabriel Jackson, *The Spanish Republic and the Civil War, 1931–1939* (Princeton: Princeton University Press,1965); Richard Herr, *An Historical Essay on Modern Spain* (Berkeley: University of California Press, 1974).

18 Víctor Pérez-Díaz, *The Return of Civil Society: The Emergence of Democratic Spain* (Cambridge, MA: Harvard University Press, 1993); Paloma Aguilar, *Memoria y olvido de la guerra civil española* (Madrid: Alianza, 1996).

19 See the testimony of a Catalanist witness, as corroborated by Josep Tarradellas, in Elisa Chuliá, "La evolución silenciosa de las dictaduras: El régimen de Franco ante la prensa y el periodismo," Ph.D. thesis, Universidad Complutense de Madrid, 1997, 219.

20 *Massnahrenstaat* versus *Normenstaat;* see ibid., 174.

21 Amparo Almarcha et al., *Estadísticas básicas de España 1900–1970* (Madrid: CECA, 1975), 446.

22 More in some parts of the country and less in others; in many cases it continued until the late 1960s. See Ronald Fraser, *In Hiding: The Life of Manuel Cortés* (New York: New American Library, 1972).

23 Linz, "La realidad asociativa de los españoles."

24 Víctor Pérez-Díaz, *Structure and Change in Castilian Peasant Communities: A Sociological Enquiry into Rural Castile, 1550–1990* (New York and London: Garland, 1991).

25 Edward Banfield, *The Moral Basis of a Backward Society* (Glencoe, IL: Free Press, 1958).

26 CECS, *España 1995. Una interpretación de su realidad social* (Madrid: CECS/Fundación Encuentro, 1996), 196–97.

27 CECS, *España 1994. Una interpretación de su realidad social* (Madrid: CECS/Fundación Encuentro, 1995), 687.

28 Almarcha et al., *Estadísticas básicas.*

29 Chuliá, "La evolución silenciosa de las dictaduras."

30 Ibid., 330.

31 Enrique Fuentes Quintana, "El modelo de economía abierta y el modelo castizo de desarrollo económico en el desarrollo económico de la España de los 90," in Julio Alcaide et al., *Problemas económicos españoles de la década de los 90* (Barcelona: Círculo de Lectores, 1995), 123.

32 Juan Velarde, "Evolución del comercio exterior español: del nacionalismo económico a la Unión Europea," in Julio Alcaide et al., *Problemas económicos españoles de la década de los 90* (Barcelona: Círculo de Lectores, 1995), 392.

33 Almarcha et al., *Estadísticas básicas.*

34 Chuliá, "La evolución silenciosa de las dictaduras," 443.

35 Ibid., 445.

36 Susan Tax Freeman, *Neighbors: The Social Contract in a Castilian Hamlet* (Chicago: University of Chicago Press, 1970); Stanley Brandes, *Migration, Kinship and Community* (New York: Academic Press, 1976); Víctor Pérez-Díaz, *Estructura social del campo y éxodo rural. Estudio de un pueblo de Castilla* (Madrid: Tecnos, 1972); Michael Kenny, *A Spanish Tapestry: Town and Country in Castile* (London: Coehn, West, 1961); M. Weisser, *The Peasants of the Montes* (Chicago: University of Chicago Press, 1972).

37 Quoted in Chuliá, "La evolución silenciosa de las dictaduras," 329.

38 CECS, *España 1995,* 196.

39 Juan Muñoz et al., *La Economía Española 1974* (Madrid: Cuadernos para el Diálogo, 1975).

40 See, for instance, Joan Subirats' introductory remarks in Joan Subirats, ed., *¿Existe sociedad civil en España? Responsabilidades colectivas y valores públicos* (Madrid: Fundación Encuentro, 1999). For a different view, see Víctor Pérez-Díaz, *Spain at the Crossroads: Civil Society, Politics and the Rule of Law* (Cambridge, MA: Harvard University Press, 1999), 46ff.

41 Lester Salamon et al., eds., *Global Civil Society: Dimensions of the Nonprofit Sector* (Baltimore: The Johns Hopkins Center for Civil Society Studies, 1999), 480.

42 Ibid.

43 José Ignacio Ruiz Olabuénaga et al., "Spain," in Lester Salamon et al., eds., *Global Civil Society: Dimensions of the Nonprofit Sector* (Baltimore: The Johns Hopkins Center for Civil Society Studies, 1999), 163ff.

44 Salamon et al., *Global Civil Society,* 478.

45 The authors of the estimates included in the Spanish chapter of the Johns Hopkins Project give only a vague and most general reference to their sources and their proceedings (Salamon et al., *Global Civil Society,* 490). So far this leaves open to debate the basis of their very estimates, since most of the original sources (particularly the registers of the Ministry of Interior and others) are of very poor quality. Their work will have to be

corroborated (or not) by further research. See also Fabiola Mota, "La realidad asociativa en España," in Joan Subirats, ed., *¿Existe sociedad civil en España? Responsabilidades colectivas y valores públicos* (Madrid: Fundación Encuentro, 1999), and for some subsectors, Gregoria Rodríguez Cabrero and Julia Montserrat, eds., *Las entidades voluntarias en España* (Madrid: Ministerio de Asuntos Sociales, 1996) and Luis Cortés Alcalá, María José Hernán, and Óscar López Maderuelo, *Las organizaciones de voluntariado en España* (Madrid: Plataforma para la Promoción del Voluntariado en España, 1999). Some work is currently being done to systematically map out the sector of social service associations under the auspices of the Cruz Roja (Red Cross) Foundation and the Ministry of Social Affairs. Increasing interest in societal associations seems corroborated by survey data in the mid-1990s; see Francisco Andrés Orizo, *Sistemas de valores en la España de los 90* (Madrid: CIS, 1996).

46 Víctor Pérez-Díaz, "Sociedad civil, esfera pública y esfera privada: tejido social y asociaciones en España en el quicio entre dos milenios," ASP Research Papers 39(a)/2000, 2000.

47 For an elaboration of this point, see Pérez-Díaz, *Spain at the Crossroads,* 16–33.

48 Depending on the estimates. See Richard Gunther and José Ramón Montero, "Los anclajes del partidismo: Un análisis comparado del comportamiento electoral en cuatro democracias del sur de Europa," in Pilar del Castillo, ed., *Comportamiento político y electoral* (Madrid: CIS, 467–548) and Rafael Prieto-Lacaci, "Asociaciones voluntarias," in Salustiano del Campo, ed., *Tendencias sociales en España,* vol. 1 (Madrid: Fundación BBV, 1993).

49 Pérez-Díaz, *Spain at the Crossroads,* 137.

50 Pérez-Díaz, *The Return of Civil Society.*

51 Manuel García Ferrando, *Aspectos sociales del deporte. Una reflexión sociológica* (Madrid: Alianza, 1990), 183; INE, *España. Anuario estadístico 1969* (Madrid: INE, 1970), 363; INE, *Panorámica social de España* (Madrid: INE, 1994), 748; INE, *España. Anuario estadístico 1995* (Madrid: INE, 1996), 325.

52 Mario Gaviria, *La séptima potencia: España en el mundo* (Barcelona: Ediciones B.Gaviria, 1996), 170 (source: UNESCO, *Statistical Yearbook* [Paris: UNESCO, 1991]).

53 Pérez-Díaz, Chuliá, and Álvarez-Miranda, *Familia y sistema de bienestar;* Víctor Pérez-Díaz, Elisa Chuliá, and Celia Valiente, *La familia española en el año 2000: Innovación y respuesta de las familias a sus condiciones económicas, políticas y culturales* (Madrid: Fundación Argentaria-Visor, 2001).

54 INE, *Panorámica social de España,* 136–38.

55 Inés Alberdi, ed., *Informe sobre la situación de la familia en España* (Madrid: Ministerio de Asuntos Sociales, 1995), 313.

56 EUROSTAT, *Demographic Statistics 1996* (Luxembourg: Office for Official

Publications of the European Communities, 1996), 215ff.

57 CIRES, *La realidad social en España* (Bilbao: Fundación BBV, Bilbao-Bizkaia-Kutxa y Caja de Madrid, 1992).

58 Gaviria, *La séptima potencia,* 159, 387.

59 For a more elaborate discussion concerning the "civilization" of normative conflicts around the themes of religion and the church, the left/ right dichotomy, and the rule of law and the nation in Spain (particularly in regard to Basque nationalism) in the last about sixty years, see Víctor Pérez-Díaz, "Iglesia, economía, ley y nación: la civilización de los conflictos normativos en la España actual," in Peter Berger, ed., *Los límites de la cohesión social: Conflictos y mediación en las sociedades pluralistas* (Barcelona: Galaxia Gutenberg–Círculo de Lectores, 1999), 547–625 (English version: "The Church, the Economy, the Law and the Nation: The Civilization of Normative Conflicts in Present-day Spain," ASP Research Papers 32(b)/1999, 1999.

60 Alicia Garrido, "Autoridad," in Salustiano del Campo, ed., *Tendencias sociales en España (1960–1990)* (Bilbao: Fundación BBV, 1993), 2:98.

61 Javier Elzo et al., *Jóvenes españoles 94* (Madrid: Fundación Santa María, 1994).

62 Pérez-Díaz, *The Return of Civil Society,* 140–83.

63 CIS, "Demanda de seguridad ciudadana. Estudio CIS 2200, diciembre 1995-enero 1996," *Boletín del Centro de Investigaciones Sociológicas* 4 (1996): 2-4.

64 Leaving aside the issue of Basque terrorism, even though there has developed a fairly impressive peace movement during the nineties. See Víctor Pérez-Díaz, "Iglesia, economía, ley y nación."

65 Francisco Andrés Orizo, *Los nuevos valores de los españoles: España en la Encuesta Europea de Valores* (Madrid: Fundación Santa María, 1991), and Orizo, *Sistemas de valores en la España de los 90.* See also Pérez-Díaz, *Spain at the Crossroads.*

66 José Ramón Montero, "Las dimensiones de la secularización: Religiosidad y preferencias políticas en España," in Rafael Díaz-Salazar and Salvador Giner, eds., *Religión y sociedad en España* (Madrid: CIS, 1993), 180.

67 INE, *España. Anuario estadístico 1969;* INE, *España. Anuario estadístico 1995.*

68 In his *De la division du travail social,* Durkheim describes with a certain anxiety the emergence of a more fragmented but interdependent society, cemented on organic solidarity; he wishes to institutionalize this new type of solidarity in professional corporations of national or international dimensions suited to contemporary markets. In a society based on the interdependence of economic activities, professional interest groups would be expected to provide the moral discipline needed to avoid open conflicts of interests or anomie, as well as the main channel of communication between society and the state.

69 Leaving aside the Basque question. See Pérez-Díaz, *Spain at the Crossroads,* and "Iglesia, economía, ley y nación."

70 BBV, *Informe económico 1995* (Bilbao: BBV, 1996), 238.

71 Ibid., 274.

72 European Commission, *Employment in Europe 1995* (Luxembourg: Office for Official Publications of the European Communities, 1996), 192. In 1997, the rate stayed around 21–22 percent.

73 See, for instance, Gaviria, *La séptima potencia.*

74 See also *The Economist,* May 3, 1997.

75 Pérez-Díaz, *Spain at the Crossroads,* 103–21.

76 European Commission, *Employment in Europe 1995,* 92, 192.

77 Pilar del Castillo, "El comportamiento electoral español en las elecciones al Parlamento Europeo de 1989," in Pilar del Castillo, ed., *Comportamiento político y electoral* (Madrid: CIS, 1994), 389ff.; Manuel Justel, "Composición y dinámica de la abstención electoral en España," in Pilar del Castillo, ed., *Comportamiento político y electoral* (Madrid: CIS, 1994), 90; and the newspaper *Anuarios El País,* several years

78 Manuel Justel, "Edad y cultura política," *Revista Española de Investigaciones Sociológicas* 58 (1992): 83.

79 Ibid.; CIS, "Los ciudadanos y el estado. Estudio CIS 2206, enero 1996," *Boletín del Centro de Investigaciones Sociológicas,* 4 (1996): 6.

80 CIS, "Los ciudadanos y el estado," 6.

81 CIS, "Los españoles ante la Constitución y las instituciones democráticas: 11 años de Constitución (1978–1989)," *Estudios y encuestas* 23 (1990); CIS, "Demanda de seguridad ciudadana."

82 Orizo, *Los nuevos valores de los españoles,* 150

83 Ibid.

84 Manuel Navarro, "Juventud," in Salustiano del Campo, ed., *Tendencias sociales en España (1960–1990)* (Bilbao: Fundación BBV, 1993), 1:125.

85 Public officials involved in this kind of behavior included the governor of the Bank of Spain and the general director of the Guardia Civil.

86 CIS, "Los españoles ante la administración de justicia," *Estudios y encuestas* 13 (1988).

87 CIS, "Informe sobre la encuesta de victimización (julio de 1978)," *Revista Española de Investigaciones Sociológicas* 4 (1978): 223–78; CIS, "Demanda de seguridad ciudadana."

88 For an elaboration of the argument in regard to the "civility" of the firm, see Víctor Pérez-Díaz, "Legitimidad y eficacia: Tendencias de cambio en el gobierno de las empresas," ASP Research Papers 28(a)/1999, 1999.

89 Norbert Elias, *The Court Society,* trans. Edmund Jephcott (Oxford: Basil Blackwell, 1983 [1969]), 339–44.

90 Michael Polanyi, *The Tacit Dimension* (London: Routledge and Kegan Paul, 1967).

91 For a more detailed analysis of the combined changes in actual practices

and in the ideational contents of the Catholic Church, see Pérez-Díaz, *The Return of Civil Society*, 108–83.

92 Victor Turner, *Dramas, Fields and Metaphors* (Ithaca: Cornell University Press, 1974).

93 Pitt-Rivers, *The Fate of Schechem*, 72ff.

94 See Pérez-Díaz, *Structure and Change in Castilian Peasant Communities*.

7   Sweden

Ylva Norén has been a very helpful and skilled research assistant in this project. My colleagues in the Department of Political Science at Göteborg University, especially Mikael Gilljam, Sören Holmberg, and Maria Oskarson, provided me with more good comments than I could handle. Many thanks to Thorleif Pettersson, who generously gave me access to the Swedish sections of the World Value Studies data, and also to Torsten Österman, who provided me with data from the FSI surveys. Nils Elvander, Lauri Karvonen, Michele Micheletti, Robert Putnam, Jonas Pontusson, Dietlind Stolle, and Filip Wijkström provided constructive comments on an earlier version of this report.

1 See e.g., Wallace Clement and Rianne Mahon, eds., *Swedish Social Democracy* (Toronto: Canadian Scholars' Press, 1994); Tim Tilton, *The Political Theory of Swedish Social Democracy* (Oxford: Clarendon Press, 1990); and Jan-Erik Lane, ed., *Understanding the Swedish Model* (London: Frank Cass, 1991).

2 See, e.g., Andrew Shonfield, *Modern Capitalism* (Oxford: Oxford University Press, 1965), and Peter J. Katzenstein, *Small States in World Markets: Industrial Policy in Europe* (Ithaca: Cornell University Press, 1984).

3 John Platt, "Social Traps," *American Psychologist* 28 (1973): 641–51. This type of problem has many other names in the social sciences. In game theory, a social trap is known either as a "n-persons prisoner's dilemma" or an "assurance game." Other terms are "social dilemmas," "tragedy of the commons," "the problem of collective action," and "the public goods problem." See Elinor Ostrom, "A Behavioral Approach to the Rational Choice Theory of Collective Action," *American Political Science Review* 92 (1998): 1–23.

4 There are of course some agents who always prefer to be free riders, hoping that all the other ones pay their taxes and sort their garbage, while they themselves just benefit from the public good that is produced, without having to pay the costs. However, most of the empirical research shows that a majority does not confirm to this type of "homo economicus." See David Sally, "Conversation and Cooperation in Social Dilemmas: A Meta-Analysis of Experiments, 1952–1992," *Rationality and Society* 7 (1995): 58–92, and Ostrom, "A Behavioral Approach to the Rational Choice Theory of Collective Action."

5 For a superb (and short) overview of the debate, see E. J. Dionne Jr., "Why Civil Society? Why Now?" *The Brookings Review* 15 (1997): 4–8. According

to a recent large-scale project about the Swedish welfare state, the twentieth century in Sweden has been a lost century for the civil society because the welfare state has colonized civil society; see Hans Zetterberg and Carl-Johan Ljungberg, *Vårt land—den svenska socialstaten* (Stockholm: City University Press, 1997), 253. However, the project does not present any data to support their hypothesis.

6 See, e.g., Jean L. Cohen and Andrew Arato, *Civil Society and Political Theory* (Cambridge, MA: MIT Press, 1993).

7 See, e.g., Michele Micheletti, *Civil Society and State Relations in Sweden* (Aldershot: Avebury, 1995).

8 Bo Rothstein, *The Social Democratic State: The Swedish Model and the Bureaucratic Problems of Social Reforms* (Pittsburgh: University of Pittsburgh Press, 1996).

9 Robert D. Putnam, "Bowling Alone: America's Declining Social Capital," *Journal of Democracy* 6 (1995): 65–78; and Robert D. Putnam, *Bowling Alone: The Collapse and Revival of American Community* (New York: Simon and Schuster, 2000).

10 See Donald Granberg and Sören Holmberg, *The Political System Matters* (Cambridge: Cambridge University Press, 1988), 5–7.

11 Shonfield, *Modern Capitalism;* Katzenstein, *Small States in World Markets.*

12 For a very good case study, see Steven Kelman, *Regulating America, Regulating Sweden* (Cambridge, MA: MIT Press, 1981). See Jörgen Hermansson, *Politik som intressekamp* (Stockholm: Norstedts, 1993).

13 *Demokrati och makt i Sverige* (Stockholm: Allmänna förlaget, 1990).

14 Leif Lewin, "The Rise and Decline of Corporatism," *European Journal of Political Research* 26 (1992): 59–79.

15 Bo Rothstein et al., *Demokrati som dialog* (Stockholm: SNS Förlag, 1995); Olof Petersson et al., *Democracy and Leadership* (Stockholm: SNS Förlag, 1997).

16 Pippa Norris, ed., *Critical Citizens: Global Support for Democratic Governance* (Oxford: Oxford University Press, 1999).

17 Sören Holmberg, *Välja parti* (Stockholm: Norstedts, 2000), 34; see Sören Holmberg, "Down and Down We Go: Political Trust in Sweden," in Pippa Norris, ed., *Critical Citizens: Global Support for Democratic Governance* (Oxford: Oxford University Press, 1999).

18 Sören Holmberg and Lennart Weibull, *Det nya samhället.* SOM-report 24. (Göteborg: Göteborgs Universitet, 2000).

19 Ola Listhaug and Matti Wiberg, "Confidence in Political and Private Institutions," in Hans-Dieter Klingemann and Dieter Fuchs, eds., *Citizens and the State* (Oxford: Oxford University Press, 1996), 320.

20 Holmberg, "Down and Down We Go."

21 See e.g., *Demokrati och makt i Sverige,* and Åke E. Andersson et al., *70-talister om värderingar förr, nu och i framtiden* (Stockholm: Natur och Kultur, 1993).

22 Source: Data received from Statens Ungdomsstyrelse (National Board for Youth), Stockholm.

23 Source: SCB, *Politiska resurser och aktiviteter 1978–1994* (Stockholm: Statistics Sweden, 1995), 66. It should be mentioned that data from the Swedish sections of the World Value Studies show no decline in party membership between 1981 and 1996, but the sample is much smaller.

24 Mikael Gilljam and Tommy Möller, "Från medlemspartier till väljarpartier," in *På medborgarnas villkor: en demokratisk infrastruktur* (Stockholm: Fritzes, 1996).

25 Rothstein et al., *Demokrati som dialog.*

26 Lars Pettersson, "In Search of Respectability: Popular Movements in Scandinavian Democracy," in Lars Rudebeck and Olle Törnqvist, eds., *Democratization and the Third World* (Uppsala: Uppsala University, Seminar for Development Studies, 1995).

27 The "free churches" were organized in opposition to the Church of Sweden, which was a state church.

28 See Micheletti, *Civil Society and State Relations in Sweden.*

29 Gunnar Olofsson, *Mellan klass och stat* (Lund: Arkiv, 1979).

30 Tommy Lundström and Filip Wijkström, *The Nonprofit Sector in Sweden* (Manchester: Manchester University Press, 1997); Michele Micheletti, "Organisationer och svensk demokrati," in *På medborgarnas villkor: en demokratisk infrastruktur* (Stockholm: Fritzes, 1996).

31 Kurt Klaudi Klaussen and Per Selle, "The Third Sector in Scandinavia," *Voluntas* 7 (1996): 99–122; Bo Rothstein, *Den korporativa staten* (Stockholm: Norstedts, 1992); Bo Rothstein, "State Structure and Variations in Corporatism: The Swedish Case," *Scandinavian Political Studies* 14 (1991): 149–71. This is not to say that this close collaboration with the state did not cause problems for the organizations; see Per-Ola Öberg, *Särintresse och allmänintresse. Korporatismens ansikten* (Uppsala: Almqvist and Wiksell International, 1994).

32 Quote from Rothstein, "State Structure and Variations in Corporatism," 162; see also Rothstein, *Den korporativa staten*, 89.

33 Qoute from Rothstein, "State Structure and Variations in Corporatism," 164.

34 Rothstein, *Den korporativa staten;* see Öberg, *Särintresse och allmänintresse.*

35 Quotes from Rothstein, "State Structure and Variations in Corporatism," 163–65.

36 Gunnar Heckscher, *Staten och organisationerna* (Stockholm: KF Förlag, 1946).

37 Rothstein, *Den korporativa staten.*

38 Per Selle, "The Transformation of the Voluntary Sector in Norway: A Decline of Social Capital?" in Jan Van Deth et al., eds., *Social Capital and European Democracy* (London: Routledge, 1998); see Öberg, *Särintresse*

och allmänintresse.

39 Lewin, "The Rise and Decline of Corporatism"; Rothstein, *Den korporativa staten.*

40 Per Selle and Bjarne Øymyr, *Frivillig organisering og demokrati* (Oslo: Samlaget, 1995); see Selle 1998.

41 Pettersson, "In Search of Respectability."

42 Lennart Lundquist, *Fattigvårdsfolket. Ett nätverk i den sociala frågan 1900–1920* (Lund: Lund University Press, 1997), 137–94; Tommy Lundström, "The State and Voluntary Social Work in Sweden," *Voluntas* 7 (1996): 123–46.

43 John Boli, "Sweden: Is There a Viable Third Sector?" in Robert Wuthnow, ed., *Between States and Markets: The Voluntary Sector in a Comparative Perspective* (Princeton: Princeton University Press, 1991).

44 SCB, *Välfärd och ojämlikhet i 20–årsperspektiv 1975–1995* (Stockholm: Statistics Sweden, 1997), 327–29.

45 Barbara A. Misztal, *Trust in Modern Societies* (Cambridge: Polity Press, 1996), 95.

46 *Folkbildningen—en utvärdering* (SOU 1996:159) (Stockholm: Fritzes, 1996), 18. Figures from 1994.

47 Ibid., 35.

48 Rothstein et al., *Demokrati som dialog,* 59.

49 *Folkbildningen—en utvärdering,* 37, 123.

50 Ibid., 19.

51 Ibid., 134.

52 Olof Petersson et al., *Medborgarnas makt* (Stockholm: Carlssons, 1987), 216.

53 Ibid., 251.

54 Lars Häll, *Föreningslivet i Sverige* (Stockholm: Statistics Sweden, 1994), 11.

55 Michael Woolcook, "The Place of Social Capital in Understanding Social and Economic Outcomes," *ISUMA: Canadian Journal of Policy Research* 2 (2001).

56 The same goes for Norway (see Selle and Øymyr, *Frivillig organisering og demokrati,* 173) and also for Denmark (see Jorgen Goul Andersen, Lars Torpe, and Johannes Andersen, *Hvad folket magter* [Copenhagen: JoF Förlag, 2001]).

57 The study asked if respondents were members of unions, political organizations, sports organizations, temperance organizations, religious organizations, and "other" organizations. See Marek Perlinski, "Livet utantör fabriksgrinden och kontorsdörren," in Rune Åberg, ed., *Industrisamhället i omvandling* (Stockholm: Carlssons, 1990), 228.

58 See Olof Petersson, *Politikens möjligheter* (Stockholm: SNS Förlag, 1996), and Micheletti, "Organisationer och svensk demokrati."

59 Rothstein, "Labor Market Institutions and Working-Class Strength," in Sven Steinmo et al., eds., *Structuring Politics: Historical Institutionalism in*

a Comparative Perspective (New York: Cambridge University Press, 1992).

60 Johan Fritzell and Olle Lundberg, *Vardagens villkor. Levnadsförhållanden i Sverige under tre decennier* (Stockholm: Brombergs, 1994), 241.

61 Rothstein et al., *Demokrati som dialog*, 59.

62 Häll, *Föreningslivet i Sverige*, 63. In sum, this would mean that the degree of mobilization for the whole population by these organizations has gone down by about 20 percent. There is, however, one reason why one should be careful about drawing conclusions from comparing these two studies. Although the questions were identical, these were two different types of surveys. The 1987 survey was about power and democracy, and the 1992 survey was about the standard of living. It may be that because of these different contexts, activity in volunteer organizations was overreported by respondents in the former one. See Häll, *Föreningslivet i Sverige*, 27.

63 Micheletti, "Organisationer och svensk demokrati," 205, and Petersson, *Politikens möjligheter*, 57–59.

64 *Demokrati och makt i Sverige*, ch. 11.

65 Olof Petersson et al., *Medborgarnas* makt (Stockholm: Carlssons, 1989), 262.

66 The SOM Institute at Göteborg University conducts an annual national survey on the topics of society, opinion, and media (hence the name SOM). The institute is managed in part by the Department of Political Science at Göteborg University. For this project, questions about trust were added to the five surveys done between 1996 and 2000. For information about sampling, response rates, etc., please visit www.som.gu.se or contact som@jmg.gu.se.

67 Bo Rothstein, "Förtroende för andra och förtroende för politiska institutioner," in Sören Holmberg and Lennart Weibull, eds., *Ljusnande framtid* (Göteborg: Göteborg University, 1999); Eva Jeppsson Grassman and Lars Svedberg, "Medborgarskapets gestaltningar. Insatser i och utanför föreningslivet," in *Civilsamhället* (Stockholm: Allmänna förlaget, 1999).

68 Thorleif Pettersson, "Välfärd, värderingsförändringar och folkrörelseengagemang," in Sigbert Axelsson and Thorleif Pettersson, eds., *Mot denna framtid* (Stockholm: Carlssons förlag, 1992), 51.

69 Thorleif Pettersson and Kalle Geyer, *Värderingsförändringar i Sverige. Den svenska modellen, individualismen och rättvisan* (Stockholm: Brevskolan, 1992), 13. The investigation defines a generally individualistic attitude as one marked by the possession of at least three of the following four characteristics: (1) recommending personal freedom over economic equality, (2) being inclined to hold firm and try to convince others, (3) desiring a stronger emphasis on individual development, and (4) wishing no greater respect for authorities.

70 Ibid. Having an individualistic view of working life means that one embraces at least three of the following four statements: (1) it is fair that a more efficient secretary earns more; (2) employees should only follow

their supervisors' instructions when they accord with their own convictions; (3) it is important to be able to take personal initiative on the job; and (4) it is important to be able to take responsibility on the job.

71 Ibid., 28–31. Emphasis on last sentence removed. That these are two different dimensions among Scandinavian citizens is demonstrated as well by Jörgen Goul Andersen, "Samfundsind og egennytte," *Politica* 25 (1993).

72 Pettersson and Geyer, *Värderingsförändringar i Sverige*, 28–30. This is also supported by a Finnish study, Helena Blomberg and Christian Kroll, "Välfärdsvärderingar i olika generationer—från kollektivism mot en ökad individualism?" *Sosiologia* 32 (1995): 106–21.

73 D. G. Barker et al., *The European Value Study, 1981–1990* (Tilburg: Gordon Cook Foundation of European Values Group, 1992), 5.

74 Andersson et al., *70-talister om värderingar förr*, 144–46.

75 Häll, *Föreningslivet i Sverige*, Table 2:10.

76 Selle and Øymyr, *Frivillig organisering og demokrati*, 241.

77 Rothstein, "Labor Market Institutions and Working-Class Strength."

78 Ibid.

79 Rothstein, *Den korporativa staten*.

80 Ibid.

81 Rothstein, "Labor Market Institutions and Working-Class Strength."

82 Sven Nelander and Viveka Lindgren, *Röster om facket och jobbet. Facklig aktivitet och fackligt arbete* (Stockholm: LO, 1994).

83 SCB, *Välfärd och ojämlikhet i 20-årsperspektiv 1975–1995*, 335–39.

84 Ibid.

85 See Boli, "Sweden: Is There a Viable Third Sector?"

86 Zetterberg and Ljungberg, *Vårt land—den svenska socialstaten*, 266.

87 Alan Wolfe, *Whose Keeper? Social Science and Moral Obligation* (Berkeley: University of California Press, 1989), 22.

88 Ibid., 142.

89 Perlinski, "Livet utantör," 231–33.

90 SCB, *Välfärd och ojämlikhet i 20-årsperspektiv 1975–1995*, 287–301 (significant levels are .05).

91 See e.g., Zetterberg and Ljungberg, *Vårt land—den svenska socialstaten*; see also Wolfe, *Whose Keeper*.

92 Karin Busch Zetterberg, *Det civila samhället och välfärdsstaten* (Stockholm: City University Press, 1996).

93 Wolfe, *Whose Keeper*, 258.

94 Kontrollstyrelsen, *Alkoholstatistik* (Stockholm: SCB, 1968).

95 Socialstyrelsen, *Alkoholstatistik* (Stockholm: SCB, 1997). Figure from 1997 by personal communication from Anders Edin at the National Alcohol Board, January 8, 1998.

96 Personal communication from Anders Edin at the National Alcohol Board, January 8, 1998.

97 SCB, *Välfärd och ojämlikhet i 20-årsperspektiv 1975–1995*, 119.

98 Fritzell and Lundberg, *Vardagens villkor,* 256.

99 SCB, *Välfärd och ojämlikhet i 20–årsperspektiv 1975–1995,* 303.

100 Katherine Gaskin and Justin Davis Smith, *A New Civic Europe? A Study of the Extent and Role of Volunteering* (London: The Volunteer Center, 1995), 28.

101 The other countries were Belgium, Bulgaria, Germany, Ireland, the Netherlands, Slovakia, and the United Kingdom.

102 The interviewers prompted those who answered no to the question by showing them a list of the types of unpaid work that people do and checking whether they had done any of them. The unprompted figure for Sweden was 32 percent and the average for the other countries was 23 percent.

103 Gaskin and Smith, *A New Civic Europe,* 35.

104 Ibid., 50.

105 Lundström and Wijkström, *The Nonprofit Sector in Sweden;* see also Lester Salamon et al., *The Emerging Sector: A Statistical Supplement* (Baltimore: Johns Hopkins Institute for Policy Studies, 1996).

106 Lester Salamon and Helmut Anheier, *The Emerging Sector: An Overview* (Baltimore: Johns Hopkins Institute for Policy Studies, 1994), 35.

107 Lundström and Wijkström, *The Nonprofit Sector in Sweden.* The study included France, Italy, Japan, Hungary, Sweden, the United States, the United Kingdom, and Germany. The nonprofit sector in this project was defined as formal, private, self-governing, and voluntary organizations in the following areas: culture, recreation, education, health, social services, environment, development and housing, civic and advocacy, philanthrophy, business, professional, and "other." Religious congregations, political parties, cooperatives, mutual savings banks, mutual insurance companies, and government agencies were excluded. See Salamon and Anheier 1994, p. 13–16. One problem with the economic measures from this study is that unions have been included. In Sweden, the state has given unions a great deal of power over working conditions for employees, such as choosing who loses their jobs first when there are layoffs. In practice, local unions have this power over employees whether or not they are union members. In many cases, this makes membership voluntary only from a rather formal point of view. As the unions' share of the economic size of the voluntary sector in Sweden is, according to this study, 17.6 percent, the Swedish figures may be exaggerated to some extent. But even if unions were not counted, the relative economic size of the Swedish nonprofit sector would still be as large or larger than in, for example, France, Germany, or Italy.

108 British data from Office of Population Census and Surveys, Monitor 17, *General Household Survey: Careers in 1990* (London: The Government Statistical Service, 1992), quoted here from Busch Zetterberg, *Det civila samhället och välfärdsstaten,* 197.

109 See Bo Rothstein, "The Universal Welfare State as a Social Dilemma," *Rationality and Society* 13 (2001): 213–33.

110 Stein Kuhnle and Per Selle, *Government and Voluntary Organizations* (Avesbury: Aldershot, 1992); see also Lundström and Filip Wijkström, *The Nonprofit Sector in Sweden.*

111 Ronald Inglehart, *Modernization and Postmodernization: Cultural, Economic and Political Change in 43 Countries* (Princeton: Princeton University Press, 1997), 172–75.

112 The same goes for Denmark; see Goul Andersen, Torpe, and Andersen 2001.

113 Bo Rothstein, "På spaning efter det sociala kapital som flytt," in Sören Holmberg and Lennart Weibull, eds., *Det nya samhället?* (Göteborg: Göteborg University, 2000).

114 The multiple regression model is presented in Bo Rothstein, "Social Capital and Institutional Legitimacy," working paper presented at the annual meeting of the American Political Science Association, Washington, DC, Aug. 28–Sept. 2, 2000.

115 Eric Uslaner, *The Moral Foundations of Trust* (New York: Cambridge University Press, forthcoming).

116 Data from the 1996 SOM survey.

117 The statistical analysis is presented in Rothstein, "Social Capital and Institutional Legitimacy."

118 Game theorists usually use the term "opportunistic behavior," which I think is a much too nice term to describe what this is all about.

119 See Sidney Tarrow, "Making Social Science Work Across Space and Time: A Critical Reflection on Robert Putnman's *Making Democracy Work,*" *American Political Science Review* 90 (1996): 389–97, and Margaret Levi, "Social and Unsocial Capital," *Politics and Society* 24 (1996): 45–55.

120 Bo Rothstein, *Just Institutions Matter: The Moral and Political Logic of the Universal Welfare State* (Cambridge: Cambridge University Press, 1998). See also Inglehart, *Modernization and Postmodernization,* 173.

121 See John Brehm and Wendy Rahn, "Individual-Level Evidence for the Causes and Consequences of Social Capital," *American Journal of Political Science* 41 (1997): 999–1023. Dietlind Stolle has shown that at the micro level, there is no evidence that over time, participation in voluntary organizations (in Sweden) increases generalized trust; see Dietlind Stolle, "Clubs and Congregations: The Benefits of Joining Associations," in Karen S. Cook, ed., *Trust in Society* (New York: Russell Sage Foundation, 2001).

122 Rafael LaPorta et al., "Trust in Large Organizations," *American Economic Review* 87 (1997): 333–38. See also Ronald Inglehart, "Trust, Well-being and Democracy," in Mark E. Warren, ed., *Democracy and Trust* (New York: Cambridge University Press, 1999).

123 World Value Studies, 1981 and 1990.

124 I have elaborated this theme in Rothstein, *Just Institutions Matter.*

125 Theda Skocpol, "America's Incomplete Welfare State: The Limits of New Deal Reforms and the Origins of the Present Crisis," in Martin Rein et al., eds.,

Stagnation and Renewal in Social Policy (Armonk, NY: M. E. Sharpe, 1987).

126 Cohen and Arato, *Civil Society and Political Theory,* 664. AFDC stands for Aid to Families with Dependent Children, which has been a major means-tested social assistance program in the United States. The "man-in-house rule" is a provision in the program that states that if an able-bodied, grown man lives in the household (as husband or cohabitant), then no assistance shall be rendered to that family. This rule has, according to critics of the program, created an incentive for the man to abandon the family and has contributed thereby to a very sharp increase in the rate of family breakup in socially disadvantaged groups.

127 See Johan P. Olsen, *Organized Democracy: Political Institutions in a Welfare State—The Case of Norway* (Oslo: Universitetsförlaget, 1992).

128 Klas Åmark, "Social Democracy and the Trade Union Movement: Solidarity and the Politics of Self-Interest," in Klas Misgeld et al., eds., *Creating Social Democracy: A Century of the Social Democratic Labor Party in Sweden* (University Park: Pennsylvania State University Press, 1992), 73.

129 Gary D. Miller, *Managerial Dilemmas* (Cambridge: Cambridge University Press, 1992); see also Adam Przeworski and Michael Wallerstein, "The Structure of Class Conflict in Democratic Capitalist Societies," *American Political Science Review* 76 (1992): 215–18.

130 Bertil Kugelberg, *Från en central utsiktspunkt* (Stockholm: Norstedt, 1986), 95.

131 Some historians have even spoken of this as a "secret addition" to the agreement, e.g., Klas Åmark, *Facklig makt och fackligt medlemskap* (Lund: Arkiv, 1989).

132 Åmark, "Social Democracy and the Trade Union Movement."

133 Kugelberg, *Från en central utsiktspunkt,* 52.

134 Göran Therborn, "Socialdemokratin träder fram," *Arkiv för studier i arbetarrörelsens historia* 41 (1988): 1–46; see also Åmark, "Social Democracy and the Trade Union Movement," and Sven-Anders Söderpalm, *Arbetsgivarna och saltsjöbadspolitiken* (Stockholm: Swedish Employers' Federation, 1981); Bertil Kugelberg, *Upp i vind* (Stockholm: Norstedt, 1985), 301–4.

135 See, e.g., Kugelberg, *Upp i vind,* 302–4.

136 Rothstein, *Den korporativa staten.* For a very instructive comparison between Germany and Sweden, see Sheri Berman, "Path Dependency and Political Action: Re-examining Responses to the Depression," *Comparative Politics,* forthcoming.

137 One of the reasons for this conviction was that a large part of the famous crisis package of 1933 between the Social Democrats and the Agrarians, which was intended to curb unemployment, could not be implemented because of a nine-month conflict in the construction industry, which was seen as provoked by the militant, partly communist, unions in this sector; see Åmark, "Social Democracy and the Trade Union Movement," and

Anders L. Johansson, *Tillväxt och klassamarbete* (Stockholm: Tiden, 1989).

138 Kugelberg, *Från en central utsiktspunkt*, 112.

139 It should be added that they received tremendous help in 1945 from a large conflict in which the communist-led Metalworkers Union had a central role and which ended in defeat for the union. As Olofsson has pointed out in *Mellan klass och stat*, the reformist strategy inside the union movement was to see to it that the communists' militant strategy lost such battles, thereby "proving" that only their own cooperative strategy could be successful.

140 Tilton, *The Political Theory of Swedish Social Democracy*, 224; see also Nils Elvander, *Den svenska modellen* (Stockholm: Publica, 1988). TCO is the confederation of the white-collar unions.

141 Rudolf Meidner, *Employee Investment Funds* (London: George Allen and Unwin, 1978).

142 Tilton, *The Political Theory of Swedish Social Democracy*, p. 229.

143 Mikael Gilljam, *Svenska folket och löntagarfonderna* (Lund: Studentlitteratur, 1988), 176.

144 Bo Stråth, *The Organisation of Labour Markets: Modernity, Culture and Governance in Germany, Sweden, Britain and Japan* (London: Routledge, 1996), 99–106.

145 Bert-Olof Svanholm, interviewed in *Svenska Dagbladet*, October 23, 1994.

146 Assar Lindbeck, *The Swedish Experiment* (Stockholm: SNS Förlag, 1999).

147 *Svenska Dagbladet*, May 6, 1996.

148 Elvander, *Den svenska modellen*; see also Lewin, "The Rise and Decline of Corporatism."

149 Jonas Pontusson and Peter Swensson, "Labour Markets, Production Strategies and Wage Bargaining Institutions," *Comparative Political Studies* 29 (1996): 223–50.

150 Jonas Pontusson, *The Limits of Reformism: Investment Politics in Sweden* (Ithaca: Cornell University Press, 1993).

151 Jon Elster, "Rationality and Social Norms," *Archives Europennées de Sociologie* 31 (1991): 233–56.

8   Australia

Since I first drafted this chapter, Sydney, Australia, has hosted the 2000 Olympic and Paralympic Games. For those four weeks in September, the fifty thousand volunteer guides, the concentration of attention on the Games, and the free public transport to the venues brought about an openness between strangers more common in times of disaster or war.

The Games worked well because they reminded us of the better parts of our history. The visible cross-party support from government and the opposition combined with the diversity celebrated in the opening and closing ceremonies and with spontaneous generosity to outsiders to build an ethos of shared goodwill. This view fits with the proposition of this chapter—that social capital in Australia is the legitimate offspring of a peculiar mix of government and nongovernment intersections.

However, reports from the previous Olympic Games in Atlanta did not note any increased civility or goodwill, so the effect could have been something peculiarly Australian. Unfortunately, despite government rhetoric hailing a new era of citizenship and calling for continuity of the volunteer spirit, the effect faded, leaving the same political bickering, the same conflict between the rural and urban populations, and the same dispute over reconciliation with the Aborigines. Even so, in November 2000, close to one million people staged a walk across bridges in support of reconciliation with indigenous peoples.

1 In Australia, the term *electorate* refers to a geographical area that elects one member.

2 Australian National University, Social Science Data Archives, Referendum Study no. 1018, 1999. When asked to choose whether government, by its nature, is the best instrument for promoting the general interests of society or threatens the rights of people and must not be trusted, 70.5 percent chose the first.

3 F. G. Castles, *The Working Class and Welfare* (Wellington: Allen and Unwin, 1985).

4 Australian Bureau of Statistics, *Australian Social Trends* (Canberra: Australian Bureau of Statistics, 1998), 2.

5 H. Eisenstein, *Inside Agitators* (Sydney: Allen and Unwin, 1996).

6 P. Adams, ed., *The Retreat from Tolerance: A Snapshot of Australian Society* (Sydney: ABC Books, 1997).

7 R. Eckersley, "Perspectives on Progress," in R. Eckersley, ed., *Measuring Progress: Is Life Getting Better?* (Collingwood, Victoria: CSIRO, 1998), 4–9.

8 Australian Bureau of Statistics, *Voluntary Work Australia,* Cat. No. 4441.0 (Canberra: Australian Bureau of Statistics, 1995), 1.

9 Australian Bureau of Statistics, *How Australians Use Their Time,* Cat. No. 4153.0 (Canberra: Australian Bureau of Statistics, 1992).

10 Australian Bureau of Statistics, *South Australian Community and Voluntary Work Survey* (Canberra: Australian Bureau of Statistics, 1988).

11 Australian Bureau of Statistics, *How Australians Use Their Time.*

12 Australian Bureau of Statistics, *Aspects of Literacy,* Cat. No. 4228.0 (Canberra: Australian Bureau of Statistics, 1996).

13 P. Hughes and J. Bellamy, "The Distribution of Social Capital," unpublished paper, 1998.

14 F. Baum et al., "Volunteering and Social Capital: An Adelaide Study," *Volunteer Journal of Australia* 23, 3 (1998).

15 Hughes and Bellamy, "The Distribution of Social Capital."

16 Unpublished student surveys, University of Technology, Sydney, 1998.

17 M. Lyons and S. Hocking, *Australia's Non-Profit Sector: Some Preliminary Data* (Sydney: Centre for Community Management, University of Tech-

nology, 1998).

18 P. Kaldor et al., *Winds of Change: The Experience of Church in a Changing Australia* (Lancer: The National Church Life Survey, 1994).

19 Hughes and Bellamy, "The Distribution of Social Capital."

20 Australian Bureau of Statistics, *Australian Social Trends,* 1994, 109.

21 Australian National University, Social Science Data Archives, *Australian Election Survey* (Canberra: Australian National University, 1996).

22 Ibid.

23 Ibid.

24 Baum et al., "Volunteering and Social Capital."

25 Australian National University, *Australian Election Survey,* 1996, 1998.

26 Roy Morgan Research Centre, Morgan Poll No. 2892, April 1996.

27 D. Weatherburn, E. Matke, and B. Lind, "Crime Perception and Reality," *Crime and Justice Bulletin* (NSW Bureau of Crime Statistics and Research) 2 (1996).

28 H. Brownlee and P. McDonald, "A Safe Place for Children," *Family Matters* 33 (1992): 22–26.

29 D. de Vaus and S. Wise, "The Fear of Attack," *Family Matters* 43 (1996): 34–38.

30 Unpublished student surveys, University of Technology, Sydney, 1998.

31 AGB McNair Pty. Ltd., Australian National University, Social Science Data Archives, 1989.

32 Australian National University, *Australian Election Survey.*

33 National Centre for Social and Economic Modelling, University of Canberra, *Income Distribution Report,* May 1996.

34 United Nations Development Programme, *Human Development Report* (London: Oxford University Press, 1998).

35 Davis and Associates, "News Ltd Submission to Media Ownership Inquiry," *The Australian,* business section, Dec. 3, 1996.

36 Australian Bureau of Statistics, *How Australians Use Their Time.*

37 Davis and Associates, "News Ltd Submission to Media Ownership Inquiry."

38 Roy Morgan Research Centre, *World Values Study* (Melbourne: Roy Morgan Research Centre, 1983, 1995).

39 Roy Morgan Research Centre, Morgan Poll No. 2877, 1996.

40 S. Knack and P. Keefer, "Does Social Capital Have an Economic Payoff?" *Harvard Journal of Economics,* December 1997, 1253–88.

41 Lyons and Hocking, *Australia's Non-Profit Sector.*

42 R. D. Putnam, *Making Democracy Work* (New Haven: Yale University Press, 1993).

9   Japan

This study has benefited enormously from the assistance provided with data analysis by Shiro Harada, Emiko Iwasaki, and Yoko Matsuba. I am most grateful to them. I am also very grateful to Ikuo Kabashima, Nobuo Takahashi, Aiji Tanaka, and Yutaka Tsujinaka for their enlightening studies on elections, organizations, and networks. Advice I received from the Management and Coordination Agency and the Economic Planning Agency was also most helpful. I also note that Table 9-4 derives from the Asia-Europe Survey data conducted by the Gallup Associations (led by the Nippon Research Center) in the fall of 2000 in eighteen societies in East and Southeast Asia and Western Europe. The survey was designed by the Democracy and Political Cultures Project, financially supported by the Japanese Ministry of Education, Science, Cultures, Sports, Science and Technology for the period 1999–2003 (project number 11102001, project leader Takashi Inoguchi). Above all, I am most grateful to the participants of the project for their critically constructive discussions on earlier drafts of this paper. I must express my particular gratitude to Robert Putnam and Then Volker for their immensely useful comments.

1   Robert Putnam, "Bowling Alone: America's Declining Social Capital," *Journal of Democracy* 6, 1 (1995), 65–78; Robert Putnam, "Tuning In, Tuning Out: The Strange Disappearance of Social Capital in America," *PS: Political Science and Politics*, December 1995, 664–83; Robert Putnam, "Democracy in America at Century's End," in Axel Hadenius, ed., *Democracy's Victory and Crisis* (Cambridge: Cambridge University Press, 1997), 27–70.

2 Yutaka Tsujinaka, "Interest Group Structure and Change in Japan," University of Maryland, College Park/University of Tsukuba Papers on U.S.-Japan Relations, November 1996.

3 Yasusuke Murakami, *An Anti-Classical Political-Economic Analysis* (Stanford: Stanford University Press, 1996); Takashi Inoguchi, *Gendai Nihon seiji keizai no kozu* [Contemporary Japanese political economy], (Tokyo: Toyo Keizai Shimposha, 1983); Takashi Inoguchi, "The Political Economy of Conservative Resurgence Under Recession: Public Policies and Political Support in Japan, 1977–1983," in T. J. Pempel, ed., *Uncommon Democracies: The One-Party Dominant Regimes* (Ithaca: Cornell University Press, 1990), 189–225.

4 Chikio Hayashi and Akira Iriyama, *Koeki hojin no jitsujo* [The reality of nonprofit organizations] (Tokyo: Diamond Sha, 1997).

5 "Jidai ni tachimukau shimin undo no suimyaku—networking keisai dantai zen list" [Currents of civic action groups confronting the times: organizations described in the feature articles], *Asahi Journal*, December 9 and 12, 1988.

6 See Takashi Inoguchi, *Nihon: Keizai taikoku no seiji un'ei* [The governing of an economic superpower 1974-1993]. Tokyo: University of Tokyo Press, 1993 (English edition forthcoming).

7 Ministry of Education, Institute of Statistics and Mathematics, *Kokuminsei no kenkyu* [Studies of national character] (Tokyo: Government of

Japan, Ministry of Education, 1953–96).

8 Gabriel Almond and Sidney Verba, *The Civic Culture* (Princeton: Princeton University Press, 1963).

9 Joji Watanuki, "Japan: From Emerging to Stable Party System?" Research Papers Series no. A-67, Institute of International Relations, Sophia University, 1997.

10 Takashi Inoguchi, "Social Capital in Japan," *Japanese Journal of Political Science* 1, 1 (2000), 73–112.

11 Claus Offe, "Social Capital: Concepts and Hypotheses," Humbolt University, July 1997.

12 Association for the Promotion of Clean Elections, *Dai sanjuhachi-kai Shugiin sosenkyo no jittai* [The 38th general election for the House of Representatives] and *Dai sanjukyu-kai Shugiin sosenkyo no jittai* [The 39th general election for the House of Representatives] (Tokyo: Association for the Promotion of Clean Elections, 1987 and 1991).

13 Joji Watanuki and Ichiro Miyake, *Kankyo henka to tohyo kodo* [Political environment and voting behavior] (Tokyo: Bokutakusha, 1997).

14 Robert Putnam, *Making Democracy Work: Civic Traditions in Modern Italy* (Princeton: Princeton University Press, 1993).

15 Ibid.

16 On the discrepancy, see, for example, Susan Pharr, "Japanese Videocracy," *Press/Politics* 2, 2 (1997); Susan Pharr, "Public Trust and Democracy in Japan," in Joseph S. Nye Jr., Philip D. Zelikow, and David C. King, eds., *Why People Don't Trust Government* (Cambridge, MA: Harvard University Press, 1997), 232–57.

17 Joji Watanuki, "Japan," in Seymour Martin Lipset and Sten Rokkan, eds., *Party System and Voter Alignments: Cross-National Perspectives* (New York: Free Press, 1967); Joji Watanuki, "Political Generations in Post–World War II Japan: With Some Comparisons to the Case of Germany," Research Papers Series A-64, Institute of International Relations, Sophia University, 1995; Watanuki, "Japan: From Emerging to Stable Party System?"

18 Inoguchi, *Gendai Nihon seiji keizai no kozu;* Inoguchi, "The Political Economy of Conservative Resurgence Under Recession."

19 Takashi Inoguchi and Tomoaki Iwai, *Zoku-giin no kenkyu* [A study of "legislative tribes"] (Tokyo: Nihon Keizai Shimbunsha, 1987).

20 Ibid.

21 Ellis Krauss, "Portraying the State: NHK Television News and Politics," in Susan Pharr and Ellis Krauss, eds., *Media and Politics in Japan* (Honolulu: University of Hawaii Press, 1995); Susan Pharr, "Media and Politics in Japan," in Susan Pharr and Ellis Krauss, eds., *Media and Politics in Japan* (Honolulu: University of Hawaii Press, 1995).

22 Benedict Anderson, *Imagined Communities* (London: Verso, 1972).

23 Pharr, "Public Trust and Democracy in Japan."

24 It must be noted, however, that especially since January 2001, when the

new Administrative Law came into force, cabinet members have come forward to answer questions from the floor much more directly than before.

25 Takashi Inoguchi, *Sekai hendo no mikata* [Global change] (Tokyo: Chikuma Shobo, 1994) (English edition, *Global change: A Japanese Perspective* [New York: Palgrave, 2001]).

26 Takashi Inoguchi, "The Pragmatic Evolution of Japanese Democracy," in Michelle Schmiegelow, ed., *Democracy in Asia* (Frankfurt: Campus Verlag and New York: St. Martin's Press, 1997), 217–32; Takashi Inoguchi, "The Japanese Political System in Historical Perspective: Political Representation and Economic Competitiveness," *Asian Journal of Political Science* 4, 2 (1997): 58–72.

27 Richard Fenno Jr., *Home Style: House Members in Their Districts* (Boston: Little, Brown, 1979); Inoguchi and Iwai, *Zoku-giin no kenkyu*.

28 Shigeki Nishihira, *Yoron kara mita dojidaishi* [Contemporary history as seen from opinion polls] (Tokyo: Brain Shuppan, 1987).

29 Nishihira, *Yoron kara mita dojidaishi*.

30 Joseph S. Nye Jr., Philip D. Zelikow, and David C. King, eds., *Why People Don't Trust Government* (Cambridge: Harvard University Press, 1997).

31 Susan Pharr and Robert Putnam, eds., *Disaffected Democracies* (Princeton: Princeton University Press, 1999).

32 Toshio Yamagishi, *Shakaiteki jiremma no kenkyu* [A study of social dilemma] (Tokyo: Science Sha, 1990).

33 Ibid.

34 Michael Taylor, *Anarchy and Cooperation* (New York: Wiley, 1979); Michael Taylor, *Community, Anarchy, and Liberty* (New York: Cambridge University Press, 1982).

35 Eshun Hamaguchi, *Kanjinshugi no shakai: Nihon* [Japan as a society of relationism] (Tokyo: Toyo Keizai Shimposha, 1992).

36 D. T. Campbell and J. C. Stanley, *Experimental and Quasi-Experimental Designs for Research* (Chicago: Rand McNally, 1963).

37 Albert O. Hirschmann, *Exit, Voice, and Loyalty* (Cambridge, Mass.: Harvard University Press, 1970).

38 Robert Putnam, comments on draft of this chapter, October 1997.

39 Eiko Ikegami, *The Taming of the Samurai: Honorific Individualism and the Making of Modern Japan* (Cambridge: Harvard University Press, 1995).

40 Richard Samuels, *Rich Nation, Strong Army* (Ithaca: Cornell University Press, 1991).

41 Inoguchi, *Global Change;* Takashi Inoguchi, "Dialectics of World Order: A View from Pacific Asia," in Hans-Henrik Holm and Georg Sorensen, eds., *Whose World Order?: Uneven Globalization and the End of the Cold War* (Boulder: Westview Press, 1995), 119–36.

42 Ronald Inglehart, *The Silent Revolution* (Princeton: Princeton University Press, 1971); Ronald Inglehart, *Culture Shift in Advanced Industrial Society* (Princeton: Princeton University Press, 1990).

43 Watanuki, "Political Generations in Post–World War II Japan."

44 Francis Fukuyama, *Trust: Social Virtues and the Creation of Prosperity* (New York: Simon and Schuster, 1995); Toshio Yamagishi, "The Provision of a Sanctioning System in the United States and Japan," *Social Psychological Quarterly* 51, 3 (1988): 265–71.

45 Ikegami, *The Taming of the Samurai;* Emile Durkheim, (Anthony Giddeas, ed.) Selected Writings (Cambridge: Cambridge University Press, 1985).

46 Paul Krugman, "The Myth of Asia's Miracle," *Foreign Affairs* 73, 6 (1993): 62–78; Robert Reich, *The Work of Nations* (New York: Knopf, 1995).

47 Takashi Inoguchi, "The Political Economy of Japan's Upper House Election of July 12, 1998," presentation at Public Seminar, Australian National University, August 12, 1998. See also Takashi Inoguchi, "The Japanese General Election of 25 June 2000," *Government and Opposition,* 35:4 (Autumn 2000) 484-498. This line of interpretation of the 2001 Upper House Election is done most cogently by Kuniko Inoguchi. See Kuniko Inoguchi, " Kaikaku, Shimin Sankaku Unagase" (Promote Civic Participation for Reform), *Yomiuri Shinbun* July 31 (evening edition).

48 Takashi Inoguchi, Edward Newman, and John Keane, eds., *The Changing Nature of Democracy* (Tokyo and New York: United Nations University Press, 1998). Ian Marsh, Jean Blondel and Takashi Inoguchi, eds., *Democracy, Governance and Economic Performance: East and Southeast Asia* (Tokyo and New York: United Nations University Press, 2000).

Appendix

Social Capital–Related Indicators
(Economic Planning Agency, 1980–1995)
Dwelling (household)

1. Percentage of persons who own their own homes
2. Percentage of persons whose houses are dangerous or irreparable
3. Percentage of persons whose houses are above the so-called minimum standard of living
4. Real rent per tatami-unit size (house)
5. Percentage of garbage and refuse processed to satisfactory sanitary standards
6. Percentage of fires per 100,000 houses
7. Traffic accidents per 100,000 persons
8. Recognized penal-law violations per 1,000 persons
9. Received complaints about pollution per 100,000 persons
10. Ratio of housing loans paid off versus those still outstanding
11. Ratio of medical doctors to number of dwellings within a 500-meter radius
12. Gini index of property assets
13. Purchase price of house vis-à-vis annual income
14. Proportion of for-rent dwellings being constructed among all houses
15. Ratio of houses receiving sunshine

more than 5 hours per day vis-à-vis all houses with residents

16. [Average size of dwelling per person] Number of tatami mats per person

17. Square meters of urban public parks per citizen

18. Kilometers of pedestrian roads and bicycle paths versus kilometers of automobile thoroughfares

19. Percentage of persons living in houses equipped with flush toilets vis-à-vis those without flush toilets

20. Ratio of houses within a 1-kilometer radius of the nearest train/subway station versus number of households

21. Amount of garbage and waste per person

Spending

22. Annual income

23. Consumer price index

24. Savings over annual income

25. Liabilities in annual income

26. Number of life-insurance policies

27. Individual bankruptcy announcements accepted by local courts per 100,000 persons

28. Amount of consumer-risk-related collected per 100,000 persons

29. Ratio of welfare-program families among all families

30. Gini index (income inequality)

31. Percentage of service expenditures versus consumption (goods and services) expenditures

32. Retail shops per 100,000 persons

33. Department stores per 100,000 persons

34. Consumer credit outstanding per person

35. Number of credit cards issued per person

36. Percentage of household budget for dining out

37. Number of home-delivery services used per person

38. Proportion of durable consumer goods expenditures in all consumption expenditures

39. Automatic teller machines per 10,000 persons

40. Convenience stores per 10,000 persons

41. Amount of mail-order sales per person

Work

42. Proportion in the workforce who have changed jobs within the last year per 10,000 persons

43. Number of publicly financed occupational training facilities per 1,000,000 persons 15 years and older

44. Percentage of fully unemployed persons in working population

45. Number of workers injured or killed in work-related accidents per 1,000,000 working hours

46. Real wages

47. Percentage of businesses that extend retirement age or reemploy older persons against [number of] businesses with fixed retirement system

48. Number of workers on sick leave (longer than four days) per 1,000 workers under the Labor Standards Law

49. Ratio of workers who live separately from their spouses because of work-related assignments

50. Ratio of workers with disabilities among new employees

51. Ratio of job-seekers per job announcements for young people (20–24 yrs.) vis-à-vis ratio of job-seekers per job announcements for older people (60–64 yrs.)

53. Average worker salary over GNP

54. Wage gap between men and women

55. Percentage of women among management personnel of executive rank

56. Ratio of successful job seekers to job announcements
57. Number of workers who have changed workplaces within the past year
58. Number of vacation days taken of paid annual leave
59. Number of workers taking advantage of flex-time work schedules
60. Real number of work hours
61. Ratio of overtime work hours to real work hours
62. Percentage of families whose main income-earner spends more than one hour commuting in one direction
63. Percentage of workers who have two days off per week
64. Number of hours women not employed outside the home devote to household matters and child rearing per day
65. Square meters of office space per person

Nurturing

66. Percentage of children being looked after in day-care centers (*hoikuen*)
67. Percentage of children who died under 1 year old
68. Number of pupils/students per class in school
69. Number of juvenile patients suffering from adult illnesses
70. Number of pupils/students absent from school for more than fifty days because they dislike school
71. Percentage of junior high school students who go on to senior high school
72. Number of minors age 14–19 arrested for crimes per 1,000 persons in general population
73. Average family expenditures for education
74. Incidences of school violence per 1,000 persons age 13–18

75. Percentage of primary-school pupils whose eyesight is below 1.0
76. Number of juvenile reformatories
77. Ratio of consultants for problems of fatherless families per 1,000 persons
78. Percentage of children attending kindergarten
79. Number of senior high schools
80. Percentage of expenditures for preparatory classes in overall educational expenditures
81. Number of public recreational facilities for children and youth
82. Number of children's recreation centers (*jidokan*)
83. Number of paper diapers (annual production in terms of tons)

Health

84. Ratio of elderly who are accommodated in public care facilities
85. Number of beds in general-care hospitals
86. Number of emergency-care hospitals
87. Number of nurses and nurse trainees
88. Percentages of persons who died of adult ailments
89. Percentage of persons hospitalized
90. Number of medical doctors
91. Percentage of [household] expenses for health and medical care
92. Ratio of medical expenses covered by public funds
93. Average life span
94. Percentage of persons who suffer from senile dementia over those 65 years and older
95. Number of elderly who can be accommodated in special-care nursing homes
96. Average hours ambulance service
97. Number of places in facilities for rehabilitation and training of persons with disabilities

98. Number of places in special-care nursing homes
99. Ratio of extra-charge hospital beds whose cost is covered by medical insurance schemes
100. Number of persons employed by facilities for the elderly not including welfare facilities
101. Number of helpers who visit and provide home care for the elderly
102. Number of helpers who visit and provide home care for people with disabilities
103. Number of home helpers for the elderly
104. Ratio of the elderly who are bedridden

Recreation

105. Number of persons who suffer from accidents or are victims of crimes
106. Number of continuous days of summer vacation
107. Ratio of corporate expense-account spending to individual consumption expenses
108. Number of movie theaters
109. Number of newly published books
110. Percentage of culture/leisure expenditures per consumption expenditures
111. Number of rental vehicles
112. Number of pachinko parlors
113. Number of local-government-sponsored horse-racing, bicycle-racing, or motorboat-racing concerns
114. Number of persons who go abroad for sightseeing
115. Number of video rental shops
116. Number of restaurants
117. Number of sports facilities
118. Number of satellite television subscribers
119. Number of karaoke box units
120. Average hours for leisure or recreation activities

Learning

121. Percentage of college entrants to college aspirants (high-school students)
122. Number of senior-high night school attendees
123. Percentage of Ikueikai scholarship recipients
124. Number of college graduates who enter graduate school
125. Ratio of foreign students per 10,000 citizens 15 years or older
126. Percentage of students entering colleges, junior colleges, polytechnic and vocational/technical schools
127. Percentage of students studying in colleges, junior colleges, polytechnic and vocational/technical schools
128. Number of bookstores and magazine stands per 100,000 persons
129. Enrollment in adult-education classes
130. Enrollment in privately run adult-education classes
131. Number of libraries
132. Number of museums
133. Number of employees in adult education
134. Length of studying and learning (minutes per 1,000 persons)

Association

135. Percentage of first marriages that end in divorce
136. Percentage of people who marry
137. Percentage of people who do not marry
138. Proportion of expense-account expenditures in consumption costs
140. Amount (yen) donated to volunteer (social welfare) activities
141. Percentage of people who volunteer for social welfare activities
142. Percentage of persons belonging to seniors clubs
143. Ratio of high-school students

from abroad received per 100,000 persons

144. Ratio of persons joining youth overseas volunteers corps age 20 to 39 per 1,000,000 population

145. Percentage of international marriages

146. Ratio of persons who correspond with people overseas per 10,000 persons

147. Number of persons an individual can come in contact with within

two to three hours over entire population

148. Percentage of blood donors in population age 16 to 64

149. Percentage of members of women's associations over total population

150. Minutes of social activity

151. Number of public halls per 1,000,000 persons

Conclusion

1 He also hypothesizes that a deterioration in economic conditions may have contributed to the decline in social trust.

2 See Susan J. Pharr and Robert D. Putnam, *Disaffected Democracies: What's Troubling the Trilateral Countries?* (Princeton: Princeton University Press, 2000).

3 Robert Wuthnow, *Loose Connections* (Cambridge, MA: Harvard University Press, 1999).

4 Eurodata TV, *One Television Year in the World: Audience Report,* April 1999.

5 For further evidence confirming this decline in trust, see Ian Winter, "Major Themes and Debates in the Social Capital Literature: The Australian Connection," in Ian Winter, ed., *Social Capital and Public Policy in Australia* (Melbourne: Australian Institute of Family Studies, 2000), 37.

6 Because of peculiarities in the available French data on associations, we can be confident of the "birthrate" of organizations, but we lack any information on the "death rate," so a substantial margin of uncertainty surrounds estimates of the net change in the size of the associational universe.

7 All the authors emphasize that the available evidence is much less good regarding trends in less formal social networks than trends in formal organizational membership. Thus, strictly speaking, the hypothesis that enhancement of informal networks is counterbalancing any deterioration in formal networks remains yet to be tested.

8 This effect is well known in other Western countries, including the United States, though ironically the first important study of this effect was conducted in Germany in the early 1930s: Marie Jahoda, Paul Lazarsfeld, and Hans Zeisel, *Marienthal* (Chicago: Aldine-Atherton, 1971 [1933]).

9 For confirmation of all these patterns in the United States, see Robert D. Putnam, *Bowling Alone: Collapse and Revival of American Community* (New York: Simon and Schuster, 2000).

10 For additional evidence on trends in American social capital, largely

though not entirely consistent with the chapters in this volume, see Putnam, *Bowling Alone*.

11 For a subsequent development of this argument, see Theda Skocpol, Ziad Munson, Bayliss Camp, and Andrew Karch, "Patriotic Partnerships: Why Great Wars Nourished American Civic Voluntarism," in Ira Katznelson and Martin Shefter, eds., *Shaped by War and Trade: International Influences on American Political Development* (Princeton: Princeton University Press, 2002).

12 Wuthnow, *Loose Connections*.

13 Mark Gray and Miki Caul, "Declining Voter Turnout in Advanced Industrial Democracies, 1950 to 1997: The Effects of Declining Group Mobilization," *Comparative Political Studies* 33 (2000): 1091–122; Martin P. Wattenberg, "The Decline of Party Mobilization," in Russell J. Dalton and Martin P. Wattenberg, eds., *Parties Without Partisans: Political Change in Advanced Industrial Democracies* (New York: Oxford University Press, 2000), 64–76; Peter Mair, "In the Aggregate: Mass Electoral Behaviour in Western Europe, 1950-2000," in Hans Keman, ed., *Comparative Democracy* (London: Sage, 2001); Hazen Ghobarah, "The Decline in Voter Turnout Across the Advanced (Post-) Industrial Democracies, 1980–1998," paper presented at the annual meeting of the American Political Science Association, Boston, September 1998.

14 Wattenberg, "The Decline of Party Mobilization," 71.

15 Mair, "In the Aggregate."

16 Wattenberg, "The Decline of Party Mobilization," 69.

17 Gray and Caul, "Declining Voter Turnout."

18 Russell J. Dalton, "The Decline of Party Identifications," in Russell J. Dalton and Martin P. Wattenberg, eds., *Parties Without Partisans: Political Change in Advanced Industrial Democracies* (New York: Oxford University Press, 2000), 19–36.

19 Mair, "In the Aggregate"; Dalton, "Decline of Party Identifications."

20 Susan E. Scarrow, "Parties Without Members? Party Organization in a Changing Electoral Environment," in Russell J. Dalton and Martin P. Wattenberg, eds., *Parties Without Partisans: Political Change in Advanced Industrial Democracies* (New York: Oxford University Press, 2000), 88.

21 Peter Mair and Ingrid van Biezen, "Party Membership in Twenty European Democracies, 1980–2000," *Party Politics* 7 (2001).

22 Wattenberg, "The Decline of Party Mobilization," 66.

23 Russell J. Dalton, Ian McAllister, and Martin P. Wattenberg, "The Consequences of Partisan Dealignment," in Russell J. Dalton and Martin P. Wattenberg, eds., *Parties Without Partisans: Political Change in Advanced Industrial Democracies* (New York: Oxford University Press, 2000), 58. See also Putnam, *Bowling Alone*.

24 Russell J. Dalton and Martin P. Wattenberg, "Unthinkable Democracy: Political Change in Advanced Industrial Democracies," in Russell J. Dalton

and Martin P. Wattenberg, eds., *Parties Without Partisans: Political Change in Advanced Industrial Democracies* (New York: Oxford University Press, 2000), 3.

25 L. Griffin, H. McCammon, and C. Botsko, "The Unmaking of a Movement? The Crisis of U.S. Trade Unions in Comparative Perspective," in Maureen T. Hallinan, David M. Klein, and Jennifer Glass, eds., *Changes in Societal Institutions* (New York: Plenum, 1990), 172. See also Bernhard Ebbinghaus and Jelle Visser, *Trade Unions in Western Europe Since 1945* (London: Macmillan Reference, 2000).

26 I am grateful to Peter Hall and Theda Skocpol for this formulation of our shared perspective on the role of history.

27 Putnam, *Bowling Alone,* ch. 14; Skocpol, Munson, Camp, and Karch, "Patriotic Partnerships."

28 See Putnam, *Bowling Alone,* ch. 6.

29 Cf. Pharr and Putnam, *Disaffected Democracies.*

30 On Japan, see Jun'ichi Kawata, "Socialization for Citizenship: Civic Education and Political Attitudes in Japan," in Ofer Feldman, ed., *Political Psychology in Japan* (Commack, NY: Nova Science Publishers, 1999), 41, who concludes that "de-politicization and cynicism arose among the younger especially after the mid-1970s in Japan. The degree in which young Japanese people take an active part in political events has also become recently astonishingly low compared to most modern countries."

31 Compare Putnam, *Bowling Alone,* ch. 14, with Frederick D. Weil, "Cohorts, Regimes, and the Legitimation of Democracy: West Germany Since 1945," *American Sociological Review* 52 (1987): 308–24.

32 This thesis has been widely argued in the American debate; see, for example, Francis Fukuyama, *Trust* (New York: Free Press, 1995).

33 On the U.S. debate about whether government programs crowd out philanthropy and volunteering and erode social capital, see Paul L. Menchik and Burton A. Weisbrod, "Volunteer Labor Supply," *Journal of Public Economics* 32 (1987): 159–83; Susan Chambre, "Kindling Points of Light: Volunteering as Public Policy," *Nonprofit and Voluntary Studies Quarterly* 18 (1989): 249–68; Richard Steinberg, "The Theory of Crowding Out: Donations, Local Government Spending, and the 'New Federalism,'" in Richard Magat, ed., *Philanthropic Giving* (New York: Oxford University Press, 1989), 143–56; Marvin Olasky, *The Tragedy of American Compassion* (Washington, D.C.: Regnery Gateway, 1992); Peter Dobkin Hall, *Inventing the Nonprofit Sector* (Baltimore: Johns Hopkins University Press, 1992), 1–83; Robert Moffitt, "Incentive Effects of the U.S. Welfare System: A Review," *Journal of Economic Literature* 30 (1992): 1–61.

34 Suzanne Mettler, "Bringing the State Back In to Civic Engagement: Policy Feedback Effects of the G.I. Bill for World War II Veterans," manuscript, Syracuse University, 2001.

CONTRIBUTORS

Eva Cox is senior lecturer, Faculty of Humanities and Social Sciences, University of Technology, Sydney. Her main current areas of research involve social capital and social ethics as part of what makes societies more civil; other interests involve policy issues such as child care, superannuation, tax, workplaces, communities, and the use of research as a tool for change. She is involved in a range of related projects, including working with the Body Shop (Australia), piloting the concept of social and ethical auditing, and the development of social audit indicators for community organizations. She was one of the first members of Women's Electoral Lobby and retains a strong interest in feminism as a means for creating more just societies. Her publications include the 1996 book *Leading Women*.

Susanne Fuchs is a researcher at the Social Science Center in Berlin, Germany. Her dissertation was a study of Georg Simmel and social integration. Her publications include "Niklas Luhmanns Aufklärung der Soziologie und andere Wege der Erleuchtung," in *Berliner Debatte Initial* (1996); "Wie schöpferisch ist die Zerstörung?" (with Claus Offe), in *Blätter für*

deutsche und internationale Politik (1998), "Germany" (with Ronald Schettkat) in Gøsta Esping-Anderson and Mario Regini, eds, *Why Deregulate Labor Markets?* (2000), and "Tristesse banale," in *Simmel Studies* (2001).

Peter A. Hall is Frank G. Thomson Professor of Government and director of the Minda de Gunzburg Center for European Studies at Harvard University. His publications include *Governing the Economy* (1986), *The Political Power of Economic Ideas* (1989), and *Varieties of Capitalism* (with D. Soskice, 2001) as well as many articles on European politics, political economy, and policy making.

Takashi Inoguchi is professor of political science at the Institute of Oriental Culture, University of Tokyo. He received his Ph.D. in political science from Massachusetts Institute of Technology, and has taught at Sophia University, Tokyo, as well as held visiting positions at many universities worldwide. In 1995–1997 he was assistant secretary general of the United Nations at the United Nations University Headquarters, acting as senior vice rector of the University. He has published more than thirty-five books and numerous articles in English and in Japanese, including *The Changing Nature of Democracy* (1998), *Democracy, Governance and Economic Performance: East and Southeast Asia* (2000), *Citizens and the Environment* (1999), *Global Change* (2001), *American Democracy Promotion* (2000), and *Japanese Foreign Policy Today* (2000). He is president of the Japan Association of International Relations and the editor of two journals, *Japanese Journal of Political Science* and *International Relations of the Asia-Pacific.* He often provides comments on Japan and international affairs to such mass media as the BBC, CNN, and the *International Herald Tribune.*

Claus Offe is a professor of political science at Humboldt University, Berlin. He has held teaching positions in Frankfurt, Konstanz, Vienna, Bielefield, Boston, and Berkeley. Offe is the author of *Industry and Inequality* (1976), *Contradictions of the Welfare State* (1984), *Disorganized Capitalism* (1985), and *Modernity and the State: East, West* (1996).

Víctor Pérez-Díaz received his Ph.D. from Harvard University and is professor of sociology at the Complutense University of Madrid and director of the ASP Research Center (Madrid). He has been a visiting professor at Harvard University, the Massachusetts Institute of Technology (MIT), the University of California, San Diego, the Institut d'Etudes Politiques of Paris; the New School for Social Research; and New York University. His books include *The Return*

of Civil Society (1993) and *Spain at the Crossroads* (1999).

Robert D. Putnam is Peter and Isabel Malkin Professor of Public Policy at Harvard University. The founder of the Saguaro Seminar on Civic Engagement, he is the author of *Bowling Alone,* which has been hailed as "powerful" (*Wall Street Journal*), "a remarkable achievement" (*Los Angeles Times*), and "wide-ranging...luminous...unpretentious and frequently funny" (*The Economist*).

Bo Rothstein is August Röhss Professor in Political Science at Göteborg University in Sweden. He received his Ph.D. from the University of Lund in 1986 and was an assistant professor in the Department of Government at Uppsala University from 1986 to 1995 and associate professor from 1992 until 1994. He served as professor in labor market policy at the Swedish Institute for Work Life Research in Stockholm 1994–1995 and as adjunct professor at the University of Bergen from 1994 to 1996. He has been a visiting scholar at the Russell Sage Foundation, Cornell University, Harvard University, the London School of Economics and Political Science, and the University of Washington in Seattle. Among his publications in English are *The Social Democratic State: The Swedish Model and the Bureaucratic Problems of Social Reforms* (1996) and *Just Institutions Matter: The Moral and Political Logic of the Universal Welfare State* (1998) as well as articles in *Comparative Politics, Governance, European Journal of Political Research, Scandinavian Political Studies, Com-*

parative Political Studies, and *Politics & Society.* He is a regular contributor to the Swedish public debate about politics, the welfare state, and labor market policy.

Theda Skocpol is Victor S. Thomas Professor of Government and Sociology at Harvard University, where she also serves as the director of the Center for American Political Studies. She is the author or editor of dozens of articles and sixteen books, including *States and Social Revolutions: A Comparative Analysis of France, Russia, and China* (1979), winner of two major scholarly prizes; *Bringing the States Back In* (1985); *Protecting Soldiers and Mothers: The Political Origins of Social Policy in the United States* (1992), winner of five major scholarly prizes; and *Civic Engagement in American Democracy* (1999). Skocpol is a member of the American Academy of Arts and Sciences; served as president of the Social Science History Association in 1996, and will be president-elect of the American Political Science Association in 2002 and president in 2003. Her current research focuses on voluntary associations and social movements in the United States from the nineteenth century to the present.

Jean-Pierre Worms is a professor and researcher at the Centre de Sociologie des Organisations. His interests include local development, the local political system, and decentralization. He has held several local, regional, national, and European political and advisory positions, as well as responsibilities in various voluntary organizations at these different levels, through which he has facilitated local development and cooperation between the state, the private sector, and the intermediaries between them. He has published several works on the state, political and civil society and its representation, the French model of social cohesion, and the guarantee of minority rights in international law.

Robert Wuthnow is Gerhard R. Andlinger '52 Professor of Sociology and director of the Center for the Study of Religion at Princeton University. The author of numerous books and articles on American religion, culture, and civil society, his publications include *Loose Connections: Joining Together in America's Fragmented Communities* (1998), *After Heaven: Spirituality in America Since the 1950s* (1998), and *Creative Spirituality: The Way of the Artist* (2001).

INDEX